REVENUE MANAGEMENT
FOR THE HOSPITALITY INDUSTRY

DAVID K. HAYES

ALLISHA A. MILLER

WILEY

John Wiley & Sons, Inc.

Photos were taken by the author unless otherwise noted.

This book is printed on acid-free paper. ⊗

Copyright © 2011 by John Wiley & Sons, Inc. All rights reserved.

Published by John Wiley & Sons, Inc., Hoboken, New Jersey.

Published simultaneously in Canada.

Evaluation copies are provided to qualified academics and professionals for review purposes only, for use in their courses during the next academic year. These copies are licensed and may not be sold or transferred to a third party. Upon completion of the review period, please return the evaluation copy to Wiley. Return instructions and a free of charge return shipping label are available at www.wiley.com/go/returnlabel. Outside of the United States, please contact your local representative.

For general information on our other products and services, or technical support, please contact our Customer Care Department within the United States at 800-762-2974, outside the United States at 317-572-3993 or fax 317-572-4002.

Wiley also publishes its books in a variety of electronic formats. Some content that appears in print may not be available in electronic books. For more information about Wiley products, visit our Web site at http://www. wiley.com.

Library of Congress Cataloging-in-Publication Data:

Hayes, David K.
    Revenue management for the hospitality industry/David K. Hayes, Allisha Miller.
        p. cm.
        Includes index.
    ISBN 978-0-470-39308-6 (pbk.)
1. Hospitality industry–Management. 2. Hospitality industry–Economic aspects. I. Miller, Allisha. II Title.
TX911.3.M27H395 2010
647.94068'1–dc22

Printed in the United States of America
10 9

CONTENTS

PREFACE

Revenue Management for the Hospitality Industry is a book that we were particularly privileged and challenged to create. This is the first textbook that has been developed specifically to examine what revenue managers in the hospitality industry must know and do to be successful.

Revenue Management is an emerging field of study. Because that is true, there are honest differences of opinion about what revenue management actually is today—and what it will become in the future. Despite some philosophical differences among revenue management experts, we believe all of them would agree that a good way to describe the goal of revenue management is to say that it is *"to charge the right price, to the right customer, for the right product, through the right channel, at the right time."* Doing that well is not as easy as it looks—and as experienced revenue managers will attest, it doesn't look all that easy. This book was developed to teach its readers exactly how it is done.

It is important to note that *Revenue Management for the Hospitality Industry* is intended for readers with prior knowledge and understanding of the hospitality industry. We believe revenue management should be a unique and separate area of study and is an area best studied by those with a solid understanding of how products and services are sold in the exciting hospitality industry.

As it continues to evolve, revenue management will certainly develop more of its own theory, principles, and practices. For the present, much of the information revenue managers need to know is taken from the various fields upon which it has been built. This can be confusing to some. For example, some marketing professionals believe that because revenue managers must understand much about marketing, the terms *revenue management* and *effective marketing* are the same. They are not the same. In fact, one very good way to avoid any confusion about what this book *is* intended to be would be to carefully describe what it is not.

Revenue Management for the Hospitality Industry is not a principles of economics textbook, despite the fact that it is critical for revenue managers to understand how and why consumers use scarce financial resources to make purchasing decisions. Concepts such as supply, demand, consumer rationality, and pricing are foundational topics for revenue managers and as a result these and other very specific economic concepts are presented in the book. Neither is this a pricing theory text, despite this book's strong emphasis on the critical relationship between strategic pricing and effective revenue management. Revenue managers must be experts at understanding how businesses determine prices and how their customers perceive prices. As a result, the principles and concepts revenue managers must know to grasp the intricacies of effective pricing do make up an essential part of this book.

This is not a book about managerial accounting although it addresses those accounting principles and practices that revenue managers must be aware of if they are to do their jobs effectively. It is not a textbook about marketing or e-marketing/information technology. Certainly, revenue managers must know a great deal about marketing concepts. As well, the extensive use of the Internet to sell hospitality products requires specialized knowledge to use that tool effectively. As a result, marketing and e-marketing information make up a significant portion of this text.

It is not a text about how to manage the front desk in a lodging operation. This is so despite the fact that in a large number of U.S. hotels the revenue manager and front office manager position will often be held by the same individual. Effective front office administration, however, is critical to revenue optimization in hotels. As a result, the book includes a great deal of information about effective front office management.

It is not a textbook about leadership, yet experienced revenue managers agree that the ability to communicate goals and build teams who are inspired to achieve those goals is one of a revenue manager's most critical tasks. As a result, information about the leadership skills that revenue managers must acquire and exhibit are included. Similarly, the book is not about managerial ethics or those laws that directly affect pricing. This is so despite the fact that employees, customers, and society at large care deeply about the ethical aspects of a business's pricing tactics and strategies. Also, it is important that revenue managers understand that there are very specific legal requirements related to pricing products, and these requirements must be well known. In any industry, the prices charged and the selling methods used must be perceived to be fair, and they must follow the law. As a result, ethics in pricing and the legal aspects of pricing are topics that must be addressed. This book does that.

In summary, the book is not an economics, pricing theory, marketing, e-marketing/ information technology, managerial accounting, front office management, leadership, ethics, or hospitality law textbook. *Revenue Management for the Hospitality Industry* is a book about revenue management. Revenue management is an independent area of hospitality study that draws from a variety of established academic areas to yield a subject of management inquiry as unique as it is exciting.

TO THE STUDENT

Learning revenue management will not be boring. It is an easy statement to make because revenue management is an exciting subject. It is fun and it is challenging. *Revenue Management for the Hospitality Industry* will be fun and challenging as well.

The book has been carefully designed to include information taken from inside the hospitality industry as well as from a variety of external sources. If you work hard and do your best, you will find you do have the ability to master all of the information in this text. When you do, you will have gained an invaluable skill that will make you one of the rare individuals with a thorough understanding of revenue management in the hospitality industry. That knowledge will enhance your company's performance and thus help you advance your own hospitality career.

TO THE INSTRUCTOR

Teaching in a new subject area can be much more challenging for an instructor than teaching in an area that is more well-established. It requires dedicated, innovative, and inspired teachers to organize relevant information and to make that information easy to understand

and interesting to study. In a new instructional area the teaching resources available may be few, while at the same time there are myriad initial pedagogical decisions to be made about what to teach, how best to teach it, and it what order it should be taught. *Revenue Management for the Hospitality Industry* was carefully designed to serve you as a technically accurate and highly flexible teaching resource. In addition to the content presented in the chapters, we believe revenue management instructors will be pleased to find:

- The material was written in an especially reader-friendly style. Both upper-division undergraduate students and graduate students will find its reading level suitable to them, and they will find the material is presented in a way that makes reading it highly enjoyable. Revenue management is not a dull topic, and this book ensures students will recognize that.

- The book was designed to provide hospitality instructors in a variety of curriculum settings with maximum teaching flexibility. Its separation into four distinct parts allows, for example, lodging management instructors the freedom to include or exclude from their courses detailed information about revenue management in the foodservice segment of the hospitality industry. Similarly, it allows food management instructors the ability to exclude detailed front office management-related guest room sales information from their culinary and foodservice-related revenue management courses.

- The many cases and practical examples used to illustrate revenue management concepts are taken directly from real-world situations. They are challenging and exciting to read. The issues raised in these practical application scenarios provide students ample opportunity to practice their newly acquired revenue management skills and to evaluate their mastery of the material.

- Questions and problems at the end of each chapter are demanding because they are extremely practical. They allow students the chance to perform the calculations and practice the decision-making skills that are used daily by those revenue managers actually working in the industry. In these chapter-ending questions, as well as in the main body of this book, the authors assumed only a working knowledge of basic algebra as the level of math proficiency required for material mastery.

- Most hospitality instructors want their graduating students to possess practical industry knowledge that can be immediately applied on the job. They also want their students to be aware of future trends that predict industry changes students will encounter as their careers progress. This book does both of those things. Students who master the information presented in it will be prepared to assume the day-to-day duties of a revenue manager. They will also understand the managerial philosophy and actions required to create a customer-centric revenue optimization plan and culture in their own organizations.

Revenue management will continue to evolve in the hospitality industry and, as a result, in the hospitality classroom as well. As the sophistication of the field grows and as the emphasis moves from the management of revenues to their optimization, the shift from a tactical focus to a strategic focus creates broader responsibilities for revenue management. As the renaissance unfolds, hotels and restaurants will look to revenue management to help understand how customers respond to offerings in the marketplace. This customer-centric thinking will focus leading hospitality firms on the essential issues of pricing and customer value, which are fundamental topics of this book.

TEXT CONTENT

Revenue Management for the Hospitality Industry is a detailed examination of the hands-on skills revenue managers must know to effectively manage their inventories and prices. As a result, readers will learn how to use those tools that professional revenue managers simply must know and understand. Thus, RevPAR, Flow-through, RevPASH, ADR, Occupancy %, Net Yield %, and Occupancy Index are but some of the industry metrics detailed in the book. Few industry professionals would object to the authors' inclusion of these important assessment tools. Similarly, most hospitality educators know the value of providing their students with professional skills that can be immediately applied on the job.

In addition to developing hands-on skills, the book includes a substantial amount of revenue management–related theory. A theory is simply a tool managers use to better understand what is happening today and to better predict what will happen tomorrow. Many decisions made by revenue managers must be based on what the revenue manager thinks or believes will happen in the future. As a result, they simply must be theoretically well-grounded. Internationally known management consult William Edwards Deming, famous for his work in advancing manufacturing methods in Japan after WWII, succinctly stated the value of theory in management when said that "Rational behavior requires theory." The authors believe the purpose of well-developed theories is to explain, predict, or advise others. The theory-related content of this book was carefully reviewed and included only when it clearly helped readers achieve one or more of these three critical objectives.

As a result, the book is practical, because practicality enhances learning by allowing students to apply new information from a variety of fields to a setting (hospitality) that is interesting and familiar to them. But it is also unabashedly theoretical because practical advancements in any endeavor, including revenue management, will only result from carefully examining old theories and improving on them.

With the goal of effectively aiding in teaching the practical skills and the theoretical principles revenue managers must know to be effective, *Revenue Management for the Hospitality Industry* is presented in 13 chapters that are divided among four major parts:

Part I: Revenue Management Principles

Part I introduces readers to the foundations of revenue management and contains the following chapters:

1. Introduction to Revenue Management
2. Stratgetic Pricing
3. Value
4. Differential Pricing
5. The Revenue Manager's Role

In Chapter 1 of this underpinning section, readers will learn about the history of revenue management and gain an understanding of the material that is included in the remaining chapters of the book. In Chapter 2 the concept of price is examined and in Chapter 3 readers will learn how customers assess value when making their purchases. Differential pricing is the sole topic of Chapter 4. In it readers will learn how revenue managers combine the concepts of price and value to develop pricing strategies based on customer willingness to buy. In Chapter 5, the role of the professional hospitality revenue manager within a business entity is examined in detail.

Part II: Revenue Management for Hoteliers

Part II of the text addresses the principles and practices applied by revenue managers working in the lodging segment of the hospitality industry. It includes the following chapters.

6. Forecasting Demand
7. Inventory and Price Management
8. Distribution Channel Management
9. Evaluation of Revenue Management Efforts in Lodging

In Chapter 6, readers learn how to forecast future demand for their hotel rooms and services. In Chapter 7, the techniques utilized to manage rooms inventory and to price hotel rooms are examined in detail. Chapter 8 addresses management and evaluation of the various distribution channels utilized by revenue managers when pricing and selling lodging products and services. These include both non-electronic and electronic distribution channels. In Chapter 9, readers will learn the various techniques used by revenue managers to assess and evaluate the quality of their revenue management decision making.

Part III: Revenue Management for Foodservice Operators

Part III of the text addresses the principles and practices applied by revenue managers working in the food and beverage segment of the hospitality industry. It includes the following chapters.

10. Revenue Management for Food and Beverage Services
11. Evaluation of Revenue Management Efforts in Food and Beverage Services

Although they may be applied in unique ways, foodservice professionals can and should utilize effective revenue management strategies to optimize sales. Many of the strategies they can use are presented in Chapter 10. In Chapter 11, readers learn the techniques foodservice operators use for assessing and evaluating the quality of their revenue management decision making.

Part IV: Revenue Management in Action

In the concluding section of the text readers will learn how they can apply what they have learned in a variety of professional settings and under varying economic conditions. The section consists of the following two chapters.

12. Specialized Applications of Revenue Management in Hospitality-Related Organizations

13. Building Better Business

In Chapter 12, readers are shown how the revenue optimization principles they have learned can be utilized by those hospitality-related entities possessing the same organizational characteristics as hotels and restaurants. Examples include golf courses, cruise ships and amusement parks. The chapter addresses the role of the multiunit revenue manager as well as the revenue manager employed by a franchise company and concludes with an examination of the revenue manager's role in destination marketing.

Chapter 13 concludes the book by examining how revenue managers can use their detailed knowledge of inventory management and pricing to improve their organizations' income levels. The chapter's primary focus is on the customer-centric revenue management strategies and tactics revenue managers can use to generate more income and improved profits regardless of the economic conditions faced by their businesses.

TEXT FEATURES

From a reader's perspective the features of a textbook often are as important as its content. Thoughtfully designed textbook features make the content presented easy to read, easy to understand, and easy to remember. Readers will find that ***Revenue Management for the Hospitality Industry*** is especially reader friendly. The following features help readers learn and practice the concepts of revenue management:

- *Chapter Outline*: The outline preceding each chapter shows the listings for each topic in order of their introduction and provides a simple way to quickly find material within the chapter.

- *Chapter Highlights*: Each chapter utilizes this three-point feature to explain in short and clear terms (and before any content is presented), exactly what readers will know when they have mastered the chapter's content. This feature makes it easy for readers to see what the chapter is about and the skills they will acquire by reading it.

- *RM in Action:* Unlike some other fields of study, revenue management-related issues are frequently described, debated, or clearly exemplified in the current news articles reported by the hospitality and general press. In this entertaining feature, students will see how the revenue management principles presented in the book can be clearly illustrated using real-world examples reported in various news outlets.

- *RM at Work*: Each chapter contains multiple mini-cases designed to make readers think about how they would personally use the information they have learned to respond to an on-the-job revenue management-related issue or challenge. These thought-provoking and realistic cases allow readers to practice the type of revenue management problems solving methods they will use as professional revenue managers.

- *RM on the Web*: This feature uses sites listed on the Internet to provide readers with detailed supplemental information about a topic or issue presented in the book.

This feature identifies pertinent Web sites to visit and gives readers specific instructions about what they should do, consider, and learn when they visit the site.

- *Essential RM Terms*: As is true with many areas of specialization, revenue managers often speak their own language. Readers needing help in remembering these key vocabulary terms and concepts will appreciate this feature because it clearly defines important terms where they are first introduced in the text. The terms are also listed at the conclusion of each chapter (in the order in which they were presented) to provide a valuable study aid.

- *Apply What You Know*: This end-of-chapter feature provides opportunities for readers to solve common revenue management problems using the information presented to them in the chapter. Some of the questions require a conceptual answer, while others can be answered only after making appropriate calculations and computations. Each of the *Apply What You Know* questions was carefully designed to be fun, to be challenging, and to reinforce important concepts presented in each chapter.

- *Key Concept Case Study*: This entertaining capstone feature allows readers to follow, via a running case study, the actions of Damario. Damario is the newly appointed revenue manager at the fictitious Barcena Resort. He reports directly to Sofia Davidson, the resort's general manager. Each case was designed to illustrate a key chapter concept and allows readers to see how revenue managers actually apply the concepts presented in the chapter in their everyday work activities.

INSTRUCTOR RESOURCES

To help instructors effectively manage their time and to enhance student learning opportunities, an on-line *Instructor's Manual* as well as several significant educational tools have been developed. The *Instructor's Manual* includes:

- Lecture outlines for each chapter
- Suggested answers for *RM at Work* case study questions
- Correct answers for *Apply What You Have Learned* end-of-chapter questions
- Suggested answers to all chapter-ending *Key Concept Case Study* questions
- A Test Bank including exam questions and answers

The *Test Bank* has been specifically formatted for **Respondus**, an easy-to-use software program for creating and managing exams that can be printed to paper or published directly to Blackboard, WebCT, Desire2Learn, eCollege, ANGEL, and other e-Learning systems. Instructors who adopt *Revenue Management for the Hospitality Industry* can download the test bank for free. Additional Wiley resources also can be uploaded into your LMS course at no charge.

A password-protected Wiley Companion Instructor's Web site devoted entirely to this book (www.wiley.com/college/hayes) provides access to the Instructor's Manual and the text-specific teaching resources. PowerPoint lecture slides are also available on the Web site for download.

Acknowledgments

Revenue Management for the Hospitality Industry has been designed to be the most comprehensive, technically accurate and reader friendly learning tool available to those who wish to know more about revenue management. We would like to acknowledge the many individuals who assisted in its development.

Very special appreciation goes to Peggy Richards Hayes, the individual singly most responsible for ensuring that this text would be easy to read, easy to understand, easy to apply, and easy to remember. In this project she performed as flawlessly as we have come to expect. Her insightful, sometimes kindly, but often brutally offered reactions to each originally drafted page of the manuscript will no doubt ensure the success of this book. She is a relentless and zealous crusader against the kind of writing designed to impress academics rather than to enlighten readers. As a result of her careful manuscript scrutiny, the presentation of complex and challenging revenue management concepts was continually revised, simplified, and improved until it resulted in a text version we believe will be much appreciated by student readers, as well as by those in the academic community. For her energy and passion for clarity we are most appreciative.

One of the most challenging aspects of producing a book designed for students as well as practicing professionals is ensuring its industry relevance. In addition to our formal cadre of academic and industry reviewers, the authors are greatly indebted to Michelle Davis, director of revenue management for Hospitality Ventures. Hospitality Ventures is a privately owned, fully integrated hotel ownership and management organization located in Atlanta, Georgia. The company currently owns and/or operates 20 hotels in 12 states. Eighteen of its properties operate under the Hilton or Marriott brands. Prior to undertaking the writing process, we recognized the wisdom of enlisting a talented and innovative revenue manager, and especially one with multiunit responsibilities who daily faces the challenges and opportunities we would be examining and describing in the book. We knew that such an individual could provide key guidance and address complex questions about the evolving roles and responsibilities of practicing revenue managers. Michelle agreed to fill that role for us, and she did so beautifully. Her tireless and rapid responses to our myriad queries added greatly to the practicality of this text. A cum laude graduate of the hospitality program at Johnson and Wales University, her thoughtful reflections on the topics we presented to her display her keen intellect, outstanding training, and varied experience. For her willingness to share her insight with us, and by doing so impart it to the many students and industry professionals who will read this text, we are deeply grateful.

We also wish to thank Sofianna A. Pastrana, who provided the ongoing motivation for writing the text. In addition, we wish to thank Laura and David Miller, and Herodina and Joseph Chandler, all of whom displayed extraordinary patience and unrelenting support during the long writing process.

Long-time restaurant professional David Berger was especially helpful in critiquing those chapters addressing foodservice-related revenue management issues. North Texas University's Dr. Lea Dopson's accounting-related insight was invaluable as well.

Particular mention is appropriate for those academic and industry professionals who reviewed the original drafts of each chapter. For their comments, collaboration, and constructive criticisms we wish to thank our external reviewers:

Eric Browning, Boston University; William Frye, Niagara University; John F. Mulrey, Florida International University; Charles Day, Marriott; Melissa Dallas, Missouri State University; Peter Ricci, Florida Atlantic University; Manisha Singal, Virginia Tech; Eric T. Brey, University of Memphis.

Experienced authors know the value of a quality publisher in transforming a very good manuscript into an outstanding book. We remain continually impressed with the high standards exhibited by JoAnna Turtletaub, Wiley vice president and publisher, and by the tremendous support she has shown for this project. Special thanks also go to Julie Kerr, the Wiley expert who served as this project's developmental editor. Always professional and insightful, Julie's efforts helped keep the project on track and ensured all the myriad details required for the production of a new text were addressed. James Metzger at Wiley deserves special recognition because of his efforts to organize the feedback received from our reviewers and because of his work in ensuring the quality and clarity of the *Instructor's Manual* produced for this text. Finally, the authors were delighted to again team with Wiley Senior Production Editor Richard DeLorenzo in this book's final production. Richard's painstakingly detailed efforts ensure this book reflects only the very best of our efforts. We are deeply grateful, as will be the students who read this text, for all of the other production staff at Wiley for their intellect, skill, and patience, in the manuscript layout, design, proofing, and printing of this exciting new book.

It is a truism that real joy is not found in finishing an activity but in doing it. Certainly for us, the journey taken to produce the first comprehensive textbook on this topic was as memorable and fascinating as the destination. We invite readers to begin their own personal expedition into the new, constantly changing and always exciting world that can be discovered by exploring *Revenue Management for the Hospitality Industry*.

David K. Hayes, Ph.D. Allisha A. Miller
Okemos, MI   Lansing, MI

PART I

REVENUE MANAGEMENT PRINCIPLES

CHAPTER 1

Introduction to Revenue Management

CHAPTER OUTLINE

CHAPTER HIGHLIGHTS

1. Explanation of why an excessive internal focus on profits or owner's return on investment is detrimental to the long-term success of a hospitality business.

2. Explanation of why businesses exist to create wealth for their customers and how effective RM helps them do that.

3. Overview of the RM-related information contained in the remaining chapters of this book.

INTRODUCTION

In increasing numbers, professionals in the hospitality industry are coming to the realization that management of their **revenue** (revenue management) is critical to their organizations' success.

Essential RM Term

Revenue: The total amount of sales achieved in a specified time period. Revenue is calculated as:

$$\text{Number of units sold} \times \text{Unit price} = \text{Revenue}$$

It may seem surprising that only recently has the full-time position of revenue manager (RM) been created by forward-thinking hospitality organizations. What is really surprising is that it has taken so long. What these progressive entities are discovering is that every member of their organization has a role to play in revenue management.

Even the professional hospitality associations that normally provide up-to-date information to their members have only in the past few years (or still have not!) created coursework, certification programs, and continuing education/professional development classes focusing on revenue management. The materials used for instruction are few, and the majority of these materials have been developed primarily for the lodging rather than foodservice segments of the hospitality industry.

Similarly, only recently have professional hospitality educators felt that *revenue management* was a topic of sufficient depth and complexity to warrant its own course content. They are now discovering that virtually the entire hospitality curriculum could (and perhaps should) be designed around the basic tenants of revenue management.

This book has been developed to assist hospitality organizations, associations, educators, and most importantly, those professionals who wish to become very highly skilled at managing revenues in the hospitality industry. The book emphasizes the importance of strategic pricing as a key tactic in effective revenue management, simply because the prices charged by a company communicate much information to its customers and determines the total sales revenue the company will achieve.

Because of the importance of a business's revenues, it would seem that implementing effective business strategies designed to optimize revenues would be crucial and fairly straightforward. It is crucial, but for a variety of reasons, it is not easy. The most significant of these reasons is that most traditionally trained hospitality managers do not understand the basic tenants of revenue management, nor do they fully appreciate the large number of organizational misconceptions, biases, and misunderstandings that actually work against them when implementing effective revenue management strategies. This book is designed to address and dispel many of those misconceptions, biases, and misunderstandings. The reasons it is important to do so are fundamental to business success because, in the final analysis, effective managers of an organization's revenues simply *must* do three things:

1. Understand the importance of revenue management
2. Understand the many complex factors that influence revenue management strategy and tactics
3. Become better at making revenue management decisions than their competitors

Interestingly, these goals should not be new. Those in business have, since the beginning of commerce, grappled with the complexity of how to best price the products they made and the services they provided, especially in the face of competition from others offering similar products and services. These early entrepreneurs understood the importance of strategic pricing because of a simple mathematical truth; in a service business, the *sum* of prices paid by the business's customers equals the total *revenues* received by that business.

Unfortunately, despite all that has been learned over hundreds of years of commerce and in many academic disciplines, the question of how much to charge for hospitality products has too often been viewed as one best answered by mathematical formula or rule-of-thumb; and thus, it has been addressed primarily by those who specialize in hospitality accounting. The rationale for doing so has been the widely held belief that prices for hospitality products should be directly related to those products' costs. Knowledgeable revenue managers understand that costs and price are related, but that the latter is not dependent on the former (nor should it be). Yet the firmly ingrained idea that costs should dictate price is just one good example of the misconceptions held by those who do not truly understanding the complexities of selling hospitality products to consumers in today's post-Internet economy.

Readers of this book will find that it presents hospitality professionals with a significant number of additional concepts that may, at first, appear counterintuitive or just plain wrong. Consider this sentence taken from a later portion of this chapter:

It is important to recognize that if an organization's primary focus is the generation of profits, it will inevitably go out of business because it will lose out to organizations that know enough not to focus on profitability.

Statements such as this might seem controversial, but they will be presented only when supported by fact, illustrated with real-world examples, or failing those two, proposed for debate based on a preponderance of evidence garnered by the lead authors' 35-plus years as a hotel owner, foodservice director, professor, writer, and most importantly, life-long student/observer of the fascinating field of hospitality management.

The preliminary response to controversial ideas (those that have the potential to change the status quo of revenue management thought to status "Go!") may be the informed reader's initial disbelief or disagreement. If, however, that is followed by vigorous debate and open-minded and spirited discussion and ultimately by increased sophistication in the application of revenue management strategy in hospitality, then the industry and its customers can only benefit from the exchange. It is the authors' hope that, in concert with open-minded readers, we can together begin a meaningful exploration of the intriguing topic of revenue management in the hospitality industry.

THE PURPOSE OF BUSINESS

We start our examination at the very beginning. If you are reading this book, it is most likely because you are now, or in the future want to be, in the **hospitality business**. If that is true, it would be fair to ask: What will be your purpose? Stated differently, if you plan to go into business, what is the purpose of your business? Even more specifically, what is the purpose of a hospitality business? Ask that question to many hospitality professionals and you are likely to get one of two reasonable answers;

1. To achieve profits
2. To generate returns on investment for the business's owners

Both answers are flawed and if you hope to successfully manage revenues in a hospitality business, you need to understand why.

The Profit Fallacy

If you want to be in the hospitality business, you likely want to be involved in a profitable hospitality business. That would be a logical choice because, in the long run, only profitable organizations will stay in business. It is important to recognize, however, that if an organization's primary focus is the generation of profits, it will inevitably go out of business because it will lose out to organizations that know enough not to focus on profitability.

The two previous sentences are not contradictory. The critical nature of profits should not lead those in business (and especially those in the hospitality business) to focus their efforts on maximizing their companies' profit levels. The organizational focus must be elsewhere. To understand precisely where organizations should direct their primary attention, you must first analyze the commonly accepted (but unsatisfactory) definition of *profits,* and then come to a deeper understanding of the concept of profits.

To many hospitality owners and managers, profit is defined as a firm's total revenue minus its total cost or expense. That seems logical. If you know basic accounting, you also know that, with a very few exceptions, hospitality accountants and managers use the words *expense* and *cost* interchangeably. Specific types of costs (expenses) may be identified in a variety of ways. Some common terms for various types of costs include fixed costs, variable costs, controllable costs, and noncontrollable costs, but they are all considered costs.

Similarly, the terms *sales* or *income* are often used as a substitute for revenue. The result is that it is not unusual for accountants to define profits utilizing one of the following two versions of the accountant's profit formula:

Accountant's Profit Formula

$$Sales = Costs + Profit^{1}$$

Applying basic algebra, and substituting more familiar and commonly used terms, the accountant's formula becomes:

$$Profit = Revenue - Expense$$

As you will learn in this book, the accountant's formula (as well as the economist's profit formula, which you will study later in this chapter) is not completely on target, although it does touch on some aspects of truth regarding profits. You likely are fairly familiar with this commonly accepted but inadequate meaning of the word *profit*. But being familiar with a concept does not necessarily mean that the concept is fully understood or is useful. To actually *generate* significant profits in a hospitality business, and to be a successful manager of a business's revenues, you must comprehend profits both *completely* and *differently*. You must acquire a revenue manager's understanding of the meaning of *profits*.

Essential RM Term

Profit: The net value achieved by a seller *and* a buyer in a business transaction.

To begin, you should recognize that successful businesspersons understand that in any rational business transaction, both the buyer and the seller seek a **profit**.

A careful reading of this definition reveals that, in a successful business transaction, both buyer and seller gain. If you are reading this book because you are interested in becoming an outstanding manager of your business's revenues, it is critical that you stop reading now and memorize this profit definition. It is the crucial foundation of effective revenue management and yet it is most often neglected when organizations, in the quest for profits, establish their prices.

This somewhat-unorthodox definition of profit is not a new concept. Consider the advice given in the early 1900s by retail business legend Herbert Marcus (co-founder of Neiman Marcus) to his son Stanley when he said: "There is never a good sale for Neiman Marcus unless it's a good buy for the customer."[2]

Think about it and you will recognize it is true. Buyers seek a profit as much as sellers. To illustrate; if you have ten dollars and purchase an item priced for that amount, you (the buyer) seek to acquire something that you want *more* than you want to keep the ten dollars you already have. If you *willingly* part with your ten dollars, it is only because you see a value in exchanging the ten dollars for something worth more than ten dollars *to you*.

To keep this illustration very clear, consider Figure 1.1, a recap of a typical buyer's likely interest in three alternative business transactions (propositions) that have been offered by a business organization whose stated goal is to make profits for itself. In this illustration, the prospective buyer is holding one ten-dollar bill.

Note that in this example (as in the real-world), the informed buyer would have a high interest only in proposition #3, the trade that results in a clear profit for the buyer. That

Figure 1.1	Three Business Propositions Related to a Ten-Dollar Buyer/Seller Transaction	
Seller's Proposition	**Resulting Profit**	**Informed Buyer's Willingness to Accept and Repeat the Trade**
#1. Trade nine $1.00 bills for the buyer's $10.00 bill.	$1.00 to the seller	Zero
#2. Trade ten $1.00 bills for the buyer's $10.00 bill.	$ 0.00 to seller and buyer	Possible, but unlikely
#3. Trade eleven $1.00 bills for the buyer's $10.00 bill.	$1.00 to the buyer	Highly likely

same buyer will likely have zero interest in proposition #1; which would result *only* in the seller's profit. It is important to understand that it matters not that the item traded in this example is money. In fact, the use of money as the item to be exchanged in this example illustrates clearly a fundamental truth about the twenty-first-century economy; namely that our current technology-driven economy still operates in much the same way as every other **barter system** in the history of mankind. Revenue managers can learn important lessons from that time-tested system.

Essential RM Term

Barter system: A trading system in which goods and services are exchanged without the use of money.

All business transactions have evolved from the barter system. Bartering is an economic activity that consists simply of two individuals *trading* one item for another. In such a system, the terms *buyer* and *seller* are essentially irrelevant because both individuals participating in the trade take on the dual roles of buyer *and* seller.

To illustrate a barter economy that does not use money as a medium of exchange, assume a baker trades two loaves of bread for a poultry farmer's single chicken. As you can readily see in this example, the baker as well as the farmer takes on the role of buyer *and* seller. Just as a barter system erases the lines between buyer and seller, it erases the lines between sellers' costs and their profits. If both participants in this transaction were voluntary participants in the trade, it could be said that they agree the *cost* of a chicken is two loaves of bread. The *cost* of a loaf of bread is half a chicken.

A *profit* in such a trade is not a major consideration of the baker or the farmer. This is so because *both parties involved in this trade achieved a profit*—which you will recall is *the net value achieved by a seller and buyer in a business transaction.* The profit of the farmer is ownership of desired bread; the baker's profit is ownership of a desired chicken.

Barter economies work well but do have built-in problems. For example, perhaps the farmer in this example would really like to begin eating one of the loaves of bread today but would prefer to receive the second loaf next week, when the first loaf has been eaten and the second loaf will be freshly baked. Similarly, the baker may want to cook only half a chicken today with the remaining half desired for cooking in a coming month. The limitations of a barter system in this example are evident. There are others. For example, in a barter system, an apple grower who wished to obtain shoes would have to not only locate a shoemaker who wanted apples but also find a shoemaker who wanted to own apples at the time the grower's crop of apples were available for trading. The invention of **money** solved both these type problems (and made the construction of Figure 1.1 much easier)!

Essential RM Term

Money: An acceptable medium of exchange used as the measure of the value of goods and services.

It is important to recognize that money has no inherent value. You cannot eat coins or currency, nor can the owners of money do much of anything useful with the metals, paper, or other items people generally accept as money. Money is highly useful, however, because if those who have it can agree on its value, it greatly facilitates the many trade transactions that can take place in a money-based economy. Its use is more efficient and more convenient than a barter system.

It should now be clear to you, however, that money is not a measure of value, nor does it represent stored-up value. Money is simply an easy way to quantify the amount of one item its owner will give up in order to get another item. Applying this truth to the hospitality industry, it would be foolish to think that simply because a chicken dinner is offered for sale by a restaurateur for ten dollars, its value is ten dollars. If, in fact, a guest willingly purchased the ten-dollar chicken dinner from the restaurateur, it would simply mean that both parties in this trade valued the new item each received (chicken for the diner and money for the restaurateur) *more* than they valued keeping what they originally had. If the trade of the chicken dinner for the money were actually made, it would be a historical fact that, at a certain time and place, this trade between two trading partners occurred. This historical fact would not necessarily establish the intrinsic "worth" or "value" of a chicken dinner to you or to me. In fact, if you are a vegetarian, you would not likely place any personal value on the chicken dinner. If you were extremely hungry, you might value the chicken dinner at much more than ten dollars. The point to remember is that one consumer's view of a chicken dinner's value may, or may not at all, be influenced by what other buyers would exchange for it. This variance in buyers' willingness to trade is another concept that will be fully explored in this text.

To further make the important point about the variable worth of items, let's return to our barter economy example. Assume that the baker awoke one day to discover he had become extremely allergic to chicken. In such a case, would the worth of one chicken still be equivalent to that of two loaves of bread? Not to that baker. Not surprisingly, an incredibly large number of factors work to influence the willingness of two individuals to take part in a specific trade. The critical point for those in hospitality businesses to remember is that in each case of a willing exchange, an independent decision will made by *both parties* regarding what will be given up and what will be received in exchange.

In today's Internet-influenced economy, never have so many potential trading partners had more trade-related information available to them. As a result, never have consumers been able to more carefully consider their alternative trade options. In fact, the wealth of information about potential trades available to the average consumer has changed our money-based economy as radically as money changed the barter-based economy (a fact that is especially true for those trades taking place in the lodging segment of the hospitality business; a phenomena directly addressed later in this book).

Now that you fully understand barter systems, money, and the roles of the parties to a trade transaction, you are in a better position to reexamine the information in Figure 1.1. Note first that the terms *buyer* and *seller* seem less important. In fact, you now likely would be just as comfortable if the terms used were trading partner A and B, rather than buyer and seller. If that is true for you, then you have come to a realization that consistently eludes many in the hospitality business. There are no buyers (customers). There are no sellers (businesses). There are only potential trading partners. Profit (whatever that term may mean to either party) is not the trader's main concern. What is given up versus what is gained is the main concern. Lest, however, you begin to think the author is proposing that the hospitality business consists simply of one happy group of organizations blissfully seeking to assist like-minded trading partners, read the Red Lobster story presented in *RM in Action 1.1*.

In this Red Lobster example, a hospitality business simply found that its trading partners behaved very normally and maximized what they got in exchange for what they gave up. Alternatively, the Red Lobster company did not; and for that mistake, experienced industry observers would conclude its former president paid dearly.

Now that you understand that profit (value) is a factor of interest to those who *buy*, as well as those who sell, products and services it should be easier to understand the limitations of the accountant's rather one-sided formula for profits. It should also be easier for you to revisit and understand the wisdom of the statement of Herbert Marcus: "There is never a good sale for Neiman Marcus unless it's a good buy for the customer."

RM IN ACTION 1.1: ALL-YOU-CAN-EAT CAN BE TOO MUCH

Some believe that Red Lobster's chief executive was ousted after a crab promotion lost money. The parent company says that wasn't the reason.

In 2003, television commercials for the nation's biggest chain of seafood restaurants invited diners to "*Red Lobster's Endless Crab: A celebration of all the hot, steaming snow crab legs you can eat.*" What top management of the 645-restaurant chain apparently never expected was a plethora of customers who would eat so much crab that they ate up all of the chain's profits, as well!

Management vastly underestimated how many Alaskan crab legs customers would consume during the promotion that ran from July 21 through Sept. 7 (2003). As a result, Darden Restaurants of Orlando replaced the president of Red Lobster; its biggest chain.

"It wasn't the second helping, it was the third one that hurt," company chairman Joe R. Lee said in a conference call with analysts. "Yeah, and maybe the fourth," added Dick Rivera, Darden's chief operating officer. Rivera has taken over as president of Red Lobster.

The former president, who had been in the job only 18 months, and who personally approved the Crabfest promotion, has left "to pursue other interests," the company said.

Many of the chain's locations reportedly started out by charging about $20 for an entree of all-you-can-eat crab and side dishes. When profits started slipping, managers raised the price by as much as $5 per diner, depending on the market, but it wasn't enough!

Excerpted on 11/11/2007 from www.stpetersburgtimes. com/2003/09/26/State/All_you_can_eat_was_t.shtml.

The Return on Investment Fallacy

Experienced businesspersons having read the previous portion of this chapter may (if somewhat reluctantly) agree that maximizing company profits should not be the primary purpose of a business. They would recognize that customers are equal parties to every trade, and thus it is part of their job to ensure their own customers make a profit (gain value) on every transaction. These same businesspersons may steadfastly maintain, however, that maximizing returns on an owner's investment, or increasing a business owner's wealth, is the true purpose of a business. Actually, the question of the purpose of business as it relates to the creation of wealth has occupied the thoughts and writings of countless bright and insightful individuals; including many studying in the field of **economics**.

As part of their study of wealth, economists study businesses and business profits. Like those in the field of accounting, economists have a formula for profits that should be understood by revenue managers:

Essential RM Term

Economics: The area of study concerned with the production, consumption, and transfer of wealth.

Economist's Profit Formula

Profit = The reward for risk

What an economist wishes to communicate by using this formula is simply that business organizations are not guaranteed a profit. Stated another way, profit is *"the compensation accruing to entrepreneurs for the assumption of risk in (a) business enterprise."*[3] Thus, business owners who actually do achieve a profit have done so as a result of their willingness to accept the very real risk of not making a profit.

Economics is the area of knowledge that describes how humans earn and spend their resources (money). When business owners elect to spend their own money by investing in a business, they do so to achieve investment returns that, when added to their original investment amount, increase these investors' total wealth.

A simplified formula for expressing an owner's **return on investment (ROI)** is stated as a percentage related to the owner's initial investment. ROI is commonly calculated as:

$$\frac{\text{Owner's investment return}}{\text{Owner's original investment}} = \text{Owner's return on investment (ROI)}$$

Essential RM Term

ROI: The short version of "Return on investment": ROI is the reward to investors for taking an investment risk.

To illustrate ROI, if an owner invests $800,000 in a business, and achieves $200,000 in investment returns (defined as revenue in excess of all expense), that owner's ROI would be 25 percent ($200,000 investment return/$800,000 original investment = 25% ROI).

In reality, calculating ROIs can be quite complex. When performing ROI calculations, legitimate questions about the process include whether investment returns before or after taxes should be considered, as well as how to accurately determine the amount initially invested (e.g., questions arise about whether the investment should include debt and equity financing and how to value assets).

Regardless of the finer points of ROI calculation, certainly it would *seem* it could be safely stated that *"the purpose of business is to increase the wealth of the business's owners."* In fact, the opposite is true.

The only legitimate purpose of a business is to increase the wealth of its *customers*. In fact, the only thing that can safely be said about a business is that it will not continue to exist simply because it is efficient, does a good job controlling costs, or creates many jobs. It should and will continue to exist *only* to the degree that it creates wealth for its customers. Noted management consultant Peter Drucker put it another way; *"The purpose of business is to create and keep a customer."* Businesses do so by ensuring that each customer transaction results in an increase in wealth *for the customer*. Sometimes managers of a company lament that their customers do not appreciate the fact that their business must make a profit (or earn investment returns) if it is to survive. Actually, this is not surprising when you recognize that customers are absolutely indifferent to the profit or ROI needs or goals of a business. Nor do customers care about a business's costs, its long-term financial goals, or internal workings, excepting for how those factors affect the value (wealth) gained by the consumer in a transaction with that business.

In fact, when asked, most customers would likely maintain that the lower the profits of a business, the *more* its customers benefit in a seller/buyer exchange. As a result, if a business-person bemoans the fact that they are not making a profit on a specific sale, or desired levels of ROI, that information will most often be met with the customer's glee, not sympathy.

Just as a focus on operating profits is a short-sighted business strategy, so too is overemphasis on maximizing owner/shareholder investment returns. If it seems to you that an inordinate amount of time in this chapter has been devoted to examining what businesses should *not* do, it is because much too often the same philosophical errors that confuse business professionals' views of their own purpose also affect their views about the purpose of revenue management.

THE PURPOSE OF REVENUE MANAGEMENT

Profits are the result of two tasks: generating revenue and controlling expenses. This could be a legitimate argument for those in management spending 50 percent of their time in each of these two processes. However, revenue managers who purchased this book thinking they would learn how to cleverly increase their prices to unsuspecting customers and thus maximize their own company profits by that clever pricing likely recognize by now that that is not the approach that we will be taking.

Thus far, you have learned that the purpose of a successful hospitality business is to provide profits to its customers (not itself), and as a result, increase those customers' wealth (not the wealth of the business's owners). Businesses that effectively service their customers' needs will prosper, achieving high levels of their own operating profits and producing attractive ROIs for the owners of the business. Henry Ford nicely summarized this:

> A business absolutely devoted to service will have only one worry about profits. They will be embarrassingly large.

> **Henry Ford**

It is a concept well understood by outstanding hospitality leaders as well. Ray Kroc, founder of McDonald's, put it this way:

> If you work just for money, you'll never make it; but if you love what you're doing and you always put the customer first, success will be yours.

> **Ray Kroc (Founder of McDonald's)**

The purpose of professional revenue management is to significantly increase company profits and owners' ROIs through advanced revenue management and strategic pricing techniques. These techniques are *always* customer-needs driven, not company-needs driven.

Revenue managers effectively manage revenue. What does it mean to *manage* revenue? The answer is too complex to provide in one or two sentences. In fact, it will take the entire contents of this book for you to learn what it truly means to become a professional at managing revenue in a hospitality setting.

This book will teach you to be a **customer-centric manager** of revenues.

Essential RM Terms

Revenue manager: The individual or team responsible for ensuring that a company's prices match a customer's willingness to pay. Abbreviated in this book as RM.

Customer-centric revenue management: A revenue management philosophy that places customer gain ahead of short-term revenue maximization in revenue management decision making.

You have already learned that only those businesses that provide their customers true value will stay in business. As a result, one way to consider the overall purpose of successful revenue managers is to recognize that their role is to help their businesses succeed by ensuring that customers receive true value in every transaction made with that business. For hospitality businesses, that means employing pricing strategies that result in charging prices that informed customers will willingly pay for the right products, in the right quantities, through the right **channels,** and at the right times.

Essential RM Term

Channel: A source of business customers. Also, a vehicle used to communicate with a source of customers.

Also known as a distribution channel.

Revenue management can be thought of as the entire set of strategies addressing the issue of value offered to customers. Strategic pricing is concerned with establishing a selling price that best *communicates* the value provided to customers.

When businesses set prices at levels that customers choose to freely and *willingly* pay, they acknowledge that customers are seeking the value provided by what they are buying and also that their own wealth increases when the customers buy. The process of setting that price, however, is complex. It requires revenue managers and those responsible for marketing to understand their customers well and to apply and communicate sophisticated pricing strategies with great skill. This book will show you exactly how to do just that.

THE PURPOSE AND DESIGN OF THE BOOK

If you can agree that your primary role as a revenue manager is to make your company, its owners, and you prosper by *first* making your customers prosper, you are ready to learn how revenue managers create prices that customers are willing to pay.

To help you learn how to make your customers rich, this book is divided into four major parts.

- Part I: Revenue Management Principles
- Part II: Revenue Management for Hoteliers
- Part III: Revenue Management for Foodservice Operators
- Part IV: Revenue Management in Action

Each part contains information that all revenue managers must understand. This is so because just as hoteliers initially learned much about rooms pricing from other businesses (e.g., the commercial airline industry), today's hoteliers can learn a good deal about RM and pricing from professionals in the foodservice industry. Likewise, restaurateurs can learn much about pricing from those in the lodging business. All revenue managers need to understand the application and evaluation of revenue management strategies and tactics.

The following will give you an overview of the specific information that is contained in this book's remaining chapters, as well as why it is important for you to know about it.

Part I: Revenue Management Principles

Part I of this book consists of five chapters. These chapters will introduce you to the foundational principles of revenue management. In business, managing revenue means accomplishing the very complex task of establishing and managing prices for the products and services the business offers for sale. Understanding how to do this well is critical to the success of your business.

You have now completed most of Chapter 1 (Introduction to Revenue Management).

In Chapter 2 (Strategic Pricing), you will learn about the important role that thoughtful pricing plays in business, as well as the serious limitations of utilizing either a supply and demand-based or a cost-based, rather than customer value-based, approach to pricing.

While it is easy to take the position that a hospitality operation's prices should be based on the economic theories of supply and demand, a closer look at those theories reveals that they are not a solid foundation for establishing prices or for managing revenue. In Chapter 2, you will learn why this is so.

In Chapter 2, you will also learn that the rationale for the traditional cost-based pricing approach was that, because revenue minus costs equal profits, costs were the single most important consideration in the creation of business profits. As a result, to maximize profits, it was believed, an organization should carefully manage its costs. It would then be following the advice given by U.S. Steel company founder Andrew Carnegie, who stated that a business should *"Watch costs and the profits take care of themselves."*[4] As reasonable as Carnegie's statement appears, you will discover why an undue focus on costs, as well as relating production costs directly to selling price, are both woefully inefficient and ineffective revenue management strategies.

In Chapter 3 (Value), you will come to know what all successful sellers must learn—namely, that individual consumers' own perceptions of the value and worth of a product is the primary reason they are willing to buy it. In addition, you will discover why consumer perceptions of value are more important to them than the supply of your product, its scarcity, your production costs, or your planned profits. This chapter carefully examines the profound but frequently unrecognized truth: *Value (like beauty) is in the eye of the beholder.*

In this same chapter, you will see why lessons you can learn from public auctions such as those held on eBay are critical to your understanding of consumer buying behavior and, ultimately, to your strategic pricing. In an eBay auction, there are many bidders when the

▶ RM ON THE WEB 1.1

Establishing prices strategically is a challenge for businesses in every industry. The Professional Pricing Society (PPS) is an association made up of individuals responsible for managing prices and revenues in many business segments. PPS offers its members workshops, conferences, training, and certification. You can learn more about this very specialized professional organization by exploring their site at: www.pricingsociety.com

When you arrive, click on *Pricing Experts Directory* to see a list of consulting companies that specialize in providing pricing-oriented advisory services.

price is low. As the amount bid increases, the number of potential buyers decreases. Finally, all but the winning bidder drops out. The resulting lesson is *not* that only a few consumers are willing to pay high prices. Rather, the lesson to be learned from an eBay auction can be briefly summarized as follows: *Different people, with identical information, about identical products, but under different buying circumstances, assign different personal values to the same product.*

For virtually every product on earth, different customers will hold different opinions about what that product is worth. This is why some buyers are willing to pay over $1,000 for a pound of Tsar Imperial Beluga caviar, while others would not consider paying even $1.00 to eat it, but might be willing to part with $1,000 rather than to be forced to eat it.

Applying lessons from an eBay auction to your own revenue management (hereafter called RM) activities will allow you to differentiate among your customers and your prices. Doing so will help you identify the customers who *willingly*, and gladly, pay the prices charged for your products and services, as well as those who would resist buying from you regardless of the prices you charge.

In this important chapter you will also learn about the four key buyer-types who purchase hospitality products and exactly what motivates each of them to buy. You will explore how variations in quality, service level, and price directly impact these buyers' views of value and the importance of communicating the value of your own products and services to them.

In the hospitality industry, some professional revenue managers (RMs) emphasize the importance of data management in the revenue optimization process. As a result, mathematical formulas and models take on great importance to them. Other RMs emphasize the importance of their own insight, skill, and experience in making good revenue-optimization decisions. Chapter 3 concludes with a detailed examination of the role data collection and analysis will play in your effort to optimize revenue. It then contrasts the importance of these processes with the equally important task of successfully applying your own insight, experience, and intuition to your future RM-related decision making.

Chapter 4 (Differential Pricing) begins with a review of revenue management principles you will have studied thus far. The chapter then investigates in detail precisely how consumers' differing perceptions of value lead logically to the practice of charging different prices to different customers. You will learn that the best revenue managers do not seek to establish a single price for their products but, rather, establish a set of prices that best satisfies the desires of all of their potential customers. In fact, effective revenue managers utilize a variety of well-established *differential* pricing techniques that allow them to increase their company's own profitability by charging different prices to customers with different willingness to pay. Of course, price differentiation must be carefully planned and implemented. As a result, you will learn about the limits associated with differential pricing, as well as eight specific techniques you can use to apply differential pricing effectively.

With thoughtful planning and understanding, differential pricing strategies such as offering unique prices based on customer characteristics (e.g., student or senior citizen discounts), the location at which a sale is made, the timing of the sale, and the quantity of product purchased can all be implemented. The specific ways RMs can utilize these approaches will be examined in detail.

The distribution channel in which a sale is made (e.g., a third-party Internet site, franchisor web site, or travel agency) can also be used to affect pricing, as can the unique version of product sold. In addition, the concept of bundling (combining) items for special pricing and the practice of altering price based on payment terms will be presented as effective strategies that can be utilized when implementing differential pricing.

Perhaps just as importantly, in Chapter 4 you will discover why differential pricing serves to benefit all of the members of society by ensuring that the maximum number of customers have access to fairly priced hospitality goods and services that can enhance their lives. The chapter concludes by examining the conceptual difference between an RM who practices revenue management and one who practices revenue *optimization*, which is superior.

In Chapter 5 (The Revenue Manager's Role), you will examine the rationale for making *"Revenue Management in the Hospitality Industry"* a specialized field of study. The chapter poses and answers this simple question:

> "Why is specialized knowledge required to effectively price and manage the sale of hospitality industry goods and services?"

Essential RM Term

Constrained supply: The condition that exists when sellers cannot readily increase the amount of products or services available for sale when consumer demand for them increases.

As you will discover in the chapter, lodging and foodservice products and services must be managed differently from other consumer products because of their **constrained supply**.

The effect of constrained supply is evident when you consider that many consumer products industries can react to increased demand for their products simply by making more of them. If, for example, the demand for Apple's newest iPhone version increases significantly, more of them can be manufactured. In contrast, a hotel that consists of 400 rooms simply cannot sell more than 400 rooms in one night, regardless of how many potential guests want to buy a room. In a similar manner, a restaurant with 200 seats can only offer that same number of seats for sale during its busiest, as well as its slowest, periods of customer demand. The RMs in both these hotel and restaurant examples will find their ability to meet the demands of their customers is restricted; or constrained due to limited supply. Because that is true, the pricing strategies best used in such situations are highly specialized.

Even after mastering the conceptual complexities of pricing **hard constraint** supply and **soft constraint** products explained in Chapter 5, RMs will find that they are not free to charge whatever they wish for the products and services they sell.

Essential RM Terms

Hard constraint: A supply constraint that cannot be removed regardless of product demand.
   Examples include hotel rooms and the capacity of natural gas pipelines.

Soft constraint: A supply constraint that can, with sufficient lead time, and/or a reasonable expense, be removed or lessened.
   Examples include the commercial airline and car rental industries, as well as the taxi business and many foodservice operations.

In the United States, businesses have great latitude in setting prices for the things they sell. RMs must recognize, however, that they do not have the unrestricted, unregulated ability to determine the fairness of their product and services prices. Nor should they have it. For example, no legitimate case could be made for charging customers different prices based on religion, race, or national origin. Doing so would be morally wrong. It would also be a violation of federal law.

Society at large, working through its various governmental entities, now has and will continue to have a direct influence on the prices that may be charged in the hospitality industry. Legislation enacted at the federal, state, and local levels currently influences pricing and revenue optimization decision making in the hospitality industry. This chapter presents and explains the societal rationale for implementing, and the penalties for ignoring, the most significant pieces of pricing-related legislation.

All RMs would likely agree that effective revenue optimization must be achieved in a legal manner but the authors argue further that it should also be achieved in an ethical manner. Because of this position, in Chapter 5, you will also examine in detail the significant issues related to ethical aspects of revenue management.

Chapter 5 concludes with an examination of the tasks and responsibilities commonly assigned to RMs working in the hospitality industry. As you will learn, the duties performed by RMs and the business titles they hold vary, but commonalities among their jobs do exist. This is because all RMs follow a crucial five-step process, explained in this chapter.

Another commonality among RMs in hospitality is the fact that often they will be only one member of a larger group that impacts revenue management decision making. Members of this important group (which also includes customers) do not necessarily share the same

---

RM IN ACTION 1.2: THE ROOM RATE WAS . . . HOW MUCH?

Are RMs free to price their products in any manner they choose? Not in Texas. Consider what happened in that state when some Houston area residents sought to escape the threat posed by the rapidly approaching Hurricane Rita. Some travelers escaped the wind and rain, only to find themselves exposed to hotel rooms offered for sale at twice their normal price. The resulting news headline and brief excerpt summarizes what happened next.

Texas Attorney General Settles Price Gouging Complaint. San Antonio's St. Anthony Hotel Will Pay $190,000 in Consumer Restitution

"Hotels cannot take advantage of Texans during a disaster," said Texas Attorney General Greg Abbott. "Today's agreement ensures Texans fleeing a disaster area will have access to standard room rates. We will remain vigilant and will enforce state price gouging laws."

The Texas Deceptive Trade Practices Act prohibits any business from taking advantage of a declared disaster by selling or leasing fuel, food, lodging, medicine, or other necessity at an exorbitant rate. Violators can face penalties of up to $20,000 per incident.

The St. Anthony was not the only hotel fined, and as you will learn in Chapter 5, Texas is not the only state that carefully watches the pricing decisions made by hospitality industry RMs.

Excerpted on 8/25/2009 from Texas Attorney General press release posted at www.oag.state.tx.us/consumer/lawsuits.php?id=2192.

agenda, but they do greatly influence the day-to-day decision making of any hospitality industry RM. As a result, it is important that you understand the roles and goals of these diverse group members. Upon completing this last introductory chapter, you will be ready to apply what you have learned, and what you will learn, to the fascinating challenge of managing revenues in the exciting hospitality industry.

Part II: Revenue Management for Hoteliers

Part II of this book contains four chapters that present the specific revenue management strategies and tactics used by RMs working in the lodging segment of the hospitality industry. Despite its title *Revenue Management for Hoteliers*, this part's content is applicable to those RMs working in full-service hotels, condo-hotels, limited-service hotels, bed and breakfasts, motels, cruise ships, and any other housing facility facing constrained supply of their product, as well as for limited-seating capacity events (e.g., concerts, movies shown in theaters, banquet halls and sporting events).

In Chapter 6 (Forecasting Demand), you will learn why it is so important for RMs working in the lodging industry to create accurate estimates of the guest demand for their products. Knowing the number of guests who will be staying in their hotels, or seeking to stay on specific future dates, directly affects both the operation of the property and the specific revenue optimization strategies the hotel will choose to implement.

To create accurate demand forecasts, RMs evaluate their hotels' past performance as well as the current buyer demand for their products and service. They, then, analyze a variety of additional factors to estimate future demand. In this chapter, you will learn about the specific tools RMs use to forecast demand. You will also learn how to analyze and respond to the data these tools produce. This chapter will also explain to you why it is generally counterproductive for an RM to allow guest demand to dictate the prices that will be charged for hotel rooms. Although the authors recognize that implementing *yield management* as a pricing strategy has long been very popular in the hotel industry, in this chapter you will learn why it can no longer be considered an effective pricing technique.

Essential RM Term

Yield management: A demand-based revenue management strategy, first initiated by commercial airline companies. It seeks to maximize income via manipulation of selling prices.

Although the process has been described and practiced in myriad ways, **yield management** has been defined in the hospitality industry as "a technique used to maximize the revenue or yield, obtained from a service operation, given limited capacity and uneven demand."[5]

Because of this book's view that all revenue management strategies must be customer driven, *yield management*, a term sometimes mistakenly used interchangeably with *revenue management*, will be examined chiefly from its historical perspective and its use by the airline companies that originally developed it. You will learn in Chapter 6 that while yield management was an innovative concept when first introduced by the commercial airline industry, it worked best when consumers' price-related knowledge was limited. Today, a lodging consumer's price-related knowledge is clearly not limited. As a result, this chapter presents the case that yield management, as hoteliers have practiced it in the recent past, is not at all an effective strategy for building customer loyalty and repeat business. In fact, honest industry professionals would admit that the practice is now widely viewed by the general public as an opportunistic and excessively greedy business strategy.

RM IN ACTION 1.3: DIRTY WORDS?

USA Today has published its travel team's 25 pivotal changes that "transformed the way we travel." Number 14 on the list was "yield management." This is how it was described:

> "Yield management—dirty words to travelers . . . now is used universally by airlines, hotels and car rental companies."[6]

The article describes how the identified industries adjust prices based on various factors that affect demand for the products they sell.

Dirty words?

Based on this article, it would appear the hotel industry has not done a good job explaining its pricing rationale to the traveling public. This is an industry communication and marketing problem, not a consumer understanding problem.

If you are having difficulty appreciating the very real perception problem consumers frequently have with a pricing system designed to vary prices based on demand rather than on increased operating costs or the value delivered to customers, consider your own reaction to the following *hypothetical* article if it appeared in today's edition of *USA Today*:

Gasoline Companies Raise Prices for the Weekend

Major gasoline suppliers announced today that, in anticipation of large numbers of drivers hitting the roads for the upcoming holiday weekend, they would be increasing their fuel prices an average of 35 percent for all the grades of gasoline they offer for sale.

Said Tom Jones, spokesperson for the Acme Oil Company, one of the country's largest suppliers of gasoline, "Our historical records and future forecasts tell us there will be big demand for gasoline this weekend so we will sell lots of it. Because so many people will want gas, we decided it would be a good idea for us to raise our prices $1.00 per gallon effective at 8:00 A.M. Friday morning, but we'll reduce our prices again after the weekend is over and travel returns to normal.

If *you* had just finished reading the article and you were a driver planning a long holiday trip, would you too have dirty words for Mr. Jones and his company?

In Chapter 6 you will also learn that accurate demand forecasts have a significant impact on legitimate pricing tactics used by lodging industry RMs. This is so because nearly all RMs working in lodging will be managing a hard constraint supply, while their restaurateur counterparts typically encounter soft constraint supply. As a result, the pricing strategies undertaken by lodging RMs who create and analyze various types of demand forecasts are different from their restaurant industry counterparts. For lodging industry RMs, the impact of demand on price, the impact of price on demand, and the impact of demand forecasts on revenue optimization strategies are all important concepts. After reading Chapter 6, you will know why and how you can forecast future demand for your business.

In Chapter 7 (Inventory and Price Management), you will learn how lodging-industry RMs monitor the number of rooms available for sale and the prices to be charged for them. By doing so, they can maximize income and actually increase the amount of revenue generated by their properties *without* raising their prices. In fact, effective inventory management can even allow an RM to increase total revenues when reducing prices!

The way RMs ultimately manage room availability is affected by the type of customer who purchases the room. In this chapter, you will learn the inventory-control techniques RMs use when reserving rooms for their individual guests and for guests who are part of a group or those who have a special contractual arrangement with the hotel.

Essential RM Term

Overbook: To accept reservations for more rooms than a hotel has available or in inventory.

Sometimes referred to as *overselling* or being *oversold*.

One of the biggest issues facing lodging industry RMs relates to selling rooms when none are available for sale. The **overbooking** of hotel rooms is a controversial issue within the hotel industry and can be the cause of significant customer and hotel staff frustration. In Chapter 7 you will examine the financial, legal, and ethical aspects of overbooking.

RMs must thoroughly understand the concept of pricing. In Chapter 7 you will review the most important of the hospitality industry's *traditional* room pricing theories and strategies. Looking backward prior to looking forward is important in many areas of knowledge, because, as Aristotle stated; *"If you would understand anything, observe its beginning and its development."*[7]

In this chapter, you will also learn how hoteliers currently establish their room rates as well as how they can impose special restrictions on guests' purchases to impact the amount of income generated from room sales. The chapter concludes with a summary of inventory and price management principles important to RMs.

Hoteliers seek to make it as easy as possible for guests to make room reservations. As a result, today's hotel guests can reserve a room using a variety of different methods. In Chapter 8 (Distribution Channel Management), you will learn how RMs administer various sources of room reservations. As an RM you will manage different channels in different ways because each is unique. For example, in some distribution channels a representative of the hotel is in direct contact with the guests. This is true, for example, of the guest who arrives at a hotel without a room reservation and immediately seeks information about room availability and rates. Alternatively, for those guests making reservations using the Internet, no direct personal contact takes place but critical information is exchanged nonetheless.

In Chapter 8, you will learn that distribution channels can be classified as either electronic or nonelectronic. Nonelectronic channels include those designed to make room sales to individuals who are physically on the hotel property, as well as to those who may call the property. In addition to those hotel staff who greet guests in person or answer phone calls, a hotel's sales and marketing staff represents an additional distribution channel. In nearly all cases, another important additional source of room sales will be the locally funded nonprofit entity responsible for promoting travel and tourism to the area in which the hotel is located. In this chapter, you will learn how each of these nonelectronic channels can help you optimize your property's revenue.

Direct customer contact is important, but increasingly, guests utilize one or more electronic sources to secure information about hotels and to make their sleeping room or meeting room reservations. The Internet is a well-known distribution channel but in this chapter you will learn that there are at least three distinctly different distribution channels housed on the Internet, and each must be managed differently. RMs know that there are important electronic distribution channels that operate in addition to the Internet, and these must also be well understood by you. In this chapter, you will learn about all of the major channels of distribution and the rationale associated with using each one. As well, you will learn specific principles related to managing each of these channels to optimize your revenues.

In Chapter 9 (Evaluation of Revenue Management Efforts in the Lodging Industry), you will learn how a hotel RM's performance can be evaluated. The assessment of a revenue management team's efforts can be internal or external, scheduled or sporadic, and in-depth or cursory, but all RMs need to understand the tools commonly used for their evaluations, as well as the strengths and weaknesses of each measure.

The chapter begins with an examination of the RM paradox of balancing **average daily rate (ADR)** maximization with that of **occupancy percentage** maximization.

Essential RM Terms

Average daily rate (ADR): The average (mean) selling price of guest rooms during a specific time period, such as a day, week, month, or year.
The formula for ADR is:

> Total room revenue ÷ Total rooms sold = ADR

Occupancy percentage: The number of rooms sold during a specific time period; expressed as a percentage of all rooms available to sell during that same period.
The formula for occupancy percentage is:

> Total rooms sold ÷ Total rooms available for sale = Occupancy percentage

In most hotel markets, it is easy for an RM to significantly increase room rates (ADR); however, doing so will most often reduce occupancy rates. In a similar manner, achieving high occupancy rates is relatively easy, but only if ADRs are significantly reduced. This paradox has resulted in the lodging industry's development of a variety of sophisticated measurements that will be used to evaluate your revenue management-related decision making. In Chapter 9 you will learn about all of these. Knowing about them is important because in many cases the measurement tools are used to appraise your personal performance. As well, they are the same ones used by internal and external reviewers to evaluate the financial results achieved by your hotel.

Today, RMs are most often evaluated by using one or more of the following industry-standard revenue generation assessment tools:

RevPAR

RevPOR

GOPPAR

Essential RM Terms

RevPAR: Short for "revenue per available room." It is the average revenue generated by each available guest room during a specific period of time.

The two formulas for RevPAR yield identical results and are:

$$\text{ADR} \times \text{Occupancy percentage} = \text{RevPAR}$$

or

$$\frac{\text{Total revenue}}{\text{Total rooms available for sale}} = \text{RevPAR}$$

Unless otherwise stated, the revenue figure utilized for RevPAR calculations is "rooms revenue" only.

RevPOR: Short for "revenue per occupied room," the average revenue generated by each occupied guest room during a specific period of time.

The formula for RevPOR is:

$$\frac{\text{Total revenue}}{\text{Total occupied rooms}} = \text{RevPOR}$$

Unless otherwise stated, the revenue figure utilized for RevPOR calculations consists of "all rooms and non-rooms revenue."

GOPPAR: Short for "Gross operating profit per available room." This is the average gross operating profit (GOP) generated by each available guest room during a specific period of time. Also written as GoPAR.

The formula for GOPPAR is:

$$\frac{\text{Total revenue} - \text{Management controllable expense}}{\text{Total rooms available for sale}} = \text{GOPPAR}$$

The revenue figure utilized for GOPPAR calculations consists of all rooms and nonrooms (total) operating revenue.

In addition, you will learn how managerial accountants assess the ability of a hotel and its RM team to convert increased revenue dollars to increased gross operating profit dollars. This ability to cause added revenue to *flow through* to increased profits is crucial and can reveal much about an RM's effectiveness in generating incremental revenues.

The hotel industry is highly competitive. In Chapter 9, you will also learn how to evaluate your own property's revenue producing performance relative to that of your

> ► **RM ON THE WEB 1.2**
>
> The Educational Institute, the nonprofit training organization that is part of the American Hotel and Lodging Association (AH&LA), provides educational materials and professional certification in a variety of lodging-related specializations.
>
> One of EI's newest certification programs is for revenue managers. You can learn more about the requirements for certification by exploring its site at: www.ei-ahla.org
>
> When you arrive, click *Certification* to see a list of specializations for which certification is offered. Click on *Manager*, then select *Certified Hospitality Revenue Manager* (CHRM) to review the requirements for EI's RM-oriented certification.

Essential RM Term

Competitive set: A group of similar and directly competing lodging properties to which an individual hotel's operating performance is compared.

Frequently referred to as the individual property's *comp set*.

Essential RM Term

Market segment: A subset of a customer group that can be readily identified by one or more common but individual customer characteristics (for example, the customer's income, gender, or purpose of travel).

Essential RM Term

User-generated content (web site): A web site in which the content is produced by the site's end users. Typical content includes news, information, opinion, gossip, and customer reviews of businesses.

Commonly shortened to UGC.

competitive set via analysis of the Smith Travel Research (STR) company's various Smith Travel Accommodations Reports (STAR reports).

Smith Travel Research and other organizations like it produce a variety of specialized hotel revenue assessment reports. These reports evaluate a hotel or group of hotel's performance *relative* to its competitors.

The ability to read and properly interpret STAR reports and others like them is critical to hoteliers' understanding of their own revenue management challenges and successes. This chapter presents the hands-on information needed to read, analyze, and interpret relative performance on key revenue-generation measures including occupancy, ADR, RevPAR, and market share. You can learn a great deal about your own market and the effectiveness of your rate strategies by assessing the revenue-generating performance of those hotels with which you compete. Chapter 9 will show you exactly how to do that.

Experienced RMs know that the revenue-generating potential of their hotels is determined in great part by the features or attributes of the property and the appeal those attributes have for a particular **market segment** traveler.

RMs who seek a complete understanding of how revenues are generated in their hotels know they must carefully monitor the source of their various customers, as well as the costs incurred when selling to them. Thus, source of business and distribution channel assessment are important and the chapter addresses how to evaluate each of these critical concepts.

Chapter 9 concludes with an examination of how RMs can monitor the increasingly important impact of customers who post negative or positive comments about their hotels on **user generated content (UGC)** Internet sites such as Twitter, TripAdvisor, Facebook, My Space, and others like them.

Armed with a complete evaluation of their current performance, RMs can assess their properties' **pace reports** and may reconsider financial targets and goals. Using solid information and their own professional insight, they can then make appropriate decisions about future prices to be charged for their rooms and the best distribution channels for selling them.

Modern hoteliers communicate the value their hotels offer through a variety of creative pricing strategies. The value message presented to guests is a complex one and depends on a variety of crucial factors:

- Franchise affiliation
- Location
- Distribution channel
- Facility
- Services offered

These characteristics affect the strategic pricing of guest rooms, including the determination of **rack,** discounted, and other room rates.

As a professional RM, you will continually be evaluated on how well you understand your business and how you use available information to improve your decision making. Because that is so, a thorough understanding of how industry professionals assess the revenue optimization performance of a hotel will be critical to your own professional success. Chapter 9 has been written to provide you with that understanding.

RM AT WORK 1.1

"How can you be unhappy?" asked Charles Lohr. "Our occupancy last month was 76 percent; that's almost 5 points higher than the same month last year. And our ADR was $144.85—that's about $4.00 more than last year. And our guest satisfaction scores for the month were higher than ever. We had a great month!"

Charles was the front office manager at the Branchwater Hotel, a 225 room full-service property located near a busy industrial park. Charles also served as the leader of the hotel's revenue management team. The

team's role in the hotel was to establish room rates and manage rooms inventory based on the data generated by the hotel's property management systems (PMS), as well as the information provided by the hotel's sales department. He was in his own office, talking with Sara Argote, the GM of the property.

"Well, I'm not looking at how we did compared to last year," replied Sara, "I'm comparing our change to our comp set's change. It's true we were up 5 occupancy points from last year, but the comp set was up just over 10 points."

RM AT WORK 1.1 *(continued)*

"But what about their rates?" asked Charles. "What happened there? Did their rates go up or down, and by how much?"

"Well, let's take a look at that," replied Sara, "and then we can assess what happened last month and see if we need to make our own rate strategy adjustments in the future."

RM Considerations:

1. Assume the ADR of the competitive set increased significantly (e.g., more than 7 percent) last month. What would be your assessment of the Branchwater's revenue

management performance compared to its comp set?

2. Assume the ADR of the competitive set decreased very significantly last month (e.g., more than 10 percent). What would be your assessment of the Branchwater's revenue management performance compared to its comp set?

3. Assume you were the hotel's GM. What additional revenue-related information would you want to have before assessing whether your property's revenue management team did a *good* job last month?

▶ RM ON THE WEB 1.3

The Hospitality Sales and Marketing Association International (HSMAI) is a nonprofit organization of marketing professionals who work in the hospitality industry. Its mission statement proclaims that it intends:

> "To be the leading source for sales and marketing information, knowledge business development, and networking for professionals in tourism, travel, and hospitality."

Through its HSMAI University, the association provides its members with professional development activities, including those related to RM. You can learn more about this specialized professional organization and the RM training resources it provides by exploring its Americas site at: www.hsmai.org/Americas.cfm

Part III: Revenue Management for Foodservice Operators

In this unique section of the book you will learn how food and beverage professionals can implement and assess their own version of revenue management and strategic pricing.

Like lodging customers, those guests who frequent a foodservice operation do so in a quest to satisfy their own value-based needs. Those restaurants that consistently meet their guests' needs will flourish, while those that do not simply cease to exist. A consistent theme of this introductory chapter, and this entire book, is that a business exists only for the purpose of providing value to its customers. By successfully doing that, it also creates profits for itself. In the two chapters contained in this part of the book, you will learn how successful foodservice operators strategically manage pricing to increase their customer's view of value and, as a result, increase their own profits.

It is interesting to note that hoteliers and restaurateurs have historically used very different pricing methods for optimizing revenues and profits. In Chapter 10 (Revenue Management for Food and Beverage Services), you will learn about the three most popular methods used to determine a foodservice operation's menu prices, as well as the philosophic rationale put forth by the proponents of each method. You will also learn that in each of these traditional pricing systems, the *cost* of the food or beverage product to be sold is the major factor influencing prices charged to customers. Understanding these traditional approaches to foodservice pricing is important because RMs will so frequently encounter their use.

Understanding traditional cost-based menu pricing systems is also important because it will help you better understand why foodservice operators should carefully *avoid* using any menu pricing method, including the three systems historically used, that is based solely on the prices paid for products sold. Instead, modern RMs in foodservice, just like their lodging industry counterparts, should employ a differential pricing system to optimize revenues. This is not because an operator's costs are unimportant to pricing but because costs are merely *one* among many factors that directly affect customers' perceptions of value they receive.

To better understand the traditional relationship between product costs and pricing in the foodservice industry, it is important to recognize that in the minds of many food and beverage professionals, the terms food *quality* and food *value* are synonymous. These operators would argue, for example, that because a USDA Prime steak is of greater *quality* than an identical USDA Select steak, the *value* of the prime steak is higher. That's simply not true. The reason it is not true is that for many, and perhaps most, of the foodservice industry's customers, the terms value and food quality are not synonymous.

You can prove this easily simply by considering whether those non–hospitality industry friends with whom you most frequently dine could accurately explain the actual difference between a USDA Prime and a USDA Select steak without first asking you! Your friends represent typical customers.

What is very true today is that foodservice customers are diverse. Within this diverse population, each customer subgroup possesses its own value perceptions and definitions of personal profit in a foodservice transaction. Certainly, for some foodservice customers, the highest-quality levels of food and drink are critically important. For other customers a foodservice operation's convenience, low prices, atmosphere, or speed of service are much more important. What you will learn as you complete this chapter is that your product costs may influence the prices you charge but the influence of at least ten other factors will be *more* critical to your customers and to your own revenue optimization efforts. In Chapter 10, you will closely examine these ten critical factors and you will learn why each must be thoughtfully taken into account prior to establishing your menu prices.

In Chapter 11 (Evaluation of Revenue Management Efforts in Food and Beverage Services), you will learn how F&B professionals monitor and evaluate the revenue-generating characteristics of their own operations. Doing so is a three-part process that includes the following:

- The examination of revenue-generating sources
- The measurement of change in revenue generation
- The evaluation of revenue-generating efficiency

Examination of Revenue-Generating Sources

In some foodservice operations, there would appear to be only one area or source of revenue generation. A small diner, for example, would likely contain only one dining area. It does not follow, however, that the revenue manager for such an operation would consider the diner to have only one revenue source. While it is true that in this example only one physical dining area exists, the revenues generated during different periods of the day (e.g., breakfast, lunch, or dinner) and through different delivery methods (e.g., dine-in versus carryout) may vary greatly. In a similar manner, RMs working in the QSR industry are very much aware that revenues generated from their operations' drive-through customers should be assessed separately from that of their dine-in guests if they are to optimize operational revenues in both areas.

Increasingly, revenue managers in foodservice find that the examination of their unique **revenue sources** must be undertaken in new and innovative ways.

Increased guest adoption of changing technology (such as text-messaging and use of cell-phone-based e-mail) will no doubt continue to challenge RMs to define their operations' revenue sources in meaningful ways.

Essential RM Term

QSR: Short for "quick-service restaurant," an operation that provides a limited menu and usually, limited at-the-table services. QSR customers typically order food at a counter or drive-through window. When serving menu items, single use product wrappings, dishes, flatware and beverage containers are most common.

QSR restaurants are commonly referred to by those *outside* the hospitality industry as *Fast Food* restaurants.

Essential RM Term

Revenue source (foodservice): A subsection of an operation that contributes a definable portion of the operation's total income. Typical factors used in foodservice to differentiate revenue sources include product sold, time of day, and the method of product ordering or delivery.

Measurement of Revenue Change

Are foodservice unit sales increasing? Decreasing? By how much? In which sources of revenue? Why? RMs must be experts within their organizations at accurately answering questions such as these. In this section of Chapter 11, you will learn about the formulas and calculations RMs use to address such complex questions.

Evaluation of Revenue-Generating Efficiency

All foodservice units generate some level of revenue. Of most interest to RMs, however, is the issue of how efficiently that revenue is generated. A variety of important factors can affect this assessment. For example, larger foodservice units typically produce more income than smaller units. Effective RMs would want to know, however, if the increased revenue generated justifies the larger building and operating costs associated with maintaining the bigger unit. In a similar manner, one foodservice operation may generate a higher level of revenue than another, but it incurs significantly more labor cost in doing so. Is the revenue vs. cost trade-off beneficial in meeting the operation's profit goals? RMs should know how to answer such a question and in this chapter you will learn how.

Finally, the efficiency with which a foodservice operation is managed greatly affects its revenue generating capability. There are a variety of useful performance traits and

RM IN ACTION 1.4: RESTAURATEURS MANAGE NEW CHANNELS TO MANAGE REVENUE

While channel management is most often associated with revenue managers working in hotels, as the following excerpt shows, the changing world of channel management is important to revenue managers in all areas of the hospitality industry.

ANN ARBOR, Mich. (Nov. 27) Domino's Pizza, based here, says a Web-enabled cell-phone ordering service using text messaging is boosting sales by a mid-single-digit amount at the approximately 2,700 U.S. restaurants now accepting such orders.[8]

To use the system, Dominos cell-phone users simply log on to *www.mobile.dominos.com* and enter their choice of pizza, side items, and soft drink, along with a delivery address.

Once orders are placed, a "store locator" capability built into the system determines which Dominos unit should receive the order, based on the address associated with the customers' mobile number.

The lesson to be learned? As always, innovation in customer-focused order-taking methods will mean new sources of business and new challenges for those RMs who price products and manage their operations' revenues.

indices currently used to evaluate the effectiveness of foodservice managers. From the perspective of an RM, however, the calculation and interpretation of **RevPASH** is one of the very best.

Essential RM Term

RevPASH: Short for "Revenue Per Available Seat Hour." It is the revenue generated during a specified time period divided by the number of seat hours available during that period.

The formula for RevPASH is:

$$\frac{\text{Total period revenue}}{\text{Number of available seats} \times \text{Hours of seat availability}} = \text{RevPASH}$$

In Chapter 11 you will learn how to calculate and interpret results from this new, innovative, and foodservice-specific revenue management tool developed by Dr. Sheryl E. Kimes.[9]

Part IV: Revenue Management in Action

In this final section of the text, you will learn how RMs in hospitality and hospitality-related industries can apply innovative revenue optimization strategies to creatively achieve their own unique RM-related objectives.

In Chapter 12 (Specialized Applications of Revenue Management), you will discover that a variety of organizations providing goods and services to their customers can use the revenue optimization principles presented in this book. Examples include golf courses, nightclubs, ski resorts, and concert venues, to name but a few such businesses. Those RMs working in businesses possessing specific and readily identifiable characteristics will find that they can apply the concepts of demand forecasting, inventory allocation, and differential pricing just as effectively as their colleagues working in hotels and restaurants. In this chapter, you will learn to identify the specific organizational characteristics that allow the application of revenue management principles.

As you progress through this book, you will no doubt recognize that it has been written primarily for RMs who are responsible for the sales optimization efforts at a single business site. Increasingly, however, talented and effective RMs are being given the responsibility for overseeing the revenue optimization efforts in organizations that operate multiple business units. Thus, for example, a company operating several hotels or restaurants may choose to assign one RM the task of overseeing the revenue management-related work undertaken at each of its individual properties. In this chapter, you will learn about the unique responsibilities and challenges of those RMs assigned multiunit responsibilities.

Yet another specialized revenue management role is that of assisting franchisees in utilizing revenue management-related resources provided by their franchisors. The hospitality industry is heavily franchised. In this chapter, you will learn how those RMs employed by franchise companies work to support their franchisees, as well as other important partners located inside and outside their companies.

Essential RM Term

Destination marketing: The advertising and promotion of travel and tourism activities in a specifically designated geographic area.

The chapter concludes with an overview of the responsibilities and challenges faced by those professionals working in the area of **destination marketing**; yet another specialized application of revenue management.

Anyone who has ever heard the city of New York referred to as *The Big Apple* or Florida as the *Sunshine State* understands well the power of a cleverly designed and professionally implemented campaign to promote travel and tourism to a specific geographic area, rather than to a single business in that area.

Because geographic areas have many of the same characteristics as do hotels and restaurants (e.g., constrained supply of goods and services available, seasonal demand that can vary widely, and a diverse range of potential customer types), you will learn that the skills you will have acquired when you reach this chapter can be directly applied to an array of destination marketing settings and jobs.

Chapter 13 (Building Better Business), is the final chapter of the book. The chapter begins by emphasizing the importance to RMs of high-quality revenue. Not all revenue is created equally. Some sources of revenue are simply better for business than are others. For example, $1,000 in revenue from one customer source might generate $100 in profits, while that same amount of revenue from another customer type might generate $200 in profits. It is the goal of an RM to optimize, not merely maximize, revenues. In this chapter, you will learn about four key strategies RMs use to build better business within their own organizations.

Building better business in very good economic times can be easy because RMs may choose the best one among several potential buyers of their products (it is usually more difficult in slower economic times because buyers are scarce). In this chapter, you will learn techniques RMs use to differentiate and choose among various pieces of potential business based on the amount and quality of revenue offered by each alternative. Using such information, RMs can immediately assess the impact of replacing one source of revenue with another. The chapter examines two additional management concepts that RMs must also consider as they seek to optimize their revenues during periods when business is very good.

Due to the cyclical nature of business, most RMs will find they must try to build better business in periods of weak economic activity, as well as in times of strong activity. When customers are scarce, some RMs turn to price discounting in an effort to maintain high revenue levels. In this chapter, you will learn how such a discounting strategy negatively affects an operation's bottom line. You will also learn how to utilize a tool designed to evaluate the impact on a business of price discounting.

2008 and 2009 were very poor years in the hospitality industry. During that time, some companies maintained or even surpassed revenue levels achieved in prior years. For most companies, however, the global recession experienced during that time resulted in significantly reduced sales. While such a significant industrywide revenue slowdown is not common, it is likely that during your career you will encounter strong, moderate, and weak demand for the products and services you sell. For that reason, the chapter examines two concepts (in addition to discounting) that all RMs must consider when seeking to build better business during a weakened business climate.

Throughout this book, we will make the case that applying revenue optimization strategy to the hospitality industry is both an art and a science. The art lies in knowing your customers so well that it is possible to discover ways in which your **target market** can be divided into unique segments such that higher prices can be charged to the high-willingness to pay segments and lower prices charged to the low-willingness to pay segments.

Essential RM Term

Target market: The potential customers to whom a business's marketing activities and message are directed.

The science involved in RM requires the application of various analytical techniques used to set and update prices and control product inventories in a way that optimizes revenues from each of the various willingness-to-pay segments. The science, and especially the mathematics background, required to utilize advanced analytical techniques can be significant. In this text, however, the mathematical background required to utilize the analysis tools presented will be limited to basic and advanced algebra.

In all cases, the information presented in this book was selected to help RMs do their best work. The authors recognize that information is not the same as knowledge. Today's RMs can easily find themselves drowning in information. It will be those RMs' understanding of how to sort, analyze, and apply that information that determines their success. As a result, the book takes both a conceptual and very hands-on approach to RM.

In selecting all of the content for this book, the authors were ever mindful of management scholar W. Edward Deming's insightful observation: "It is not enough to do your best; you must know what to do, and then do your best."[10]

Let's get started!

RM AT WORK 1.2

"According to my calculations, it's about $2.55 per delivery," said Connie.

"That's includes everything?" asked Chad. "Labor costs, vehicle, . . . packaging?"

"Everything" replied Connie.

They were discussing the additional costs associated with starting their new on-campus pizza delivery service. Connie and Chad were partners in one of the country's largest franchised pizza chains.

Business was good, their product tasted great and because their store was adjacent to the campus, the University supplied a large, hungry and built-in market. It was service to that market Connie and Chad wanted to expand by offering their new "*To Your Dorm Room*" delivery program.

"Well, I guess that means we need to charge at least $2.55 more per pizza," said Chad.

"Not necessarily" said Connie. "One dorm room might order two or more pizzas. Maybe we should charge a flat $2.55 delivery fee instead?

"Connie, maybe it should be $3.00 per delivery," said Chad. "We need to make a profit on this service or we shouldn't offer it. Right?"

RM Considerations:

1. Assume Connie discovered a mathematical error in her calculations that, when corrected, increased the estimated cost of the pizza delivery program from $2.55 to $3.55 per delivery. Would such a discovery also immediately increase by $1.00 the value to students of the pizza delivery program? Explain your answer.

2. Do you think that the value students would associate with the "*To Your Dorm Room*" delivery service is directly related to the costs incurred by Connie and Chad? In what way(s)?

3. What factors do you think would most affect student perceptions of the value provided by the "*To Your Dorm Room*" delivery service? What steps would you advise Connie and Chad to take if they wished to learn more about the importance of those factors?

❖ ESSENTIAL RM TERMS

Revenue

Hospitality business

Profit

Barter system

Money

Economics

ROI

Revenue manager

Customer-centric revenue management

Channel

Constrained supply

Hard constraint

Soft constraint

Yield management

Overbook

Average daily rate (ADR)

Occupancy percentage	Pace report
RevPAR	Rack room rates
RevPOR	QSR
GOPPAR	Revenue source (foodservice)
Competitive set	RevPASH
Market segment	Destination marketing
User-generated content (web site)	Target market

▷ APPLY WHAT YOU KNOW

1. Some professionals think that RM techniques are not important for those managers working in *nonprofit* segments of the hospitality industry. They cite the fact that operating budgets in many such facilities are low and their customers constitute a captive audience.

   Other RMs would maintain that these type of customers, because of their captive audience status, require more, not less, of an organization's attention to the prices the customers must pay, as well as the value they receive in their business transactions. With which group would you agree? Illustrate your position by using a hospitality-specific example.

2. This chapter posed several variations of the word *profit*, but noted that in a barter situation, profit is gained by both parties involved in the exchange. Do you agree or disagree that equality of profit is also a valid concept in a money-based trading system? What implications does this have for consumers who seek to purchase hospitality products and services as well as for those hospitality professionals responsible for establishing prices?

3. This chapter introduced you briefly to the concept of a hard constraint. In the short run, all hotels face hard constraints if demand for rooms exceeds the number of rooms available to sell. In such sell-out situations, the per-unit selling costs of guest rooms would typically decline (due to a hotel's fixed operating costs). In such a situation, however, room prices typically increase, not decrease. Assume you were a hospitality accountant attempting to explain your hotel's pricing strategy to a potential guest. How would you defend the notion that increased costs justify selling price increases for your rooms but decreased costs should not result in decreased prices? Assume you were the potential guest. How would you likely react to this cost-based pricing explanation?

4. Assume you own and operate a hotel near a busy international airport. Your property caters directly to business travelers. Assume also that your historical records indicate a complete rooms sell-out every Tuesday and Wednesday night for the past six months. Your hotel's director of sales (DOS) informs you that she forecasts Tuesday and Wednesday night sell-outs for the coming six months as well. What does that information tell you about business traveler's willingness to purchase rooms on those specific nights?

Would you encounter an ethical dilemma instituting a differential pricing strategy that valued the rooms you have available for sale on Tuesday and Wednesday nights higher than those rooms you sell on other nights? Explain your position.

5. When consumer demand for hotel rooms increases, the average selling prices for those rooms typically increase as well. In the foodservice business that has not historically been the case. Fluctuations in consumer demand (e.g., volume differences between high demand Saturday nights and lower-volume Sunday nights) in restaurants do not typically result in menu price changes. Given that both hotels and restaurants are part of the hospitality industry, how do you account for these fundamental differences in approach toward strategic pricing? As a customer, which approach do you believe sends you the better *value* message? Explain your position.

KEY CONCEPT CASE STUDY

"So Damario, what do you think now?" asked Sofia Davidson, the GM at the Barcena Resort. Damario was the newly hired revenue manager at the 480-room Barcena Resort, a five-year-old, *Four-Star* vacation property located on a pristine Caribbean beach. The physical setting was stunning. To date, the resort's financial results had also stunned its owners, but not in a good way.

Sofia Davidson, the resort's GM, was also new. She had only recently been selected by the property's owners and had arrived at the resort just eight weeks earlier. Damario was one of her first hires and was the first individual at the resort to hold the title of *revenue manager.* He had just completed his first week on the job.

"Well, here's what I have learned so far," replied Damario. "The resort opened five years ago, had decent volume, but didn't perform as well financially as the owners planned. Two years later, there was a new GM, a reorganization of the staff, and some strategic cost cutting. Revenues improve some. But profits not so much. So another

new GM is brought in. This one was a real efficiency expert. Big on cost control. Reorganizes again, downsizes the staff, changes some department heads, cuts budgets, reduced costs—must have been the type that really excels at financial controls.

The problem was, revenues declined along with the costs, and as a result, the profits declined as well. The owners liked the operating ratios, but were even more upset with the results than before—and then you were brought in."

"We do have some real challenges," replied Sofia.

Sofia had just finished her weekly staff meeting with the hotel's executive operating committee. As the property's newly appointed revenue manager, Damario had attended and been introduced. As Sofia and Damario walked back to her office, they were discussing the highlights of that meeting.

"I think you did a good job explaining our owner's disappointment over the current performance of the property and how that could affect all of our hotel departments' operating budgets next year," said Damario.

"Thanks," replied Sofia. "I knew the managers wouldn't be happy about it. But here's what I have observed so far in the eight weeks I've been on site. On the food side, our food and beverage product cost percentages are right where they should be."

"So Sam's department is doing great?" asked Damario, referring to the hotel's food and beverage director.

"Not really," replied Sofia, "It's operating break-even at best. The food quality and service is outstanding, but his labor cost is so high it eats up all of his departmental profit. It's the same thing on the rooms side," continued Sofia. "Beverly has her amenities costs per occupied room right on target and room cleanliness inspection scores are superb.

"So Bev's area is O.K.?" asked Damario, referring to the resort's very experienced executive housekeeper.

"Well, there are problems in that area, too. Bev's cleaning times per occupied room are great—35 minutes per room; right at her targeted budget. But you know how we sell out nearly every weekend? Well, Bev often has to pay her employees overtime on Saturday, Sunday, and Monday to take care of the weekend stayovers and then get the rooms back in shape for the coming week. That really drives up our cleaning costs per occupied room. In that area, we are way over budget.

"Why doesn't she just hire more staff"? asked Damario, "that would eliminate the weekend overtime."

"What would she do with them through the week?" replied Sofia. "In the eight weeks I have been here, we have only had two weeks where our Monday through Thursday occupancy exceeded 55 percent."

"Hire them part-time?" asked Damario.

"Good luck in this labor market," said Sofia. "Besides, I have real concerns about our ability to maintain high-quality room cleanliness standards with large numbers of part-time room attendants. Especially when we are extremely busy."

"So, do I hear you saying that those two departments are doing a good job?" said Damario. "Or a bad job?"

"They are controlling what they can with what they have. And remember, between them they employ over 80 percent of the resort's entire staff," said Sofia. "And account for most of the property's operating budget."

"And that's why they reacted like they did when you told them the owner's were considering asking you to submit operating budgets for next year that reflected 10 percent across-the-board cuts in all department budgets?" asked Damario.

"Right," replied Sofia. "No one likes budget cuts. And from what I can see, this group has been downsized, reorged, and outsourced to the point that there is not much fat left to cut. I think we are already down to muscle. And bone. I'm concerned that more budget cuts will have a really negative effect on our guests' experience. I don't know of any hotel that has had great success expanding its market share by reducing the quality of its guest services. Our problem isn't inefficiency, its insufficient income."

"So what do we do now?" asked Damario.

"Now that you have met the executive committee, that's where you and the entire revenue management task force I want you to assemble comes in," said Sofia.

For Your Consideration

1. Under what scenarios could a foodservice operation achieve excellent food and beverage cost percentages, yet incur excessively high labor costs? Which of these different scenarios do you think is occurring at the Barcena Resort? Upon what case facts do you base your assessment?

2. Assume you were Beverly. What specific actions would you likely undertake if you were given a 10 percent cut in your operating budget for the coming year? What impact would each of these actions likely have on your guests' view of the value they receive for the money they spend while staying at the property?

3. Assume Sofia is an experienced and talented GM. From the point of view of new guests arriving at the resort, how important to them will be her ability to reduce the resort's operating costs? Alternatively, how important to them will be her ability to find ways to increase the number and quality of the resort's guest service offerings?

4. As a savvy GM, what do you think Sofia will seek to gain from the work of Damario and the revenue management task force she has asked him to assemble?

ENDNOTES

1. Paul Dittmer and Desmond Keefe, *Principles of Food, Beverage, and Labor Cost Controls*, 8th ed. (Hoboken, NJ: John Wiley and Sons, 2005), 81.

2. http://thinkexist.com/quotes/herbert_marcus/ Retrieved 11/15/2007.

3. http://www.m-w.com/cgi-bin/dictionary?book = Dictionary&va=profit. Retrieved 11/27/2007.

4. http://www.pbs.org/wgbh/amex/carnegie/ peopleevents/pande01.html. Retrieved 11/30/2007.

5. Robert Reid and David Bojanic, *Hospitality Marketing Management*, 4th ed. (Hoboken, NJ: John Wiley and Sons, 2006), 561.

6. *USA Today*, August 27, 2007 (page 8B: Money section).

7. http://hnn.us/articles/1328.html. Retrieved 11/28/2007.

8. http://www.nrn.com/landingPage.aspx?menu_id=1398&coll_id=696&id=348128. Retrieved 11/27/2007.

9. Sheryl E. Kimes, Richard B. Chase, Sunmee Choi, Elizabeth N. Ngonzi, and Philip Y. Lee, "Restaurant Revenue Management," *Cornell Hotel and Restaurant Administration Quarterly*, 39 (3) (June 1998): 32–39.

10. http://www.brainyquote.com/quotes/authors/w/ w_edwards_deming.html.

CHAPTER 2

Strategic Pricing

CHAPTER OUTLINE

CHAPTER HIGHLIGHTS

1. Examination of the concept of price from the perspective of a seller and a buyer.

2. Detailed assessment of why RMs who consider only supply and demand or costs when determining their prices will inevitably make poor pricing choices.

3. Discussion of the concept of strategic pricing and the role of the RM in it.

WHAT IS A PRICE?

The ability to price products and services effectively is one of an RM's most important skills. In the previous chapter, you learned that an RM is the individual or team responsible for ensuring that a company's prices match its informed customers' willingness to pay. When this is done, customers perceive value and fairness in the prices they pay. As a result, the business's revenue and profitability are maximized. To achieve this goal, however, RMs must fully understand the meaning of *price*. Doing so is a bit more complex than it first appears.

First, you should know that in the hospitality industry, there are some very specialized terms that are used when referring to prices. The various terms commonly used to indicate selling price are based primarily on what is being sold. Common examples illustrating this variance in pricing terminology are shown in Figure 2.1.

In this book we will use the generic term *price* when referring to the amount a buyer pays for a hospitality industry seller's product or service because this term is universally understood even by those who work outside a specific hospitality industry segment. When pricing within a specific industry segment is addressed, however, the term most commonly used in that segment will be utilized. Thus, for example, the term *room rate* will be used when referring to guest room pricing in the lodging industry and *menu price* will be used when referring to pricing in the foodservice industry.

Unfortunately, RMs who wish to better understand what the term *price* means based on a dictionary definition will face a dilemma. This is so because the meaning of the word *price* varies based on one's perspective. An economist views price as "*the cost at which something*

Figure 2.1	Common Pricing Terms Used in Hospitality and Hospitality-Related Industries	
Industry Segment	**Product Sold**	**Price Referred To As**
Lodging	Guest rooms	Rate or room rate
Lodging	Meeting rooms	Room rental
Lodging	Telephone services	Toll charge
Foodservice	Food and beverages	Menu price
Foodservice	Special guest services	Service charge
Special events/theaters	Admission	Ticket price
Golf resorts/courses	Rounds of golf	Greens fee
Amusement parks	Park admission	Pass price or admission fee
Ski resort	Ski area access	Lift ticket price
Parking areas/lots	Parking space	Hourly rate or overnight charge
Taxi	Transportation	Fare
Airlines	Transportation	Airfare
Car rental	Use of vehicle	Daily or weekly rental rate
Casino	Games of chance	Minimum bet

is obtained."[1] The accountant prefers to define price as *"the amount of money something would bring if or when it is sold.*[2]

Hospitality professionals with a marketing background will no doubt have encountered a definition of price similar to one of the following:

Price: The value placed by a firm on its products and services.[3]

Price: The amount of money charged for a good or a service.[4]

Each definition has merit. But for RMs, each also has shortcomings. When faced with seeming contradictions about business, or any other ideas, it is always good to remember the quote from Buddha: "Believe nothing, no matter where you read it, or who said it, no matter if I have said it, unless it agrees with your own reason and your own common sense."[5]

Essential RM Term

DOSM: Short for director of sales and marketing. This is the individual responsible for managing the organization's entire sales and marketing effort.

Essential RM Term

Price: *Noun:* A measure of the value given up (exchanged) by a buyer and a seller in a business transaction. For example: *"The price of the room is $245.00 per night."*

Verb: To establish the value to be given up (exchanged) by a buyer and a seller in a business transaction. For example: *"We need to meet with the revenue management team to price the New Year's Eve dinner package."*

RMs should understand the meaning of *price* at a much deeper level. In fact, because effective pricing is the foundation of successful revenue management, it can be reasonably said that RMs should understand *price* and pricing theory better than any other individuals in the hospitality organization—better than the controller; better than the **DOSM**; better than the general manager; better than the owner.

Surprised? You shouldn't be. The hotel chef should understand the art and science required to make a crème brulé better than the hotel's front office manager. In a similar manner, a hotel's chief engineer should be able to diagnose the cause of an electrical malfunction in the boiler system better than the food and beverage director. Just as understanding the purpose of business first required an appreciation of the buyer *and* seller in a business transaction, mastery of the term **price** requires specialized knowledge and understanding of a seller's perspective and a buyer's perspective. Effective RMs must possess that knowledge and understanding.

To begin, it is important to understand that, for an RM, the term *price* is both a noun and a verb.

A very careful examination of price as defined in this text will reveal two important details:

1. Both the seller and buyer are part of the definition.

2. The concept of value "given up" is present whether price is used as a noun or a verb.

Notably missing from this definition of price is any mention of cost recovery, profit, return on investment (ROI), or supply and demand. This is by design. Too many RMs believe that a price, whether noun or verb, is synonymous with a numerical calculation. It is not.

To illustrate the importance of proper price determination in a hospitality setting, consider the hotel RM who is asked to establish a room rate to be quoted for 100 group hotel rooms to be sold on a specific Friday night. If that RM believes that arriving at a suitable price is a matter of applying the appropriate mathematical formula or calculation, they likely have missed the basic fact that an effective and strategic price is a *concept*, not merely a number. Consider the following questions that would be fair to ask such an RM after he or she had determined the rate (price) to be charged to this group:

- How will the price we offer to this group buyer today affect his or her decision to buy from us in the future?
- If this price is accepted by the group, what impact will that have on the number of room reservation requests for that same night that we will likely be required to refuse to individual buyers because all of our rooms have been sold?
- Does the price take into account the specific type of room desired by the group?
- Does the price consider the probability that this group will:

  - Cancel at the last minute?
  - No-show?
  - Arrive early?
  - Stay more than one night?

- How has this price been influenced by the prices our competitors are likely to quote to the same group?
- What are the likely secondary sources of revenue (i.e., food and beverage sales, meeting room rentals, and the like) that this group could provide if they accept our price?
- What, if any, is the hotel's historical relationship with:

  - This group?
  - Other groups of this same type?

- Has the quoted price been influenced by the payment form to be utilized by the guest? By the estimated timeliness of the group's payment?
- How has the recommended price been influenced by the source or channel from which this business originated?

Note that most of the questions cannot be adequately addressed by mathematics alone. Despite that, the RM in this example must be able to answer all of these type questions, and more, if they are to establish an appropriate price. To do so, they must completely understand the concept of price.

Seventeenth-century writer Jonathan Swift is best known for penning *Gulliver's Travels*. RMs seeking to fully understand pricing should consider his perceptive statement: "The art of vision is to see what others do not."[6] What too many pricing managers do not see is that price can be truly understood only by exploring the two very different, but complementary, price-related perspectives of the seller and the buyer.

Interestingly, some pricing managers believe they have already mastered pricing from their own (the seller's) perspective, despite the fact that many have not. One of the major themes throughout this text is that RMs must equally consider their customer's pricing decisions if they are to ensure that the buyer benefits as much as the seller. Thus, while the buyer's perspective will be presented second in the following examination, that is not a reflection on its relative significance. Rather, it recognizes that it is imperative for RMs to understand themselves before they seek to understand their customers.

The Seller's Perspective of Price

All sellers must set their prices. To begin your examination of price from the perspective of a sophisticated seller in the hospitality industry, however, consider the following question:

> Why do restaurants charge their customers so much for wine at dinner when by lowering the price they could sell more of it?

Put another way, why do we not see aggressive price competition among restaurants that sell bottled wine? The same wines are commonly available to consumers in retail stores at one fourth to one third of the price usually found on a restaurant's menu. Industry observers are likely to offer one of six answers:

1. There is no competition. The restaurant has a captive audience that cannot bring its own wines in with them.
2. It costs the restaurant a lot in licensing, inventory, storage space, equipment, and staff training to make the wines available.
3. Wine sales are a significant profit center for the restaurant.
4. Only high-quality wines have been selected by management, thus the chances of a guest making a mistake when purchasing a wine is greatly reduced and customers will pay a significant amount to avoid choosing a poor wine.
5. Drinking wine with dinner adds to the overall dining experience.
6. Many guests will pay the prices charged.

All of these answers appear to make sense, but let's examine each more closely. The first and most common response—that customers are a captive audience with no available alternatives—would seem to imply that restaurants should also install pay toilets. Surely their guests are a captive audience in that regard, as well. They do not install them, of course, because they, like you, probably recognize that any extra income derived from pay toilets would be insignificant compared to the number of guests they would lose if they did install them.

Second, it does cost a restaurant a significant amount to offer wine. Licensing, storage, and wine inventory costs are real. But that does not fully explain the higher prices charged, because the operator must also buy, store, and even cook the food. Yet food items are typically sold at a price much closer to the price the restaurateur paid for them.

Third, wine sales may well be a profit center, but so are food sales. Surely restaurants make a profit on meals sold to nonwine drinkers. So, it would seem to make just as much sense to charge a bit more for the food, reduce the markup on wine, and, most likely, sell more of it.

Fourth, if ensuring that a quality product is selected and served makes customers happy, why not charge less for it and make these customers even happier?

If the fifth rationale is correct, and wine does in fact add significantly to the dining experience, why not include wine in the price of all the dinners served, thus maximizing the number of guests with an enhanced dining experience? And if the sixth option is true, why not charge even more?

The fact is that restaurateurs who successfully sell wine to maximize their revenue and profits know something important and deceptively elegant in its simplicity. What they know is that *some of their diners like wine more than others do.* This is a fact understood by sophisticated price setters in all industries. The fact is that lower wine prices would undoubtedly encourage more diners to buy wine, even if these diners had to pay a bit more for the food they order. But to encourage these diners, the restaurateur would have to increase food prices, and doing so might discourage those diners who prefer to come only to eat food. If there were enough nonwine drinkers, that pricing strategy might backfire.

Sophisticated restaurateurs understand how revenue is generated. The real purpose of high wine prices is *not* to increase the average amount of money spent by each customer. That goal would be better achieved simply by selling wine for a bit less and raising menu prices to cover the reduction. The reason wine can be sold in restaurants for prices far beyond what the wines could be purchased for and drunk at home is that wine drinkers are not just buying wine. Read that again. They are not just buying wine. What they *are* buying is a valuable enhancement to an elegant dining experience. Some guests desire that enhancement and are willing to pay for it. They are certainly not forced to pay for it. In fact, those wine drinkers who truly seek and then value the experience of having wine with their dinners are pleased to pay more to get that experience. Satisfying these customers' desire to experience elegance is the job of the restaurateur. If the elegant experience is provided, the guests will return. But they will not be returning merely to purchase wine. That product could, in most cases, be purchased and consumed more inexpensively at home. These guests are looking for, and will willingly pay for, the experience of fine dining.

The end goal of a sophisticated restaurateur's wine-pricing strategy is to recognize that different amounts should be charged to different customers because differing customers have different dining goals. Subsequently, there is an increase in the amount of money spent by some, but not all, of the restaurant's customers.

There is no way a restaurateur can easily determine, upon their arrival, which customers are willing to spend more. Many diners—for example, large families, students, and those with lower incomes—may not be likely candidates for spending large amounts on wine. The restaurant needs these customers, and increasing the menu prices charged to them might drive these guests away. Thus, in an effective pricing system, all arriving diners get two choices: enjoy the meal alone, or enjoy the meal with wine. Those who manage revenue will recognize this as a **two-tiered price**.

Two-tiered pricing is effective and very common; you have no doubt experienced it. Country clubs routinely charge a one-time initiation fee, as well as regular monthly dues. In many amusement parks where country fairs are held there is a fee for entrance to the fair and additional fees for the purchase of rides, games, food, beverages, or souvenirs. Airlines charge one price for a traveler's ticket and add baggage charges for those travelers who check their luggage.

Essential RM Term

Two-tiered price: A pricing strategy in which the buyer must pay a price for the ability to make additional purchases.

Broadway theater owners charge one price for admission and another for drinks served during intermission. Condominium hotels charge one price for the individual unit its owner buys, as well as an additional monthly maintenance fee. Transient hotels charge a fixed price for a guest room, but add charges for any items purchased from the in-room mini bar and for movies watched on the pay-per-view system.

Successful business author (and founder of the Body Shop*) Anita Roddick said, "Business is not financial science; it's about trading: buying and selling. It's about creating a product or service so good that people will pay for it."[7] In a two-tiered pricing system, customers are free to choose whether an additional product or service is so good they will pay for it.

Two-tiered pricing serves both the business and its customers. Consider the situation that would exist if two-tiered pricing were prohibited by law. To maintain their current revenue and profit levels, businesses would have to increase the prices paid by all of their customers—those who value the additional products and services offered, as well as those who do not. The result would not really affect the wealthiest customers. In fact, those who would be hurt the most are those least able to pay higher prices. Lower-income families, senior citizens, and children are some of the groups that would be hurt by a system that prevents businesses from employing a pricing strategy that provides multiple purchasing options to all of their customers.

If you think that the answer to the question of why restaurateurs charge their customers so much for the wines they sell them at dinner has more to do with customers and their buying behavior than the cost of the wines offered, you are correct. And you will likely have an interest in learning more about the strategic pricing and customer-centric revenue management concepts found in the rest of this book. Before you can fully understand strategic pricing from the sellers' perspective, however, it is imperative that you first consider price from a buyer's perspective.

The Buyer's Perspective of Price

If sophisticated sellers can use price to, among other things, determine the willingness of a buyer to buy, how do buyers perceive price? To gain an understanding of the buyer's perspective of price, it is important to first understand the concept of **consumer rationality**.

Essential RM Term

Consumer rationality: The tendency to make buying decisions based on the belief that the act is of personal benefit.

Consumer rationality assumes that buyers consistently exhibit reasonable and purposeful behavior. That is, in the overwhelming majority of cases, buyers make purchase decisions based on the sincere belief that it benefits them to do so. For RMs, the implications of accepting as true the concept of consumer rationality are huge. By adopting the rationality assumption, RMs are pledging to treat each customer's behavior as worthy of respectful consideration. By doing so, RMs will discover possibilities and develop insights that would never arise if they dismissed as "irrational" any customer behavior they did not immediately understand. By rejecting the easy way out, effective RMs can move directly to a careful and creative

---

*The Body Shop International PLC is a global manufacturer and retailer of naturally inspired, ethically produced beauty and cosmetics products. Founded in the UK in 1976 by Dame Anita Roddick, it now has over 2,100 stores in 55 countries, with a range of over 1,200 products, all animal cruelty free.

RM IN ACTION 2.1: BUYERS BEHAVING RATIONALLY?

RMs must exercise care in analyzing consumer behavior. In fact, as experienced RMs know, some buyers make purchase decisions that appear to be completely irrational. But what looks like irrational behavior to an RM may be completely rational to the consumer. Understanding complex consumer behavior is always a challenge. Want proof? How would you explain the rationality exhibited by these recent buyers of sports-related memorabilia?

Item Sold	Price Paid
Used chewing gum from Arizona Diamondback baseball player Luis Gonzales	$ 10,000
Ty Cobb's False teeth	$ 8,000
Nolan Ryan's jock strap	$ 25,000
O. J. Simpson's white Bronco	$ 75,000
Stocking worn by Marilyn Monroe the day she married Joe DiMaggio	$ 5,600

Irrational? Not to these buyers. But perhaps buyer decisions such as these do help explain why so much of marketing research is geared toward better understanding buyer behavior.

_____

Excerpted on 12/21/2007 from: http://sports.espn.go.com.

http://sports.espn.go.com/espn/page2/story?page=rovell/050413 retrieved 4/22/2010

consideration of why their customers behave the way they do. That is a trait consistently exhibited by effective RMs.

The acceptance of the concept of consumer rationality involves no less than a willingness to look beyond the obvious and seek to understand, in an open-minded manner, exactly how buyers believe they will benefit from a business transaction. In some cases, this is not so easy. RMs must resist the temptation to declare that buyers are most often quite irrational. Despite its potential limitations, those who refuse to accept the validity of consumer rationality must be prepared to offer an alternative and equally useful explanation of buyer behavior.

Of course, the assumption of rationality is a seller's trait as well. When we earlier addressed the question of why restaurateurs charge so much for wine, the immediate response might be that they are behaving irrationally, because they could sell more wine if it were offered at a lower price. The actual rationale behind this approach to wine pricing, however, is that it serves, in a very rational manner, as a means of separating different types of customers.

Effective RMs understand that all rationale buyers do seek to gain an increase in **value** when they are assessing a potential purchase.

Essential RM Term

Value: In a buyer or seller transaction, the amount of perceived benefit gained minus the price paid. Expressed as a formula:

Perceived benefit − Price = Value

To illustrate how the concept of value actually works, consider that, if a customer is used to paying $9.99 for a medium pizza, a larger pizza for the *same* price represents an increase in value. A small pizza for the same price represents a *decrease* in value. Similarly, a reduction in price from $9.99 to $6.99 for a medium pizza represents an increase value. As a rule, buyers make a value judgment regarding the wisdom of a purchase based on their very personal assessment of a seller's **value proposition.**

Essential RM Term

Value proposition: A statement describing the good or service to be received and the price to be paid for it.

For example, the following common menu item listing states clearly the item to be sold and the price to be paid for it:

> 20-ounce T-bone steak $29.99

From a buyer's perspective, price is an important part of the seller's value proposition. When a seller states, "I will give you this, if you will give me that," a buyer will make an assessment that will lead to one of three purchase decisions. These three possible reactions to a seller's value proposition are shown in Figure 2.2.

In most cases, it is the seller, not the buyer, who initiates the value proposition. (*Note:* We will closely examine the special case of buyer initiated value propositions in the next chapter.) It is also important to recognize that rational buyers *do not* automatically equate a seller's price with the amount of value they will receive in an exchange. In fact, conventional wisdom advises them not to do so. From a common sense and even from a legal perspective, buyers assessing a value proposition are cautioned not to trust sellers. As a result, "*Caveat Emptor*," the Latin phrase for "Let the buyer beware," is known and understood by most consumers.

Because most buyers are naturally leery of a seller's value proposition, an important part of an RM's job is ensuring that buyers understand the answers to their very rationale: "*What do I get?*" and "*Why is it of value?*" questions just as much as they understand the price they will be charged. Only then can buyers, who are today very sophisticated and Web-savvy

Figure 2.2 **Buyer Assessment of a Seller's Value Proposition**	
Buyer Assessment	**Purchase Decision**
1. Perceived Benefit − Price = A value less than "0"	Do Not Buy
2. Perceived Benefit − Price = A value equal to "0"	Do not buy in most cases*
3. Perceived Benefit − Price = A value greater than "0"	Buy

*Note that this is the situation illustrated in Figure 1.1 of Chapter 1, in which a seller proposed to "trade" ten one-dollar bills for a single ten-dollar bill.

consumers, be convinced they will consistently receive *more* than the worth of the money they must part with when making the purchase.

We conclude this important portion of the chapter by reemphasizing that it is only when both parties to a transaction feel they have received value in excess of what they have given up that a mutually beneficial exchange can occur. Value must always exceed price paid if rational buyers are to become repeat buyers. It is important to recognize that from a buyer's perspective, your prices do not automatically represent the buyer's personal opinion of your product's true value. Your prices do, however, provide a quick and convenient way for your customers to rationally evaluate and assess your value proposition.

RM AT WORK 2.1

"What would you like to drink with that?" asked the counter person to Tamara Hendricks. Tamara was in Metropolitan airport, and because the time between her connecting flights was short, she had stopped in at a busy deli outlet for a prewrapped sandwich that could be purchased and eaten quickly.

"Give me a small bottle of water . . . the 12 ounce . . . not the 20," replied Tamara.

"This looks great . . . and I'm starved," thought Tamara happily, as she left the busy counter. As the newly appointed district manager for Copy Plus business centers, there was a lot of travel involved in her position, but she loved her job.

"How much was that?" asked Jerome Odde as Tamara joined him at the stand-up counter that served as the deli's small designated dining area. Jerome had been with Copy Plus for over ten years and also held a district manager's title. Jerome, who was traveling with Tamara to a Copy Plus regional sales meeting had also ordered a sandwich and a drink from the same vendor and was now staring intently at the tray she was carrying.

"My sub?" asked Tamara.

"No" replied Jerome, "the water."

"$2.50" said Tamara, "the same as your soda."

"That's crazy. There's a drinking fountain right over there" he said, pointing to a water fountain located between the entrance to the men's and ladies' restrooms just across from the area in which they were standing. "Why would you ever pay good money for something you can get for free?"

1. What did Tamara buy for $2.50? At the time of purchase, do you believe she was pleased with her transaction?

2. Do you think Jerome would be more likely to value and buy bottled water from this sandwich vendor if its price were reduced by 10 percent? If it was reduced by 50 percent?

3. Jerome is 55 years old and Tamara is 25. Do you believe a person's chronological age, or any other demographic characteristic, can affect how a buyer views a seller's value proposition? What are some specific examples from your own life experience, or those of your customers, that support your position?

THE IMPORTANCE OF PRICE IN THE 4 P's OF THE MARKETING MIX

Thus far, you have learned that price plays a large role in the interactions between buyer and seller. As a result, price is considered to be an important part of an organization's overall marketing effort. The American Marketing Association, the professional association for marketers, defines marketing as *"the activity, set of institutions, and processes for creating, communicating, delivering, and exchanging offerings that have value for customers, clients, partners, and society at large.*[8]

How important is marketing to the success of a business? Consider management consultant Peter Drucker's perspective on marketing: *"Marketing and innovation are the two chief functions of business. You get paid for creating a customer, which is marketing. And you get paid for creating a new dimension of performance, which is innovation. Everything else is a cost center."*[9]

Marketing, as used in this text, will be defined simply as the entire set of activities required to communicate a business's value proposition to a specific **market.**

Although price is one important part of every business's effort to convey the value of what it offers for sale, there are other critical components of that effort. Collectively, these components are known as the "4 P's" of the marketing mix:[10]

Essential RM Terms

Marketing: The process of providing a seller's value proposition to a market.

Market: The set of current and potential buyers for a seller's product or service.

Product: The product or service delivered to the buyer

Promotion: The means of communication between buyer and seller

Place: The location or means of delivering the product or service to be sold

Price: What is given up in exchange for the product or service

Figure 2.3 lists some of the many specific elements associated with each of the 4 P's of marketing.

Despite some criticism that the 4 P's are overly simplistic and that they may apply better to the exchange of products than to services, the 4 P's do address buyer-related questions of great importance:

Product: What is the product or service offered?

Promotion: How will the seller's value proposition be communicated?

Place: If accepted, where will the value exchange take place?

Price: What will be the financial terms of the exchange?

In the hospitality industry, product is important. Hoteliers rightly pay a good deal of attention to the color, shapes, sizes, and even textures of the products that make up their guest rooms and public spaces. They know that in the lodging industry, the physical characteristics of the "Product" they sell are vitally important to their guests. The importance of product in the lodging industry was illustrated well when, in 1999, Westin hotels introduced its "Heavenly Bed." Guests loved the significantly improved quality of this product offering. Competitors at all **price points** were forced to copy it, and it forever changed guests' perceptions of what constituted a quality sleep experience.

Essential RM Term

Price point(s): The specific point at which a price falls on a range of low to high prices.

Figure 2.3	The 4 P's of the Marketing Mix
Marketing Mix Component	**Component Elements**
Product	Features and benefits
	Brand name
	Quality
	Safety
	Packaging
	Service
	Warranty
Promotion	Advertising
	Personal selling
	Sales promotions
	Public relations
	Direct marketing
Place	Units (foodservice)
	Properties (lodging facilities)
	Locations (all)
	Facilities
	Channels of product distribution
	Inventory management
Price	Pricing strategy
	Room rates
	Menu prices
	Discounts
	Allowances
	Credit terms
	Payment terms

Similarly, in the foodservice industry, a tremendous amount of management effort and thought is focused on the products (menu items) sold. Chefs and other foodservice professionals of all types spend a great deal of their time concentrating on the production techniques required to produce and serve high quality food and beverage products. As a result, the advancement of cooking skills, cook books with extensive recipe files, the interest in

Essential RM Term

Oenology: The study of wine and winemaking.

microbrewed beers, and even entire fields of study (e.g., *oenology*) related to the service of food and beverages in the hospitality industry are considered important because they focus on maintaining or improving the quality of the products sold.

Promotion is the second P of marketing. Promotion, especially via advertising, has taken on ever greater importance in the hospitality industry as brand consolidation, unit expansion, and the Internet have allowed more and more companies to directly and cost-effectively communicate with their target markets.

The reverence with which both hoteliers and restaurateurs view "Place" as an important part of the marketing mix can easily be seen in the tongue-in-cheek answer to the often asked question:

What are the three most important factors to consider when choosing a restaurant or hotel site?

The answer always given is: Location, location, location!

Of course, in the hospitality industry, "Place" is more than the physical site of a hospitality operation. It includes the facility itself, the design of that facility, its ambience, and even the people in the organization who deliver the products and services sold. As a result, designers of restaurant and hotel facilities constitute a highly specialized and very important group of hospitality professionals.

Product, promotion, and place have always commanded a great deal of management's attention. Interestingly, however, it is only within the past decade that hospitality professionals have begun to truly understand the power and significance of "Price" in the marketing mix.

This text is one of the first designed to clearly communicate the importance of strategic and effective pricing. In pursuing its objectives, it does not seek to downplay the importance of quality food, beverage, and lodging products that are properly marketed and professionally delivered in a pleasant environment. Product, promotion, and place are certainly important.

Effective RMs understand, however, that from the perspective of the customer, price is easily the most noticeable, powerful, and understandable part of the entire marketing mix. You can understand this as well if you have ever decided not to go to a restaurant simply because of the prices charged for its menu items or if you have ever elected not to stay at a particular hotel based on the advertised price of that hotel's guest rooms.

In most cases, sellers are free to decide what products they sell, where they will sell them, and how they communicate with potential customers. Are sellers just as free to determine their own prices? It is a common thought among managers that they are not, in fact, free to establish prices. Price, these managers would argue, is determined by specific factors that dictate what can and cannot be charged.

Thus far, we have examined price from the perspective of sellers who do enjoy the complete freedom to establish the prices they believe are appropriate. Such sellers are free to enter the marketplace and utilize the 4 P's of the marketing mix to design and promote their products. The marketplace will then respond to their efforts. As it does, they will experience the maxim first attributed to Pubilius Syrus, the first-century-BC Roman writer: *"Everything*

RM IN ACTION 2.2: NO PIGEONS IN PIGEON FORGE

One definition of a *pigeon* is somebody who is *easily swindled or deceived*.[11] Increasingly, local governmental entities are moving to ensure their business communities do not prey on pigeons. In Pigeon Forge, Tennessee, home of the famous Dollywood attraction, hoteliers who promote a price must make that price available or face the prospects of a court appearance.

Pigeon Forge community leaders recently passed a law requiring hotels to honor the rates posted on their outdoor signs. Undercover police investigations revealed that, prior to the passage of the ordinance; over 20 percent of the hotels in Pigeon Forge routinely advertised a lower rate on their outdoor signs than was made available to guests seeking the rate. The ordinance was in response to tourist's complaints that some hotels were advertising rates on outdoor signs that differed from rates actually assessed. In an area dependent on tourism, it is not surprising that community leaders demanded corrective action.

"It's a consumer protection issue for us. The city is enforcing this. It's going to force people to honor the rates they have posted," said Leon Downey, tourism director for the city of Pigeon Forge.

In Pigeon Forge, tourists who are refused a room at the rate posted on an outdoor sign are encouraged to call the Pigeon Forge Police Department.

So, how important is it that hoteliers ensure promotion is in sync with the price they charge? In Pigeon Forge, it's pretty important if they want to stay out of court.

Excerpted on 1/04/2008 from: http://www.hotel-online.com/News/PR2008_1st/Jan08_SignRates.html.

is worth what its purchaser will pay for it."[12] Stated differently, sellers are free to propose their prices, but they also must face the real possibility that their value propositions will *not* be embraced by purchasers. If it is true that everything is worth what a purchaser will pay for it, then it also follows that when a sale is not made, the purchaser simply did not believe the item was worth the seller's asking price; or that a lower cost alternative that was worth its asking price was also available.

▶ RM ON THE WEB 2.1

Increasingly, enlightened RMs seek professional assistance when considering how to best price their products and services. Given the complexity of effective pricing, it is not surprising that some companies have developed sophisticated software programs to assist in the process. To view the offerings of one such company, go to: www.zilliant.com

When you arrive, click on "About Zillant" to learn more about their pricing programs' capabilities.

Those managers who believe they are not free to charge what they wish question whether sellers do indeed have the freedom to set their own prices. For example, some managers believe that, to a large degree, the laws of supply and demand will dictate a seller's price. Alternatively, a good number of hospitality professionals firmly believe that it is the costs incurred by a seller in producing their products and services that must dictate the prices to be charged.

Both observations seem reasonable, but neither observation is valid. Actually, in the hospitality industry, RMs must understand the two alternative observations that are valid:

1. Supply and demand should not be a major determinate of price.

2. Costs should not be allowed to be a major determinate of price.

Essential RM Terms

Supply (law of): The higher the demand for product, the more of it will be produced by sellers.

Demand (law of): The higher the price of a product, the less of it will be wanted by buyers.

Despite their truth, these two observations are likely to be viewed by some with initial skepticism. Because these two statements may appear to be counterintuitive, especially to those who have studied economics and accounting, it is important that RMs understand them well. When the reasons these two concepts cannot be allowed to dictate a seller's price have been explained, it will then be possible to consider those important factors that should in fact affect the determination of selling prices.

THE ROLE OF SUPPLY AND DEMAND IN PRICING

Economists and others who study how people spend their money have consistently observed several interesting phenomena related to the value buyers place on a seller's goods, as well as the prices they are willing to pay for them. Those who have studied introductory economics are likely familiar with two of these time-tested buyer/seller realities that have come to be known as the laws of **supply** and **demand.**

These two age-old truths or laws were first combined graphically in the late 1800s by Alfred Marshall, a Cambridge University economics professor. His visual depiction of supply (how much of a product is available) and the level of buyer interest in purchasing it (see Figure 2.4) looked somewhat like a pair of scissors, with one blade (S) representing the available supply of a product and the other blade (D) representing buyer demand for it.

Marshall was most interested in the point at which the two scissor blades would naturally intersect. It was at this natural intersection that Marshall felt the optimum price of a product (P_o) on the price (P) line would match the optimum quantity supplied of it (Q_o) on the quantity (Q) line. To better understand the significance of Marshall's natural price (which has now come to

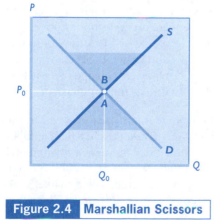

Figure 2.4   **Marshallian Scissors**

Essential RM Term

Equilibrium price: The point at which the amount of a product supplied and the amount of it demanded are in balance.

be better known as the **equilibrium price**), consider that if the price of a product is *lower* than the equilibrium price (represented by shaded area A), demand for the product, at that price, would exceed its supply, and a shortage would soon exist.

Conversely, if the price of a product is *higher* than the equilibrium price (represented by area B in Figure 2.4), demand for the product, at that price, would be less than the supply of it and a surplus would soon exist.

Later economists altered the Marshallian model somewhat (changing the scissor blades from straight to somewhat arched) and created the supply and demand "curve" common in introductory economics and business textbooks (see Figure 2.5).

Unlike Marshall, these later economists were most interested in what would happen to the price of an item (P_1) at a specified demand level (D_1), if demand for that item increased (D_2), or decreased. As seen in Figure 2.5, in a situation where demand increases, the law of supply and demand predicts the new price (P_2) would be higher than the previous price (P_1).

Airfares in the airline industry provide an excellent illustration of how the law of supply and demand illustrated in Figure 2.5 actually works in the real world. If, for example, the consumer demand for airline seats arriving at a specific destination increases, two things will likely happen:

1. The new and higher demand level (D_2) will result in higher ticket prices.
2. At the higher price (P_2) it is likely that the supplier of airline seats (the airlines) will increase the number of seats available for sale, either by adding additional flights or by increasing the size of the plane used on its current number of flights.

In either case, it would be the natural inclination of the seller to produce, and sell, more.

Although supply and demand curves are a very useful way of observing the manner in which changes in demand affect prices, they are much less useful in initially determining prices that should be charged. Recall that Marshall was most interested in depicting how supply and demand identified, rather than dictated, an equilibrium price. It is extremely unlikely that the average RM in the hospitality industry will create a supply and demand curve to actually determine the specific prices they will charge. This is true for two important reasons that RMs must understand:

1. *The supply of a product is fairly easy to measure; the demand for hospitality products is not.* The number of seats in a restaurant, hotel rooms in a city, or rental cars available at an airport can be readily counted. Knowing the supply of a product in a market is an important concept. As you will learn in Chapter 9, knowing the amount of available supply can be very helpful in evaluating the effectiveness of an

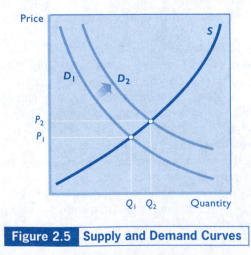

Figure 2.5 **Supply and Demand Curves**

RM's pricing strategies. An accurate measurement of *demand* for hospitality products, however, would require the consideration of three separate factors affecting buyers:

- Desire

- Ability to pay

- Willingness to pay

It is not enough for buyers of hospitality products to want to buy a product or a service. Many people would like to eat in fine dining restaurants and stay in expensive resort hotels. Those potential buyers, however, must have the *ability* to pay as well as the *willingness* to pay. If all three conditions are not met, then the demand does not truly existent. Experienced sellers know that while many buyers may *desire* a product, it is quite another issue to be willing to pay for it. Advertising is one method used by sellers to attempt to move consumers from merely wanting an item to the action of willingly buying it. Effective pricing can certainly help in this endeavor, but ineffective pricing often detracts from it. In all cases, however, the complexity of demand and the factors that influence it make it very difficult to accurately measure, or graph, demand for a single business's products. The result, unfortunately, is that too many hospitality pricing professionals equate demand with the prices their competitors are charging. As a result, when their competitors' prices are lower than these professionals charge, they conclude that "supply and demand" requires a reduction in their own price in order to "stay competitive."

In addition to being more complex to measure, demand in the hospitality industry, unlike supply, can and does change quickly. For example, in 2009, the recession caused demand for some hospitality products to drop as much as 30 percent or more from the prior year.

To complicate this issue even further, there are two distinctly different types of change in demand. The first is the change in the demand for a product that occurs when the price drops. If, for example, $9.99 pizzas go on sale for $4.99, demand for those pizzas will likely increase and more will be sold. The second type of change relates to demand for a product virtually regardless of its price. For example, every year there will be an increase in the demand for hotel rooms in the city that hosts the National Football League's Super Bowl game. As a result, hotel room prices in those areas will also increase. Those hoteliers operating seasonal resorts; for example, ski resorts in Vermont, are quite accustomed to this type of predictable change in demand.

Because of the complexity of its measurement, its varied components, and its continual tendency to change, it is only when demand is defined as "number sold" that an equilibrium price can be easily graphed, and of course, that must take place *after*, not before, the product's price has been established.

2. *An equilibrium price does not establish the value of a product. Only buyers can do that.* RMs know that the price buyers are willing to pay for a product is subjective and constantly changing. Those familiar with the Planet Hollywood restaurant

chain, a movie-themed restaurant group that entered Chapter 11 bankruptcy protection in 1999, will recognize this fact. Planet Hollywood offered upscale, higher-priced hamburgers, the single most popular (highest demand) menu item in the United States. In addition, it sold sandwiches and merchandise to diners in a restaurant decorated with movie memorabilia. With its highly publicized openings, the concept at first appeared wildly successful. Revisiting the marketing mix concept, the "Product" was highly popular, the "Promotion" well executed, the "Place" was quite unique. However, guests seldom returned and food quality was often not in keeping with the prices charged. Excited guests, after one or two visits, felt they had "seen" the concept, much like you would have "seen" a Hollywood movie, and did not return. The fact that hamburgers were a high-demand item was not nearly enough, in the long term, to ensure this chain's success or to justify the costs incurred in operating it. Economists tracking "Demand for Hamburgers" at the original Planet Hollywood company would have a difficult time determining if it were very high or very low.

An intersecting demand curve does not indicate the amount a customer is willing to pay for a product, but, rather, it is an estimate of the amount that will be purchased *at a known price and at a point in time*. Hospitality prices vary, but only because of the actions of buyers and the reactions of sellers to those initial actions. Hotels open, restaurants close, and supply and demand curves can give an *approximate* picture of market behavior. It is important to recognize, however, that the picture presented is the *result* of the actions of buyers; the picture does not cause the actions. Recall again the maxim of Pubilius Syrus:

Everything is worth what its purchaser will pay for it.

The role of supply and demand in pricing is not to dictate price but to serve as a pricing guide. For example, should an excessive supply of regularly unsold hotel rooms in a particular geographic market indicate to hotel developers that they must be cautious when considering the addition of new rooms to that market? Of course it does. If they decided to add the rooms, however, does the higher level of supply indicate that the selling price of each hotel room in the market will inevitably go down? It does not. The hospitality industry is not analogous to the farming of a commodity item such as wheat. The cultivation of additional acres of wheat in an agricultural area may well serve to reduce the value of each bushel of wheat grown and shipped to market in that area, as would be predicted in a supply and demand curve. A new hotel in a market may, in fact, serve to *raise* the selling prices of all rooms in that market because it may actually result in an increase in the number of visitors to an area. For example, few hoteliers would argue that the addition of the several thousand rooms of the Gaylord Opryland Resort and Conference Center located in Nashville, Tennessee, served to reduce the selling prices of rooms in the Nashville area. The resort served as a significant draw to many conventions, and as a result increased the value (and selling prices) of all hotel rooms in the Nashville area.

Finally, when assessing the supply of, and demand for, hospitality products RMs should be careful not to assume that "greater scarcity equals greater value" and thus

RM IN ACTION 2.3: NEW YORK

New York City hotels often hit record levels of occupancy. Consistently averaging over 85 percent, New York occupancy rates are typically a full 20 percent higher than the rest of the country. Is that when the supply/demand curve indicates rates should be *reduced*? Absolutely. Note the following information taken from a recent New York City hotels' promotion.

Make Sunday Special

NYC Sunday Stays is a new program that gives you a City Sunday at one of many hotels offering discount rates and special value-added amenities. Take advantage of room rates reduced from 20 to 30 percent, discounted room service and restaurant dining, complimentary breakfast, and more.

Sundays are "slow" in New York. New York City hoteliers respond to the reduced demand level, quite predictably, with reduced pricing. This is a reminder that price, like promotion, has the power to change consumer demand. With the advent of the Internet, price changes such as these can be instantaneous, as can the resulting changes in demand.

Excerpted on 01/01/2008 from: http://nycvisit.com/content/index.cfm?pagePkey=2005&CFID=13667792&CFTOKEN=42462516.

increased selling prices. That may be true for ancient sculptures and many fine wines, but if it were universally true, the pictures you drew in third grade would now be worth tremendous sums. They were, after all, certainly one-of-a kind and are now scarce.

The more common situation is that the scarcity of a product, in the long run, may actually reflect a lack of interest in it, thus indicating consumers value it less, not more, and its price will be low. If, over the long run, product scarcity actually does yield increased value, the laws of supply and demand would indicate that producers will make more of that product. That may not be possible with diamonds and Picasso paintings, but it certainly is the case with hospitality products. Scarcity of hospitality products does not last long in a free-market economy.

THE ROLE OF COSTS IN PRICING

Although it should now be apparent to you that, in the hospitality industry, the "laws of supply and demand" do not dictate specific prices that should be charged, experienced hospitality professionals would correctly point out that, regardless of the supply of a product, the demand for it, or the price consumers are willing to pay for it, unless a seller receives more money when selling a product than was required to produce it, that seller will ultimately go out of business and stop producing. As a result, they would insist that a firm's costs must dictate its prices. Such individuals are certainly correct about cost sustainability, but they misunderstand pricing.

To maintain that businesses, as well as consumers, must profit in a sales transaction is certainly not a new concept. The notion that producers must make a profit to keep them interested in future production was, perhaps, most famously stated by Adam Smith in his book *Wealth of Nations*. Smith wrote, *"It is not from the benevolence of the butcher, the brewer, or the baker, that we expect our dinner, but from their regard to their own interest. We address ourselves, not to their humanity but to their self-love, and never talk to them of our necessities but of their advantages."*[13]

Like the butcher, the brewer, and the baker, all businesses seek to benefit in the seller/buyer transactions they initiate. Businesses desire profits. Those businesses that cannot sell their products for more than it costs to produce them will ultimately cease operations regardless of their production efficiency. It is their legitimate concern that income (revenue) must ultimately exceed costs that cause some to overstate the role of costs in price determination.

Essential RM Term

Cost: The price paid to obtain the items required to operate a business.

For purposes of this text, a business **cost** will be defined simply as a business expense.

Although it does complicate matters to some degree, it is important to understand that there are actually many types of cost. As a result, cost accountants have identified several useful ways to classify business costs. Among the most important of these are:

- Fixed and variable costs
- Mixed costs
- Step costs
- Direct and indirect (overhead) costs
- Controllable and noncontrollable costs
- Other costs including:
  - Joint costs
  - Incremental costs
  - Standard costs
  - Sunk costs
  - Opportunity costs

These various types of cost are listed simply to demonstrate that the term *cost*, especially as used by those working in the area of **cost accounting**, must be well understood before the effect on pricing decisions can be examined.

Essential RM Term

Cost accounting: The specialized branch of accounting that focuses on recording and analyzing the expenses incurred by an organization.

Before examining those costs that most affect pricing, it is important for RMs to understand that not all business costs can be objectively determined in an easy manner. In fact, in some cases, cost can be very subjective. For example, the food and beverage director at a Country Club who orders and takes delivery on $1,000 worth of

USDA Choice strip steak to be served at a golf outing knows exactly what those steaks cost. The invoice states the amount.

In other cases, however, cost is more subjective. Assume in this example that the golf outing is held as planned. After the event, a final invoice is prepared and sent to the entity sponsoring the outing. Upon receiving the invoice, this buyer has a question about the invoice. Consider now, the salary of the person at the Country Club who originally prepared and sent the bill for the golf outing to the buyer paying it. The cost of *"talking with customers regarding invoice questions"* is an example of an activity performed inside many hospitality companies and one for which a clear-cut cost cannot be so easily assigned. Some customers will have invoice questions. Others will not. How then can the true cost of *"talking with customers regarding invoice questions"* be assigned? A related question would be, "Is knowing the exact cost of such an activity, on an invoice-by-invoice basis, even worth the time it might require to calculate such a cost?"

The calculation of costs such as those in the golf outing example can, of course be undertaken. Cost accountants facing such issues could, for example, assign each hospitality employee's time to different activities they perform. They could use surveys to have the workers themselves assign their time to the different activities they perform (such as food preparation, guest service, invoicing, and the like). A cost accountant could then determine the total time and cost spent on each activity by summing up the percentage of each worker's time and pay that is spent on that activity. This process is called activity-based costing, and it seeks to assign objective costs even to the somewhat subjective items such as the payment for various types of labor, as well as the even more subjective management tasks involved with planning, organizing, directing, and controlling a hospitality business. Using activity-based costing when examining expenses is an example of the actions undertaken by accountants to help managers make better decisions and to operate more successful businesses. This is especially true as managers seek to identify their **break-even points.**

Identification of the break-even point in a sales transaction is critical because, as we have seen, businesses that do not consistently generate revenue in *excess* of expenses will cease to exist. It is important to note, however, that each of a business's *individual* sales transactions need not result in more revenue than expense. The sum of all a firm's transactions over the long run, however, certainly must do so.

The Break-Even Point

In Chapter 1, you learned that a common profit formula used by accountants is:

$$Profit = Revenue - Expense$$

Upon initial examination, this seems like a straightforward formula. Experienced RMs, however, know that the profitability of a sale is changeable because, for many hospitality businesses, some sales are simply more profitable than others. One reason for this is the fact that many businesses experience busy periods and slow periods. For example, a Colorado ski resort may experience tremendous sales volume during the ski season, but have a greatly reduced volume, or may even close, during the summer. Similarly, a country club manager working in the Midwestern part of the U.S. may find that revenue from green fees, golf outings, and food and beverage sales are very high in the summer months, but the golf course will likely be closed for several months in the winter.

Hoteliers in many cities also frequently experience varying levels of sales volume. For those hotels that cater to business travelers, the periods around the major holidays result in reduced business travel and as a result, reduced hotel room revenue. Those hotels that cater to family-oriented leisure travelers often find their busiest months to be in the summer when school has traditionally been out of session and families take their vacations. Even year-round travel destinations such as Cancun and Florida's coast experience spikes in volume during special events such as college spring break or the Christmas holidays.

It is also important to recognize that many cost percentages change as volume changes. Costs, when expressed as a percentage of revenues (calculated as: Expense/Revenue = Expense %) are typically *reduced* when sales are high, and *increase* when sales volume is lower. This is so because while some costs are **variable**—for example, food and beverage costs—other costs—for example, rent, insurance, and some labor—are **fixed,** and thus are the same when revenues are high as they are when revenues are low.

The result, in these cases, is greater profits from each dollar's sale during high volume periods, (when a firm's total expense percentages are lower) and lesser profits in lower volume periods (when the total expense percentages are higher). This relationship between sales volume or revenue, costs, and profits is easier to understand when you examine it, as shown in Figure 2.6

The *x*-axis (horizontal axis) represents sales volume. In a restaurant, this is the number of covers (guests) served, or dollar volume of sales. In a hotel, it is the number of rooms sold. The *y*-axis (vertical axis) represents the costs associated with generating the sales.

The Total Revenues line starts at 0 because if no guests are served or no rooms are sold, no revenue dollars are generated. The Total Costs line starts farther up the *y* axis because fixed costs are incurred even if no guests are served or rooms are sold. The point at which the two lines cross is the break-even point; the point at which operating expenses are exactly equal to sales revenue. Stated in another way, when sales volume in a business equals the sum of the total fixed and variable costs required to produce those sales, its break-even point has been reached. Below the break-even point, costs are higher than revenues, so losses occur. Above the break-even point, revenues exceed the sum of the fixed and variable costs required to make the sales, so profits are generated.

While most managers do not calculate the break-even point on each individual sale, those managers would certainly like to know the break-even point of their businesses on a daily, weekly, or monthly basis. In effect, by determining the break-even point, those

Essential RM Terms

Variable (cost): An expense that generally increases as sales volume increases and decreases as sales volume decreases.

Also known as a variable expense.

In the hospitality industry, examples include the cost of food, beverages, and hotel guest room supplies.

Fixed (cost): An expense that remains constant despite increases or decreases in volume.

Also known as a *fixed expense.*

In the hospitality industry, examples include the costs of illuminating exterior signage, overhead music and liquor liability insurance premiums.

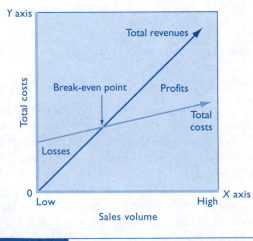

Figure 2.6 Cost/Volume/Profit Relationship

managers are answering the question, *"How much sales volume must I generate before I begin to make a profit?"* Beyond the break-even point, the manager will want to answer another question, *"How much sales dollars and volume must I generate to make my target profit level?"* To answer these questions, they must conduct a cost/volume/profit analysis to predict the sales dollars (volume) required to achieve a break-even point; which is their desired profit based on known costs.[14]

RMs should know how to compute or analyze their break-even points. If they prefer, RMs working in foodservice could compute or analyze their minimum sales point (MSP).[15]

Essential RM Term

Minimum sales point (MSP): The revenue level required to archieve the break-even point within a specific time period.

A **minimum sales point (MSP)** is simply defined as the dollar sales volume required to break even or justify staying open for a given period of time.

When the costs incurred in a sale are known and break-even points are determined, RMs can certainly utilize that information when establishing their prices. The best RMs, however, understand that the identification of costs and the control of costs, as important as they may be, cannot be allowed to unduly influence pricing decisions.

The Confusion over Cost

Perhaps because they have been taught how to compute costs and calculate break-even points, hospitality managers have traditionally utilized cost-based pricing when establishing their prices. The rationale seems straightforward. If a firm knows its costs and has established its break-even point, it can use an established formula, or rule-of thumb, to price its products and services in such a way as to consistently exceed their cost of production and to ensure a profit. It seems like a good way to determine prices. It is not. Sir Rocco Forte, chairman of Rocco Forte (hotel) collection, put it nicely; *"A lot of hotels companies tend to be run by accountants these days, who spend their time looking at costs. You need to make a profit these days. If you don't have a top line, you can control costs all you want, but you won't make a profit.*[16]

Before examining why Forte's reasoning is sound, it will be helpful to examine why **cost-based pricing** has in the past dominated the price setting philosophy of so many hospitality professionals.

Essential RM Term

Cost-based pricing: A pricing philosphy that involves summing product (or service) costs incurred, with a desired profit, to arrive at an item's selling price.

Also known as cost-plus pricing.

The cost-based (cost-plus) pricing formula is:

$$\text{Expenses} + \text{Desired profit} = \text{Selling price}$$

There are likely several reasons for the popularity of cost-base pricing in the hospitality industry. They include:

- The relative accuracy with which skilled accountants can calculate costs, thus the relative ease of calculating what are deemed to be accurate prices
- The belief that it is a just system since reasonable profits determined by the firms' owners are legitimized by the business's real costs
- The fact that, thus far, using the system has resulted in little government interference related to unfair pricing
- The belief that, if prices were *higher* than those calculated using this system, customers would buy less product and revenues would decline, thus reducing profitability
- The belief that, if prices were *lower* than those calculated using this system, an industrywide price war could result and profits would decline
- The fact that the system is very easy to use and teach to others

Despite its popularity and the logic that initially seems inherent in cost-based pricing, it is useful to recall General George Patton Jr.'s famous observation, "If everyone is thinking alike, someone isn"t thinking."[17]

Experienced RMs recognize that a cost-based approach to pricing is simply ineffective. The reasons why are fundamental. First, it is virtually impossible to determine a product's cost before determining its price. Read that line again. Experienced RMs (and honest accountants) know that unit costs change with volume. This is so because a significant portion of any hospitality business's costs are fixed. As a result, a portion of those fixed costs must be allocated to the total cost of each unit sold. That allocated amount depends on the number of units sold. As Marshall pointed out so well, with changes in price, the concept of a true *unit cost* inevitably varies based on the unit's selling price.

RMs recognize that prices dictate revenues and revenues affect costs. In markets where consumer demand is weak, cost-based pricing leads to higher prices than most customers are willing pay. In markets where demand is high, cost-based pricing leads to lower prices than most customers are willing to pay. If you immediately recognize that this is exactly the *opposite* of the pricing logic that should be used by effective RMs, you are absolutely correct.

The second fundamental flaw in cost-based pricing is the assumption that businesses can charge more for their goods and services simply because the business has added costs to them. Thus, for example, a hotel might assume that because a room has two beds instead of one, it can legitimately charge more to recover the cost of the second bed. In a similar manner, a restaurateur might assume that because cheese has been added to a hamburger, it is reasonable to recover that cost by charging more for cheeseburgers.

Unfortunately, for business owners, however, increased costs do not automatically equate to increases in consumer perceptions of value; a fact recognized by any business owner whose operating costs continually exceed his or her revenues. An increase in costs cannot be automatically allowed to decree an increase in selling price. In fact, the opposite should be true. An appropriate selling price for a product or service must dictate its allowable cost.

It is only when selling prices accurately reflect consumer perceptions of value that a business can ascertain the costs it can incur while still generating the profit levels it requires for long-term sustainability. If you recognize that diamonds of the same size and quality will have equal value even if one was discovered accidentally on the ground and the other took the expense of a year's labor and equipment to uncover, you understand that costs cannot be allowed to dictate price; rather, it is value, as measured by price, which must dictate a firm's costs.

The third and perhaps most fatal flaw of an overdependency on cost-based pricing is the tendency of its proponents to focus on themselves (internally) rather than their customers (externally). This is so because many hospitality managers confuse cost efficiency with business effectiveness. Big mistake. The difference is clear and can be readily illustrated by an example outside of, but related to, the hospitality industry. Consider the rental of audiovisual (AV) equipment, an activity undertaken by many hoteliers whose properties contain meeting space and thus whose meetings clients have need for various pieces of audiovisual equipment. Assume that, five years ago, through hard work, conscientious cost control, and superior managerial skill, an audiovisual rental company became the most efficient source of rental and repair services for the DVD players and recorders used by many of the AV departments of hotels at that time. The result of their efforts was that the company did its work better, faster, and cheaper than anyone else. It owned the market. Today, it still excels at providing DVD-related services. But its customers are few. The problem, of course, is that the company is now very good at doing the wrong thing. In today's competitive meetings market, DVD players are out; and have been for some time. Today, digital video projection units are in (or at least were at the time of this book's initial printing!).

The best of AV service companies will survive only if they keep an eye out for what their customers, in this case the hotels, will seek to buy in the future. If they do not, they will go the way of the DVD, VHS, slide projectors, and buggy whip manufacturers. It is a simple truth that cost-effectively doing what your customers do not care about is a sure sign of a business that will not long be in business. Time after time, experience shows that a company's undue focus on the internal cost of operations ultimately leads to a focus on cost containment; more often than not then followed by cost cutting, and all typically enacted at the expense of the customer. Despite the pressure to do so, a reality you must face as an RM is that it is simply not possible to shrink a business to greatness.

Notwithstanding a great deal of lip service to the contrary, there is only so much that can be cut and controlled before a hospitality business begins to compromise product or service quality and as a result causes a perceptible decrease in their customers' assessment of value received. To believe a business can significantly reduce services or quality with no customer impact is simply naïve. This fact was well stated by Ron Shaich, executive chef for the very successful Panera Bread chain. In the midst of the slowdown in sales experienced by most restaurant chains in 2009, *The Wall Street Journal* asked Shaich why he felt Panera's customer counts continued to increase. Replied Shaich: *"Every chain is cutting something—portion size, quality, hours of labor. The result is that ultimately the customer feels it. We are increasing our quality."*[18]

As an effective RM, it is important to your success that you focus more on increases in customer value, and thus the long-term profitability accruing to you and your customers, than on reductions in your costs. The confusion about the role of costs in pricing can be cleared up if you understand that costs must perform a *supporting* role in price determination, but never a starring role.

RM AT WORK 2.2

"You're our food guy. How can they do that? asked Kevin Gustafson to Dominick Carbonne, the Director of Operations for the seven-unit Brooklyn Pizza House restaurants. The Brooklyn Pizza House was known for its mid-priced, but very high quality, New York-style pizza. Located near the main campus at State University, its target market was the students attending the University. The marketing programs created by Kevin, the chain's director of marketing, were clever and effective. Business and profits were good. But now they were discussing the new $5.99 pizza promotion that had just been rolled out by their major competitor.

"They changed their cheese topping formulation Kevin," replied Dominick. "They increased their use of pizza cheese by another 25 percent. One of my buddies works in their central production kitchen. That's where they process and prepackage the ingredients for delivery to the stores. She says they changed their 75/25 mozzarella/pizza cheese ratio to a 50/50 ratio. We still use 100 percent mozzarella.

Why would they do that?" asked Kevin.

"Well," replied Dominick "the increased use of corn for ethanol production in this country may be good for gas prices, but it's made the price of dairy cattle feed skyrocket. Add to that a continued drought in Australia that has limited their contribution to the world market and you now have about a 40 percent increase over last year's cheese prices. Pizza cheese is a

processed, pasteurized cheese food. Melts O.K., but it can't compare to real mozzarella. Actually, it can conatin as little as 51 percent real cheese. Using a Higher percentage of pizza cheese means a lower per-pizza cost. That's how they can reduce the price of their large pizza to $5.99. I have been considering an increase in our own pizza prices just to maintain our profit levels."

"Whoa!!! We need to talk about that first. When they were at $6.99 and we were at $7.99 for the same size, we were still O.K.," said Kevin. "But now, since they reformulated, reduced their price, and are at $5.99, I think they are really going to cut into our sales. That's a major problem. If we raise our prices now, that could absolutely kill us in the marketplace."

1. How large a role do you believe "costs" played into the decision of this competitor to reduce its pizza prices?

2. Do you think "increased cheese costs" have directly reduced the quality of pizza sought by the students at the University? What is your general assessment of the wisdom of the "reduced costs and reduce price" strategy as used by this competitor? Would your opinion change if you knew that, in the near future, the cost of cheese would be reduced to its normal levels?

3. Assume you were the RM of Brooklyn Pizza House. What specific price-related decision making challenges do you now face? How would you respond to them?

RM IN ACTION 2.4: CONSUMER-BASED PRICING

Hospitality is not the only industry awakening to the importance of consumer behavior when determining price. Look at the approaches now utilized by retail firms in this report on price optimization software.

Pricing Software Could Reshape Retail

For all the sophistication of the retail industry, prices often have been set with a simple formula: the cost to the retailer plus a set markup to ensure a profit. Sometimes there's even less math. Retailers often match a competitor's price or replicate what they charged last year. The problem with marking all items up by roughly similar percentages is that some products are more "price sensitive" than others. For many everyday items, like milk, stores can't get away with a high markup. On specialty products, however, the stores might be leaving money on the table by charging only their set markup. They probably could demand more.

With advanced data collection methods, expect stores of the future to adopt variable pricing. More often than happens now, goods will be priced higher in certain neighborhoods and lower in others. That's because price-optimization software gives fine-grained views of how demographic and regional factors influence demand. Also, as companies uncover products that tend to be bought together—buyers of some expensive wine, let's say, grab a certain kind of cheese—expect retailers to be sharper about promotions. Instead of deals in which "anyone who walks in the door gets a buck off mayonnaise," says DemandTec CEO Dan Fishback, a store can focus on promoting the items it knows its best customers buy.

Recall that retail stores include such direct hospitality industry competitors as grocers and convenience stores. Does anyone really believe that those hospitality industry professionals who remain convinced that, for example, a "4 times food costs" (or $1.00 per thousand of construction cost when selling guest rooms) approach is the best way to price products can compete effectively against professionals in other industries not so tied to the past? Those satisfied with today's status quo of pricing should ponder the insightful statement of Charles Kettering (for 27 years the vice president of research for General Motors), "If you have always done it that way, it is probably wrong."[19]

Excerpted on 01/01/2008 from: www.demandtech.com.

IMPLEMENTING STRATEGIC PRICING

In this chapter you have learned that to be properly understood, a price must be viewed from the perspective of the seller and the buyer. Sophisticated RMs do just that. Regarding price, these RMs understand that:

- *Prices act as signals to buyers and sellers.* When prices are low enough, they send a "buy" signal to buyers (customers), who can now afford the things they want and are able and willing to pay for. When prices are high enough, they send a "sell" signal to producers who seek to optimize their profit by offering more products and services for sale.

■ *Prices encourage efficient production.* Prices encourage businesspeople to produce their goods at the lowest possible cost. Despite the illogic of using costs to dictate prices, it is true that the less it costs to produce an item, the more likely it is that its producers will earn a profit. Firms that are cost efficient can produce more goods with fewer materials and lower labor costs than can firms that are inefficient. While these efforts are clearly in the best interests of sellers, buyers also benefit directly because they are provided with the things they want at the lowest sustainable prices.

■ *Prices help ration scarce resources.* Prices help determine who will receive the entire economy's, or a single business's, output of goods and services. The prices charged for some goods are greater than some buyers are willing or able to pay. As a result, prices ensure that goods and services go primarily to those buyers who value them most.

Savvy RMs also appreciate that buyers' perceptions about price are *more important* than those of sellers. Above all, buyers seek value in what they buy. They are absolutely disinterested in the profits achieved by a business (unless those profits are perceived as too high), and are completely indifferent to a firm's costs or cost structure. Buyers attach importance only to their personal perception of the value they receive for the prices they pay.

Price is an important (and this book will maintain it is the most important) part of a company's marketing mix. As a result, those responsible for establishing the prices of a firm's products and services are critical to the company's success. But who in the firm should be responsible, and accountable, for its **strategic pricing** efforts?

Because "Price" is a crucial "P" in the 4 P's of marketing mix, some hospitality *marketing* professionals feel that pricing is a task best assigned to those in charge of the firm's marketing effort. Some marketing professionals even go so far as to maintain that it is a significant mistake when "*Prices are a decision of management, not marketing.*"[20]

Essential RM Term

Strategic pricing: The application of data and insight to effectively match prices charged with buyer's perceptions of value.

Not surprisingly, hospitality cost accountants generally disagree. Citing the tendency for those in marketing and sales to view pricing as affected chiefly by what the competition charges, many of these financial professionals view pricing as a cost-based activity best left to those who can effectively "crunch the numbers."

Both groups often ignore the fact that while pricing is indeed one of the 4 P's of the marketing mix and that costs should be considered when determining prices, pricing is far too important to be left solely to either a firm's marketing or accounting experts. This is so because, when it is properly performed, pricing actually drives the company's entire business strategy and communicates to consumers its overall business philosophy.

Today's professional hospitality industry RMs must understand well the products their companies create and the customers they serve. As a result, effective RMs can come from a number of diverse areas within the industry. No operational area within hospitality has a monopoly on sensitivity to customer needs. In fact, the closer a hospitality professional is to the actual customer, the better RM he or she will likely become. For example, in 2007, the individual holding the title of Corporate Director of Revenue Management for Hyatt Hotel's 122 properties began his career 27 years earlier as a floor supervisor in the Housekeeping department of the New York Hyatt.[21]

Clearly, effective RMs may have a background in sales, marketing, finance, or operations. In a properly structured revenue management system, the RM provides valuable insight and data that assists in determining whether a specific price will optimize revenues and/or profitability. Typically, he or she is not the sole decision maker. Every significant pricing decision should be reviewed by a team (or individual) capable of representing sales and marketing, finance, operations, strategic planning and the owners of the business. The key to pricing strategically is not the background of RMs but an understanding of a firm's customers and what they value most. For that reason, the next chapter of this book is devoted solely to understanding consumer perceptions of value and the impact of those value perceptions on strategic pricing.

▶ RM ON THE WEB 2.3

A serious examination and explanation of the power of strategic pricing in the hospitality industry is now well established. Cornell University is just one of several entities that now offers a seminar on the topic. Cornell advertises revenue management and strategic pricing seminars at locations in the United States, Belgium, and Singapore. To learn more about the sessions go to www.hotelschool.cornell.edu/industry/executive/pdp/course-desc.html?id=SPH.

Topics examined in these seminars include:

- What is price and how to change prices
- Components of value and how to increase the perceptions of value in order to earn higher prices
- How to use consumer research to determine consumers' willingness to pay
- Consumer psychology and decision making and how firms can use this knowledge to make better pricing decisions
- How to understand market positioning and the competitive framework within which the firm operates
- How to easily explain the concepts of revenue management to others in your firm

At a cost of approximately $2,000–$2,500 per participant, the course is not cheap, but as those involved in education are fond of pointing out, "If you think training is expensive, try ignorance!

❖ ESSENTIAL RM TERMS

DOSM	Demand (law of)
Price	Equilibrium price
Two-tiered price	Cost
Consumer rationality	Cost accounting
Value	Break-even point
Value proposition	Variable (cost)
Marketing	Fixed (cost)
Market	Minimum sales point (MSP)
Price point	Cost-based pricing
Oenology	Strategic pricing
Supply (law of)	

⮕ APPLY WHAT YOU KNOW

1. Assume that you need a single room at an independent (non-branded) hotel such as the Roger Smith Hotel in New York for the first Friday and Saturday night of next month. You will be staying in New York to attend the wedding of a friend. Price the two-night room rates (including all taxes and fees) for your stay by searching the following travel seller's Web sites:

   i. www.orbitz.com

   ii. www.expedia.com

   iii. www.rogersmith.com

   iv. www.priceline.com

   Which site offered the lowest rate for the two nights? Which offered the highest? Calculate the percentage difference between the lowest and highest price you found. Why do you think the prices varied?

2. The marketing mix and its 4 P's have been likened to a recipe in which each of these four "ingredients" must be combined with a skilled hand if an acceptable end-product is to be produced. The proper use of any one of the ingredients will not, on its own, ensure success. Each of the P's is an important ingredient and extremely poor execution in any one of these areas can, in many cases, mean failure of the business. If asked, however, which one of the 4 P's do you feel would be the *most* important ingredient for success in the lodging industry? Why? Which would be the *most* important ingredient in the foodservice industry? Why?

3. It is generally agreed that, in the hospitality industry, consistently outstanding service is a key factor in generating repeat business. In light of the three major components of consumer demand: (desire, ability to pay, willingness to pay) do you believe "Promotion" (one of the 4 P's) is more or less important than service levels when seeking to increase the number of a company's *repeat* customers? Give an example from your own life experience.

4. Experienced RMs in the hospitality industry know that the price paid (value given up) by their customers buys those customers more than the elimination of their hunger and thirst, or a safe place to sleep at night. If that is so, what exactly *are* these customers buying? List some of those items that you believe constitute the *profit* these customers receive in their seller/buyer transactions.

5. In this chapter you learned that one function of price is to help allocate scarce resources. The inevitable result is that the prices charged for some goods and services are greater than some buyers are willing, or able, to pay. How would you respond to a customer who maintains that he would very much like to buy your product or service but that it is simply "too expensive"? If possible, practice your response on a classmate; then ask her how, as a potential customer, she would have reacted to your approach and rationale. Why do you think the challenge of explaining pricing is so difficult for some hospitality professionals? Do you believe a thorough understanding of the real value inherent in your product or service would help you handle a situation such as this? Would a lack of knowledge about your product or service tend to impair your effort?

KEY CONCEPT CASE STUDY

"You said it would be interesting, but I didn't realize just how interesting it was going to be," said Damario.

"Well," replied Sofia, "This resort is not unique. In a lot of properties I've worked, there is an ongoing conflict between managers in charge of covering costs and those directly responsible for getting and satisfying guests.

"Like Mark and Pam," interrupted Damario.

"Yes, like Mark and Pam. That's why things got a little animated. I'm convinced they both have the resort's best interests at heart; they just come at our challenges from their own perspectives."

Damario, the Barcena Resort's recently appointed RM, and Sofia, the property GM, were recapping the first meeting of the newly formed *Strategic Pricing and Revenue Management* committee. Sofia had chaired the first session and had informed the group that Damario would lead their efforts in their future.

In the initial meeting that had just concluded, conversations between Mark, the property controller, and Pam, the DOSM had gotten quite spirited at times. Mark's position was that prices needed to stay high if the hotel was to cover its operating costs and return adequate profits to the resorts owners. Pam was in favor of using price as a tool to maximize income, even if that meant lowering prices to attract more business.

"Look," continued Sofia, "if we are going to make significant improvements in our revenue and profitability, then strategic pricing in this property will have to involve an integration of costs and customers. Mark, Pam and all the others will have to come together."

"You mean a compromise?" asked Damario.

"No, definitely not a compromise," replied Sofia. "A compromise on our pricing would mean that we couldn't fundamentally agree about our objectives or the value we offer our guests. That would just to lead to a lot of "Let's find the middle-ground" pricing decisions. That's unacceptable.

"But based on what they each said in the meeting, I'm not sure we could even find a middle ground," said Damario. "And I think the conflict made everyone else a little uncomfortable."

"That may be true now," replied Sofia, "but each of them, and perhaps some others, are going to have to let go of their preconceived notions and recognize that times have changed. We need everyone on this committee to understand and agree about what drives profitability in our industry today."

"Is that even possible?" asked Damario.

"Of course it is. I have great faith in you to get the job done." said Sofia. "And by the way, being uncomfortable in a meeting will be the least of all our problems if we don't move quickly to right our pricing ship."

"Aye, Aye, Captain," replied Damario. "Will do."

For Your Consideration

1. Assume you were Damario and that Mark, the controller, was privately discussing with you Pam's meeting suggestion that, due to extremely competitive market conditions, prices at the resort needed to be reduced in order to increase the revenues needed to ensure its profitability. What would Mark's response likely be? Would you agree with him?

2. Assume you were Damario and that Pam, the DOSM, was privately discussing with you Mark's meeting suggestion that, due to the extreme financial difficulties faced by the resort, prices needed to be maintained or even increased, and the extra expenses earmarked for guest "freebies" offered so frequently by Pam's department needed to be scaled way back to ensure the resort's profitability? What would Pam's response likely be? Would you agree with her?

3. Assume that the Barcena Resort operates three restaurants and a lounge as well as its 480 rooms and related amenities. In addition to the departments operated by the controller and DOSM, what other areas within the resort do you believe should be represented in Damario's new committee? Explain your reasoning for the inclusion of each area.

4. Sofia is convinced that a "Let's find the middle ground" pricing strategy would be detrimental to the resort. Based on what you know about prices, do you agree with her assessment? Explain your answer.

ENDNOTES

1. http://www.bartleby.com/61/22/P0552200.html. Retrieved 12/18/2007.

2. http://www.ventureline.com/glossary_P.asp. Retrieved 12/18/2007.

3. Robert Reid and David Bojanic, *Hospitality Marketing Management*, 4th ed. (Hoboken, NJ: John Wiley and Sons, 2006), 17.

4. James Kotler, Philip Bowen and John Makens. *Marketing for Hospitality and Tourism*, 4th ed. (Upper Saddle River, NJ: Prentice Hall, 2005), 447.

5. http://en.proverbia.net/citastema.asp?tematica= 1264. Retrieved 12/02/2007.

6. http://thinkexist.com/quotes/jonathan_swift/. Retrieved 12/18/2007.

7. http://www.debtconsolidationlowdown.com/ 2007/03/talking_dollars.html. Retrieved 12/21/2007.

8. http://www.marketingpower.com/content4620. php. Retrieved 12/27/2007.

9. http://www.marketingprinciples.com/articles. asp?cat=397. Retrieved 12/27/2007.

10. In 1948, James Culliton, former Dean of the Notre Dame Business College, said that a marketing decision should be a result of a "mixing" of ingredients, somewhat similar to a recipe. This idea was expanded in 1953 when Neil Borden, a Harvard Professor of Advertising, took the recipe idea one step further and coined the term *marketing mix*. E. Jerome McCarthy is credited with organizing the ingredients into the 4 P's.

11. http://encarta.msn.com/encnet/features/ dictionary/DictionaryResults.aspx?refid= 1861726142. Retrieved 8/15/2009.

12. http://en.proverbia.net/citastema.asp?tematica= 1264&page=2. Retrieved 12/28/2007.

13. http://www.adamsmith.org/smith/quotes. htm#jump1. Retrieved 1/02/2008.

14. For a detailed description of the required methodology, see Lea R. Dopson and David K. Hayes, *Food and Beverage Cost Control*, 5th ed., pp. 419–420(Hoboken, NJ: John Wiley and Sons, 2011).

15. Ibid., pp. 425–428.

16. *Hotels* magazine (August 2008), p. 22.

17. http://www.military-quotes.com/Patton.htm. Retrieved 01/02/2008.

18. www.online.wsj.com/article/ SB125055615200338805. Retrieved 8/19/2009.

19. http://www.wisdomquotes.com/cat_changegrowth. html. Retrieved 1/03/2008.

20. Reid and Bojanic, 405.

21. *Ibid.*, 373.

Value

CHAPTER HIGHLIGHTS

1. A detailed examination of how buyers utilize personal value formulas when considering a purchase.

2. A discussion of the roles of quality, service and price in a buyer's value formula.

3. A rationale for the use of data analysis and personal insight when implementing strategic pricing.

THE ROLE OF VALUE IN PRICING

In the previous chapter, you learned that strategic pricing is defined as "the application of data and insight to effectively match prices charged by a seller with their buyers' perceptions of value." In Chapter 1, you learned that in any successful business transaction, both the buyer and seller achieve a profit. For buyers, a profit is the perceived benefit they receive in the transaction minus the price paid for that benefit.

Many business writers use the term *benefit* or *value* to describe buyer profit, and those are useful ways to consider buyers' gains in a buyer/seller transaction. Similarly, for sellers, the prices they charge less the costs they incur equal their profits. In a service industry, a buyer's profit—or value received less price paid—most often results in an intangible benefit. A business's profit is a very tangible benefit, and it is easily measured monetarily.

The difference between a seller and a buyer's view of a sales transaction can be expressed by the two following formulas:

Seller's view of a sale:

$$\text{Selling price} - \text{Costs} = \text{Organizational profit (a tangible benefit)}$$

Buyer's view of a purchase:

$$\text{Perceived value (an intangible benefit)} - \text{Selling price} = \text{Personal profit}$$

Essential RM Term

Intangible (benefit): Lacking material qualities, not able to be touched or seen, but nonetheless received.

It is very important for sellers to recognize that neither their costs nor their desire for the tangible benefit of a profit are considerations in their buyers' view of a successful sales transaction. Rational buyers are concerned only with their own perceptions (an **intangible** factor) and the price they pay, as these two factors directly determine the personal profit they receive.

Some RMs view the concept of buyers' perceived benefits as synonymous with buyer expectations. It is easy to see why. Because a buyer must assess benefits *prior* to making a purchase, buyers expect to receive a specific benefit as a result of their decision to buy. For example, the hotel guest expects a clean room. That is only reasonable. The restaurant customer expects tasty food. In some cases, however, buyer expectations may not be realistic, given the prices they are charged. A hotel guest charged a resort's lowest room rate should not reasonably expect to receive the property's most upscale and spacious room (unfortunately, as experienced hoteliers know, guests are *always* reasonable—except when they are not). In fact, the difference between what buyers expect and what they actually receive is the source of many buyer/seller conflicts. You could likely recount your own instances of making a purchase only to find that what you received for your money did not match your pre-purchase expectations. To avoid such situations, it is imperative that sellers clearly communicate their value propositions to buyers. That way it is plain to buyers what they must pay and what they will receive in return.

Prices should be based on a buyer's view of value delivered. Because the specific intangible benefits perceived by a purchaser of goods and services are difficult to quantify, however, sellers often revert to an assessment of their own costs and profit needs as a justification for their prices. Effective RMs must resist this tendency and instead focus on better understanding buyer behavior. This is so they can better apply data and insight to effectively match the prices they charge with their buyers' perceptions of value. When they do so, they quickly discover that different customers often perceive different values for the same products and services. Reasonable or not, the perspectives of these customers are all important because they will determine the ultimate success of a business. This fact, and the challenge it presents to RMs, was well-stated by the Austrian economist Ludwig von Mises:

> ... [consumers] make poor people rich and rich people poor. They determine precisely what should be produced, in what quality, and in what quantities. They are merciless bosses, full of whims and fancies, changeable and unpredictable.[1]

This fundamental truth about the power of buyers means that effective RMs should not, in most cases, view price merely as a number (i.e., a noun). Rather, price charged by a seller should be viewed as a verb; a series of strategies designed to identify and communicate the true value of what they sell to each of their potential buyers. This is especially challenging when those buyers have divergent views of what constitutes value to them.

Lessons from eBay

When you eat dinner at the Masa sushi restaurant (Columbus Circle, New York), the chef and owner, Masayoshi Takayama, does not present you with a menu or choices. You are fed what he elects to feed you. The menu price fluctuates with the season and the availability of the delicacies selected by the chef. The price now stands at about $400 per person before wine, sake ($18.00 per drink), tax, and tip.[2] Masa is arguably the most expensive restaurant in New York. Lunch or dinner for two can easily exceed $1,000. Will rational buyers pay that much without knowing exactly what they will get in return? Yes. They will also pay $129.7 million for Vincent van Gogh's "Portrait of Dr. Gachet," painted in 1890.[3] What do these two seemingly unrelated examples prove? Simply this; that while some might disagree; there are buyers who would consider dining at Masa or acquiring a Van Gogh portrait to be a very rational way to spend their money because both transactions provide good value to them.

The Van Gogh painting of Dr. Gachet was sold at Christie's auction in New York. For an RM, an auction, such as the millions held daily on eBay, can teach much about buyers' perceptions of value. In an auction, many people are willing to bid when the price is low. Understandably, these potential buyers exhibit a high level of willingness to buy at a low price. The most intriguing aspects of an auction, however, are the forces that cause individuals to *stop* bidding.

As the posted price of an item on eBay increases, participants in the auction begin to drop out. Increasing numbers of bidders simply assess their perceived benefit and determine that, as the price increases, the value received is too low to constitute a rational purchasing decision. Stated differently, these potential buyers say, "At *that* price, the item is not worth it *to me.*" Of course, the item will ultimately be sold to a buyer who, by placing the highest bid, states, *"I am willing to pay more for this item than anyone else. To me, the benefits I receive are greater than the price I will pay."*

Consider that, in an online auction, every bidder reads the same information about the item to be sold. Everyone is bidding on exactly the same thing. What is different among the potential buyers is that each has made his or her own assessment of perceived benefit and value. As a RM, it is important for you to recognize that the reasons for each buyer dropping out are not identical. Stated differently, not all buyers drop out because the price is too high to pay. This is a critical point to understand.

Recall that in the previous chapter you learned a buyer's purchase decision is influenced by desire to buy, ability to buy, and willingness to buy. Desire refers to how much the buyer wants the item. Ability to pay refers to price and even to payment terms. Willingness to pay is affected by the presence and desirability of reasonable alternatives.

In an eBay auction, potential bidders will stop bidding at the point that their desire, ability, or willingness to buy ceases to convince them their purchase is a rationale one. From a strategic pricing perspective, this is perhaps the single most important buyer-related truth RMs must recognize. Think about a consumer item that you recently purchased on sale. Why did some other buyers elect to pay full price for it while you waited for the price to drop? Now consider your answer in terms of your desire, ability, and willingness to buy.

The stock market is another example of lessons learned from an eBay auction. For every stock transaction, both the buyer and the seller believe that, at the time of the stock exchange, each has received what they most value. The sellers sell because they are convinced that, in the future, it is best not to own the stock. The buyers, of course, have the opposite point of view. They believe that, of all the stock purchase alternatives available to them (and there are thousands!), this stock represents the best use of their money. As a RM, understanding lessons from an auction helps you appreciate just how powerful price is in the buyer's value equation. Lessons from an auction also clearly point out the fallacy of a fixed price, or one-price-fits-all customers pricing approach. In fact, different customers should be charged different prices. This is a concept that will be fully explored in the next chapter; but all RMs must recognize that an appropriate price for an item is a as varied as the desires of those who seek to buy it. As a result, price is not best viewed as a single number, but rather, as a series of numbers and selling terms designed to optimize revenue.

Because all buyers perceive benefit in their own way, prices that are too low may leave business profits on the table, while prices that are too high excessively limit the number of potential buyers and, as a result, reduce business revenues. A price "in the middle" may seem to make sense, but that is also a strategy that tends to underprice many of the products and services you will sell.

The Buyer's Multiview of Value

Buyers calculate their own value equations when considering a purchase. Interestingly, most buyers are happy to buy, but strongly resent being sold. Few buyers, for example, would announce a new purchase by proudly stating, "Look what I was just sold!" Rather, they proudly state, "Look what I just bought!"

The best RMs, and salespersons, understand this well. They succeed by helping their customers see the benefits inherent in the products and services they sell. By doing so, they permit customers to make their own "buy" decisions. Effective RMs do not focus on their selling. They focus on their customers' buying. That is a good idea, but it is not so easy to do.

In their book *Free to Choose: A Personal Statement*,[4] economists Milton and Rose Friedman point out the complexity of understanding buyer behavior when they note that buyers utilize not just one but rather four different and unique value formulas when considering a purchase. The specific value formula utilized depends on whose money is being spent and who receives the benefit of the transaction. Because so many buyers in the hospitality industry are

Figure 3.1	Four Alternative Value Formulas	
Whose Money	**Spent On**	
	You	**Someone else**
Yours	A	B
Someone else's	C	D

not buying products and services for themselves (a fact that, interestingly, is rarely addressed in most hospitality marketing textbooks), the Friedmans' observations provide particularly valuable insight for hospitality industry RMs. The value formula alternatives suggested by the Friedmans are graphically summarized in Figure 3.1.

Value Formula A

In this form of the equation, buyers are spending their own money by purchasing goods and services for themselves. In this case, the greatest amount of personal profit, or value, possible is their goal. The use of this value formula explains, for example, why vacation travelers spending their own money often invest a great deal of time researching the best (often defined as the lowest) price for airfare, hotel rooms, and restaurant meals. These are the buyers who want to get a good deal on whatever they are buying, and are very proud of themselves when they are successful. Often willing to compromise, for example, on flight arrival or departure times or the designated times in which specially priced meals can be purchased in a restaurant, effective RMs understand the flexibility inherent in these buyers. They are a prime market for strategic pricing decisions related to off-season or off-hour buying.

Value Formula B

In this equation, buyers use their own money to buy for another. The purchase may be made for a spouse, child, parent, significant other, or just a friend. While value is still of great importance to these buyers, so too are perceptions of quality and even pride. While a buyer utilizing Formula A might boast of paying the lowest price possible for their purchase, few gift givers want the recipient to believe they were given the cheapest item possible. Consider your own gift giving. Would you want your gift recipient to believe you spent great amounts of time seeking to pay the absolute lowest possible price for a dozen roses or similar gift item where variation in quality exists?

This is not to imply that all gifts chosen are or should be selected for their high prices. Rather, in this scenario, the buyer's hope is that the gift recipient is pleased, or at least not disappointed, with the gift given. Interestingly, fulfilling this need is so strong that, increasingly, gift givers elect to give gift cards, the equivalent of money, rather than take the risk of choosing poorly. RMs marketing to these buyers must help ensure that the products and services they sell can meet their buyers' specific expectations and personal needs related to pleasing others. When they do, the increases in revenues that can be achieved are significant.

RM IN ACTION 3.1: THE GIFT THAT KEEPS ON GIVING

Every revenue manager should ensure a gift card program is in place at the hotel or restaurant in which they work. Note this information from an article in *Seafood Business.*

According to the National Restaurant Association (NRA), restaurant gift cards are number one among consumers who were asked to rate their interest in receiving certain gifts including clothing, books, CDs, DVDs, flowers, perfume and candy. They are popular with businesses too; 62 percent of gift card recipients spent more than the face value of the card.

Gift cards are big business in the hotel industry as well. And creative marketing opportunities abound. For example, creating a swipe-and-win sweepstakes when the gift card is redeemed is an excellent way to drive additional sales. Think about it: Buyers are purchasing a gift card that has a certain value, and the person they give it to has the opportunity to not only redeem their gift card for your product or service, but also to potentially win a prize. Who wouldn't want to give a gift card that just might make the recipient a big winner?

Excerpted on 1/8/2008 from http://seafoodbusiness. texterity.com/seafoodbusiness.

Value Formula C

In this equation, buyers use someone else's money to buy something for themselves. From the perspective of buyers, this is about as good as it gets. The use of this particular value formula was perhaps best stated by an observation attributed to Diogenes the Cynic who, in 350 B.C. when responding to the question of what type of wine he found most pleasurable to drink, replied: "I like best the wine drunk at the expense of others."[5]

Essential RM Term

Reimbursable expense account: An arrangement in which a buyer is fully reimbursed by another entity for agreed upon purchases that have been made by that buyer.

Buyers applying value Formula C are extremely common in the hospitality industry. Corporate expense accounts that allow buyers to directly charge lodging and meals to their businesses are an excellent example. **Reimbursable expense accounts** are another. In both of these situations, there is often less incentive for buyers to economize than to increase the level of their purchases. When value Formula C buyers can upgrade to the next highest hotel room type, purchase appetizers, drinks, and desserts without undue concern for price, or make significant purchases from a hotel's highly priced in-room mini-bar, they frequently will do so. Experienced RMs know that routine use of value Formula C when considering purchases is one of the buyer characteristics that make corporate clientele so desirable to restaurants and hotels and, because of the propensity of these buyers to purchase upgrades, to rental car agencies and airlines as well. In fact, when considering all of the industries in the entire world's economy, the hospitality and travel industries are those that benefit most from value Formula C buyers.

RM IN ACTION 3.2: AT $1,000.00 PER HOUR, AND $1,000 PER OUNCE, IT'S A STEAL!

What would a night's stay in one of the world's most expensive hotels cost?

The Bridge Suite at The Atlantis Paradise Island, Bahamas is $25,000 per night.

That's about $1,000 per hour.

How about the most expensive wine?

Wine collectors agree that the most expensive wine ever made in the United States was the 1941 Inglenook Cabernet Sauvignon Napa Valley.

The 1941 Inglenook goes for about $25,000 a bottle, or approximately $1,000 per ounce for a standard 750 ml bottle.

Can those purchases represent good value? Or are those who make such purchases foolish? If you truly understand buyer behavior, the answers, respectively are yes and no. Typically, those who can afford these type purchases didn't get in that position by being foolish.

So who has stayed in the Bridge Suite at the Atlantis? In their article titled "Most Expensive Hotel Rooms in the World," www.Forbes.com reported the Bridge Suite's past guests included Oprah Winfrey and Michael Jackson. Forbes did not report whether either guest had wine delivered to the room!

The serious lesson for RMs is clear. Value is determined in the eyes of those who have the desire to buy, ability to buy and willingness to buy. And those who make these determinations do not consider themselves foolish.

_____

Excerpted on 8/15/2009 from www.stylecrave.com.

Value Formula D

In this equation, buyers are spending someone else's money on others. Every DOSM in the hospitality industry recognizes that this value formula describes purchases made by professional **meeting planners** and travel agents, as well as by many others.

Meeting planners and similar buyers may be employed by corporations, associations, or governmental entities. They may even be independent service providers. In all cases, however, these buyers are seeking value for their clients or group members. In addition, because the choices they make are subject to scrutiny by each member of the group attending the meeting, delivery of the seller's promised quality is critical to their personal and professional image and, as a result, to their becoming repeat customers of the seller.

Understanding buyer usage of these four value formulas is critical to understanding strategic pricing. Regardless of the formula they use to assess value, however, all buyers making purchases will ultimately evaluate three factors that affect their perceptions of value received:

1. Quality
2. Service
3. Price

Essential RM Term

Meeting planner: An individual responsible for securing the meeting space, sleeping rooms, food, and other services required by those attending group meetings.
Also known as a meeting(s) professional.

> ▶ **RM ON THE WEB 3.1**

Based in Dallas, Texas, the Meeting Professionals International (MPI) group is the professional trade association and certification entity for meeting planners. Its goal is to make its members successful by building human connections to knowledge and ideas, relationships, and marketplaces. You can view its web site at:

www.mpiweb.org

Understanding the needs and expectations of professional meeting planners is a critical job function of any hotel revenue manager responsible for strategically pricing meetings-related products and services and for those foodservice professionals who benefit from meetings in their area.

A company must also determine exactly how it will combine each of these factors to create its unique value proposition.

Every business maintains that it provides its customers with excellent quality and service at a very competitive price. The reality, of course, is that when a company elects to increase quality or service levels, that action will, in nearly all cases, result in higher prices to buyers. A guest room reserved at the Hilton Corporation's Waldorf Astoria will provide its buyer with a higher-level lodging experience than a room purchased at one of its Hampton brand hotels. That higher-level experience, however, comes with a price. Quality/price trade-offs produce price variation and, in fairness to buyers, these variations can cause hospitality consumers to become particularly challenged. This is so because, in the case of a restaurant meal or hotel stay, the product will not actually be experienced until after it is purchased (i.e., the meal is consumed or the room reserved).

RMs and those they work with must understand and appreciate the fact that it is much more difficult for a buyer of hospitality services to evaluate the quality of a future hotel stay, for example, than for the same buyer to evaluate the quality of a car in a dealer's showroom or the quality of a container of fresh strawberries in a grocery store.

The car and strawberries can be touched, smelled, and experienced prior to purchase. The room typically cannot. Because this is so, it should not be surprising to RMs that their buyers will be extra cautious when making a hospitality industry purchase. The difference between these buyers is clear if you understand the sheer faith that must be exhibited by the diner at Masa's, mentioned earlier in this chapter, and the feelings of the van Gogh portrait's buyer. The Masa's guest relies on the business owner to provide value based only on trust. The van Gogh buyer knows ahead of time exactly what he or she will get. It is this trust level that RMs in the hospitality industry must remember when they consider the very complex relationships between quality, service, and price in the hospitality industry.

THE RELATIONSHIP BETWEEN QUALITY AND PRICE

Much has been written about delivering quality in the hospitality industry. As a result, articles about how to best provide "quality foods" and "quality service" are commonplace. For RMs who are responsible for strategic pricing, it is important to recognize that from their customers' perspectives, the terms **quality** and **value** are not synonymous.

Essential RM Term

Quality: The degree of excellence of something as measured against other similar things. Examples include the USDA grade assigned to a cut of meat or the thread count of bed sheets.

In the hospitality industry, the relationship between quality, price, and value is complex. High quality does not necessarily represent good value, nor does a low price necessarily represent good value.

For example, few food managers would suggest that the $1.00 McDoublecheeseburger offered on the McDonald's value menu represents the highest degree of hamburger excellence possible; or even the highest available when compared to the Angus Third Pounder burger offered at that restaurant chain. In fact, many diners might agree that neither of these items would be placed on the very high end of the entire "quality hamburger" scale. As the chain's strong sales indicate, however, a great many QSR customers do view these lesser-quality items as representing tremendous value received *relative to the price* they pay for them.

Similarly, it is important to recognize that a low price for a hospitality product or service does not automatically translate into consumers' perceptions of high value. In fact, when prices are perceived as too low, the opposite customer perception often results. Miguel de Cervantes, the sixteenth-century Spanish author of *Don Quixote*, pointed out this very human reaction quite plainly when he wrote *"That which costs little is valued less."*[6] If you were driving across country and saw a roadside motel offering rooms for $19.99 per night, you might well be wary of the value that motel owner could deliver to you at that price.

Essential RM Term

Service: Intangible activities or benefits provided to buyers either alone or in conjunction with the purchase of a product.

An example is the concierge services that are provided to registered hotel guests.

In the hospitality industry, it might not be either the highest quality or the lowest price that represents greatest value. For hospitality industry RMs, it is the relative quality of products and services sold that must be well understood if the strategic pricing goal of matching prices charged with buyer's perceptions of value is to be achieved. While some exceptions are certainly possible, as a general rule, variation in quality levels, **service** levels, and price affect buyer perceptions of value, as shown in Figure 3.2.

Figure 3.2 | **The Impact on Value Resulting from Changes in Quality, Service, or Price**

- If quality is constant and price increases, then value decreases.
- If quality is constant and price decreases, then value increases.
- If quality increases and price decreases, then value increases.
- If quality decreases and price increases, then value decreases.
- If service is constant and price increases, then value decreases.
- If service is constant and price decreases, then value increases.
- If service increases and price decreases, then value increases.
- If service decreases and price increases, then value decreases.

RM AT WORK 3.1

"How much will it cost to make the change?" asked Tamara Stevens.

Tamara owned the 50-Yard-Line Steakhouse. She was meeting with Stacy Black, the restaurant's executive chef, and Faye Cavanaugh, the sales representative for Broiler Meats, a potential vendor that Stacy had gotten very excited about.

"Well, it depends on the cut," replied Stacy. "Faye can give you the details. But the point is, when we print on our menus that we serve only *Certified Angus Beef* instead of the USDA Choice we now advertise, I think our customers will be happy to pay more for it."

"Because they will be getting better quality for their money," said Faye.

"Are you saying that all Certified Angus Beef is of higher quality than USDA Choice?" asked Tamara.

"Not exactly. Some Certified Angus Beef is equivalent to high-grade Choice, but most of it is equivalent to USDA Prime," said Faye.

"And you believe our customers will readily accept paying more for a *Certified Angus Beef* steak?" asked Tamara.

"Absolutely," replied Faye.

"I agree," said Stacy.

1. As a hospitality professional, could you in response to a customer's query, explain the difference between a USDA Choice New York Strip steak and a *Certified Angus Beef* New York Strip steak?

2. How important would it be to know if this proposed quality enhancement would in fact be readily accepted by the 50-Yard-Line's customers *before* the decision to implement it has been made?

3. What inherent difficulties do RMs face when specialists in an area; such as Stacy in this example, are allowed to alter quality parameters *independent* of their effect on strategic pricing decisions?

THE RELATIONSHIP BETWEEN SERVICE AND PRICE

Essential RM Term

Four Is of Service: Four unique characteristics of services. These are: (1) intangibility; (2) inconsistency; (3) inseparability; and (4) inventory.

In most cases, hospitality *product* characteristics and their relative quality levels are easy to communicate to customers. A 20-ounce beer is larger than a 16-ounce beer. A guest room with an ocean view is perceived by most guests to be different and more desirable than one without such a view. When product characteristics can be clearly communicated to buyers, it helps RMs match prices with perceived benefits.

Communicating variations in service levels is more difficult than in product levels, and that makes strategically pricing them more difficult as well. You have learned that services provide intangible benefits to buyers. They are intangible because they cannot be held, touched, or even seen before they are purchased. In most cases, a service is a performance rather than a product. As a result, RMs face unique challenges in communicating the benefits of services offered to those who buy them. *Intangibility*, however, is only one of four service-related challenges commonly known as the **Four I's of Service**.

Inconsistency refers to the fact that the quality of service often depends on the individual who supplies it. Inconsistency when providing services is much greater than when providing products. For example, the sports bar customer will usually find that the quality of several bottled Heineken beers purchased while watching a game is constant; however, the skill level, appearance, and attitude of the beer's server can vary greatly. That variation in delivery has a direct effect on the quality of that customer's beer purchase experience. Due to the importance of consistency when providing hospitality goods and services, it follows that RMs should have a significant amount of input related to their own firm's training and standardization efforts.

Inseparability refers to the tendency of consumers to equate the quality of service provided with the actual person who provides it. As a result, the *surly* desk clerk is perceived by guests as providing poor check-in service, while the *cheerful* desk clerk is perceived as providing good service; even when the precise tasks performed by the two are similar or identical. It is for this reason that so many hospitality service managers hire for attitude rather than skills. They understand that the real job of a professional service provider is to:

- Make guests feel important
- Make guests feel special
- Make guests feel comfortable
- Show a genuine interest if guest expectations have not been met and corrective action must be taken
- Correct service shortcomings promptly and with a positive attitude

Inventory is one of the Four Is of Service because of two difficulties it creates for service providers. The first of these is inventory perishability; the second relates to providing services during periods of little demand. To illustrate the first of these difficulties, consider, for example, the retailer who sells shoes. Any pair of shoes not sold on a Monday will still be available for sale on the following Tuesday. Contrast that situation with a 100-room hotel. That hotel has the potential to sell 36,500 rooms per year (100 rooms × 365 nights per year = 36,500 room nights available for sale). If however, 50 rooms go unsold on a given Sunday night, those unsold rooms will disappear from the hotel's inventory of rooms available to be sold just as if they had been sold. The hotel's inventory disappears, but no revenue has been collected for it.

Essential RM Term

Idle production capacity: The condition that exists when a service is available but there is little or no consumer demand for the service offered. One example is the time period between lunch and dinner in a foodservice operation that is open continually from lunch time until dinner time.

Restaurateurs with a fixed amount of available seating face similar constraints. For all service providers, unused production capacity is the same as a loss from inventory. This **idle production capacity** can cost a hospitality operation a tremendous amount of money.

Providing this potentially vanishing inventory when there is little consumer demand requires service companies to pay, despite lack of buyer demand, for the persons needed to provide the service, as well as to pay for needed equipment. Thus, for example, commercial airlines with relatively high costs of labor (their pilots) and very costly equipment (their planes) will spend a great deal when they experience idle production capacity (when planes are parked on the ground or fly only partially full). Alternatively, a small corner tavern paying one or two staff members the minimum wage during slow periods may experience only modest idle production capacity

Figure 3.3	The Four Is of Service
"I" of Service	**Characteristic**
Intangibility	A service cannot be touched or seen before it is purchased.
Inconsistency	Uneven performance results from variations between the skills of those who are actually delivering the service.
Inseparability	It is often impossible to make a distinction between the individual delivering the service and the service itself.
Inventory	Unsold inventory vanishes if not sold and the costs associated with idle production capacity can be high.

charges. In both of these cases, however, it is important that the service providers not understaff during these time periods. This is so because—as any customer knows who has waited an excessive time for food in a restaurant whose single server was "in the weeds" due to an unexpected rush—most people intensely dislike waiting for the things they want to buy now!

Figure 3.3 provides a snapshot of the Four Is of Service. For RMs it is the characteristic of each specific "I" that is of critical importance to understanding the delivery and pricing of services.

THE LINK BETWEEN QUALITY, SERVICE, AND PRICE

Despite the fact that it is most often classified as a service industry, sellers in the hospitality industry seek to provide quality products as well as quality services. Clearly, the steaks and glasses of wine served to guests in a fine-dining restaurant are products. The in-room movie purchased by a hotel guest is a product. The presentation of the steaks and wine in a fine-dining restaurant, as well as the electronic delivery of the in-room movie are clearly services. Perhaps the reason hospitality is most often classified as a service industry is related to the importance of product quality and service quality to guests' perceptions of value and to the prices they are charged.

Effective RMs understand that the following statement is true:

In the hospitality industry, service quality is perceived by most guests as more critical to value than is product quality.

Hospitality organizations can offer excellent service to all their customers, even when the product they are selling is not perceived as being of the highest quality available. Not every hotel is a four-star hotel. Not every restaurant uses the most expensive ingredients or sells the highest-priced wines. The hospitality industry provides products for those customers on tight budgets, as well as for those able and willing to buy the best. All products must, of course, meet minimum levels of acceptability. Thus, for example, all food products served must be safe and wholesome. Hotel guest rooms must be clean. But beyond those basics, the variation in quality of hospitality products available for sale is wide to reflect the varying desires of customers.

During your career as an RM, you may be assigned the responsibility of pricing products that are in the middle, at the higher, or at the lower end of the product quality scale.

RM IN ACTION 3.3: COKE OR PEPSI?

In the United States, soft drinks are overwhelmingly the most popular category of beverages sold. Coca-Cola Classic is the number-one selling soft drink, followed by Pepsi-Cola. Both Coke and Pepsi are excellent products. Both companies would argue that their product tastes the best. It does not follow, however, that RMs should base their soft drink pricing decisions on the fact that their operation sells one or the other of these products. It makes little sense to sell Coke for a higher price than Pepsi. While that fact may seem obvious, it is important to recognize that the same principle holds true with respect to many other hospitality products that they sell.

Only when a product's quality is truly unique and it clearly exists at either end of the product quality range should the product's quality level be allowed to dictate a strategic pricing decision. Extremely high-quality products most often should carry higher price tags, and lower-quality products may be most salable only at discounted prices.

For the majority of RMs, however, it will be service quality, not product quality, that most heavily influences strategic pricing. The good news for RMs is that service quality is a significant factor that they themselves, not a distant product manufacturer, can directly influence!

_____

Coke vs. Pepsi market share information accessed on 1/25/2008 from www.energyfiend.com/2007/03/top-10-soft-drinks.

The prices charged by some of your competitors will likely be higher than yours while others will be lower. The prices you choose must take into account the quality of the tangible product you provide as well as the intangible services you provide. As product quality and service quality increase, guests making purchases at all product quality levels may perceive greater value for the money they spend.

Despite a sincere interest in serving excellent products, the reality for most RMs in the hospitality industry is that significant changes to product quality are not a realistic means of affecting their customer's value perceptions. Read that line again; then consider the operations managers or the RMs offering the following products for sale:

McDonald's sandwiches

Olive Garden entrees

Chili's appetizers

KFC bone-in chicken combinations

Dominos pizzas

Consider, also, the typical room construction, furnishings, and amenities offered by RMs responsible for pricing guest rooms at:

The Four Season's hotels

Hyatt hotels

Comfort Inns

Hampton Inns

Holiday Inn Express hotels

Red Roof Inns

America's Best Value Inns

In both the foodservice and lodging examples cited, an organization's actual product offerings, the franchise requirements it must meet, and even the construction standards of its facilities are among those items that act to significantly restrict RMs' abilities to substantially move the level of product quality offered to guests up or down the product quality scale. This is not to imply that talented managers of franchised or highly structured operations cannot significantly impact revenue generation. They can and they do. The means by which these managers can most impact revenue, however, is via an emphasis on changing and improving service levels; not by introducing variation in product quality.

Experienced managers working in foodservice know that the number one complaint in restaurants is not bad food; it is lousy service. Similarly, in the lodging industry, guests do not typically complain most about the size of their room or its age. They complain most about lack of expected services such as cleanliness, timing of room cleaning services, or security.

In the hospitality industry, most buyers' assessments of value are determined by their individual perceptions of benefits derived from product quality and service quality, less (minus) the price they must pay. This relationship was presented mathematically in the previous chapter as follows:

$$\text{Perceived benefit} - \text{Price} = \text{Value}$$

Because you now know that hospitality service provides intangible benefits, a variation on this original buyer's view of value formula can easily be created, as shown in Figure 3.4

Readers with a background in basic algebra will recognize that the revised buyer's view of value formula can also be expressed as:

$$(A + B) - C = D$$

Where:

A = Perceived tangible product benefit

B = Perceived intangible service benefit

C = Price

D = Value (profit)

Figure 3.4 Alternative Buyer's View of Value Formulas

Original buyer's view of value formula:	Perceived benefit − Price = Value (profit)
Revised buyer's view of value formula:	(Perceived tangible product benefit + Perceived intangible service benefit) − Price = Value (profit)

Utilizing the formula and again applying basic algebra it can be stated that:

As A increases: Value (D) increases

As B increases: Value (D) increases

As A and B increase :   Value (D) increases

As C decreases: Value (D) increases

Given the consistent and significant impact on value of variations in product (A) and service (B), it is unfortunate that so many RMs and other managers focus only on utilizing the power of reduced price (C) to affect changes in buyer's perceptions of value (D).

It is important to recognize that changes in product quality and service may only be noticed by guests over a period of time. Price, however, has the incredible power to immediately influence consumer perceptions of value. Unfortunately, the extraordinary power of price is too often misunderstood and thus misused; frequently with damaging effects.

Price is easily the most dynamic of the 4 Ps of Marketing. RMs know that in most consumer transactions price behaves exactly like a super action hero (think Spiderman). It is truly all-powerful and produces extraordinary results in an incredibly short time period. Strategic pricing can optimize a business's revenues regardless of the business's product or its place. Best of all, strategic pricing is a tool that is available to RMs instantaneously and at all times.

As illustrated by the buyer's view of value formula, reductions in price should lead most buyers to believe the value they received has increased. Problems occur, however, when RMs erroneously conclude that lower prices *automatically* result in higher value perceptions. In a tidy algebraic formula it does. In the real world of buyer's perceptions of value, it frequently does not, and, in fact, may even have the opposite effect.

In large part, the confusion about the relationship between quality, service, and price is a direct result of the awesome power of pricing. Excessively high prices will *not* result in equally high levels of consumer value perception. Most RMs understand that. Similarly, low prices are not always synonymous with higher buyer perceptions of value, or with a seller's profitability. This fact was stated well by A. G. Lafley, CEO of Procter & Gamble who, when asked how he would respond to the notion, popularized by Wal-Mart and others, that price rules the world replied:

> It's value that rules the world. There's an awful lot of evidence across an awful lot of categories that consumers will pay more for better design, better performance, better quality, better value, and better experiences. Price is part of it, but in many cases not the deciding factor.[7]

Do customers unswervingly prefer to pay low prices? Of course they do. So do you. A low price is a powerful buyer stimulant. When McDonald's entered the specialty coffee field and elected to price its offerings at 40 cents to 80 cents less than the similar Starbucks product but include fewer choices, the decision was certainly an instance of strategic pricing.[8]

You have learned that strategic pricing requires RMs to match the prices they charge to their customers' perceptions of value. Stated differently, RMs match their

RM AT WORK 3.2

"How many rooms do we have left for next weekend?" asked Ben Humphrey, GM of the Lennox Suites.

"165," replied Hillary, the Lennox Suites' Front Office manager.

"We got too aggressive," said Ben.

It was Thursday afternoon, and Ben and Hillary were discussing room pricing for the Friday, Saturday, and Sunday that were now only eight days away. The three weekend days they were discussing coincided with the International Cattle Breeders Association meeting, which was to be held at the convention center in the city where the Lennox was located.

Together, Ben and Hillary filled the role of revenue manager for their property, and they were discussing room rates.

"The organizers claimed their attendance would be higher," said Ben. "That's why I felt we should keep the rates at full rack, plus 20 percent, for so long. If we had known their attendance was going to be this soft, we could have backed our rates off earlier. But since we have only 200 rooms reserved as of today, we need to move quickly if we are going to sell our remaining 165 rooms."

"What do you think we should do?" asked Hillary.

"Let's take the rates from $299.00 per night to $199.00 per night. Put that on our Web site. If we aren't fully booked by next Thursday, drop the rates another $50.00 per night. That should allow us to sell out any remaining rooms."

1. Consider the buyer's value formula. Do you think Ben's pricing strategy will significantly increase value offered and thus help the hotel sell out?

2. What impact will Ben's pricing strategy likely have on the value perceptions of those guests who have already booked at the Lennox?

3. Is it likely that those guests who have already booked rooms at the Lennox will find out about the new room rates? How would they? If you were Hillary, how would you respond to a telephone inquiry from an "early buyer" regarding the hotel's willingness to change the rate the guest had agreed to pay previously to the newer and lower room rates?

prices with the amounts their customers are willing to pay. This can be challenging when RMs recognize that all rational customers will consistently seek lower prices. This is a market reality that, unless well understood, can very much complicate strategic pricing. In fact, one criticism of pricing based on perceived consumer value is that it is sometimes extremely difficult to know precisely what customers are, in fact, willing to pay for a product or service. This can be especially true when lower-cost alternatives are available.

The fact that learning to price strategically is a real challenge, however, is certainly not reason enough to avoid learning how it is done. In fact, as Bertrand Russell, the British author, mathematician, and philosopher pointed out: "The greatest challenge to any thinker is stating the problem in a way that will allow a solution."[9]

RM IN ACTION 3.4: THE COFFEE WARS?

In 2008, McDonald's announced it would enter the specialty coffee market in a big way. Starbucks, the industry leader in that segment immediately took notice. *The Wall Street Journal* reported the Starbucks reaction:

> Faced with growing competition from cheaper rivals, Starbucks Corp. is testing offering small cups of drip coffee for $1 with free refills in its hometown. That's about 50 cents less than the Seattle-based coffee retailer normally charges for an 8-ounce cup of joe,

The report went on to state that in the prior year, Starbucks raised the average price of its coffee and other freshly made drinks by 9 cents, citing the rising cost of dairy products. That price increase helped shore up revenue as customer traffic in U.S. stores flattened and then declined for the first time in the company's history.

Starbucks chairman Howard Schultz, who recently returned as company CEO, said he believed the company's main problem was that it lost its focus on its customers as it concentrated on growth.

Effective RMs know that rising product costs and reduced prices do not generally make for increased company profits. As Chairman Schultz points out, however, a misguided focus on growing revenues, rather than servicing core customers, can create that very unfortunate situation.

Excepted on 1/29/2008 from http://www.rimag.com/beverage briefing.

THE ART AND SCIENCE OF STRATEGIC PRICING

In the final analysis, and despite the challenges faced, RMs are responsible for assessing value and for strategically pricing their products and services. In Chapter 2, you learned that strategic pricing involves the application of data and insight to effectively match prices charged with your buyers' perceptions of value. Some RMs consider strategic pricing to be a precise science and thus these RMs emphasize the data collection and analysis aspects of it. Perhaps this is one reason why mathematical formula-driven pricing programs are popular with some RMs. Other RMs consider strategic pricing to be an art. These RMs emphasize the importance of applying their experience, intuition, and insight to revenue optimization decision making. As you will learn, these two perspectives do not necessarily conflict and each viewpoint merits thoughtful consideration.

The Science of Data Management

In many areas of human enterprise, the question of science vs. art is raised. For example; the belief that "Extraordinary chefs can be trained" implies the science of teaching can be applied to anyone who wishes to become an excellent chef. Alternatively, the belief that "Extraordinary Chefs are discovered, not made" implies these chefs have inherent artistic talents much like a gifted singer or athlete.

In a similar vein, a legitimate revenue management-related question is "Must an effective RM acquire, through advanced training in scientific theory and sophisticated mathematics, the skills needed to implement effective pricing strategies?" Many believe so.

In the Preface to his excellent text *Pricing and Revenue Optimization*, Robert Phillips writes: "This book grew out of courses in pricing and revenue optimization developed at Columbia and Stanford University. The primary audience for this book is students at the MBA, Masters or undergraduate level. It assumes some familiarity with probabilistic modeling and optimization theory and comfort with basic calculus."[10] Many RMs in hospitality do not have such a statistical and mathematical background. Can they be successful RMs? In most cases, the answer is "Absolutely!"

The majority of RMs can readily implement effective strategic pricing programs by carefully analyzing data. In fact, the specific methods utilized to do so make up a large portion of Chapters 6 to 11 of this text. Also, as you have seen in this chapter, the ability to apply elementary algebra is a useful revenue management skill. It is also true that some RMs do employ extremely sophisticated mathematical models to assist in their pricing efforts. Data management of this type can be very helpful. Unfortunately, some revenue management consultants take the position that the probabilistic models and logarithms required to effectively price hospitality products and services are so advanced that understanding them is beyond the reach of all but the most sophisticated of statisticians. Such a point of view is not valid or realistic.

For most RMs working in hospitality, the data they are called upon to generate, store, and analyze on a daily basis will be sufficient to guide their revenue management decision making. The analysis techniques required to properly apply the information collected is not, nor should it ever be, beyond the ability of the average RM to understand them because revenue management is not as complicated as rocket science. Or is it? Robert Cross, author of *Revenue Management: Hard Core Tactics for Market Domination*, believes it is more complicated than that. He writes: "From a purely mathematical viewpoint, the forecasting and optimization problems posed by revenue management are far more complicated than those involved in a space shot. The laws of physics don't change from here to the moon. . . . but the nonconformist consumers in an amoeba marketplace change constantly."[11]

A careful rereading of Cross's comment reveals that he recognizes the importance of applying data management as well as a RM's own insight to the strategic pricing process. It is precisely because consumers change constantly and because an amoeba marketplace exists that insight as well as data management is such a crucial aspect of the revenue management and strategic pricing processes.

RMs engaged in strategic pricing certainly must have the ability to collect, analyze, and apply information gleaned from relevant data. They must also appreciate what scientist Dr. Carl Sagan stated so well: "Knowing a great deal is not the same as being smart; intelligence is not information alone, but also judgment, the manner in which information is collected and used."[12] It is precisely this collection and use of pricing-related data that demands RMs utilize their experience and insight when deciding what to charge for the products and services sold by their organizations.

The Art of Insight Application

As its definition indicates, the management of data is important for strategic pricing. But bringing insight to the pricing process is equally important. Insight can be defined as *the*

> ► **RM ON THE WEB 3.2**
>
> Increasingly, hoteliers utilize advanced technology systems to enhance their ability to manage their strategic pricing-related data. One of the most innovative companies in this area is Datavision Technologies. Its technology is designed to warehouse data from a variety of on-property systems, including the property management system (PMS), sales and catering, payroll, golf, spa, and multiple point-of-sale (POS) systems. To view its web site, go to: www.datavisiontech.com
>
> Note especially how the product can combine multiunit property data into single reports for the convenience of RMs responsible for pricing in more than one operation. When data are compiled in a manner that eases its use, an RM's insight can also be more effectively applied to strategic pricing.

ability to see clearly and intuitively into the nature of a complex person, subject or situation.[13] It is the perfect word to describe the skills needed by RMs working in the hospitality industry. RMs must see clearly and intuitively into complex persons (their customers), subjects (the determination of product value), and situations (those instances in which RMs must determine strategic prices).

Fortunately, insight regarding strategic pricing increases with pricing experience. Will experienced RMs generally make better strategic pricing decisions than those who are less experienced? In most cases, the answer is yes. This is so because experienced RMs recognize that, in the final analysis, price is an objective number placed on a subjective value. While strategic pricing may be considered an art, it may also be classified as a skill. Like most skills, with practice, RMs improve. They will make the greatest improvement, however, when they recognize they must apply *both* data and their own insight to the strategic pricing process. In his outstanding book *Pricing: Making Profitable Decisions*, Kent Monroe writes, "Pricing simply cannot be reduced to a formula. There are too many interacting factors. Successful pricing requires considering all internal and external factors and adapting to changes as they occur. Successful pricing is an adaptive process."[14]

In many cases, learning how to adapt is a process best learned on the job and after acquiring basic skills. Just as a car's driver is not allowed to drive in traffic until they have learned (usually from reading a book!) the many rules of the road, so too will RMs benefit from a thorough understanding of the strategic pricing process prior to their beginning to practice it.

Now that you grasp the complex meanings of both price (Chapter 2) and value (Chapter 3), you are ready to explore *differential pricing*—the single most important economic concept you can apply to optimize hospitality revenues and the sole topic addressed in Chapter 4.

❖ ESSENTIAL RM TERMS

Intangible (benefit)   Service

Reimbursable expense account   Four I's of Service

Meeting planner   Idle production capacity

Quality

▶ APPLY WHAT YOU KNOW

1. In this chapter, you learned that both product quality and service are important in the sale of hospitality products. Consider your last hospitality purchase. Who do you believe were the key individuals within the seller's organization whose actions most influenced whether your expectations regarding these two factors were met?

2. Product quality, service, and price were the three factors identified as being major determinates of a customer's perception of value. Contrast the value formula you would use if A: You were interested in purchasing a lunch that you needed to consume in ten minutes and B: You wanted to enjoy a leisurely dinner with someone with whom you are romantically involved. Would the manner in which you evaluate value remain constant? What are the implications of your answer to RMs in the hospitality industry?

3. In this chapter you learned that a buyer's perception of benefits to be received can be viewed as the same as that buyer's expectations. Consider a time when a purchase you made did *not* meet your expectations. At the time, did you hold yourself or the seller responsible for your dissatisfaction? What specific steps could the seller have taken if it wanted to remove the disappointment you felt as a result of your purchase?

4. Researchers have found that normally frugal buyers are, when spending others' money on themselves (Value Formula C), often less cost conscious when purchasing than they otherwise would be. Identify at least three specific hospitality industry-related actions you believe these buyers might undertake that would be considered an alteration of their normal buying behavior. Why is it important that RMs recognize the existence of these types of changed behavior?

5. In the lodging segment of the hospitality industry, many hoteliers allow front desk and night audit staff to use their own judgment when deciding whether to reduce room rates to ensure room sales to call-in or walk-in customers. As a RM, what specific training regarding *prices* and *value* do you believe such staff member should have to aid them in making good decisions regarding the prices they quote? Who within a lodging organization do you believe should be responsible for providing that training?

KEY CONCEPT CASE STUDY

"Thanks for taking the time out to be here," said Damario, the revenue manager at the Barcena Resort. Damario was addressing the members of the resort's newly formed *Strategic Pricing and Revenue Management Advisory Committee.* "As you know, Sofia has asked me to chair this committee," continued Damario. "I'm looking forward to hearing your thoughts on lots of the topics that will directly affect the revenue optimization and strategic pricing decisions we will make in the coming months."

"Well, I can already tell you what I think," said Mark Chaplin, the hotel's Controller. "With our owner's expectations and the financial pressures on the property, we should be targeting customers who seek a premium product and are willing to pay a premium price. I'm talking about the top 15 percent of the resort-going public. That's the customer who won't haggle with us on rates. And that approach would allow us to increase our prices to the level we need to support our cost structure."

"Those are savvy consumers, Mark, and their standards are pretty high. I don't know if the product we can deliver will consistently match the expectations they have," replied Pam, the property's DOSM.

"I would match our rooms against any of our competitors," protested Adrian, the resort's rooms manager. "Guests don't have a problem paying a premium price if the product we deliver is outstanding."

"In my area, that means an exceptionally well-trained staff providing service that is as good as the food we make," said Sam, the resort's F&B director. "No over-cooked steaks," he continued, "and servers that are friendly, knowledgeable, and efficient. That's the secret to good food."

"I agree. Service delivery is every bit as critical as our product quality, so staff training really is important," said Damario as he looked in the direction of Shingi Rakuni, the resort's human resource director.

"Shingi," said Damario, "Have all of our departments implemented a regularly scheduled training plan for each of their staff positions?"

Shingi looked down uncomfortably at the papers she had spread in front of her as she said. "Maybe you should ask each department head. They would be more up to speed in their own areas than I would."

"When we first opened, we really stressed staff training," said Adrian quickly, "but when the budgets tightened up, I think most of us had to make cut backs." The other department heads nodded in agreement.

Damario quickly considered the other resort properties competing against the Barcena. Some were newer and had some modern guests features the Barcena did not have. Some were older properties that were showing their age, but they were all pretty well maintained and they typically priced their rooms lower than the Barcena. On the whole, he thought, some of our competitors are newer and some are older. We have some service features they don't have and some of them have some features we don't have. For a five-year-old property, he felt the product offered could hold its own in this market. But that assumed its service levels were where they needed to be.

"That's right," quickly added Amanda, the front office manager. "It's hard to implement training when you only have enough payroll budgeted to schedule the exact number of desk agents we need to handle our check-ins and departures."

"Amanda's spot on," said Bev, the resort's executive housekeeper, "and when we are short staffed, it's all we can do to get the rooms turned on time. I'd love to increase the training of my room attendants if I had the money. We would have better room quality and our room inspections could be speeded up."

"That's exactly why we need to go after the premium market," said Mark. "That's the way we will get the revenue we need to increase training budgets and fix some of these problems."

All of the department heads except Pam seemed to nod their concurrence.

"Higher prices? Now? In this economy?" she said aloud. "There're good, but I'm not sure my team can sell that," she concluded, as she gave Damario a troubled look.

For Your Consideration

1. Assume that in a recently completed competitive site survey, Damario found the physical quality of the rooms sold and food served at the Barcena to be in the mid-range of its competitors with regard to quality. Now consider the "buyer's view of value" formula you learned about in this chapter. What would be the likely impact on that formula if the resort immediately implemented Mark's suggested pricing strategy?

2. In this meeting, Damario learned about two reasons (lack of money and lack of time) typically given for not having formal staff training in a hospitality organization. Assume that Damario's ultimate goal is in fact the ability to charge a premium selling price relative to the resort's competitors. Do you think it is likely that such a goal could be achieved with the lower-than-average levels of guest service and product delivery that typically result when employee training programs are deficient? Explain your answer.

3. Assume the Barcena is currently competing for a 400-room-night contract against a newer resort whose total bid is nearly identical to that of the Barcena. What would Mark advise Pam to bid? If you were the customer in this scenario, what would be your likely reaction be to such a bid? Support your position with information you learned in this chapter.

4. Mark's pricing strategy assumes immediately increasing the resort's prices will generate the revenue needed to improve its products and services. Do you believe such an assumption is reasonable? Explain your answer using the buyer's view of value formula.

ENDNOTES

1. http://blog.mises.org/archives/005756.asp. Retrieved 8/15/2007.

2. Prices as of 1/1/2008 http://masanyc.com/.

3. http://en.wikipedia.org/wiki/List_of_most_expensive_paintings. Retrieved 1/20/2009.

4. Milton and Rose Friedman, *Free To Choose: A Personal Statement* (Fort Washington, PA: Harvest Books, 1990), pages 116–117.

5. http://www.sidewayswineclub.com/toasts.php. Retrieved 8/15/2008.

6. http://en.proverbia.net/citastema.asp?tematica= 1264. Retrieved 2/25/2008.

7. http://www.fastcompany.com/magazine/95/design-qa.html. *Fast Times* (June 2005), page 57

8. "Would You Like a Mocha with That?" www.usatoday.com. Retrieved 1/8/2008.

9. http://www.quotationspage.com/quotes/Bertrand_Russell/. Retrieved 3/3/2009.

10. Robert L. Phillips, *Pricing and Revenue Optimization* (Stanford Business Books, 2005), from Preface.

11. Robert G. Cross, *Revenue Management: Hard-Core Tactics for Market Domination* (Broadway Books, 1997), 87.

12. http://thinkexist.com/quotations/information/. Retrieved 10/2/2008.

13. http://encarta.msn.com/encnet/features/dictionary/DictionaryResults.aspx?refid=1861621532. Retrieved 2/21/2008.

14. Kent B. Monroe, *Pricing: Making Profitable Decisions*, 3rd. ed. (New York: McGraw-Hill Irwin Books, 2002), 653.

CHAPTER 4

Differential Pricing

CHAPTER OUTLINE

CHAPTER HIGHLIGHTS

1. Detailed explanation of differential pricing; the practice of charging different prices, to different customers, for the same or similar products and services.

2. Detailed examination of the eight techniques RMs use to applying differential pricing.

3. Review of the evolving terminology used to describe the activities and goals of RMs.

TEN PRINCIPLES OF MANAGING REVENUE

In Chapters 1 to 3, you reviewed the fundamental principles of price and value; two concepts that must be known and understood by all RMs. In this chapter, you will begin to learn the strategies, tactics, and decision-making processes required for the effective management of business income. Before you are introduced to those techniques, however, it is important that you are prepared for them. Having come this far, you already understand a great deal about the foundations of effective revenue management. A review of the key information you have learned can be summarized in the following *Ten Principles of Managing Revenue*.

Ten Principles of Managing Revenue

1. Businesses exist only to create wealth (value) for their customers.
2. Successful businesses are careful to focus externally; on their customers' needs, rather than internally; on their own needs.
3. Consumers make rational buying decisions based on their perceptions of the value they receive for the prices they pay.
4. The true value of a product or service is equal to what a buyer will willingly pay for it.
5. Product quality is important, but service quality is just as important when delivering value to buyers of hospitality products and services.
6. Any change in product quality, service quality, or price will have a direct impact on buyers' perceptions of value.
7. While it may be viewed simply as a number, a *price* is a very powerful message sent by sellers to buyers.
8. Different buyers place different values on the same products or services, and as a result are willing to pay different prices for them.
9. Strategic pricing is the application of data and insight to effectively match prices charged with buyers' perceptions of value and willingness to pay.
10. Revenue managers are those individuals or teams directly responsible for optimizing a business's income and profits.

Knowing these ten key revenue management principles is good—but not good enough. RMs must also have the skill and knowledge needed to apply them. Consider Principle #9:

Strategic pricing is the application of data and insight to effectively match prices charged with buyers' perceptions of value and willingness to pay.

Being ready to make informed data-related decisions assumes RMs have a solid understanding of financial accounting, managerial accounting and cost control as well as of the basic mathematics and algebra need to organize and assess revenue management-related data.

For example, assume a potential group rooms buyer would like to reserve 50 hotel rooms. This customer qualifies for a room rate of $179.99 per night. The buyer, however, asks for a room rate quote that would include a hot breakfast buffet the morning of check-out.

In this scenario, an understanding of the fixed and variable costs associated with serving 50 breakfast buffets on the specific date in question must be well understood. It is important to recognize that an accurate calculation of the food, labor, and other costs associated with this guest's request will *not* make the pricing decision needed to answer this guest's question. The correct calculation will, however, provide the decision maker with valuable information (data) that could only be obtained by managers familiar with calculating the costs related to breakfast buffets.

Structured academic courses are available in the accounting and cost areas identified in the previous paragraph and it is assumed the reader has successfully completed them or has gained equivalent knowledge through industry experience. Some specialized RMs now employ revenue management tools that require even greater quantitative skills. They utilize optimization theory, calculus, multiple regression analysis, and other advanced mathematical or statistical techniques. The authors make *no* assumptions regarding the reader's familiarity with these more advanced areas of study. In fact, they remain convinced that while an understanding of advanced mathematics can help some RMs better achieve their goals, advanced training in this area is no more a prerequisite for the effective management of hospitality revenues than is an understanding of computer programming essential to the use of a laptop computer.

In addition to the background required to organize and interpret data, Principle #9 indicates the importance of applying *insight* to price determination and the management of revenue. Doing so requires knowledge of hotel operations, food and beverage management, event management, economics, marketing as it relates to customer segmentation and the marketing of services, consumer psychology, ethics, and those laws specifically related to consumer pricing. With the exception of those laws and regulations related specifically to managing revenue in the hospitality industry (which are addressed in this book's next chapter), formal or on-the-job training related to each of these insight-related areas is also assumed.

Because the management of revenue is a topic best understood by experienced hospitality professionals, many of the terms, concepts, and techniques that will be presented in the remainder of this text assume a significant background in the industry. If you are completing this course in a formal setting, your instructor may be able to assist you in any areas in which you are not familiar. If you are studying revenue management on your own and lack some training or experience in any of the data or insight-related areas, the good news is that a wealth of educational resources are readily available to assist you.[1] When you understand prices and value and have a solid understanding of the hospitality industry, you are ready to learn how RMs apply strategic pricing to revenue optimization.

DIFFERENTIAL PRICING

Revenue Management Principle #4 states: *The true value of a product or service is equal to what a buyer will willingly pay for it*. As a result, a firm's pricing strategy should always be **value based**. The purpose of this section is to examine the synergy that results when RMs also utilize **differential pricing**.

Essential RM Terms

Value based (pricing): The practice of establishing prices for a firm's products and services based primarily on the buyer's perceived value of those products and services.

Differential pricing: The practice of a seller charging different prices to different buyers for the same product or slightly different versions of the same product.

This is sometimes referred to as demand-based pricing, segmented pricing, price differentiation, or price discrimination.

Some industry professionals do not believe pricing can or even should be value based. Those hospitality managers with a background in accounting often make the case for a numerical formula-based approach to pricing. Such an approach typically considers fixed and variable costs, desired profit level, and the costs of a business owner's initial investment. Familiar terms for these managers include the Hubbart room rate formula, contribution margin pricing (for restaurants), and investment rates of return. Readers unfamiliar with these terms and how they impact price decisions will not have difficulty locating them in the hospitality literature.

Similarly, those managers who view pricing as essentially a marketing-related task make the case for the utilization of a variety of pricing approaches depending upon the goals of management. These approaches include skim pricing, penetration pricing, neutral pricing and cost-oriented pricing, demand-oriented pricing, and competitive pricing.[2] Despite the cases that can be made for accounting and marketing-related pricing approaches, in nearly all cases they recommend the use of **fixed pricing**.

Experienced RMs understand that differential pricing is a more powerful pricing approach than is fixed pricing. This is true, in part, because price differentiation also provides the rationale to practice **inventory management**; one of the most critical tasks that can be undertaken by effective RMs.

To better understand the power of differential pricing, assume you are the revenue manager of a 500-room **branded hotel** in a mid-sized city. While you likely will have many responsibilities, as an hotelier, you are primarily interested in two fundamental pieces of information because they will determine both your RevPAR and GOPPAR:

1. How many rooms are sold each night (i.e., your occupancy rate)
2. The average room rate at which those rooms are sold (i.e., your ADR)

As a branded hotel that operates under a franchise agreement, you are free to establish the price structure for your rooms that you feel makes the most sense to you and

Essential RM Term

Fixed pricing: The practice of a seller charging the same price to all buyers.

This is sometimes referred to as *flat* or *single* pricing.

Essential RM Term

Inventory management: The process of allocating and modifying the number of products available for sale at various prices and through various distribution channels.

Essential RM Term

Branded (hotel): Industry jargon for a hotel affiliated with a national chain.

to your property's owners. This is so because in the United States it is illegal for franchisors to dictate their franchisee's selling prices.

Assume that, after you have studied the local market, your brand, and your competitors, you are convinced that the typical traveler to your city is willing to pay a room rate of approximately $150.00 per night for a room of the quality you offer and with the services you provide. Also, assume that the management controllable costs (variable rooms costs) incurred when selling one room are $75.00.

Now consider your selling alternatives. How much should you charge? You are concerned about the number of rooms sold and would, in all likelihood sell all 500 rooms each night if you sold your rooms at a price of $1.00 per night. This would maximize your occupancy percentage. In fact, you would likely achieve a 100 percent occupancy each night. Of course, you would not select such a pricing strategy for a variety of reasons, not the least of which is that you would quickly find that the revenue generated from room sales would not equal the amount required to operate your hotel.

Alternatively, if you priced your rooms at $300.00 per night, a rate twice as high as the average value buyers assign to your rooms, you would likely sell few of them, but if you did sell any of them, your ADR would be very high indeed. Using a fixed pricing strategy in this example, you might logically choose to sell your rooms for $150.00 per night, the price at which you believe you would maximize the revenue from the number of customers who feel they have received that much value for the price they would pay. This intersection of rooms sold and price to be paid is illustrated in Figure 4.1.

Assume that at a selling price $150.00 per night your hotel would sell 250 rooms on a given day. Utilizing the rooms-related formulas introduced in Chapter 1, your occupancy rate would be 50 percent (250 total rooms sold/ 500 total rooms available for sale = 50%).

Your ADR would be calculated as:

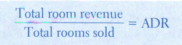

$$\frac{\text{Total room revenue}}{\text{Total rooms sold}} = \text{ADR}$$

Figure 4.1 **Potential of Price Differentiation**

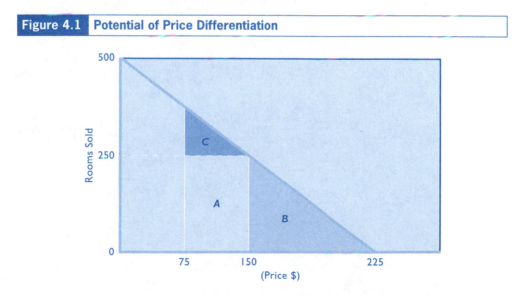

In this scenario:

$$\frac{250 \text{ rooms} \times \$150.00 \text{ per room}}{250 \text{ total rooms sold}} = \text{ADR}$$

$$250 \text{ rooms} \times \$150.00 \text{ per room} / 250 \text{ Total rooms sold} = \text{ADR}$$

or

$$\frac{\$37,500}{250} = \$150.00 \text{ ADR}$$

Utilizing the RevPAR formula:

$$\frac{\text{Total revenue}}{\text{Total rooms available for sale}} = \text{RevPAR}$$

In this scenario:

$$\frac{250 \text{ rooms} \times \$150.00 \text{ per room}}{500 \text{ rooms available for sale}} = \text{RevPAR}$$

or

$$\frac{\$37,500}{500} = \$75.00 \text{ RevPAR}$$

Thus, an occupancy of 50 percent, an ADR of $150.00, and a Rev PAR of $75.00 would be generated as a result of selling the 250 rooms shown in region "A" of Figure 4.1.

Applying the GOPPAR formula introduced in Chapter 1, you would find it to be calculated as:

$$\frac{\text{Total revenue} - \text{Management controllable expense}}{\text{Total rooms available for sale}} = \text{GOPPAR}$$

or

$$\frac{\$37,500 - (250 \text{ rooms sold} \times \$75.00 \text{ cost per room})}{500 \text{ rooms available for sale}} = \text{GOPPAR}$$

or

$$\frac{\$37,500 - \$18,750}{500 \text{ rooms available for sale}} = \text{GOPPAR}$$

or

$$\$18,750 / 500 = \$37.50 \text{ GOPPAR}$$

Note, however, that at least two problems exist with the fixed- or single-price model. First, the hotel has not generated any extra income from those guests who might have been willing to pay *more* than $150.00 for rooms. These high-end guests, indicated in Region B of Figure 4.1 perceive relatively greater value than do other guests for your rooms, and as a result, would be quite willing to pay a higher price. Recalling the lessons you learned from eBay sellers, it should not be surprising to find that some guests will value your rooms more than do other guests. The excess, or difference between what some consumers would have willingly paid (for example, up to $225.00 per night in this scenario), and what they actually paid ($150.00) is $75.00 per room ($225.00 willing to pay – $150.00 actually paid = $75.00).

As a result, those guests who would have paid $225.00 for your rooms actually saved $75.00. Economists refer to this buyer savings as **consumer surplus**.

Essential RM Term

Consumer surplus: The difference between the amount a buyer would be willing to pay for a product or service and the amount they are charged.

Consumer surplus simply represents the difference between what you were willing to pay for a product and the lesser amount you were charged by the seller. Consider, in this example, that if your hotel could capture all or even some of the consumer surplus related to the sale of your rooms, the increase in revenue you would achieve could be significant. The potential size of this market, representing all of those guests who received some level of consumer surplus at your $150.00 price, is identified in region "B" of Figure 4.1.

Note that with fixed pricing, you eliminate your ability to capture any legitimately earned consumer surplus. Thus, your hotel's extra attention to cleanliness, excellent customer service, efficiency and positive staff attitude may have created an increase in perceived customer value for buyers who seek those traits in a hotel, but you did not collect on it. As a result, your fixed pricing strategy short-changed your hotel.

The second significant issue related to a fixed price strategy on the part of the hotel in this example is the large number of customers (identified in Region "C" of Figure 4.1) who will not pay $150.00 per night for your rooms, despite the fact that they are willing to pay a price somewhat above your hotel's variable cost of providing the room. The result is that, had you charged a rate of at least $76.00 or more, each of these potential guests could be paying an amount that would cover your hotel's variable room costs and contribute revenue that could be applied toward your hotel's fixed operating costs.

Because hotels have high levels of fixed operating expense, selling to these types of customers can be very attractive and, depending on the actual rate charged, quite profitable. This is especially the case when the rooms would otherwise go unsold. Again, utilizing a fixed pricing strategy shortchanges your hotel because you did not sell rooms to those who would not pay $150.00, but would have paid a rate higher than $75.00.

Compounding the hotel's problems, this fixed-pricing strategy also provides the hotel's lower-priced competitors the opportunity to enter the market if they have not already done so, or if they have, to improve their competitive stature in it. By pricing their rooms, for example, at $149.00 or less, they may sell a large number of them.

Experienced RMs know that as a general rule, it is better to serve multiple market segments by offering multiple prices than it is to serve their property's or company's entire market at a single price point. The logical question that arises, of course, is how many submarkets should be identified and how many different price points should be established? That is a question best answered on a property-by-property basis; however, to illustrate the power of even a minimal application of differential pricing, assume you elected to implement a simple three-price strategy at your hotel. Utilizing this strategic pricing approach, you identify your rates as "Low," "Regular," and "High." You set the Low rate at $100.00 per night, and establish the High rate at $200.00 per night. The Regular rate remains $150.00

Assume that, when utilizing this approach, the hotel continues to sell 250 regular rated rooms per night. Assume also, however, that 100 low-priced rooms could be sold per day, and that with effective marketing, at least 25 high-price rooms could be sold per day. Under these assumptions, the hotel would sell a total of 375 rooms per night (250 regularly priced + 100 low-priced + 25 high-priced rooms = 375 total rooms). The hotel's occupancy would increase by 50 percent, from its current 50 percent to the significantly higher 75 percent, as shown by utilizing the *% Change in Occupancy* formula:

$$\frac{\text{New occupancy \%} - \text{Previous occupancy \%}}{\text{Previous occupancy \%}} = \text{\% Change in occupancy}$$

In this example:

$$(75\% - 50\%) / 50\% = 50\% \text{ change (increase) in occupancy}$$

The impact on the hotel's ADR and GOPPAR is shown in Figure 4.2. While ADR *declines* by 6.7 percent, due to the sale of 100 low-priced rooms, the hotel's GOPPAR increases by a very significant 30 percent!

There are two lessons that can be learned from this illustration. The first is that a thoughtful and informed analysis of changes in a hotel's ADR, whether an increase or a decrease, can only be properly undertaken in *conjunction* with a GOPPAR analysis. Note that, in this scenario, the implementation of differential pricing caused your ADR to decline by 6.7 percent. Meanwhile, GOPPAR increased by an extraordinary 30 percent. Experienced RMs know that the use of differential pricing can routinely increase a seller's profitability by 10 to 100 percent!

Figure 4.2	Single-Price versus Three-Price Strategy				
Strategy	**Rooms Sold**	**Room Revenue**	**ADR**	**GOPPAR***
Single Price				
($150.00)	250	$37,500	$150.00	$37.50
Tiered Pricing				
Low ($100.00)	100	$10,000	$100.00	$5.00
Regular ($150.00)	250	$37,500	$150.00	$37.50
High ($200.00)	25	$5,000	$200.00	$6.25
Total Tiered Pricing	**375**	**$52,500**	**$140.00**	**$48.75**
Change % Change	+ 125 + 50%	+ $15,000 + 40%	− $10.00 − 6.7%	+ $11.25 + 30%

*(Total Rooms Revenue less $75.00 controllable costs per room sold)/Rooms Available to Sell

The second lesson to be learned from this example is also tremendously important to understanding the power of differential pricing. Consider the high-priced room that sells for $200.00. Its "after costs" contribution to the GOPPAR calculation is $125.00 per room ($200.00 selling price less $75.00 per room sold cost = $125.00).

A regular-priced room contributes $75.00 ($150.00 selling price less $75.00 per room sold cost = $75.00). The difference in room profitability is $50.00, resulting in a 66.7 percent improvement in profits ($125.00 − $75.00)/$75.00 = 66.7%) when the higher priced room is sold. Where did these extra profits come from? The answer is consumer surplus. As this example demonstrates, effort expended to capture consumer surplus is extremely important because of its direct impact on profits. Consumer surplus represents 100 percent profit for a business and it can only be captured via differential pricing.

Differential pricing means charging different prices to different guests. The potential ethical issues related to differential pricing will be addressed in the next chapter, but it is important for you to recognize that your customers, as well as your hotel, clearly benefit from differential pricing. Using your 500-room hotel as an example, consider that when differential pricing was applied, the same 250 buyers purchase their room for $150.00. For them, differential pricing had no effect.

In addition, however, 100 buyers who were priced out of the market because of an inability to pay $150.00 per night are now able to purchase rooms at an affordable (for them) $100.00 per night. In this case, as in most cases, utilizing a price differentiation strategy is a win-win situation for a hotel and its guests. Recall the examination of wine pricing presented in Chapter 2. Restaurateurs who capture the consumer surplus of those diners who are willing to pay more for an enhanced dining experience (i.e., one that includes wine) allow diners who do not value that experience as much the ability to enjoy their meals at a more affordable price; while maintaining the overall profits targets established by the operation. Again, this presents a win-win situation for both restaurateurs and the wide range of guests they serve.

Returning to our hotel example, even those guests paying $200.00 per night benefit because they were able to purchase their room at a price they felt represented excellent value to *them*.

LIMITS TO DIFFERENTIAL PRICING

If different customers place different values on the same products and services, and if differential pricing is such a powerful tool, why don't all sellers aggressively practice it? The answer is simple: *It is not easy.*

Some savvy buyers who find they have been quoted higher prices have strong incentives to undermine differential pricing. The fact that a buyer is willing to pay a higher price does not mean they will be willing to do so if they can secure a lower price for the same item. You might be willing to pay $50.00 for a pair of jeans. If you find them offered for sale at $40.00 you would be pleased. If you decided to pay $40.00 but, when you were checking out, found that the buyer ahead of you in line was paying $30.00, you would not be so pleased. In addition, customers who are willing to pay higher prices do not automatically signal their intent to do so simply to improve the profitability of a seller. In fact, both types of customers may

Essential RM Term

FOM: The individual responsible for administration of a hotel's front office/front desk area. This is an industry term for front office manager.

become adept at disguising themselves as customers who prefer to pay, or qualify for, lower prices. Experienced hotel **FOM**s and desk agents will readily recognize such common guest behavior as misrepresenting their ages (to qualify for senior citizen discounts) or their membership in selected groups such as AAA or AARP to obtain discounts targeted for members of these associations.

Complicating matters further, especially in the lodging industry, is that savvy distributors and wholesalers of various types can negotiate very low prices with inexperienced RMs and then resell the products they buy to customer segments willing to pay higher prices. This type of capture of consumer surplus is especially damaging to the lodging industry and its entire customer base because, as you have learned, it is that surplus that is typically available to help support lower prices for all lodging customers. When distributors sell products at too-low prices, the consumer surplus disappears from the seller providing the product and is instead paid fully to the distributor. It is important to note that in the hospitality industry, distributors do not actually transport products from point A to point B as they would in the case of manufactured goods. Rather, they serve merely as booking agents for hotels, and in many cases, compete directly for customers with those from whom they originally secured the rooms. This makes their capture of consumer surplus even more damaging to the financial health of a hotel and its customers.

If RMs recognize that different customers value their products differently, and are willing to pay different amounts for them, it follows that prices should reflect these buyer differences. Despite the difficulties involved, those RMs working in the hospitality industry and who seek to maximize profits must learn to practice differential pricing by overcoming four pricing-related challenges:

1. *Imperfect knowledge.* Unfortunately, it simply isn't always possible to know precisely what buyers are willing to pay for what they want to buy. Professional buyers can get very good at hiding their actual intention. As a result, RMs often must base the prices for the products and services they sell on their estimate of the *average* willingness of customer segments to pay. Inevitably, some buyers' willingness will fall above that average and others below. Despite this fact, RMs must resist the temptation to structure a *one-price-fits-all* approach. RMs must do better than that simply because if they do not, their more-sophisticated competitors certainly will. Alternatively, however, pricing strategies that result in literally hundreds of different price points targeting dozens or more different groups can quickly become unwieldy. When that happens, even talented sales and marketing staff will not be able to communicate the pricing strategy effectively to guests. In the lodging segment of the hospitality industry, even with the aid of sophisticated computer software, if too many rates are offered to guests the hotel's front office professionals may find they are unable to effectively communicate or manage the property's rate strategy.

2. *Cannibalization.* A significant threat to the implementation of profitable price differentiation strategies is the tendency for "high willingness buyers" to masquerade as "low willingness buyers" and thus avoid paying higher prices. Any time an RM designs a differential pricing strategy there must be an effective way to accurately identify those who qualify for the differentiated price. Do hospitality customers actually

RM IN ACTION 4.1: THE NRA "SHOW"

Say the words: *"The NRA Show"* and hospitality industry veterans know you are talking about the National Restaurant Association's (NRA) annual convention. It is held every May in Chicago, Illinois. This is the world's largest foodservice and hospitality event, and it attracts over 70,000 attendees and 2,000 exhibitors annually from all 50 states and over 100 foreign countries.

In preparation for the event, the NRA Show staff works with Chicago's hoteliers to reserve a large number of guest rooms to be occupied by the event's attendees and exhibitors. Not surprisingly, because of the large number of hotel rooms they request, most of the guest rooms reserved for the NRA event are priced at room rates below those charged others visitors traveling to Chicago on the same dates. It is an excellent example of differential pricing based on large quantity purchasing. But, are those held rooms in danger of being reserved by non-show attendees seeking to take advantage of the lower

rates? They are. To prevent this cannibalization, note the following statement posted on the NRA's official show Web site:

> The National Restaurant Association secures discounted hotel rooms for exhibitors and restaurant/foodservice buyers attending the NRA Show. Should the NRA discover non-exhibiting manufacturers or unregistered attendees in our room blocks, we reserve the right to release those rooms with written notification to the individual or group.

Sophisticated buyers of discounted rooms (such as the NRA) understand that it is in their own best interest to assist hoteliers in identifying and preventing cannibalization. The best buyers work in partnerships with RMs to do just that.

Excerpted on 02/10/2008 from the National Restaurant Association web site (www.restaurant.org).

undertake these cannibalization activities? Yes they do. Can sellers respond with effective countermeasures? Yes they can. Read about an example of this very situation in RM in Action 4.1.

3. *Arbitrage.* If some buyers are willing to pay more than others for the same item, what would keep those buyers who are allowed to purchase at a low price from reselling to those buyers willing to pay a higher price? In many cases, the answer is *nothing*. It is easy to see, however, that **arbitrage** has a negative effect on an RM's ability to effectively maintain differential prices.

Essential RM Term

Arbitrage: The nearly simultaneous purchase of a product at a low price and reselling of it at a higher price with the intention of keeping the difference in price.

As you will learn in Chapter 8, in the time period immediately following 9/11, many U.S. hotels experienced significant reductions in volume. Some responded by selling large amounts of their rooms inventory at very low prices to the newly emerging travel resellers doing business on the Internet. The resellers offered their recently purchased rooms for resale at marked up but still very attractive (low) prices. The result, in the overwhelming majority of cases, was that the hotels were placed in a position of competing against these arbitragers for the very same customers they themselves were targeting.

4.   *Questions of legality or ethics.* Some observers of differential pricing ask a question that is both fundamental and important: *How can an organization charge different prices for what is the same, or essentially the same, product or service?* A related question is: *Is it fair to do so?* Even within the hospitality industry, there may not be universal agreement on an answer. Recall, however, that differential pricing means offering different prices to different customers based on a customer's willingness to buy. In most cases a hospitality firm would not be able to defend offering, at different prices, identical products to identical buyers. Sellers can, however, creatively vary their product and service offerings and criteria that buyers must meet to qualify for these special offers. To illustrate how this can be done, consider that a restaurant may seek to increase its revenues by offering five-dollar pizzas; but they can be purchased only if the customer agrees to buy at least three of them at a time.[3]

Similarly, a golf course may choose to offer reduced green fees for players, but only if the players are willing to tee off before 8:00 A.M. or after 4:00 P.M. This strategy, of course, is designed to encourage play during the course's less busy time periods. The price offered seeks to communicate a unique value message to those golfers willing to play at slower times in order to gain the advantage of a reduced green fee.

In the hotel industry, examples of differential pricing are plentiful. Hyatt Hotels, for example, can offer seniors (age 62 and over) saving of up to 50 percent on prevailing rates at participating Hyatt Hotels and Resorts in the continental U.S. and Canada.[4] Hyatt's pricing strategy in this case targets a unique buyer group (seniors) and offers buyers in this age group reduced pricing not available to everyone.

Essential RM Term

Price fence: The specific requirements that describes who is and is not eligible for a special pricing offer.

Also known as a *hurdle* or *barrier,* a price fence must be legal and should be rationale.

Each of these selected seller's value offers illustrate how creative sales and marketing departments can help communicate special offers intended to directly address differences in guest needs and value perception. These sales and marketing professionals then must carefully communicate to buyers the **price fences** that define those buyers eligible for the special offer.

Not surprisingly, those industries that have highly perishable inventories; for example, airlines, car rental agencies, hotels, and cruise ships, have become very adept at differential pricing. Each has suffered, however, from the sometimes perception of customers that their pricing systems are confusing, irrational, unethical, or predatory. When a differential pricing strategy is ineptly applied it can be easy to see why buyers would feel that way.

To illustrate, consider that few consumers would find it objectionable for a seller to offer price discounts for senior citizens. All consumers, however, would oppose differential pricing based upon a customer's race, ethnicity, or religious background. Such an approach would clearly be unethical and illegal. The question of ethics in pricing is an important one. The question of legality in pricing is just as important. This is so because, as you will learn in Chapter 5, some pricing practices are illegal in the United States, and as an RM, you must be well aware of these. Differential pricing when properly practiced, however, is perfectly legal.

RM IN ACTION 4.2: KISS LADIES' NIGHT GOODBYE?

Few people complain about the "early-bird" specials given to senior citizens as a means of increasing the frequency with which these individuals go out to eat. The same is true when hotels allow children 18 and under to stay in their parent's guest room at no extra charge, while instituting additional per-guest charges for those who are older or not related. What about Ladies' Nights? In this case, pricing is based on the buyer's gender. While historically popular with buyers of both sexes, gender-based differential pricing strategies are under fire, as the following ABC news report indicates:

> Den Hollander is a New York lawyer who says Ladies' Night drinks and admission specials are unconstitutional, and he says he's suffered personally. "I'm tired of having my rights violated and being treated as a second-class citizen," said Hollander, who is seeking class-action status for his suit in federal court.

In his lawsuit, Hollander said he sought to represent all men over age 21 who had entered certain Manhattan nightclubs since June 2004 and been subjected to policies that provide discounts to women of the same age.

Vanessa Elliott, a lawyer representing one of the night clubs charged with discrimination, said in court papers she filed that nightclubs recognize men might not want to visit the clubs if they fail to attract enough women. "Under this theory, male customers may actually benefit from ladies' nights in other ways and be encouraged to attend the club on those nights," she wrote.

Properly designed differential pricing strategies are legal. It is acceptable, for example, to establish a pricing structure that charges those serving in the military lower room rates than those who are not enlisted. Some pricing strategies, however, are neither legal nor ethical. For example, charging a guest more or less because of their national origin is illegal and would, of course, be inappropriate.

In still other cases, such as the one identified in this lawsuit, the appropriateness of a segmented pricing approach is subject to honest debate and to various legal interpretations that will ultimately be decided by the courts. Case law in these areas will continue to evolve and it is the job of RMs to stay up-to-date on all such debates.

Excerpted on 02/11/2008 from abcnews.go.com/TheLaw/story?id=3412561&page=1.

APPLYING DIFFERENTIAL PRICING

One of the greatest drawbacks of a fixed pricing strategy is that it assumes all customers are the same. Although it might seem very fair and even egalitarian to treat each customer as an average customer, good businesses don't do that. Instead, they treat their customers as individuals. Not all customers are the same. Some are high value. They eat in your restaurant on a regular basis or reserve a room at your hotel every time they come into town. These customers do not expect to be treated like everyone else nor should they be.

Essential RM Term

Rewards program: A formalized system of granting special pricing or other benefits for a company's best customers.

It is for that reason hospitality businesses commonly seek to identify and repay their best customers by planning and implementing sophisticated **rewards programs**.

Paradoxically, some businesses give their lowest prices to their worst customers. These customers are the buyers who feel it is their right to put extreme downward pressure on any seller's value offer, continually threatening to take their business elsewhere if the seller does not acquiesce and respond with price reductions. Continually complaining about the prices they pay, these buyers often secure price concessions granted to them by anxious sales staff who are worried business will be lost if these customers price reduction demands are not met.

Experienced RMs, however, know very well that a price should *never* be reduced for a customer simply because that customer feels the price is too high. Doing so cheats the businesses' best customers; those who value a product so much they are willing to pay more for it. At the same time, discounting prices to those who are not willing to pay a fair price subsidizes a firm's worst customers; those who make the purchase based upon low price only.

Customers who value only low price will not be loyal customers because they are not convinced of the value delivered by the seller. Selling too cheaply to them inevitably causes a business to suffer because, as the U.S. twenty-fifth president, William McKinley, pointed out so well years ago, "Cheap prices make for cheap goods."[5] Desirable customers seek quality, not cheapness, in the products and services they buy. When quality products and services are consistently delivered, customers willingly return.

Because customers should not be treated as *average*, it would follow that in the best of all possible worlds, individual prices should be established for each individual customer or, at least, for each individual customer with similar characteristics. Some hospitality professionals use the term "segment pricing" to describe the process of strategically pricing products especially for guests with specific characteristics. This marketing-related term can be useful, but it is important to note that differential pricing is often

▶ RM ON THE WEB 4.1

Hospitality companies go out of their way to ensure their best customers know how much their business is appreciated. The means of doing so vary, but in each case, the organization seeks to communicate to these buyers that their business is important and that if they continue buying, they will benefit in special ways. To review one hotel company's approach to communicating its appreciation to its special guests, go to www.hyatt.com

When you arrive, click *Gold Passport.com* to review the rewards Hyatt gives to its very best customers.

RM AT WORK 4.1

"There's a Rice Krispies Treat and a bottle of water near the TV in my room," said Dan Flood. He had just checked into the Best Western and had called down to the front desk, where Sybil, the Manager on Duty had taken the call.

"Is there a problem?" asked Sybil.

"Well," replied Flood, "I'm a *Best Western Rewards* member and usually my stays are perfect."

"That certainly is one reason why we are one of the world's largest hotel brands with over 4,200 hotels in 80 countries," replied Sybil.

"Right, I know that," replied Flood. "That's part of the reason why I joined your *Rewards* program. I know about the airline miles, free rooms, and the gift cards, but what I'm telling you is that somebody left a package of Rice Krispies Treats and a bottle of Aquafina on the counter near my TV."

"That would be us, sir," replied Sybil. "Welcome to our hotel. Oh, and if you prefer, we do have chocolate chip cookies."

1. When two products are identically priced, but one seller offers a frequent customer awards program, it makes the alternative seller's product to be perceived as having a higher price. Some individual hotel operators, like those who own Sybil's hotel, do more than their company or franchisor requires. The result is often customers whose expectations are exceeded. What are some other no-cost or low-cost benefits any hotel could offer to its "Rewards-type" members to provide even more value in their purchase? What are some no-cost or low-cost benefits any restaurant could offer to its "Rewards-type" members to provide even more value in these customer's purchases?

2. How do you think Mr. Flood will feel about this specific branded hotel in the future? If there were multiple Best Western franchised properties in the immediate vicinity, do you think he would return to this one on a future visit to the area?

3. It has been said that strategic pricing means providing the right price; to the right customer; at the right time and for the right product. Rewards-type programs provide incentives for guests to return, but also offer access to the names and addresses of previous customers. How can RMs use that information in ways that help them advertise right-priced special events and promotions to their best customers?

applied *within* a seller's specific market segments. For example, within a hotel's transient guest segment, prices may be greatly differentiated based on defined subsegments of this larger market segment.

Experienced RMs know that there are a wide variety of important ways rational differential pricing strategies can be applied in the hospitality industry. These strategies can be grouped into eight broad categories that can impact differential pricing. These categories are shown in Figure 4.3, and each will be examined in detail.

Figure 4.3 | **Factors Impacting Differential Pricing**

Customer Characteristics

One of the most common differential pricing strategies is that of offering the same product or service, at different prices, to selected *groups* of buyers known or assumed to have different willingness to buy. The identification of such groups requires that RMs give thoughtful consideration to the unique buyer characteristics of their specific market segments. In the hospitality industry, some common examples of such groups include:

Senior citizens

Students

Families

Frequent customers

Favored customers

Members of select organizations

Possessors of a special offer or coupon

To be successful when using customer characteristics as a differential pricing strategy it is important to ensure that:

1. *There is an accurate method of determining the customer's identifying characteristic.* I.D. cards used to verify age, seller or buyer maintained records of purchase frequency

and organizationally issued membership cards are all examples of accurate and distinct identification methods used to separate those who qualify for a special price from those who do not.

2. *The product or service sold cannot be easily exchanged among buyers.* This is necessary to avoid arbitrage. One method of doing so is to institute a "one-per-customer" restriction on purchases. That prevents a potential arbitrager from buying large quantities of a product at a low price with the intention of reselling the products at a higher price. Ticket scalping for concert and sporting events is one example of arbitrage. Some online sales of discounted hotel rooms are another.

3. *The characteristic used is defendable, and acceptable, to other buyers.* For example, consider the use of advancing age as a characteristic to grant favored pricing status to senior citizens taking their grandchildren to an amusement park. This is a common attractions-industry[6] pricing strategy. Most park visitors view it as acceptable because seniors are perceived as not as likely as others to use the park's most popular ride attractions. Thus, other park attenders do not perceive the granting of this benefit as reducing the value of their own purchases. RMs must be careful, however. A restaurant that implemented a program allowing seniors to completely bypass long waits for an open table on a busy weekend night, and thus be seated immediately, would not likely find its other waiting customers quite as accommodating or accepting of the concept. Would you be?

For many hospitality businesses, the customer characteristic of "possession of a coupon" has been an excellent way to regulate or limit the number of their special reduced price offers. Possession of the coupon also serves to definitively identify the coupon holder as entitled to the discount. Historically, distribution of coupons has been restricted to the use of print media such as magazines and newspapers. Today's RMs increasingly utilize the Internet to publicize their coupon or other special offers and they save marketing dollars by permitting buyers to self-print the coupons.

▶ RM ON THE WEB 4.2

It likely comes as no surprise that those travelers who are "coupon clippers" may have a lower willingness to pay for the products for which they clip coupons than do other buyers. Recognizing that, how can RMs target promotional materials directly at these more thrifty buyers?

One way is simply to place advertising on web sites that target travelers who clip coupons. To review one of several such sites, go to: www.travelcoupons.com

When you arrive, click on a state near you to see the businesses that have elected to target those buyers exhibiting this specialized customer characteristic.

Location

Differential pricing can often be instituted based on the location of the seller. Revenue managers for large lodging chains are well aware that hotel room buyers in Manhattan are, for a variety of reasons, likely to pay more for a guest room there than would a buyer purchasing an identical room located in Milwaukee, Wisconsin. For the same reason, a draft beer at the airport or a professional ball park can typically be sold for a higher price than the exact same draft beer purchased in a small neighborhood tavern. Product and service prices are often based on the location of the seller.

A variation of this location-based approach exists when the location of the *buyer* varies. Ski resorts utilize this approach. For an annual fee, skiers in many locations can purchase a season pass that provides unlimited skiing. The season passes are sold at a significant savings compared to the cost of buying daily lift tickets. But the procedures restricting their purchase makes it highly impractical for visiting skiers to buy one. The sale of the passes begins in late summer and ends well before the snow begins to fall. In most cases, buyers must purchase their pass in person (one per customer) and most often have an identification photo taken at the time of purchase that will be affixed to the season-long pass. The targeted segment for this pricing strategy is *local* area residents. The strategy works well on several conceptual levels and examining it closely can give RMs a good indication of how differential pricing actually works.

First, the restrictions on buying in person prior to snow falling ensures that in nearly all cases, only local skiers will purchase the passes. This is a market consisting of buyers who, because they live close to many ski options, are unlikely to pay the full-day prices charged by the resorts during their busiest periods. Second, holders of season passes actually tend to avoid the busiest times for the resort and use their passes during off-periods. They do so simply because there is no reason to wait in long lift lines when they can easily arrange to ski on other days. The result is an increased ability of the resorts to service higher-paying skiers during peak ski periods. Finally, this pricing strategy is a good one because local skiers will likely also purchase food, beverages, ski equipment, and other skiing-related services offered by the resort. The result is increased revenue generated from a buyer segment that would otherwise be priced out of the market.

Although it is less common at this time, thoughtful RMs in the restaurant business may begin to more seriously consider the location, not of their buyer, but of their buyer's *dining experience* when establishing prices. Currently only a few restaurants offer their customers significant savings for buying food and consuming it away from the restaurant (where the operation's costs are reduced). When it does occur now, it frequently takes the form of pizzas that are sold for a lowered price, but only if the buyer picks up the product and consumes it at a different (nonrestaurant) location.

In the early days of QSR drive-through windows, guests gladly paid the same prices as those eating in the restaurants because of the convenience and time savings delivered along with the food items they purchased. As today's consumers increase their use of takeout, curbside pickup, drive-through, and at-home delivery options, serious consideration should be given to implementing pricing strategies that reward some of these customers for buying in a manner that minimizes operational costs and frees seating capacity, thus providing operators the ability to optimize RevPASH—an important RM concept that will be explored in detail in Chapter 11.

Time

Incorporating time into the strategic pricing equation allows RMs to capture consumer surplus from those buyers who place a high value on securing a product or service when they want it, while providing real savings to those who are able or even prefer to wait, even though these buyers recognize they might not ultimately be able to obtain the item at a time of their choosing or for a lower price. Segmenting prices by time also helps sellers who experience idle production capacity. Movie theater owners implement this strategy when they offer highly discounted mid-day matinee prices. Airlines address variations in demand for preferred times by pricing flights higher during those periods (mid-day and evening) when most fliers prefer to fly. Of course, this strategy also permits those fliers who place a lower value on a specific departure time to benefit from the reduced prices offered to minimize the impact of the airline's idle production capacity (i.e., empty seats.)

Time-sensitive pricing is one of the most commonly used differential pricing techniques because it affects so many businesses. Hotels, restaurants, long-distance telephone companies, beauty parlors, barber shops, and parking garages are just a few examples of businesses whose products are time sensitive. Astute RMs, however, soon recognize that instituting a reduction in price for all buyers choosing to purchase during the off-peak periods is not the best pricing approach.

In a business hotel, Sunday night is traditionally a low-demand day. Those business travelers, however, arriving on Sunday for an important Monday morning meeting clearly do not value their room less than a similar business traveler arriving on Monday (a high-demand day) for a Tuesday morning meeting.

A Sunday night price reduction for all Sunday travelers only serves to reduce overall revenues. Nor will a heavy discount for Sunday night likely entice the Monday arriving traveler to book an additional night (Sunday) simply to take advantage of the lowered price. Rather, an effective strategic pricing strategy targets, for example, local residents who would not typically stay in the hotel normally, but could be enticed to do so on Sunday night via an attractive price, while maintaining higher price levels for those who value their rooms more highly.

Quantity

The quantity of an item purchased is one of the most universally accepted reasons for a seller's price differentiation. Variations, typically in the form of reductions, in price can be given in response to a buyer's increased order size; the amount purchased at one time or for the total purchase amount; or the amount purchased over a defined time period.

As a seller, offering lower prices for large purchases serves three purposes. First, it rewards those good customers who buy a great deal of product or services from you. Second, it encourages buyers to buy more. Customers who buy in large volume are often price sensitive and knowledgeable because they buy so much. They also typically have significant experience in the negotiation of prices. These buyers appreciate the lower prices resulting from quantity buying. For this reason, a barbeque restaurant that offers its customers six beers sold in a "bucket" at a price lower than that of six individual beers knows that its customers benefit by paying a lower price per beer purchased, while the operation benefits as well because it sells more product. Third, while large volume customers may be harder to obtain, when their business is won they are generally easier and less costly to service than other buyers. This is so because the costs of selling and servicing an account do not increase proportionately with the volume of purchases made. This makes the per-unit cost of selling to high-volume buyers less than the cost associated with low-volume buyers.

Every customer who has purchased a large bag of potato chips, or any other item, because they cost less per ounce or serving than do smaller bags understands the buyer's rationale for buying in larger quantity. The more customers buy, the more they save. While in actuality these buyers are spending more, their perception and their reality is that they are spending less per unit purchased.

Interestingly, in different segments within the hospitality industry, sellers react differently to customers who buy in volume. For example, hoteliers treat their volume buyers much differently than do restaurant operators. A guest seeking to reserve ten or more guest rooms for a specific night would likely be referred to a hotel's group sales department and the price per room quoted by that department would likely be less than the price charged if the customer sought to buy only one room on the same night. That same buyer entering a restaurant with nine fellow diners and suggesting to the manager on duty that a price discount should be granted because she plans to purchase ten steak dinners for her fellow diners would not find many restaurateurs receptive to that suggestion. In fact, while most food service operations are menu-price neutral regarding a customer's order size, some actually implement policies that can discourage quantity buyers. These operations assess a mandatory **service charge** on tables larger than a certain size; often six to eight diners.

Essential RM Term

Service charge: A mandatory amount added to a guest's bill for services performed by the seller.

Realistically, this service charge constitutes an *increase* in price paid based on a larger-sized purchase. It is a practice defended on the basis of ensuring that guest tips are an appropriate amount or to compensate the restaurant for the additional costs of servicing a larger group. Regardless of the validity or necessity of such charges, however, when service charges are assessed to large dining groups the increase amounts to an increase in the price charged to the customer and thus should be implemented only after careful consideration.

Many restaurants do reward customers for volume purchases made over time through a customer rewards programs. An additional and very popular discounting techniques employed by restaurateurs is that of offering a volume-related price reduction, but only for an incremental, not the initial, purchase. Thus, a promotion that allows guest to "buy one meal at full price, get the second meal at half price" illustrates how sellers can apply a quantity discount to the second, but not the first, purchase price. This approach works well because it increases the number of total diners served, while maintaining the integrity of full pricing for those who are dining alone.

Two-tiered pricing, a strategy introduced in Chapter 2, is a variation on the quantity discount concept. Recall that a two-tier pricing strategy allows buyers the option of electing or declining to make additional purchases after their initial purchase has been made. Two-tiered pricing also permits those businesses offering more than one distinguishable product the benefits that result from differential pricing. To illustrate, consider a comedy club that offers its customers both a stand-up comedy show and the ability to purchase alcoholic beverages.

One pricing option for such a club would be to offer free admission and then to factor the cost of the entertainment into the price of the drinks it sells. Such a strategy would inevitably penalize quantity drink buyers because it would charge them more, while subsidizing the low-volume drink buyers who would benefit from the "almost free" entertainment.

Under such a pricing strategy, volume drink buyers would likely be inclined to go elsewhere and the club operator might ultimately find it difficult to recover the operation's entertainment cost relying only on those remaining patrons who prefer to buy a smaller number of few drinks. To address this problem, entertainment clubs of many types implement both a cover charge and a charge for drinks or food items consumed in the club. Utilization of this strategy helps ensure that those who buy more are not penalized for doing so.

Distribution Channel

Recall from Chapter 1 that a distribution channel is a source of business customers or the vehicle to communicate with a source of customers. Most hospitality sellers advertise their products or offer them for sale through a number of distribution channels. These typically include their own operations, other brick and mortar locations (for example, travel agencies) or electronic "stores" (e.g., the seller's web site).

Figure 4.4 illustrates some of the distribution channels typically used by hotels to deliver reservations to their **central reservation system (CRS)** or directly to a hotel's **property management systems (PMS)**.

The number and type of different distribution channels available to hoteliers and the management of these channels

Essential RM Terms

Central reservation system (CRS): The structure used to accept hotel guests' reservations and communicate them to an individual hotel's property management system (PMS).

Property management systems (PMS): The hardware and software used to record reservations, guest stay information, and payments, as well as to record and store other relevant hotel operations data.

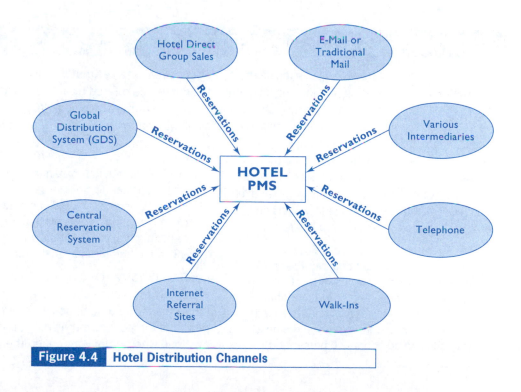

Figure 4.4 | **Hotel Distribution Channels**

are so important they will be examined in detail later in Chapter 8. From a differential pricing perspective, however, it is important to recognize that the use of distribution channels increases the number of a seller's locations (points of distribution), and as a result, it increases the options and complexity of pricing and selling.

Different distribution channels exist because they appeal to different types of buyers. Distribution channels in the hospitality industry may generally be classified as either direct or indirect. A **direct channel** is one in which the ultimate product or service user buys directly from the seller. In a direct marketing channel, no **intermediaries** are utilized.

For example, when guests call a hotel directly to make a reservation, they are utilizing the telephone as a direct distribution channel. When customers enter a pizza parlor and place a to-go pizza order, they are using the direct channel of face-to-face selling. In many respects, direct distribution channels are superior because they place sellers in one-on-one meetings with buyers. In such a circumstance, sellers have the opportunity to learn much about their buyers. Also, in many cases, the costs associated with utilizing direct distribution channels are less because no intermediate is involved and thus no payment is made by either buyers or sellers for any effort expended on their behalf by an intermediary.

Indirect channels utilize one or more intermediaries and may take a variety of forms. Figure 4.5 lists the terms most commonly used to describe these intermediaries as well as who they are.

Essential RM Terms

Direct channel: A system of selling to consumers without the use of an intermediary.

Intermediary: An entity that acts as a communication or service link between buyers and sellers that are unable or unwilling to deal directly.

Essential RM Term

Indirect channel: A system of selling to consumers utilizing one or more intermediaries.

RM IN ACTION 4.3: THE "LOWEST" PRICE?

With the hundreds of travel-related sites on the Internet, it is not surprising that lodging customers become confused about where they should go to book the rooms they want at the lowest possible rate. In response to this buyer confusion, most hotel chains have rolled out their own version of a "Lowest Rate Guarantee." The one offered by Choice Hotels International, managers of the Comfort Inn and Clarion as well as other brands, is a good example. Its web site states:

> We guarantee the best online rates at any Choice hotel. Just book your room here. If you find a lower published rate for the same hotel and accommodations for the same dates at any other qualified online source, . . . we'll give you the best rate, plus an additional 10 percent off![7]

Sounds reasonable—that is, until you read the guarantee offered by a third-party room reseller, www.ratestogo.com. Its guarantee, similar to that offered by many room resellers, reads:

> If you find a rate lower than the best available Rates To Go Internet rate on another Web site for the same hotel/ accommodation, . . . we will honor that rate for the night(s) for which the lower rate was found and refund you the difference.[8]

Confused? You are not alone. Only in extremely few cases should any profit-seeking intermediary be able to sell standard-quality products for less than the selling price offered by those who actually produced the product.

Figure 4.5	Terms Used For Marketing Intermediaries
Term	**Function**
Agent or broker	Any intermediary with legal authority to act on behalf of the seller
Wholesaler	An intermediary who sells to other intermediaries
Retailer	An intermediary who sells directly to consumers
Middleman	Any intermediary between seller and buyer

In the lodging industry, travel agents and travel agencies are a form of an indirect distribution channel. Web sites such as Travelocity.com, Expedia.com, and Hotels.com are additional examples of indirect distribution channels that hotels can elect to utilize.

From a differential pricing perspective, distribution channels are important for two key reasons. The first is that some buyers prefer to use a specific channel when making their purchases and they are willing to pay more; or may feel they should pay less, when they use that channel. To illustrate, consider the local couple who wishes to reserve a hotel room for use on the night they are celebrating their twentieth wedding anniversary. Such local buyers could physically drive to several area hotels, inquire about rates, view many different guest rooms and their features, return to the hotel that best meets their needs, and then make their room reservation in person. Alternatively, they could call several hotels directly, receive price quotes, and then call the selected hotel back to make the preferred reservation. Both approaches are time consuming.

Today's computer-savvy rooms buyer would likely find it much more convenient to simply search the Web using one or more available intermediary search sites, compare alternatives, and then electronically book their preferred room. Would such a buyer likely be willing to pay a different price than that quoted by the hotels directly simply for the convenience and cost savings associated with the Web-based room selection process? In most cases, the answer is yes.

Buyers may utilize a variety of distribution channels because their use allows for buying the products they want when they want them. As a result, marketing channels often add value to the products and services purchased by these buyers. When they do, differential pricing can be applied to these value-adding distribution channels utilized by customers.

Many of the indirect distribution channels in use today are Internet based. That is good news for most hospitality industry RMs, because while the Internet often makes it possible for buyers to find lower prices, it also makes it easier for sellers to find buyers who are willing to pay higher prices. In addition, utilization of the Internet as a way to advertise a seller's prices reduces almost to zero the **communication costs** associated with changing prices.

The second reason why distribution channels affect pricing is that channel operators, including intermediaries of all types, charge sellers for their services. Intermediaries in any business certainly have a right to charge for the services

Essential RM Term

Communication costs (pricing-related): The cost of printing and distributing new prices to buyers (for example, on brochures, flyers, or price lists).

Essential RM Term

Net ADR yield: The proportion of the standard rate (ADR) for a room sale that is actually realized by a hotel after subtracting the cost of fees and assessments associated with the specific distribution channel responsible for the room's sale.

The formula for net ADR yield is:

$$\frac{\text{Net room rate}}{\text{Standard ADR}} = \text{Net ADR yield}$$

Where:

$$\text{Standard ADR} - \text{Distribution channel costs} = \text{Net room rate}$$

they provide. In some cases, these charges are levied on the buyer of products sold. In other cases, however, it is the seller who is charged for use of the distribution channel.

For sellers, the costs related to selling in different channels can vary dramatically. Experienced RMs recognize that these costs can and must be managed. The careful selection of distribution channels chosen to be used by RMs is one way of managing these costs. There are other ways. For example, one important channel-related task facing RMs in the lodging industry is that of managing pricing in such a manner as to move repeat buyers from higher-cost channels of distribution to those that have a better **net ADR yield**.

Effective RMs understand that due to distribution channel costs, all revenue dollars are *not* created equally. Figure 4.6 illustrates typical net ADR yields associated with six hypothetical distribution channels.

Note in Figure 4.6 that a $299.99 room sold by a high net ADR yield channel (Channel 1) will be more *profitable* than the same rate sold on a channel with a significantly lower net ADR yield (Channel 6) because it yields more net revenue per room.

RMs must understand the channels of distribution available to them and price their products strategically on those channels. As well, they should seek, where possible, to maximize net revenue via the movement of repeat buyers from higher- to lower-cost distribution channels.

Figure 4.6	Net ADR Yields by Distribution Channel				
Source	Net ADR Yield	Rate	Net Per Room	Rooms Sold	Net Revenue
Channel 1	98%	$299.99	$293.99	100	$29,399
Channel 2	95%	$299.99	$284.99	100	$28,499
Channel 3	90%	$299.99	$269.99	100	$26,999
Channel 4	88%	$299.99	$263.99	100	$26,399
Channel 5	85%	$299.99	$254,99	100	$25,499
Channel 6	80%	$299.99	$239.99	100	$23,999
Total				600	$160,794

Product Versioning

Thus far, we have examined how differential pricing can be used to charge different prices to different buyers for *identical* products. Product versioning refers to the practice of varying the form of the product or service and then varying price. Drivers know that gasoline stations routinely practice price differentiation through product versioning when they offer premium gasoline for sale at a price 10 to 20 cents higher than the price charged for regular grade gasoline. This is done even though the station may pay only 3 to 5 cents more per gallon for premium themselves. Product versioning is a powerful differentiation technique because often the difference in seller costs between the product versions offered is slight, but the impact on buyers is significant. To make the tactic work best, the lower-priced version should be inadequate to meet the desires of less-price-sensitive buyers, such as those who own high-performance cars, while fully satisfying the needs of more-price-sensitive buyers.

Tickets for sporting events provide another excellent example of product versioning. While some novice ticket buyers might believe that any one ticket to a New York Yankees baseball game is the equivalent of any other, those sitting in the right field seats truly have purchased a different version of admission ticket than have those who are sitting behind home plate. In football, the price premium is placed on "50-yard line" seats, in boxing, "ringside" seating is preferred, and in basketball, it is "center court" seating that is most highly prized.

Any time sellers offer products in a quality range from *good* to *better* to *best*, they are engaging in product versioning by offering buyers varying purchase opportunities. It works well because inevitably, some buyers value the very best product or service available while others are quite satisfied with merely "good" quality and service. Versioning also permits sellers to repay loyal buyers of their good and better products by strategically upgrading them to the seller's "best" product for the same price. This not only rewards customer loyalty but may also help move the customer in the future to buy a higher-level, higher-priced product since the guest will now have sampled a higher-quality version of the product they had purchased in the past.

Airlines use product versioning by offering both First Class and economy seating. Some airlines offer Business Class seats as a mid-grade option. Car rental agencies practice versioning by offering various levels of car size and perceived quality. Food operations routinely practice product versioning when they sell "half-sized" portions for a price numerically equal to, or slightly greater than, one half the selling price of a full portion.

Interestingly, restaurants themselves are the beneficiaries of product versioning when chefs buy brand-name vegetables or fruits that have been canned and sold to distributors to be resold, for a lower price, under these distributors' own private labels (e.g., Sysco, Gordon, or US Foodservice brands).

Essential RM Term

Room types: A lodging term used to identify specific guest room configurations. For example, king bed versus queen bed rooms, suites versus standard rooms, and ocean view versus garden view or standard view rooms.

Product versioning works when nearly all of a seller's customers can easily determine the quality difference in the products or services offered. Hotels use product versioning extensively. Figure 4.7 illustrates this concept by listing the **room types** and their associated prices at the hypothetical Hotel Pastrada, a full-service hotel located in a beach community.

It is important to note that variations in the room selling, cleaning, and maintenance costs associated with

Figure 4.7	Hotel Pastrada Room Rates

Hotel Pastrada Room Rates: Effective 1/1/20XX	
Room Type	**Rate**
Single Queen	$199.99
Double Queen	$209.99
King	$229.99
King Parlor Suite	$249.99
King Parlor Suite with Ocean View	$299.99
Honeymoon Suite	$349.99

the various room types at the Hotel Pastrada are likely minimal. Those RMs working in hotels where room types provide natural versioning opportunities are wise to take advantage of them. Room sizes, features, and amenities all provide grounds for creative product versioning. The authors are familiar with one rectangular-shaped hotel that billed its west-facing rooms as "Sunset Rooms," and its east-facing rooms as "Sunrise Rooms," leaving only the few rooms on each end of this North/South running building to be promoted as its "Standard Rooms."

Essential RM Term

Price band: The span from lowest to highest price in a range of prices.

Restaurant wine lists provide yet another excellent example of product versioning. Prices on traditional wine lists fall within a **price band** that offers lower-cost wines for those who prefer them, while providing the opportunity to purchase the very best wines for those discriminating guests who value fine wines highly.

Some RMs are unduly concerned that offering lower-priced versions of their products will encourage all buyers to purchase only the "stripped down" versions. In fact, the opposite is most often true. Despite the universal interest in paying the lowest possible prices *for what they want*, few buyers actually are comfortable defining *what they want* as the cheapest product offered for sale. Recall that these products are known to be selling for a lower price because they unmistakably lack desirable features or valuable characteristics provided by the seller's higher-priced product alternatives. Put simply, albeit in a nonhospitality context, would you prefer to own the cheapest car manufactured in the United States or one that rightly sells for more because of its better quality or features? Put in another context, would you really like your own heart transplant surgery performed by the cheapest surgeon in town? Or one of the best?

Product versioning offers talented RMs many chances to employ creativity and flexibility. Those considering versioning as a way of instituting differential pricing may choose to do one or more of the following:

- **Add features:** This may include increasing quality, quantity, or the service levels provided to customers.

- **Subtract features:** Doing so may allow the product or service to appeal to new customers while leaving current customers unaffected.

■ **Add a service to a product:** In some cases, the service may be permitting the customer to save time by avoiding a wait, or to feel pampered, or even to circumvent having to perform a less-than-pleasant task related to the purchase (e.g., the effective "We'll Pick You Up" promotion offered by Enterprise Car Rentals.) Versioning a product or service to save customers' time is an effective strategy because so many of them will have more money than time. Some of these are the buyers described by American author/businessman Paul Hawken when he observed: "We are speeding up our lives and working harder in a futile attempt to buy the time to slow down and enjoy it."[9] Helping your customers actually slow down and enjoy their life is not just a good thing to do, it is something they count on you to do and they are quite willing to pay you for doing it.

■ **Offer a menu of choices:** In many cases, product alternatives can be easily mixed and matched by the customer. Allowing guests to create their own definition of good, better, and best maximizes the chances of offering a product that is a perfect fit for its buyer. Pizza prices established based on the number of ingredients selected is one very common example of this practice.

RM AT WORK 4.2

"Twenty bucks! I can't believe that," said Ralph.

"Believe it. I heard him," said Karen.

"You're telling me," Ralph said, "that when Mr. James was checking in and asked our desk clerk the difference between our King Suite and our Deluxe Suite, our guy told him . . ."

"Twenty bucks," interrupted Karen.

Mr. James, a new guest, had just checked into the Lamar Hotel. When he arrived, he asked Mike, the desk agent checking him in, the room rate for the King Suite he had reserved. Mike replied "$179.99," the rate shown in the PMS.

When Mr. James then asked the price of a Deluxe Suite he had seen advertised, Mike had quoted the approved rate of $199.99. When Mr. James then asked what the difference was between the two suites, Mike replied, "Twenty bucks."

Karen, the hotel's front office manager had overheard Mike's comment and was now discussing the incident in the office of Ralph Blount, the hotel's GM.

"But the Deluxe Suite has an oversized desk, ergonomic chair, 48-inch high-def flat-screen TV, and a whirlpool tub." protested Ralph. "It's an upgrade from a King Suite in a ton of ways. What did Mr. James do then?"

"He saved twenty bucks," said Karen.

1. Assume Mike wants to be a conscientious employee. Why do you think he answered this guest's question as he did?

2. How do you think Mr. James now views the pricing program in place at the Lamar hotel?

3. It is important that all employees who sell to guests understand their company's product versioning efforts. Who, in this hotel, do you think is responsible for ensuring Mike's answers to guest rate inquiries support the total revenue management efforts of this property?

Bundling

Offering products and services for sale both individually and in combinations allow sellers to increase revenues while reducing prices for those who purchase multiple items. This **bundling** concept is most effective when the price of the items included in the bundle is less than if the same items were purchased individually.

Most consumers are quite familiar with bundling as it is practiced in the QSR industry. In that segment, combo-type meals offer a sandwich, fries, and drink bundle at a price less than the cost of those same three items purchased separately.

Actually, bundling occurs many more times than some RMs realize. Hotels that offer free overnight parking to its guests are engaging in a form of bundling (i.e., room + parking at one price). Full-service restaurants have traditionally offered **prix fixe**, or *table d'hôte* menus, which are complete meals consisting of, for example, appetizer, soup or salad, entrée with vegetable and dessert, all for one price.

Theater and sports venues bundle by offering buyers season tickets at a price much lower than the sum of the prices that are charged for individual game tickets.

Hoteliers most often use the term **package** when referring to the bundles they create.

Thus, for example, a hotel resort with a golf course might create a "golfer's package" that for one price includes overnight accommodations, dinner upon arrival, breakfast the next morning, and 18 holes of golf. Figure 4.8 is an example of a hotel package that targets couples.

Essential RM Term

Bundling: Combining individual products and/or services into groupings that are sold for a single price, usually lower than the sum of the prices charged if the same included items were purchased individually.

Essential RM Term

Prix fixe: French for *fixed price*. A meal offered with several courses for sale at a single price. Also know as *table d'hôte*.

Essential RM Term

Package: The lodging industry term for a group of bundled products and services offered at one price.

Figure 4.8	Barcena Hotel and Resort

ROMANCE and RELAX PACKAGE ®

Through December 27, 20xx   Starting from $349 per night

This signature package provides unique memories for guests visiting our resort and beach.

Package includes:

Deluxe room, Club room, or Suite accommodations for one evening

Welcome basket and Champagne in room at arrival

In-room dining special menu

Romantic breakfast for two in-room or beach-side

One in-room movie

Package rates are per room and are based on single or double occupancy, including breakfast gratuity but excluding tax. Packages may not be combined with any other offer and are subject to availability. Blackout dates apply. Packages are not applicable to groups of 10 or more rooms. For group reservations, please contact the hotel at 1+ (767) 123–4567.

> ▶ **RM ON THE WEB 4.3**
>
> Bundling serves customers in ways beyond price savings. The Ritz Carlton hotel chain sells its rooms at some of the highest prices of any hotel group. Its customers are not extremely price sensitive. Does the chain still offer one-price packages? Absolutely. To view its current package offerings, go to: www.ritzcarlton.com
>
> When you arrive, click *Packages*. Why create packages for affluent guests? These individuals are often time pressed. Creating a package saves them the time and effort required to create a complete travel or vacation experience. These buyers value their time, and they are willing to pay for the privilege of preserving it.

Note that the package clearly states the items included as well as the fences (restrictions) associated with the offer.

While bundling certainly can save time on the part of the buyer by, for example, reducing the time and effort required to select individual menu items when ordering, it is important to recognize that for the majority of buyers, bundling is most powerful when it is very easy to calculate the savings associated with purchasing the bundle. When these savings are perceived as significant, buyers are more inclined to purchase the items in the bundle. When they do, they increase the total sales revenue achieved by the seller from that sale.

Payment Terms

In the hospitality industry, payment terms are an often-underused means of differentiating prices. Experienced lodging industry RMs seeking to optimize GOPPAR recognize that the method and timing of payments for goods and services directly impact the profits of the operation. Food service RMs also know that payment form affects their income directly. Hospitality businesses typically pay a fee of 1 to 5 percent of the selling price charged when their customers utilize payment cards (i.e., credit, debit, and entertainment) rather than cash to pay for their purchases. These **discount fees** can be significant on large purchases and always impact the net profitability of a sale.

Essential RM Term

Discount fees: Charges assessed to sellers for their customers' use of a credit, debit, or entertainment card to pay for purchases.

Nearly all lodging operations and most restaurants (including QSRs), routinely allow guests to pay with "plastic" today, despite the real costs to these sellers of accepting these payment forms. Some restaurateurs (for example, the famous *Carnegie Deli* on Seventh Ave. at 55th Street, New York City[10]), however, still insist on "cash only" for payment because cash is the least expensive way for sellers to receive what they are owed. The advantages of a cash-only operation, of course, is that there are no disputes or chargebacks from the credit card company, no card fees, and no bounced checks.

Most buyers, however, prefer options when choosing how to pay for their purchases and they should of course be accommodated. It is important for RMs to recognize, however, that some alternative payment options are more costly to sellers than others. As a result, the payment method selected can be reasonably used, in some cases, to establish variations in product or services pricing.

How buyers pay matters a great deal. So does when they pay. RMs should note that it is a fact of life for most buyers that consuming products and services is more fun than paying for them. Thus, selling a product or service and collecting the money for it after it has been consumed is more costly and difficult than if the payment were collected prior to the sale.

Most consumers are unlikely to complain about the price paid for an airline ticket or a movie theater ticket even if they did not enjoy the flight or the movie. That's because these buyers paid first, and then experienced what they paid for. A higher percentage complain when they receive the experience first; but pay for it later. This so because few people really love to pay their bills, even when they are legitimate ones. Experienced hospitality managers know that a small percent of customers even refuse to pay for products and services after they have consumed or used them, citing a variety of reasons why they should not be required to do so.

In most cases, payment resistance can be minimized by ensuring customers understand fully the products and services they will receive and the prices they will be charged before they agree to the purchase. In the best-case scenario the purchase price is communicated and collected prior to product or service delivery. This is so because buyers do not like to discover the prices they will charged *after* they have committed to a purchase. When buyers do understand, ahead of time, the prices they will be charged as well as their payment terms, the differences between payment options offered to these buyers can easily be used to differentiate prices.

To illustrate the impact of payment timing on the buyer/seller interaction, consider Figure 4.9. It summarizes some of the risk differences that exist due to the time frames in which lodging customers pay their bills. It provides a rationale for price differentiation

Figure 4.9 Variations on Time of Payment for Lodging Products

Time of Payment	Risk to Buyer	Risk to Seller	Impact on Price
Payment in Advance (partial to full deposit)	Complete. Totally dependent on the integrity of the seller to deliver	None	May indicate a reduction is in order
Payment Upon Delivery of Product or Service (at check out)	Slight. Product or service may not be delivered as promised	Slight. Buyer may refuse to pay	May indicate a price neutral approach is in order
Credit Account (pay well after delivery of product or service)	None	Complete. Totally dependent on the integrity of the buyer to pay	May indicate an increase in price is in order

based on those differences in lodging and other industry segments that routinely allow guests various time of payment options.

Payment disputes are among the most common forms of litigation in the hospitality industry. While the application of strategic pricing cannot be expected to prevent all product and service performance-related conflicts from occurring, experienced RMs understand that the payment method utilized by buyers can and should be permitted to influence the prices that buyers pay.

Experienced RMs also know that the effective use of differential pricing is the key to maximizing operational profitability. In most cases, the secret to inducing buyers to reveal their true willingness to pay is to begin with full price and then to implement price variation in response to buyer characteristic or behaviors that more fully reveal their buying preferences. The strategic use of the eight price-differentiating factors presented in Figure 4.3 and detailed here allows RMs tremendous flexibility in creating and pricing products and services their buyers will perceive as fulfilling their personal perceptions of great value.

REVENUE MANAGEMENT OR REVENUE OPTIMIZATION?

It may seem unusual that as you near the end of this fourth chapter of the book, the term *revenue management* has yet to be formally defined. There is good reason. To truly understand revenue management, an RM must first have a full understanding of value, the meaning of strategic pricing, inventory management, and the deft utilization of differential pricing techniques. When you understand these concepts, you are prepared to evaluate the many and varied definitions of revenue management typically offered by those in the hospitality industry. You are also now prepared to assess the usefulness of each proposed definition.

Some industry professionals have defined revenue management as:

> The combining of people and systems in an attempt to maximize revenue by coordinating the processes of pricing and inventory management.[11]

Others prefer:

> The act of skillfully, carefully, and tactfully managing, controlling, and directing capacity and sources of income, given constraints of supply and demand[12]

Still others prefer:

> The methodological approach to allocating a perishable and fixed inventory to the most profitable customers[13]

Each definition no doubt contains useful perspectives. Collectively, they stress the importance of people, systematic procedures, control of product inventory, and purposeful pricing as RMs seek to best manage their business income. While there certainly would

Essential RM Term

Revenue management: The application of disciplined tactics that predict buyer response to prices, optimize product availability, and yield the greatest business income.

not be universal agreement with the authors' **revenue management** definition, most industry professionals would agree that the revenue management process can be identified by four significant characteristics:

1. It is an active, strategic process requiring extensive, tactical, and insightful decision making on the part of RMs.

2. It requires a focus on buyers and predicting buyer demand in response to strategic pricing decisions made by RMs.

3. It entails the effective management of available product inventory to maximize potential revenue.

4. Its primary goal is increasing a business's income.

Despite its widespread usage, the authors predict that the term or concept of revenue management will soon give way to an improved term. It will be a good change, but as British Novelist Arnold Bennett pointed out well: "Any change, even a change for the better, is always accompanied by drawbacks and discomforts."[14]

Just as the earlier used industry term *yield management* has been replaced, albeit with some inevitable confusion and discomfort, by the broader scoped term *revenue management*, increasingly RMs will be employing the term **revenue optimization** to describe their chief activity of strategically pricing and selling their products and services.

Essential RM Term

Revenue optimization: The application of disciplined tactics that predict buyer response to prices, optimize product availability, and yield the greatest business profits.

In nearly all cases, revenue optimization is simply a better description of what RMs should do than is revenue management. This is so because the effort to maximize income as undertaken by some RMs leads to undue emphasis on the formulas and procedures used to calculate rates and manage inventory *in response* to current guest demand. As a result, traditional revenue management techniques too often teach RMs to maximize the business they already have.

Revenue optimization is more proactive. Instead of simply responding to current demand, revenue optimization asks: "How can we use information to create business we do not already have?" Instead of a focus on RevPAR, revenue optimization focuses on GOPPAR. The distinction will be readily recognized by insightful RMs who understand success in business. They realize that increasing market share to maximize revenues without thought to the profits associated with the increase is foolhardy. It is nice to use sophisticated RM techniques to get more business, but the goal should be to get *better* business.

Simply acquiring more customers or making more sales should not be the goal of any revenue manager. Herb Kelleher, co-founder, chairman, and former CEO of Southwest Airlines, the most profitable and arguably the best managed of all the U.S.-based airline companies, said it best: "Market share has nothing to do with profitability. Market share says we want to be big; we don't care if we make money doing it. In order to get an additional 5 percent of the market, some companies increased their costs by 25 percent. That's really incongruous if profitability is your purpose."[15]

Experienced hospitality professionals know that increased market share does not automatically increase company profitability. If it did, General Motors would not have entered bankruptcy while owning the title of the world's largest auto maker. Instead, as you learned in Chapter 1, only a focus on increasing the wealth of your customers will result in gaining more of them, thus increasing your market share, and ultimately, increasing your company profits. RMs would do well to remember that:

> Increased profitability is not a result of increased market share. Rather, market share increases as a result of increasing the amount of value delivered to your customers.

This concept is difficult for some professionals to grasp. In their view, after a firm's fixed costs have been covered, any incremental revenue in excess of variable costs goes to the bottom line. While that may be true in the accountant's equation, it rarely works so cleanly in the real world. This is so because, in the quest for increased market share, both a firm's fixed and variable costs often increase substantially.

Recall from Chapter 2 that an item's actual unit cost inevitably varies based on the item's price and how many of it are sold. Experienced RMs recognize that prices dictate revenues, and revenues affect costs. As Herb Kelleher points out, in too many cases, additional unit sales can cause increases, not decreases, in total costs.

Also, as you will learn in later chapters of this book, the irrational pursuit of market share costs business in a variety of nonfinancial as well as financial ways. The impact on profits of seeking to maximize revenue *only*; is as dramatic as it is negative. It is for that reason the authors believe the concept of *revenue optimization,* with its superior focus on profitability (GOPPAR), must inevitably supplant that of *revenue management* and its emphasis on income maximization.

In the remaining chapters of this text, the authors will take the liberty of using the common term *revenue management* because of its familiarity and common usage, while simultaneously reinforcing the concepts of *revenue optimization*—the key to maximized profitability that can only be achieved by customer-centric RMs.

❖ ESSENTIAL RM TERMS

Value-based (pricing)	Price fence
Differential pricing	Rewards program
Fixed pricing	Service charge
Inventory management	Central reservation system (CRS)
Branded (hotel)	Property management systems (PMS)
Consumer surplus	Direct channel
FOM	Intermediary
Arbitrage	Indirect channel

Communication costs (pricing-related)	Prix fixe
Net ADR yield	Package
Room type	Discount fees
Price band	Revenue management
Bundling	Revenue optimization

IIIⅢ➡ APPLY WHAT YOU KNOW

1. Sharon Cronin is the revenue manager for a hotel company that owns and operates five full-service hotels operating under the Holiday Inn brand. Each is located on an interstate highway exit, and the average age of the properties is 20 years. As newly built limited-service hotels located near her own properties have chipped away at the occupancy levels of the company hotels, Sharon is seeking to identify characteristics of travelers who still seek the amenities offered by mid-sized full-service properties.

   A. List five identifying characteristics of room buyers you believe Sharon should target as her potential rooms buyers.

   B. Describe a distinct distribution channel you feel Sharon could use to communicate and sell to each of her targeted groups.

   C. Do you believe Sharon should sell to these groups at room rates higher or lower than the rates offered by her newer limited-service competitors? Explain your answer.

2. Tom Rodgers is the director of purchasing of Dart Industries. Tom is responsible for booking 1,000 rooms per month in the city that houses his company's corporate office. Tom approaches you, the DOSM/RM of the local Hawthorne Suites hotel, with a proposition. Instead of paying $159.99 per night; your hotel's normal room rate for corporate travelers, he proposes the following rate structure:

   A. Calculate the room revenue your hotel would receive if Tom booked:

      I.   250 rooms in a month
      II. 350 rooms in a month
      III. 401 rooms in a month

   B. Assume the variable cost associated with selling each room is $65.00. Calculate the "after variable costs" revenue your hotel would receive if Tom booked:

      I.   250 rooms in a month
      II. 350 rooms in a month
      III. 401 rooms in a month

Rooms Purchased	
Per Month	**Room Rate**
1 to 100	$159.99
101 to 400	$139.99
401 to 600	$119.99
601 to 1,000	$109.99

C. As the DOSM/RM for the Hawthorne Suites, would you be in favor of this quantity discount program? Explain your answer.

3. Sandy Miley owns Fox Meadows golf club. The current greens fees for playing one round (18 holes) of golf on her course is $75.00 per player. To increase sales, Sandy partners with six different area hotels that have created golf packages marketed to their own customers. Each hotel pays Sandy a different amount for the rounds of golf included in their package. Sandy wants to calculate a net round yield for each hotel using the formula:

$$\frac{\text{New Round Fee}}{\text{Standard Fee}} = \text{Net Round Yield}$$

Where:

$$\text{Standard Fee} \ (-) \ \text{Distribution Costs} = \text{Net Round Fee}$$

Fox Meadows Weekly Sales Recap:

Source	Standard Fee	Net Round Fee	Dist. Costs	Net Round Yield	Rounds Sold	Net Revenue
Comfort Suites	$75.00	$69.00			40	
Hampton Inn	$75.00	$67.00			30	
Hilton Garden	$75.00	$65.00			30	
Springhill	$75.00	$61.00			20	
Sheraton	$75.00	$60.00			40	
Hyatt Place	$75.00	$59.00			20	
Total	$75.00				180	

A. Calculate Sandy's "distribution cost" for each channel.

B. Calculate Sandy's "net round yield" for each channel.

C. Calculate Sandy's "net revenue" for each channel.

D. Calculate the overall average "net round fee" for the 180 rounds of golf Sandy received during the week from these six channels.

E. Which channel(s) do you believe are Sandy's best partners? Explain your answer.

4. Lara is the managing owner of the "The $\frac{1}{2}$ Pound Char-burger" kiosk at Metro Airport. Her menu is limited. She sells burgers, fries, and drinks. Last week, she served 1,000 customers. Most of her guests order at least a burger and a beverage. Some order a burger, fries, and beverage, while still others order only fries and a beverage. Sales data from last week are presented in the following table.

"The Char-burger" 1,000 Customers Served					
Item	# Sold	Selling Price	Item Cost	Item Cont. Margin	Total Cont. Margin
Burger	822	$2.99	$1.45	$1.54	
Fries	640	$1.49	$0.44	$1.05	
Drink	972	$1.19	$0.22	$0.97	
Total					

Item Contribution Margin (Item Cont. Margin) is defined as:

Selling price – Item cost = Item contribution margin.

Given the data presented, what is the *lowest* price at which Lara could sell a burger, fries, and a drink combination and still equal the "per customer" served contribution margin she currently achieves? Do you think she could sell the bundle for more? Explain your answer.

5. Keith is the group sales manager at the 400-room full-service Tripletree Hotel. Carla is the front office manager. Together with Leona, the GM, they make the revenue management decisions for their property. For the Saturday night that is just one week away, they have 180 unsold rooms remaining. Keith would like to accept an available group contract for the entire 180 rooms. "We'll sell out," he proclaims, "and have a great RevPAR."

Carla would like to reduce the room rates to $159.00 per night; which is a $20.00 reduction from the hotel's normal rate of $179.00.

"How many rooms do you forecast we can sell at that rate?" asks Leona.

"I believe we can sell about 120 of them," is Carla's reply.

"That means we'll leave 60 empty rooms, and a lower RevPAR," protests Keith.

It costs $35.00 to prepare, sell, and clean (prepare for resale) a room at the Tripletree. Review the data and then answer the following questions:

Room Sold	ADR	RevPAR	GOPPAR
Keith's Plan			
220	$179.00	$	$
180	$109.00	$	$
Total		$	$
Carla's Plan			
220	$179.00	$	$
120	$159.00	$	$
Total		$	$

a. What will be the hotel's occupancy % under each of the plans?

b. What will be the hotel's ADR under each of the plans?

c. What will be the hotel's RevPAR under each of the plans?

d. What will be the hotel's GOPPAR under each of the plans?

e. If you were Leona, whose plan would you support?

f. The Tripletree is a full-service hotel. Would your position change if the hotel were a limited-service property? Explain your answers.

KEY CONCEPT CASE STUDY

"If anyone should be able to afford our regular rates, it's seniors," said Adrian, the rooms manager at the 480-room Barcena Resort. "You're our revenue manager, don't you follow economic trends? People today have *more* money when they get older, not less. And with the Baby Boomers starting to turn 60, they're going to have even more to spend than previous generations. All I'm saying is that I think a senior discount for this package just leaves money on the table."

Adrian was having coffee in the resort's restaurant with Damario, the resort's revenue manager. They were discussing an idea Damario had presented at the last *Strategic Pricing and Revenue Management Advisory Committee.* Essentially, Damario had worked with the hotel's sales and marketing department to devise a "thru-the-week" package targeting active senior travelers.

Adrian wasn't convinced it was a good idea.

"I'm at the desk when they check in," continued Adrian. "Those folks *do* have money."

"You're right," said Damario. "Senior travelers are typically among the wealthiest of all the markets that we target."

"Then why offer them special discounts?" asked Adrian.

"Because we have empty rooms," replied Damario. "Seniors have money, but they have something even more important to us. They have time."

"Time?" said Adrian.

"Time. They have worked all their lives and have had longer to save, so they have more disposable income. That's still true, even after the most recent economic downturn. And lots of them love to travel. Of course, seniors also love discounts. Every group does, and that includes those with plenty of money. But seniors are also in a position to book with us at the last minute. They can vary their travel plans. They have no kids to worry about taking out of school. No limit on when they can get off work, because they already are off work. Permanently. And weekend travel is nice, but weekday travel is just as nice for most of them." They have the freedom to choose. Let me ask you, when is our hotel least used?" said Damario.

"Weekdays," replied Adrian. "We're booked solid most weekends. You know that."

"O.K. When do we need flexible date travelers?" asked Damario.

"Through the week," said Adrian slowly. "Now I get it."

For Your Consideration

1. Assume Damario is successful in "selling" the idea of a discounted thru-the-week package for seniors to the rest of the revenue committee. What specific fences would you recommend he construct to optimize the hotels' revenues from this program?

2. Assume the hotel also hosts senior travelers currently paying full price for their visits. Some visit on the weekend, but others visit during the week. What specific actions could the hotel undertake to ensure these full-paying guests felt they also received excellent value for each travel dollar they spent at the Barcena?

3. Assume you were Damario. What are specific price differentiation tactics you could implement in regard to this specific discount program? Explain why each tactic you selected was chosen.

4. Prices strongly communicate to customers the value a company places on its own products and service? In some cases, prices that are too low can cause some customer perceptions of quality to decline. How can Damario ensure the customers he targets do not respond to his value proposition with the thought that his new package is "too cheap" to truly represent a good value?

ENDNOTES

1. For texts related to the variously mentioned hospitality-related topics, visit: www.wiley.com/ WileyCDA/Section/id-300834.html.

2. Robert Reid and David Bojanic, *Hospitality Marketing Management*, 4th ed. (Hoboken, NJ: John Wiley and Sons, 2006), 547–558.

3. YUM Brands, Pizza Hut offer. In effect 2/15/2008 shown at http://www.pizzahut.com/pizzamia/.

4. Hyatt Hotels Senior Citizen Travel rates. In effect 2/15/2008. http://www.hyatt.com/hyatt/specials/offers-details.jsp?offerId=25&category=25.

5. http://thinkexist.com/quotes/with/keyword/cheap/4.html. Retrieved 02/16/2008.

6. http://www.tia.org/express/ntlcouncil_of_attractions.html. Retrieved 5/12/2009.

7. http://www.choicehotels.com/ires/en-US/html/BestRate. Retrieved 8/18/2009.

8. http://www.ratestogo.com/RateGuarantee.asp. Retrieved 8/1/2008.

9. http://quotes-motivational-inspirational.blogspot.com/search/label/Time. Retrieved 2/23/2008.

10. Confirmed as of 2/18/2008.

11. Reed and Bojanic.

12. Kimberley Tranter, Trevor Stuart-Hill and Juston Parker, *An Introduction to Revenue Management for the Hospitality Industry: Principles and Practices for the Real World* (Upper Saddle River, NJ: Prentice Hall, 2009), 325.

13. James Kotler, Philip Bowen and John Makens. *Marketing for Hospitality and Tourism*, 4th ed. (Upper Saddle River, NJ: Prentice Hall, 2005), 918.

14. http://thinkexist.com/quotation/any_change-even_a_change_for_the_better-is_always/220763.html. Retrieved 2/21/08.

15. Kevin Freiberg and Jackie Freiberg, *Nuts! Southwest Airline's Crazy Recipe for Business and Personal Success.* (Austin, TX: Bard Press 1996), 49.

CHAPTER 5

The Revenue Manager's Role

CHAPTER OUTLINE

CHAPTER HIGHLIGHTS

1. Explanation of the hard and soft supply constraints faced by RMs in the hospitality industry.

2. Examination of the legal and ethical aspects of revenue management.

3. Presentation of the typical job responsibilities and reporting relationships of RMs.

THE REVENUE MANAGER IN THE HOSPITALITY INDUSTRY

As the very existence of this book demonstrates, revenue management in the hospitality industry has taken great strides since its early and simplistic days of applying *yield management*, the concept defined in Chapter 1 as one seeking to maximize revenues by varying prices in response to buyer demand. A truly effective hospitality revenue manager must do much more than merely react to guests. Today, revenue management in the lodging industry is an overarching approach that considers total dollars spent on rooms as well as across all other areas of a property. In foodservice, revenue management means optimizing revenues through strategic pricing and the effective management of production and service capacity.

Revenue management has advanced from a focus on variable demand for those products offered for sale to a focus on how customers and channels respond to pricing and how to use that information to direct and shape consumer behavior. This means RMs must increasingly focus on forecasting demand, distribution channel management, internal communications, and training staff in modern revenue management concepts and strategies. Doing so makes good sense for many businesses; thus, a reasonable question to be asked is, *"Why is revenue management in the hospitality industry any different from revenue management in other fields?"*

The rationale for revenue management as a *distinct* field of study within the hospitality industry stems from the fact that, unlike revenue managers in many other industries, RMs in hospitality must manage both hard and soft supply constraints. Recall from Chapter 1 that a hard supply constraint is a restriction on product availability that, in the short run, cannot be remedied at any price; while a soft supply constraint can at some cost allow for additional product availability. Understanding the implications inherent in managing hard and soft constraints makes the hospitality RM's job quite unique.

Hard Constraint Management

In some cases, sellers can produce as much of a product as they can possibly sell. In such a situation, producers calculate their production costs, forecast buyer demand, and seek to charge a price that exceeds their costs, maximizes their income, and ensures a profit. To illustrate, consider the maker of a breakfast cereal. To optimize revenues the selling price chosen by the manufacturer is of critical importance. In all likelihood, as the price of the cereal is reduced, sales will increase but profits per box sold would decline. As the cereal's selling price increases, sales will likely be reduced—however, profits per box sold would increase.

The challenge for the cereal seller is to determine the optimal price at which to sell the product, producing more if more cereal were sold and making less if fewer boxes were sold. Consider further that such a producer could, at the end of each day, assess the amount of cereal produced and sold and then use that information to adjust the next day's cereal production. In such a business, the job of the revenue manager would not be extremely complex. It would essentially consist of establishing the optimum price, monitoring cereal sales, and then adjusting the amount produced (inventory) each day to equal buyers' demand.

Assume, however, that our cereal producer encountered the following set of interesting circumstances:

■ Once the cereal factory was built, the amount of cereal produced each day could not be increased or decreased each day regardless of how much was or was not sold on previous days.

- Demand for the cereal produced will vary widely, based on the time of year or even the day of the week.

- Any cereal not sold on the day it was made could not be sold the next day; rather it would disappear from inventory forever at the end of that day.

To summarize, consider that production levels cannot change, demand for the product will vary greatly and no unsold product from today can be sold tomorrow! Clearly, this cereal producer now faces a world filled with significant challenges. That world is the daily world of RMs in the lodging industry. This is true because, for hoteliers:

- The number of rooms offered for sale each day cannot vary.

- Demand for rooms varies widely, based on the time of year or even the day of the week.

- Any **room night** not sold on a given day disappears forever at the end of that day.

Essential RM Term

Room night: The single night's use of a guest room.

For example, one room sold for three consecutive nights yields three *room nights*.

RMs in the lodging industry face hard supply constraints because the number of rooms they have available for sale cannot be increased, at any price, in response to increased short-term demand. Nor can the number of rooms offered for sale be reduced in periods of slackened demand. In addition, while the cereal producer in our hypothetical example can keep enough unsold stock on hand to supply buyers in short-term periods of heightened or unanticipated demand, while reducing production during periods of weak demand, the hotelier cannot.

The lodging industry is not the only one in which hard supply constraints are encountered. A business selling gas through its pipelines is constrained by the capacity (size) of the lines. Hair salons are constrained by the number of chairs and hair stylists available to service their customers. In each of these businesses, as well as in other businesses facing hard supply constraints, RMs are forced to implement one of three income-management alternatives when demand for their products is high:

1. Establish one fixed price, then sell to customers on a first come-first served basis until they have exhausted their supply of products.

2. Allocate the limited supply to selected customers who meet established criteria (i.e., they are volume buyers, repeat buyers, or they hold other favored buyer status).

3. Raise their prices until demand is reduced sufficiently to equal the available supply.

Of course, RMs have the option of A, B, or C mentioned above, as well as that of fashioning a strategy that combines aspects of B and C into a customized approach because these two strategies are not mutually exclusive. As you learned in the previous chapter, one effective approach would be to implement a differential pricing strategy and allocate the limited supply to those market segments who value the product most highly. In fact, doing just that in a manner that maximizes operational profits is the goal of all effective RMs working in the lodging industry.

Soft Constraint Management

Lodging industry RMs face hard supply constraints. Most foodservice operators face soft supply constraints. As a result, the revenue management challenges faced by foodservice operators are different from those encountered by hoteliers. The first of these differences relates to capacity. Consider the fact that limited-service hotels, which make up over 75 percent of the hotels in the United States, essentially sell just one product: guest rooms.

Full-service hotels sell additional products and services, but their guest room night sales are as constrained as are those of their colleagues in the limited-service lodging segment. On any given night, hoteliers simply cannot increase their number of room nights available for sale at any price. Unlike the supply of hotel rooms foodservice supply is based on two factors, rather than one product. In this context, foodservice supply in a sit-down restaurant can be defined with the following formula:

Number of seats available $\times$ Hours of seat availability = Total available seat supply

Thus, for example, a restaurant with 150 seats that is open for 12 hours per day would have a total available seat supply of 1,800 seat hours (150 seats $\times$ 12 hours = 1,800 total available seat hours). With 1,800 seat hours available, longer dining times reduce the number of customers that can be served in that number of seat hours, while shorter dining times increase the number of guests that can be served.

Excluding, for this illustration, the ability of the foodservice operation to increase supply via the use of carry-out or delivery sales, the manager of this business could also increase the available supply of seat hours by increasing the number of seats in the operation or by extending its operating hours. Thus, for example, a restaurant currently closing its doors at 10:00 P.M. could elect to increase available seat supply by extending its closing time until 11:00 P.M. Doing so would increase its operating costs somewhat but it would also increase the seat hours available and thus its supply capacity. In response to reduced demand, the operator could, of course, elect to reduce operating hours. That's the good news. The less good news is that demand for dining between 10:00 P.M. and 11:00 P.M. will likely be quite limited.

Recall that a hard or soft supply constraint affects an RM's decision making primarily when demand exceeds supply. Also, it is important to recognize that despite its importance, restaurateurs do not gain increased revenues merely from increasing seat capacity or supply, but rather from the amount of money spent by those guests occupying each available seat. Thus, RMs in the foodservice industry should be especially concerned with RevPASH (revenue per available seat hour), a concept that will be explored in detail in Chapter 11.

From a revenue management perspective, it is also interesting to note that hotels and restaurants vary greatly in their knowledge about their customer's spending. Hoteliers know that a guest occupying a room will pay the room rate agreed upon in advance and confirmed at check-in. In contrast, restaurateurs do not know the income-producing capacity of an occupied seat until the guest has placed his or her order. This, of course, presents an additional challenge for RMs working in the foodservice industry. Even with this setback, foodservice operators benefit from a positive difference between themselves and those in the lodging industry. Recall that an unsold room night is lost forever. The restaurateur, however, who does not sell an aged Porterhouse steak on a given night will likely have the opportunity to sell that same item the next day. Again, some additional costs may be incurred due to product shrinkage, spoilage, and the like, but the ability to recover at least some of the business's lost revenue-generating capacity related to products sold is retained.

A final difference between the lodging industry and the foodservice industry is that of daily price variation. RMs working in the lodging industry are accustomed to price changes made on a monthly, weekly, daily, and even hourly basis in response to changes in demand. Their foodservice counterparts have not adopted this custom and thus do not typically

Figure 5.1	Revenue Management Characteristics in the Hospitality Industry		
Issue	**Cereal Maker**	**Hotelier**	**Restaurateur**
Supply constraint	None	Hard	Soft
Ability to increase supply	Unlimited	None	Limited
Ability to decrease supply	Unlimited	None	Limited
Ability to carry over excess supply to the next day	Yes	Service capacity: No Product: No	Service capacity: No Product: Yes
Practice price modification in response to variation in short-term demand	Optional	Almost always	Almost never
Can benefit from effective Revenue Management practices	Yes	Yes	Yes

adjust their prices in a similar fashion, although some restaurateurs do vary prices between meal periods—for example, a lunch price versus dinner price for the same menu item.

Figure 5.1 summarizes some of the significant differences, similarities, and common practices that distinguish hospitality industry RMs from those in other businesses, such as, in this example, the breakfast cereal industry.

This chapter began with the posing of a reasonable question: *"Why is revenue management in the hospitality industry any different from revenue management in other fields?"* Having, we hope, satisfactorily addressed that question, it now remains for you to learn about the societal restraints placed on you as an RM when you utilize techniques and tools to address the hard and soft supply constraints you will encounter when performing your job.

LEGAL ASPECTS OF REVENUE MANAGEMENT

Those who understand economics recognize that business and **capitalism** go hand in hand.

In a pure capitalist system, RMs would be completely free to establish and then manage the prices they felt would best serve the interests of their business's owners. Such an approach would be in keeping with the observations of Kenneth Minogue, Emeritus Professor of Political Science at the London School of Economics. Minogue stated, "Capitalism is what people do if you leave them alone."[1]

Although the certainty of Minogue's observation may be subject to debate there can be no debate about the fact that there are indeed societal limitations and governmental restrictions placed on the activities of all RMs. RMs are not left alone when it comes to pricing. The restrictions they face take the form of legal and ethical constraints that must be well understood before RMs begin to practice their profession.

RMs must be aware of the laws that affect their actions but the ethical behavior of RMs must be understood as well. Although some laws dictate precisely what RMs can

Essential RM Term

Capitalism: An economic and political system in which a country's trade and industry are controlled by private owners for profit, rather than by the state.

and cannot do, ethics regulate what they should and should not do. The inclusion of revenue management-related ethics is in keeping with the view of Thomas Jefferson who wrote, "I consider ethics, as well as religion, as supplements to law in the government of man."[2] It is to the legal and ethical aspects of revenue management that we now turn our attention.

Federal Antitrust Legislation

In the late 1800s, economic conditions in the United States led to the emergence of some very large businesses and some very wealthy business owners. Such familiar names as Andrew Carnegie (steel), John Jacob Astor (real estate), J. P. Morgan (finance), John D. Rockefeller (oil), and Cornelius Vanderbilt (railroads) gained much personal wealth during this period, and were revered by some as "Captains of Industry." But these same individuals were reviled by others as *robber barons*, a term that came to be used to describe a business leader applying unscrupulous practices and even bribery of public officials to gain personal power and wealth.

In 1890, Congress passed the Sherman Antitrust Act in an effort to ease public suspicion of business activities seen as damaging to the country. This would be only the first of several pieces of **antitrust legislation** that directly affect you as an RM.

The term *antitrust* was originally formulated to combat business *trusts*, a type of business arrangement that is now more commonly referred to as a **cartel**.

Identifying and breaking up cartels is an important part of the antitrust legislation in most industrialized countries. Illegal cartel activities include price fixing, bid rigging, and customer allocation. Price fixing occurs when two or more competing sellers agree on what prices to charge, such as by agreeing that they will increase prices a certain amount or that they will not sell below a certain price. Bid rigging most commonly occurs when two or more firms agree to bid in such a way that a preselected firm submits the winning bid. This typically occurs when businesses seek local, state, or federal government contracts. Customer-allocation agreements involve some arrangement between competitors to split up customers, such as by geographic area, to reduce or eliminate competition.

Cartel agreements are generally made in secret thus the participants mislead and defraud customers by continuing to hold themselves out as competitors despite their agreement with other cartel members not to compete against them. Cartel activities and other unfair business practices harm consumers by causing them to pay more than the market would suggest for products and services. It has been estimated that such practices can raise the price of a product or service 10 percent or more, thus in most countries there is a governmental interest in prohibiting these kinds of business actions. In the United States, the following federal antitrust laws most affect the day-to-day activities of RMs:

- The Sherman Antitrust Act
- The Federal Trade Commission Act

Essential RM Term

Antitrust legislation: Laws and regulations aimed at preventing abusive business behavior or anticompetitive practices, including those related to unfair pricing.

It is also known internationally as *competition legislation*.

Essential RM Term

Cartel: A consortium of independent organizations formed to limit competition by controlling the production, distribution, and pricing of a product or service (also known as trusts).

For example, the Organization of the Petroleum Exporting Countries (OPEC) is often referred to as a cartel because it controls oil production and pricing.

- The Clayton Act (1914)
- The Robinson-Patman Act

The Sherman Antitrust Act

The Sherman Antitrust Act, named after its author, Senator John Sherman of Ohio, was passed in 1890. It outlaws all contracts and conspiracies that unreasonably restrain interstate trade. This expressly includes any agreements among competitors to fix prices, rig bids, or allocate customers. Sherman Act violations are punished as criminal felonies. The **Department of Justice** enforces the Act.

Individual violators can be fined up to $350,000 and sentenced to up to three years in federal prison for each offense. Corporations can be fined up to $10 million for each offense. Department of Justice attorneys, often working with the Federal Bureau of Investigation (FBI), may use court-authorized searches of businesses, consensual monitoring of phone calls and e-mails, and informants equipped with listening devices to gather information that could lead to convictions for antitrust violations such as bid rigging or price fixing.

It is this act that prevents groups of hoteliers from different companies, for example, from meeting (even in cyberspace) to agree on the room prices that will be charged for upcoming events or charged to specific groups of customers.

Essential RM Term

Department of Justice: The federal government entity with control over all criminal prosecutions and civil suits in which the United States has an interest. This department also enforces all federal laws.

The Federal Trade Commission Act

Passed in 1914, the Federal Trade Commission Act created the Federal Trade Commission (FTC), which was established for the express purpose of enforcing the Sherman Antitrust Act. The FTC can prevent businesses from engaging in certain activities simply by declaring them illegal, thus avoiding the often slow response times that would result if the courts were used to challenge a questionable business activity. Thus, the FTC can order a firm or group of firms to "cease and desist" any practice that it deems unfair, even if the practice has not been declared illegal by a court. It is this power that should make RMs aware that the defense of "there is no law against it" will not hold up if the FTC feels a business practice unfairly restricts competition.

The Clayton Act

Named after its author Henry Clayton, a congressman from Alabama, and passed in 1914, the Clayton Act was implemented to modify the Sherman Act. It addresses many issues related to trade, unions, and corporate mergers. For RMs, the most important portions of this act are those provisions related to pricing. Specifically, the Clayton Act mandates that a business must apply its prices fairly—that is, it cannot illegally discriminate in its pricing policies.

The Robinson-Patman Act

The Robinson-Patman Act of 1936 again addressed pricing and it modified the requirements previously detailed in the Clayton Act. The Robinson-Patman Act is also known as the *Small Business Protection Act*. Passed during President Roosevelt's New Deal[3] period, the law aimed to assist smaller businesses in their competition against larger companies. It prevents sellers from giving discount prices to volume buyers if the volumes required for the discount are so high that only one or two buyers could meet them. This act also outlaws **predatory pricing**, an illegal practice but one that is often difficult to prove in court.

RMs must understand that while federal law clearly prohibits **collusion** among sellers and the practicing of discrimination in pricing, it does *not* prohibit differential pricing. It is also important to recognize that most federal legislation regarding price relates to fairness in the prices charged by producers for identical products. The pricing of dissimilar products or versions of the same product, as well as the pricing of services, is not addressed in Federal legislation.

In general, two buyers can pay different prices for the same product or service as long as the seller does not violate any other law in doing so. For example, hospitality industry RMs charging buyers different prices based on the buyer's race, religion, or ethnic background would be in violation of the Civil Rights Act of 1964, a bill introduced by President John F. Kennedy in a civil rights speech in which he asked Congress for legislation "giving all Americans the right to be served in facilities which are open to the public—hotels, restaurants, theaters, retail stores, and similar establishments."[4]

> **Essential RM Term**
>
> **Predatory pricing:** The practice of a firm harming consumers by selling its products below costs or at a price developed with the intent of driving competitors out of the market, thus creating a monopoly and the ability to raise its own prices significantly in the future.

> **Essential RM Term**
>
> **Collusion:** A secret agreement between people or firms to do something illegal.

State and Local Constraints

U.S. state and local governments are heavily involved in dictating, controlling, or monitoring the prices charged for a variety of goods and services, including those purchased and sold by hospitality businesses. For example, prices for electricity, gas, water, and sewage rates are among those that are governmentally controlled and/or regulated. Wholesale prices of alcoholic beverages are another area in which some level of governmental price control is common. Although in most cases sellers are allowed to charge what they wish for their products and services, many states have laws prohibiting **price gouging**.

In most cases, consumer protection legislation authorizes a state's Attorney General to investigate claims of price gouging during a declared state of emergency and allows for financial or criminal penalties, as well as restitution if it is found that an illegal act was committed. Figure 5.2 summarizes a sample of price gouging-related legislation in effect in several states.

> **Essential RM Term**
>
> **Price gouging:** The increasing of prices, often in response to a natural disaster or emergency, beyond a level deemed reasonable by society.

RM IN ACTION 5.1: HOTELIERS DENY THE EXISTENCE OF ANY KIND OF CARTEL

Due to federal legislation, cartels are illegal in the United States, as they are in most countries. But sometimes it is not clear what constitutes a cartel. Also, proving the existence of a cartel is rarely easy, as businesses understandably are unwilling to commit their cartel-related agreements to writing. The result can be an ambiguous situation, as this news report about India's lodging industry clearly demonstrates.

MUMBAI, India—Hoteliers are veering around to the view that cartelization is the best way to stem rampant price undercutting. Says a leading hotelier based in Mumbai; "There is (price) information sharing among us. I won't

agree that it is cartelization. It's an arrangement between the hotel groups."

Internationally, in some markets like Dubai and Kuwait, cartelization is perfectly legal. Senior managers meet once per year to fix room rates and that is strictly followed, sources said.

The actual existence and legality of cartels may be in the eye of the beholder, but most countries do address cartels in some fashion. As a result, RMs working in the international environment must clearly understand the local pricing rules they will be expected to know and follow.

Excerpted on 02/20/2008 from www.hotel-online.com/News/PR2008_1st/Feb08_Cartels.html.

Figure 5.2	Sample Revenue Management-related State Law[5]			
State	**Covered**	**Authority**	**Prohibited Act**	**Penalty**
California	Goods and services vital and necessary for the health, safety, and welfare of consumers	Cal. Penal Code § 396	Upon proclamation of a state of emergency by president, governor, or county or city executive officer, no price may be raised more than 10% above the price charged immediately prior to the proclamation unless directly attributable to increased costs.	$2,500 per violation when brought by district attorneys or city prosecutors, plus injunction and restitution. Misdemeanor is up to one year in jail or $10,000 or both.
Hawaii	Rental or sale of essential commodities	HRS 209–9	When the governor declares a state of disaster, or when the state is the subject of a "severe weather warning."	Violator is subject to penalties of $500 to $10,000 per violation.
Iowa	Merchandise needed by disaster victims	Regulation I AC 63–31.1(714) IC 714.16(2)a	During time of disaster and subsequent recovery period (60 day max.), in declared disaster zone, period declared to be disaster, charging unjustified prices.	$40,000 per violation plus restitution, injunctive relief. There is an additional penalty of $5,000 on top of the $40,000 if elderly was defrauded.

(Continued)

Figure 5.2	*(Continued)*			
State	**Covered**	**Authority**	**Prohibited Act**	**Penalty**
Michigan	Property or services	UDAP Statute MCL 445.903(1)(z)	Not specifically targeted at disaster/gouging. Prohibits charging a price in gross excess of the price for which similar products or services are sold.	Up to $25,000.
Virginia	Sale, lease, or license of necessary goods or services	Va. Code §§ 59.1–525 et seq	Upon declaration of state of emergency, no supplier can sell, lease or license necessary goods or services at an unconscionable price.	$2,500 per willful violation of Virginia Consumer Protection Act.

RM IN ACTION 5.2: GROWING STATE OVERSIGHT AND INFLUENCE

State legislatures give hospitality managers wide latitude in establishing their prices, but that latitude is not absolute. Consider hoteliers working in the state of Florida during an event such as the Super Bowl. Historically, in each city that hosts the game, hotel room rates in the area near the stadium skyrocket. Despite the usual freedom to raise room rates to virtually any level desired by a hotel's owners, there are some restrictions. Those restrictions typically come about in response to news headlines such as the following printed by the Florida Sun-Sentinel:

"Innkeepers Unapologetic About Rate Boosts of up to 100%."

> A room at the Hampton Inn in Hallandale Beach will set you back about $2,400.

> That's a rate of $599 a night for a minimum of four nights. Earlier this month, the same room went for between $179 and $229.

When asked about the significant rate increase, the Hampton Inn GM made no apologies. "It's just the demand in the market," he was quoted as saying. The article goes on to detail other hotel rate increases resulting from the Super Bowl, as well as what the State of Florida was doing to protect consumers.

In the 1990s, price gouging by hoteliers caused the National Football League (NFL) to create a policy under which they would only agree to pay a hotel's full rack rate plus a maximum 10 percent premium for the 17,000 rooms they reserve during the Super Bowl. Typically, however, hotels not reserved by the NFL are not limited in what they can charge. In Florida, however, they are required to file their rates with the state five days before they become effective. Failure to file, or exceeding the filed rate, is a second-degree misdemeanor.

As rooms buyers, state legislatures and state agencies increase their awareness of pricing strategies used by RMs, hoteliers can expect additional pricing-related scrutiny and oversight. This is likely to be especially so in those states and during times in which large numbers of consumers may share the opinion that hotel pricing is unfair. Newspaper articles with titles such as this one are clearly a factor in shaping that opinion.

Excerpted on 01/18/2007 from South Florida Sun-Sentinel.

ETHICAL ASPECTS OF REVENUE MANAGEMENT

Essential RM Term

Ethics: Moral standards of right and wrong conduct toward others.

RMs must, of course, obey all of the laws that directly affect their decision making. In the majority of cases, however, decisions made about prices and selling are affected more by **ethics** than by the law.

Certainly, RMs should ensure the prices they charge, as well as the way those prices are managed is fair. The difficulty, of course, comes in making the determination of exactly what constitutes a fair price. The question is important for a variety of reasons:

- Buyers must be convinced the prices they are paying are fair if they are to become repeat customers.

- Employees of a business must be convinced the prices charged by their employers are fair if they are to be effective salespersons for the business.

- Business owners must be convinced the prices they receive for the products and services they sell are fair or they will not continue their businesses.

- Regulatory agencies must be convinced prices charged are fair or they will be motivated to increase their oversight and control over any industry (including hospitality) that is perceived as pricing its products unfairly. RMs in hospitality need look no further than those lawmakers vocally supporting legislation that would tax airlines if they charged carry-on luggage fees to see the legal and public relations impact of pricing that appears to be unfair.

The question of what constitutes a fair price is closely related to the question of who should determine the fairness of prices. As you have learned, in the long run it is always the buyer who will ultimately determine the fairness of a price. The decision to buy, or not to buy, not only shapes the answer to what is a fair price but also affects the continued existence of a product or service in the marketplace. Just as buyers will not continually pay more for a product than they believe it is worth, sellers will not continue to sell for a price that does not return a sufficient profit for the risk they undertake in operating their businesses.

In most cases, it is not the actual price charged for an item that makes consumers question the fairness of the price. Rather, it is the perception of profit made by the seller that cause the accusations of price gouging or unconscionable selling prices that can result in government regulation. It is interesting that excess profits are often identified as the reason for too high prices, yet if the average investor elected to invest in the U.S. businesses that comprise the **S&P 500**, he or she would have achieved the returns displayed in Figure 5.3. The average capital gain (excluding dividends) for that entire period is 10.16.[6]

Note that, while the annual average return for the 20-year period was just over 9 percent, the volatility of returns is significant. Any consumer group or governmental agency protesting the excessive business returns achieved

Essential RM Term

S&P 500: A group of 500 very large, diverse, and mostly American, companies whose stock values are calculated daily to provide a benchmark, or baseline, comparison for the performance of other stocks. S&P stocks are traded on the two largest U.S. stock markets, the New York Stock Exchange and NASDAQ.

RM IN ACTION 5.3: IS TURNABOUT FAIR PLAY?

The airline industry has long been identified as one of the pioneers of "yield management," the basic concept of maximizing revenues by varying prices charged in response to consumer demand. A very similar idea is "Congestion Pricing," the concept of charging planes more to land at airports during their busiest times, and less during slower landing periods. The concept was supported in *The Wall Street Journal* (WSJ) as a way of reducing passenger flight delays resulting from too many planes scheduled to land and take off at peak periods.

During his second term, then President George W. Bush instructed Mary Peters, U.S. Secretary of Transportation, to begin hearings on how congestion pricing could be implemented. Were the airlines, champions of yield management pricing, supportive?

Note the following excerpts from the letter dated September 2007 by James May, CEO of the Air Transport Association (ATA), the professional trade association of the airline industry and written to Ms. Peters:

> The Air Transport Association (ATA) and its member airlines remain solidly

opposed to congestion pricing as a solution to flight delays. "Congestion pricing amounts to higher prices to drive away average travelers in favor of just those who can pay top dollar." "It is. . . . bad public policy."

On May 18, 2009, *USA Today* reported the Department of Transportation (DOT) was dropping the proposed congestion pricing plan. The DOT issued a statement that auctioning the slots to the airline willing to pay the most for them "was highly controversial and that most of those who filed comments opposed the slot auctions." The paper reported that transportation trade groups "applauded" the decision.

Hotel RMs should take special note of the ATA's stance on demand-based pricing. Increased pricing justified only by demand for a product is rarely popular with any group of customers, even those who practice it regularly in their own businesses.

Excerpted on 12/17/2007 from www.airlines.org/government/letters/ATA+Letter+to+DOT+Secretary+Peters+on+Congestion+Pricing.htm.

Figure 5.3   **S&P 500 Rates of Return 1989–2009**

Year	% Return	Year	% Return	Year	% Return
2009	27.11	2001	−13.04	1992	4.47
2008	−36.55	2000	−10.14	1991	27.25
2007	3.81	1999	19.51	1990	−6.85
2006	12.80	1998	26.67	1989	27.25
2005	3.01	1997	31.02		
2004	9.00	1996	20.27		
2003	26.39	1995	34.11		
2002	−23.37	1994	−1.47		

in 1995 would also be required to address the dismal returns of 2002 and 2008. Few critics of business, however, could seriously argue that a 9 percent average return on investment over a 20-year period is excessive. Ultimately, in nearly all cases, the prices charged by businesses simply cannot be excessive or buyers will simply reject the products and services sold by that business. In many cases, they will reject the business as well. From the perspective of an RM, there are four pricing-related ethical issues that must be considered:

1. Are the actions I am taking ethical?
2. Are the profits resulting from my actions ethical?
3. Are my prices presented fairly?
4. Are my prices perceived as fair by customers?

Are the Actions I Am Taking Ethical?

The first question; *"Are the actions I am taking ethical?"* simply addresses the fact that RMs face ethical dilemmas on a regular basis. Consider, for example, the RM whose hotel consists of 300 rooms. On a specific night, the hotel has 200 arriving reservations (reserved rooms) and 100 occupied rooms. As a result, each room has been sold. The RM knows, however, that historically 5 percent of all reservations made for any given night will be **no-shows**.

Essential RM Term

No-show: A guest who makes a reservation but fails to cancel the reservation or arrive for check-in on the date of the reservation.

At two in the afternoon, the RM is approached by a member of the hotel's sales and marketing department to make a decision regarding a repeat customer's request to reserve 11 rooms, at full rack rate, for that night. Would you advise the RM to approve the sale? When you do the required calculations, you can see why for many RMs the answer to this question may be as much an ethical one as a financial one.

Most questions related to ethical behavior are, by their very nature, of two types. The first are those where the decision is easy, and the great majority of RMs would follow the same course of action. For example; *"Should RMs accept money (a kickback) for themselves in exchange for giving a customer a price-reduction?"* Such a course of action would, in the opinion of nearly all RMs, be a clear violation of professional ethics.

The more difficult ethical questions are of the second type. In these cases, there are no clear-cut answers. RMs must examine their own moral conduct codes and then make their own decisions. Answers to what is ethical behavior in such situations may be unclear. Although there often are no easy or universal answers to many ethical dilemmas, RMs questioning the ethics of a decision or course of action can be guided in their decisions by utilizing the following questions:

- Is the intended action legal?
- Would my boss be O.K. with the action and advise me to do it?
- Would potential future employers of mine be pleased to learn I had initiated the activity?

- Would I be content if my decision/action were reported on the front page of the next day's local newspaper?
- Would I be satisfied if the action taken were directed at me or my own family members?
- Is the action fair to all parties involved?

If you can answer yes to each of these, the proposed action is likely ethical. If you cannot, it indicates that great care should be taken before you engage in the activity or make the decision because the ethics of it are clearly suspect in your own mind.

Are the Profits Resulting from My Actions Ethical?

The second question posed, *"Are the profits resulting from my actions ethical?"* is unfortunately one that is not addressed often enough. Its answer is not easy. The notion of what constitutes a "fair" or "just" profit has for centuries vexed philosophers, religious leaders, politicians, and businesspersons. Throughout this book we have taken the position that it is the free market that determines fair prices, with buyer's willingness to pay as the true measure of an item's worth.

As you have learned, price gouging (the charging of unreasonably high prices for goods and services) is sometimes illegal, but it is universally considered unethical. The difficulty, of course, lies in addressing the question of who gets to decide if a price is fair and thus if the profit resulting from it is, in fact, reasonable or unreasonable.

Some in business would argue that it is no more immoral for a producer to charge premium prices than it is for a consumer to pay low prices. Others state that the fairness of a price depends on the alternatives available to the buyer. For example, to charge $10.00 for a 12-ounce bottle of spring water during a normal time period would simply be bad business because few bottles would be sold. To charge the same $10.00 per bottle in the aftermath of a hurricane when no alternative water sources are available would clearly be unethical (and illegal in some states).

A customer willing to pay a high price simply because they have no reasonable alternative is not truly a willing customer, and RMs must recognize that. It is also true, however, that a legitimate function of a price is to allocate scarce resources. When for example, only one hotel ballroom in a city is available for hosting a June wedding, the value of that space is legitimately higher than during alternative months when fewer weddings take place and thus more alternative rental space is available.

The question of what constitutes ethical pricing is one that RMs will encounter frequently. This is especially true of those working in hard constraint industries such as lodging. It is critical, however, that RMs are able to defend and justify their pricing policies. It has been said that ethics is doing the right thing when no one is watching. For RMs, the fact is that their customers, their supervisors, and their employees *are* watching, and they are watching closely.

Despite lip service to the contrary, experienced businesspersons recognize the simple truth that *"honesty and integrity often do not pay off in the short run."* There are frequently real costs involved with maintaining these values. These costs may take the form of lost business or in reduced profits resulting from charging prices lower than those that could feasibly be charged. For ethical reasons alone, however, these costs are worth paying. For business

RM AT WORK 5.1

"Did the Austin wedding contract you were working on go out yet?" asked Tonya Roberts, the executive director of the downtown convention center operated by the city of Springdale.

"Yes, I mailed it to them yesterday after we talked about it," replied Lara, the Center's DOSM and revenue manager for space rental. "Why do you ask?

"I just got off the phone with the mayor's office. They want to hold a big fundraiser for his reelection campaign in the ballroom the same night the Austin wedding wanted to reserve it. The wedding was for 200 people right?" continued Tonya.

"That's right. 200 people at about $150 a head; it's a nice piece of business. About $30,000." said Lara.

"Well the mayor expects 1,000 people, at $100 per person. And don't forget, he's the boss. We can't hold both events. I need you to call the Austins and tell them you made a mistake. Tell them the room is already booked that night. They'll need to find another space".

1. How much additional revenue would the Mayor's event bring to the city convention center?

2. What would you advise Lara to do if she asked you for advice on how to respond to Tonya's directive?

3. Would the fact that the second space request came from the mayor's office affect your advice to Lara? Should it have an effect?

reasons, it is unquestionable that, in the long run, honesty and integrity yield tremendous payoffs. This is so because the value to RMs and their businesses of ethical behavior and impeccable integrity is priceless. Customers expect sellers to act with integrity every time, not just sometimes. This was summed up nicely by Tom Peters, the best selling author of *In Search of Excellence*, when he stated, "There is no such thing as a minor lapse of integrity.[7]"

Are My Prices Presented Fairly?

The question of *"Are my prices presented fairly?"* is an important one. Certainly it is fair for RMs to use their knowledge of consumer behavior to take advantage of the known ways consumers react to prices. Thus, for example, it makes sense for all RMs working in the lodging industry to add $0.99 to the end of their advertised room rates because they know that consumers perceive very little difference between a rate of $299.00 per night and $299.99 per night. This phenomenon exists even at lower rates (i.e., a rate of $59.00 per night is perceived about the same as $59.99). In a similar manner, restaurateurs whose menu prices end in $0.95 or $0.99 can do so fairly because they know that buyers tend to overweight the first digits in a price[8] and lower numbers are perceived as providing more value. Thus, for example, a $7.99 menu item seems to be a much greater savings from an $8.00 price than $7.92 is from $7.99. In both of these examples, the prices are presented openly with no intent to disguise them. That should always be the case. RMs must be fully

RM IN ACTION 5.4: SURCHARGE MAY MEAN NO CHARGE

Periodically, even well-intentioned businesses fail to follow principles of fairness in pricing. Consider the early 1990s pricing decisions made by some hotel chains when their energy costs were high. In many cases the hotels added a previously undisclosed energy "surcharge" to each of their guest's bill at the time of the guest's check out. The result?

Consider this Reuters news report from Los Angeles Superior Court:

> Four more hotel companies have reached tentative settlements in lawsuits stemming from energy surcharges they had surreptitiously imposed on guests under the settlement, Marriott International, Starwood Hotels & Resorts, Hilton Hotels Corp. and Hyatt Corp. could be liable for more than $60 million in future discounts.

According to Reuters, the amount of future discounts to be given by Marriott was estimated at $21 million, Starwood's $13 million, Hilton's $26 million, and Hyatt's $1.5 million. Over 6 million guests qualified for the discount coupons.

While the hotels maintained the charges were justified, the courts found the hotels failed to notify customers in advance of the fee; effectively quoting them one rate and charging another.

Today energy surcharges may be gone, but in-room safe charges, resort use fees, Internet access fees, pool use fees and other hidden charges still exist in some hotel companies. If charges of this type are not disclosed to guests at the time they make their reservation (i.e., *not* at the time of arrival or departure) they are clearly unethical, sometimes illegal, and always bad for business.

Excerpt on 8/25/2009 from http://www.allbusiness.com/transportation-communications-electric-gas/4220035–1.html.

aware that, regardless of the justification, their customers will react to hidden charges or charges revealed after the fact in much the same way they themselves would. They will dislike them. How intensely will they dislike them? And how will they react to them? For one hospitality example, consider the information presented in *RM in Action 5.4*.

Are My Prices Perceived as Fair by Customers?

The final question, *"Are my prices perceived as fair by customers?"* is the most difficult of all. Because customers naturally seek to pay low prices, they have a tendency to feel nearly any price is "too high." That is, their preference, much like your own, would always be to pay a lower price for all of the things they want or need to buy. Seasoned RMs understand this natural tendency. As stated earlier, however, the simple fact that a potential customer feels a price is too high is not a legitimate reason for granting that customer a price reduction. The issue of too high a price, however, is vastly different from that of an unfair price. Prices can often be beyond a customer's willingness to pay; but prices should never be unfair.

RMs will have little control over the inherent tendency of buyers to seek low prices. They have a great deal of control, however, over buyer perceptions of price fairness. In general, customers evaluate price fairness based on two different perspectives. The first relates to the perceived profit that the seller will earn. The second relates to the price a buyer believes other buyers are being charged.

Essential RM Term

Dual entitlement (theory): The idea that consumers feel (1) They are entitled to a reasonable price, and (2) Businesses are entitled to a reasonable profit.

Most buyers believe that it is simply unfair for sellers to charge excessively high prices, even if the majority of buyers are willing to pay those prices. **Dual entitlement** theory explains why.

Consumers feel they have a right to a reasonable price just as sellers have a right to a reasonable profit. Prices that appear to customers as having been established for the sole purpose of increasing profits beyond *reasonable* levels will be viewed as being unfair. Thus, if prices are raised in response to a business's increased costs, the higher prices will likely be perceived as fair. Raising prices simply to increase profits excessively is most often viewed as unfair. Ignoring this customer viewpoint can often be the cause of pricing fiascos.

To illustrate, consider the hardware store normally selling snow shovels for $25.00. The morning after a major snowstorm, the store raises the price on its ten remaining snow shovels to $35.00. Is such an action and the resulting new price "fair"? The overwhelming majority of buyers (over 82 percent of respondents in one study) found such an action to be unfair. Interestingly, in an identical study, 76 percent of University of Chicago economics students found raising the prices of the shovels to be "fair," a strong indicator that pricing debacles and the strong consumer reactions they generate will not disappear in the foreseeable future. Buyers found the hardware stores new prices unconscionable. The economics students saw strong demand as the justification for a significant price increase.

RMs must remember that buyers will sympathize with a seller's cost increases much more than with the seller's supply shortages. Thus a seller who finds that it has only one or two of an extremely popular item in stock (e.g., the season's most popular new video game release, or a single hotel room) must be careful. While the price of the item could,

Essential RM Term

Reference price: The price perceived by consumers to be the normal price for a product or a service.

of course, be raised significantly, or even auctioned to the highest bidder, doing so would certainly be perceived as unfair by the majority of consumers. Buyers use a variety of information to establish a **reference price** or the selling price they believe to be fair. They will then evaluate all other prices for that same item in comparison to that reference price.

It is for this reason that discounts from "normal" prices—even those normal prices that are set very high—are popular with buyers. Experienced sellers know it pays to keep reference prices high, and when it is advantageous to them, to offer discounts from those regular prices.

The second consumer view of price fairness relates to perceptions of the prices that are paid by *others*. Buyers who are perfectly happy with the price they paid for an item can instantly become irate if they find that another buyer has paid less for the same item. This phenomenon is familiar to many professionals, including those professionals working in human resource management. They know that a specific employee may be quite satisfied to be paid a salary of $50,000 per year, but if that employee discovers another worker is doing exactly the same job for $60,000 per year, he (or she) will likely become angry.

Similarly, the employee who gets a $5,000 raise may be thrilled with it, but not if a co-worker doing similar work was granted a $10,000 raise. Astute readers will recognize that from a purely economic perspective, this price-related reaction is irrational. A buyer's own consumer surplus is dependent only on what that buyer has paid for an item, not what someone else has paid. But RMs must also remember that the axiom *"Consumers will always behave rationally, except when they don't"* is all too often true.

The implications of the importance of fairness perception to pricing and revenue optimization are several, and they dictate six important pricing concepts that RMs would do well to remember:

1. Prices should be presented fairly. Hidden or after-purchase charges will be perceived as unfair.

2. Buyers prefer rewards to punishments. Rewarding guests for buying more or more frequently, is preferable to penalizing them for buying less or less frequently.

3. Discounts are viewed more favorably then surcharges.

4. Price increases justified only by supply shortages (or even increased consumer demand) are likely to be viewed unfavorably.

5. Lower prices (when offered) should be available to all buyers willing to meet the low price criteria or fences established for them. When lower prices are offered to all, potential buyers can decide for themselves whether they wish to meet the qualifying criteria.

6. If they do vary from traditional pricing approaches, a seller's pricing offer must be easily explained and understood. Deviations from traditional pricing approaches must be presented carefully and fully to consumers who must then perceive them to be fair.

If these concepts appear to be self-evident, consider the case of Douglas Ivester, past chairman of the Coca-Cola Corporation. In 1999, he proposed the idea of a temperature-sensitive vending machine that would automatically vary the price of soft drinks in response to changing outdoor temperatures. When the temperature would rise, so would the product's price, at lower temperatures, soda would cost less. He explained the rationale in an interview with Brazilian magazine *Veja* by saying:

Coca-Cola is a product whose utility varies from moment to moment. In a final summer (soccer) Championship, . . . the utility of a chilled Coca-Cola is very high. So it is fair it should be more expensive. The machine will simply make this process automatic."[9]

Ivester's idea violated several of the six fairness-related pricing concepts. The response from the U.S. and Canadian press was predictable:

"A cynical ploy to exploit the thirst of faithful customers" (*San Francisco Chronicle*)

"A lunk-headed idea" (*Honolulu Star-Bulletin*)

"Soda jerks" (*Miami Herald*)

"Latest evidence that the world is going to hell in a handbasket" (*Philadelphia Inquirer*)

"Ticks me off" (*Edmonton Sun*)[10]

Ivester's tenure as Chairman of Coca-Cola ended shortly thereafter, with some pointing directly to the *Veja* interview as a significant contributing factor. Ivester was no doubt sincere in believing the proposed idea was fair, but RMs must always remember that it is their customers' perceptions of pricing fairness, not their own, that matters most.

THE REVENUE MANAGER POSITION

This book was written for hospitality industry RMs. While the jobs of many hospitality professionals impact the management of their business's income, increasingly, more individuals are assigned full time to the position of "RM." The past decade has seen great change in the way hospitality professionals view revenue management. The change has affected the vocabulary and job duties of designated RMs. The future will likely bring additional change. Rather than be overwhelmed by the rate of change, however, today's RMs would do well to recall Abraham Lincoln's statement that "the best thing about the future is that it comes only one day at a time."[11] Because the position of RM will no doubt continue to evolve, it should not surprise you that today both the job duties and reporting relationships of RMs vary widely. Despite that, many RM practitioners (and some educators) persist in the belief that the way they personally perceive RM is the only way it can be perceived. It would be better if these RMs considered their personal views of revenue management to be correct "from their own perspectives"; because, as British politician John Lubbock pointed out so well: "What we see depends mainly upon what we look for."[12]

Job Duties

To understand just why it is so difficult to precisely define the role and job duties of RMs, consider that even the job title for this position varies greatly within the hospitality industry and even within industry segments. Figure 5.4 presents a baker's dozen of alternative titles for the hospitality RM position. Note that these titles are currently in use by hoteliers. These titles were taken from a list compiled and distributed by the sponsors of a popular **customer relations management (CRM)** travel conference held annually in the United States.[13]

Essential RM Term

Customer relations management (CRM):
A term applied to a variety of processes, often computerized, implemented by companies to handle their direct contact with customers.

Notice that while some of the job titles are very similar, each title likely reflects the unique philosophy of the organization adopting it. It is also likely that as management's vision of an RM's role in their organization varies, so too will the specific job duties assigned to RMs by leaders of those organizations.

Whatever the job title, RMs in all segments of the hospitality industry perform similar tasks designed to achieve similar results. These tasks can be viewed as a continuous five-step revenue management process, as summarized in Figure 5.5.

Figure 5.4   **A Baker's Dozen Different Names for Revenue Managers**

Job Title	Organization
Director of Revenue Management	Harrah's
Revenue Manager	Gaylord Opryland Resort & Conference Centre (Nashville, TN)
Manager, Yield Management Systems	Princess Cruises
Corporate Director of Revenue Optimization	Destination Hotels and Resorts
Manager, Hotel Yield & Revenue Management	Four Seasons Hotels & Resorts
Senior Revenue Management Consultant	Amadeus North America
Senior Director—Brand Pricing	Accor North America
Sales and Revenue Manager	Best Western (Listel Whistler; BC, Canada)
Revenue Optimization Manager	ResortQuest, Hawaii
Inventory Manager	Vail Resorts
Manager: Pricing	Via Rail Canada
Director of Marketing Analysis	Hyatt Hotels Corporation
Customer Centric Revenue Management*	Walt Disney

*It will not surprise readers of this text that the authors clearly support the "Customer-Centric" approach to RM expressed in the job title utilized by the Walt Disney Company. Properly practiced revenue management is first and foremost about understanding and benefiting customers.

Figure 5.5   **The Revenue Management Process**

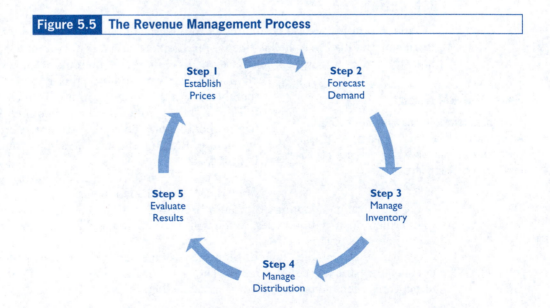

Step 1
Establish
Prices

Step 2
Forecast
Demand

Step 3
Manage
Inventory

Step 4
Manage
Distribution

Step 5
Evaluate
Results

RMs seeking continuous improvement in their revenue optimization efforts undertake the following steps:

Step 1: Establish prices. The importance of price and strategic pricing has been extensively addressed in earlier chapters of this text. Because the word *price* communicates strongly to potential customers the value placed on a product or service by its seller, the ability to properly establish pricing is a critical aspect of every RM's job. Some readers might suggest that this step should only follow that of forecasting demand (Step 2), but the authors would remind such readers that, as explained in Chapter 2, consumer demand is a function of how much of a good or service is desired by buyers at *a specific price*. As a result, it is extremely difficult, if not impossible, to assess demand for a product independent of its price.

Step 2: Forecast demand. After a price has been established, customer demand for products and services can be estimated or forecasted. Of course, if prices are changed, forecasts of demand may be changed as well. Some RMs specialize in this task and use sophisticated mathematical modeling tools to help them. All RMs seeking to optimize revenue, however, must have the ability to forecast demand for their products and services.

Step 3: Manage inventory. This crucial step requires RMs to understand how to withhold or make available to specific buyers the products and service capacity held in inventory. This task is made more challenging by the fact that revenue optimization must be viewed from a long-term as well as a short-term perspective.

Step 4: Manage distribution. In nearly all segments of the hospitality industry intermediaries are used to assist in the selling process. The portion of the selling price paid to intermediaries should vary, based on the value the intermediary adds to the process. As a result, channels of distribution must be carefully managed to maximize revenue while minimizing selling-related costs.

Customers themselves will vary in the amount of revenue they generate. For example, some hotel guests will reserve their rooms and stay longer than do other guests. Similarly, some identifiable types of restaurant customers purchase more food and beverages while dining than do others. When it is known that specific distribution channels deliver guests whose buying patterns are significantly higher or lower than that of guests produced by other channels, RMs must consider and manage these source-related factors.

Step 5: Evaluate results. The thoughtful evaluation of results is one of an RM's best tools for improving performance. Assessing the outcome of revenue management-related decisions that have been made in the past helps improve the quality of future decisions.

Often, a precise evaluation of an RMs' efforts can be challenging. The best metrics for ascertaining success in revenue optimization decision making may be uncertain. As well, success in some measures may mask a lack of success in others; thus providing RMs with conflicting information. The best RMs, however, understand the importance of evaluating their performance—and the very best RMs do it well. As Winston Churchill pointed out "True genius resides in the capacity for evaluation of uncertain, hazardous, and conflicting information."[14] Despite the inherent difficulties of assessing uncertain and conflicting historical information RMs must learn to modify their future actions in direct response to

> ▶ **RM ON THE WEB 5.1**
>
> Smith Travel Research (STR) is a company well known to RMs in the lodging industry. This company has enjoyed great success in helping hoteliers evaluate the effectiveness of their revenue management efforts, which is Step 5 of the revenue management process.
>
> Some of the tools they have developed to aid RMs will be examined in detail in Chapter 9.
>
> To get a preview of some of the performance information they can provide RMs, go to: www.strglobal.com
>
> When you arrive at their site, click *Products,* then click *Revenue, Sales, and Marketing.*

the outcomes they have achieved, the actions of their customers, their competitors and the general business environment.

While it would no doubt be pointless to argue that any one step in the five-step revenue management process is the most important, simply recognizing that revenue management *is* a process should help you better understand some of the reasons why RMs' jobs vary so much among different companies. Because of the segment in which they work some hospitality professionals may place greater emphasis on any one of the steps than they do on another. In addition, some businesses are large enough to have revenue management specialists who work only in one or two of these processes while other companies employ a single RM to perform all of these tasks.

Lastly, as the importance of revenue management has grown, some advisory companies have been formed specifically to assist RMs in one or more of their specialized duties. The decision by a business to utilize these companies' services can also have a significant impact on the daily tasks assigned to their own RMs.

Reviewing a sample **position description** is a good way for you to become more familiar with the typical duties of an RM. Figure 5.6 is an example of a position description for an RM working in the **full-service** segment of the hotel industry

RMs in full-service hotels manage revenues related to guest rooms, foodservices, meeting space, and other hotel services. RMs in **limited-service** hotels will focus more of their efforts on guest room sales.

Essential RM Terms

Position description: A human resource (HR) management tool that summarizes a job position, lists the essential tasks holders of that position would perform, and identifies the skills required to do the job.

Full service (hotel): A hotel that offers guests rooms as well as an extensive range of food and beverage products and meeting services.

Essential RM Term

Limited service (hotel): A hotel that offers very limited or no food, beverage, and meeting services.
Increasingly referred to as Select Service or Focused Service.

Figure 5.6	Position Description, Revenue Manager: Full Service Hotel

Job Title: Revenue Manager

Job Description: The primary responsibility of the Revenue Manager is to optimize the hotel's revenues by working closely with the GM, DOSM, and FOM and implementing strategies agreed upon by this team.

Job Duties: The following are specific responsibilities and contributions critical to the successful performance of the position:

- Optimize RevPAR by analyzing and forecasting demand and establishing effective selling strategies.
- Work with the director of sales and marketing and hotel team to establish strategies to increase room revenue.
- Manage and update current selling strategies and product information in all available internal and external distribution channels and reservation sources.
- Facilitate weekly revenue strategy meetings.
- Conduct ongoing competitor price analysis to ensure proper rate positioning relative to the competition.
- Generate and distribute daily, weekly, and monthly revenue management reports.
- Maintain historical data from all distribution channels in all market segments.
- Continually monitor all pertinent travel related web sites to ensure competitiveness in both availability and price.

Job Requirements:

- Prefer previous revenue management experience
- Strong analytical skills
- Ability to identify relevant data and use it to draw inferences with reference to impact on hotels revenues
- Excellent communication skills and interpersonal skills
- Ability to use PMS/reservation/revenue management systems to forecast, implement, and evaluate optimization strategies

Figure 5.7 summarizes some of the hospitality industry segments currently employing RMs, as well as the products and services those RMs are typically responsible for monitoring.

As you can see from the information presented in Figure 5.7, RMs may be responsible for managing revenues related to many hospitality products and services. It is true, however, that the lodging segment of the hospitality industry is a leader in implementing RM techniques. As a result, their specific activities, as well as those of RMs working in food and beverage operations, will constitute a significant portion of the remainder of this text.

▶ RM ON THE WEB 5.2

Specific job descriptions for RMs vary greatly. To review a large number of different position descriptions for RMs, go to: www.hcareers.com

When you arrive, click:

1. Management positions, and then click on
2. "Revenue Manager"

Note specifically those positions that indicate the reporting relationship of the RM as these too vary widely within the industry.

Figure 5.7	Typical RM Responsibilities by Industry Segment
Hospitality Industry Segment	**Areas of RM Responsibility**
Full-service resorts	Guest rooms
	Meeting space
	Food and beverage operations
	Resort activities
Full-service hotels	Guest rooms
	Meeting space
	Food and beverage operations
Limited-service hotels	Guest rooms
Condominiums/time shares	Guest units
	Food and beverage operations
Cruise ships	Cabins
	Food and beverage operations
	Activities
Commercial restaurants	Food services
	Beverage services
	Meeting space
Private clubs (Golf)	Tee times
	Food and beverage operations
	Meeting space
Private clubs (Dining)	Food and beverage operations
	Meeting space

Figure 5.7	*(Continued)*
Hospitality Industry Segment	**Areas of RM Responsibility**
Convention centers	Meeting space
	Food and beverage operations
Sports and entertainment venues	Tickets
	Meeting and/or event space
	Food and beverage operations
Casinos	Guest rooms
	Food and beverage operations
Theme/amusement/water parks	Admission tickets
	Food and beverage operations
	Rides/activities
Spas	Spa services
	Salon services
Intermediaries/service organizations	Services designed to inform/advise RMs

It is important for you to recognize that the same principles and practices applied by RM in lodging and foodservices can be applied to many other of the specialized segments within the hospitality industry. This is so because the hard constraint RM techniques utilized by RMs in lodging and the soft constraint RM techniques applied by foodservice industry RMs can be directly applied to any hospitality product or service in which these same supply constraints are encountered.

▶ RM ON THE WEB 5.3

The Educational Institute of the American Hotel and Lodging Association (E.I.) has developed a certification in revenue management. Titled the Certified Hospitality Revenue Manager (CHRM), on its web site, E.I. states:

The primary objective for earning the CHRM designation is to raise the professional standing of the hospitality revenue manager professional. Participation in the CHRM program recognizes an interest in professional development and a commitment to excellence in the industry.

You can learn more about the E.I. certification program at: http://www.ei-ahla.org/content.aspx?id=29346

> **▶ RM ON THE WEB 5.4**
>
> The Hotel Sales and Marketing Association International (HSMAI) has also developed a certification in revenue management, titled the Certified Revenue Management Executive (CRME). It was developed for individuals working in revenue management in the lodging industry and who meet the qualifications established by HSMAI.
>
> Candidates for certification can take an online examination offering them a chance to confirm their knowledge, experience, and capabilities in their field. You can learn more about this certification effort at: www.hsmai.org/resources/certification.cfm

Reporting Relationships

Just as there is no single job description that would address the activities of all RMs, there is no single best organizational structure representing an RM's ideal **reporting relationship.**

In fact, even within the same industry segment, the reporting relationships of RMs vary greatly. This can reflect the objective of the business employing the RM, the specific revenue management philosophy of its managers, or both. In most cases, RMs will find that their reporting relationship will be to one of the following individuals:

Essential RM Term

Reporting relationship: The person assigned to exercise power and authority over another.

■ **The director of sales and marketing (DOSM):** Organizations utilizing this structure emphasize the RM's role in demand forecasting and in the selling process. Because the DOSM is typically responsible for **group room** sales, this scenario is also common in those lodging properties in which group room sales constitute a significant portion of total rooms revenue. The title of the customer may change from guest, to diner, to client, to attendee, but the RM in this scenario plays a supporting role to the DOSM.

Essential RM Terms

Group room (sale): Hotel room sales in which an individual reservation is part of a larger, multiguest reservation.

Rooms manager: The individual in a hotel responsible for management of both the Front Office and the Housekeeping departments.

Transient room (sale): A room sale made to an individual who is not part of a larger group.

■ **The rooms manager:** Exclusive to the lodging industry, in this scenario, the RM reports to the **rooms manager,** the individual traditionally responsible for the management of a hotel's front office and the housekeeping departments. In other properties, the RM may report directly to the FOM. This scenario is common in those lodging properties in which **transient room** sales constitute a significant portion of total rooms revenue. In this role, the RM supports the efforts of the hotel's front office in establishing room prices, managing reservations, and maintaining relationships with the property's various intermediaries and distribution channels.

■ **The controller:** The controller is responsible for a hotel's on-property accounting procedures. Those entities selecting this placement for the RM's position emphasize the pricing and results analysis duties of RMs. Typical in this role are activities related to the forecasting and evaluation of the organization's financial results as well as preparation of financial reports related to the management of revenues.

■ **The property GM:** In some properties, the RMs position is valued so highly the reporting relationship is directly to the general manager or even the owner of the business.

■ **A corporate-level executive:** In multiunit organizations, it is common for property-level RMs to report directly to an area or regional RM. This structure helps ensure revenue management consistency across properties and where more than one property exists in the same geographic market, allows for cooperative revenue management activities.

Those intermediaries and service companies advising or supporting the efforts of property-level RMs are also likely to be structured in this way.

Is there a "most common" RM reporting relationship or organizational structure in the hospitality industry? It was to address that very question that the Hospitality Sales & Marketing Association International (HSMAI) commissioned a study by Michigan State University. The study results are presented in RM in Action 5.5, and clearly indicate that at this time there is no industry consensus on the ideal organizational structure or reporting relationship for the RM's position.

RM IN ACTION 5.5: WHO REPORTS TO WHO?

There is little agreement in the lodging industry about the best organization structure for revenue management or the best reporting relationship structure for RMs. This is illustrated in the results of an RM-related survey undertaken by the Hospitality Sales & Marketing Association International (HSMAI). Their findings are revealing:

The HSMAI study reported the following responses to the question:

"To whom do you directly report?"

36 percent to general manager

23 percent to "other" on property (DOSM, rooms manager, or FOM)

16 percent to corporate VP (vice president)

16 percent to regional DRM (director of revenue management)

9 percent to owner/CEO (chief executive officer)

The study was conducted by researchers from The School of Hospitality Business at Michigan State University. The survey reflects 250 valid responses from professionals engaged in revenue management.

It is not surprising that in a newly emerging field, a variety of approaches to organizational structure will be undertaken. The lesson for you as an RM is that flexibility and adaptability to various reporting and organizational structures will be important keys to your advancement and career success.[15]

THE REVENUE MANAGEMENT TEAM

Given the diversity of duties, responsibilities areas, and reporting relationships encountered by RMs an extremely useful way of reviewing the RM's role is that of a vital member of the revenue management team. Figure 5.8 illustrates the important team relationships held by virtually all RMs.

Figure 5.8 | **The Revenue Management Team**

Each member of the revenue management team plays an important role:

Revenue manager: As an RM, your own role in the revenue management team will likely be one of planning, organizing, directing, and evaluating your team's revenue manager activities.

Organization administrators: Business owners, corporate or property level managers, and department heads all will have input into your revenue management decision making. They must be kept informed about your actions and their own goals must always be kept foremost in your mind.

Sales and marketing staff: Pricing and revenue management activities are closely related to sales and marketing activities. In nearly all cases, members of the sales and marketing departments will be part of the revenue management team and their specific goals will strongly influence the actions of your team. As well, in many cases an RM may report directly to an individual holding a position within this area of their organization.

Financial administrators: An organization's financial accountants and controllers as well as those department heads responsible for the financial management of their own areas will most often be important members of your revenue management team. Historically many of these individuals have viewed pricing and revenue management from a cost-based, not value-based perspective, yet their insights and points of view should always be among those you understand and fully appreciate.

Essential RM Term

Line-level employees: Employees who jobs are primarily nonsupervisory. These employees perform most of the tasks directly related to providing guests the products and services that generate revenues for the business.

Line-level employees: **Line-level employees** as well as those holding mid-supervisory positions interact directly with guests. In many cases, revenue management plans fail because these individuals have not been given the information and training they need to properly communicate those plans to guests. It will be part of your responsibility as an RM to ensure these individuals are prepared to implement the strategies and tactics you devise.

Intermediaries and channels: Although not directly employed by your organization, these professional partners in your RM efforts are crucial to your success. Coordinating information exchange with them, understanding their own needs, and working hard to maintain good relationships with them are all crucial aspects of your own success as a revenue management team member.

(Continued)

Figure 5.8	*(Continued)*

Guest and buyers: A recurring theme of this book has been the importance of guests in the revenue management process. It is only by keeping the needs of your guests, clients, customers, and buyers clearly in focus that your revenue management team can achieve its goals. Whether purchasing your products and services for themselves or for others, continuous feedback from these individuals will be essential to the quality of your own future decision making.

Essential RM Term

Strategy meetings (revenue management): Regularly scheduled and formal meetings in which the pricing and revenue management strategies and tactics of an organization are developed and evaluated.

An additional and important team member role of many RMs is the coordination of revenue management **strategy meetings**. Often headed or chaired by the RM, these monthly, weekly, daily, and in some cases even hourly meetings are essential for coordinating the efforts of those team members with direct revenue management-related responsibilities.

Which member of the revenue management team is most important? All of them! Few individuals understood this as well, or embodied the concept of teamwork more, than Vince Lombardi, legendary coach of the championship Green Bay Packers football team. Understanding his statement, "Individual commitment to a group effort—that is what makes a team work, a company work, a society work, and a civilization work,"[16] is critical to your success as an RM. It is only through the efforts of talented *individual* RMs, serving at the center of the revenue management *team*, that organizations will achieve the financial success they desire. The next chapters of this text will teach you the individual skills you will need to make an outstanding contribution to your own revenue management team.

RM AT WORK 5.2

"This blizzard is incredible," said Shaniqua, the desk clerk on duty at the Quality Suites located at exit 15 on Interstate 96. Our phone hasn't stopped ringing for the past 30 minutes."

"How many rooms do we still have left to sell?" asked Tara, the Front Desk supervisor on duty.

"45 rooms and 3 suites" replied Shaniqua.

"And what rate are you quoting?" asked Tara.

"Rack, just like you told me. But I think you could double that and we would still sell out!

The Interstate will be closed down within an hour, and this lobby will be packed with folks wanting rooms."

1. If you were Tara, would you increase the room rates at your hotel above the normal "rack" rate? How much?

2. Are there ethical issues in play in this scenario? Explain your answer.

3. How would Tara know if there are state or local laws that could directly affect the room rate decision she is about to make?

❖ ESSENTIAL RM TERMS

Room night	Reference price
Capitalism	Customer relations management (CRM)
Antitrust legislation	Position description
Cartel	Full service (hotel)
Department of Justice	Limited service (hotel)
Predatory pricing	Reporting relationship
Collusion	Group room (sales)
Price gouging	Rooms manager
Ethics	Transient room (sales)
S&P 500	Line-level employees
No-show	Strategy meetings (revenue management)
Dual entitlement (theory)	

APPLY WHAT YOU KNOW

1. This chapter introduced the concept of congestion pricing for airlines. Assume you were the president of a major air carrier and that during a televised national news program, you were asked your opinion about the fairness of it. How would you respond? What applications would your answer have regarding the decision-making process of a lodging company RM?

2. Chuck Stout is the RM for the Holiday Inn Express. His 220-room property normally sells 85 percent of its rooms on Tuesday nights at an ADR of $141.50. All variable costs related to selling his rooms are $55.00 per room. The DOSM at his Holiday Inn Express is proposing to place a bid to sell 125 rooms for a Tuesday night next month at a rate of $109.00 per room. Chuck believes that if the hotel wins this group rooms bid, the transient room sales for that day will ensure a sell-out at the rate of $141.50.

   A. What would be the total amount of revenue the hotel will achieve if:

      It makes the group sale? _____

      It does not make the group sale? _____

   B. What would be the total amount of after-variable costs rooms' revenue the hotel will achieve if it wins the group rooms contract? _____

   C. What would be the after-variable room's income if the hotel does not win the contract? _____

   D. What additional factors might Chuck and the DOSM take into account before determining whether to bid on this piece of group rooms business?

3. The Brookshire Country Club rents its ballroom for weddings and provides food and beverages services for those using its facility. Last year, the Club hosted 25 wedding events.

The total revenue derived from these events was $225,000. The product (food and beverage) costs associated with each wedding averaged 31.5 percent. All other variable costs for each event averaged 48.5 percent. What was the average after-costs revenue (in dollars and percent) achieved by the Club for each wedding event?

4. Gene Monte is president of the five-unit El Ray Taqueria chain of restaurants. His quick-service operations offer both dine-in and carry-out (drive through) service. Gene is considering keeping his operations open one additional hour per night. Based on his revenue estimates, the following data represent the incremental sales he believes he will achieve in each of his restaurants:

Assume Gene's product cost is 30 percent and all other variable costs equal 45 percent of sales.

Unit Number	Additional Revenue
1	$850
2	$700
3	$650
4	$750
5	$900

A. What is the additional amount, per unit, that Gene could contribute to his fixed costs by extending his operating schedule by the additional hour?

B. What is the total amount of contribution to fixed costs he would achieve?

C. What additional factors should Gene take into account before implementing the extended schedule?

5. John Flowers owns Keneally's Irish Pub. On the upcoming St. Patrick's Day, John expects a capacity crowd. John normally operates with four servers. Because of seating limitations, John can only add a total of four more servers to his staff for St. Patrick's Day. Each server costs John $12.00 per hour. His beverage costs are 25 percent. Each added server can generate an additional $600.00 in beverage sales per hour if they work a full 8-hour shift. Prepare a spreadsheet that details the increased revenue, labor costs, beverage costs, as well as the revenue remaining after John pays his product and labor costs if he places an additional one, two, three, or four full-time servers on his St Patrick's Day employee schedule. What additional factors might John take into account before determining how many additional servers he should add?

KEY CONCEPT CASE STUDY

"So just what is it you do all day long? Try to figure out how to raise our prices so no one notices?" asked Sam with a good-natured smile.

Sam, the F&B director at the Barcena Resort, was having coffee in one of the property's restaurants with Damario; the resort's newly appointed Revenue Manager and a colleague that Sam had quickly grown to like very much.

"Trust me," replied Damario. "Guests always know when we raise prices!"

"Well that's the problem with you roomies. You just change prices too much," said Sam.

"What do you mean?" asked Damario.

"Well, as long as I've been here, whenever the resort gets busy, our room rates go up. And the people managing our room rates think it is O.K. to jack up the prices. Can you imagine how my guests would react if I raised our dinner prices whenever my restaurant was full? It wouldn't stay full very long, I can bet you that!" said Sam.

"It's true that the pricing of rooms and food in most hotels are pretty different," said Damario.

"Yes, but why is that?" asked Sam.

"Why is what?" asked Damario.

"Now I know you have a future as a consultant," laughed Sam, "they usually answer a question with a question. What I meant was; why do you feel like our room prices have to be managed so much? In my department, my motto for prices is *Set 'em and then forget 'em.* At least until the next menu reprint. I think changing prices all the time would be too confusing for my customers, and I think it would drive my servers crazy trying to remember exactly what *today's* prices are if I changed them all the time!"

For Your Consideration

1. Assume you were Damario. How would you explain to Sam the differences inherent in pricing hard supply constraint products, soft constraint products, and those with no supply constraints?

2. Consider your answer to the previous question. Do you think that guests of the Barcena Resort, if they overheard your conversation with Sam, would think your explanation to him reflects a fair and ethical pricing philosophy on the part of the resort?

3. Is it ever fair and ethical for a revenue manager who is responsible for the pricing of hard (or soft) constraint products to increase prices by 10 percent in response to increased consumer demand? 50 percent? 100 percent or more? Who within a hospitality business should be responsible for answering questions such as these?

4. Consider your answers to question 3. What, if any, role should the government play in influencing the decisions made by pricing managers? Is it reasonable to assume that politicians without a background in business will understand the challenges of hard and soft constraint pricing? Who within the hospitality industry do you feel should take a leadership role in ensuring that government policy makers at the local, state, and national level do understand?

ENDNOTES

1. http://thinkexist.com/quotes/kenneth_minogue/. Retrieved 2/08/2008.

2. http://thinkexist.com/quotation/i_consider_ethics-as_well_as_religion-as/144509.html. Retrieved 2/08/2008.

3. For detailed information on Franklin Roosevelt's "New Deal," visit http://www.geocities.com/Athens/4545/.

4. http://en.wikipedia.org/wiki/Civil_Rights_Act_of_1964. Retrieved 3/25/2008.

5. http://www.ncsl.org/programs/energy/lawsgouging.htm. Retrieved 3/25/2008.

6. http://www.moneychimp.com/features/market_cagr.htm. Retrieved 3/25/2008.

7. http://thinkexist.com/quotations/ethics/2.html. Retrieved 4/1/2008.

8. Jack E. Miller and David V. Pavesic, *Menu Pricing and Strategy* 4th. ed. (New York: Van Nostrand Reinhold, 1996), 126.

9. http://crab.rutgers.edu/~goertzel/cokeprice.htm. Retrieved 8/29/2009.

10. http://www.argmax.com/mt_blog/archive/1999_11_mean_vending_ma.php. Retrieved 3/15/2008.

11. http://www.brainyquote.com/quotes/authors/a/abraham_lincoln.html. Retrieved 3/15/5008.

12. http://thinkexist.com/quotes/john_lubbock/. Retrieved 3/20/2008.

13. http://events.eyefortravel.com/crm/past-attendees.asp. Retrieved 8/1/2008.

14. http://www.brainyquote.com/quotes/quotes/w/winstonchu144998.html. Retrieved 3/20/2008.

15. Study Results Excerpted from Press HSMAI Press Release MCLEAN, VA. Retrieved June 26, 2007.

16. http://thinkexist.com/quotation/individual_commitment_to_a_group_effort-that_is/15114.html. Retrieved 8/24/2009.

PART II

REVENUE MANAGEMENT FOR HOTELIERS

CHAPTER 6

Forecasting Demand

CHAPTER OUTLINE

CHAPTER HIGHLIGHTS

1. Explanation of why collecting and analyzing data about customer demand for lodging products and services are essential when forecasting future sales.

2. Presentation of the tools RMs use to track historical, current and future demand for their rooms inventory.

3. Examination of how demand forecasts affect decisions on hotel room and services pricing.

THE IMPORTANCE OF DEMAND FORECASTING

As an astute reader, you will quickly become aware that in this and the chapters that follow, the focus of this book changes. In the first five chapters, you learned about important revenue management principles. In this and all future chapters you will learn RM practices and exactly how RMs apply what they know to their daily job duties. The goal for you is to become a customer-centric revenue manager who is skilled at revenue optimization.

Why is a focus on customers so important in revenue management? Because developing customer loyalty is more important than maximizing short-term revenue. Loyal customers come back again and again. And they tell others about their experience. In fact, the only way to maximize *long-term* revenue generation is to develop loyal customers who prefer to buy from you, *even when lower-cost alternatives are available to them.* The reasons why this is true are many, but the importance is summed up nicely in the title of *New York Times* bestselling author Jeffery Gitomer's book, *Customer Satisfaction Is Worthless; Customer Loyalty Is Priceless: How to Make Customers Love You, Keep Them Coming Back, and Tell Everyone They Know.*[1] The best RMs naturally prefer loyal customers over those customers who seek only to buy from a seller offering the lowest prices.

To obtain and retain loyal customers, businesses must perform well. Most RMs intuitively understand that accurate estimates of future sales help to better manage pricing. But an effective RM's accurate sales forecast does much more. It helps the entire lodging team make management decisions that aid the hotel in developing loyal customers.

It is critical that you collect and properly assess your hotel's operating data. Effective data analysis leads to an accurate assessment of **demand**; the number of buyers seeking to purchase what you have for sale at its current price. Estimating the number of potential buyers allows for accurate sales forecasts.

Essential RM Term

Demand (customer): The number of potential buyers with the interest and ability to purchase the products sold by a business at the specific price offered.

For hoteliers, an accurate estimate of future room demand is essential to the effective operation of their hotels because:

- Accurate revenue forecasts allow hotel department leaders to more efficiently schedule the departmental staff needed to serve guests. Proper staffing is required to ensure that guests are provided with the service levels intended. Customer-centric RMs are *just as concerned* with ensuring guest satisfaction as they are with revenue optimization.

- Accurate revenue forecasts give those responsible for purchasing supplies the information required to buy needed items in the correct quantities. The impact on guest satisfaction of ensuring the presence of necessary products and supplies upon guest arrival is significant.

Essential RM Term

Capital improvement: An addition to a property that will enhance its value or increase its useful life. Examples include roof replacement and the purchase of new furnishings.

- Accurate revenue forecasts allow managers and owners to estimate the future profitability of their properties. Doing so provides the information needed to make decisions about profitability and cash flow that directly affect decisions related to **capital improvements** and capital expenditures.

RM AT WORK 6.1

Dee Hardy was angry, and Randy Moran was just as angry.

"They said it was an absolute disaster. Bad service and we ran out of food," said Dee.

"What did you expect," replied Randy. "It's your fault. We did our best!"

Dee and Randy were discussing the previous day's breakfast at the 500-room hotel where Dee served as DOSM and Randy as the F&B director. Between 6:30 A.M. and 7:30 A.M. the previous morning, over 500 guests had attempted to enter the hotel's 250-seat dining room. With too few servers scheduled and too little food preprepared, guest waits were long, service slow, and the kitchen ran out of several key breakfast items.

"Those rooms weren't on the forecast you passed out at our revenue management meeting last week," said Randy. "When you add 150 rooms, with four people to the room, and you don't tell me about it, what do you expect?"

"We only got the business three days ago," replied Dee. "And at a good rate. Were we supposed to turn it down because we couldn't serve a few extra people a decent breakfast?"

"We can serve 1,000 extra," said Randy as he stalked off, "and we can serve them well—but only if you do your job!"

1. Assume Randy had known about the 600 extra guests two days prior to their arrival. What steps might he have taken to ensure the guests received a quality breakfast experience on the day of their departure?

2. Would you define 600 unexpected guests as "a few extra"? What was Dee's responsibility to the hotel in this situation? As a customer-centric revenue manager, what was Dee's responsibility to her arriving guests?

3. Part of an RM's responsibility must include ensuring that guests get what they pay for. Assume you were this hotel's GM. What would you expect from your RM team in a future and similar circumstance?

■ Accurate demand forecasts allow RMs to make better decisions about how to modify and manage the prices of their products and services.

To create accurate and ultimately useful demand forecasts, RMs look to three sources of data: historical, current, and future. Figure 6.1 presents the type of information each data category describes.

Figure 6.1	Data Types
Type of Information	**Describes**
Historical data	Events that have already occurred
Current data	Events occurring now or in the very near term
Future data	Events that will occur in the future

Figure 6.2 **Four Components of Effective Demand Forecasts**

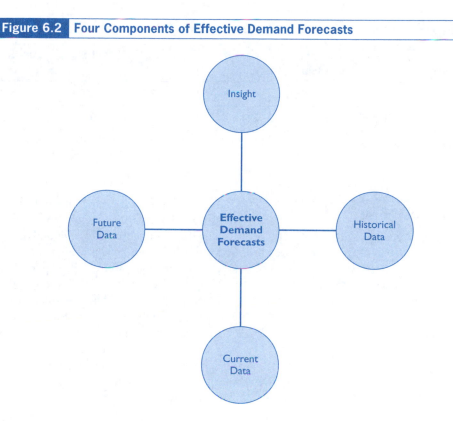

RMs use data to create forecasts or estimates of customer demand. Figure 6.2 graphically illustrates the four components of an effective demand forecast.

Each data type is important to accurate demand forecasting. Insight involves the skillful analysis of what each data type reveals.

HISTORICAL DATA

To begin the data collection and demand forecast process, it is important to understand that every operating hotel generates **historical data** even if the data are not recorded or analyzed.

Understanding historical data is essential because a key aspect of any RM's job is to see into the future. Understanding a hotel's past (historical) performance is one of the best ways to make good decisions about future performance. Put another way, RMs "*study the past to define the future*."[2] This is true regardless of whether the past performance was good or bad. In fact, experienced RMs know that in many cases, the errors of the past provide wisdom for future decision making.

Essential RM Term

Historical data: Data describing events that have already occurred. Such data are also known as *actual* data and *results data*.

Figure 6.3	Your Hotel Operating Data (Trailing 8 week average)						
Average	Last 8 Mon	Last 8 Tues	Last 8 Wed	Last 8 Thurs	Last 8 Fri	Last 8 Sat	Last 8 Sun
Occ.%	88%	91%	78%	67%	45%	51%	29%
ADR	$158.75	$188.75	$148.75	$138.75	$155.75	$159.75	$129.75
RevPAR	$139.70	$171.76	$116.03	$ 92.96	$ 70.09	$ 81.47	$ 37.63

Essential RM Term

Trailing period: A data collection method characterized by the act of discarding the oldest piece of data in a data set when the newest data are added, thus updating the set's information while keeping the set size constant. Data contained in a trailing period are often used in calculating a rolling average.

To illustrate the importance of historical data to RMs, assume that for the past eight weeks you had carefully collected and sorted the daily ADR and occupancy information for the 200-room hotel at which you are the RM. The data covering this eight-week **trailing period** are in Figure 6.3.

The data in Figure 6.3 present the average (mean) Occupancy % and ADR you calculated for your hotel for each night of the week based on its actual performance over the past eight weeks. For example, the average occupancy % on Mondays, as calculated from the actual occupancy rates achieved on the prior eight Mondays, was 88 percent.

Why are historical data important? Assume that, as this 200-room hotel's RM, you are now confronted with the following question:

Do you recommend that the hotel fill a tour operator's request to reserve 100 rooms on the Monday night that is three weeks from now, if the room rate requested by that tour operator is $109.00 per room?

To determine the answer to this and other questions similar to it, RMs use the following three-step procedure:

Step 1: Calculate the forecasted RevPAR* based on the estimated demand for rooms that does *not* include the new piece of business.

Step 2: Calculate the forecasted RevPAR based on the estimated demand for rooms that includes the new (proposed) piece of business.

Step 3: Assess the difference between the two RevPAR estimates and make a recommendation

To illustrate the process:

Step 1: Lacking any additional information or data, one of the best predictors of what will happen in the future is what has happened in the past. Based on the average performance

*Some RMs choose to assess GOPPAR as an alternative to RevPAR (see Chapter 9). The rationale for doing so is compelling. Currently, however, RevPAR is the most commonly utilized revenue statistic reported in the lodging industry and thus it will be used for the majority of the revenue management decision making illustrations presented in the text.

of your hotel over the past eight weeks, your estimate for the RevPAR[3] you would likely achieve on the Monday three weeks from now is:

$158.75 (trailing ADR) × 0.88 (trailing Occupancy %) = $139.70 RevPAR forecast

Step 2: If 100 rooms are sold at $109.00, it is reasonable to assume a sellout of all remaining available rooms. The estimated RevPAR generated in such a case would be calculated as:

$109.00 (proposed tour operator rate) × 0.50 (Occupancy % @ 100 rooms) = $ 54.50

Plus

$158.75 (trailing ADR) × 0.50 (Occupancy % with sellout) = $ 79.38

Total RevPAR $ 133.88

Step 3: The difference between the two RevPAR estimates is $5.82 ($139.70 − $133.88 = $5.82). Thus, your hotel would actually achieve a *lower* RevPAR by accepting the tour operator's proposal and selling out the hotel than it would if the proposal was rejected. Experienced RMs, however, recognize that additional factors must be considered before a proper recommendation to accept or reject the tour operator's proposal could be made. Among these additional factors are:

- Revenue impact
- Expense impact
- Impact on future pricing

Let's look at the importance of these three areas when applied to the current example:

- **Revenue impact.** This refers to the impact on *total* hotel revenue of the additional rooms sales. If the hotel offers additional services such as food, beverages, in-room services, spa services, or other opportunities for guest purchases, the additional revenues that could be generated from a sellout (200 rooms sold in this example) compared to the 88 percent occupancy (176 rooms sold) might affect the decision you would make. In this specific example, it is unlikely that the additional revenue would cause you to want to accept the group. Knowing exactly how to make this critical calculation is important, however, and in Chapter 13 of this book you will learn how to do it.

- **Expense impact.** This refers to the additional costs that would be incurred through the servicing of the additional 24 sold rooms (200 rooms − 176 rooms = 24 additional rooms). Room cleaning costs, in-room supplies, and amenities used and additional labor costs required in other areas of the hotel may be additional expense factors to consider.

- **Impact on future pricing.** This refers to the impact on the remaining rooms' selling prices if in fact 100 rooms are "presold" on that specific Monday. Note that the ADR estimated for your property is $158.75 (see Figure 6.3) at a forecasted occupancy of 88.5 percent. If, however, a sellout is forecast, discounts that may have been offered to guests unwilling to pay full rack rate for your remaining rooms should likely be scaled back or eliminated. Taking the tour group could result in the elimination of discounted rates and thus an *increased* ADR for all unsold, non–tour-committed rooms. As a result, a higher RevPAR may be achieved for those nongroup rooms and, as a result, the entire property.

This example illustrates that total revenues, operating expenses, and impact on future selling prices should be assessed by RMs when they utilize historical as well as other types of data in their revenue management decision making.

The specific historical data that may be of interest to RMs and thus should be regularly collected for future analysis will vary somewhat by property but would typically include the data related to the following:

Essential RM Terms

Denied (reservation): The situation that occurs when a hotel is unable to accommodate a guest's reservation preference due to the unavailability of the room or service at the price, or on the date requested by the guest. Also known as a *denial*.

Walk-in: A guest that arrives at the property seeking a room but without an advanced reservation.

■ Number of reservations/ room nights booked per day
■ Number of reservations/ room nights **denied** per day
■ Number of daily reservation cancellations
■ Total number of room nights canceled
■ Number of check-ins (arrivals)
■ Number of check-outs (departures)
■ No-shows
■ **Walk-ins**
■ ADR achieved

■ Occupancy % achieved
■ By the property
■ By room type
■ Average number of guests per room
■ Average length of guest stay

Essential RM Term

Track (data): To continually monitor a set of data.

In many cases, RMs who have collected historical data will want to summarize it. Thus, for example, an RM may seek to monitor, or **track**, historic ADR levels or any other relevant measurement on a daily, weekly and/or monthly basis.

In many cases, RMs track their data by calculating mathematical averages. Inexperienced RMs seeking to summarize data often make a mistake when calculating their averages. To better understand why they sometimes have difficulty and to avoid such mistakes yourself, consider the hotel that achieves a $300.00 ADR on Monday and a $320.00 ADR on Tuesday.

In this scenario, the RM seeks to summarize the Monday and Tuesday ADR data by calculating an average ADR for the two days. Such an RM would *not* add the Monday ADR to the Tuesday ADR and arrive at a $310.00 two-day average ADR.

Figure 6.4	Mean ADR Calculation Average		
Date	**Revenue Sold**	**Rooms Sold**	**ADR**
Monday	$ 60,000	200	$300.00
Tuesday	$ 96,000	300	$320.00
Mean ADR	**$156,000**	**500**	**$312.00**

$310.00 is *not* likely to be the two-day ADR average for that hotel. To understand why, recall that the formula for ADR is:

$$\frac{\text{Total room revenue}}{\text{Total rooms sold}} = \text{ADR}$$

Figure 6.4 illustrates the proper method used to calculate the hotel's actual *average* or *mean* ADR.

Recall from Chapter 3 that an arithmetic mean is the mathematical average of a set of numbers. A mean is calculated by adding up two or more values (scores) and dividing the total by the number of values (scores). Note that the proper denominator in the calculation of mean ADR in this example is 500 (the number of rooms sold), not 2 (the number of days' ADR included in the average)! Properly calculating the mean produces an average ADR of $312.00, not $310.00.

For RMs, two additional types of means, or averages, are important to understand. These are the **fixed average** and the **rolling average**.

A fixed average is an average in which an RM would determine a specific time period—for example, the first 14 days of a given month—and then compute the average amount of revenue generated, rooms sold or other relevant data based on results for that defined period.

Note that this average is called *fixed* because the first 14 days of the month will always consist of the same days (days 1–14 of each month). To illustrate, consider the RM of the Lafayette-Lincoln Lodge, a small hotel property that wishes to calculate a fixed average of revenue generation for the first 14 days of the month. Figure 6.5 details the revenue generated for this period and the average (mean) revenue generated per day.

Essential RM Term

Fixed average: An average calculated by using historical data generated during a specific and unchanged time period.

Rolling average: An average calculated by using historical data generated during a changing time period.

This average revenue is calculated as: Total revenue ÷ Number of days. In Figure 6.5, $19,980/14 = $1,427.14 per day. It is a fixed or constant average because the RM at the Lafayette-Lincoln Lodge has identified the 14 specific days that are used to make up the average.

The number $1,427.14 may be very useful because it might, if the RM decides it makes sense to do so, be used as a good predictor of the revenue volume that should be expected for the first 14 days of *next* month.

The rolling average is the average amount of sales revenue, rooms sold, or other data over a *changing* time period. Essentially, while a fixed average is computed using a specific and constant set of data, the rolling average is computed using trailing data that will change regularly.

Figure 6.5	14-Day Fixed-Average Revenue Calculation

Lafayette-Lincoln Lodge	
Day	**Daily Revenue**
1	$ 1,350.00
2	1,320.00
3	1,390.00
4	1,440.00
5	1,420.00
6	1,458.00
7	1,450.00
8	1,460.00
9	1,410.00
10	1,440.00
11	1,470.00
12	1,460.00
13	1,418.00
14	1,494.00
14-day Total	**$19,980.00**

To illustrate a rolling average, consider the case of the RM who manages the Douglas Lodge, also a small hotel property. She is interested in knowing the average revenue dollars generated by her property for each prior seven-day period. Obviously, in this case, the prior seven-day period changes or *rolls* forward by one day, each day. It is important to note that this RM could have been interested in calculating her average daily revenue last week (a fixed average), but she prefers to know her average sales for the last seven days.

This means that she will, at times, use data from both last week and this week to compute the most up-to-date (current) seven-day average. Using the trailing revenue data recorded in Figure 6.6, the seven-day rolling average for this RM would be computed as shown in Figure 6.7.

Note that each seven-day period is made up of a group of daily revenue numbers that change over time. The first seven-day rolling average is computed by summing the first seven days' revenue (revenue on days 1−7 = $9,828) and dividing that number by seven to arrive at a seven-day rolling average of $1,404.00 ($9,828 ÷ 7 = $1,404.00). Each day, the RM would *add* the day's revenue to that of the prior seven-day total and *subtract* the revenue from the day that is now eight days past. This gives her the effect of continually *rolling* the most current seven days' data forward.

Figure 6.6 14-Day Revenue Generation

Douglas Lodge

Date	Revenue	Date	Revenue
1st	$1,350	8th	$1,460
2nd	1,320	9th	1,410
3rd	1,390	10th	1,440
4th	1,440	11th	1,470
5th	1,420	12th	1,460
6th	1,458	13th	1,418
7th	1,450	14th	1,494

Figure 6.7 Seven-Day Rolling Average

Douglas Lodge

Date	Seven-Day Period							
	1–7	2–8	3–9	4–10	5–11	6–12	7–13	8–14
1	$ 1,350	—						
2	1,320	$ 1,320	—					
3	1,390	1,390	$ 1,390	—				
4	1,440	1,440	1,440	$ 1,440	—			
5	1,420	1,420	1,420	1,420	$ 1,420	—		
6	1,458	1,458	1,458	1,458	1,458	$ 1,458	—	
7	1,450	1,450	1,450	1,450	1,450	1,450	$ 1,450	—
8		1,460	1,460	1,460	1,460	1,460	1,460	$ 1,460
9			1,410	1,410	1,410	1,410	1,410	1,410
10				1,440	1,440	1,440	1,440	1,440
11					1,470	1,470	1,470	1,470
12						1,460	1,460	1,460
13							1,418	1,418
14								1,494
Total	$9,828	$ 9,938	$10,028	$10,078	$10,108	$10,148	$10,108	$10,152
7-Day Rolling Average	$1,404.00	$1,419.71	$1,432.57	$1,439.71	$1,444.00	$1,449.71	$1,444.00	$1,450.29

> ▶ **RM ON THE WEB 6.1**
>
> In the previous chapter, you learned that Smith Travel Research (STR) offers RMs a variety of informational reports. STR also reports weekly and monthly demand for rooms (and room rates paid) in a variety of geographic locations both nationally and internationally. You can view the most recent demand reports at: www.strglobal.com
>
> When you arrive, click *News*.

The use of the rolling average, while more complex and time consuming than that of a fixed average, can be extremely useful in recording the historical data that will help you make effective predictions about the sales levels, rooms sold or other data you might expect in the future. This is true because in many cases, rolling data are more current and thus more relevant than some fixed historical averages.

As you design your revenue management program, you may choose to compute fixed averages for some data and time periods and use rolling averages for others. For example, it may be helpful to know your average rooms sold for the first 14 days of last month and your average rooms sold for the past 14 days. If, for example, the larger number was from last month, you may be experiencing sales decline. If the most recent number is larger, you are likely experiencing an increase in room sales. Either way, the data you have collected and analyzed can help you better predict your future room sales.

Regardless of the type of averages they utilize, RMs must track their historical data because it is from sales histories that they will be better able to predict current and future operating data.

CURRENT DATA

Historical data help RMs understand what has happened in the past. **Current data** aid in understanding the present.

Essential RM Term

Current data: Data describing currently occurring events.

Current data can be examined best when it is divided into its three main reporting areas:

Occupancy and Availability Reports

Group Rooms Pace Reporting

Nonrooms Revenue Pace Reporting

Occupancy and Availability Reports

As you learned in Chapter 3, for the great majority of RMs working in hospitality, the data that they are called on to generate, store, and analyze on a daily basis will be sufficient to guide their revenue management decision making. Failure to collect and manage that data, however, gives rise to the industry saying:

Average RMs know what has just happen, good RMs know what is happening now, and outstanding RMs know what will happen in the future.

What is happening now is best communicated by the monitoring of four key areas:

1. The number of rooms available to sell
2. The number of rooms reserved
3. The number of rooms held or **blocked**
4. The estimated ADR resulting from currently reserved or blocked rooms

Essential RM Term

Block(ed): Rooms reserved or removed from a hotel's sellable inventory exclusively for members of a specific group. Such rooms are said to be "blocked" (from being sold to alternative buyers) especially for that group. Also referred to as a *group block*.

Detailed data related to each area are routinely maintained in a hotel's CRS and its PMS. To illustrate, consider Figure 6.8. It presents the PMS print-out detailing the rooms sold or held during a 14-day period (6/2/20XX through 6/16/20XX) at the 1,400-room McAllister Plaza.

The data contained in Figure 6.8 can be interpreted as follows:

1. The *Run Date* indicates when the report was prepared.
2. The *Date* (column 1) identifies the numerical day of the month.
3. The *Day* column identifies the day of the week.

Figure 6.8	McAllister Plaza: 14-Day Occupancy Detail					
June 2 to June 16: 20XX						
1. Run Date: May 1, 20XX						
2. Date	**3. Day**	**4. Rooms Available**	**5. Reserved**	**6. Blocked**	**7. Total Held**	**8. Current Occ. %**
6/2/xx	Mon	1,400	825	60	885	63.2%
6/3/xx	Tues	1,400	715	250	965	68.9%
6/4/xx	Wed	1,400	610	210	820	58.6%
6/5/xx	Thur	1,400	800	700	1,500	107.1%
6/7/xx	Fri	1,400	475	1,100	1,575	112.5%
6/8/xx	Sat	1,400	450	650	1,100	78.6%
6/9/xx	Sun	1,380	275	125	400	29.0%
6/10/xx	Mon	1,380	925	0	925	67.0%
6/11/xx	Tues	1,380	850	250	1,100	79.7%
6/12/xx	Wed	1,400	725	400	1,125	80.4%
6/13/xx	Thur	1,400	875	400	1,275	91.1%
6/14/xx	Fri	1,400	550	50	600	42.9%
6/15/xx	Sat	1,400	500	50	550	39.3%
6/16/xx	Sun	1,400	325	75	400	28.6%
9. Total		19,540	8,900	4,320	13,220	67.7%

4. The *Rooms Available* column is the total number of salable rooms in the hotel (1,400 in this example).

5. The *Reserved* column represents the number of rooms for which there is *currently* (as of the run date) a confirmed reservation.

6. The *Blocked* column represent the number of rooms being held by the property for one or more groups whose members have not yet individually reserved the rooms.

7. The *Total Held* column represents the sum of the Reserved plus the Blocked rooms (i.e., the number of rooms *not* available for public sale).

8. *Current Occ. %* indicates the percentage of the hotel's rooms that are currently reserved and/or blocked from sale. It is the occupancy percentage the hotel would experience if all currently reserved rooms and currently blocked group rooms were in fact sold on that date. This percentage can exceed 100 percent.

9. *Total* is the column totals (sums) for each category during the 14-day period covered in the report.

Some RMs prefer to analyze their current data based on rooms *availability* rather than on reserved and blocked rooms. These RMs use the formula:

> Rooms available – Total held = Available for sale

Figure 6.9 details a PMS print-out that indicates the rooms yet to be sold (available for sale) at the McAllister Plaza for the period 6/2/20XX through 6/16/20XX.

The data contained in Figure 6.9 can be interpreted as follows:

1. The *Run Date* indicates when the report was prepared.

2. The *Date* (column 1) identifies the numerical day of the month.

3. The *Day* column identifies the day of the week.

4. The *Rooms Available* column is the total number of salable rooms in the hotel (1,400 in this example).

5. The *Reserved* column represents the number of rooms for which there is currently a confirmed reservation.

6. The *Blocked* column represent the number of rooms being held by the property for one or more groups whose members have not yet individually reserved the rooms.

7. The *Total Held* column represents the sum of the Reserved and Blocked cells (i.e., the number of rooms *not* available for sale).

8. *Available for Sale* indicates the total number of rooms that remain unsold as of the report's run date. This can be a negative number, indicating an overbooking situation.

9. *Total* is the sum for each category during the 14-day period covered in the report.

Essential RM Term

Out-of-order (OOO): A room that is unrentable for reasons other than normal cleaning. Also referred to as an *OOO* room.

Figures 6.8 and 6.9 demonstrate four concepts important to RMs:

1. The number of *Rooms Available* in a property may vary due to repairs or renovation. Note the dates of 6/9/20XX thru 6/11/20XX. On those dates 20 rooms have been placed in **out-of-order (OOO)** status due to planned renovations.

Figure 6.9	McAllister Plaza: 14-Day Availability Detail					
1. Run Date: May 1, 20XX						
2. Date	**3. Day**	**4. Rooms Available**	**5. Reserved**	**6. Blocked**	**7. Total Held**	**8. Available for Sale**
6/2/xx	Mon	1,400	825	60	885	515
6/3/xx	Tues	1,400	715	250	965	435
6/4/xx	Wed	1,400	610	210	820	580
6/5/xx	Thur	1,400	800	700	1,500	−100
6/7/xx	Fri	1,400	475	1,100	1,575	−175
6/8/xx	Sat	1,400	450	650	1,100	300
6/9/xx	Sun	1,380	275	125	400	980
6/10/xx	Mon	1,380	925	0	925	455
6/11/xx	Tues	1,380	850	250	1,100	280
6/12/xx	Wed	1,400	725	400	1,125	275
6/13/xx	Thur	1,400	875	400	1,275	125
6/14/xx	Fri	1,400	550	50	600	800
6/15/xx	Sat	1,400	500	50	550	850
6/16/xx	Sun	1,400	325	75	400	1,000
9. Total		19,540	8,900	4,320	13,220	6,320

2. Both reserved and blocked rooms must be considered when calculating the total number of rooms committed or available for sale.

3. In some cases, the number of reserved and blocked rooms (*Total Held*) may *exceed* the number of the hotel's room count (*Available for Sale*) as seen on 6/5/20XX and 6/7/20XX. The causes of this oversold situation, as well as solutions to it will be addressed in detail in this book's next chapter.

4. Regardless of an RM's preference to evaluate occupancy (Figure 6.8) or availability (Figure 6.9), knowledge of the number of rooms yet to be sold on a specific date is the most important information that can be gained from current data.

While the data presentation format of any hotel's PMS may vary somewhat from that of other hotels, the conceptual issue regarding the use of current data can be easily expressed mathematically. The following formula provides RMs the information they need for analyzing each future date for which rooms are available for sale:

$$\text{Total rooms available}$$

Less   Total unsellable rooms

Less   Presold/blocked rooms

Sellable (Available) rooms

Essential RM Term

On-the-books: An industry term referring to the number of currently reserved and/or blocked rooms committed for any future date. The term originated in the days when hotel reservation data was stored in a bound reservations book, rather than in a software program.

Used, for example, in: "We currently have 200 rooms on the books for September 8."

Because most hotels do not typically accept individual room reservations for dates further than one year in the future, RMs in most cases will need to continually monitor approximately 52 weeks, or one year of current data. In some cases, the number of current reservations **on-the-books** for dates far into the upcoming 52-week period will be small. Effective RMs, however, know that all future dates for which reservations are currently being taken must be carefully and regularly monitored to avoid major errors in revenue management strategy and pricing.

An effective PMS is a vital aid in monitoring current data and in identifying future dates that require an RM's special attention. In fact, sophisticated mathematical programs that help hoteliers manage revenues are available to interface with most CRSs and PMSs in use in the industry today.

RM AT WORK 6.2

"You've got to be kidding me!" said Basil Bakal, owner of the 200-room Holiday Inn Express in Baytown.

"No, I'm not kidding. He sold them all," replied Sandy Lamia, the hotel's director of sales and marketing.

Together, Basil and Sandy served as the hotel's revenue management team.

It was February 6. Sandy had just informed Basil that Mike Brennan, the hotels' new night auditor, had, late last night, taken 17 separate reservations. Each reserving guest had purchased nine rooms. Each reservation was for one night, and all were scheduled to arrive November 22.

Because the buyers had purchased in quantity, Mike had given each a 10 percent room discount; the normal amount permitted by Basil and Sandy when a reservation agent was quoting rates for a multiroom sale. Mike had sold every remaining available room for that date.

"But that's the weekend of the Annual Sailboat Show. The city will be packed! We always sell out that weekend. We never sell at discount, and we always require a three-night minimum stay on each room.

"I know," replied Sandy. "But Mike's new. He said he didn't know. No one told him."

1. As experienced RM, why do you think Basil and Sandy would require a three-night minimum stay for guests reserving rooms during the Annual Sailboat Show?

2. Given what you know about differential pricing, why would they eliminate discounts on the rooms sold during the weekend of the Annual Sailboat Show?

3. How could Basil and Sandy ensure that all desk agents at their hotel were aware of all special future sale dates? How could they themselves stay abreast of the future dates they should be carefully monitoring?

The Fidelio company, now owned by Microsoft, was a German pioneer in producing computerized hotel systems, including those designed to manage revenue. This is how they now describe their currently popular Opus Revenue Management System (ORMS). Note the specific reference to historical data:

> ORMS seamlessly interfaces with most major PMS, CRS and S&C (sales and catering) systems. At the heart of the ORMS solution is an accurate and automatic forecasting model. Our world class systems use automatic trend recognition and historical data to dynamically forecast transient stay patterns and to optimize rates."[4]

Whether purchased as stand-alone programs or directly interfaced with the CRS or PMS, by utilizing information gleaned from the hotel's historical and current sales data, these programs can:

- Recommend room rates that will optimize the number of rooms sold
- Recommend specific room rates that will optimize sales revenue
- Recommend special room restrictions (e.g., **minimum length of stay (MLOS)** requirements) that serve to optimize the total revenue generated by the hotel during a specific time period
- Identify special high consumer demand dates that deserve special management attention in pricing

Essential RM Term

Minimum length of stay (MLOS): A revenue management strategy that instructs reservationists to decline any room reservation request that does not equal or exceed the predetermined minimum number of nights allowed. For example: "We need to put an MLOS of two nights on any room requests that include October 17."

Evaluating current data can help RMs estimate room demand, and as you will learn, serves to assist in pricing rooms. A hotel's computer system can "remember" more important dates than can an individual hotelier or revenue manager, but those dates must first be carefully identified and then monitored on a regular basis via the use of current occupancy or availability data. Truly effective RMs review each future sales period by day; for every upcoming day (*that's right; for every upcoming day the property is accepting reservations!*).

Less effective RMs review reservation activity and current data weekly. Even less effective RMs review only selected future dates, and even then, only on a monthly or even less frequent basis. Of course, RMs who do not use the data in their systems to evaluate current occupancy or availability on a consistent basis simply will not have the information they need to prevent errors made by themselves and others when making revenue management decisions.

Groups Rooms Pace Reporting

As you can see from the data presented in Figure 6.10, many major hotel companies—and thus the great majority of all hotels operating in the United States—do not accept individual room reservations for dates that are more than one year in the future. Although not every chain is listed, those not included employ similar policies. Thus, in over 295,000 U.S. hotels it might appear that RMs need only concern themselves with monitoring current data related to the upcoming 365 days. In fact, in most of these hotels that would not be

Figure 6.10	Days Into the Future Reservations are Accepted by Selected Hotel Chains	
Hotel Brand	**Number of Operated and/ or Franchised Hotels[5]**	**Accepts Reservations**
Choice	5,376	364 days out/52 weeks out
Best Western	3,952	350 days out/50 weeks out
IHG	3,741	350 days out/50 weeks out
Hilton	2,935	364 days out/52 weeks out
Accor	4,121	404 days out/57 weeks out
Marriott	2,832	350 days out/50 weeks out
Wyndham Hotel Group	6,473	Varies with brand; typically 6 months to 1 year out
Total	29,430	

true. This is so because RMs in most properties must also carefully monitor current data related to group room and group pace sales.

In Chapter 1, you learned that a pace report is a summary description of future demand for a lodging property's rooms or other services. A **group rooms pace report** summarizes future demand for group rooms. It is important to understand that this is also considered current (not future) data because the rooms identified in these reports, regardless of the number of years in advance, represent rooms that are already sold or are being held for sale. They are not rooms considered available to be sold in the future.

Perhaps one of the greatest misunderstandings an inexperienced lodging industry observer has about the hotel business relates to how reservations for rooms are made. Many think that the majority of hotel room sales in a typical hotel are made to individuals. In some cases this may be true, but in many more cases, the majority of room sales are made to groups of individuals or to individuals reserving large numbers of rooms for a specific group. In most cases, these rooms will be reserved and held for purchase at a date in the future that can easily range from a few weeks to several years in the future.

Although some PMS systems can accommodate recording and reporting the data related to far-in-advance group sales, most cannot. As a result, in most cases information about them will be compiled in a group rooms pace report, will be updated regularly, and will be maintained in the property's sales and marketing files. As a result, RMs should monitor these pace reports just as closely as they monitor current data reports from the PMS.

To better understand the rationale for creating and regularly analyzing group rooms pace reports, consider the RM whose hotel is located in a city that houses a university that is a member of the South East Conference (SEC). This university plays a home football game each year against a major rival and the following year plays the game in the rival's home

Essential RM Term

Group rooms pace report: A summary report describing the amount of future demand for a lodging property's group rooms and the rate(s) at which that group business has been captured. Also referred to as a group rooms booking pace report.

city. Hotel rooms in both cities sell out when the game is held in the local stadium. In this example, the RM's hotel has secured a contract to house the visiting football team on those alternating years it comes to town. In such a case, this hotel will need to block the required rooms, two, four and/or even six years in advance of the game. These blocked rooms would not be entered as a sale in the PMS because that system can only record reservations made one year in advance. The group room commitment made to this visiting university would instead be identified on the hotel's group rooms pace report.

In hotels that host extremely large meetings and conferences group rooms pace reports may indicate blocked rooms for dates that are up to ten (or even more) years in the future. Identifying those days on which rooms have already been reserved helps RMs better make their pricing and rooms inventory-related management decisions regarding remaining rooms that will be sold to transient guests. Properly prepared and monitored, however, group rooms pace reports can do even more.

In all cases RMs should ensure that confirmed group sales made by their property's sales and marketing team during the month, for all future months, are recorded and reported regularly. Of course, some of these sales may be made during the month, for that current month; but many more will likely be made for a future date that is several months or years in the future. Each of these sales has the potential to significantly impact revenue management decision making. Thus, each should be included in any consideration of pricing and rooms inventory allocation decisions related to the dates affected by those specific sales. In addition, if the hotel experiences any group cancellations or significant room block reductions on previously made group sales these should also be reflected in the updated group pace reports.

Essential RM Term

Tentative (sale): The situation that occurs when a hotel blocks group rooms for a specific date in anticipation of a future confirmed contract or sale.

Many RMs, working in conjunction with their sales and marketing team will, on a monthly basis, also assess **tentative sales**.

While individual room reservations are almost never held in tentative sale status, tentative group room sales occur often and for a variety of reasons. For example, a client seeking to purchase 500 room nights for a specific time period two years in the future may ask to review a sales contract before signing. During the agreed-on review period, the requested rooms may be held in anticipation of the customer's contract signature. This ensures they cannot mistakenly be sold to another client during the original customer's allotted contract review period. When tentative sales (contracts) are reported as part of the hotel's group rooms pace report, the number of days the rooms have been held in tentative sale status, as well as the agreed-on signing or release date of the rooms, should also be noted and enforced.

Similarly, if a hotel has submitted a bid for a room sale to an entity requesting rooms on a future date, those rooms may be held (in tentative sales status) during the agreed bid evaluation period identified in the **request for proposal (RFP)**. This ensures that, should the hotel win the group room's contract for which they have bid, the rooms promised in the bid will not have mistakenly been committed or sold to other customers. It also means that if the hotel does not win the group room's contract or if the group's decision is not made by the agreed upon date, then the hotel reserves the right to release those rooms for sale to other buyers.

Essential RM Term

Request for proposal (RFP): An official request by a potential rooms or space buyer that a hotel quote, in writing, its rates and contract terms in response to the buyer's specifically identified rooms or space needs.

RMs assessing future rooms sales are interested in two issues:

1. How many rooms have been sold at this point?
2. How quickly are we selling our remaining rooms?

Essential RM Term

Position report: A simplified form of a pace report that summarizes rooms sold or held for a future date or time period.

Some RMs record the number of rooms or group rooms that have currently been sold or held for a future date using a **position report**. A position report states the total rooms sold for a future date of interest but does not compare that number to sales levels achieved in a prior time period.

Position reports are important because they indicate the amount of sales volume already achieved. Pace reports, however, help RMs answer the second question: *"How quickly are we selling our remaining rooms."*

As you learned in Chapter 1, the rate or speed at which unsold rooms are being purchased compared to a previous time period is documented in a hotel's pace report. To assess the pace at which group room sales take place, RMs should rely on an up-to-date, accurate, and monthly or more frequently prepared group rooms pace report.

Figure 6.11 is an example of such a summary group rooms pace report for the McAllister Hotel. Note that it that also includes a comparison to group rooms sales achieved during the same

| Figure 6.11 | McAllister Plaza Group Rooms Pace Report for DECEMBER, 20XX |

ROOM SALES FOR USE IN 20XY				
1. Month	**2. Rooms Sold for This Month**	**3. Total Sold for This Month YTD**	**4. Rooms Sold for This Month Last Year**	**5. Rooms Sold for This Month Last YTD**
Jan	150	950	50	100
Feb	800	2,250	600	2,000
Mar	950	3,500	1,150	3,750
Apr	725	2,900	850	3,100
May	600	1,800	900	1,600
June	150	1,400	600	1,200
July	10,800	22,800	8,800	19,500
Aug	1,900	18,500	1,825	16,500
Sept	1,500	15,500	1,400	22,500
Oct	1,300	9,000	1,200	10,500
Nov	1,850	9,800	1,900	9,600
Dec	1,200	17,500	1,400	15,550
TOTAL	**21,925**	**105,900**	**20,675**	**105,900**

period in the previous year. This report details the number of group rooms sold in the month of December 20XX for use by guests in 20XY (next year). It also includes year-to-date (YTD) data indicating the total number of rooms sold for that month during all prior sales periods.

Where:

> Column 1: Identifies the month for which rooms have been committed (via sale or block).
>
> Column 2: Identifies the rooms sold *within* the reporting month (sold in December 20XX) for all dates in 20XY.
>
> Column 3: Identifies the total rooms sold in all prior time periods for all dates in 20XY.
>
> Column 4: Identifies the room sold *within* the reporting month (sold in December of the previous year) for all dates in 20XX.
>
> Column 5: Identifies the total rooms sold in the previous year for all dates in 20XX.

The value of a pace report can readily be seen by applying a percentage change in sales formula to the data found in Figure 6.11, calculated as:

$$\frac{\text{Total sales this year} - \text{Total sales last year}}{\text{Total sales last year}} = \%\text{ Change in sales}$$

To illustrate, consider the fact that, in this year, total group room sales for the month of December 20XX increased 6 percent over last year. Using the basic change in sales formula:

$$\frac{\text{Total rooms sold this year} - \text{Total rooms sold last year}}{\text{Total rooms sold last year}} = \%\text{ Change in room sales}$$

$$\frac{\$21,925 - 20,675}{20,675} = 6\%\text{ increase in room sales}$$

Thus, in terms of group rooms sales, this month might be considered a better month for group sales than was last December. Note also, however, that, the total number of presold or blocked rooms for next year is unchanged from the previous year (105,900 this year and 105,900 last year).

$$\frac{\text{Total sold YTD} - \text{Rooms sold last YTD}}{\text{Rooms sold last YTD}} = \%\text{ Change in room sales}$$

$$\frac{105,900 - 105,900}{105,900} = 0\%\text{ Change in room sales}$$

Astute RMs carefully reviewing pace reports can learn a great deal. A close examination of the specific data reported in Figure 6.11 suggests at least two important facts:

1. *Demand for rooms in July and August of the coming year is strong relative to the prior year.* It would likely be important to determine the specific days within those months

where demand has increased for the purpose of reviewing pricing and inventory allocation to the property's various channel alternatives during those high demand dates.

2. *Demand for rooms in September of the coming year appears to be weak relative to the prior year.* It would be helpful to determine, if possible, the cause of the demand reduction and to review pricing and inventory allocation strategies to be used during those reduced demand dates.

A pace report can be prepared based on the number of rooms sold, the sales value (in dollars) of the sales made, or both. It can also be produced to include any period of time in the future. In Figure 6.11, the pace report was prepared based on the number of group rooms sold in December for the 12-month period that ends in December of the following year.

Most RMs prefer that group cancellations be reported separately and in the month the sales are canceled (not when the group was slated to arrive). That is, if a group of 100 rooms canceled, in January, their contract for rooms in the coming June, that value should be noted in the January (not June) pace report. Tentative contracts, which should also be monitored, are not typically considered to be a final sale until a signed contract has been returned and thus are not generally included in a group rooms pace report until a signed contract or rooms commitment has been secured.

Essential RM Term

Pick up: The proportion of previously reserved rooms that are ultimately occupied.

Thus, for example, if 200 group rooms are reserved, and only 100 are ultimately occupied, the pick-up rate is 50 percent (100 occupied/200 originally held = 50 percent pick up).

Pace reports help tell RMs where future pricing opportunities or challenges may exist. Of course, the number of rooms reserved by group guests is most often only an estimate of the rooms to be sold until those rooms are actually occupied. Therefore, it is important that the group sales reported by the hotels sales and marketing team be realistic in regard to the number of rooms that will actually be sold. If a sales team significantly overestimates the **pick up** on a group sale, the pace report will be artificially inflated and poor revenue management decisions based on the report will likely result.

Nonrooms Revenue Pace Reporting

While many lodging industry RMs concern themselves primarily with guest room pricing, those RMs working in full-service hotels should also carefully monitor the sale of other hotel products and services. This can be done via the use of pace reports designed especially for nonrooms revenue areas such as sales and catering, which generate significant food and beverage or meetings income and thus may impact guest room pricing decisions.

To better understand why this is so, consider a 300-room full-service hotel that has a ballroom which seats 1,000 guests. Assume that the sales and catering team reserves this ballroom space for a newly engaged couple. The couple's wedding and dinner reception is to be held in 14 months. A full 1,000 guests are expected, and most of these will arrive from out of town, as the hotel was selected because it is equally distant from the hometowns of the bride and groom. The bride and groom maintain that out-of-town guests will all likely need lodging, but that these attendees will be "on-their-own" regarding their needs for guest rooms. In this case, the number of sleeping rooms that will likely be utilized by those attending the dinner/reception for this couple may be significant. Most guests would likely prefer to stay at the hotel where the reception is being held. Unless the communication among the revenue management team in this property is very good, revenue optimization decisions for this date may be poorly made because the impact of this sale would not likely be detected by CRS or PMS reports (because the date is more than 12 months out), or even by reviewing a group rooms booking pace report (because no firm guest room sales or room reservations resulted when the ballroom was reserved).

Many RMs in full-service hotels work with their sales and catering departments team members to create a banquet or catering pace report detailing the monthly food and beverage and/or meeting room sales made by the sales and marketing staff. In fact, a position or pace report should be prepared for any identifiable segment of business that the RM feels it is important to monitor because of its potential impact on room sales.

In too many cases, revenue management in the past has been seen as a "guest rooms only" issue. But a thriving hotel's revenue stream also includes income derived from restaurants, bars, conferences, banquets, spas, and a variety of other operating departments. All too often, the monitoring of activity, as well as the tools to do so, which is so carefully devoted to the rooms side of the business, are completely or largely absent from the rest of the business.

Effective RMs understand that answers to these questions are indeed revenue management essentials:

- Who are our key buyers of conferences?
- What is their lead time for reserving space?
- What is the role of price in converting a prospect to a customer?
- What is the best utilization of each meeting room?
- What is the most profitable configuration (set-up) of those rooms?
- What meetings business has recently been lost, and why?
- What meetings or conference business has been denied, and why?

The same questions, of course, apply to the hotel's restaurant business, to its bar business, and for the wedding or meetings market.

Regardless of their assigned areas of responsibility experienced RMs know that very strong (increasing) rooms and nonrooms revenue position and pace reports show that sales made by the sales and marketing team are rising on a monthly and/or annual basis. Weaker reports would show they are level or declining. By comparing the pace report data in any given time period with the pace report results of the same period in the prior years, an RM can gain valuable information that may not be available from the current data found in the property's PMS reports.

FUTURE DATA

The careful and continual monitoring of historical and current data help RMs better understand previous and existing demand for their hotel's guest rooms. This data also are essential because of their ability to help guide decision making and estimates related to future room demand. Of course, even the best of RMs will find their crystal balls to be a bit fuzzy at times. These same RMs understand, however, that the essence of their job is to learn from the past, manage the present, and by doing so shape the future. The importance of preparing for the future was captured nicely by American engineer Charles F. Kettering, who sagely observed, "My interest is in the future because I am going to spend the rest of my life there."[6]

Factors Affecting Future Demand

In Chapter 2, you learned that an important job of an RM is the application of data and insight to the revenue management process. Precisely estimating future room demand data certainly requires insight and experience as well. This is so because a variety of factors directly impact the future demand for a hotel's guest rooms and services. While the variation in individual properties makes it difficult to precisely identify the factors that will most affect the future demand for any single hotel's guest rooms, for most properties these factors include:

- Demand generators
- Demand drains
- The strength or weakness of the local as well as state or national economy
- The property's addition or elimination of specific services
- The opening or closing of competitive hotels
- Predictable factors such as planned road construction or seasonality
- Unpredictable factors such as unplanned events, road construction, or severe weather

- The pricing decisions made by the property's competitors
- The pricing decisions made by the property

Essential RM Terms

Demand generator: An entity or event that produces a significant increase in business. For example, in a college community, "spring graduation" would likely be a significant demand generator (i.e., the direct cause for an increase in the use of overnight rooms).

Demand drain: A circumstance that produces a significant decrease in business. For example, in a hotel catering to businesspersons, holidays typically represent demand drains (because few business travelers travel on the holidays).

Essential RM Term

Future (forecast) data: Data describing events that will occur in the future. Also know as *forecast data* (recall, however, that all three data types—historical, current, and future—are used in forecasting).

Forecasting Future Demand

RMs forecast future demand utilizing **future (forecast) data**.

To illustrate the importance of future data and information, consider the RM working in the 500-room Plaza Place hotel. The property is attached to the convention center of a large southern city. Because it caters primarily to groups and business travelers, it is busy during the week but slow on the weekends when business travel is light. It manages to achieve a 50 to 60 percent occupancy on Friday and Saturday nights. But it can do so only by heavily promoting a "Romantic Getaway" package to local city residents.

The getaway package includes rooms offered at 30 percent off rack rate. The hotel's general manager learns from the local **convention and visitors' bureau (CVB)** that the city has just been selected to host, in three years, the International Hospitality Educator's Association convention.

This will be the first time the group has met in this city, so no historical data exist related to any previous stays. The group has 5,000 members. The convention's meetings will all be held at the convention center on the third weekend in July. It is anticipated that the Plaza Place hotel next to the convention center, will be a desirable location for attendees.

Area rooms will likely sell out at full rack rate. Given this information, should the RM immediately designate the weekend of the educator's convention as one in which the "Romantic Getaway" package will not be offered?

Most talented RMs would indeed eliminate the "Romantic Getaway" package that weekend because the educators will likely fill the hotel. This decision would be made despite the fact that:

- There is *no historical data* in the PMS related to this educator's convention.
- The PMS shows that *not a single current reservation exists* at this time for the actual days on which the convention will be held.
- No contract for group rooms has been signed, nor is a contract currently in tentative sale status.
- The date in question is three years away.

It is not possible to identify every event that could impact an RM's estimation of demand, but careful monitoring of historical and current data—as well as upcoming demand generating and draining entities and events—should be a regular activity. To this end, RMs must:

- Know about special citywide or areawide events in the area that affect demand for their properties.
- Have an understanding of the demand for competitive hotel properties in the area.
- Consider any the opening or closing of competitive hotels in the area.
- Adjust demand forecasts very quickly when faced with significant demand-altering events (i.e., unusual events, inclement weather, power outages, and airport or highway closings).

In some unique situations, future demand simply cannot be anticipated. Consider the impact on area hotels immediately following the announcement that there would be a memorial service held at the Staples Center in Los Angeles, California, for world-renowned artist Michael Jackson following his untimely death:

> "The magnitude of this event is 10 to 100 times of any other event we've had," said John Kelly, general manager of the Holiday Inn across the street from the Staples Center. "Within 48 hours of Thursday's announcement . . . all 195 rooms at the hotel were booked."[7]

Essential RM Term

Convention and visitorsbureau (CVB):
The local entity typically responsible for promoting travel and tourism in a specifically designated geographic area.

Figure 6.12	Basic Forecast Types

Forecast Type	Characteristics/Purpose
Occupancy forecast	■ Forecasts at least 1, 2, 7, 14, 21, and 30 days out ■ Produces daily and weekly occupancy percentage estimates ■ Unlikely to exceed 100 percent ■ Helps improve employee scheduling ■ Shows guest arrival and departure patterns
Demand forecast	■ Identifies periods of 100 percent or more occupancy demand for rooms ■ Identifies periods of very low demand ■ Forecasts 30, 60, 90 days out ■ Produces at least weekly occupancy percentages ■ Used to help establish room rate selling strategies
Revenue forecast	■ Forecasts 30 days out or more ■ Estimates RevPAR ■ Matches revenue forecasts to preestablished budgets ■ Advanced versions help estimate the hotel's cash flows ■ Should not exceed the revenue that can be generated by selling 100 percent of available rooms

Regardless of the uncertainty involved, forecasting future demand in the lodging industry is crucial for several reasons, including the determination of long-range revenue budgets, planning for the hiring and training of new staff, and the scheduling of needed hotel renovation and repairs. The most important rationale, however, for the development of extended forecasts is the impact such forecasts will have on rooms pricing, a factor significantly affecting total room revenue. With experience, those responsible for forecasting demand for a hotel's rooms can produce room revenue forecasts that will be within 1 to 5 percent of actual hotel room revenues.

Experienced RMs often produce extended demand forecasts of one year or more, but then alter those forecasts monthly as new information, data and insight becomes available. In this manner, a hotel's 7-, 30-, 60-, and even 90-day future demand forecasts can become increasingly accurate. As shown in Figure 6.12, effective RMs are typically called on to produce not one but three different types of future forecasts. Note the characteristics and main purpose of each. Note also that each forecast type still relies on historical, current, and future data to maximize their accuracy.

The actual development of a forecast of any type and for any period begins with an RM's clear understanding of the forecast's component parts and why each is included. To illustrate, consider Figure 6.13, the forecast format in use at a typical 300-room hotel. This sample occupancy forecast is for the single day of October 1.

Figure 6.13	Occupancy Forecast for Monday, October 1

Date: October 1   Day: Monday

Total rooms available	300
(less) Out-of-order (OOO) rooms	−0
Net Availability	**300**
Stayovers	40
(plus) Reservations (Arrivals)	+150
Rooms Sold or Reserved	**190**
Forecasted Adjustments:	
(less) No-shows	−15
(less) Early departures	−5
(plus) Overstays	+10
Total Forecast Sold or Reserved After Adjustments	**180**

Forecast

Rooms sold 180

Occupancy % (180/300) **60 %**

Rooms available 120

Availability % (120/300) **40 %**

Forecast @ ADR = $185.00

Forecast Room Revenue ($185.00 ADR × 180 rooms) **$ 33,300.00**

RevPAR Forecast ($33,300/300) **$ 111.00**

Essential RM Terms

Stayover: A guest (room) not scheduled to be vacated on the forecasted day. That is, the guest will be staying and using the room(s) for at least one more day.

Early departure: A guest who checks out of the hotel *before* his or her originally scheduled check-out date.

Overstay: A guest who checks out of the hotel *after* his or her originally scheduled check-out date.

Important terms in Figure 6.13 include the following:

- **Stayover:** Guests not scheduled to check out of the hotel on the day his or her room status is assessed. That is, the guest will be staying and using the room(s) for at least one more day.

- **No-show:** A guest who makes a room reservation but fails to cancel the reservation (or arrive at the hotel) on the date of the reservation.

- **Early Departure:** A guest who checks out of the hotel *before* his or her originally scheduled check-out date.

- **Overstay:** A guest who checks out of the hotel *after* his or her originally scheduled check-out date.

In most hotels, room usage and room availability will be forecast by individual room type (see Chapter 4), as well as by the total number of hotel rooms available. Clearly this makes accurate forecasting more difficult and more important. To illustrate its critical nature, consider a mother and father traveling with their two young boys who have reserved a room with two queen beds. How satisfied are they likely to be if they arrive at their designated hotel and find that the only room available to them is one with a single king bed? In as similar manner, consider the difficulty encountered by a hotel that contains a single bridal suite but finds that the room has been promised to two different brides on the same night!

The monitoring of room type sales is an important job for RMs. It follows that forecasted ADRs will often vary by room type sold and, as a result, RMs find it helpful to forecast these rates separately. It is important to recognize, however, that the basic forecast procedure is identical whether an RM is forecasting availability by room type or by total availability.

It is also important for you to understand that much of the data in Figure 6.13 are maintained by the PMS and thus should be readily available to you. The number of salable rooms available, the number of out-of-order rooms, the number of stayovers, and the number of reservations currently booked are all recorded by a hotels reservation and rooms management system. Thus, one of an RM's first tasks upon assuming revenue management responsibility for a new hotel is to meet with the property's FOM to determine exactly which occupancy and revenue reports and statistics are readily available from the property's rooms management system.

▶ RM ON THE WEB 6.2

Whether income generated from penalty charges assessed to no-show guests should be counted as rooms revenue or accounted for in another manner is an ongoing debate within the hospitality industry accounting community.

Not surprisingly, in most cases franchisors instruct franchisees to include no-show revenues when calculating rooms revenue totals because these totals are subject to franchise fees.

The attitude of different state entities toward taxing this type revenue, however, varies a great deal. For example, in Texas if the full room rate is assessed as a no-show charge, the revenue is subject to the state's occupancy tax. If a partial rate is charged (for example 50 percent) then no tax is due. To see an example of how detailed states are in defining rooms revenue, go to: www.window.state.tx.us/taxinfo/hotel/matrix/hotel_rm_rev.pdf

Although the positions of franchisors and taxing entities are important to know, the most important point for RMs to remember is that all income considered by their property to be rooms revenue should be part of any rooms revenue forecast, including no-show charges or penalties if they are counted as rooms income.

Data for the three forecast adjustments (no-shows, early departures, and overstays) shown in Figure 6.13 predict events that will occur in the future and thus actual data regarding them will not exist. Historical data on these items, however, is routinely maintained. Thus these numbers can usually be forecasted accurately by RMs who carefully track the hotel's historical data related to them.

The Misuse of Forecasts

Accurate forecasts lead to better decision making. But not all forecasts are accurate, and in some cases, the inaccuracy is intentional. To better understand how forecasts can be intentionally misleading, assume that on a specific day, the RM at a 1,000-room property truly believed that 800 rooms would be sold that night. What might cause that RM to produce a forecast estimating that 700 rooms or that 900 rooms would be sold instead?

The answers to those questions relate to the misuse of forecasts. As you have learned, there are a variety of reasons RMs seek to produce highly accurate rooms sales and revenue generation forecasts. Unfortunately, there are often real pressures on RMs to produce inaccurate forecasts. This pressure can take the form of encouraging the production of forecasts that are of one of the following types:

- Forecasts that are unrealistically low
- Forecasts that are unrealistically high

Unrealistically Low Forecasts

When forecasts are set too low, it is usually because a significant incentive exists for exceeding or *beating* the forecast that has been developed. The approving audience in such cases is often external to the hotel property's revenue management team. This group may include, for example, the hotel's individual ownership, its stockholders, or its management company. When entities such as these distribute financial or other rewards for exceeding forecasted revenue levels, RMs may feel pressure to provide a lower forecast.

Similarly, a hotel's GM or the hotel's **executive committee** may make the internal decision to reward those individuals they feel were responsible for the hotel exceeding planned, budgeted, or forecasted revenues. When such rewards are significant, the internal pressures on RMs to create artificially low forecasts may also be significant.

Essential RM Term

Executive committee: Members of a hotels' administrative team charged with the responsibility of achieving propertywide goals.

Unrealistically High Forecasts

Like unrealistically low forecasts, those forecasts that are unrealistically high may be produced to achieve either external or internal goals. It is important to understand that those who purchase, lend to, or invest in hotels are vitally interested in the future sales volume of the properties with which they are involved. Revenue and occupancy estimates are routinely used to gauge the desirability of owning or investing in a hotel property, as well as the value of the property itself.

Most often, the forecasted future revenues of a lodging facility will be one of the critical considerations in determining whether to buy it, its purchase price, or its estimated worthiness as a continued investment. In such cases, there can be significant pressure by property sellers or current operators to produce revenue forecasts for dissemination to these investor groups that forecast significantly more income than would normally be realistic. Consider the situation that occurred in late 2009. U.S. RevPAR rates were down as much as 15 percent or more from the previous year. Many hotels fell behind in their mortgage payments and the owners were forced to sell. Potential buyers were basing the amount they were willing to pay for these distressed assets on the property's revenue-generating potential. It is easy to see that in these cases the hotels' owners could exert tremendous pressure on RMs to produce overly optimistic, inflated, or even severely inflated revenue forecasts.

In far too many cases, such overly optimistic revenue forecasts have been produced to encourage investment in hotels by local governmental entities, many of which are unfamiliar with the manner in which accurate lodging revenue forecasts should be produced and thus lack the sophistication needed to knowledgably assess the validity of the forecast.

Artificially high revenue estimates may also serve an internal human resource-related purpose. Some lodging professionals feel that budgets or forecasts that represent a significant *stretch* or *reach* will spur those responsible for generating revenues to greater levels of effort. Thus, for example, if a 75 percent occupancy is the realistic expectation for a given

---

RM IN ACTION 6.1: CAN A REVENUE FORECAST BE "LUDICROUS?

Forecasting future occupancy and ADR levels can be serious business for a hotel or for an entire city. Consider the controversial revenue forecast submitted to the city of Lexington, Kentucky, as reported in the *Lexington Herald-Leader* under the heading:

Lexington, Kentucky, Hoteliers claim projections for a taxpayer financed $90 million Westin Hotel and Conference Center are ludicrous
A new Westin hotel is proposed for Lexington. The Westin's developers expect it to open in 2010 with 81 percent occupancy and an average room rate of $195.

The article goes on to describe the situation in Lexington. In that city, the Marriott is a fine hotel and has averaged a 64 percent occupancy and $136.00 ADR. Yet the hotel's developers claim their new hotel will significantly outperform the Marriott. "To

think they can outperform the Marriott to that degree is ludicrous," Mike Curd, general manager of the Holiday Inn Lexington-North, was quoted as saying in the article.

Why was the Westin's success a concern to taxpayers? Because in this case, the original plan called for the hotel's owners to pay back the city for loans received—but if they failed to do so, Lexington taxpayers would be required to make up the difference.

Was the Westin's revenue forecast accurate? Or ludicrous? Was Mike Curd a better forecaster than the one employed by the proposed hotel's owners? Whose forecasts would Kentucky taxpayers accept? The example illustrates the critical importance of producing accurate and realistic revenue forecasts!

Excerpted on 2/24/2008 from *The Lexington Herald-Leader*.

month, the forecast for that month may instead be set at 80 percent in an effort to encourage those involved in selling the property to work harder.

If forecasts are indeed set artificially high in an effort to motivate staff to greater sales efforts, it is important for RMs to understand that the forecast has then become a motivational tool and not purely a revenue management tool. There is certainly nothing inherently wrong or unethical about utilizing a difficult-to-achieve target, goal, or budget as a means of motivating those individuals responsible for an organization's revenue generation. However, making inaccurate forecasts should never be the goal of a professional RM. Rather, these RMs should make it clear that their own goal is to produce revenue forecasts that truly reflect their best interpretation of available data and the application of their honest insight to that data.

An accurate forecast simply should not be based on hope, deception, or greed as an overriding forecast strategy. Although it would be naïve to say that RMs should refuse to modify their forecasts in the face of the direct orders of their supervisors, it is important to recognize that RMs placing their approval on such sales estimates do so only at the peril of their long-term professional reputations.

DEMAND FORECASTS AND STRATEGIC PRICING

In Chapter 2, you learned that the economic law of supply indicates that the higher the demand for a product, the more of it will be produced by sellers. Interestingly, in the lodging industry, that law is simultaneously valid and invalid. In the long run, those areas of the world that exhibit high demand for lodging services will certainly experience a rapid increase in the number of available hotel rooms. For example, hotel expansion in the increasingly popular tourist area of Dubai, in the United Arab Emirates (UAE) in the eastern Arabian Peninsula exceeded 20 percent each year during the five-year period 2005–2009. Thus, in the long run, sellers of hotel rooms will indeed build more rooms in the face of increased demand for them.

For most RMs, however, the law of supply simply does not hold true. That is, in the short run, the number of rooms available to sell at their hotels cannot be increased simply because demand for those rooms has increased. This hard constraint supply situation is one faced by many hospitality industry RMs, including those working in traditional hotels, time-share hotels, bed and breakfasts, cruise ships, and other housing facilities. In fact, it is a situation faced by all RMs managing a finite product supply.

It is often said that great minds think alike, and perhaps that is so. But it is certainly true that "great minds like a think." If you, too, "like a think," then you can now clearly see that three critical issues confront the RM who seeks to optimize revenue in a highly constrained supply setting:

1. Impact of demand on price
2. Impact of price on demand
3. Impact of demand forecasts on an RM's pricing strategy

Impact of Demand on Price

RMs that are honest recognize that very few buyers are pleased to pay a higher-than-normal price for the same product simply because it is temporarily in short supply. This is especially so when the buyer realizes the supply shortage has not resulted in an increase in seller's cost.

To illustrate; if you arrived at a grocery store on a Saturday morning seeking to buy a gallon of milk but were told that, because so many shoppers wanted to buy milk that day the grocer had decided to double its price, your reaction would likely not be a happy one. The grocer might well justify his or her action as a logical one given a limited supply of milk and a virtually unlimited number of milk buyers. The typical buyers' reactions, however, will not be positive because it will be difficult for them to see how they profit in such an exchange. In fact they (like you) would probably feel they were being unjustly taken advantage of.

It is, of course, possible for a business or even an entire industry to decide that it is best to establish its selling prices directly in response to buyer demand. In fact, *yield management*—the name given to the technique first used by commercial airlines to maximize the revenue or yield obtained from selling their limited capacity service in the face of uneven demand—was just such a strategy. Although the approach may have had merit when first introduced, the advent of the Internet has rendered this pricing strategy largely obsolete.

For yield management (essentially using sophisticated algorithms to continually reprice products to maximize revenue) to be effective, buyers must be unaware of seller alternatives. In the early days of the airlines' yield management efforts, it was not possible for flyers to easily compare rates among carriers. This was so because in the pre-Internet age such information simply was not directly available to them. Few observers of the myriad Internet travel sites would today maintain that either flyers or room buyers are unaware of their lower-cost alternatives. This is bad news for any industry where the products or services offered by various sellers are considered to be identical. This was a point poignantly made by Robert Crandall, former CEO of American Airlines and the man often credited for developing yield management, when he, speaking of the airline industry, stated, "The customer considers one airline to be exactly the same as another airline. The customer always chooses the lowest price."[8]

It is likely true that most consumers perceive a trip on one airline to be identical to a trip on another if the departure and arrival times and locations offered by each airline are approximately the same.

▶ RM ON THE WEB 6.3

Today, hotel room buyers have more access to room rate information than ever before. Not only can they review room rates across different brands (hotels), but by visiting only one site they can also review the prices charged by the same hotel on alternative travel sites. To see an example, choose a night you wish to stay in Manhattan (New York). Then go to: www.kayak.com

When you arrive, enter the date of your room request. When you have selected the hotel you prefer (the Clarion Hotel Park Avenue was chosen for this example) click on "All Prices" to see the various rates charges by different sellers on that day. On the date this was written, prices offered at the Clarion Park for the night we chose ranged from $287.99 (at www.choicehotels.com) to $331.11 (at www.agoda.com)—a difference of $43.12, or 15 percent.

For RMs working in the lodging industry the best practice is one of *not* permitting demand to have a direct impact on price. Yes, *the authors fully realize this statement amounts to lodging industry heresy.* Careful readers, however, will recognize that this pricing principle was first introduced in Chapter 2 (Price) and illustrated again in Chapter 5 (remember the snow shovels?).

Demand *can* and should, however, be permitted to affect discounts. While these two ideas may seem at odds with each other, controversial, or even wrongheaded to some RMs, the authors contend that allowing demand for hotel rooms to directly dictate their selling prices is as disastrous to optimizing revenue in the lodging industry as it ultimately proved to be in the airline industry.

Our position was summed up well by Dr. Robert L. Phillips, author of *Pricing and Revenue Optimization* and the instructor for the "Pricing and Revenue Optimization" course taught in the Stanford University Business College's MBA program when he wrote:

> If the desired action is to raise overall revenue then the least controversial way to do so is by eliminating or restricting discounts. This is the concept behind revenue management. . . . To lower prices for some segments but not others it is best to do so via . . . channel specific discounts. [9]

For RMs working in hospitality, Phillip's philosophy can be restated simply as:

To optimize ADR and RevPAR in periods of temporarily heightened demand RMs should seek to eliminate discounts rather than increase their rack rates.

The question of exactly how RMs should manage price in response to increased room demand is a complex one and will be addressed in greater detail in Chapter 7 (Inventory and Price Management).

Impact of Price on Demand

Recall from Chapter 2 that demand for a product or service is a function of a buyer's:

- Desire
- Ability to pay
- Willingness to pay

Although demand should not be allowed to dictate price, it is certainly true that a change in price will often result in a shift in buyer demand. To illustrate the concept, it is likely that your own desire, ability, and willingness to pay for a seven-night stay (including airfare, lodging, and meals) in Paris will be at one level should the trip cost you $4,000. It would likely be quite another thing if you could buy the trip for $2000, a full 50 percent discount.

In this illustration, a significant change in price would likely result in a change in your willingness to buy. Buyer demand is affected by price. RMs need to understand how buyer demand is influenced by:

- Reductions in price to be paid
- Increases in price to be paid

Reductions in Price to Be Paid

For RMs, pricing lodging services this issue can be phrased as follows:

Will reducing the selling price of my rooms result in increased demand for them?

In most cases, the answer is simple. It is a resounding *no!*

Given what you have learned thus far, the idea that reducing room rates will *not* lead to increased revenues (or profits) may seem counterintuitive. It is important for RMs selling guest rooms to understand why price reduction does not stimulate overall demand and why inexperienced RMs have a tendency to misunderstand the impact of their room rates.

During periods of low demand, some RMs operate under the misconception that lower rates generate incremental revenues. That is a myth. Unfortunately, it is a myth believed by many in the hotel industry. Belief in it explains, to a large degree, why industry-wide ADRs fall so rapidly in times of reduced occupancy levels.

It is important to understand that in only a very few cases is a hotel, by itself, a demand generator. In the overwhelming majority of cases, people decide to travel to a specific area, then select their hotel, not the other way around.

Astute RMs understand that most guests need a reason to visit their hotels. Because that is true, these RMs learn those reasons why people travel to their areas and then develop targeted marketing tactics to get the message about their hotel to those travelers. Increased knowledge and targeting of demand generators build incremental revenues, not reduced room rates. To illustrate the point, assume that rooms at the Comfort Suites in West Lafayette, Indiana, were selling for $199.00 per night this coming Saturday. Would you travel to Indiana to stay in that hotel? Now assume the RM of the property reduces room rates to $99.99 per night (again a full 50 percent discount). Would that make *you* change your mind about reserving a room at the hotel? Not likely.

The reason why your responses to Paris and middle-Indiana (which is lovely by the way!) travel likely varied is due to inherent demand. Most travelers would *already* like to go to Paris. Many don't, however, because the price is too high. When the price is reduced, it satisfies their *preexisting* demand for the trip and they, like you, might gladly take the trip because their willingness to pay increases significantly.

The same may not be true regarding a specific city in the Midwestern United States. As a result, even significantly reducing the price for a hotel's guest rooms in those cities will not increase demand for them if that demand did not already exist. At best, price reduction by a single property ignites a "race to the bottom" among its competitors causing the majority of properties in the area to excessively reduce rates; each in a futile attempt to maximize revenues through price reduction.

If the concept that reduced price does not increase demand is now clear to you, read "RM in Action 6.2." You will then be ready to continue this chapter because you will have fully grasped one of the most fundamental principles of revenue management and strategic pricing:

Room rate reduction does not increase demand for a hotel's rooms, its revenue, or its profitability.

Some RMs may counter that while they understand price reductions do not stimulate incremental demand, their own revenues can be increased if, by lower their prices, they can capture a larger share of existing demand. To illustrate this rationale, assume that 1,100

RM IN ACTION 6.2: REPEAT AFTER ME . . . .

Some RMs feel they can significantly increase demand for their rooms by implementing a price reduction strategy. Most lodging industry experts, however, agree that the reduction of room rates during times of weak demand is almost always a bad idea.

Consider the main point of a recent article written by Jeff Weinstein: editor in chief of *Hotels*, the magazine of the worldwide hotel industry. In the article's first sentence, Weinstein humorously advises hoteliers to chant the following mantra during times of reduced demand for rooms:

> Repeat After Me. . . .
> "I will not cut prices nor panic sell because it does not stimulate incremental demand and only serves to drive down prices."

Weinstein goes on to explain precisely why he believes room rate reduction is the wrong approach in an economic downturn or period of soft demand. Weinstein concludes the article by advising RMs to remember to chant the mantra:

> "I will not cut prices nor panic sell because it does not stimulate incremental demand and only serves to drive down prices."

Believe it.

———————————
Excerpted on 2/8/2008 from "Hotels" February 2008 (Editorial).

visitors per day sought lodging in a specific area. Assume further that the number of travelers then dropped by 10 percent. Now 990 travelers seek accommodations. Is it logical to assume that a room rate reduction will result in greater income because more of the 990 travelers will select the hotel that has reduced its rates? History and research say no. The reason for this is that in most cases, a rate reduction initiated by one hotel will be immediately matched by rate reductions at its competitors. The result is an ever-decreasing size of the revenue "pie." Those who seek to get a larger slice of that pie must recognize that the very act of seeking a greater share actually causes the pie to shrink.

Increases in Price to Be Paid

If *reducing* room rates does not increase demand (or RevPAR) does it logically follow that *increasing* room rates also has no effect? *No.*

In fact, an increase in room rates can have significant and quite varied effects on demand. Recall that in an eBay auction, as price increases some bidders drop out. Similarly, as the cost of securing a given hotel room increases, the number of "bidders" for that room will decrease. This will be true in times of low, medium, or high demand for rooms. In high-demand situations, where the aggregate demand for available rooms far exceeds the supply of rooms, the total number of bidders will be so high that even a significant decrease in the number of potential buyers will still result in the sale of all available rooms. Because the price actually paid for each room is increased, total revenues (RevPAR) achieved on those high-demand days will be increased. In periods of low or moderate demand, however, when prices increase, *too many* buyers drop out, and as a result, total revenues decline.

Figure 6.14 | **Impacts of Alternative RM Rate Strategies**

RM's Pricing Strategy	Effect on Demand for Rooms	Effect on ADR	Effect on RevPAR (Total Revenue)
1. Reduction in average rate	Negligible effect on increasing the number of new buyers	Lowered	Generally lowered
2. Increase in average rate in response to high demand	Reduces number of potential buyers choosing the property	Increased	Generally increased because demand exceeds supply
3. Increase in average rate in times of average or low demand	Reduces number of potential buyers choosing the property	Increased	Generally lowered because supply exceeds demand

To illustrate the effect of various rate strategies resulting from assessing demand forecast data, assume an RM has created an accurate forecast for a specific date. Figure 6.14 summarizes the possible outcomes related to the RM's decision to reduce or to increase the average rate to be paid for rooms on that date.

As Figure 6.14 demonstrates, it is important that RMs forecast accurately to identify the periods of high demand that permit them to achieve increased levels of ADR and RevPAR and thus optimize revenue. This is so because, if rate paid (ADR) is increased in a time of low or moderate (average) demand (row #3 in Figure 6.14) the RevPAR achieved will actually be lower, not higher, than if no rate increase were implemented.

When demand forecasts indicate the number of available buyers will greatly exceed the supply of available rooms, RMs should *not* automatically increase their rack rates. *Again, the authors understand the heresy inherent in that sentence.* When demand for rooms exceeds supply RMs should review their RM teams' answers to ten key questions:

1. What type guest is generating the increase in demand?

2. Which of our products would these guests prefer to buy?

3. From which distribution channel do these guests typically buy, and how can these channels best be managed?

4. How can changes in price best be communicated to these guests?

5. When do these guests typically book (reserve their rooms)?

6. Who, if anyone, is offering similar products to these guests? Why would guests select our product rather than our competitor's?

7. What inventory management strategies can be effectively employed during this period?

8. What rate management strategies can be effectively employed during this high-demand period?

9. How will our loyal (repeat) guests be treated during this period of high demand?

10. As a property committed to customer-centric revenue management, how can all of our guests' perceptions of value be maintained or increased during this period of higher demand and selling price?

During periods when demand is forecast to be high, answers to questions of this type are critical to ensuring a proper customer-centric pricing strategy is employed. Those RMs who, in times of high demand, ignore these questions and simply increase room rates across the board do no service to their hotels, to the profession of the RM, or to the lodging industry.

Impact of Demand Forecasts on RM Strategy

Demand forecasts are the singlemost important piece of data RMs will review and evaluate when seeking to optimize rooms revenue. Only by creating an accurate forecast can RMs know when room demand is strong (or weak) enough to dictate significant changes in the pricing strategies designed to help their hotels achieve their unique RevPAR and RevPOR goals.

If no active and accurate forecasting program is in place, RMs will consistently make misinformed decisions and continually lead their properties in directions that are detrimental to both the property and its guests. Such a consistent but misguided course of action will yield consistent results, just as was predicted by the Chinese proverb that states, "If we don't change our direction we're likely to end up where we're headed."[10]

RMs who want to be continually headed in the proper direction do the following:

- Understand the unique property features that affect demand for their hotels
- Know about special citywide and areawide events that affect room demand
- Understand the demand for competitive hotels in the area
- Consider the pricing strategies of competitive hotels in the area
- Include weather, road construction, season of the year, special occurrences, and any other relevant factors when making demand assessments
- Adjust forecasts quickly when confronted with significant demand-affecting events
- Keep the interest and reactions of guests foremost in all decisions related to rooms pricing

Analysis of historical forecast data helps RMs understand what has happened. Current data help RMs understand what is happening. Future data predict what may happen. Understanding each of these data forms and using the information they provide helps RMs influence and shape what will actually happen. They can help shape the future of their properties by applying their own insight to their data collection efforts and to their revenue management decision making. This is so because experienced RMs understand that not all revenue is created equal.

Simply put, some revenue is good revenue and some revenue is bad revenue. Good revenue generates profits. Bad revenue often does not. Bad revenue comes with a high-channel distribution cost or even prevents the alternative sale of rooms for good revenue, because inventory has been presold for too low a price or with too high a cost of acquisition. Thus, it is vitally important that RMs who have completed their forecast next implement inventory management—the determination of the specific rooms products that will be sold and the prices at which they are to be sold. These two important topics are addressed in Chapter 7 (Inventory and Price Management). After they learn to do that, these RMs must determine *where and how* their products will be sold. You will learn to do just that in Chapter 8 (Distribution Channel Management).

RM IN ACTION 6.3: FRIEND OR FOE?

Savvy RMs around the world increasingly recognize the difference between "good" and "bad" revenue; or put differently, between "good" and "better" revenue, where "better" can be defined as revenue booked through lower-cost distribution channels. RMs now working in Australia provide an excellent example, as the following article illustrates.

Hoteliers Attack Net Booking Fees [11]
Hoteliers. . . . are putting pressure on third-party websites to lower commissions. The region's largest hotel group, Accor Asia Pacific, said its properties were now "pushing back" against demands from some popular websites for commissions of up to 20 per cent.

The article details the efforts of Australian hoteliers to maintain commission rates paid to intermediaries at their historic level of 10 percent. The article reports that Accor, one of the world's largest hotel groups, had pulled out of a preferred distribution agreement with U.S. travel giant Expedia over commission levels in excess of that amount.

The debate regarding the amounts that should be paid to third-party room re-sellers will likely continue. An RM's understanding of the difference between "good" and "better" (i.e., lower cost) revenue must continue as well if those RMs are to effectively stand watch over the best interests of their properties and their guests.

❖ ESSENTIAL RM TERMS

Demand (consumer)	Group rooms pace report
Capital improvement	Tentative (sale)
Historical data	Request for proposal (RFP)
Trailing period	Position report
Denied (reservation)	Pick up
Walk-in	Demand generator
Track (data)	Demand drain
Fixed average	Future (forecast) data
Rolling average	Convention and visitors bureau (CVB)
Current data	Stayover
Block(ed)	Early departure
Out-of-order (OOO)	Overstay
On-the-books	Executive committee
Minimum length of stay (MLOS)	

▐▐▐▶ APPLY WHAT YOU KNOW

1. Lea Ray is the revenue manager at the 200-room Hilton Garden Inn. She tracks her occupancy and ADR on a daily basis. The following data represent her hotel's Thursday-night performance for the past seven weeks.

Thursday	Week 1	Week 2	Week 3	Week 4	Week 5	Week 6	Week 7
Occ. %	69.5	73.5	66.5	72.0	72.5	69.0	77.0
ADR	$151.50	$145.95	$161.50	$178.50	$179.95	$129.95	$159.95

Using that historical data, calculate her Occupancy %, ADR, and RevPAR for these trailing periods:

   A. For weeks 1–4

   B. For weeks 2–5

   C. For weeks 3–6

   D. For weeks 4–7

   E. What do you think would be Lea's best estimate of next Thursday night's RevPAR? Explain your answer.

2. Amanda Sipe is the RM at the 500-room Doubletree Hotel. She also heads her property's RM committee. Amanda is preparing for the committee's weekly meeting and wants to present them with an updated occupancy forecast for the first two weeks of May. Unfortunately, some of the information on the report did not print out. Help Amanda get ready for her meeting by completing her occupancy forecast report, including the "Total" row at the bottom.

Occupancy Report: The Doubletree Hotel For Dates May 1–14
Run Date: Today

Date	Day	Rooms Available	Reserved	Blocked	Total Held	Current Occ. %
5/1	Mon	500	210	60		%
5/2	Tues	500	175		420	
5/3	Wed	500	200			50.0%
5/4	Thur	500	90	110		
5/5	Fri	500	220		300	
5/6	Sat	500	100			75.0%
5/7	Sun	500	275	25		
5/8	Mon	500	100		350	

(continued)

Occupancy Report: The Doubletree Hotel For Dates May 1–14
Run Date: Today (*Continued*)

Date	Day	Rooms Available	Reserved	Blocked	Total Held	Current Occ. %
5/9	Tues	500		250		90.%
5/10	Wed	500	60	210		
5/11	Thur	500		175	420	
5/12	Fri	450	210	60		
5/13	Sat	450	175		420	
5/14	Sun	450	200			50%
Total						

Some of the members of Amanda's RM team prefer to review the number of rooms available to sell, rather than those already reserved. Because she has the data needed to do so, complete the Doubletree's Availability Report for the same 14-day period.

Availability Report: The Doubletree Hotel For Dates May 1–14
Run Date: Today

Date	Day	Rooms Available	Reserved	Blocked	Total Held	Available for Sale
5/1	Mon	500	210	60		
5/2	Tues	500	175		420	
5/3	Wed	500	200			250
5/4	Thur	500	90	110		
5/5	Fri	500	220		300	
5/6	Sat	500	100			125
5/7	Sun	500	275	25		
5/8	Mon	500	100		350	
5/9	Tues	500		250		50
5/10	Wed	500	60	210		
5/11	Thur	500		175	420	
5/12	Fri	450	210	60		
5/13	Sat	450	175		420	
5/14	Sun	450	200			225
Total						

3. Wendy Parker works in the sales and marketing department at the Hawthorne Suites. As part of her duties, Wendy updates the hotel's group room sales pace reports. These reports record the number of rooms that have been sold, by month, for all upcoming years in which groups have reserved rooms. Wendy prepared such a report for next year at the end of August, but because it is now the end of September, that report must be updated to include September's group rooms sales results. Help Wendy create an updated group rooms pace report by revising the August report to include the following September sales information given to Wendy by the hotel's director of sales and marketing.

September This Year: Group Room Sales

Sale To:	Cancels	Nights Reserved For	Rooms per Night	Total Nights Sold
California Firefighters		2–5 and 2–6	75	150
Antique Cup Collectors		5–2 and 5–3	50	100
NRC Corp.		4–15 thru 4–20	60	360
Little Sluggers Softball Tournament		6–10 thru 6–14	80	400
Sate Mental Health Advisors		8–2 and 8–3	150	300
Real Estate Investment Seminar		6–6 thru 6–9	40	160
Eastern Star Conference		10–31 thru 11–2	100	300

Hawthorne Suites Hotel
Group Rooms Pace Report For Jan-Dec Next Year

Month	Sold in August (This Year)	Total Committed Group Rooms (Jan-Dec Next Year)
Jan	40	1,250
Feb	60	1,800
Mar	140	5,620
Apr		850
May	600	975
June	220	850
July		2,200
Aug		3,400
Sept	180	1,900

(continued)

Hawthorne Suites Hotel
Group Rooms Pace Report For Jan-Dec Next Year (*Continued*)

Month	Sold in August (This Year)	Total Committed Group Rooms (Jan-Dec Next Year)
Oct		2,800
Nov		5,500
Dec	440	620
TOTAL	**1,680**	**27,765**

Last Update: 8/31/This Year   Prepared By: Wendy Parker

Hawthorne Suites Hotel
Group Rooms Pace Report For Jan-Dec Next Year

Month	Sold in September (This Year)	Total Committed Group Rooms (Jan-Dec Next Year)
Jan		
Feb		
Mar		
Apr		
May		
June		
July		
Aug		
Sept		
Oct		
Nov		
Dec		
TOTAL		

Last Update: 9/30/This Year   Prepared By: Wendy Parker

4. Nigar Patel prepares a daily Rooms Forecast Report that is shared with the housekeeping, food and beverage, and front desk managers of the 200-room Comfort Inn she both owns and manages. Today is Monday. Help Nigar complete Tuesday's Rooms Forecast Report using the following information she has compiled from historical records, current PMS data, and her own insight into rooms sales-related events likely to occur today. When you have completed the forecast, answer the questions that follow.

Rooms Forecast Report for:	**Tuesday (This week)**
Date: June 3rd.	**Day: Tuesday**
Total rooms available	200
− Out-of-order (OOO) rooms	0
Net Availability	200
Stayovers	85
+ Reservations (Arrivals)	60
Rooms Sold or Reserved	___
Adjustments:	
Overstays	15
Early departures	10
No-shows	5
Total Forecast Sold or Reserved After Adjustments	___

A. How many rooms does Nigar forecast will be occupied on Tuesday night?

B. What is Nigar's occupancy % forecast for Tuesday night?

C. Assume Nigar's forecasted ADR for the night is $160.99. What would be her estimated total room revenue for this date?

D. Given her forecasted ADR, what would be forecasted RevPAR for this date?

5. A 400-room hotel located near Boston's Logan International airport (BOS) normally discounts very heavily (sometimes as much as 50 percent off the rack rate) on Sunday nights because, historically, it has sold an average of 100 rooms on that night. Historical data taken from the PMS indicates that over the past two months, occupancy percentage on Sunday nights averaged slightly less than 25 percent. Today is Sunday, and the PMS shows the property currently has 110 reservations on the books. The weather forecast, however, is for extremely heavy snowstorms of the type that have, in the past, significantly delayed flights or closed the airport. On nights such as these, the hotel has experienced a sell-out as airlines seek housing for their stranded passengers and delayed flight crews. Should the hotel's RM immediately revise their demand forecast and also eliminate the heavy discounts on the rooms remaining to be sold on this Sunday night? Do you feel any ethical issues are in play in this scenario? Explain your answers.

KEY CONCEPT CASE STUDY

"Hello. Adrian? Have you read the paper today?" asked Damario, the revenue manager at the 480-room Barcena Resort as he spoke into his cell phone. It was 9:00 A.M., and Damario had just placed a call to Adrian's office.

"You've got to be kidding me!" replied Adrian, the Barcena Resort's rooms manager. "Who's got time to read the local paper? I can barely get through my e-mails!"

"Well, there's an article in the Business section that I think we need to talk about," said Damario. "I know I'm pretty new here, but I think this will really affect us."

"What is it?" asked Adrian. "I have a hard time believing that anything happening locally will affect us. Our guests all fly in." As a resort located on a Caribbean island, most of the hotel's guests were vacationing Americans, Canadians, South Americans, or Europeans, coming either in charter groups or as individual travelers.

"That's just it. The article is about InterContinental Airlines. It says that due to higher fuel costs and slackening demand, it will be reducing the number of flights to our island by 20 percent, starting in the third quarter of this fiscal year." Damario paused and let Adrian consider what he had just said.

"That could be really bad," said Adrian, as he recognized the importance of the information. "I bet InterContinental currently has 20 to 30 every weekend."

"Most of the InterContinental flights are scheduled to arrive Thursday and Friday, right?" asked Damario.

"Right," replied Adrian. "Their arrivals are mostly couples, mostly two to three night stays, mostly requests for King-bedded rooms. We already have tons of reservations for the third quarter. Some of those must be on InterContinental Airlines flights. What will happen to those?"

"The article says flyers with previous reservations will be contacted to be rescheduled on different flights or to get a refund. How many rooms do you think will be affected?" asked Damario.

"Well, we certainly do more with charter flights than transient-oriented flights like InterContinental's, but if their flights are reduced by 20 percent for half the year? A lot!" said Adrian.

"Let's get together to talk about this," said Damario.

"I'm on my way," said Adrian, as he hung up the phone.

As he walked to Damario's office, Adrian tried to assess the impact of InterContinental's decision. It would affect the number of rooms sold to the type of clients arriving on InterContinental, that was for sure. And also the room types requested. And the start of the third quarter was only 30 days away. No doubt, this was big news!

For Your Consideration

1. What impact will the reduction of the number of flights to the Barcena's island likely have on the previous demand forecasts that have been created by the resort's revenue management team?

2. What specific historical data would be helpful to them as the RM team evaluates the potential impact of the airline's decision?

3. What specific current data would be helpful to them as the RM team evaluates the potential impact of the airline's decision?

4. In this scenario, the number of potential guests delivered to this destination by this air carrier will likely be reduced. If that is so, what impact would significantly reducing room prices in an effort to stimulate demand likely have on the resort's third- and fourth-quarter RevPAR performance? Explain your answer.

ENDNOTES

1. Jeffery Gitomer, *Customer Satisfaction Is Worthless; Customer Loyalty Is Priceless: How to Make Customers Love You, Keep Them Coming Back, and Tell Everyone They Know* (Austin, TX: Bard Press, 1998).

2. Quote from Confucius (551 B.C.–479 B.C.) http://www.quotationspage.com/search.php3?Search=the%20past%20&Author=&page=30. Retrieved 5/5/2008.

3. Utilizing the RevPAR formula presented in Chapter 1.

4. http://www.micros-fidelio.co.uk/product-information/opera/rms/. Retrieved 8/29/2009.

5. http://www.hotelsmag.com/article/CA6518833.html. Retrieved 7/7/2008.

6. http://thinkexist.com/quotes/charles_f._kettering/. Retrieved 5/5/2208.

7. hotelsmag.com/articleXML/LN1001935903.html?nid=3457&rid=14115930. Retrieved 7/8/2009.

8. http://query.nytimes.com/gst/fullpage.html?res=9806E0D6103DF93AA35751C1A9659C8B63&sec=&spon=&pagewanted=all/. Retrieved 7/22/2008.

9. Robert L. Phillips, *Pricing and Revenue Optimization* (Stanford Business Books, 2005), 321.

10. http://thinkexist.com/quotation/if_we_don-t_change_our_direction_we-re_likely_to/10544.html. Retrieved 7/12/2008.

11. http://www.theaustralian.news.com.au/story/0,20867,21821573–25658,00.html. Retrieved 7/25/2008.

CHAPTER 7

Inventory and Price Management

CHAPTER OUTLINE

CHAPTER HIGHLIGHTS

1. Detailed examination of how RMs optimize revenue when applying inventory management strategies.

2. Candid presentation of the pros and cons of overbooking as an inventory management strategy.

3. Detailed examination of how RMs optimize revenue when applying price management principles.

THE MARKETING MIX REVISITED

In the previous chapter you learned how to measure and anticipate the number of guests and customers who want to buy from you. In Chapter 2 you learned that *marketing* can be defined as the complete process of exchanging products and services between you and your buyers. You also learned that one way to describe how marketing is done is to consider the 4Ps of the marketing mix. Recall that three of these Ps are:

Product: What will be sold?

Price: What are the financial terms of the sale?

Place: Where/how will the exchange take place?

Promotion, the final P, refers to the process of communicating all of the information to your market, or your pool of potential buyers. While very important, promotion is a topic best addressed in a text that emphasizes marketing—a management process that is clearly related to, but distinctly different from, revenue optimization.

The focus of the first part of this chapter will be how an RM addresses *product*, or inventory management. The second half of this chapter will focus on *price* management. In the hospitality industry, *place* is both the location of a hotel and that property's commonly used *distribution channels*. The management of these channels is so important that it will be the sole focus of the next chapter.

INVENTORY MANAGEMENT

In the lodging industry, sleeping rooms are the primary item sold. As a result, lodging industry RMs seek to optimize their facility revenue through the aggressive management of their unique products—the guest rooms that make up the hotels' **rooms inventory**.

In the common industry vocabulary *rooms inventory management* is also known as *inventory management*, which is simply a shortened term for the same concept.

Essential RM Term

Rooms inventory: All of the unique forms of guest room products offered for sale by a lodging facility.

Recall from Chapter 4 that inventory management is the process of allocating and modify the number of products available for sale at various prices and through various distribution channels. For RMs, inventory management is the process of allocating room types, room rates, and restrictions among the hotel's various distribution channels. Inventory management can best be viewed as the control of product availability and its nonavailability.

Essential RM Term

DD room: The common CRS and PMS code for a guest room containing two full-sized (double or queen) beds.

To better understand exactly why and how RMs can effectively manage their inventories via the application of availability strategies, consider the case of Shanna and Luis. Both operate a 200-room franchised hotel. Each of their hotels consists of 100 rooms containing one king-sized bed and 100 **DD rooms**.

Each room type is sold at the same rack rate of $199.99 per night. Figure 7.1 displays the room revenue, ADR, and RevPAR each hotel would generate at full rack rate on a sold-out night.

Typically, both Shanna and Luis offer 20 percent discounts on their weekend room rates because occupancy percentages for weekends at their hotels are low—typically averaging only 50 percent. On a weekend date in the future, both Shanna and Luis produce demand forecasts that estimate they will achieve 75 percent occupancy on Saturday night. Luis produces his demand forecast based on PMS-provided information about his hotel's total estimated room sales. Shanna creates her forecast based on demand for each of her two different room types. In doing so, she determines that the current demand for DD rooms is very strong, while current demand for king bed rooms is not above its normal levels.

Luis and his RM team make the decision that for that specific date, his discounted rate of $159.99 will remain unchanged. His rationale is that, since his hotel is not sold out, and in fact is forecasted to have 50 unsold rooms on that night, offering discounted rates will help encourage travelers to stay at his hotel.

Shanna halts the sale of discounted DD rooms for this particular weekend night only. She does so because the transient pace reports she has reviewed indicate a 2 to 1 current booking preference for DD rooms by those guests who have reserved for that night. Shanna recognizes that the demand generator causing increased interest in DD rooms for that Saturday is a state-wide gymnastics competition among 10–14 year old girls. Demand for DD rooms far exceeds demand for king-bed rooms because most of the girls competing in the

Figure 7.1	Alternative Room Revenue Results at Rack Rate				
	Shanna's Hotel			**Luis's Hotel**	
Rack ADR	**Rooms Sold**	**Revenue**	**Rooms Sold**	**Revenue**	
$199.99	100 Kings	$ 19,999.00	100 Kings	$ 19,999.00	
$199.99	100 DD	$ 19,999.00	100 DD	$ 19,999.00	
Total	**200**	**$ 39,998**	**200**	**$ 39,998**	
Occupancy	100 %		100 %		
RevPAR		$199.99		$199.99	

Figure 7.2	Alternative Room Revenue Results with Optimization Effort			
	Shanna's Hotel		**Luis' Hotel**	
Rate	**Rooms Sold**	**Revenue**	**Rooms Sold**	**Revenue**
$159.99	50 Kings	$ 7,999.50	50 Kings	$ 7,999.50
$159.99	50 DD	$ 7,999.50	100 DD	$ 15,999.00
$199.99	50 DD	$ 9,999.50		
Total	**150**	**$ 25,999.50**	**150**	**$ 23,998.50**
Occupancy	75 %		75 %	
ADR	$ 173.32		$ 159.99	
RevPAR		$ 129.99		$ 119.99

tournament are traveling with their parents. These parent travelers place a high value on having two beds in their room.

As the Saturday approaches, Luis sells out of DD rooms quickly due to the nearly 25 percent discount offered on them. Not surprisingly, rooms buyers like his low prices! Shanna also eventually sells all of her DD rooms due to the very high demand for them. Both hotels achieved their forecasted 75 percent occupancy rates. However, 50 of Shanna's DD rooms were sold at a higher, full rack rate because her RM team had earlier decided to eliminate the availability of discounted DDs. Figure 7.2 details the rooms-related statistics generated by each property on that Saturday.

The difference in this scenario is an increased RevPAR achieved by Shanna's hotel. The increase on this particular Saturday night is a significant 8.3 percent. That difference can be calculated as:

$$\frac{\text{RevPAR Shanna's Hotel} - \text{RevPAR Luis's Hotel}}{\text{RevPAR Luis's Hotel}} = \text{RevPAR difference}$$

In this example it is calculated as:

$$\frac{\$ 129.99 - \$ 119.99}{\$119.99} = 8.3\%$$

Recall that rooms inventory refers to all of a hotel's unique, or distinct forms of guest room products available for sale. In this scenario, four distinct rooms exist. They are:

1. King
2. Discounted king
3. DD
4. Discounted DD

It is important to recognize that Shanna did not vary the price of her rooms inventory, but rather, its *availability* only. The rooms inventory available at the two different hotels on this Saturday night is tabled in Figure 7.3.

Figure 7.3	Shanna and Luis Rooms Inventory Availability: Saturday Night		
Rooms Inventory Item	**Rate**	**Available at Shanna's Hotel**	**Available at Luis' Hotel**
King	$ 199.99	Yes	Yes
Discounted king	$ 159.99	Yes	Yes
DD	$ 199.99	Yes	Yes
Discounted DD	$ 159.99	No	Yes

In this case, Shanna's ability to better manage inventory, based primarily on her superior forecasting techniques, resulted in decision making that generated an improved RevPAR. Shanna did not change her room rates on this Saturday. She did, however, recognize that a DD made available at a discounted rate is a different room product from the same room offered at rack rate. Her success was the result of her decision to **close out** discounted DDs on this specific Saturday.

Essential RM Term

Close out: To remove from sale or to stop selling.

For example: "We need to close out kings for August 3rd."

CHARACTERIZING ROOMS FOR OPTIMUM INVENTORY MANAGEMENT

Professional rooms inventory management requires that RMs know their guest rooms' distinctive characteristics and that they match them to potential guests who value those same characteristics. The number of unique rooms products offered for sale by a hotel can be quite large, and as a result so can the number of **room codes** utilized in the property.

The specific factors that create these unique room products will vary by property but the factors most often utilized by RMs are quite similar to those used in establishing differential pricing strategies (see Chapter 4):

Essential RM Term

Room code: A property-specific, shortened description used to identify a specific room product in a hotel.

For example, NSDD to identify a nonsmoking, double-double room, or SSP to identify a smoking permitted suite that faces the swimming pool, and created by using the first letters of the words smoking, suite, and pool.

Location of room

Room size or type

Bed configuration

Package

Location

In many hotels, the concept that all rooms are created equal is simply not true. In a beach resort, those rooms with a beach view will be perceived by most guests as having a higher value than those that do not possess that view. Within a hotel, a room located by an elevator may be perceived as having a lower value than one that is not located by the elevator. In a mountain resort, rooms on a higher floor may, because of the view they afford guests, have greater value. In a beach resort, lower-level rooms (and thus rooms that are closer to the beach) may have a higher perceived value. Rooms in remote sections of a hotel may be perceived by guests to have a lower or higher value. Some hotels make maximum advantage of the fact that location affects perceived value by creating VIP or **concierge floor** rooms. These hotels provide special amenities to guest reserving rooms in these areas and then permit access only to those guests staying in them.

Creative RMs should closely examine their property to identify rooms perceived to be located in desirable areas of the hotel. These rooms should be given their own room codes, their unique characteristics should be communicated specifically to those guests that will value those most, and they should be priced accordingly.

Essential RM Term

Concierge floor: An area (often an entire floor) located within a hotel, access to which is limited only to those guests staying in rooms located within that restricted area. In most cases, specialized amenities and services are provided to guests staying on concierge floors.

Also known as a concierge level or VIP level.

Room Size or Type

Most guests perceive larger guest rooms to be of more value than smaller rooms. RMs can respond to that fact by identifying their property's largest rooms and supplying additional amenities that support the room configuration. They can then assign unique room codes to these rooms and offer them for sale as a distinctly different room product and at prices that reflect guests' greater willingness to buy them. Common examples of doing so include rooms that are designated as whirlpool suites, parlor suites, bridal suites, or junior suites (to indicate that these are large rooms but smaller than even larger, *regular-size* suites), or rooms identified with other similar names and titles.

RMs must understand how larger rooms affect guests' perspectives, but it is also important for RMs to understand larger rooms from the perspective of their housekeeping departments. The property's **executive housekeeper** will be able to inform RMs about the amount of additional time it may take to clean and restock these larger rooms. RMs seeking to optimize their revenue and GOPPAR should take these additional operating costs and labor-related factors into consideration when making rooms allocation, **upgrade**, and pricing decisions.

Because of the importance guests place on the number and types of beds their rooms contain, a hotel's larger-sized rooms are typically given a special, two-part product designation that identifies both their size (type) and their specific **bed configuration**.

For example, a hotel that offers an ocean-view suite containing a king-sized bed might be designated in the CRS or PMS as an OVSK—an ocean-view suite with a king bed. A similarly sized suite facing the beach but containing

Essential RM Terms

Executive housekeeper: The management professional responsible for providing guests and employees a clean, safe, and healthy environment in all of the areas for which they are assigned accountability.

Upgrade: The act of assigning a guest to a higher-priced and more desirable room product at the selling price of a lower-valued product. Upgrades are typically undertaken to reward a valued customer or to atone for a service-related property shortcoming.

Essential RM Term

Bed configuration: The number and size of beds contained in a specified hotel guest room.

> **▶ RM ON THE WEB 7.1**
>
> New York's Waldorf Astoria hotel is an excellent example of a property that recognizes the importance of room size to its customers. To see how it communicates this information to its guests, go to its web site at www.waldorfnewyork.com
>
> When you arrive click *Waldorf Accommodations*, chose any date for a future reservation, then note the price variations on that date between the following three room types.
>
> 1. 1 King Bed Deluxe Room (230 square feet)
> 2. 1 King Bed Mini Suite (315 square feet)
> 3. 1 King Bed; 1 Bedroom Suite (450 square feet)
>
> Note the meticulous listing of square footage within each room type to reinforce the point that some of their rooms are larger and as a result justifiably more expensive than are others.

two double beds might be designated in the PMS as an OVSDD—an ocean-view suite with two double beds.

Bed Configuration

Even in identically located and sized rooms, bed configuration plays such an important role in product inventory that it dictates room type in nearly all hotels. Thus, for example, two rooms located adjacent to each other and consisting of the same square footage will still be designed as either a "K" (king) room if it contains that bed type or as a "DD" (double-double) room if it contains that bed type.

Package

The creation of a package is one of the most common forms of product versioning used in the lodging industry. The bundling of products and services such as a room, dinner for two, and breakfast the following morning creates a unique product for both accounting and room-selection purposes. For example, a hotel's "Honeymoon" package in all likelihood will be perceived as having higher value when the bed configuration includes one large rather than two smaller beds.

Where the unique characteristics of a package call for special pricing or room selection, that package becomes a unique rooms product and thus is subject to inventory control and management strategies.

DESIGNATING UNIQUE ROOM CODES

Unique room products are designated in a hotel's CRS and PMS with their unique room code. Figure 7.4 lists ten room codes that might be used in a resort hotel that is located on a beach and that has a selected number of rooms directly facing the ocean, with the remaining rooms facing the resort's pool area.

When devising room codes, RMs should strive to create the optimal number of them. Individual room codes should help hotel sales and front desk staffs clearly understand the significant differences between the hotel's various room types. The use of too few room codes typically means a hotel has not done a good job in versioning its room products.

Figure 7.4	Sample Beach Resort Room Codes	
Room Description	**Bed Configuration**	**Room Code**
1. Standard room; view of pool, Approx. 300 square feet	King	KP
2. Standard room; view of pool, Approx. 300 square feet	Double-Double	DDP
3. Standard room; Ocean view, Approx. 300 square feet	King	KO
4. Standard room; Ocean view, Approx. 300 square feet	Double-Double	DDO
5. Jr. Suite; Ocean view, small parlor (sitting area) and 2 TVs. Approx. 400 sq. feet	King	JKO
6. Jr. Suite; Ocean view, small parlor (sitting area) and 2 TVs. Approx. 400 sq. feet	Double-Double	JDDO
7. Grand Suite; large parlor area, 2 TVs. Ocean view, Approx. 600 sq. feet	King	GKO
8. Grand Suite; large parlor area, 2 TVs. Ocean view, Approx. 600 sq. feet	Double-Double	GDDO
9. Grand Suite; large parlor area, 2 TVs. Ocean view, Approx. 600 sq. feet VIP Floor	King	GKOV
10. Grand Suite; large parlor area, 2 TVs. Ocean view, Approx. 600 sq. feet VIP Floor	Double-Double	GDDOV

The use of an excessive number of room codes should be avoided as well. It is important to recognize that a modern CRS/PMS can be programmed to record data about a virtually unlimited number of room codes, but the hotel's human staff must still be able to sell and distinguish between them. An excessive number of room codes can make effective rooms demand forecasting and the room assignment process cumbersome and error prone.

CLASSIFYING GUESTS BY MARKET SEGMENT

Superior rooms inventory management is the result of knowing the unique features of the rooms that make up the rooms inventory and then making available the right rooms products for the right guests. The specific tactics RMs use to do so are many. One good way to better understand these tactics is to examine how they are applied to rooms sought by potential guests. Although the specific rooms buyers utilizing a hotel will vary based on the property's location, service level (full or limited), and target market, in most hotels, guests can be generally classified as belonging to one of three market segments:

Transient

Group

Special contract and negotiated

As a result, RMs apply specific revenue optimization strategies to their transient rooms, their group rooms, and those rooms sold on a contract basis.

Transient Rooms

Transient guests are best defined simply as those who are not part of a group or contract sale. Strategies for optimizing rooms revenue relative to transient rooms inventory management can best be understood by examining those tactics applied prior to arrival and those that are applied at the time of the guest's arrival at the property.

Prearrival Strategies

Prearrival strategies for maximizing room revenues via inventory management consist of clearly communicating to potential buyers the availability of the hotel's various room types and then accurately recording these guests' purchases. When the number of distribution channels used is large, these two tasks alone can be quite challenging. They are made even more challenging when one considers the practical matter of rooms-related data management within a hotel.

To illustrate, assume that a property is located in Orlando and offers king-bed rooms. On a given day, five such rooms are available for sale at a price predetermined by the hotel's RM team. The property uses a variety of intermediaries that assist the hotel in selling its rooms. At noon on this day, an intermediary (a travel agent) located in New York reserves the five rooms. The precise methods used by the hotel to receive news of this sale, remove the five rooms from available room inventory, and communicate the hotel's newly revised rooms inventory information to all of its other intermediaries, many of which are located across the entire world are varied, but it is easy to see that the timeliness of that information exchange is critical.

The same is true with regard to information about room cancellations. If rooms are not removed from inventory as they are sold, the hotel risks selling rooms it does not have.

Similarly, if availability and rate-related decisions are not communicated to a hotel's intermediaries, the wrong rooms may be sold to the wrong guests at the wrong rates. For these reasons, RMs should strive to ensure that, to the greatest degree possible, their transient rooms inventory is updated and the updates communicated in **real time**.

Essential RM Term

Real time (inventory update): The term used to identify rooms inventory availability that is designed to be updated in the CRS/PMS immediately upon the taking or canceling of a room reservation.

Essential RM Term

Interfaced: To be electronically connected.

The difficulty with maintaining real-time inventory relates to the inability of some intermediaries' reservations systems to be **interfaced** with the CRS or PMS in use at the property. This is made especially difficult when you recognize that each hotel chain mandates that its franchisees and company-operated facilities use its own uniquely designed and proprietary PMS. As a result, an intermediary selling rooms for a variety of hotel brands must ensure that its own control system is interfaced with each of those brands.

The degree of connectivity between a hotel's available rooms data and its channels of distribution greatly affect the prearrival revenue management strategies that can be employed. In the least desirable of all possible cases there is simply no interface between a distribution channel and a hotel's inventory management system. This situation could be termed a no-way, or noninterfaced system.

In the recent past, noninterfaced intermediaries would fax or e-mail reservations and cancellations to a hotel as they were taken or, even worse, at the end of the intermediary's own business day. Modifications to inventory availability were then made at the hotel property level by manually entering the data contained in the fax or e-mail into the hotel's CRS or PMS. The number of inventory management errors typically resulting from the use of a noninterfaced communication model is significant. Although the method is still in use in many independent and non–brand-affiliated hotels, even when frequent inventory updates are made, using this communication system will always result in the potential for errors—misspelled names, double bookings, and incorrect arrival dates. As well, erroneous no-show billings can increase, and the final outcome in too many cases is unhappy guests and reduced rather than increased rooms revenue.

Essential RM Term

Third-party resellers: Intermediaries that purchase hotels rooms for resale to their own customers. Current examples include intermediaries such as hotels.com, expedia.com, and Travelocity.com.

One-way connectivity is a vast improvement over the "no-way" interface model. Essentially, one way connectivity is achieved when a hotel's intermediaries—including wholesalers and **third-party resellers**—all have Internet access to the hotel's updated rooms inventory.

Because the flow of information is from the hotel's various distribution channels *to* the hotel's record system, it is one-way communication. The greatest benefit of this arrangement is that it eliminates the untimely and error-prone data entry of a no-way system.

The downside of the one-way configuration is that it requires RMs to provide rooms inventory levels in a form that is usable by each intermediary's booking system. Because these booking systems are not standardized (i.e., the actual reservation system used by American Airlines to reserve the rooms of its partner hotels is likely to be different from that used by some of the hotel's other intermediaries), they are not easily interfaced directly with a hotel's CRS or PMS. The result is that an RM must manage and maintain, at a minimum, two availability inventories. One availability record contains the updated inventory per the hotels reservations management system and another must be made available for intermediary booking entities. More commonly, 3, 4, or in some cases, as many as 20 or more duplicate inventories must be maintained. In addition, the hotel incurs significant per-reservation-made charges for the privilege of distributing these secondary inventories on a global basis.

The best situation is that of a *two-way* communication model. In this arrangement, all of the inventory and rates are communicated, in real time, utilizing data in the property's reservation management and availability system. When a reservation is made by any entity, that entity's system actually checks with the CRS or PMS, to ensure room availability. As a result, if the room is available locally, it is available globally. When a reservation is made, the interface communicates that the room has been sold (even if it was sold halfway across the world!) and the hotel immediately removes it from the room's available inventory. Only this arrangement provides an RM with real-time inventory management ability. In this situation, an RM must manage only one room and rate inventory. An additional advantage in such a system is the ability to offer rooms sellers the option of communicating to potential buyers an alternative room choice if the initially requested room product is unavailable. Continued advancements in third-party booking systems, as well as hotel reservation system upgrades, will be required to make seamless (two-way) connectivity an industry standard.

Currently, identity theft concerns related to third-party site security breaches have delayed full deployment of two-way interfacing. In such breeches, computer hackers would have access to all customer credit card and future stay information contained in a hotel's PMS. This continues to cause hotel information technology (IT) managers to exercise extreme caution in creating seamless, two-way interfaces. Until such concerns are fully addressed, RMs must do what they can to ensure their room inventory availability is communicated to all of their intermediaries as quickly, safely, and fully as is reasonably possible.

In the foreseeable future, most RMs will likely encounter intermediaries with booking capabilities that fall into each of the three communications options detailed in Figure 7.5.

Figure 7.5	**Prearrival Rooms Inventory Communication Options**		
Communication Option	**Advantages**	**Disadvantages**	**Impact on Inventory Management**
No-way communication	No third-party interface fees.	Inventory updates are not made in real time.	Availability-related decisions are communicated manually to all intermediaries. Real-time updates are not possible.
One-way communication	Improved intermediary access *to* a hotel's CRS or PMS.	Significant third-party interface fees. No intermediary access *from* a hotel's CRS or PMS.	Multiple nearly real-time inventories must be maintained and are communicated.
Two-way communication	Eliminates most third-party interface fees. Real-time inventory availability.	Cost of equipment development and upgrade. Concerns related to data security.	Availability/inventory decisions can be made and communicated in real time.

It is also important to recognize that the group sales efforts undertaken by most hotels will affect the number of rooms an RM makes available for sale. This is especially true when significant numbers of group rooms are held in tentative sales status during the agreed-on bid evaluation period identified in a potential group room buyer's request for proposal (RFP).

You have learned that making rooms available for sale or withholding them from sale is a powerful prearrival revenue management tool. The number of times per day that an RM makes an inventory availability-related decision affecting transient guests can be quite large. It should be clear that these decisions and the timely communication of them are critical because they determine the exact number, type, and price of the rooms' products offered for sale by the hotel, as well as by all of its intermediaries.

Upon Arrival Strategies

An RM's revenue optimization strategies related to transient guest inventory do not stop when a room has been reserved and thus taken from inventory. If the reservation is not canceled or no-showed, the guest will ultimately arrive at the hotel. In nearly all cases, the responsibility for greeting, registering, and assigning guests to their chosen rooms upon their arrival rests with the front office and its front desk staff. The ability of the front office to implement revenue optimization strategies upon guest arrival will have a tremendous impact on a hotel's RevPAR generation. It is yet another example of the dependency of effective revenue management on the performance of a hotel's individual operating departments.

Upselling is the single most significant RM-related effort that can be undertaken by a front desk staff upon a guest's arrival at a hotel.

To better understand the potential impact of upselling, consider the hypothetical case of Jerri's and Ben's hotels. Both properties have 150 rooms. Each hotel offers room products in one of three versions and price. The most desirable and thus highest priced rooms sell for $159.99 per night, the middle priced rooms for $129.99, and the lowest priced rooms for $99.99. Assume that on a specific night, 110 guests arrive (without reservations) at each hotel.

At Jerri's hotel, all 110 rooms that are sold to these arriving guests are sold from the **top down**—that is, each arriving guests is sold the highest priced room available at the time of that guest's arrival. At Ben's hotel, each of the 110 rooms is sold from the **bottom up**. As a result, each arriving guest is sold the lowest-priced room available at the time of arrival.

Figure 7.6 shows the operating results that would occur in each of these two alternative selling scenarios.

Note that while the number of rooms sold and the pricing structure at each hotel is identical, the difference in RevPAR generated is 18.3 percent ($103.33 − $87.33)/$ 87.33 = 18.3%). This example is also one of the clearest illustrations of why revenue managers are so important. Note that in this case Jerri achieved significantly increased revenues *without* increasing the hotel's rack rates.

Essential RM Term

Upsell: To increase seller revenues: (1) by selling the buyer a higher cost item than that which was originally intended to be purchased, or (2) by increasing the number of items purchased by the buyer.

Essential RM Term

Top down (selling): A selling approach that seeks to sell an entity's highest priced items prior to the sale of its lower priced items.

Bottom-up (selling): A selling approach that seeks to sell an entity's lowest priced items prior to the sale of its higher priced items.

Figure 7.6	Top-down versus Bottom-up Sales Results				
Available Rooms	**Room Rates**	**Jerri Sold: Top Down**	**$ Revenue**	**Ben Sold: Bottom Up**	**$ Revenue**
50	$159.99	50	$ 7,999.50	10	$ 1,599.90
50	$129.99	50	$ 6,499.50	50	$ 6,499.50
50 150	$ 99.99	10	$ 999.90	50	$ 4,999.50
	Total Sold	110	$ 15,498.90	110	$13,098.90
	Occ. %	73.3%		73.3%	
	ADR		$ 140.90		$ 119.08
	RevPAR		$ 103.33		$ 87.33

The implementation of effective upselling strategies is the single most effective way to increase transient RevPAR generation without increasing the number of room versions offered in inventory or the price of rooms. In nearly all cases, significant upsell efforts are in place wherever RMs are achieving above-average RevPAR generation.

It is important to understand that upselling is *not* a process designed to sell guests what they do not want. Instead, it is a customer-centric process designed to offer guests the rooms they do want at a price they are willing to pay. Some RMs discount the potential impact of upselling by taking the position that the guests have already (at the time of his or her reservation) made the choice of the room product they desire most. The argument is weak, for three reasons.

The first reason relates to the communication method used to make the hotel's inventory options available to potential room buyers. The features and amenities that RMs in different hotel companies use to version their products are quite varied. Thus, a buyer evaluating the desirability of a business suite versus a regular guest room can be understandably confused about exact differences between those two room products, as these differences are not likely to be uniform across hotel brands.

For example, assume that a room buyer making a reservation utilizes the services of one of a hotel's intermediaries when selecting his or her preferred room type. In such a case, it is very possible that the distinctive features and amenities used to differentiate available room types may not have been fully communicated. Recall that the "Grand Suite" described in Figure 7.4 consisted of four product versions. The unique room features, amenities, and direct benefits to the guest of buying each version of this room type may simply not have been effectively communicated by an intermediary who offers for sale this room as well as the rooms of many other hotel brands.

Effectively designed and professionally implemented upon arrival upselling techniques provide a hotel the opportunity to make the room features of higher priced and thus higher valued room products available to guests at the time of check-in. It also allows the hotel to communicate, if desired, reductions in rates charged for higher-priced room options that may present greater perceived value to arriving guests while still serving to increase a hotel's RevPAR generation. Thus, for example, a hotel guest may have reserved a $99.00 standard room rather than a $199.00 suite because at $199.99 the suite did not represent value to that guest. If, upon arrival, however, the guest is offered the chance to upgrade to the suite at $149.00, the guest may then perceive great value and purchase the upgrade—and as a result, the hotel will achieve an extra $50.00 in revenue.

The second rationale for the implementation of a well-designed upsell program relates to normal vacillation in rooms inventory availability. To illustrate, assume that a vacationing guest, at the time of her reservation, expressed a preference for a room facing the hotel's pool area. At the time of booking, no such room was available in inventory, thus the guest reserved an alternative room that sold at a lower rate but that did not have a pool view. Because rooms are sold and canceled on a continuous basis, assume a pool view room was indeed available (due to a cancellation) at the time of this guest's arrival. Unless an effective upsell program were in place, this arriving guest would not be given an opportunity to purchase what she had originally preferred to buy even though that room product is available for purchase at the time of this guest's arrival. The result would be a less than fully satisfied guest, as well as lower-than-optimal RevPAR generation.

The third strong rationale for a well-designed upsell effort relates to changes in guests themselves. Arrival and departure dates for many travelers vary from the time of their original reservations, and so do the circumstances of their travel. Travel companions, trip purposes, the buying formula applied (see Chapter 3), and their personal value assessments are among the many factors that can change for guests between the time they reserve a room and the time they arrive to take possession of it. When room products options that are generally perceived to be of higher value are offered to arriving guests, they have the opportunity to reassess the quality/service/price propositions that RMs have made available to them. The result, in many cases, is an upsell opportunity.

Some RMs have achieved excellent results by designing upsell programs that begin with a description of rooms that are *two* quality/price levels above the room originally reserved. If, upon presentation of the initial higher offering, the guest exhibits price resistance, then the lower cost of the two upgrades, which still represents a one-level upsell from the originally reserved room, is then offered to the guest.

It is not realistic, of course, to assume that a hotel can be successful at upselling every arriving guests. Neither is it rational to assume that zero arriving guests can be upsold. RMs must work with their front office managers and DOSMs to ensure that upon arrival, upsell programs and tactics put into place at their properties are well-designed and professionally delivered, and that their effectiveness is measured and assessed on a regular basis.

Group Rooms

The best RMs are very adept at managing rooms inventory related to group room sales. Inventory management of group rooms is different from that of transient rooms simply

Essential RM Term

Attrition: The difference between the purchases a group pledges to make and the purchases it actually makes. Also referred to as wash, wash down, or slippage.

In the case of guest rooms, when the differences between blocked and picked-up rooms are significant, attrition penalties may be imposed by a hotel. The courts have ruled, however, that these penalties must be disclosed to the group in advance, in writing, and at the time the group signs its agreement with the hotel.

Essential RM Term

Cut-off date: The last day on which rooms may be picked up from a group block. It is also the date after which any unreserved rooms remaining in the block are to be released for public sale.

Essential RM Term

Group history: Details about the number of rooms blocked and ultimately purchased by a group holding an event similar to one held in the past.

because of the way group rooms are sold. Recall that the sale of a group room is a two-step process. In the first step, rooms are blocked, or removed from available inventory for future use by the group. In the second step, rooms are picked up (i.e., individually reserved) by group members.

The impact of this two-step process on rooms inventory availability should be apparent. If rooms are blocked for a group but not ultimately picked up by the group's members, the rooms may go unsold. If this occurs, the hotel can lose significant revenue—especially on those dates when demand for rooms was high but potential buyers were denied reservations due to the hotel holding excessively large room blocks for excessive periods of time. For this reason, among the many important issues to be negotiated when developing terms for a group rooms contact are the details about how many rooms will be blocked, exactly how long those rooms will remain in the block before they are released for sale to others, and what kinds of **attrition** penalties (if any) are to be imposed on the group by the hotel.

Even when the number of group rooms to be blocked and the **cut-off date** to be applied to the rooms are known, experienced RMs recognize that the effective management of group room blocks is often affected by several important factors:

Group Histories
Unrealistic Buyer Expectations
Buyer's Negotiation Tactics

Group Histories

A hotel's PMS can provide detailed information about a specific guest's previous hotel stay. In a similar manner, a **group history** can provide valuable information about an entire group's previous date(s) of stay, its room preferences, room rates paid, and forms of payment used.

In some cases, groups will meet at the same hotel year after year or on a rotational basis. When this occurs, information about the group can be retrieved from the hotel's PMS. In many cases, however, group history information will not be available because the group's previous event(s) will not have been held in the same hotel. When they have not been, RMs may be able to obtain group history information provided by other hotels or by the group itself. Figure 7.7 is an example of a group history for a group that has held a similar event for each of the last three years.

The group blocked fewer rooms last year than were blocked in previous years (575 last year versus 650 in the two prior years). A careful review of the data contained in Figure 7.7 makes it easy to see that RMs who have this group's prior three-year history of block

Figure 7.7	Sample Group History		
Event Date	**Rooms Blocked**	**Picked-up**	**% Utilized**
Three Years Ago			
Wednesday	100	85	85.0 %
Thursday	150	130	86.7 %
Friday	200	171	85.5 %
Saturday	200	166	83.0 %
Total	**650**	**552**	**84.9 %**
Total Years Ago			
Wednesday	100	82	82.0 %
Thursday	150	117	78.0 %
Friday	200	169	84.5 %
Saturday	200	167	83.5 %
Total	**650**	**535**	**82.3 %**
Last Year			
Wednesday	100	81	81.0 %
Thursday	125	115	92.0 %
Friday	175	171	97.7%
Saturday	175	162	92.6 %
Total	**575**	**529**	**92.0 %**

Note, that in this example, the group's historical *peak night* is Friday, although Saturday night's pick up is also strong.

Essential RM Term

Peak night: The night of a group's heaviest room pick-up and use in a multi-night block.

Essential RM Term

Host hotel: The hotel that has been chosen as the headquarter hotel for a group that must utilize multiple properties to house all of its group members.

size, total pick-up, **peak night** production, and decreasing room pick-up would be in a stronger position to manage this group's room block than would be an RM who does not have access to such information.

Experienced RMs know that a variety of factors can affect a group's actual pick-up in a specific year. If, for example, the group is one that holds its meetings in a variety of cities, the individual group members' perceptions of the desirability of each city in which the group meets may affect meeting attendance and thus room pick-up. Selection as the **host hotel**, meeting program content, local attractions, and available family activities are additional factors that may impact group demand for a hotel's rooms. The careful consideration of these factors is simply one more example of how RMs must apply personal insight to the process of revenue optimization.

Unrealistic Buyer Expectations

Upon initial examination, it would seem that managing inventory in group room blocks would be easy. Group rooms buyers indicate the rooms they need and then individual group members ultimately pick up the rooms. In fact, managing group rooms block inventories is very challenging. This is so because more often than not, group rooms buyers overestimate the number of rooms they will need from a hotel. In many cases, rooms buyers are simply optimistic. These buyers have a tendency to sincerely believe the maximum numbers of group members possible will attend their events. They seem to overlook the wisdom exhibited by Margaret Mitchell, author of *Gone With the Wind*, who stated, "Life is under no obligation to give us what we expect."[1]

In addition to overly optimistic attendance projections, group rooms buyers can feel the prospect of not having enough total rooms available for their group members is so unpleasant that they overestimate their projected usage on purpose. Of course, in some cases, group rooms buyers' estimated usage of rooms is unrealistically low. They may do this to avoid potential attrition penalties. This underestimate often leads to last-minute requests from the buyer to increase the size of room blocks. These requests can sometimes be difficult or even impossible to accommodate when additional rooms needed to fill the request are simply unavailable due to their prior sale to transient guests or to other group guests.

Buyer's Negotiation Tactics

In some cases, the size of room block a group rooms buyer requests is one part of their greater overall room rate negotiation strategy. The strategy is based on the assumption that a hotel will be more inclined to grant lower room rates to a higher volume of rooms buyer than to a lower volume buyer. When buyers perceive this to be true (and often it is!), buyers may feel it is in their group's best interest to inflate their potential room usage.

When managing the rooms inventory in group room blocks, cut-off dates can be just as important as block size. In most cases, group rooms buyers seek to negotiate cut-off dates that are as close to the date of their event as is possible. This gives their group members the maximum amount of time possible to pick up their blocked rooms. RMs, however, generally seek earlier cut-off dates because this increases the number of days available to sell to other buyers any unpicked-up rooms that will be returned to rooms inventory. Even after they have been established by contract terms, requests to extend cut-off dates are common occurrences. They may be requested by the buyer directly, but are often presented and supported by the hotel's sales and marketing team as it seeks to maximize goodwill with the group rooms buyer requesting the extension.

Special Contract and Negotiated Rate Rooms

In addition to inventory issues related to transient and group rooms, RMs face unique challenges when managing **contract** and **negotiated rate** inventories.

To illustrate the inventory management challenge of negotiated rates consider the travel needs of a large corporation. The

---

Essential RM Terms

Contract rate (room): A long-term room rate whose availability is agreed to in advance and for the duration of the contract agreement.

For example, the agreement by a hotel to house every night for one year an airline's ten-person flight crew.

Negotiated rate (room): An agreement to provide a select group of travelers, subject to availability, rooms at an agreed on and discounted rate. The discounted rate is in effect for the term of the negotiated rate agreement.

For example, a special given to all travelers employed by the Ford Motor Company.

Also referred to as a *volume discount rate*.

RM IN ACTION 7.1: ALLOWABLE ATTRITION

Meeting planners and group rooms buyers often request larger room blocks than they ultimately need. If blocked rooms are not picked up and the blocked rooms go unsold, the hotel's revenue-generating ability is clearly diminished. As a result, RMs must assure their hotels clearly indicate allowable attrition rates. Allowable attrition refers to the amount of downward variance that may be permitted in a group rooms contract before some type of penalty is incurred on the part of the rooms buyer. The only legally enforceable way to communicate a hotel's attrition policy is to include it, in written form, in the group rooms contract. The following is a sample allowable attrition clause, but each RM should ensure its own contract clause is enforceable in the state within which its hotel is located.

Allowable Attrition:

The hotel agrees to hold ample rooms inventory to accommodate the rooms requested in this group block contract. The hotel, however, limits the amount of attrition allowable (reductions) in block size that will be permitted as follows:

90 days prior to arrival	50% of room block
30–90 days prior to arrival	25% of room block
Less than 30 days prior to arrival	2% of room block

Attrition in excess of the above amounts will be billed at 100 percent of the contracted room rate plus applicable tax.

It is also important to recognize that attrition disputes are becoming more common as meeting planners increasingly insist that group room contracts also include clauses that hold the hotel accountable for using their best efforts to resell any rooms that were not picked up and for which attrition charges could be assessed.

corporation, which is headquartered in city A, sends a large number of overnight corporate travelers each month to city B. To minimize room and travel planning costs the corporation's rooms buyer negotiates with one of city B's hotels to offer rooms to its traveling employees at an agreed on rate. The benefit for the company is that all of its travelers know in advance where they are to stay and the rate they are to be charged. The hotel benefits from capturing all of this company's business. The practical RM issues to be addressed in participating in such an arrangement include:

- Must a specific number of rooms be held in reserve daily for the company?
- Which room type or types will be offered at the agreed on rate?
- Are there dates within the year when the contract's terms will not be honored?

Essential RM Term

Run of the house: A contract stipulation that permits the hotel to apply its contractually agreed-on rate to any room of its own choosing, determined at the time a contracted guest arrives to claim his or her reservation.

Contracts to house airline crews are an example of an arrangement where a hotel does agree to hold a specified, but often variable, number of rooms daily for the duration of the contract. These kinds of agreements may dictate that only certain room types are to be included in the rooms offered to arriving guests. In other arrangements, the hotel may be permitted to supply **run of the house** rooms.

RM AT WORK 7.1

"How many rooms do we still have available on those three days?" asked Josephine Cico, the manager of the 300-room Holiday Inn Capitol Plaza hotel.

"52 left on Thursday and Friday, 50 Saturday," replied Erick, the hotel's front office manager.

"And my client wants to add 40 more rooms to her block each of those days. They have already picked up the 150 rooms we previously blocked for them each day, and registrations for their meeting are still coming in. The client text messaged me with the request about an hour ago," said Elizabeth, the hotel's DOSM.

"So we have the rooms. What's the problem?" asked Josephine.

"The problem is their rate. The group rate we gave them was $129.00, but I can sell all of the remaining rooms to transients at $199.99," said Erick.

"But," protested Elizabeth, "we all agreed to that discount rate last year when I bid for the group. We bid it at $129.00 because they were bringing us 450 room nights. They picked up all the room nights they promised. I think we should give them the extra rooms they want."

"That's right. I did agree with our original bid and I had no problem with that," said Erick, "but if we can't get rack rate for our unsold rooms on a weekend we know we can sell out, when will we ever get it? Your group missed their estimate. That's not *our* fault. Let them buy their additional rooms at rack. It's continually doing things like adding rooms to discounted group blocks on sell-out dates that keep us from hitting our monthly RevPAR targets and making our bonuses. And I'm tired of missing my bonus!"

1. What are some possible reasons you believe would motivate Elizabeth to support granting her group's request?

2. Mathematically, it should be easy for Erick to prove the superior short-term RevPAR impact of his position. What, if any, impact would those same mathematical results have on the likelihood of future sales to Elizabeth's group?

3. Assume you were Josephine. How important would data management be to your decision to increase or to maintain at present levels the size of this group's room block? How important would insight be to the process? Would you favor adding rooms to the group's block at the discounted rate?

Essential RM Term

Last room available: A contract stipulation that requires a hotel to apply its contractually agreed on rate to any room type (suites typically excluded) available at the time a contracted guest makes his or her reservation.

Blackout date: Any date on which a hotel will not honor a contracted (negotiated) rate. Common blackout dates include New Year's Eve, holidays, and special events dates.

Room buyers naturally seek to have their contract terms extend to the **last room available** at a hotel, while RMs often seek terms that allow them to close negotiated rate rooms when occupancy levels or forecasts reach predetermined thresholds.

In addition, RMs must know if any of their hotels' contracts and agreements identify agreed-on **blackout dates**, as these have the effect of closing out a negotiated rate in advance and on agreed-on days.

As an RM, your hotel may have dozens (or even hundreds!) of individually negotiated room rates, as well as a large number of contracts. It is easy to see why it is essential that you exercise care and diligence when considering the impact of these arrangements on your rooms inventory management decision making. Variations in contracted room types, availability requirements, and blackout dates make contracted and negotiated rate management an important part of every RM's job because errors made in calculating inventory availability related to these agreements could put the future resigning of these mutually beneficial sales arrangements at considerable risk.

OVERBOOKING AS AN INVENTORY MANAGEMENT STRATEGY

In Chapter 6 you learned that demand forecasting seeks to answer an RM's question of how many buyers want to purchase a hotel's available rooms. Rooms inventory management seeks to answer the question of how many rooms actually remain available for sale. Except in those cases where a hotel is operating at 100 percent occupancy, demand for rooms is generally less than the number of rooms available for sale. In some cases, however, the demand for rooms is equal to or greatly exceeds their supply. In these situations, the temptation for RMs to intentionally overbook a hotel can be very strong.

Essential RM Term

Walk(ed): To relocate a guest with a confirmed reservation at a hotel to an alternative property.

Upon initial examination, overbooking a hotel would seem to be an illogical RM strategy because the compensation policies mandated by most hotel chains for those guests who are involuntarily **walked** *are significant.*

Although hotels are not currently faced with a federal law (like the airlines) that says they must compensate for walking a guest, most RMs recognize that it makes good business sense to say more than simply: *"We're sorry,"* if a guest is walked.

Various state innkeepers' laws mandate legal responsibilities toward walked guests and, as a result, in many cases a hotel that walks a guest with a confirmed reservation will be held responsible for the following:

- Securing for the guest a room at a comparable alternative hotel
- Paying in full for the guest's first night stay at the selected alternate hotel
- After the first night, paying the per-night difference in rate if the alternative hotel is more costly than the originally reserved property
- Providing or paying for transportation to and from the alternative hotel
- Providing reimbursements for telephone tolls used to inform relatives/friends about the use of the alternative hotel

Given these significant costs, a very reasonable question for RMs to ask is *"Why overbook?"* It is a question deserving of a carefully considered, reasonable, and balanced answer.

The Case for Overbooking

All hotels overbook. In some cases, the overbooking is unintentional while in other cases it is intentional. The reasons for unintentional bookings can vary but include the following:

- *Damaged rooms.* Guest rooms flood, air conditioners malfunction, carpets are damaged, and unexpected maintenance-related issues arise and can causes a room to be placed in out-of-order (OOO) status. As a result, a room that was previously included in the available rooms inventory count is no longer available. The hotel sold the room for us on a future date in good faith because it was presumed to be available on that date. Because the room is now damaged, however, the result can be an overbooked guest.

- *Staff errors.* While most reservation management systems are programmed to alert staff when potential errors are about to be made when making or canceling reservations, human errors still occur. When they do, rooms that seemed to be available for sale are not due simply to human error made in the spelling of names, the recording of proper dates, or even the management of specific room types.

- *Inventory availability errors.* You previously learned in this chapter that not all intermediaries have two-way communication with a hotel's PMS. As a result, real-time updates of a hotel's rooms inventory simply may not be possible with all of a hotel's rooms sellers. Because that is true, the possibility for unintentionally double-booking one or more rooms can exist.

- *Guest overstays.* Assume that a guest reserves a room for two days. Upon check-in, the guest again indicates the intention of checking out of the hotel in two days. If subsequently, due to illness, changes in travel plans, or a variety of other circumstances the guest does not check out as planned and decides to stay one or more additional nights, that guest's room may have been reserved for an incoming guest but it will not be available for that arriving guest. Experienced RMs know that hotels face tremendous restrictions on their ability to immediately remove overstay guests. While the number of these overstays can be estimated with some degree of accuracy, an underestimate of overstays on a sold-out night will result in an overbooking.

In all of these cases and more, the end result is an overbooked hotel—but the hotel's intent was not to overbook. Good management can minimize, but never eliminate, all overbookings of this type. Experienced RMs who find themselves in an overbooked situation seek to implement strategies that minimize the damage to their properties and the harm to guests that could result if walks are handled poorly.

Experienced RMs know it is best not to walk:

- Members of their hotel or brand's loyalty (frequent guest) programs
- Group meeting or event attendees
- Contracted rooms such as airline crew rooms
- Couples celebrating special occasions
- Families arriving late at night

The ideal walk situation is to find a rooms buyer spending their own money on themselves (see Chapter 3). In such a case, paying for the guest's stay at an equally high-quality property nearby may be perceived positively, not negatively, by that guest.

Some RMs intentionally overbook their hotels. The reasons to do so range from the reasonable to the ethically questionable. To illustrate the rationale typically given for overbooking, assume you are the RM for a 500-room property. On the average sold out, or fully reserved, night, your hotel historically experiences a no-show rate of 5 percent of all incoming arrivals.

These data are carefully maintained in the hotel's PMS. On this night, your PMS shows all available rooms committed and that there are 200 planned arrivals.

Question: Do you have rooms available for sale?

If your position is that you do have rooms to sell because your best estimate is that 10 rooms, (200 arrivals × 0.05 no-show rate = 10 no-show rooms) will become available due to no-shows, you likely view overbooking as a financial issue and one that is ethically justifiable. You are not alone.

Those RMs who carefully calculate estimated no-show rates and utilize the resulting data to overbook their properties would argue that they are not actually taking a reservation for a room they do not have. Rather, they would maintain that because they are taking a reservation for a room that they believe will in fact, based on historical data, be available for arriving guests, they are simply utilizing overbooking as a legitimate revenue optimization strategy.

RMs who take this position will find a wealth of support for their view, as well as detailed information including a variety of academic papers outlining strategies designed to teach RMs how they can *best* employ their overbooking strategies. In most cases, *best* as used in this context is defined as those overbooking-related revenue optimization strategies designed to maximize short-term (nightly) RevPAR by ensuring the hotel sells out.

Essentially, advanced overbooking procedures teach how to calculate the cost of an overbooked room and weigh that cost against the revenue gain that will be achieved by overbooking. The end goal of these procedures is to employ those strategies that maximize revenue, minimize costs, and mitigate customer impact. Pressed to justify an action that many would find objectionable, those RMs who intentionally overbook also argue (some more convincingly than others), that overbooking in anticipation of no-shows is an **act utilitarian**.

Essential RM Term

Act utilitarian: A theory of ethics that states that the morally correct action is one that results in the greatest good for the greatest number of people.

Those familiar with the writings of Adam Smith, whose 1776 publication of *An Inquiry into the Nature and Causes of the Wealth of Nations* presented the first rationale for free markets and can be argued to be the first book of modern economics, may recognize the phrase "greatest good for the greatest number." The phrase describes an act utilitarian and it is often used to justify a course of action that may result in harm to a few members of society but benefits a larger number.

Is overbooking an act utilitarian? Possibly. Certainly, if an RM's no-show predictions are accurate and no guest is ultimately walked, it could be argued that no one is directly harmed and the hotel gains. Honest RMs who routinely overbook, however, would admit that guest walks will occur from time to time because even the best estimates and forecasts of damaged rooms, overstays, and no-shows will not predict the future perfectly every time.

Even in cases where a guest is walked, those who intentionally overbook often take the position that the only one directly inconvenienced is the guest. The hotel's owners certainly achieve their greatest good—at least in the short run. The owners have maximized RevPAR by having filled all of their rooms. The hotel to which the guest is relocated gains as well because they have now sold an additional room.

Finally, some RMs would argue, all of those guests who were successfully accommodated because of the RM's skill in overbooking benefit. In the final analysis, these RMs truly believe overbooking is indeed an act utilitarian and a financially profitable one as well.

The Case against Overbooking

Despite its widespread industry prevalence, some RMs do not intentionally overbook, citing the fact that in their own industry segment, doing so would be, as a professional hotelier pointed out "too much of a risk to a . . . hotel's reputation."[2]

Open-minded readers might, at this point, legitimately question how an industry activity that purports to be ethically permissible and is often financially beneficial could actually cause some hoteliers to feel that doing it would pose a risk to their hotel's reputation. The authors can suggest several risk-related reasons why this is so.

Ethical

Defending intentional overbooking on the basis that, from an ethical perspective, it is an act utilitarian may be popular in business circles, but astute readers will recognize it as a variation on the phrase *"the ends justify the means."* That is, the legitimacy of an act is judged by its ultimate outcome. An opposing view states that the ethical evaluation of an act should be based on its inherent rightness or wrongness and not the rightness or wrongness of the consequences of the act. This view takes the position that a promise made with the expectation that it will, or may, be broken is inherently wrong.

This philosophy is perhaps best summarized by the famous line: *"Let justice be done though the heavens fall"*—a phrase most often attributed to Lucius Calpurnius Piso Caesoninus, a statesman of ancient Rome and the father-in-law of Julius Caesar.[3] The statement supports the view that the right thing to do is always the right thing to do, regardless of the act's consequences. Similarly, the wrong thing to do is the wrong thing to do regardless of its immediate benefit. Are certain acts inherently right or wrong or in the business world do the ends indeed justify the means? The issue is certainly open to honest difference of opinion and it is not unreasonable for RMs to fully consider their personal views in this area. Oscar Wilde put the legitimacy of questioning conventional wisdom nicely when he observed, "A man who does not think for himself does not think at all."[4]

Legal

In Chapter 5 you learned that an act may be legal despite its being ethically questionable. From a strictly legal perspective, intentionally overbooking can be considered analogous to the act of entering into a contract in which one of the parties (the hotel) knows it cannot fulfill its obligations.

It is fair to state that few businesses would think it is a good idea to create contracts with their clients knowing in advance they will not be able to fulfill the contracts' terms. Legally, however, nonperformance by a hotel in an overbooking situation is considered to be a minor breach or partial breach. Minor and partial breeches, in the legal sense, mean contract nonperformance, a situation in which the non-breaching party is entitled to collect only the actual dollar amount of their proven damages. In most cases, these damages amount only to a traveler's increased costs, and not to their emotional or inconvenience-related damages.

As a result, while they could do so, it is quite rare that walked guests will actually sue the hotels that walk them. This is because of the relatively small amount of provable damages incurred by a walked guest and to the high cost of litigation. The fact remains, however, that any time a hotel can be proved in court to have intentionally overbooked rooms and then denied a room to a guest with a **guaranteed reservation**, that hotel will indeed be held liable for breach of contract and will be ordered to pay appropriate damages. Intentional overbooking and resulting breech of contract are difficult to defend on a strictly legal basis.

Essential RM Term

Guaranteed reservation: A contract in which the hotel agrees to hold a room until the reserving guest arrives, and the guest agrees to pay for the room if they arrive to claim it or if they no-show.

Reputation

Are there reputation damaging consequences that may result in a hotel that aggressively overbooks? In the past some hoteliers have made arguments against overbooking based not on its guest impact, but on its staff impact. These hoteliers were concerned about the consequences that result if employees view overbooking as an example of management's inconsiderate treatment of guests. Despite the common complaint by managers that employees don't pay attention to what they are told, experienced hoteliers know that employees pay a great deal of attention to what they see. Employees take their cue from their supervisors.

When management engages in its own questionably ethical behavior toward customers, say hoteliers who are opposed to overbooking, the housekeeper might well decide that the bathroom already looks "clean enough" for guests. The bell person might decide to charge a guest for calling a taxi and the bartender might decide that since the hotel's managers' do not pay enough, taking liquor from the storeroom for personal use is O.K. In the past, such arguments no doubt may have swayed some RMs against overbooking.

Essential RM Term

Social network (online): A group of individuals with common interests or characteristics who joined together to share information. When using the Internet for information exchange, these are commonly referred to as a "virtual community." Current popular examples include Facebook, MySpace, LinkedIn, and TripAdvisor.

Today, the reputation impact issue is completely different. Any notion an RM may have that walked guests can be compensated for their inconvenience and then will simply go away clearly does not understand the powerful influence of online **social networks** on the travel industry. Today's walked guest is nothing like the walked guest of 1970, 1980, 1990, or 2000.

Those RMs or other hoteliers who remain unconvinced of the potential damage to a hotel's reputation caused by overbooking in the Internet age need only log on to a popular traveler review site such as TripAdvisor.

com; type the word "overbook" in the search engine and then examine the many experiences and opinions that overbooked travelers have shared with the 15 million + members

> ▶ **RM ON THE WEB 7.2**
>
> One of the newest examples of a social network focusing on traveler-shared views of their experiences is "Where Are You Now?" To view this innovative travel booking and review site, go to: www.wayn.com.
>
> Most travelers place more credence on travel reviews written by friends and others they know than on the advertisements placed by businesses. When you arrive read more about this site that proclaims itself the best place to *"Find travel guides and information and make new friends."*

of this virtual community. They would also do well to consider why Janine Hills, the chief executive of Vuma Corporate Reputation Management, quoted U,S, billionaire business owner Warren Buffett's warning to his own managers when he said: "If you lose money for the firm, I will be very understanding . . . If you lose reputation for the firm, I will be ruthless."[5]

RevPAR Generation

Those RMs who steadfastly maintain the practice of overbooking in the face of its many potential drawbacks ultimately justify it based on the revenue generating power of the practice more than its customer-centric orientation. Simply put, these RMs calculate the monetary costs associated with overbooking and if these costs are less than revenue generated from overbooking, implement an overbook strategy. That seems a curious and somewhat needless approach when it is recognized that a room that has been sold on a guaranteed basis has in fact, regardless of guest no-shows, been sold. As a result, payment should be collected. In the overwhelming majority of cases (industry estimates exceed 75 percent no-show collectability), those RMs who elect to legitimately bill no-show customers will collect payment for the rooms their hotels have held. When that is not the case, the problem typically relates to failures in the hotel's reservations, cancellation, or no-show billing procedures, not in its revenue management processes.

In some cases, internally developed bonus programs that pay staff premiums for "sell-outs" can be to blame for overbooking. These programs can, in some cases, result in the motivation of reservation and/or front desk staff to put their own short-term interests ahead of the interests of the hotel's guests, as well as the hotel's long-term customer-centric revenue optimization efforts.

In the final analysis, the overbooking debate will no doubt continue with vocal proponents on both sides. As a result, individual RMs must continue to make their own determinations about the desirability of the practice and its impact on their guests, their hotels, and the industry. Regardless of the mental and mathematical sophistication that can be applied to the overbooking process, however, today's customer-centric RMs might do well to consider a second quote by billionaire Warren Buffett, who sagely observed, "If something is not worth doing at all, it is not worth doing well."[6]

RM AT WORK 7.2

Two weeks before their granddaughter's wedding, Ester and Greg Barnes booked a room at the Lakeside Plaza hotel. Ester received a confirmation number when she gave the hotel her credit card information and agreed to its mandatory 24-hour cancellation policy.

When they arrived at Lakeside Plaza, much to their dismay, they were told that their room was not available because the hotel was overbooked and as a result they would be put up at the Clarion Hotel, which was only ten miles away.

Mrs. Barnes felt a little better when she was told that the Lakeside Plaza would pay for the room at the Clarion the first night. The Lakeside's front desk clerk then informed Mrs. Barnes that the Lakeside Plaza did have openings for the second night, and thus the Barnes would have to return to the Lakeside for their second-night stay because on that day, the Clarion had sold all of its rooms.

After checking in at the Clarion, the Barnes unpacked, showered, and arrived at their granddaughter's rehearsal dinner one hour late. The next day, they had to leave a family function in the morning, return to the Clarion, repack their belongings, check out before noon, and drive back to the Lakeside, where the somber clerk on duty informed them that their room would not be ready until 3:00 P.M. because the hotel had sold out the night before and also because, the clerk stated, *"3:00 P.M. is our normal check-in time."*

"But," protested Mrs. Barnes, "the wedding begins across town at 2:30 this afternoon and I still have to get ready!"

1. What did the Lakeside do wrong in the case of Mr. and Mrs. Barnes?

2. If the RM at the Lakeside Plaza intentionally overbooked on the night of the Barneses arrival, was his or her action ethical in your opinion?

3. Assume these were your grandparents and the wedding they wished to attend were your own. Would you share details of this incident with those you know? Would you use the Internet to share the details with them? How would your comments reflect on the Lakeside Plaza?

PRICE MANAGEMENT

When RMs have accurately forecasted buyer demand and monitored their product availability, their next task is **price management**. Recall from Chapter 5 that the establishment of an initial price is the first step in revenue management. This is so because the demand forecast for a hotel's rooms reflects buyer response to an established price. Price management is the process of adjusting that initial price to influence demand.

To illustrate, consider your own personal interest in purchasing a five-night stay in Miami, Florida, to visit South Beach. If you are like most buyers, your interest in purchasing the five-night stay can only be determined

Essential RM Term

Price management: The strategies and tactics employed by revenue managers to best match rates or prices charged with prospective customers' willingness to pay.

after you know its price. At a very low price, your interest will likely be high. At a higher price, your interest will likely decline. Thus, it is an RMs' *response* to forecasted demand and supply levels at initially determined rates or prices that is the essence of price management.

Hoteliers may establish their initial rate offerings based on a variety of factors including the season, their hotel's location, its operating costs, and the service levels it provides. Understanding exactly how hoteliers historically determined their initial room prices is helpful in understanding how it is done today, as well as how a hotel's initial rates can be price managed to optimize revenues.

Historical Perspective

In the past, surprisingly little was written about the complexity of hotel room or food and beverage pricing. In the hotel industry, most of the available literature focused on the relative pros and cons of using different cost-based mathematical formulas. These formulas were all developed to establish initial room prices. The conceptual basis for the individual formulas varied, but the Hubbart room rate formula, named after a Chicago hotelier of the 1950s, the $1.00 per $1,000 Rule, and other rate development methodologies[7] all shared a cost-based orientation. Each sought to establish a hotel's ideal or target ADR.

In addition, the hotel accountants of the time developed fairly sophisticated formulas designed to measure the percentage or proportion of that targeted rate that was actually achieved by a hotel. Thus, for example, a hotel having calculated that its ideal (some writers used the terms *target* or *potential*) initial room rate was $100.00 per night would likely achieve, due to normal discounting, a lower rate over any given time period. If the hotel actually achieved an ADR of $90.00 for example, its achieved room rate or achieved potential ADR would be 90 percent ($90.00 actual rate/$100.00 target rate = 90% achievement).

Based on season or a variety of other factors, hotel managers and their sales departments were initially judged on their ability to achieve high percentages of their targeted initial rates. As you have learned, however, while costs certainly must be considered in rooms pricing, cost cannot be allowed to be the primary consideration in a differential pricing system designed to maximize RevPAR. Yet, prior to the 1980s a handful of 1950s and 1960s era cost-based price management systems were in use by the great majority of hoteliers. It would be these same hoteliers, as it would turn out, who would be completely unprepared for the business environment they would face in the 1990s and 2000s. To understand why this was so you must recognize that as late as 1989 students reading the most highly respected "Introduction" to the hotel industry textbooks published in that year would find no mention of the terms *revenue optimization, revenue management,* or even *RevPAR* in the index of topics."[8]

In fact, only in the early to mid-1990s did the term "yield management" begin to appear with regularity in the hospitality industry literature. To understand why, recall that in Chapter 1 you learned yield management is a common term used for the demand-based revenue management strategies first initiated by commercial airline companies. These strategies were designed to maximize income via manipulation of selling prices. In the mid- to late-1980s, yield management was introduced at Delta and American Airlines as a response to their industry's *yield/load* paradox.

An airline's performance is measured by two factors. These are yield—the amount the airline is paid per passenger flown—and load, which is the percentage of seats filled by those paying customers. The paradox and challenge faced by airlines is that high prices could result in flight yields that were also high, but as a result, loads would often be low. Alternatively, low pricing might result in higher loads, but, of course, lower yields.

Yield management pioneers such as Robert Cross at Delta Airlines reasoned that if an airline could anticipate those flights for which demand would be high, prices on those flights could be maintained at high levels or even increased. In a similar manner, on those flights for which demand was projected to be low, reduced priced tickets could be used to increase the flights' load factors. In the days leading up to the flight's departure, further reasoned Cross, appropriate and immediate ticket price adjustments could be made based on the actual demand levels experienced by each flight.

Thus, on those flights where demand exceeded projections, prices would be maintained or increased. On those flights where demand was less than originally forecast, ticket prices could be reduced. A variety of restrictions would be used to ensure only new flyers (i.e., those without a previous reservation on the flight) would be permitted to obtain the new fares. Thus became common the purchase restrictions, change fees, cancellation fees, and other ticket-change limitations now common in the airline industry.

The end goal of the airlines' price management strategies, of course, was maximization of the airlines *total yield*, which they calculate easily using the formula:

$$\text{Yield} \times \text{Load} = \text{Total yield}$$

The initial financial results achieved by the application of yield management strategies to pricing airline tickets were nothing short of dazzling, chiefly because, as its proponents pointed out, each incremental revenue dollar achieved was gained without an increase in the cost of flying the planes.

If you see the similarity between an airlines "yield" and a hotel's ADR, as well as the similarity between a planes "load" factor and a hotel's occupancy percentage, you can better understand why the lodging industry was fascinated when, in the early 1990s, some hoteliers began to apply the 1980s-developed yield management strategies to their own businesses.

In fairness to these insightful operators who were moving from a cost-based to demand-based pricing system, they were exploring what for them was completely uncharted territory. Unfortunately for them, most industry observers now admit that the earliest yield management systems used in hotels, as copied directly from the airlines, were rather crude efforts, in many cases were quite flawed, and in even the largest of hotel companies would ultimately prove to be applied naively.

Interestingly, as hotels increasingly embraced the new yield management philosophy in the early 1990s, airlines were at the same time discovering the complex realities and difficulties associated with applying yield management. Consider that, having been a pioneer in the area and having utilized yield management techniques for over half a decade, Robert Crandall, chairman and CEO of American Airlines, called a press conference in April 1992 where he announced:

> We have said for some time that our yields are too low. Yet. . . . an ever growing array of
> discount fares surrounded by an ever-changing plethora of restrictions, simply does

not work. . . . In our unsuccessful pursuit of profits, we have made our pricing so complex that our customers neither understand it nor think it is fair[9]

Crandall then stated that American would abandon complex yield-management generated fares and simplify its ticket pricing. It would immediately institute a new and simplified pricing approach with only four prices for each flight (first class, coach, 7-day advance, and 21-day advanced). He was too late. Despite positive public response, his unchanging ticket prices allowed American's competitors to yield manage their prices around his. American's logical and easily understandable prices were, quite literally, sitting ducks for yield management's increasingly sophisticated pricing systems. By October 1992, Crandall stated that his new pricing program was "dying a slow death." By November 1992, American, like its competitors was back to reluctantly manipulating thousands of fares throughout its system.

Meanwhile, in the hotel industry, hoteliers were reading with fascination articles containing information such as the following that appeared in the winter 1999 edition of *Decision Sciences* journal. The article introduced readers to the power of pricing using yield management strategies:

> Yield management is the dynamic pricing, overbooking, and allocation of perishable assets across market segments in an effort to maximize short-term revenues for the firm. Yield management provides some success stories and a few nonpublicized failures. For example, American Airlines increased its revenues by an estimated $1.4 billion over the 1989–91 time frame.[10]

Had they continued reading they would have come across less encouraging sections of the same article:

> However, these benefits are not easy to obtain (Hanks, Cross, & Noland, 1992; Lieberman). One hotel chain spent over $1 million in implementing a yield management system, only to discontinue using the system because it was not appropriate for their properties. One airline attributed losses in excess of $10 million due to errors in its yield management models.[11]

Unfortunately, the euphoria that initially surrounded yield management focused on it advantages over cost-based pricing, rather than its real challenges and potential pitfalls. Regardless of its still largely unknown shortcomings, in the hotel industry the application of yield management strategies continued to increase. As a result, respected industry professionals writing popular accounting texts as late as 2002 would write in newly released editions that:

> In the past few years, hoteliers have become aggressive in pricing rooms by using a concept popularly referred to as "Yield Management."[12]

It is important to recognize that despite the fact airlines had by now been practicing yield management for over a decade, in the early 2000s yield management was still a relatively new concept for many in the lodging industry. In July 2001, this state of affairs prompted John Palmer, sales manager for technology provider Fidelio (now Micros-Fidelio), to state, "Small-to-medium hotels understand the yield management concept intuitively but without sophistication and certainly without applying any controls or logic to it."[13] As you will learn in the next chapter, two months after the publication of Palmer's comments, hoteliers would pay dearly for this lack of sophistication. They would suffer as they sought to respond to the events of 9/11. And they would struggle to understand the growing impact of those Internet travel sites owned and operated by the more yield-management experienced airlines.

Today, most hoteliers still understand cost-based rooms pricing best, but many have gained a much better understanding of the logic related to yield management. In fact, it is that improved understanding of yield management that has today begun to move very experienced hoteliers (as it did Robert Crandall after he better understood it) *away* from an unwieldy approach to yield management and toward price management practices designed to optimize revenues in a customer-centric manner.

Establishing Room Rates

Today, RMs must decide the best prices at which to sell their rooms. This requires that they answer the question, *"What is my hotel room worth?"* You have learned that the question is not easily answered. Cost-based approaches to the question ignore the fact that buyers are indifferent to a seller's costs. However, simply allowing demand for a product to determine its price can lead to charges of price gouging and extreme customer dissatisfaction. In addition, that practice inevitably leads to the development of unwieldy pricing systems that can easily become so complicated only statisticians with advanced mathematical training and computer programmers well-educated in the intricacies of logarithms truly understand how they work.

Today a major difficulty in establishing the proper selling price of hotel rooms relates to the curious tendency of the hotel industry's revenue management experts to introduce the topic by relating it directly to pricing as it is practiced by the airline industry. Many then go on to use the airlines as an example of how sophisticated pricing programs can be developed to continually adjust room rates charged in response to fluctuations in demand.

Sophisticated RMs (and you are becoming one!), however, will recognize that pricing hotel rooms is completely different from, and inherently more difficult than, pricing airline seats. Despite the seemingly advanced manner in which many of the airlines mange their prices, hoteliers seeking to model their price management strategies after those of the airlines would do well to recognize four important price-related differences between pricing airline seats and hotel rooms:

1. *An airline reservation is a confirmed sale with a substantial financial penalty for any subsequent change in the flyer's reservation.* In most cases, however, a hotel room may be reserved at one price and then that reservation cancelled (with no penalty) if subsequent prices are reduced. Airline tickets are purchased, hotel rooms are merely reserved. The difference is significant, as anyone who has ever tried to change an airline ticket after it was purchased can readily attest.

2. *Airlines company executives are responsible for establishing prices; thus they can ensure logic and consistency in their product pricing.* In the hotel industry, neither Wyndham, Starwood, Choice, IHG, Hilton nor Marriott, for example, establish room prices. In fact, it is illegal for them to do so except in the very small number of hotels they actually own or manage.

In the lodging industry, each individual hotel owner sets his or her own price. This means that RMs in any given market will encounter both logical and illogical competitor pricing. Fixed costs, variable costs, and yield curves displayed beautifully in marketing texts applicable to companies that have the ability to set prices for their own products, mean absolutely nothing to a single hotel owner whose primary motivation may be pricing in such a manner as to assure enough revenue is generated this weekend to fund next week's payroll!

3. *Airlines facing changes in demand for flights routinely increase or decrease the size of their planes.* If continued demand is very high or low, flights may be added or subtracted. Once its construction is complete, however, individual hotels cannot utilize this approach.

4. *An airplane that takes off with empty seats incurs virtually identical costs to an airplane that leaves with no seats empty.* Especially today, when free services such as meals and beverages are eliminated or minimal, allowing a plane to take off with an empty seat makes very little sense. Hotels, however, incur real costs when the decision is made to sell a room. These costs include cleaning the room, stocking it with guest room supplies and amenities, and wear and tear.

For all of these and a variety of other compelling reasons, the approach the authors take to room price management is not one currently in use by the airlines, nor will it be dependent on impenetrable mathematics that are beyond the understanding of all but a few RMs.

On the contrary, the approach presented is, we believe, a superior one, both in terms of conceptual foundation and practical application. Most importantly, it is an approach designed to be decidedly customer-centric in its implementation. This is not a claim often made by those nonhospitality experts busily applying differential equations to the question of how RMs can best price their hotel rooms.

Rack Rates

In Chapter 2 you read that "*an effective price is a concept, not a number.*" Lodging industry RMs make their initial value proposition to room buyers via the development of their rack rates, the price of rooms when no discounts of any type are offered to guests purchasing the rooms. In retail industries this price would be considered an item's list price. Experienced RMs know that the management of a hotel's rack rates, however, is much more complex than a retailer's management of list prices.

Regardless of the specific method used to establish rack rates, the appropriateness of a hotel's rack rates should be continually assessed and the rack rates modified as needed. In Chapter 9, you will learn exactly how that is done.

RMs keep a record of their current rack rates, as well as discounted rates, in their hotel's CRS and PMS via the use of **rate codes**.

The typical hotel will establish not one, but numerous, rack rates. Figure 7.8 lists the rack rates associated with the various room types offered for sale at the sample beach hotel previously presented in Figure 7.4.

Essential RM Term

Rate code: A property-specific notation used by a hotel's PMS to specify the price of a unique room product. Also known as a rate plan.

Figure 7.8	Rack Rates at Sample Beach Hotel		
Room Description	**Room Code**	**Rate Code**	**Rate**
1. 2. Standard room; view of pool, Approx. 300 square feet	KP	Rack	**$ 199.99**
2. Standard room; view of pool, Approx. 300 square feet	DDP	Rack	$ 199.99
3. Standard room; Ocean view, Approx. 300 square feet	KO	Rack	**$ 249.99**
4. Standard room; Ocean view, Approx. 300 square feet	DDO	Rack	$ 249.99
5. Jr. Suite; Ocean view, small parlor (sitting area) and 2 TVs. Approx. 400 sq. feet	JKO	Rack	**$ 299.99**
6. Jr. Suite; Ocean view, small parlor (sitting area) and 2 TVs. Approx. 400 sq. feet	JDDO	Rack	**$ 279.99**
7. Grand Suite; large parlor area, 2 TVs. Ocean view, Approx. 600 sq. feet	GKO	Rack	**$ 399.99**
8. Grand Suite; large parlor area, 2 TVs. Ocean view, Approx. 600 sq. feet	GDDO	Rack	**$ 389.99**
9. Grand Suite; large parlor area, 2 TVs. Ocean view, Approx. 600 sq. feet VIP Floor	GKOV	Rack	**$ 499.99**
10. Grand Suite; large parlor area, 2 TVs. Ocean view, Approx. 600 sq. feet VIP Floor	GDDOV	Rack	$ 499.99

Those rack rates that are underlined and bolded represent the seven unique rack rates maintained in the CRS/PMS at this hotel.

Rate codes are used to simplify price management and reservation management. To illustrate, assume that on a given Saturday night this hotel's RM has determined that all KP rooms will sell at rack rate. The reservationist providing information about the cost of such a room reserved for that day would find that the reservation system displays a rack rate of $199.99.

The RM may or may not dictate that other room types sell at their rack rates on that same day. It is easy to see that in a hotel with multiple room types, with each representing a unique room product, the number of rack rates recorded for use at one time can be very large indeed. Because demand for various room types will vary, it is not unusual for an RM to make the decision that, on any given day, some rooms will sell at their rack rates, while others sell for less, or for more. It is a fundamental principle of revenue optimization in hotels, however that:

RMs should strive to sell as many rooms as possible at rack rate.

Rack rated rooms are those sold with no discount. It may seem obvious that RMs would want to sell their rooms at nondiscounted rates. What may be less obvious is exactly why they should do so. In a customer-centric revenue management system, the first reason relates to a hotel's guests.

Recall that a price is both a *concept* and the value proposition offered by a seller. Because that is true, a hotel's rack rate should clearly state to room buyers this concept:

"Our rack rate represents the value we truly believe *buyers* (just like you) place on our room products."

Note that the rack rate does not represent what a hotel *needs* it rooms to be worth, what it *wishes* its rooms were worth, or what it *hopes* they are worth. As interesting as the concepts of needed, wished, and hoped-for revenue may be for a hotel's owners and managers, you have learned that it is the room buyer who dictates the worth of a room. Because that is true, it is unrealistic to assume that this worth will change on an hourly, daily, or even weekly basis unless the product offered changes as well. Those RMs who continually tweak their rack rates typically do so not in response to their buyers' perceptions of value, but rather, in response to changes in buyer demand for their rooms.

The industry-accepted rationale for this practice is that increased guest demand for rooms justify their higher price. That approach might seem reasonable to them (but not necessarily to their guests) during times of high demand. However, the industry pays a significant price for that philosophy during periods of reduced demand. For example, when the recession of 2008/2009 occurred, demand for U.S. rooms was severely reduced. Occupancies fell approximately 8 to 10 percent, and room rates declined at an equal level, with industry predictions that it would be 2012, or four years, before prices recovered to their 2007 levels.[14] Such radical swings in pricing are not the norm for other industries and are not inevitable, as the pricing philosophy of restaurateurs (which is not predicated on demand-based price changes) readily attests.

As you learned in Chapter 5, price increases implemented by any seller due only to short-term increases in demand will inevitably be met with dislike, suspicion, and resistance by nearly all buyers and in nearly all industries, including the lodging industry.

In addition to the impact on guests of selling at rack rate, it is important for RMs to understand that reductions in rack rate that are not based on sound reasoning have a direct and negative impact on a hotel's staff. This is so because rack rate reductions send the clear message to hotel employees that management's own view of room value provided to the hotel's guests is diminished. Approximately 80 percent of U.S. hotels have 150 rooms or less. In these properties, many of the reservations made for the hotel are made by front desk staff. Some RMs ignore or discount the difficulties inherent in directing front desk staff to sell, or to understand the rationale for selling, a specific room type at $199.99 one day, $159.99 the next day, and then $209.99 the following day. Others believe that because many guests book rooms online, the attitudes of on-property desk staff are unimportant. It is essential for you to understand that RMs who think they can frequently and drastically manipulate room rates with no residual impact on hotel staff morale simply do not understand the impact of their actions.

Reductions in rack rate send the clear message to employees that RMs have no faith in the original value proposition which should be:

"Our rack rate represents the value we truly believe *buyers* place on our room products."

Indeed, if this statement is true, a reduction in rack rate is clearly *not* a message RMs should send to those employees who must be enthusiastically enlisted to support their property's revenue optimization efforts by selling at a full and undiscounted price. Nor is it a message the lodging industry as a whole should send potential guests during times of diminished demand because the difficulties inherent in returning rates to their previous higher levels are significant.

Rack Rate Discounts

While it is always most desirable to sell rooms at rack rate, you have learned that implementing effective price differentiation strategies not only means selling different versions of products (room types) at different prices; it also means selling the same room types to different market segments at prices that reflect those market's willingness to pay. For this reason, offering rooms at price points below rack rate can make perfect sense. For example, in any of the following situations, effective price management strategies may indicate that rates other than rack may be appropriate:

- *When the length of a guest's stay offsets the rate reduction.* For example, extended-stay guests requesting a reservation for a 21-night stay may be offered a rate lower than another corporate guest requesting only a one-night stay. If extended-stay guests constitute a significant market for a hotel, effective price management would dictate that a separate rate code (e.g., "EXT" for "Extended Stay") be developed for each extended stay room product offered. Figure 7.9 is an example of how such a rate could be implemented. Note that in this example, unique EXT rates are developed within this non–rack rate code.

- *When the date(s) requested by the guest includes one or more days for which minimal demand is forecast.* In a hotel with minimal demand for weekend rooms, a guest arriving on a Friday night for a two-night stay may be offered a lower rate than a guest arriving on a Tuesday (a high demand day) for a two-night stay.

- *When the number of rooms purchased is large.* A group rooms buyer seeking to purchase 150 rooms for a three-night stay (450 total room nights) may receive a lower rate than a guest wanting to reserve one room for a three-night stay.

- *When the buyer has special status.* A guest seeking to reserve a two-night stay every week for the next 25 weeks may be offered a lower rate than a guest seeking to reserve a two-night, but only for a one-time stay.

- *When the total revenue generated by the sale offsets the reduction in rack rate.* For example, consider the governmental agency that seeks to reserve, in a full-service hotel, 100 rooms for each of the three days of a training session. The agency also wants to purchase three meals daily for the attending trainees. That agency may be offered a lower rate than a different buyer seeking to reserve 100 rooms for the same three days but without food and beverage purchases.

Figure 7.9 **Extended Stay Rates at Sample Beach Hotel**

Room Description	Room Code	Rate Code	Rate
1. 2. Standard room; view of pool, Approx. 300 square feet	KP	EXT	$ 169.99
2. Standard room; view of pool, Approx. 300 square feet	DDP	EXT	$ 169.99
3. Standard room; Ocean view, Approx. 300 square feet	KO	EXT	$ 219.99
4. Standard room; Ocean view, Approx. 300 square feet	DDO	EXT	$ 219.99
5. Jr. Suite; Ocean view, small parlor (sitting area) and 2 TVs. Ocean view Approx. 400 sq. feet	JKO	EXT	$ 269.99
6. Jr. Suite Ocean view, small parlor (sitting area) and 2 TVs. Ocean view Approx. 400 sq. feet	JDDO	EXT	$ 269.99
7. Grand Suite; large parlor area, 2 TVs. Ocean view, Approx. 600 sq. feet	GKO	EXT	$ 369.99
8. Grand Suite; large parlor area, 2 TVs. Ocean view, Approx. 600 sq. feet	GDDO	EXT	$ 369.99
9. Grand Suite; large parlor area, 2 TVs. Ocean view, Approx. 600 sq. feet VIP Floor	GKOV	EXT	$ 409.99
10. Grand Suite; large parlor area, 2 TVs. Ocean view, Approx. 600 sq. feet VIP Floor	GDDOV	EXT	$ 409.99

These examples of non–rack room sales are presented simply to illustrate three important price management concepts:

1. Non–rack room rates and the codes required to identify them can be developed any time the RM seeks to implement one or more of the following price differentiation strategies you learned about in Chapter 4:

- Customer characteristic
- Location
- Time
- Quantity
- Distribution channel
- Product versioning
- Bundling
- Payment terms

2. *Uniformity in the number of unique prices across rate codes need not be maintained.* Recall that the rack rate code in this sample beach hotel consisted of six unique prices, while the EXT code consisted of five unique prices.

3. *Room rates (prices) identified by unique rate codes must be easily understood by employees.* They must be easily explainable to room buyers, and, if required, they must be defendable to other guests who become aware of the rates paid by their fellow travelers.

In some hotels, RMs and their revenue management teams have created dozens of rate codes resulting in hundreds of room rates. Unfortunately, that is easy to do for a variety of reasons. The creation of some rate codes will be mandated by a hotel's franchisor. For example, the rate code "AAA" identifies special room rates offered to members of the American Automobile Association. The use of this rate code is mandatory for franchisees in several hotel chains. It is important to note that while the use of a specific rate code may be mandatory, the rates (prices) associated with that rate code are determined by the owners of a hotel via their RMs, *not* by the hotel's franchisor. In other cases, unique room codes offering selected "percent off" rates may be mandated. Thus, for example, a chain may require its franchisees to offer a special "10 percent off rack rate" to members of the American Association of Retired Persons (AARP).

In other cases, room buyers who have developed contracted or negotiated rates with a hotel may seek to have a unique rate code identifying their rate loaded into the hotel's reservation system. They do so because the unique rate code eases their own ability to identify room availability and to book (reserve) rooms at that rate. In hotels with large numbers of negotiated rates, this results in a large number of unique rate codes.

To identify special products, RMs may create their own rate codes. Hotels should, of course, create only the unique rate codes that make the most sense for their own operations. Thus, for example, a hotel in Orlando, Florida, may create a package rate that includes a guest room and tickets to local Disney attractions. Such a package, could, in this scenario sell for a price identified by the rate code "DSNY" (Disney). If the hotel offered multiple room types, the DSNY rate code would be programmed in the PMS to identify the varying rates to be paid for each room type offered for sale with this package. This same DSNY rate code would not, of course, be used by a hotel located in New Mexico. That hotel would, however, develop its own appropriate rate codes.

For many lodging industry RMs, the following groups represent market segments that are generally large enough to justify the development of unique rate codes:

- State government employees
- Federal government employees (including military)
- Corporations
- American Automobile Association (AAA) members
- American Association of Retired Persons (AARP) members
- Rates for those booking rooms via the Internet
- Senior citizens
- Weekend travelers
- Package buyers

The list is not exhaustive, but is presented to illustrate the fact that price managers, even in a hotel with a minimal number of rates codes, will find that the number of individual room rates resulting from the use of those rate codes is large indeed. The resulting rates become numerous quickly. If you recognize, for example, that in the beach hotel example (Figure 7.7) the ten room types offered can yield a large number of individual room rates then you understand the sheer number of prices that must be managed. You may also better understand the folly of calculating only one "cost-based rate" that represents what a hotel should charge for its rooms. Note that if the beach hotel in our illustration utilized only ten unique rate codes, each of which resulted in only five unique rates, the RM of that property would, on a daily basis, be managing 50 individual room prices (10 rate codes × 5 unique rates per code = 50 unique prices). If reservations can be made 365 days in advance, the RM in that property is responsible for monitoring a minimum of 18,250 pricing opportunities (365 days × 50 unique prices = 18,250 total prices) each and every day of the coming year. Consider the following:

- The average hotel establishes a different room rate for each of its unique room types.
- The number of rate codes in use (including negotiated rates) at the average hotel will likely number in the dozens or more.
- In seasonal hotels, all rack rates will be adjusted up or down at least one or more times of the year.

Based on that, it is easy to see that RMs typically manage not dozens or even hundreds, but thousands or even hundreds of thousands of unique room prices during any 365-day period. When these prices are changed or modified on a regular basis, the complexity of their management obviously increases. As a result, some RMs feel that the only way they can effectively establish and then manage this number of room prices is via the use of highly advanced and automated revenue optimization programs, and the rationale for this position can be compelling. Despite the huge task of price management, however, the authors simply do not believe the exclusive use of such programs is superior to data analysis and insight on the part of an experienced and talented RM.

Why is that? Recall that in a customer-centric revenue optimization system a price should represent a *buyer's* view of value delivered. Is it truly realistic for RMs to assume that their own buyers' value perceptions of the same room offering change hundreds and thousands of times per year? Or even several times in the same week? The answer is no.

When RMs believe effective price manipulation is dependent on the constant adjustment and readjustment of room rates, those modifications are usually defended as a response to changes in buyer demand for rooms and an effort to maximize short-term revenue. As stated (and restated!) earlier, however, despite its strong economic rationale, that is a tactic that almost always represents an ineffective approach to customer-centric pricing management.

Those RMs who steadfastly insist that continual price manipulation as practiced by some companies in the airline industry represents a desirable price management model for the lodging industry would be well advised to become familiar with Frederick Reicheld, a management researcher whose work relates to the ways companies seek to acquire and maintain a dedicated customer base. His research is published by the Harvard Business

School Press. Arguably the U.S. leader in the study of maintaining customer loyalty, in one of his popular books Reicheld writes, "The pricing game does little to build customer trust or improve convenience. One of the few airlines that has avoided this approach is Southwest, which concluded that the yield management systems are unfair, complicated, and expensive to administer."[15]

With all due respect to the brilliant Mr. Reicheld, the RMs at Southwest *do* practice their own version of yield management, as they should. The number of different fares offered, however, is very small, and the few reasons (restrictions and fences) that account for the differences in fares are clearly communicated to and understood by their customers.

For example, on the day this portion of the text was written, Southwest offered three fares from Chicago to Dallas for a date two months in the future. Their "Business Select" fare was $20.00 higher each way than their "Anytime" fare, but it allowed for priority boarding and one free alcoholic beverage during the flight. The "Wanna Get Away" fare was lower than the "Anytime" fare, but was nonrefundable. Interestingly, this information was easily accessible simply by clicking the "Compare Fare Benefits" button prominently displayed on its web site (www.southwest.com). Astute readers will immediately recognize the product versioning efforts (priority boarding and a free drink) and the erection of a price fence (no refund) by the RMs at Southwest who, in this instance, are clearly practicing forms of differential pricing, the powerful revenue optimization strategy you learned about in Chapter 4.

By contrast, on the same day, one of Southwest's larger competitor's web site listed four different prices for the exact same flight class; with no difference in the product purchased (i.e., identical services offered and ticket purchase restrictions). Interestingly, there was no explanation of why these prices varied. Returning to each airline's web site on the following day, the ticket prices at Southwest remained unchanged, while rates for the other air carrier's flights varied by an average of $2.00, a clear indication that, overnight, the RMs at that company felt the value of their flights had changed. It is most likely, of course, that this minimal price management change was enacted by a computer-generated response to an overnight-updated forecast of buyer demand. The improved accuracy of the forecast is not in doubt, but which pricing approach do you believe best builds customer loyalty?

Perhaps there are two pricing lessons lodging RMs can learn from Southwest. The first is that customers (and employees) must be able to understand a company's prices. The second is that the pursuit of revenue obtained at the expense of frustrating, alienating, or disappointing customers is not a good long-term strategy in any business. Generating this less-than-desirable revenue should never be the goal of a customer-centric RM.

The price management approach implemented by lodging RMs seeking to optimize revenue related to price management of hotel rooms could be summarized as follows:

Strive to sell the maximum number of rooms possible at rack rate. Offer easily explainable and defensible discounted rates as needed to fill rooms; then close out discounts and use appropriate stay restrictions when forecasted demand is strong.

The end result of such an approach has the effect of optimizing revenue (via ADR increase) while minimizing rack rate pricing adjustments. The quality of an RM's decision making regarding the opening and closing of discount room rates can and should be regularly evaluated and will be examined in detail in Chapter 9.

RM IN ACTION 7.2: YOU'RE WITH THE GOVERNMENT AND WE'RE HERE TO HELP YOU

RMs without a strong hotel front office background often underestimate the real difficulties inherent in implementing new rate codes. Consider the hotel RM that seeks to implement a basic "government" rate designed to appeal to this unique market segment. Government room rates are very common and are a good example of price differentiation based on a readily identifiable group.

In this example, the RM chooses an abbreviated rate code (GVT), and establishes appropriate rates for each of the hotel's room types. The rate code is then programmed into the hotel's CRS/PMS. A memo is routed to the hotel's FOM announcing the new rate program. From the RM's perspective, so far, so good.

At the front desk, however, confusion reigns. Some desk clerks are not sure who qualifies for the rate. Clearly, federal government employees seem to qualify. The military is federal, however, so do individuals in the military qualify? How about retired military? Veterans? How about state workers? County?

City? Police? Firemen? Employees hired by the government to do temporary work such as cut grass or paint buildings? How about these employees' families? Can government workers reserve only one room per employee? Two? Ten?

Most importantly, what is to be done with the guests who believe the term "GVT" rate is synonymous with their own governmental agency's per diem? If you have a front desk background, you already know the difficulty. Per diem rates vary by government entity. If you are not sure of the issue, go to www.gsa.gov and click *Per Diem Rates* to see what the *federal* government will reimburse its employees staying in your own area of the country. Is the federal per diem going to equal that applied to state government employees staying in the same area? Maybe, maybe not. Will it be the same for County or City employees? Maybe, but it is pretty unlikely.

Is the confusion directly related to the implementation of this particular rate code unique? Unfortunately, not at all.

Special Event Rates

Even RMs who generally maintain rack rate integrity sometimes change their rack rates temporarily in the face of overwhelmingly strong demand forecasts. Examples of times such **special event** rates make good sense include Mardi Gras, for New Orleans hoteliers; the Indianapolis 500, for Indianapolis, Indiana hoteliers; and the ever-changing, but very crowded, Spring Break locations favored by U.S. college students.

For most RMs, however, special event rates are put in place to coincide with *local*, but for them very major, sporting events, concerts, festivals, graduations, meetings, holidays, and other special occasions that are sure to fill their areas' hotels.

Special event rates make good sense during these high-demand periods because guest willingness to pay will be

Essential RM Term

Special event (rate): An above-rack room rate typically implemented during single day or multiday periods of extremely high demand for rooms. Also referred to by some RMs as a *premium* rate, *premium rack* rate, or *super rack* rate.

increased during these events and as you have learned an RM's job is to match prices with buyer willingness to pay. That is a central theme of this book. That same rationale, however, does not extend to all high-demand situations and at all times.

Few hoteliers would argue, for example, that room rates for Florida residents fleeing a hurricane bearing down on that state should pay triple the hotelier's rack room rates. This should be so despite the fact that the hotels would very likely find plenty of terrified buyers willing and able to pay their tripled rates. It should be pointed out, however, that any hoteliers who would raise their rates to those levels would find themselves subsequently prosecuted by state governmental officials, who themselves believe such inflated rates violate good public policy as well as Florida's consumer protection laws.

In most nonemergency cases, the fact is that RMs are free to establish special event rates at nearly any level of their choosing. What is also true, but too often overlooked, is that unjustifiable special event rates affect more than just the pocketbooks of individual room buyers. To cite just one typical example, consider the mid-sized community's CVB staff who work hard to bring, for the first time, a major special event to their area. The event organizers are pleased with the city, the area hotels, and the promises of hospitality made by the CVB staff in their sales presentations. The hotels are pleased, also. In fact, so pleased are the hotels that some of their RMs, in their euphoria, immediately double room rates for the time period of the special event. The newly initiated special event rate is justified on the basis of the very strong demand forecast for the dates of the just-acquired special event. The reaction of the event organizers to the new rates, of course, is as predictable as it is negative.

In some cases, the use of a special event rate for a specific time period can be warranted. The percentage amount by which the special event rates should exceed a hotel's rack rate, however, is difficult to determine. Some RMs feel that special event rates developed to take advantage of high-demand dates must be very hefty to help make up for the many days of the year in which ADRs are driven down by the large numbers of guests who balk at paying the hotel's normal rack rates. Creating very high special event rates, these RMs reason, can offset the impact of these low-priced buyers and thus help enhance their hotel's overall RevPAR performance. If you carefully consider this rationale, however, you recognize that this strategy actually subsidizes those hotel customers who are not willing to pay rack rate, the rate indicating the value placed on the hotel's rooms by the typical buyer. As well, it penalizes those who are willing to pay full price by extracting an even greater rate premium from them.

Those RMs who argue that it is their duty to the hotel's owners to establish special event rates or to increase rack rates based on *"what the market will bear,"* when in fact the market will bear two or three times rack rate, should also be willing to justify and defend their pricing decisions in terms of being customer-centric. The customer-centric case must be made to both these RMs' external audiences (guests) and their internal audiences (front desk staff). Doing so is not as easy as it looks—and it doesn't look that easy.

The authors fully recognize the fact that many RMs are so conditioned to the legitimacy of a "what the market will bear" pricing philosophy that it is difficult for them to view it objectively. In an effort to try and help them do so, assume you are serving as an advisor to the owner of a hair salon in a small town. The salon has four chairs and normally charges $40.00 to style a young woman's hair. The local high school's senior prom is next month. The salon owner indicates to you that demand for hair style services on the Saturday of the prom will easily be five times that of a normal Saturday. The salon owner believes that if prices are increased to $120.00 per style session the salon's four chairs would still be filled by those young ladies whose families are wealthy enough to be willing and able to pay the increased prices charged on that day. After all, contends the salon owner, the prom is certainly a special event, and thus the salon's clients will understand why the charges on that day need to be increased. My customers, states the salons owner, will readily accept the higher prices as reasonable. The salon owner wants you to develop the explanation of the new pricing that will be shared with the salon's customers as they call for appointments for the Saturday of the prom.

If you are initially at a bit of a loss on how to defend this salon owner's proposed pricing program to its prom-bound customers, you would not be alone.

Some RMs reading this chapter will still take exception with any philosophical approach that seeks to limit the increasing of rack room rates in times of temporary high demand. These RMs would argue that the essence of revenue optimization is the identification of unique market segments seeking to buy a hotel's rooms and the proper pricing of those rooms in response. The difference of opinion might be summarized in the meaning of the term "proper pricing." As with all pricing decisions these should be made from a customer-centric position and with a long-term goal of generating positive, not negative, forms of revenue and of building, not reducing, customer loyalty levels.

It is important to recognize that raising rack rates in direct response to sustained increases in guest demand is a perfectly legitimate customer-centric strategy because it is guest driven and reflects an increase in the number of guests willing to purchase rooms and, as a result, the prices they will be willing to pay. In such a situation guest are telling you your rooms are worth more. The best RMs also recognize, however, that selling the exact

▶ RM ON THE WEB 7.3

The sophistication of group rooms buyers continues to increase. That is certainly having an effect on RMs' price management decision making. To see just one example of how this is occurring, go to www.realtor.org

When you arrive click on "Meetings and Expo." Then click on "Hotel rates."

What you will find on the site is a listing of room rates approved for use by members of the National Realtors Association. Note that the association lists a maximum that can be charged to its members during their annual meeting. Hotels hoping to capture part of this market are, of course, free to charge what they wish but they must also be prepared to defend their rates if they are higher than the ones listed on the association's web site.

It is clear that sophisticated buyers increasingly do understand hotel room pricing. Those RMs who price hotel rooms increasingly need to understand their buyers.

Essential RM Term

Stay restrictions: Duration rules and limitations related to guests' arrival dates, departure dates, and minimum stay lengths. Also known as *stay controls.*

same product at higher prices due solely to temporarily increased consumer demand is almost always a bad idea. Instead, these RMs take advantage of periods of higher demand to *enhance* their product offerings, thereby giving room buyers more products and/or services than they would normally receive—at justifiably higher room prices.

This is a price management strategy that can be appreciated and well-understood by room buyers and a hotel's employees, as well as one fully endorsed by the authors. But the very best RMs know that in periods where forecasted demand is extremely high, the selection and implementation of appropriate **stay restrictions** is a much better method of optimizing revenues than are the implementation of excessively high special event rates.

STAY RESTRICTIONS

If rack rates should only be increased in response to sustained increases in demand, if discounts should be offered to specific market segments, and if special events should not be used as an excuse to inflate rack rates, how can talented RMs optimize revenues via the combination of inventory and price management? The answer in most cases involves the implementation of well-planned stay restrictions.

To better understand how RMs use stay restrictions to optimize revenue, consider the lodging industry RM working in a 300-room property. On a weekend that is 30 days out (into the future), that RM analyzes the data in the hotel's PMS and calculates the hotel's available rooms inventory as shown in Figure 7.10.

In this case, demand for rooms is very strong on Saturday night, is weaker on Friday, and is much weaker on Sunday. Some RMs would undoubtedly raise the rates on the 45 remaining Saturday night rooms. A more experienced RM would implement a stay restriction. This is done by identifying Saturday as a day that has a minimum length of stay (MLOS) attached to it or, alternatively, by designating Saturday as a day that is **CTA**.

Essential RM Term

CTA: Short for *closed to arrival.* A date on which guests are not permitted to *begin* their hotel stays.

In this situation the hotel's RM does not inflate room prices but, rather, identifies Saturday as a day that will have a MLOS of two days attached to it. As a result, only reservations from guests requesting arrival on Saturday with the intention of staying for two (or more) days are accepted. Those guests requesting a reservation for a one-night stay with arrival on Saturday night will be denied their reservations. By managing the length of stay required for a Saturday arrival, the RM optimizes revenue by selling only to potential guests who seek to purchase two room nights (Saturday and Sunday or Friday and Saturday).

Figure 7.10	Forecasted Room Availability: 300-Room Hotel		
	Friday	**Saturday**	**Sunday**
Rooms Available to Sell	180	45	250

In this scenario, the hotel has only 45 rooms remaining to be sold on Saturday night. The RM has made this inventory/pricing decision based on the belief that although the proportion of potential guests who want to stay two nights is significantly smaller than those who merely want one night, it is large enough to allow the hotel to sell all of its remaining Saturday rooms only to those guest staying two or more nights. An alternative stay restriction strategy of designating Saturday as a CTA day would deny reservations for Saturday arriving guests in favor of those arriving Friday and planning to stay two or more days.

Some RMs who frequently utilize a MLOS strategy employ a CTA strategy only rarely because, as they point out, the hotel (as in this example) that implements a CTA approach could run the risk of denying a reservation to a guest who may have wished to arrive on Saturday and stay 30 (or more!) days. In most cases, of course, the hotel would want to accept such a reservation—however, a rigid CTA strategy would prevent it.

MLOS, CTA, maximum length of stay, and other stay restrictions, in addition to payment related restrictions, can all be applied as revenue optimization strategies. To see how such restrictions can be combined to be of even more effect, consider the following price quote obtained (online)[16] from the South Bend, Indiana, Marriott on the extremely high-demand day that occurs when the University of Notre Dame plays its home football game against the University of Michigan. On a normal day, rooms at this hotel sell for approximately $199.00 per night. Special event prices, stay, and rate restrictions have been bolded by the authors to make them more easily identifiable.

Note how the RMs at this Marriott combine enhanced product offerings (a welcome reception and a free program), a special event rate, stay restrictions, and payment restrictions to maximize the revenue received for the room products they will sell on this very busy weekend. Even in a unionized situation where service levels may not easily be enhanced without negotiations, creative RMs like those in South Bend can devise product enhancements to delight their guests.

The question of when it is best to maintain rack rates, offer discounts, or use a stay, rate, or payment restriction is one that should be subject to open discussion among members of a hotel's revenue management team. This is because in most cases, the actual rooms demand

---

Marriot Hotel: South Bend, Indiana
Date: Notre Dame vs. Michigan (football)

Marriott.com $469.00 king or double; $60.97 estimated taxes

Total **$539.97** per night

Conditions applied to room (Note: inserted from Marriott web site)

Rate includes*

OVERNIGHT ACCOMMODATIONS—**FR & SA NT STAY REQUIRED**

WELCOME RECEPTION IN THE LOBBY

COMPLIMENTARY FOOTBALL PROGRAM

A FULL ADVANCE DEPOSIT IS DUE FOR ALL NIGHTS 30 DAYS BEFORE

ARRIVAL. DEPOSIT WILL BE CHARGED BY HOTEL 30 DAYS BEFORE ARRIVAL

THE DEPOSIT IS NON-REFUNDABLE AFTER THE 30 DAY CUT OFF DATE

IF A RESERVATION IS CHANGED FROM A 2 NIGHT STAY TO A 1 NIGHT STAY, NO REFUND WILL BE MADE AT ANY TIME

ARRIVAL TIME IS 3PM—NO EARLY ARRIVALS

3 ROOMS PER GUEST LIMIT

RM IN ACTION 7.3: PRICE MANAGEMENT . . . AFTER THE FACT

What if a hotel sells all of its rooms inventory but subsequently finds that demand for the sold-out dates is so strong that ADRs were not optimized and a great deal more revenue could have been generated had room rates been increased or restrictions implemented? It does happen. The following news release examines what happened during the National High School Rodeo finals. Demand for rooms was exceptionally strong. In the small county hosting the event, 10,000 extra people sought hotel rooms. Guests who made reservations early and at rates that were normal were surprised upon arrival to find that the rates they would be charged for their rooms had been increased significantly. The result?

Hotel Chains Investigate Alleged Price Gouging

Some guests were charged hundreds more than what they were told they would pay when making reservations months before the rodeo. Hotel managers of (the local) Days Inn and Rodeway Inn said prices were increased to make money amid soaring demand for rooms.

One guest from Idaho reported that he was charged $231 more per day than the rate originally quoted. He would have paid more when he reserved the room earlier in the year he was quoted as saying, *"but hotels shouldn't jack rates up and gouge."* Not surprisingly, the franchisors of the Days Inn and Rodeway brands announced they would investigate the actions of the local hotels.

RMs must recognize that a confirmed room reservation taken at a confirmed rate constitutes a legal contract. Efforts to change the terms of the contract "after the fact" will undoubtedly, and rightly so, be met by strong negative reactions from guests and from a hotel's franchisor.

Excerpted on 8/1/2008 from www.hotel-online.com/News/2008 _Jul_31/k.FJH.1217521805.html.

for a date or set of dates is not clearly known, but instead must be estimated in a forecast. This is especially true when one-time or first-time events held in an area are projected to strongly affect local room demand but the extent of the impact is unknown.

PRINCIPLES OF INVENTORY AND PRICE MANAGEMENT

It is not surprising that it is challenging to develop a set of inventory and price-management principles that would be applicable to all hotel RMs. Hotels are different, their markets are different, and the operating philosophies of their owners vary greatly. Despite those limitations there are some guiding principles that can help direct an RM's inventory and price management decision making. With the intent of stimulating discussion, but admittedly at the risk of inviting the ire of those RMs who see things differently and in the spirit of asking readers to think with us, not like us, the following 12 principles are presented as a guide to those RMs who can forecast well and who are committed to implementing customer-centric revenue optimization programs in their own properties.

12 Principles of Inventory and Price Management

1. Maximize the number of logical room codes utilized in the property, minimize the number of rate codes utilized.

2. Carefully monitor and minimize errors resulting from communication gaps between the property and its intermediary sales partners that can affect room inventories.

3. Institute an aggressive upon-arrival upsell program.

4. Carefully and continually monitor the impact of group contracts and contracted rooms on inventory levels.

5. Avoid intentional overbooking; use payment restrictions (e.g. non-fundable advanced payment) to ensure sell-outs on high-demand dates.

6. Establish rack room rate based on *buyer* behavior, and always (e.g. never close out) the rack rate.

7. Utilize sound differential pricing strategies to create multiple, but easily defensible, rack rate discounts.

8. If special event rates are utilized, increase via product and service enhancements the value offered to guests to help justify the higher rates internally and externally.

9. Close out discount rates aggressively and institute appropriate stay restrictions when forecasted demand is very strong.

10. Implement and maintain effective training programs to ensure staff understand and can explain to guests the meanings of all room and rate codes.

11. Drive rates up by continually monitoring the appropriateness of rack rate levels via competitive set analysis (a procedure you will learn to do in Chapter 9).

12. Minimize channel distribution costs to maximize GOPPAR.

It is easy to see that principles 1–11 flow rationally from what you have learned in this chapter. The last principle, however, is one of great importance to RMs. In fact, distribution channel management is so critical to the optimization of GOPPAR, and thus a hotel's profitability, that the entire next chapter will be devoted to this crucial topic.

❖ ESSENTIAL RM TERMS

Rooms inventory	Real time (inventory update)
DD room	Interfaced
Close out	Third-party resellers
Room code	Upsell
Concierge floor	Top-down (selling)
Executive housekeeper	Bottom-up (selling)
Upgrade	Attrition
Bed configuration	Cut-off date

Group history

Peak night

Host hotel

Contract rate (room)

Negotiated rate (room)

Run of the house

Last room available

Blackout date

Walk(ed)

Act utilitarian

Guaranteed reservation

Social network (online)

Price management

Rate code

Special event (rate)

Stay restrictions

CTA

▐▐▐▶ APPLY WHAT YOU KNOW

1. Sherri Lamar is the RM at the 200-room Kingston Harbor Inn. The Inn has five different room types, each with a rack rate that reflects its guests' view of each room type's value. Sherri knows she cannot upsell guests who stay in her highest rated rooms; however, she feels there is good potential to impact her hotel's revenue performance via upsells to guests who originally reserved one of the four lower-priced room types. Sherri created and implemented a comprehensive upsell training program for her hotel's front desk. The cost of providing the upsell training to the Inn's eight desk staff was $100.00 per employee. At the end of the first week of the program's implementation, Sherri found that her clerks were successful at upselling approximately one of every ten guests arriving at the hotel. A summary of the Inn's guest reservation/actual stay records is displayed here. Complete the summary for her and then provide Sherri with answers she needs for the questions that follow.

Kingston Harbor Inn Upsell Results: Week 1

Room Type	Rack Rate	Nights Reserved	Reserved Revenue	Actual Night Usage	Actual Revenue
Superior Parlor Suite	$ 299.99	75		75	
Parlor Suite	$ 249.99	100		110	
Jr. Parlor Suite	$ 219.99	125		140	
Deluxe	$ 159.99	250		275	
Standard	$ 109.99	450		400	
Total Nights		**1000**		**1000**	
Total Revenue					
ADR					
RevPAR					

Based on Sherri's first week data:

A. What would the Inn's ADR have been if all arriving guests had been assigned to their originally reserved rooms?

B. What was the ADR actually achieved by the Inn as the result of the upsell program?

C. What would the Inn's revenue have been if all arriving guests had been assigned to their originally reserved rooms?

D. What was the revenue actually achieved by the Inn as the result of the upsell program?

E. What was the amount of the increased revenue that resulted from Sherri's upsell program?

F. What was the percent increase (rounded to one decimal place) in revenue achieved by the Inn as a result of the program?

G. Assume this first week represents the typical week for the upsell program. What would the hotel's 52-week revenue increase be as the result of implementing it?

2. Poco Miller is the RM at the Hampton Inn. Mark is the property's FOM and Latisha is the DOSM. All three serve on the hotel's RM committee. The hotel has 175 rooms. Next month the hotel will serve as the host hotel for the Retired Firefighters Association. The Association originally blocked 90 rooms per night for Thursday, Friday, and Saturday nights at a rate of $99.00 per night. All the rooms in their block have been picked up. The current rooms availability forecast for the three days of the meeting is as follows:

Date:	Thursday	Friday	Saturday
Reserved			
Firefighters' rooms @ $ 99.00/night	90	90	90
All Other rooms @ $149.99/night	55	35	45
Total Reserved	145	125	135
Total Rooms Available	30	50	40

The group has requested that Latisha add 20 rooms each night to its block at the originally contracted rate of $99.00. It states that its members will use all of the additional rooms if they are made available, but if not, they will move their remaining 20 attendees down the street to the Comfort Inn. Latisha is in favor of increasing the block and keeping the group together. Mark is opposed. He is convinced he can sell 20 more rooms on Thursday, 40 rooms on Friday, and 30 rooms on Saturday at the normal rack rate of $149.99. Under his plan, he states, "The hotel can maximize its ADR."

Based on Mark's estimate of future sales to be made at rack rate, Poco knows the hotel will sell out and maximize its occupancy percentage under Latisha's plan. Help Poco analyze the data she needs to answers the questions that follow by filling in the chart.

	Under Latisha's Plan	Under Mark's Plan
Rooms sold		
Group revenue		
Transient revenue		
Total revenue		
Occupancy %		
ADR		
RevPAR		

    A. What would the hotel's ADR be under Mark's plan?

    B. What would the hotel's RevPAR be under Mark's plan?

    C. What would the hotel's ADR be under Latisha's plan?

    D. What would the hotel's RevPAR be under Latisha's plan?

    E. Who's plan would you advise Poco to support? Explain your rationale.

3. Tonya Stephani is the front office manager/RM at the 200-room Hilton Garden hotel. Tonight, she has 100 stay-over rooms and 100 arrivals. Based on her own forecasts, she anticipates 10 no-shows tonight. The average rate to be paid by each arriving guest is $199.99. Tonya has a signed agreement with the local Sheraton hotel that states each property is willing (subject to blackout dates) to accept the other's walks at the rate of $99.00 per night.

   Tonight, the Sheraton has available rooms and has agreed to take up to ten walked guests. The cost of transporting guests to the Sheraton and back, as well as other walk-related costs incurred by the Hilton, average $15.00 per room. Assume Tonya decides to overbook by ten rooms.

   A. Excluding any potential no-show billings, how much extra room revenue will be gained from overbooking if Tonya indeed experiences ten no-shows but overbooks by ten rooms and thus achieves a 100 percent occupancy? _____

   B. How much extra cost will the hotel incur if it sells out, but ultimately walks:

       1 guest? _____

       5 guests? _____

       10 guests? _____

   C. In addition to added room revenue and potential costs, what are at least three other factors Tonya should consider as she makes this overbook/no-overbook decision for her hotel?

4. Due to a weak local economy, business is slow at the Haymen House, a 300-room property owned by the Haymen family. Last month's ADR was $159.00. Occupancy was 58.5 percent—down from the prior year's same month occupancy of 65 percent. Bill Zollars, RM for the Haymen House, and Rebecca Mornay, the hotel's GM, forecast that this month's occupancy will also be approximately 58.5 percent and at the same ADR.

"We're down six and half occupancy points from last year! That's a 10 percent decline. We need to cut prices so we can fill these rooms," says Andrew Haymen. "If we increase our discounts, I think we can shoot for a $139.00 ADR, sell more rooms, and get our revenue back up to where in needs to be."

Assume Mr. Haymen mandates his new rate strategy and that he is correct in his prediction that the next month's overall ADR is $139.00.

A. What would be the percentage decrease in ADR experienced by the Hayman House?

B. Assume that this month and last month each contained 30 days. How many total rooms would have to be sold at an ADR of $139.00 to equal the rooms revenue achieved last month?

C. What would be the percentage increase in occupancy required to equalize the rooms revenue achieved last month?

D. Why does a 10 percent decrease in ADR require more than a 10 percent increase in occupancy percentage to equalize room revenue?

E. What additional factors would you suggest Bill and Rebecca might mention to this owner as they discuss the advisability of his proposed pricing strategy?

5. Josiah Prentiss is the VP of RM for the ten-unit Mahler's Hotel Management Company. Mahler's has contracts with various hotel owners to operate the hotels. The properties are flagged with brand managed by three different franchisors (Marriott, Hilton, and Choice). Josiah has been approached by a salesperson for *Revenue Concepts Inc.*, a company that has developed revenue optimization software that it promises will:

■ Accurately forecast business demand

■ Manage rooms inventory

■ Improve control over group business

■ Determine the correct pricing for hotel rooms

■ Manage and control distribution channels

Assume you were Josiah:

A. What connectivity/communications issues would be important for you to discuss with *Revenue Concepts Inc.?*

B. What training and support issues would be important for you to discuss with it?

C. Are there pricing philosophy-related issues you feel would be important to discuss?

KEY CONCEPT CASE STUDY

"Let me make sure I understand this. You want to set the rates for the third week in October at full rack, close out all discounts, and immediately block any inventory we are not contractually obligated to provide our discount intermediaries," said Amanda, the front office manager at the Barcena Resort.

"That's right," said Pam, the resort's DOSM. "We really have to. The bid I just submitted to the International Association of Academic Authors for their annual meeting in October was at full rack rate for all our currently available rooms."

"That event will sell out our entire area," said Damario. "We certainly don't want to offer transient rates lower than our group rates for that week."

Amanda and Pam were members of the Barcena Resort's *Strategic Pricing and Revenue Management Advisory Committee,* which was headed by Damario. They were finishing the last agenda item for the week's meeting. It concerned a group rooms bid submitted by Pam's department as part of an area-wide effort coordinated by the local Tourism Development Bureau. The Bureau was the entity charged with the task of generating sales leads, primarily for group and meetings business, for all of the hotels in the area. Pam had submitted her bid through the Bureau and had appealed to Damario not to let the hotel advertise low room rates during the period of the projected convention. "If we do," said Pam, "the academics will book outside the group block and we'll never hit the occupancy targets we can make if the group accepts our bid.

"Do you feel you have a good chance to get it?" Damario had asked.

"We have an excellent change. I would say 90 percent or more," Pam had replied.

"When will we know?" Damario asked.

"The group will be making its decision in the next 90 days," Pam had replied.

Based on Pam's confidence about the bid, Damario supported the approach that, for the next 90 days, the hotel would eliminate all discounted rates for the time period of the Author's convention and remove all rooms from sale.

Amanda was not happy with the decision.

"Well, I do hope we get the bid," said Amanda, "because if we close all our discount rates for 90 days, shut down all our room sales, and then we don't get the bid, this hotel will be empty the third week in October. That's all I have to say!"

For Your Consideration

1. Why do you believe Amanda is concerned about the elimination of discount rates during the period of this convention?

2. Assume the tactic proposed by Damario is implemented. What will be the likely outcome if Pam's bid is accepted by the Author's group?

3. Assume the tactic proposed by Damario is implemented. What will be the likely outcome if Pam's bid is rejected by the Author's group?

4. What are the dangers to the future success of this revenue management team if Amanda is not brought "on board" with the decision made by Damario and Pam? Whose job is it to see that Amanda and her entire front office team actively support the final decision?

ENDNOTES

1. http://www.quoteland.com/topic. asp?CATEGORY_ID=378. Retrieved 8/8/2008.

2. http://www.caterersearch.com/ Articles/2006/11/02/309801/overbooking-a-balancing-act-for-the-budget-chains.html. Retrieved 8/13/08.

3. http://en.wikipedia.org/wiki/Lucius_Calpurnius_Piso_Caesoninus. Retrieved 8/15/2008.

4. http://thinkexist.com/quotations/thinking/. Retrieved 10/15/2008.

5. http://www.eturbonews.com/226/airline039s-true-crisis-loss-reputation-warn-public-relations-experts. Retrieved 8/18/2008.

6. Warren Buffett (http://www.squarewheels.com/content/busquotes.html). Retrieved 8/18/2008.

7. For a thorough presentation of the calculations required to compute these and other well-known room rate formulas, see Lea Dopson and David Hayes, *Managerial Accounting for the Hospitality Industry* (Hoboken, NJ: John Wiley and Sons, 2010).

8. See Donald E. Lundberg, *The Hotel and Restaurant Business*, 4th. ed. (New York: Van Nostrand Reinhold, 1989).

9. Robert L. Phillips, *Pricing and Revenue Optimization* (Stanford Business Books, 2005).

10. A comparative revenue analysis of hotel yield management heuristics: http://findarticles.com/p/articles/mi_qa3713/is_199901/ai_n8828483. Retrieved 8/18/2008.

11. A comparative revenue analysis of hotel yield management heuristics: http://findarticles.com/p/articles/mi_qa3713/is_199901/ai_n8828483. Retrieved 8/18/2008.

12. Raymond S. Schmidgall, *Hospitality Industry Managerial Accounting*, 5th. ed. (The Educational Institute of the American Hotel and Lodging Association, 2002), 374.

13. http://www.caterersearch.com/ Articles/2001/07/26/19931/playing-the-yield.html. Retrieved 8/18/2008.

14. http://money.cnn.com/2009/08/21/pf/starwood_stock_analysts.fortune/index.htm. Retrieved 9/1/2009.

15. Frederick Reicheld, *The Loyalty Effect: The Hidden Force Behind Growth, Profits, and Lasting Value* (Cambridge, MA: Harvard Business School Press, 2001), 144.

16. www.marriott.com. Retrieved 8/17/2008.

CHAPTER 8

Distribution Channel Management

CHAPTER OUTLINE

CHAPTER HIGHLIGHTS

1. Explanation of how distribution channels affect revenue optimization.

2. Details about the way lodging industry RMs manage non-electronic distribution channels.

3. Details about the way lodging industry RMs manage electronic distribution channels.

MANAGING DISTRIBUTION CHANNELS

In previous chapters you learned how to assess rooms inventory availability and how to use differential pricing to establish appropriate rack room rates based on market segmentation. Market segmentation is the process of dividing your market into distinct subsets or segments, which will respond positively to the value propositions presented via your differential pricing strategies. This process leads to consumer targeting and the selection of distribution channels that best deliver your price/value proposition to your target market. As a result, it is possible to communicate full rack rate or even special event rates to those segments that are less sensitive to price while offering discounted prices to those segments with lower willingness to pay.

If you strategically manage the availability of rooms inventory allotted to each channel used to help sell your rooms, it is possible to increase your revenue exponentially. Distribution channel management is the process by which RMs target customers by promoting room sales among their various selling alternatives and, as a result, optimize revenues.

In Chapter 1 you read that a distribution channel is a source of business customers or a vehicle used to communicate with a source of customers. In a perfect world, there would be no need for hoteliers to read an entire chapter about distribution channel management. RMs would simply determine their available rooms inventory level, establish appropriate prices for those rooms, and then accept guests as they walked into the hotel to purchase their rooms. An analogous situation would be that of a theater owner who determines that a single movie will be shown one time each day. The owner would simply count the number of seats in the theater, establish appropriate ticket prices, and then open the box office for movie-goers on a first-come, first-serve basis. Life would be simple. Unfortunately for RMs in the hospitality industry, Henry David Thoreau's admonishment to *"Simplify, Simplify!"*[1] is simply not possible when it comes to distribution channel management.

To better understand why distribution channel management is so complex, assume that the previously mentioned theater owner offered movie-goers a choice of seat types when buying their tickets. Very luxurious seats in the theater sell for more than the more modest seats. Seats closer to the screen sell for more than those further away. In fact, in this theater there could be a large number of different seat types available for sale. Once the theater has been built and opened, however, the seat types and number of each seat cannot be changed. In a hotel setting, room type is analogous to this theater owner's seat type.

Assume that, on any given day, the theater owner is willing to sell tickets for any movie to be shown not just today, but any day in the coming year. To maximize attendance in the coming year, some tickets are sold at a discount to selected buyers. For example, on some days, senior citizens are allowed to pay a lower price for tickets than are other moviegoers. Teens might get discounts some days, but not others. The same could be true for families or couples.

The reasons for the discounts and the number of discounted tickets offered for sale would likely vary based on the date the movie is showing and the estimated popularity of the movie. This is so because some movie-going times and days are more popular than others, and movies starring popular actors and actresses are predicted to be more popular than others. Offering discounted tickets on days of high demand would not maximize potential revenue. If, however, certain movies were predicted to attract fewer movie goers, the theater owner may reason that the number of discounted tickets available for those shows should be increased. Given the assumptions presented, it is easy to see that this theater owner will need to be diligent if he or she is to effectively manage ticket availability and pricing for each day of the coming year.

Now, however, assume that in an effort to maximize ticket sales, the theater owner decided to open multiple box offices across the country. Each new box office would initially be allotted a certain number of tickets for each of the movies to be shown in the coming year. In the typical case, once all tickets allotted to one of the external box offices were sold, no more would be available for sale from that specific location. As it turns out, however, at some locations all allotted tickets would be sold, but some movie-goers are still lined up to buy tickets. In such cases, the theater owner might decide it was a good idea to take unsold tickets from another external box office and permit those tickets to be offered for sale in the sold-out location. Recall that not all tickets in this example are identical. Thus, for example, one box office might have sold out all higher-priced tickets while still offering for sale its allocation of lower-priced tickets. Similarly, another external location might have sold its initial allocation of lower-priced tickets, but still have higher-priced tickets available.

Add to the complexity of the scenario the fact that some of the remote box offices could be owned and managed by our theater's owner, but others would not be. In fact, some of these independently operated box offices will even sell tickets for other movie theaters, including ones that directly compete with ours. To compensate them for their efforts, assume the theater owner lets each independently operated box office retain a percentage of the ticket's actual selling price. These percentages, however, vary based on the number of tickets sold and the amount collected. Finally, assume that the majority of the external box offices are honest and well-managed, but some are not. If you assume each external box office is analogous to a distribution channel used by a hotel, you better understand the daunting task of optimizing hotel revenue via multiple channels of distribution.

There's more. In this scenario, it would not be unusual for additional complications to arise. Some of these relate to the fact that inevitably, a few box offices will sell all of their ticket allocation quickly and demand more for their customers. Others may not sell any of their allocation. In the case of extremely popular movies, the theater owner may decide to sell all available tickets internally. If you assume tickets can be sold 24/7 in most of the box offices, the constant information exchange necessary to ensure the maximum number of seats are sold, but not oversold, each day is evident.

Our theater owner will face still more challenges to revenue optimization. For example, it may be that the sold-out seats at a specific box office location are among the theater's least expensive; however, at that same box office, higher-priced seat types are still available. Should these seats be offered for sale at the lower price to that site's remaining customers? If so, how many should be offered? Should they sell at full or discounted prices? In addition, consider that our experienced theater owner knows that in some cases, those who have purchased tickets will not actually arrive on the day of the movie to claim their seats. This fact allows the owner, if desired, to sell more tickets than there are seats in the theater. Of course, there is some risk to this practice, so the owner knows it must be monitored carefully and on a day-by-day basis.

Now that you better understand the business model, assume that this theater owner— who is offering a variety of seat types for each of the next 365 day's movies, at literally hundreds of different ticket prices, utilizing dozens of differently operated box offices, asks you to "manage" the ticket sale process with a goal of optimizing the theater's ticket income. If you hesitate a bit prior to taking the job, then you appreciate the difficulty of distribution channel management as practiced in the lodging industry, because as an RM, *you* are the theater owner, your theater seats are your hotel rooms, your ticket prices are your room rates and the external box offices are your distribution channels.

Historical Perspective

Two-time Pulitzer Prize winner and Presidential Medal of Freedom recipient David G. McCullough was right when he stated, *History is a guide to navigation in perilous times. History is who we are and why we are the way we are.*[2] RMs seeking to truly understand why we are where we are today in distribution management should recognize that in the very earliest days of the hotel industry, channel distribution management was a nonissue. With no dependable mail service, no telephone, and even no guarantee of the date on which they would safely arrive, pre-eighteenth-century travelers would, at the time of their arrival, utilize the hotel's reception area as the sole means of securing a hotel room. Rates would be communicated in person and full payment collected directly from the rooms buyer.

In the United States, the advent of a governmentally operated mail service was an important milestone in the hospitality industry because, for the first time, guests could use this new distribution channel (dependable mail service) to communicate directly with hotels. Equally importantly, it allowed hotel intermediaries such as travel agents and **travel wholesalers** the ability to contact hotels in advance and book rooms on behalf of their clients.

Prior to the 1970s, the primary distribution channels used by hotels were telegraph, the mail system, and the telephone. Rooms were booked by travel wholesalers, individual travelers, or their travel agents. Communicating a hotel's rooms availability and recording sales through the available channels was slow and labor-intensive.

With the development of commercial airline service in the 1940s and 1950s, it was not surprising that U.S. airline companies developed the same traditional relationships with travel wholesalers and travel agencies as the ones used by hotels. However, these airline companies embraced changing technology faster than most of the hotel industry, and by the end of the 1970s the major airlines provided travel agents the first electronic method for verifying seat availability and making reservations. Called the **global distribution system (GDS)**, the larger airlines recognized that the electronic booking of tickets was more efficient and cost-effective than attempting to do so by the existing distribution channels of telephone, telegraph, or mail.

Advancements in the GDS soon allowed travel agents to book car rentals and hotel room reservations on the same systems. Travel agencies found using the GDS was faster and more cost-effective. They began to insist that all the products they reserved or purchased be available for booking through the GDS. Despite fierce recent competition from the Internet, the GDS still accounts for approximately 20 percent of all hotel rooms booked.

Essential RM Term

Travel wholesaler: A large-volume travel industry intermediary who sells to other, smaller-volume travel intermediaries.

Essential RM Term

Global distribution system (GDS): A group of companies that electronically connect travel-related businesses such as airlines and hotels with those individuals and companies seeking to buy from them.

▶ RM ON THE WEB 8.1

Travel intermediaries such as travel agents have a long history of positive partnering with the hotel industry. Although most airlines have drastically cut or eliminated all commissions paid to these travel advisors, the hotel industry has almost universally continued to pay its historical 10 percent commission to those working in this important distribution channel.

With the advent of the Internet, many industry observers felt the need for travel agents had passed. By 2009, however, CNN was reporting that an increasing number of travel buyers preferred to talk with a real person when buying travel services. According to a study released by Forrester Research, 46 percent of U.S. leisure travelers enjoyed using the Internet to book travel in 2009, down from 53 percent in 2007. Increasingly, travelers were finding that access to pricing information is not the same as access to value information. "What the Internet has done is given us a nation that knows the price of everything and the value of nothing," said Bill Maloney, CEO of the American Society of Travel Agents in the CNN piece.[3]

The development of Turbo Tax tax preparation software did not put accountants out of business. In a similar vein, RMs who ignore the importance of travel agents do so at their hotel's peril because despite the increased consumer use of the Internet, travel agents are still alive, well, and vitally important. To view the Web site of the American Society of Travel Agents (ASTA), the professional organization for those individuals and businesses dedicated to selling travel services, go to www.asta.org.

When you arrive, click *About ASTA*.

In its early development, each airline created its own GDS program. *Sabre* was the name given by American Airlines to its electronic booking system. *Amadeus* was the name selected by the joint GDS effort created by Air France, Lufthansa, Iberia, and SAS airlines. *Apollo* was the name chosen by United Airlines (later merged with the GDS system devised by British Airways, Alitalia, Swiss Air and others, and renamed *Galileo*).

Other airlines such as Eastern, TWA, and Delta also created and named their own electronic reservation systems. Each of these systems was initiated by competitors in the airline business. They were developed independently of each other and were not originally designed to be interfaced. The inevitable result was inefficiency and a significant amount of travel agent confusion as they were required to maintain multiple GDS terminals to monitor availability and rate information. For hoteliers, connecting to the GDS meant each hotel company had to interface its own reservation systems with each of the various airline systems found in the GDS.

Not surprisingly, the airlines were not inclined to allow hotels to have access to their GDS components without paying for it. Large hotel chains had the financial ability to develop information exchange (rate and room availability) systems that interfaced directly with each airline groups' GDS. As a result, these companies paid a GDS fee only when the system was used to make a room reservation at one of their hotels. Independent hotels and smaller hotel companies had to employ specialized entities that would, for a fee, create multiple GDS-interfaced reservations systems and manage the interface—making modifications to rooms inventory and room rates as directed to do so by the individual hotel properties. The result of paying travel agent fees, GDS access fees, and interface management fees reduced the net revenue hoteliers received from each room sold via this growing channel of distribution. Because of these fees, the room rate charged to the guest would not be the same "after expenses" amount actually realized by the hoteliers.

Because of the relatively higher costs associated with processing reservations through the GDS, the hotel industry might not have utilized it heavily had it not been for the travel agents' rapid embracing of it. Faced with an ever-expanding number of GDS companies (by 1998 there were seven) and no viable alternative, 16 of the largest hotel chains decided that if they pooled their resources they could develop a single GDS interface, called a *switch* and by using that single switch could negotiate reduced GDS reservation fees from the airlines. They created a switch and it did reduce the fees. To manage and update the switch each hotel paid a switching fee. This fee was assessed each time the switch was used in making a GDS reservation. As a result, for each reservation made using the GDS, hotels paid three fees—one to the travel agent using the GDS, another to the switching company interfaced with the GDS, and yet another to the GDS operator.

The mid-1990s would see the emergence of the next major distribution channel. In 1994, Hyatt hotels developed an integrated reservation system that utilized the Internet to bypass the GDS and allow the booking of rooms directly with their own central reservation

---

▶ RM ON THE WEB 8.2

The original GDS switch created by hotel companies was called THISCO, short for "The Hotel Industry Switch Company."

Today, Pegasus Solutions is the company that owns and maintains the original lodging industry's GDS switch. At the time of this writing, it connects the three remaining GDS companies (Sabre, Amadeus, and Galileo) to over 86,000 hotels and 63,000 travel agents. If you are a RM in the United States or any one of the 200 countries they service, your hotel is likely using Pegasus Solutions. To learn more about this RM partner, go to www.pegs.com

When you arrive, click *About Us* to read about additional revenue management-related services Pegasus Solutions now offers.

system (CRS). Information about bookings made in Hyatt's CRS was then distributed to its individual hotels. As a result, the hotel industry had its first "non-GDS" electronic reservation system.

In the late 1990s, hotels increasingly explored the option of using the Internet to sell rooms. Those hotels utilizing this new Internet-based distribution channel paid the Internet site's owners an Internet booking fee for making reservations as well as an additional fee simply for the right to have their hotels listed on the web site.

As you have learned, room availability changes every time a reservation is made or canceled. If you have concluded that to be accurate the newly developed Internet booking systems would need to be interfaced with the traditional GDS system, the CRS (if applicable), and a hotel's own PMS, you are correct. If you recognize that this important interface service would not be provided to the hotels for free, you are also correct.

Increasingly, travel agents with access to both the Internet and the GDS preferred using the Internet. As a result, the number of different booking options available on the Internet virtually exploded. In many cases, some of these Internet booking engines and sites were developed by the GDS companies themselves. As a result, the Internet did not spell the end of the GDS, but rather, it added another distribution channel for hoteliers to manage, and of course, additional booking fees to pay.

Essential RM Term

Internet distribution system (IDS): The group of online reservation systems and travel portals that utilize the Internet to connect travel-related businesses such as hotels with those individuals and companies seeking to buy from them.

Today, Internet-based reservation systems are extremely popular with travel professionals and the general public. Collectively, these sites and systems are often referred to as the **Internet distribution system (IDS)**, and they take various forms you will learn more about in this chapter.

Net ADR Yield

Good distribution channels produce room sales for a hotel. The best channels deliver those rooms with high net ADR yields. Traditional travel intermediaries, the GDS, the IDS, and fees that franchisors of franchisee-owned chain hotels pay for use of that brand's CRS all affect net ADR yield.

As you learned in Chapter 4, net ADR yield is the percentage of the normal or standard room rate that is actually realized by a hotel after subtracting from the selling price the cost of fees and assessments associated with the specific distribution channel responsible for a room's sale.

Net Room Rate

$$\frac{\text{Net room rate}}{\text{Standard ADR}} = \text{Net ADR yield}$$

In this formula: Standard ADR − Distribution channel costs = Net room rate

You now recognize that net ADR yield is directly and significantly affected by the distribution channel that delivers a room sale. The potential impact of that difference is illustrated in Figure 8.1 by comparing the selling costs associated with two different distribution channels, each of which has sold 100 rooms.

Note that in this example, a 15 percent variance in net ADR yield results in an 18.75 percent difference [($18,999 − $15,999) ÷ $15,999 = 18.75%] in revenue achieved after accounting for selling costs. Note, too, that this occurred despite the fact that *RevPAR* in both scenarios could very well be identical. These are differences of the type that RMs and their sales colleagues must understand because they are well-known to hotel GMs and to hotel owners.

Of course, it is important for RMs to know the overall ADRs achieved by their properties. It is even more important, however, that RMs know the net ADR yields produced by each of their distribution channels. This is so because the costs related to selling in different channels vary dramatically. As a result, RMs must be especially aware that in addition to the number of rooms sold, it is net ADR yield, *and ADR* that should be considered when evaluating the effect on hotel profitability of any individual distribution channel utilized. Figure 8.2 illustrates the typical fees affecting net ADR yield.

It is an oversimplification to assume that high net ADR yields are always more desirable than lower net ADR yields. This is so because a very low standard or overall ADR with a high net ADR yield can be as undesirable as a higher ADR with a lower net ADR yield. It is for this reason that RMs must recall the importance of GOPPAR. In Chapter 1 you learned the formula for GOPPAR is:

$$\frac{\text{Total revenue} - \text{Management' controllable expense}}{\text{Total rooms available for sale}} = \text{GOPPAR}$$

Figure 8.1   **Effect of Alternative Net ADR Yields on After Selling Costs Revenues**

	Distribution Channel A	Distribution Channel B
Standard ADR	$199.99	$199.99
Selling costs	$10.00	$40.00
Net ADR	$189.99	$159.99
Net ADR yield	95%	80%
Net ADR difference (Channel A vs. B)	+$30.00	−$30.00
After selling costs total net revenue with 100 rooms sold	$18,999.00	$15,999.00
After selling costs net revenue difference % with 100 rooms sold	+18.75%	

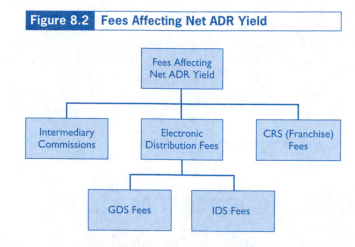

Figure 8.2   Fees Affecting Net ADR Yield

As you have now learned, *profitability* is directly affected by net ADR yield because that reflects how much of its room revenue a hotel gets to keep. As net ADR yields go down, and as ADRs go down, GOPPAR declines as well.

Given the significant fees associated with some channels of distribution, and the negative effects on GOPPAR you may be wondering why RMs utilize these channels at all. Would it not be better for the hotel to avoid franchise-related selling fees by remaining independent and then sell all of its rooms through a no-cost distribution channel, such as to walk-in guests, or through a channel with minimal additional costs, such as a hotel's own group sales department?

In fact, those would be excellent alternatives if the hotel could optimize its revenue by doing so. A select group of hotels can. The reality for most RMs, however, is that they will need to be franchised or otherwise affiliated with a CRS system and use a variety of distribution channels if they seek to maximize room sales. Thus, an assessment of the number of rooms sold via a distribution channel *and* the cost of utilizing the channel must be made. As well, because each distribution channel carries with it its own unique costs, as an effective RM you must consider how repeat buyers originally delivered to your property by low net ADR yield channels might, in the future, be moved from that original channel to one that produces a better net ADR yield at the same or at a higher room rate.

It is important to understand the individual characteristics of various distribution channel alternatives. These alternative channels could be examined in a variety of different ways—including their costs, physical location, ownership, or the amount of control that RMs can exercise over the distribution channel's operation. RMs in the lodging industry would do well to apply the words of American poet Paul Eldrige to the study of distribution channel management. Eldridge is famous for writing, "Reality is merely an illusion, albeit a very persistent one."[4] This is applicable because the *illusion* is that hotels distribute their products through various distribution channels. They do not. The *persistent reality* for RMs in the lodging industry is that, unlike manufacturers, hotels distribute only *information* about their available rooms inventory and the prices charged. The difference is significant.

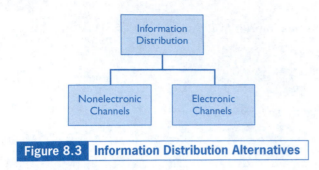

Figure 8.3 | **Information Distribution Alternatives**

Using distribution channels in which your rooms inventory and rate change information can be accurately and instantly updated will assist you in revenue optimization. As a result, it is most meaningful to examine characteristics of distribution channels based on how you will regularly exchange information with them. As shown in Figure 8.3, viewing distribution channels as being either non-electronic, or electronic, is one convenient way to do that.

NONELECTRONIC DISTRIBUTION CHANNELS

Nonelectronic distribution channels are those in which room rate and availability information is delivered to buyers *face-to-face*. Nonelectronic distribution channels tend to be lower cost in terms of fees assessed, and they enhance the accurate exchange of information and provide for easy information updating. To illustrate, consider the walk-in guest. At the time of the guest's arrival, completely up-to-date and accurate room availability information can be verified via use of the PMS. In such a scenario, real-time updated room rates can be quoted and the room sale made quickly and without unnecessary and excessive selling (distribution channel) costs.

In some hotels, nonelectronic channels of distribution supply a very large proportion of the hotel's total revenue. This is so because many hotels serve buyers who make their purchase in person. These buyers experience increased comfort levels when dealing with a bricks and mortar store. Buyers like these place great importance on live communication with a seller. Most hospitality industry observers recognize that in the future, for a variety of reasons, such buyers will likely be reduced in numbers. The trend toward increased electronic booking of rooms may continue to grow. Many enlightened RMs, however, recognize this trend is actually a negative one because it creates physical and emotional distance between the seller and the buyer. Information exchange is reduced. The result, in too many cases, are buyers who *overemphasize* price in their purchase decision. That's not good for a hotel or for the hotel industry.

For this reason, RMs should carefully nurture, not ignore, their nonelectronic distribution channels. For most RMs, this will entail devising and managing revenue optimization programs for the following distinct nonelectronic distribution channels:

- On-property transient sales
- Direct telephone sales
- On-property group sales
- CVBs

On-Property Transient Sales

It is interesting, but unfortunate, that in many hotels those programs designed to optimize future revenue from existing customers are among their weakest and least developed. In some properties sophisticated software programs monitor daily revenue generation from an array of different Internet-based room sellers and resellers. Yet, in many cases, no similar program exists to measure the hotel's effectiveness in converting its already-on-property customers into repeat customers. This is especially unfortunate when you recognize that an important revenue optimization tactic is that of moving repeat guests from higher-cost (low net ADR yield) distribution channels to lower-cost (high net ADR yield) channels.

In today's hotel environment, there is no lower-cost distribution channel than on-property transient room buyers. RMs addressing this channel should recognize that these buyers present two distinct revenue optimization opportunities. One is related to walk-in guests and the other to those guests who are checking out of the hotel.

Walk-ins

Guests arriving at a hotel without a reservation represent the least expensive distribution channel possible. Despite that, a surprising number of RMs do not pay enough attention to them. In fact, the revenue strategy utilized to address these guests is often counterintuitive. As a result, it is ultimately counterproductive. As shown in Figure 8.4, walk-in guests arrive with buyer characteristics that make selling to them easy and beneficial.

Ask any front desk staff member to recount the typical walk-in guest's conversation and this is what they will tell you is the guest's first question: *Do you have rooms available?*

If the answer is yes, the next question is invariably: *How much are they?*

It is the response to this question that differentiates the good from the bad (or even the ugly!) approach to customer-centric revenue management.

Essential RM Term

Fade rate: A lower room rate offered when a potential rooms buyer exhibits initial price resistance.

Walk-in guests seek to buy their rooms for use now. As a result, some RMs mistakenly instruct their front office staff to quote these arriving guests the hotel's full rack rate. If rate resistance is encountered, the staff are authorized to offer the guest one or more **fade rate** alternatives.

In some cases, increasingly lower fade rates are authorized for use until the sale is ultimately made. The philosophy of such hotels is one of, *"Don't let 'em leave"* without making the sale. The rationale for this approach is perceived

Figure 8.4	Characteristics of a Walk-in Guest
Guest Characteristic	**Selling Opportunity**
1. Is on the property	Stops the guest's room search immediately
2. Seeks immediate purchase	Allows the hotel to immediately satisfy the guest's desire to buy
3. Wants a room for use today	Minimizes lost rooms inventory and cancellations
4. Has already experienced part of the hotel (by merely entering the property)	Properly presented, the hotel's fairly priced value offer should be accepted a very high percentage of the time
5. Face-to-face communication exchange is possible	Permits the opportunity to directly match a guest's willingness to pay with product offerings

Essential RM Term

CPOR: Short for "cost per occupied room." The total incremental expense associated with the sale of one guest room. Examples include Amenities CPOR, Housekeeping CPOR and complimentary breakfast CPOR.

to be simple and logical. If rooms are still available for sale late in the day (when walk-in guests typically arrive), such rooms will likely go unsold that day. The walk-in guest may represent the hotel's last chance to sell a vacant room before its revenue potential disappears forever. Because that is true, continues the rationale, a room sale made at any price above the hotel's total **CPOR** represents positive revenue and thus it should be made.

If you have absorbed the lessons presented thus far in this text, you immediately recognize four revenue optimization errors associated with utilizing fade rates:

1. *They undermine the concept that the hotel's rooms have value based on the average customer's value assessment.* It replaces that concept with one that implies the room's value is equal to the price preferred by the individual walk-in guest seeking, of course, to pay the least amount possible.

2. *It requires front office staff training that is unrealistic.* Excluding those lodging facilities consisting of less than 15 rooms, there are approximately 47,135 hotels in the United States. Of those, over 40,000 have 150 rooms or less and are located in suburban areas or small towns.[5] To assume that hotels of such a size employ hourly staff fully prepared to analyze buyer's rate resistance and then skillfully negotiate price with buyers is naïve on the part of the hotel chain RMs who promote such tactics.

   It is also naïve on the part of the RMs who embrace the tactics. In most smaller (and many larger) properties, the front office staff will simply avoid confrontation by *initially* quoting the lowest authorized fade rate.

3. *It miscalculates costs.* The true cost of selling a room at a too-low fade rate is not its CPOR expense total or even damage to net ADR yield. Rather, it is the long-term damage to pricing that inevitably results when front office staff realizes management does not hold firm to the notion that the room products being sold are truly worth their asking price. These staff will retain that negative lesson.

4. *Ultimately, it seeks to establish price based only on what is best for the seller* — a strategy that you have seen does not achieve long-term revenue optimization success.

The better approach to walk-in rooms sales is one that builds RevPAR and is customer-centric. To implement such an approach, RMs can take five steps:

1. *Establish a "last-minute traveler" (walk-in) rate code appropriate for the day.* The rate, like all discounted rates, would be a discount from rack rate. It should be established for each day and thus would likely vary. For example, it may be 10 percent off rack on some days and 20 percent on others based on rooms availability and forecasted volume. Additional offer restrictions justifying the price differentiation should be communicated to staff. These may include on-site purchase only, no advance purchase and limited to "day of arrival" sales only. RMs should also ensure these differentiating characteristics are easily explained to guests by staff and are defensible to other guests.

2. *Where possible, offer alternative product versions.* This is the tactic of varying the form of the product to give reason for variance in price. This helps accommodate budget-minded rooms buyers because they inherently recognize less desired rooms justify reduced rates while higher-valued rooms justify higher prices.

3. *Train staff to explain, in detail, why the initial rate quoted represents true value to the buyer.* Emphasize room features and benefits. Make employees proud of what they sell and the rates at which their rooms are sold.

4. *Maintain the integrity of the last-minute traveler rate.* It should not be reduced despite any walk-in rate resistance exhibited by the guests. Hotel staff should be authorized to vary price only by varying room type and restrictions.

5. *Pleasantly provide unwilling buyers (those who maintain the quoted rate is still too high) alternatives.* Offer the name and travel directions to alternative lodging facilities that better fit within those travelers' budgets.

Some RMs would object to this approach. They maintain it could easily result in losing a sale to a competitor. Worse, they would maintain, it would actually mean assisting customers in buying from a competitor.

There are two reasonable responses to such a concern. The first would be for these RMs to view *Miracle on 34th Street*, the 1947 Christmas movie. In the movie, Kris Kringle (the *real* Santa Clause) is hired by Macy's flagship New York department store, located on 34th Street at Herald Square, to play Santa Clause. Ignoring his boss's instructions, Kris tells one woman shopper to go to another store (Schoenfeld's) for a fire engine for her son. She is so impressed by Kris's referral that she tells the head of Macy's toy department that she will forever be a loyal Macy's customer. Kris later informs another mother that Gimbels—Macy's archrival—has ice skates that would better fit her child's needs. Word of the referral program causes so much positive publicity that Macy's expands on the marketing concept. The message of the importance of customer-centric revenue management is not lost on Gimbels. To avoid looking greedy by comparison, that chain implements the same referral policy. Ultimately, Mr. Macy and Mr. Gimbel shake hands and smile. The story has a happy ending and the business-related lesson is the winners are clearly the customers, as well as the stores.

The second response, for nonmovie buffs, or perhaps hard-nosed realists still convinced that competitors are to be feared or fought, comes from the single most successful hospitality executive in the history of the industry. Ray Kroc, founder of McDonald's, said, "My way of fighting the competition is the positive approach. Stress your own strengths, emphasize quality, service, cleanliness and value and the competition will wear itself out trying to keep up."[6]

As a professional RM, you have choice. You can train your staff in the fine points of fade rate implementation. Or, you can train them to better understand the reasons why the rates your revenue management team has established deliver real value to your hotel's guests. It should not be hard for you to guess which approach Kroc would endorse.

Despite the significant drawbacks of using fade rates, some RMs will remain unconvinced. They have been taught that because a hotel's rooms are perishable (like airline seats), the fade rate approach makes economic sense. It would be instructive to test that theory with an airline company. That is, the RM should arrive at an airport just prior to a flight's departure. Upon arrival, they should inquire about seat availability and ticket price on the flight. If there is availability, they should politely present their case that, because the plane still has available seats, one or more seats should be sold to them at a price well below the initial fare quoted. After all, they can point out, when the plane takes off the sales opportunity will be lost forever. The airline counterperson's look of disbelief will be followed by the inevitable polite decline of this golden opportunity to sell for less. In fact, one reviewer of this text pointed out that some airlines would actually terminate any employee who offered the lower rate you request. That response may come as a surprise to some RMs. It should not be a surprise to you, however, or to any RM who truly understands customer-centric revenue optimization.

Check-Outs

In many hotels, repeat customers are a significant market segment. As a result, it makes sense that as guests depart they would be asked if they would like to rebook for a future date. Surprisingly, few front desk staff members take the time to do so. Consider your own hotel experiences—were you asked to rebook during your last hotel check-out experience?

If pressed on the issue, the FOM would likely point to the fact that morning check-out times are so busy the desk staff simply does not have the time to ask each guest about re-booking. This is especially so, they would add, when check-out lines are long and travelers are in a hurry to leave. Finally, these FOMs might add, their staff members are not in *sales* but rather they are in *operations*. RMs who work in smaller properties know such distinctions are simply an illusion. You should know that they are an illusion in larger properties, as well.

This situation is a classic example of the need for those managing a hotel's sales, marketing, revenue management, and reservations teams to come together to optimize revenue. Recall that a rebooked guest is one in which no GDS, IDS, or other non-franchisor intermediary fees are paid. The net ADR yield on such reservations is very high. Not only should adequate staffing be provided to promote rebooking, RMs should measure the effectiveness of their rebook efforts. The number of rebooked guests per guest checked out is an important statistic for evaluating the effectiveness of rebooking efforts. As that number increases, it means that additional high net ADR yield reservations have been made. It is a statistic that should be tracked regularly, and Figure 8.5 is a tool for doing so. When implementing this tool, note that the following formulas are utilized:

$$\frac{\text{Nights booked today}}{\text{Check-outs today}} = \text{Nights (booked) per check-out today}$$

$$\frac{\text{Nights booked to date}}{\text{Check-outs to date}} = \text{Nights (booked) per check-out to date}$$

Figure 8.5 | Reserved Nights Per Check-Out

Day of Month	Check-Outs Today	Check-Outs to Date	Nights Booked Today	Nights Booked to Date	Nights/per Check-Out Today	Nights/per Check-Out to Date
1st	85	85	6	6	.07	.07
2nd	144	229	15	21	.10	.09
3rd	130	359	11	33	.08	.09
4th	65	424	13	46	.20	.11
5th						

Thus, for example, the nights (booked) per check-out today on Monday is calculated as:

6/85 = 0.07 Nights (booked) per check-out today

In this example, through the fourth of the month, .11 room nights were booked per guest check-out, about one room per each ten guests checked out. The numbers required for this evaluation are easy to obtain from a hotel's PMS. What is often more difficult for RMs to obtain is the staffing level and front desk commitment required to continually increase this low-cost source of revenue.

Property Direct Telephone Sales

From the 1990s to the mid-2000s, individual hotels saw an ever-decreasing use of the telephone as a distribution channel. The advent of the fax machine and the Internet served to reduce the importance of the telephone. Today, however, expanded numbers of applications (apps) available for downloading to smart telephones has increased the importance of the telephone as a distinct distribution channel.

In the late 2000s, Choice Hotels International was one of the first hotel chains to recognize the re-emergence of the telephone's importance. In response, it introduced a free iPhone application that allowed its guests to easily search for hotels in their area by city, address, airport, or by popular attractions. After wirelessly downloading the application, guests used the application's built-in GPS function to search for Choice-affiliated hotels and then make real-time bookings.

It is important to recognize that most hotels still receive large numbers of traditional telephone reservation requests. Handling these calls properly is important for several reasons, including the fact that such calls produce high net ADR yield reservations. Some RMs think the cost of making this type of reservation is high because of the staffing costs required to take them. Smaller hotels (less than 150 rooms), however, do not typically have a full-time person designated as a telephone reservationist. Instead, the hotel's front desk staff usually assumes this important responsibility. In such cases, the incremental labor cost required to make these reservations is small. In some hotels, the front desk staff performs well—in others, it does not. Compare, for example, the following two telephone greetings

Reservationist 1:   "Heritage Hotel . . . please hold."

Reservationist 2:   "It's a great day at the Heritage Hotel. This is Rebecca. How may I help you today?"

The resulting impact on revenue optimization should be clear. Like many areas of revenue management, this one requires that RMs be actively engaged in employee training program development and implementation. Learning to take telephone reservations to maximize ADR is important, but it does not come naturally to employees. They must be trained, and it should be part of your responsibility to ensure that they are.

To evaluate the effectiveness of telephone sales efforts, RMs frequently use outside companies specializing in providing **shopper services.**

Increasingly, hotel franchise companies supply no-cost shopper services. In the typical case, a franchisor representative places a call to the hotel. During the reservation request call, key questions are asked of the reservationist. The hotel employee's answers to these questions are scored. After the call, the employee's performance is formally evaluated and confidentially submitted to the hotel's managers for review. The results of shopper calls such as this can be used to identify areas in which employee training must be improved.

Essential RM Term

Shopper service: The unannounced, anonymous and professional evaluation of an organization's employee behavior, productivity, and customer service skills. Also known as mystery shopper services.

On-Property Group Sales

A hotel's on-property group sales department is a separate distribution channel. Evaluating the revenue-producing ability of this channel requires RM's to evaluate both ADR and net ADR yield. In most cases, the ADRs associated with group room sales will be lower than

---

▶ RM ON THE WEB 8.3

Telephone skills training is important, and there are a variety of tools available to RMs seeking to improve in this area. Some of the best tools have been developed by the AH&LA's Educational Institute. To review its *"Courtesy Rules! Better Telephone Skills Now"* program addressing:

Answering promptly and politely

Effective talking and listening techniques

How to transfer, take messages, and place people on hold

Handling dissatisfied callers

Selling rooms

Responding to emergencies

Go to www.ei-ahla.org/. When you arrive, enter the program's name in the search field.

RM AT WORK 8.1

"So how is it working, Anthony?" asked Sandra, the RM at the Holiday Inn Express.

Sandra and Anthony were old classmates. They were chatting after a monthly meeting of the local hotel association. Anthony was the FOM at another hotel in the area. He was telling Sandra how he had solved the problem of dealing with telephone call reservations at his property when his front desk staff was too busy to handle the calls effectively.

"It's great," replied Anthony. "When we get busy I just have our employee tell the caller they will be transferred to *Reservations*. We have our franchisor's reservation center number on speed dial, so the call is transferred to that extension. Presto, the call is forwarded to the res center. Somewhere

in Colorado—or maybe India—I think. Anyway, they handle it. We don't."

"Any negative feedback?" asked Sandra.

"None at all," replied Anthony. "No guest complaints, and our staff just love it."

1. How should Anthony compute the cost of implementing this specific solution to his "we're too busy to take the call" problem? What is your assessment of it?

2. Do you think most hotel franchisors would encourage, or discourage, the call strategy implemented at Anthony's hotel? Why?

3. If you were Sandra, how might you solve the "we're too busy to take the call" problem if it were one that was frequently experienced by your own front office staff?

transient ADRs. Net ADR yields, however, will most often be higher. This is so because group rooms are most often sold at a significant rack rate discount but a hotel's group sales effort does not typically require the payment of distribution charges and assessments associated with many alternative channels of distribution. As a result, it is often better to discount rooms for the hotel's internal group rooms sales staff than to offer the same discount on rooms to be sold through a more costly distribution channel.

RMs working in full-service hotels face the added challenge of factoring in the impact of meeting room, F&B, and perhaps other income-producing department sales when assessing guest room revenue generation. Consider, for example, a full-service hotel that has a group willing to pay $200 per night for 100 hotel rooms. Such a sale might initially appear preferable to an alternative group's offer to pay $190 per night for the same number of rooms on the same night.

Assume, however, that the second group seeks to hold a meeting at the hotel and, as a result, will utilize and pay full price for a significant number of the hotel's meeting spaces. This second group also wants to hold a breakfast, lunch, and very formal dinner for its meeting attendees on the day of their meeting. In such a case, the *total* room revenue, meeting room revenue, and F&B revenue produced by this second group would likely be significantly greater than the room revenue that would be generated if the guest room sale were made to the group seeking to pay $200 per night for its rooms. Thoughtful RMs will recognize this to be true, despite the fact that the hotel's RevPAR would be lower with the second group.

Working with their DOSMs, RMs in full-service hotels must develop systems for ensuring that guest room and all other departmental revenue generated is properly assessed when evaluating the value of a single piece of business as well as the productivity of the hotel's entire group sales effort. When doing so, it important to recognize that the profit margins for guest room sales, meeting room sales, and F&B products are not typically identical. For example, a single dollar of guest room revenue may yield more, the same, or less profit than a dollar of meeting room revenue. This makes an RM's ability to calculate the relative worth of alternative types of income very important. In Chapter 13, you will learn how lodging industry RMs do it.

In many hotels, the pricing of meeting space and services and F&B products and services are, respectively, the responsibility of the DOSM and F&B director. In other cases, the RM may have significant impact on pricing decisions in these areas. In all cases, however, it is important that RMs in full-service hotels understand the pricing and selling philosophies that are in place regarding these two important revenue-producing areas. When they do, they can better understand how to evaluate the impact of each on the property's overall revenue optimization efforts.

For RMs, an additional aspect of managing on property group sales relates to the ability of group guests reserving blocked rooms to monitor and respond to publicly advertised room rate changes. To illustrate, consider the hotel that makes a group room sale. The group picks up its entire block, but as the group's arrival date draws near, some of the hotel's rooms remain unsold. In such a situation, the notion of utilizing the Internet to offer very significant discounts on the remaining rooms can seem to be very appealing. It should not be. If, in an effort to sell the remaining rooms, the property's RM team elects to advertise discounted rates *lower* than the rate paid by the group, the results will be as negative as they are swift.

Utilizing this ruinous RM tactic to sell unsold rooms will most often result in immediate room cancellations from the group block, followed by rebooks at the lower advertised rates. In addition, the group room buyer/rate negotiator will likely face significant criticism from his or her group members. These members will point out (rightly) that they could, booking on their own, have received a better rate than the one negotiated by the buyer. Also, because group members are now booking outside the block, it would cause the group's pick-up to appear worse (lower) than it actually was and could unjustly trigger allowable attrition clause penalties (see Chapter 7) written into the group's rooms contract. The end result is an unhappy group rooms buyer, an irate group membership, and ultimately, a hotel group room sales staff member who will be angrily confronted by the group rooms buyer. Alienating group rooms buyers is not a customer-centric approach to revenue optimization.

Some RMs facing such a situation might elect to reassess and reduce the price charged to the group so that any unsold rooms could then be advertised and sold at lower, market-driven prices. In all cases, however, the existence of a group room sales contract for a specific date affects an RM's ability to promote significantly discounted rates for that same date. This is true for RMs utilizing any alternative distribution channel that offers discounted room rates that can be easily seen by the general public.

Convention and Visitors Bureau (CVB)

RMs working in the lodging industry are fortunate to have a virtually *free* distribution channel available to them, yet many fail to take full advantage of it. This channel is the local CVB, a not-for-profit entity responsible for representing a specific travel destination and helping the long-term development of its community through the promotion of travel and tourism.

CVBs represent many businesses, including hotels and restaurants that rely on tourism and meetings for revenue. For most services, CVB do not charge their clients. These clients include visitors, business travelers, and meeting planners who seek to utilize an area's travel-related resources. Rather than charge fees, most CVBs are fully funded through a combination of hotel occupancy taxes and membership dues.

CVBs serve as a hotel's extended sales force and cost hotel owners virtually nothing. Given that, it would seem only reasonable that RMs would fully support the efforts of their CVBs. As many CVB leaders will attest, however, that is not always the case.

CVBs solicit new business and work with local hotel sales professionals to track rooms inventory, thus helping travel planners avoid conflicts with other events. Moreover, as CVBs have first-hand familiarity with the hotels and with meeting space in the area, they can help planners match lodging properties to an event planner's specific meeting requirements and budgets. Conflicts can easily arise, however, between a CVB and an individual hotel property. These conflicts typically relate to the degree with which a CVB is viewed as *fairly* representing each individual hotel property within an area. Complaints of favoritism are common, as are charges that CVBs might share a hotel's confidential sales-related information with one of the hotel's direct competitors.

As an RM, you must ensure that your property is fairly and fully represented by your local CVB. You can do so by staying active with it, serving on its board of directors if possible, and by taking all reasonable steps to promote its efforts and ensure its success.

Citing the ever-increasing importance of the Internet in rooms bookings, some RMs discount the importance of nonelectronic distribution channels. They believe that, in the future, everyone will book their rooms electronically. Those that share that feeling should reflect on the lyrics from the band Rush's song *Tom Sawyer*. The song includes the line, "*Most change isn't permanent, but change is.*"[7] The Internet has certainly changed the way today's RM considers the various distribution channels it contains. An RM's over-emphasis

▶ RM ON THE WEB 8.4

Formerly known as the International Association of Convention and Visitors Bureaus, but now by the name Destination Marketing Association International (DMAI), this professional organization for individuals working to promote travel was founded in 1914.

Its mission is to promote sound professional practices in the solicitation and servicing of meetings, conventions, and tourism. Today, DMAI provides educational resources and networking opportunities to its members and information on the CVB industry to the public.

To learn more about the services it provides to lodging industry RMs, go to www.destinationmarketing.org/

on any single distribution method, however, can in the long run prove detrimental to revenue optimization because distribution channels will continue to change and evolve.

The emergence of blogs, tweets, and sites such as TripAdvisor as well as Facebook and MySpace, combined with advanced technology in cell-phones and other devices, would indicate that social media sites and emerging technology will soon make a hotelier's excessive focus on Internet search page placement seem quaint. Electronic distribution of hotel products will remain important. It is also crucial for you to recognize that the common characteristic of all nonelectronic distribution channels is that each places the buyer and seller in close personal contact. In the long run, it is very unlikely that such channels will disappear. In fact, these channels are one of the primary ways in which RMs can help ensure they avoid the **commoditization** of their products.

Essential RM Term

Commoditization: The process by which a product (or service) reaches a point in its development where one brand has no features that differentiate it from other brands, and consumers buy based on price alone.

Effective RMs can best manage their nonelectronic distribution channels when they:

- Calculate, monitor, and manage net ADR yield indexes for each channel.
- Calculate and assess the total revenue generated by each channel on a regularly scheduled basis.
- Ensure that each channel is operating at maximum effectiveness and efficiency.
- Offer, through these channels, rate discounts that maximize GOPPAR.
- Close discount rates on these channels last, as they tend to have higher net ADR yields.
- Include a detailed evaluation of each nonelectronic channel during every revenue management optimization team meeting.

ELECTRONIC DISTRIBUTION CHANNELS

Effectively managing electronic distribution channels is increasingly important to the overall success of RMs. Given the hotel industry's centuries-old existence, however, it can safely be said that only fairly recently have electronic distribution channels affected hoteliers' revenue management efforts.

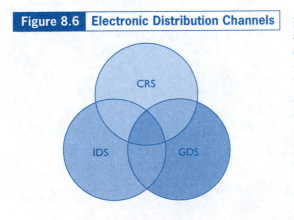

Figure 8.6 **Electronic Distribution Channels**

Three significant events have given rise to the explosion of electronic distribution channels. The first and most recent is the growth of the Internet as a means of selling travel products. As you have learned, it was not until 1994 that it became possible to easily book hotel rooms online. The second event, the airline industry's development of the GDS, preceded the rise of the Internet only by a decade or two. The third important event precedes development of the GDS by only two decades, as well. That incident occurred in 1952 when Kemmons Wilson built the first Holiday Inn in Memphis, Tennessee. By doing so, he set in motion the modern hotel chain's commitment to the development of a proprietary CRS. These three events are important to understanding electronic distribution channels because, as illustrated in Figure 8.6, they are so interconnected.

Three major components directly resulting from the three significant events mentioned make up electronic distribution channels. These are, in order of their historical appearance the CRS, the GDS, and the IDS. To understand how RMs can best manage electronic distribution channels, they must first recognize the unique characteristics of each.

CRS

If you are like most RMs, you work in a branded hotel. As well, if you are like most RMs, your brand has developed a CRS whose use is mandated by your hotel owner's franchise agreement. The CRS accepts reservations from a variety of electronic and non-electronic distribution channels and feeds those reservations to your hotel's PMS. Today, most brands accomplish this electronically. A few smaller hotel brands, however, still operate manual systems. In either case, room sales are communicated to your property while rooms availability and room rate information must be communicated from your property to the CRS.

Because you will set your room rates based on your own revenue optimization strategies, it is your responsibility to ensure that your electronic distribution channels, as well as all others you use, have up-to-the-minute information about your rates. Also, due to walk-in, check-out, group, and other on property room sales, rooms inventory availability must be continually updated in your CRS. In increasing numbers of brands, an entry in a hotel's PMS is automatically registered in the database of the franchisor's CRS, and vice versa.

If you operate an independent hotel, you will also need a way to let your electronic distribution channels know about your rooms availability and the rates you are charging. In that case, you may purchase your CRS services from a hotel representation firm offering it to you and a number of other independent hotels.

As either a franchised or independent property, you will incur charges and fees associated with your use of a CRS. These may include monthly maintenance fees, per reservation fees, and fees for connecting to other electronic distribution channels such as the GDS or IDS.

▶ RM ON THE WEB 8.5

CRSs for independent hotels are on the market. The available quality and features offered can vary tremendously. Some of the most innovative CRS companies offer nonfranchised hotels PMS, CRS, and GDS services in a single package. To view a U.S./Australian company's that has developed and markets just such a product, go to www.bookingcenter.com

When you arrive, click *Products* to learn more about its innovative approach to electronic distribution channel management.

> ▶ **RM ON THE WEB 8.6**

How important is a CRS in today's lodging industry? It can actually create a brand. It is not surprising that companies who have invested heavily in the development of their CRS would like to use it to attract independent hotels who need such a system, but who prefer to retain their independent status.

For Marriott International, the solution was the 2009 development of its Autograph Collection of independent hotels and resorts. For Choice Hotels International, the solution for these independents is the Ascend Collection of hotels.

The Ascend group was created in 2008. Independent hotels who become *members* of the Ascend Collection, like Marriott's Autograph Collection, are typically upscale, independent, unique, boutique, or historic properties with strong local brand equity. These hotels want to keep their own names and identities while securing the use of Choice's CSR.

To learn more about the Ascend Collection and how the brand works, go to www.ascendcollection.com

Beginning with the introduction in 1965 of Holidex, the Holiday Inn's initial CRS[8], additional CRSs were the inevitable outgrowth of each hotel brand's original central reservations offices. In the past, dialing *1–800 (your favorite hotel)* was great for travel agents and consumers, but difficult for RMs. This is easy to understand when you recognize that rooms inventory as maintained in a hotel's PMS was *not* electronically updated when a sale was made in a hotel brand's central reservation offices. With hundreds of reservationists working in each brand's central reservation office, and with multiple office locations, it was hard to keep inventory levels up-to-date. Rate changes were also difficult to communicate to a CRS. Consider, for example, the communication challenge faced by RMs who wished to submit a room rate code change for a single room type, on a single day, six months into the future, to thousands of travel agents. Then you can appreciate the communication difficulties faced by these early RMs.

Today, in most (but not all) hotel brands, the interface between the CRS and PMS is seamless (two-way) and accomplished in real time. Thus, when the sale of a room to a walk-in guest is made and entered into a hotel's PMS, that room's sale is automatically reflected in the CRS. Increasingly, hotel brands are interfacing their own CRS with other electronic distribution channels. This effectively establishes two-way communication between these interfaced channels and a hotel's PMS.

Today a hotel brand will utilize its CRS in the operation of its **call center** and to communicate each property's inventory and rate information on its own brand web site, as well as on a variety of distribution sites linked to the brand's own site.

Essential RM Term

Call center: A physical location, maintained by a brand, for its customers who prefer to book their room reservations via telephone.

As the cost of providing *live* reservationists continues to increase, along with buyers' comfort in using the Internet for room bookings, call-center volumes may continue to decline. They remain a significant revenue source but in most cases now generate fewer reservations than a brand's web site. When combined, however, it is common for call centers and a brand's own web site to contribute 10 to 50 percent of a franchised hotel's total rooms revenue.

Most RMs understand that the physical process of changing room rates, as well as opening and closing discount codes, in the PMS or a CRS is one that is manually undertaken. Because that is so, human error is a factor in CRS management and revenue optimization. Today, hotel brands seeking to maximize their franchisee's revenues are aggressively including automated revenue management tools within the CRS. If their properties are affected, it is important that RMs understand these tools well.

To demonstrate the effectiveness of their CRSs, most brands provide RMs with monthly or, more frequently, CRS business generation reports. These reports typically include information about a designated time period (usually a month) and the prior year's equivalent time period data. Data reported most often includes information about:

Reservations made

Reservations canceled

ADR achieved

Sales revenue generated (Reservations made × ADR)

Average length of stay (ALOS)

Source of reservation

Year-to-date (YTD) data will most often be included in these reports as well. RMs analyzing trends in the data can evaluate the effectiveness of their CRS in delivering call center–generated reservations, as well as those delivered via the brand's web sites. Increasingly these type reports provide detailed data about the revenue generation achieved by other electronic distribution channels when those channels are interfaced with the CRS.

Looking forward, as franchisors seek increased communication between their brand operated CRS and your property-based PMS, expect the differences between these two tools to become increasingly blurred. Already, several chains mandate the use of both their own CRS and a PMS system designed exclusively for it. Figure 8.7 illustrates the information exchange between a hotel's PMS and the CRS the hotel utilizes.

| Figure 8.7 | PMS/CRS Information Exchange |

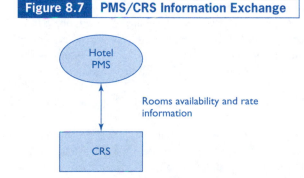

Rooms availability and rate information

GDS

You have learned that the GDS originated with the airlines. Today, the companies that make up the GDS are still an important part of the airline, car rental, and hotel industries' ability to sell their products. Though the GDS is no longer owned by the airlines, it remains a powerful distribution channel.

Lodging RMs new to the industry must recognize that the GDS survived the Internet age and, in

Effective RMs can best manage the CRS channel when they:

- Understand all fees associated with accepting a reservation via the brand's mandated CRS.

- Become familiar with all revenue optimization features included in the CRS/PMS.

- Ensure that all approved rate codes are properly entered in the PMS and are in sync with those found in the CRS.

- Spot-check room types and room rates in the CRS, especially for high-volume days.

- Make regular shopper calls to their brand's telephone call center to verify the continued accuracy and to update the property's information.

- Regularly analyze the data supplied by the property franchisor in any available CRS production reports.

- Make a review of the monthly (or more frequent) CRS report part of their revenue optimization team's regularly scheduled meeting agenda.

fact, grew because of it for a very significant reason that has not changed. To better understand that reason, consider the travel agent or corporate travel manager seeking to book a room in an unfamiliar city. Would the buyer likely make a telephone call to each hotel in the new city to inquire about rates and availability? No. Even if the buyer knew which hotel properties existed, the time required to contact each would be excessive.

Could the buyer simply contact every hotel chain's CRS, either via telephone or their Internet web site and choose a room? Not likely. That would assume the buyer knew the names of the chains operating in the city and would be willing to contact each one individually. The time required to do so would be prohibitive. Consider, further, that this rooms buyer sought to purchase airline tickets and a car rental at the same time. The buyer could go to each hotel chain's CRS, then contact each airline, and then contact each car rental company. There is a faster, better, cheaper way to do this, and it is the GDS.

After nearly 50 years of continuous operation and advancement, its member companies are very adept at providing convenient, comprehensive, *comparative*, and one-stop travel services shopping. If you now better understand why professional buyer's use the GDS, you can appreciate what Norm Rose, 26-year travel industry veteran, meant when he posted the following on his travel blog: "The power of the GDS lies in the 100,000 of travel agency desktops deployed as well as the engine behind online travel agencies (OTAs) such as Expedia. No single company, no matter how well funded can displace the dominance of the GDSs in the market overnight."[9]

Figure 8.8 illustrates the information exchange between a hotel's PMS, its CRS, and the GDS.

Astute readers will recognize that the existence of the GDS changes the RM's world. When your room types and their accompanying rates are displayed only on your PMS and a CRS whose data are displayed on your brand's Internet site, potential buyers can compare your rev-

Figure 8.8   PMS/CRS/GDS Information Exchange

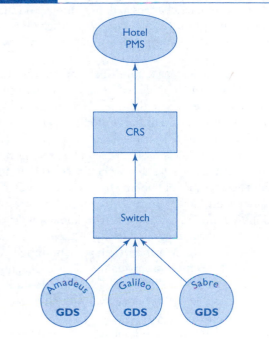

enue management decisions only with those of other hotels within your brand or perhaps within the family of brands operated by your franchisor. Figure 8.9, however, illustrates the way your hotel looks to a GDS user.

When an RM's pricing strategy is displayed on the GDS or the IDS, buyers make buying determinations based in large part on what they read and see of your property *when compared to others*. Room products that are presented clearly and priced fairly sell well. Those that are not listed or presented well do not sell as well.

At this point it is important to reemphasize that this is not a book primarily about hotel marketing, e-marketing, or advanced marketing-related technology implementation. All three of these are important topics. Best practices associated with each change rapidly. Each may be worthy of your further study if they address an area directly related to your primary RM duties and responsibilities. What is important for all RMs to recognize, however, is that with the emergence of the GDS, and later the Internet, the revenue optimization decisions made by RM teams are publicly put to the test because they are displayed directly alongside their competitors.

In Chapter 9, you will learn how RMs directly compare the performance of their own RM teams to that of their competitors. In regard to competitors, some RMs take the position of singer Celine Dion, who stated, "I'm not in competition with anybody but myself. My goal is to beat my last performance."[10]

Many in the hospitality industry, of course, see competition very differently. In a large number of organizations an RM's compensation package and promotion prospects are tied directly to his or her performance as measured against that of their competitors. Ms. Dion's philosophy might not fare so well in an environment based more on the competitive nature espoused by UCLA Bruins football coach Henry Russell (Red) Saunders who in 1950 was famously quoted as saying, "*Winning isn't everything. It's the only thing.*"[11]

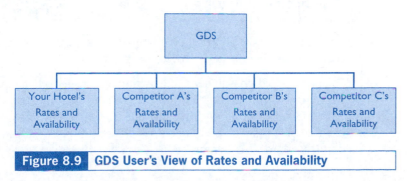

Figure 8.9   GDS User's View of Rates and Availability

Where e-commerce and the GDS are concerned, things move exceedingly quickly. Those RMs who do not keep up and make appropriate changes to their optimization strategies will be quickly left behind. As noted information technology expert Michael Hugos observed, "Agility means that you are faster than your competition. Agile time frames are measured in weeks and months, not years."[12]

It is true that the GDS primarily serves travel sellers (e.g., travel agents and travel wholesalers) and other travel-oriented businesses. The often-predicted demise of travel agents, usually by those representing distribution channels found on the Internet, is simply not supported by recent satisfaction surveys of online purchasers of travel products. The Internet has indeed led to a significant reduction in the number of travel agents. However, RMs who believe travel agents will disappear do their hotels a disservice. This is so because the travel agents who disappeared due to the Internet were those who provided their individual or corporate customers no services beyond that of booking hotel rooms. Individual room buyers can now do that just as quickly on the Internet. Those travel agencies that remain are, in the majority of cases, highly trained professionals who know how to add real value to travel transactions by using their own expertise. Many of them thrive and prosper and increasingly use Web-based tools to their own advantage. Combined with their travel knowledge, Internet tools will likely keep them very competitive, especially in the sale of corporate travel and what is often termed *complex travel* (i.e., travel to multiple foreign destinations or specialized travel such as adventure or special interest vacations) and tours.

Regardless of the location of your own hotel, travel agents booking via the GDS can be a significant source of business. They should not be ignored or too quickly be brushed aside. Despite the fees they charge for services, travel experts (like revenue management experts!) are likely to be around for quite some time. Some people do find it rewarding to personally make all of their travel plans, including choosing from airfare, hotel, and car rental options. Others, increasingly pressed for personal time, will seek someone else to take on the job of travel arrangements. If you think the average traveler's life will get busier and busier and that travel options will continue to increase and become more complex to assess, then you should not be surprised to find society's need for value-adding and knowledgeable travel agents will likely increase, not decrease.

▶ RM ON THE WEB 8.7

Perhaps no part of an RM's job changes more quickly than their tasks related to e-commerce and the effective use of technology.

To keep up-to-date with changing technology, many lodging industry IT managers and accountants rely on their professional membership in the Hospitality Financial and Technology Professionals (HFTP). Many RMs find membership in HFTP aids them as well. To learn more about this important group and the services it provides its members, go to www.hftp.org

The assessment of actual bookings generated by the GDS is just as important as that of the CRS. As was true with the CRS, there will be charges and fees associated with the use of the GDS. These may include monthly maintenance fees, per reservation fees, and fees for connecting to other electronic distribution channels. These charges may, in some cases, be reported on the hotel's income statement as a part of franchise fees. RMs should note, however, that the tenth edition of the *Uniform System of Accounts for Lodging Industry* (USALI) recommends travel agent commissions for GDS delivered-room sales reported in the *Rooms* portion of a hotel's income statement, not the *Marketing* portion.

Effective RMs can best manage the GDS when they:

- Understand all fees associated with accepting a reservation via each member of the GDS used at their hotels.
- Monitor the communication link between their property and the GDS.
- Ensure that the information included in their GDS listings is accurate and-up-to date. Review the data on a regular basis.
- Ensure all approved rate codes **loaded** for use by the GDS are accurate and up-to-date.
- Ensure that top revenue producing travel agencies and wholesalers are well informed about property product improvements and enhancements as they occur.
- Ensure travel agents commissions are paid in a timely manner.
- Regularly analyze the revenue production reports supplied by the GDS including data sorted:
  - By booking source
  - By travel agent
  - By room type
  - By room rate code
  - By country or region
- Make a review of the monthly (or more frequent) GDS report part of the revenue optimization team's regularly scheduled meeting agenda.

IDS

Despite the differences in how various IDS sites operate, for RMs it is most convenient to consider them part of a single group. Viewed in that way, 2004 was a landmark year for the IDS. It was in that year, for the first time, that the number of room reservations made via the Internet exceeded those made on the GDS.[13] Well over 50 percent of all travelers now go online to book or research room reservations. Over 80 percent of all online reservations are routed through franchisor operated web sites. As a result, the impact of IDS on revenue optimization strategies is great and will undoubtedly continue to expand.

Essential RM Term

Loaded (rate): The point at which a room rate and its companion rate code have been properly submitted for listing by one or more of a hotel's chosen distribution channels.

RM AT WORK 8.2

"Let me see if I can summarize," said Lucir, the RM at the 400-room Sheraton Civic Center hotel. "Jaymal, you think we should pay extra to move our property up on the Internet listing of our area's hotels."

"That's right," said Jaymal, the hotel's FOM. "I think we need to be listed first or second and pay what we need to pay to get that placement. If we are lower than that, I think we just lose out. We need to make it easy for travelers to book us."

"O.K." continued Lucir, "Sharon, you think we should take the same financial resources to purchase the entire back cover of the CVB's new *Meeting Planner's Guide To The City*."

"That's right," said Sharon, the hotel's DOSM. "We're adjacent to the civic center. It's a no-brainer to appeal to those groups bringing meetings to the area. Besides, I think it will help our standing with the CVB to really support their efforts."

1. Assuming similar costs and revenue generation from these two channels, what customer-related factors would likely influence Lucir's decision?

2. In addition to the actual costs associated with the two alternatives, what net ADR yield considerations should be part of this decision-making process?

3. If you were the GM of the hotel, what other factors would you want your RM team to consider before making the final decision on this issue?

Despite the plethora of information related to IDS rooms sales, RMs should first recognize that selling rooms on the Internet truly is not rocket science. Nor is it so complex it must be left only to online marketing experts who see the world strictly in terms of banner ads, search engine optimization tools, meta tags, click through rates and Web analytics. Certainly these and other unique aspects of e-commerce and webvertising are important. But it is more important to apply the fundamental principles of buying and selling to the Internet and to recognize that effective IDS channel management is not *synonymous* with effective revenue management. A hotel's revenue management efforts consist of much more than its IDS management efforts. As you have learned, revenue management consists of many areas of expertise, including of course, those related to Internet site management. But those RMs who best understand how to apply fundamental revenue management principles to IDS channel management will be the ones in the best position to utilize this important channel as it continues to grow, develop, and evolve.

Savvy RMs in the lodging industry increasingly recognize that as a distribution channel, the IDS presents as many challenges as it does opportunities. In fact, the most recent changes in Internet-related revenue management tactics used by RMs are responses directly related to challenges resulting from unique aspects of guests' online room-buying behavior. As you will learn, these were much needed responses. This is so because, despite very vocal advocates, the sale of guest rooms via some IDS channels has historically been an exceptionally *poor* means of achieving customer-centric revenue optimization goals.

A complete history of the evolution of IDS channels, from the events of 9/11 (when hotels began in earnest to utilize the Internet to sell excess inventory) to the current emphasis on the interconnectivity of Web-delivered content is beyond the scope of this text and would be hopelessly outdated before it could be printed! The fact is that the Internet makes history daily. As a result, RMs must be vigilant in monitoring developments that directly affect their properties. To better understand how to manage the IDS as a unique channel, however, it can be helpful for RMs to view it as consisting of three major divisions. These are:

- Property web site(s)
- Third-party web sites
- Web 2.0

As shown in Figure 8.10, each of these divisions shares the Internet as a home and communication vehicle. The entity in control of the site's value message, however, varies and that is what makes each a unique distribution channel within the IDS.

Property Web Site(s)

When it comes to a property's own web site, perhaps the most important consideration for RMs is the site's mere existence. In too many cases, individual hotel properties still do not have their own vanity web sites or they operate web sites that do not reflect well on their properties. In addition, Web addresses for individual franchised hotels are virtually indecipherable to guests. In many other cases, individual hotels have a presence on the Web but it is weak and ineffective. This problem is epidemic and historic. In the early 1990s, many hotels were slow to develop their own **proprietary web sites.**

The reasons for this varied from lack of on-property technical skills required to build and maintain the sites, to reservation interface difficulties, to franchisors that appeared to be more than willing to do the job for them if they could also control the site's look and content.

As an RM, you must recognize that your proprietary web site can be a tremendous marketing asset as well as an effective distribution channel. This is only true, however, if you follow six points:

1. The site's address can be easily remembered by your guests.
2. It includes a fast and easy to use CRS interface.

Figure 8.10	Components of the IDS
IDS Component	**Content Controlled By**
Property web sites	Hotel/hotel franchisor
Third-party web sites	Intermediaries
Web 2.0	Guests/rooms buyers

3. There are minimal distribution channel fees associated with its maintenance and use.

4. You have complete control over the site's content.

5. You can rapidly modify the site's content.

6. You have the ability to measure the site's effectiveness.

Essential RM Term

Search engine results page (SERP): The listing of Web pages returned by a search engine in response to a keyword query.

Essential RM Term

Conversion: The proportion of web site visitors who actually make a guest room purchase.

For example, if a site receives 100 hits that result in two bookings, the sites conversion rate is 2 percent (2/100 = 2%).

Effective Internet marketers understand that on today's web sites content is king. It is for that reason that item's 4 and 5 are so important. Yet in too many cases, RMs do not control these features. If your hotel is to have a highly effective web site, you must have quality content. This is so because having the right content will enable your web site to rank higher in a **search engine results page (SERP)** viewed by a potential rooms buyer.

As a unique distribution channel, your web site's primary function is to communicate rooms availability and pricing, get hits, and sell rooms. To do this, most RMs will find it easy to encourage the use of the hotel's web site on letterhead, stationery, business cards, newsletters, guides, e-mails, and promotional materials. When there is traffic coming to a web site, an RM's focus should turn to **conversion.**

Ease of navigation is the single most important site feature affecting conversion rates. A room buyer should never (on any page of the site) be more than one click away from a screen that allows a room reservation to be made. It is also important that this can be accomplished without excessive user instructions.

A hotel's proprietary web site is not merely an online brochure. The best web sites are interactive sales tools designed to be easily found through generic search and, once found, to produce reservations. The cost to develop a web site is largely a matter of the time it takes to research, prepare, and create it. Of most importance, however, is the ability to modify its content as needed. It is in this area that most hotel web sites fall short. In most franchised hotel arrangements, the property web site provided by the brand franchisor will be the one interfaced directly with that brand's CRS. As a result, content changes made to the site must go through and be approved by the franchisor. The process can be restrictive and is most often very slow. As a result, if RMs are to maximize the effectiveness of a franchisor provided site, they must take the time to understand any limitations placed on the site's content by their franchisor.

In all cases, if a web site is to generate significant numbers of visitors, those visitors must have a reason to come. A "set it and forget it" attitude may work well with cooking devices of questionable value, but it will not work with a hotel's proprietary web site. A web site is a communication device. Unless the franchisor permits the development of an interactive and dynamic site, then a truly proprietary site, which can display information and accept reservations directly or that can be independently linked to a franchisor's CRS, is imperative.

Effective RMs can best manage their proprietary web sites when they:

■ Research their local area to identify and utilize the most popular search key words and phrases.

Essential RM Term

Link strategy: The identification and linking of complementary sites (especially high-traffic sites) that improve a hotel's SERP ranking in response to a keyword query.

- Develop and write site content, incorporating the key words needed to maximize search results.
- Perform a comprehensive online review of competitor's sites to influence their own site's overall design.
- Incorporate good quality, high resolution, and optimized images or video into the site to maximize its effectiveness.

- Include essential content such as property contact information, location, directions, maps, facilities, nearby attractions, and special sales.
- Develop an effective **link strategy** to popularize the site.
- Build local and regional search listings to dominate local competition.
- Monitor the site's revenue production to evaluate its effectiveness.

Third-Party Internet Sites

Third-party Internet sites (TPIs) are those operated by a variety of travel intermediaries *not directly controlled* by a hotel. To best understand these, it is very important that you understand how they first came into being.

Essential RM Term

Agency model: An arrangement in which a hotel pays a commission (historically, 10 percent of selling price) to an intermediary for selling its rooms.

As you have learned, hoteliers have a long history of successfully working with traditional travel agents using a hospitality-specific **agency model**.

As the agency model's name implies, a travel agency's main function is to act as an agent, selling rooms on behalf of a hotel. As a result, they do not buy hotel rooms in advance. Rather, a room is booked when the travel agent's own client requests the booking. The hotel then supplies the room. The travel agent's income is its commission. Thus, for example, if a travel agent purchases for a client a hotel room advertised for $199.00 per night, the agent's client will indeed pay $199.00. In a typical 10 percent commission arrangement, the hotel returns $19.90 (10 percent of $199.00) to the travel agent. This represents the agent's income. The hotel then keeps the balance of the money as payment for the room. The **net rate** achieved by the hotel in this case would be $ 179.10 ($199.00 − $19.90 = $179.10).

Essential RM Term

Net rate: The amount per room actually received by a hotel when selling its rooms through an intermediary.
Also referred to as *wholesale rate*.

In this scenario, it would not be wise for the travel agency to publish the net rate received by the hotel. To do so would publicly reveal its own income level—something few businesses in any industry seek to do. Neither would the hotel want net rates publicized. This is especially true during very slow periods when they are quite willing to pay larger-than-average commissions to those travel agencies able to sell rooms during reduced demand periods.

Today, the IDS include Internet-based travel agencies, and most RMs still understand their hotels' relationship with these agency model room sellers fairly well. Despite recent changes in the amount of commissions paid (now often less than 10 percent), it is a very rational way for RMs to expand the number of entities helping to sell their rooms. Also, the cost of using this channel is known in advance. Of course, if your hotel can sell all of its rooms without the use of such agencies, it should do so. It is important to recognize, however, that a hotel utilizing an agency sales model distribution channel is not in any way competing directly against its travel agent teammates. In fact, the travel agency and the hotel are truly partners in the room sale. The hotel needs help selling rooms and the agency seeks commissions. When a room is sold, both entities benefit. As a result, most RMs should utilize effective agency model third-party Internet sites.

Historically, an equally important but lesser-known business model used by hoteliers involved the sale of rooms directly to tour operators or wholesalers. In these cases, a tour wholesaler would actually purchase a hotel's rooms before it had buyers for them. It would then market the rooms either directly to travelers or through its travel agent partners. Hotels participating in such arrangements often sold specific room types, for very specific dates, at very, very low net rates with the adamant stipulation that the tour operator *could not* publish the room's actual selling price (Net rate + Tour operator's income) unless it was bundled with other travel services such as airfares or meals.

Thus, for example, a tour operator such as Apple Vacations (www.applevacations.com) could advertise a *seven-night stay* at an all-inclusive resort in Cancun for a single price of $1,499.00. For that price, the traveler would receive booking services, airfare, hotel room, all meals, beverages, and perhaps some tours. Note that in such an arrangement, the price of the hotel room would not be listed as a separate item. Knowledgeable hoteliers knew that to permit tour operators to list rates separately would reveal prices for the hotel's rooms that could be so low the rates would, if they were widely advertised, have a significant negative effect on future, higher priced room sales made through other channels of distribution. *So far, so good.*

Unfortunately for the hotel industry, the aftermath of 9/11 resulted in hoteliers being approached in great numbers by a new and very sophisticated type of third-party Internet room seller. Most industry observers now agree that these Web-based sellers understood the power of the Internet much better than did hoteliers. In fairness to industry leaders, it is important to recognize that the new breed of Internet room seller did not initially approach franchise companies and their experienced industry executives. The reason why was simple. In 80+ percent of U.S. hotel properties, these particular industry executives controlled neither a hotel's rooms inventory nor the hotel rooms' prices. Rooms inventory and pricing decisions then, as now, are made at the hotel property level. Due primarily to a fear of too many unsold rooms and to the economic uncertainty surrounding 9/11-induced travel slowdowns, individual hotel property managers and many owners were willing to sell rooms via a newly formed IDS channel that utilized a **merchant model.**

Essential RM Term

Merchant model: A system in which an intermediary obtains rooms inventory at a wholesale rate and then acts as a merchant by selling the rooms to buyers at retail rates.

Hoteliers and RMs embraced the merchant model because online merchants promised to sell very large numbers of rooms. In their enthusiasm to embrace these sellers, the stipulation against revealing unpackaged room prices was not imposed. Merchant model sellers were allowed to advertise the retail price they preferred. *Big mistake.*

What these tech-savvy distribution channel managers recognized was that only the invention of writing and the printing press would have as big an impact on communication as would the Internet. The room prices these online sellers were to establish would, in fact, soon come to represent online buyers' reference price (the selling price the buyers believed to be fair), and the price by which these buyers would evaluate all other prices.

Following the logic employed by cost-based pricing experts who stated one or more variations on the theme that if someone helps you sell excess room inventory that you could not otherwise sell, they are putting heads in beds, a variety of industry writers and consultants were more than ready to help hoteliers learn how to sell more rooms via the Internet's merchant model. What hoteliers did not understand was that they had unwittingly entered into agreements that legitimized and promoted the age-old practice of arbitrage. As you learned in Chapter 4, sellers cannot maintain differential pricing strategies when they encounter arbitrage. Hoteliers would soon learn that lesson held true when selling via the Internet. That was bad. *It got worse.*

In many cases, online merchants convinced hotels that the online merchants themselves should not actually have to buy their rooms in advance (and thus run their own risk of not selling the rooms), but rather they would pay the heavily discounted (often 30 to 50 percent off) rates for rooms only *after* they themselves had already secured an online buyer. Thus, RMs agreed to hold rooms inventory for the site operators, in much the same way they held group room blocks. If, however, all of the rooms blocked for the merchant site were not picked up, no penalty was imposed. The net result was unsold rooms inventory, held by hotels, for sale by discount online merchant model sellers.

Facing their own competitive pressures, online merchants then elected to expand their reach by employing the services of virtually thousands of their own affiliates. These web sites assisted the online merchant in selling additional rooms. Each affiliate site, however, was free to set its own price for the rooms it tried to sell. Now instead of encountering one discount room price online, buyers could easily find dozens of prices.

<table>
<tr><td>

Essential RM Term

Referral site: A web site the searches for and reports information found on other web sites. Also known as a scrapping site or meta search site.

</td><td>

The results were as predictable as they were disastrous. No doubt, you can understand that a rooms buyer, seeing a multitude of different prices (for the same room, at the same hotel, booked on the same night) preferred to buy from the lowest cost source. You also can understand why **referral sites,** became popular. Referral sites such as Kayak and Sidestep simply search other web sites for the lowest prices, and present them on a SERP.

</td></tr>
</table>

Because the Internet is so efficient in communicating, buyers could now find the very lowest price for a room without looking very hard. As nonsensical and nonfunctional as the hotel rooms pricing process became in the early 2000s, from a customer-centric revenue management perspective, the situation would get even worse.

To understand why, it is important to recognize that about 80 percent of online travel business goes through one of three large companies. These are Travelocity, Expedia, and Orbitz. Each site has thousands of affiliates across the globe. These affiliates operate their own sites but use the big three's booking engines. In the typical case, these affiliates make their money in four ways:

1. *Higher room rates.* The affiliate site charges its customer a higher room rate than the rate negotiated with the hotel. The affiliate service keeps the difference.

2. *Fixed fees.* The affiliate site levies a set service charge per night or per booking.

3. *Variable fees.* These are most often combined and listed as part of a single line item labeled *taxes and fees*—thus, making it difficult or impossible for the customer to separate the taxes from the fees.

4. *Tax excess.* Merchant model sites estimate customer taxes based on the marked-up room rate that the customer pays. The affiliate, however, typically pays taxes on the discounted room rate it pays the hotel and keeps the difference; taking the position that the excess represents a tax handling fee. Various affiliates, of course, charged these various fees according to their own revenue goals.

RM IN ACTION 8.1: WHO OWES WHOM?

Online travel agencies (OTA) face an ever-increasing flurry of lawsuits from city taxing officials. As reported in *The Seattle Times,* these officials claim their cities have been cheated out of millions of dollars in hotel and occupancy taxes. The city of Atlanta charged in a lawsuit that Travelocity, Orbitz, Expedia, and 14 other online travel companies owe the city "untold" millions in unpaid taxes. Other cities, including Los Angeles, Philadelphia, Miami, Chicago, and Branson, Missouri, have filed similar suits. The issue is a deceptively simple one. According to the article:

> If an online travel company buys a room from a hotel at $50 and sells it for $100, the company sends the hotel taxes for the amount it paid—not the price it charged. The city isn't trying to recover any money that's not theirs," said Atlanta attorney Wade Tomlinson.

Online travel sites maintain they pay all of the taxes that are legitimately due. Taxing authorities respond that online buyers are deceptively charged the higher tax rate when they buy online. The Internet selling sites counter that the difference in amount collected and amount paid is a service fee, legitimately charged to buyers for the right to book online. Ultimately, the issue of who owes which taxes will likely be settled by the judiciary, followed by legislation that clears up the issue. But the issue is complex. In the case of *Columbus (GA) v. Expedia Inc.,* the Georgia Supreme court ruled 4–3 that the online travel service should pay lodging taxes based on the higher costs they charge customers, not on the lower wholesale room rate the hotels charge Expedia.[14]

In March 2010, the American Hotel and Lodging Association (AH&LA), the Asian American Hotel Owner's Association (AAHOA), The National Association of Black Hotel Owners, Operators and Developers (NABHOOD) and the Latino Hotel Association went on record opposing the OTA's suggested Federal legislation that would allow OTAs to pay taxes only on the lower amount.[i]

Consider your own views. If you were a federal judge responsible for deciding this issue, whose position would you support? Second, assume you were an RM on the board of directors for the New York City CVB (www.nycvisit.com), which, like most CVBs, is funded primarily by occupancy taxes. Whose position would you support?

Excerpted on 6/17/2009 from http://online.wsj.com/article/SB124519701062921181.html

Some affiliates operated legitimately, many did not. Increasingly, the major hotel chains complained that they were getting blamed for travel site affiliates' high fees and questionable marketing practices. The fees charged and practices employed by merchant model sellers did not go unnoticed by enlightened industry leaders. In 2004, at a hotel investment conference in Berlin, Germany, Hilton hotel's chairman and CEO Stephen Bollenbach was quoted as saying, "Internet intermediaries are not bad in the biblical sense. They just charge too much!"[15]

Essential RM Term

Opaque model: A system in which the room buyer does not know the name of the hotel they have chosen until after they have committed to the purchase price of the room.

The IDS spawned another innovative and equally questionable approach to the sale of excess rooms inventory. Known as the **opaque model,** it exists on the IDS in two formats—auction or bid. In the auction format, rooms at hotels that are unknown to the buyer are offered for sale at a set price, and if the price is accepted by the buyer, the name of the hotel that will be supplying the room is revealed. In the bid format, potential buyers name their own price. Thus, for example, room buyers determine a price they are willing to pay for a hotel room (e.g., $200.00 per night), typically choosing from among various quality levels (1–5 stars). Buyers verify their requests with a credit card and, if their bid is accepted, the buyer is then told the name of the hotel. Priceline.com is an example of an opaque model site.

Through the early 2000s, third-party merchant model and opaque model third-party IDS sites flourished. Hotel owners and managers liked the sites because of the revenue they produced and consumers liked the low prices. The site operators themselves enjoyed the greater levels of profits they achieved when compared to the traditional travel agent (GDS) channel. Travel agents even liked the sites because they found that these sites frequently offered room rates lower than those that could be found on the GDS and hotels would, as always, still pay the travel agent's 10 percent commission!

As a professional RM, however, if you understand that both the merchant and opaque models train guests to consider price above all else when choosing hotel rooms, you are correct. If it also seems to you that it would rapidly lead to the commoditization of hotel rooms, you are also correct. If you recognize that for the hotel industry that would be a very bad thing, then you are still correct!

While in some cases, selected third-party web-site operators can be of great value, it is important for RMs to remember that these site operators do not own hotels, do not operate hotels, and possess no rooms to sell that have not been provided by actual hoteliers. The inventory they are supplied belongs to a hotel. Since rooms are the main product sold by your hotel, controlling how your rooms inventory is presented in the market is critically important. It must be done in a way that optimizes long-term revenues. Intermediaries that do not allow you to do just that are working against your customer-centric revenue optimization efforts.

Some lodging industry experts are fond of using the airline industry as an example of how to effectively implement yield management practices. These same experts would adamantly support the extensive use of third-party web sites to sell hotel rooms. It is interesting to note that in most cases, these experts do not mention Southwest Airlines. Southwest Airlines tightly controls its flight inventory and its pricing. Its seats may only be booked on the Web through its own proprietary web site, www.southwest.com. As of 2011, you simply cannot book flights for Southwest Airlines on Orbitz, Expedia, Priceline, Travelocity, or any other third-party travel web site.[16] Thoughtful readers will recall from the previous chapter

> ▶ **RM ON THE WEB 8.8**
>
> The proportion of online rooms booked via brand CRS, the GDS and other IDS players continues to change. To stay up-to-date on the relative booking contributions of each distribution channel, go to www.travelclick.com
>
> When you arrive, click *Knowledge Center,* and then click *Hotel Bookings by Channel.*

that Southwest Airlines also practices a very customer-centric differential pricing strategy and tightly controls its inventory and pricing. Some might point to this practice as one of several reasons why it is also the only consistently profitable airline operating in the United States.

Today, nearly all major hotel brands mandate that a franchisee's lowest room prices must be offered on the brand's web site. As a result, the lowest priced IDS site should always be operated by a hotel's franchisor. Third-party sites, however, will continue to thrive for a simple reason—they allow rooms buyers to compare purchase options for rooms *across* various hotel brands. On sites such as Expedia.com or Travelocity.com, many competitive hotels are listed. Thus, far, brands such as Marriott are unwilling to list the rooms availability for the Hilton hotel brand on its web site, nor will Hilton list Marriott rooms. Each brand lists only its own rooms. That may be changing, according to Chuck Ledsinger, past CEO of Choice Hotels. He stated, "The one thing we haven't done is single-site shopping [for all brands]. That's the last piece, the last frontier. I think you'll start to see some of that."[17]

The exact manner in which hotel rooms are sold by third-party Internet site operators changes continually, and RMs must stay current with those changes. Fundamentally, there is nothing wrong with an RM using online discounters to promote its differentiated prices. But it is very wrong to turn these online services into your hotel's *primary* IDS channel. This is so because, if your hotel appears on the Internet only through highly discounted rates offered by online intermediaries, Internet users will always bump into your hotel's discounted rates and, because no other rates will be listed in their search, the discount rates will become, in your buyer's mind, the reference price and thus your hotel's default rack rate! Because this is so, RMs should continue to seek creative ways to move their customers away from heavily discounted third-party merchant model and opaque sites and onto sites offering their rooms at prices that truly reflect the quality of their product offerings.

RM's may or may not be the onsite person responsible for marketing through third-party Internet sites. This area of room marketing is changing quickly and RMs are advised to keep up-to-date on the best practices required to effectively utilize this IDS channel.

Hotel RMs considering the use of third-party Internet sites must do so carefully. Effective RMs can best manage these sites when they:

- Use third-party operated merchant model Internet sites only if it is unavoidable.
- Enter into third-party agreements only with reputable site operators who can fully and adequately control all of their affiliates.

- Monitor each third-party site's gross contribution to total rooms revenue and monitor net ADR yield on rooms sold through these IDS sites.

- Sell rooms to wholesale third-party site operators at net prices consistent with their overall revenue optimization strategy.

- Do not permit the publication of unbundled net room rates.

- Avoid selling rooms on consignment to third-party sites. Do pay for sales made on a commission basis.

- Seek to partner first with sites that simply direct users to their own (or your brand's) web site.

- Avoid opaque web site operators if they feel the sites lead to commoditization of their product. If bid systems are utilized they should be offered.

- If discounted rates are offered on third-party sites, close them first when rooms availability is low, apply the rates only to those rooms with the lowest demand, and do not agree to last room availability.

- Regularly monitor third-party sites to ensure accuracy of information about their properties.

- Monitor and report to their revenue optimization committee third-party site revenue generation and costs on a regular basis.

Web 2.0

Web 2.0 is the term commonly used to describe social-networking sites, video sharing sites, blogs, tweets, and ever-changing other Internet sites providing **consumer-generated media (CGM)**.

In the hotel industry, Web 2.0 is of critical importance because increasingly it is how consumers share, in print and via video, their hotel experiences with others. These shared experiences affect room buyer purchasing decisions much more than does "paid for" advertising. How big is the impact? According to eMarketer:[18]

- 38% of U.S. Internet users (72 million) use a social media site at least once a month.

- 89% of U.S. online buyers read customer reviews before they buy:

  43% most of the time

  22% always

Essential RM Term

Consumer-generated media (CGM): Various online venues such as forums, blogs, wikis, and reviewer sites where those seeking to research and buy products can use information and opinions posted by other consumers before making their buying decisions.

Talented hoteliers in all industry segments have always been well aware of the importance of word-of-mouth advertising. Word-of-mouth advertising builds business, year in and year out, regardless of fluctuations in the economy or the activities of the competition. In the fairly recent past, it was common for business professionals in many industries to be taught that unhappy customers would tell dozens of people about their negative experiences. The individual teaching about word-of-mouth advertising would then typically explain the importance of providing quality service to minimize the number of unhappy customers and as a result, minimize the spread of negative word-of-mouth advertising.

In the Web 2.0 world, such a concern about word-of-mouth advertising seems almost quaint. That is because today a single unhappy customer can, within minutes and with a few computer key strokes, share their negative stay experience with literally millions of a hotel's potential customers. For the hotel industry, word-of-mouth has been replaced by *word of mouse*. Because of word of mouse, RMs must increasingly monitor web sites such as TripAdvisor.com, TravelPost.com, and Kayak.com for inventory availability, rates, *and* consumers' review status.

Effective RMs can best manage social media when they recognize the growing importance of their Web 2.0-influnced activities. These include:

- A blog on their hotel's property web sites
- Photo sharing functionality on the hotel web site
- Survey and comment/feedback cards on the hotel web site
- Active participation in blogs that concern the hotel or local geographic area
- Creation of a profile for the hotel on social networks (Facebook, MySpace, and the like).
- Subscription to a reputation social network monitoring service
- Advertising, if appropriate, on selected social media and social network sites

The best practices for an RM's management of non-electronic and electronic distribution channels evolve rapidly. In the final analysis, however, any distribution channel used by a hotel is useful only to the degree that it:

- Accurately communicates a hotel's room availability
- Accurately communicates a hotel's room pricing decisions

▶ RM ON THE WEB 8.9

Online hotel reviews are estimated to influence more than 85% percent of travel site visitors' buying decisions. Over 90 percent of those booking rooms report that the reviews they read online prior to reserving rooms were accurate. Today, some innovative companies provide to RMs the service of monitoring and reporting back to them the ever changing consumer-generated information posted about their hotels. Utilizing the services of these companies allow RMs to more easily track, analyze, and react to online reviews. To review the product offerings of one such Web 2.0 monitoring company, go to www.standingdog.com.

When you arrive, click *Social Media Strategies and Monitoring* to examine the services this company can provide to RMs. One important service is that of providing summaries of reviewer information posted to selected Web 2.0 sites. As well, this company provides RMs with advice about appropriate responses to negative consumer-generated content.

RM IN ACTION 8.2: "YOURS IS A VERY BAD HOTEL"

One of the Internet's most widely distributed hotel-related incidents concerns two men trying to check into their Houston-area hotel very late at night. They had a confirmed reservation but the night clerk said no room was available. The pair was then walked to another hotel. Unhappy with their treatment, they spent the next day producing a humorous PowerPoint presentation describing their experience. They titled it, *"Yours Is A Very Bad Hotel,"* then sent it to the hotel's GM—and posted it on the Web. It got literally *millions* of hits. Among many other comments regarding the mathematical chances of various occurrences, the following tongue-in-cheek statements were posted:

1. Chance of Earth being ejected from the solar system by the gravitational pull of a passing star 1 in **2,200,000** (University of Michigan)

2. Chance of us returning to ("the hotel") in Houston: **worse than any of those!** (What are the chances you'd save our rooms for us anyway?)

Fortunately for its owners, the hotel in Houston no longer exists. Imagine today, however, if you were the RM and a legitimate or even very unfair posting criticizing your hotel appeared on a popular Internet hotel review site. What to do? Consider these positive steps:

1. Go on the review site and thank the customer for taking the time to write a review.

2. Apologize if the customer is right about the negative experience.

3. Provide a simple, short explanation of what really happened (if possible).

4. Assure the reviewer and review readers that every possible action has been taken to avoid a repeat of the problem.

5. Offer a direct line of communication between your hotel and the reviewer (via email, direct phone line, etc.) to receive an apology "in person."

6. Conclude the response by using, if possible, any elements of the reviewer's comments that are constructive (e.g., great hotel location, comfortable rooms, etc.) to end your response on a positive note.

Excerpted on 9/28/2008 from http://www.snopes.com/business/info/badhotel/frame.htm and http://www.snopes.com/business/consumer/badhotel.asp

- Easily permits room availability and rate information updating and revision
- Produces a reasonable Net ADR Yield on each room sold (see Figure 8.11)
- Does no damage to guests' perception of the price value relationship offered by the property and thus contributes to brand building; not brand eroding
- Avoids product commoditization
- Permits the hotel to retain customer ownership and thus maximize its customer-centric revenue optimization focus

It is in the *customer ownership* issue that hoteliers misunderstand the impact of some IDS sites. Too many IDS sites train customers to shop by price alone. Some even have created their own frequent buyer or points programs.[19] RMs who overutilize such sites seemingly forget that

Figure 8.11	Net ADR Yield and Information Control Summary of the Top Nine Revenue Producing Distribution Channels

Channel	Typical Net ADR Yield	Direct Control of Information
Nonelectronic Distribution Channels		
On property transient sales	90–95%	Hotel
On property group sales	90–95%	Hotel
Telephone direct	90–95%	Hotel
CVB Initiated	85–95%	Intermediary
Electronic Distribution Channels		
CRS	90–95%	Hotel/Hotel franchisor
GDS	80–95%	Intermediary
IDS (Property site)	90–95%	Hotel/Hotel franchisor
IDS (Third-party site)	65–85%	Intermediary
IDS (Web 2.0 site)	N/A	Customers/Rooms buyers

competing on *price only* severely limits their ability to attract and retain more sophisticated travel shoppers and more affluent customers. The commoditization of a consumer product is not the way to optimize revenue from its sale. A decommoditization strategy requires the creation of distinctive product offerings designed to provide a unique value proposition (e.g., suite specials, romantic getaways and hotel packages, including family packages, weekend getaways, museum packages, seasonal packages, golf packages, and spa packages).

Third-party online intermediaries have been responsible to a great extent for the commoditization of the hotel industry's products and services. Too many RMs permit this to happen and remarkably, as shown in Figure 8.11, they accept much lower than average net ADR yields from these same distribution channels that promote commoditization. RMs must seek to own their customers by building mutually beneficial interactive relationships with them. Only in that way can they increase repeat business, build customer loyalty, and optimize their revenue.

PRINCIPLES OF DISTRIBUTION CHANNEL MANAGEMENT

The management of distribution channels is the management of partnership relationships. In the lodging industry, the type and forms of these partnerships will continue to evolve. It is important to remember that a distribution channel is effective only to the degree that it helps you achieve your revenue optimization goals. Both your hotel and the channel you use must benefit. This concept was stated well by Nobel prize–winning economist Milton Friedman, who pointed out, *"The most important single central fact about a free market is that no exchange takes place unless both parties benefit."*[20] RMs managing their current and future distribution channels will continue to face many challenges as they ensure that distribution channels truly do assist their efforts to expand their customer and revenue bases. Effective RMs can best manage their distribution channels when they apply the 12 principles of distribution channel management shown in Figure 8.12.

Figure 8.12	12 Principles of Distribution Channel Management

1. Evaluate channel effectiveness based on net ADR yield as well as the channel's total revenue generation ability.
2. Use distribution partners to promote rack rates and premium rates as well as selected discount rates.
3. Regularly measure the proportion of revenue generated directly as a result of the hotel's brand affiliation.
4. Design or employ shopper services to regularly evaluate the quality and information accuracy of nonelectronic distribution systems.
5. Regularly measure the proportion of revenue delivered via nonelectronic distribution channels.
6. Develop and aggressively promote their own well designed proprietary (not brand controlled) property web site.
7. Assign one or more individuals to regularly evaluate the accuracy of those electronic distribution partners listing the property's inventory and room rates.
8. Avoid distribution channels that require manual uploads of inventory and rates.
9. Seek out commission-based IDS partners; avoid merchant and opaque model site operators if they lead to product commoditization.
10. Implement a proactive Web 2.0 strategy via CGM initiatives such as blogs, tweets, guest experience, and photo sharing.
11. Seek out specialized distribution channels to advertise unique hotel offers based on unique product attributes. Utilize sound differential pricing strategies to price the offerings.
12. Aggressively implement strategies designed to shift guests' future bookings from more expensive distribution channels to lesser expense channels.

❖ ESSENTIAL RM TERMS

Travel wholesaler

Global distribution system (GDS)

Internet distribution system (IDS)

Fade rate

CPOR

Shopper service

Commoditization

Call center

Loaded (rate)

Proprietary web site

Search engine results page (SERP)

Conversion

Link strategy

Agency model

Net rate

Merchant model

Referral site

Opaque model

Consumer-generated media (CGM)

‖‖‖➡ APPLY WHAT YOU KNOW

1. Joel Liberman is the RM at the City Center Plaza, a 300-room franchised hotel. He is evaluating alternative options regarding the allocation of 100 unsold guest rooms for the third weekend of next month. His property's group room sales department believes (but is not positive) that it can sell 80 group rooms for that date at a rate of $185.00 per room. The hotel's FOM believes that if the 100 rooms are listed on the "Deals at This Hotel" page of the franchisor operated property web site, with a 25 percent discount off the hotel's normal $229.99 rack rate, 90 rooms might sell through the CRS. The sale would apply only to buyers willing to agree that the room would be billed to the guests at the time of purchase and could not be canceled.

   Uberhothotels.com, a third-party merchant model operator, is willing to pay the hotel $160.00 for each room it purchases but wants a commitment from the hotel that it would be able to buy and then resell up to 100 rooms. It believes it can do so if it lists the rooms as open to all buyers and at a rate of $172.99 per night.

   Joel already has 200 rooms sold for this specific night at the hotel's rack rate. Assume that each distribution channel produces as projected. Complete the following revenue estimate report and answer the questions that follow.

RevPAR Estimate Worksheet: City Center Plaza
Prepared By Joel L.

Distribution Channel	Group Sales	CRS Sale	Third-Party Merchant
Previous booked revenue: 200 rooms @ $229.99			
Estimated channel revenue contribution			
Total rooms revenue estimate			
Total rooms sold			
ADR			
Occ.%			
RevPAR			

A. Based on his best estimates of each channel's performance:
   1. Which channel would produce the highest ADR?
   2. Which channel would produce the lowest ADR?

B. Based on his best estimates of each channel's performance:
   1. Which channel would generate the highest occupancy %?
   2. Which channel would generate the lowest occupancy %?

C. Based on his best estimates of each channel's performance:
   1. Which channel would generate the highest RevPAR?
   2. Which channel would generate the lowest RevPAR?

D. If you were Joel, to which channel would you allocate the 100 rooms? Why?

2. Joel knows that under his franchise agreement, he pays an 8 percent franchise fee and 3 percent marketing fee on all revenue generated from room sales. Additional fees for using the hotel's CRS are 1 percent of booked revenue plus $2.00 per each room reserved. Internet service provider (IDS) related charges paid by the hotel for rooms sold through Internet sites including uberhothotels.com are $10.00 per room sold. Given this information, help Joel complete the revenue estimate worksheet presented below.

Net ADR Yield Estimate Worksheet: City Center Plaza
Prepared by Joel L.

Distribution Channel	Group Rooms	CRS Sales	Third-Party Merchant
Rooms sold	80	90	100
(Standard) rate	$185.00	$172.49	$160.00
Gross revenue			
Franchise fee (8%)			
Franchise marketing fee (3%)			
Franchisor's CRS fee (1% + $2.00 per room))			
IDS fee ($10.00 per room)			
Net total revenue			
Net ADR yield			

A. Based on Joel's calculated net ADR yields for each of the three channels:
   1. Which channel has the highest net ADR yield?
   2. Which channel has the lowest net ADR yield?

B. Based on Joel's calculated net total revenue achieved under each of the three sales scenarios:

1. Which channel would generate the highest net total revenue?

2. Which channel would generate the lowest net total revenue?

C. Based on this information, to which channel would you allocate the 100 rooms? Why?

3. Joel estimates that the net ADR yield on the 200 rooms he has already sold will average 88 percent. He also knows that at his hotel it costs $55.00 to prepare, sell, and clean (prepare for resale) each room sold. To help him make the very best revenue optimization decision possible, complete the worksheet and then answer the questions that follow.

GOPPAR Estimate Worksheet: City Center Plaza
Prepared by Joel L.

Channel	Group Rooms	CRS	Third-Party Merchant
Previous booked rooms net revenue @ 88% net ADR yield			
Channel contributed net revenue*			
Total net revenue			
Total rooms sold	280	290	300
Rooms cost @ $55.00			
After rooms costs revenue			
GOPPAR (300 rooms available) *From Question 2: Chapter 8			

A. Based on Joel's calculated GOPPAR for each of the three channels:

1. Which channel produces the highest GOPPAR?

2. Which channel produces the lowest GOPPAR?

B. Assume you were Joel.

1. What additional customer-centric revenue optimization factors might affect your decision to utilize or not utilize the group rooms distribution option?

2. What additional customer-centric revenue optimization factors might affect your decision to utilize or not utilize the CRS distribution option?

3. What additional customer-centric revenue optimization factors might affect your decision to utilize or not utilize the third-party merchant option?

4. Carrie Thorton is the RM at the 400-room Sheraton Bay City, the highest-priced hotel in a popular summer vacation area that is home to 15 other hotel properties. Carrie has been approached by her local CVB to participate in a rooms bid for Bay City to host the organizers, participants, and attendees for next year's 30-mile "Bike-A-Thon For Kids" charity event. Over the four day event, the Bike-A-Thon will produce approximately 3,000 room nights for the host city and draw 6,000 visitors. Harbor Falls is 50 miles away from Bay City, and its CVB will also be preparing a bid for the event. One of the two cities will be chosen to host the event.

   The CVB informs Carrie that the planners responsible for choosing the site of the Bike-A-Thon are very price sensitive. As a result, the CVB would like to be very competitive with its bid. What tangible factors would you advise Carrie to consider when determining whether to commit rooms inventory for this CVB bid. What intangible factors would you suggest she consider?

5. Increasingly, information about hotels is distributed via Web 2.0 sites. Unfortunately, some of the information posted on such sites is not accurate or fair to hotels. Assume that you are the RM for a property that has just received an extremely negative customer review. The review was written by Ray Snipe, a previous hotel guest at your property. Mr. Snipe's review has now been posted on TripAdvisor.com. Some of the facts stated in this consumer's review are true, while others are not. The reviewer ends the long review by writing and posting the following:

   > The staff wasn't unfriendly, but they weren't particularly friendly either. It's in a relatively safe neighborhood, so there is that. But I would only suggest you stay here if you are absolutely desperate. Other than that, I recommend you spend your money at a nice hotel.

   As the property RM, identify the key content elements that should be included in any response to Mr. Snipe that you could post on the same consumer-generated traveler review site.

KEY CONCEPT CASE STUDY

"Well, what's your reaction to Lorenzo's proposal?" asked Damario, the revenue manager at the Barcena Resort. Damario was addressing the members of the resort's *Strategic Pricing and Revenue Management Advisory Committee*.

The committee had just finished hearing a detailed proposal from Lorenzo Monteagudo, the senior sales vice president for BidCarib.com, and a fairly new company that was operating an opaque web site specializing in Caribbean vacations. "Our target market is South Americans," Lorenzo had explained. "Our web site is written in Spanish and Portuguese. We can provide guests when your North American customers are staying home."

"Well, I like it," said Mark Chaplin, the hotel's Controller. "Lorenzo said we didn't have to provide a fixed inventory allocation in advance, or fixed rates. We can turn the service on and off like a light switch. And they don't charge a commission. It seems like a no brainer to me. The rooms they would sell for us would go empty without them. I say we use them on any day we know we will not sell out."

"I agree," said Pam, the property's DOSM. "The fact that they will only pay a net rate that is 50 percent of our rack rate is a concern, but I do like the fact that they are shielding our hotel's name from view until after the sale is made. I think it could help us generate incremental sales without tarnishing our image or affecting the higher rates we advertise on other IDS sites. That way we can discount without letting our regular customers know we are doing it."

"I'm not so sure. I was concerned about what he said regarding the customers we would attract," said Adrian, the resort's rooms manager. "I wrote it down in my notes during his presentation. Near the beginning of it, Lorenzo said, *We can help you attract guests that are not brand loyal and choose their resort based on price. Then when you get them here, you can Wow them with service and make them guests for life.*"

"That makes sense to me," said Mark, "What's the problem?"

"Well," replied Adrian, "I'm wondering why we would think those types of guests would become any more loyal to us in the future than they have to anyone else. Honestly, they just sound cheap to me. I'd rather see us offer significant discounts or rewards to our guests who are already loyal."

"I think you are missing the point," said Mark. "These would be incremental sales. Sites like Lorenzo's can help us sell rooms at a big discount without anyone knowing we are discounting."

"Not exactly," quickly added Amanda, the front office manager. "Guests may not know about the existence of extra low rates when they buy, but they sure do talk to each other about the rates they paid *after* they get here. I'm wondering what we will instruct our desk staff to say if a couple approaches them to complain that they found out they are paying twice the rate of the couple they met at dinner last night. For the exact same room type and the exact same dates?"

"Well, they bought from different sites," said Amanda. "We'll just explain that we sell our rooms for different prices based on how guests buy them."

"That's my whole concern," said Adrian. "How do we maintain that our pricing is fair, and customer-centric, if we are differentiating price based on *how* guests buy instead of what they buy?"

For Your Consideration

1. Mark's position appears to be that any room sale that can be made if the room would otherwise go vacant is a good sale. Do you agree? Explain your answer.

2. Pam's position appears to be that the use of opaque web sites allows significant discounting without harming the resort's image. Do you agree? Explain your answer.

3. Adrian's concern relates to the hotel's ability to convert low-priced buyers to higher-priced buyers in the future. Amanda's concern relates to the impact on other guests of room sales made through BidCarib.com. Do you believe their concerns are valid? Explain your answers.

4. The job of an RM is to use data and insight to optimize the property's revenue.

Assume you were Damario. Do you believe establishing a business relationship with BidCarib.com would help or harm your overall efforts to create a customer-centric revenue optimization program? What factors would be important in helping you decide? Explain your answer.

ENDNOTES

1. http://thinkexist.com/quotation/simplify-simplify-/145742.html. Retrieved 9/5/2008.

2. http://www.wisdomquotes.com/cat_history.html.

3. "Are Travel Agents Making A Comeback" excerpt retrieved from Cable News Network, CNN.com on August 12, 2009.

4. http://www.worldofquotes.com/author/Paul-Eldridge/1/index.html.

5. http://www.ahla.com/content.aspx?id=4214 Retrieved. 9/10/2008.

6. Joe Griffith, *Speaker's Library of Business Stories, Anecdotes, and Humor* (Englewood Cliffs, NJ: Prentice Hall, 1990), 66.

7. http://www.asklyrics.com/display/Rush/Tom_Sawyer_Lyrics/174801.htm.

8. http://www.ihgplc.com/index.asp?pageid=373. Retrieved 9/17/2008.

9. http://traveltechnology.blogspot.com/2008/07/gnes-and-gds-bypass.html. Retrieved 9/17/2008.

10. http://www.boardofwisdom.com/default.asp?topic=1005&listname=Competition. Retrieved 9/17/2008.

11. http://en.wikipedia.org/wiki/Winning_isn't_everything;_it's_the_only_thing. Retrieved 9/20/2009.

12. http://thinkexist.com/quotes/michael_hugos/. Retrieved 9/19/2208.

13. Stowe Shoemaker, Robert Lewis and Peter Yesawich, *Marketing Leadership in Hospitality and Tourism*, 4th. ed. (Upper Saddle River, NJ: Pearson Prentice Hall, 2006), 527.

14. Excerpted 6/19/2009 from *Columbus Ledger-Enquirer*, "Columbus Wins Expedia Lawsuit: Georgia Supreme Court Rules: Online Travel Service Should Pay Lodging Taxes."

15. M. Scovick, "Internet Wars," *Hotels* (May 2004): 40.

16. http://www.galtech.com/research/travel/airline-reservations.php.

17. http://findarticles.com/p/articles/mi_m3072/is_4_219/ai_114717379. Retrieved 9/21/2008.

18. http://www.hospitalitynet.org/news/4037310. Retrieved 9/29/2008.

19. http://www.allbusiness.com/company-activities-management/management-personal/5438629–1.html. Retrieved 6/30/2009.

20. http://www.woopidoo.com/business_quotes/partnership-quotes.htm. Retrieved 9/30/2008.

[i] Hotel Business, Vol. 19 No. 7 April 21-May 6, 2010, p. 3.

CHAPTER 9

Evaluation of Revenue Management Efforts in Lodging

CHAPTER HIGHLIGHTS

1. Detailed examination of the primary financial measures of RM performance.

2. Explanation of how to read and analyze STAR and similar reports.

3. Examination of additional RM-related performance measures and their uses.

THE LODGING REVENUE PARADOX

As you have learned in the previous two chapters, all RMs should use relevant data and their insight to make good inventory management, pricing, and distribution channel management decisions. But how do they know if they have done so? The answer will be important to how you assess your own efforts, as well as to the operating **statistics** others will use to evaluate your performance.

Essential RM Term

Statistic: A number or term used to summarize or to describe a larger collection of information. Examples include sums, averages, and ratios.

To illustrate the importance of properly evaluating operating statistics, assume you are the RM for a hotel located in a city in which last month's average occupancy rate for all hotels was 65 percent. Your hotel achieved a 90 percent occupancy last month. Should you be pleased?

Next, assume that you are the RM for a different hotel located in a city in which last month's average ADR for all hotels in that city was $199.99. Your hotel achieved a $249.99 ADR during the same period. Should you be pleased?

If your answer to each of the above questions was *"I simply don't know,"* then you are correct; and you also know one of a lodging RM's most important lessons:

Any evaluation of a hotel's occupancy percent or its ADR, without a simultaneous assessment of both, is meaningless.

To equitably assess revenue generation in a hotel, occupancy percentage and room rate must be evaluated at the same time. This revenue assessment paradox exists in the lodging industry and is quite similar to the load factor paradox faced by airlines. In both industries, RMs must carefully balance the quantity of product sold (hotel rooms or airline seats) with the prices charged (ADR or air fares) to optimize revenue. Recall from Chapter 1 that the formula for RevPAR is:

$$\text{ADR} \times \text{Occupancy percentage} = \text{RevPAR}$$

Note that this formula permits RMs to simultaneously consider the impact of ADR-related decisions and Occupancy %-related decisions on their hotels' revenue generation.

RM IN ACTION 9.1: REVPAR PERFORMANCE AS KEY TO PROFITABILITY? NOT SO MUCH.

RMs must be careful not to make the mistake of thinking that maximization of RevPAR means maximization of facility profits. To illustrate this point, consider the wording of two important parts of a press release issued by Starwood hotels:

1. Starwood Hotels and Resorts today reported that systemwide revenue per available room (RevPAR) increased 9.5 percent in the third quarter . . . compared with the same period last year.

2. Profits, however, were down. Earnings for the quarter dropped by almost 17 percent compared with last year.

How can RevPAR increase, but profitability be reduced? The simple answer is GOPPAR.

An understanding of why and how GOPPAR drives an RM's revenue optimization efforts is absolutely crucial.

_____

Excerpted on 10/15/2008 from http://www.allbusiness.com/travel-hospitality-tourism/lodging-lodging-industry/6627987—1.html

Since the mid-1990s, efforts and strategies designed to maximize RevPAR have been a major focus of lodging property RMs. Interestingly, while property RMs and a good number of management companies use RevPAR to measure their effectiveness, sophisticated hotel owners typically do not. The reasons why are many, but they relate directly to the importance of revenue optimization and profitability (GOPPAR), not revenue maximization.

RevPAR Limitations

Although hotel owners have long embraced GOPPAR (gross operating profit per available room) as a reliable indicator of the cash generating capacity of their hotels, many RMs continue to focus on RevPAR (revenue per available room) to measure their effectiveness. Because it is easy to calculate, RevPAR does provide a convenient, if not always accurate, way for hotels of different sizes to be measured against each other in terms of revenue generation. As you will learn, RevPAR is also useful in comparing the performance of a hotel against that of its competitive set. As well, RevPAR improvement and growth has been embraced by many hotel operators as an easy measure for use in RM's compensation and incentive programs. The usefulness of the RevPAR statistic is undeniable. However it is critical that RMs understand its limitations.

First, it is essential to recognize that RevPAR is typically calculated using rooms revenue _only_. Food and beverage and other sources of revenue do not affect RevPAR. This major weakness of the RevPAR statistic can be illustrated by considering the case of Michele and Amanda. These two RMs work in competitive 400 room full-service hotels. Last month, Michele's hotel achieved a $200.00 ADR and 80 percent occupancy. Her hotel's RevPAR would be computed as:

$$\text{ADR} \times \text{Occupancy percentage} = \text{RevPAR}$$

or

$$\$200.00 \times 0.80 = \$160.00 \text{ RevPAR}$$

Amanda's hotel achieved a $320.00 ADR and 50 percent occupancy. Her RevPAR would be computed as:

$$\$320.00 \times 0.50 = \$160.00 \text{ RevPAR}$$

Michele's hotel, however, is likely to have achieved higher total revenues because her F&B outlets, gift shop, and in-room product and service sales will likely be higher due to her higher occupancy and the resulting increased number of guests who stayed in her hotel. Of course, Michele's hotel will incur higher operational costs as well. As a result, it could be that Amanda's hotel will achieve a higher GOPPAR level. The important point for RMs to understand is that RevPAR measures total room revenue generation only, while ignoring revenues achieved in other areas of the hotel, the property's operational costs, and other factors that may directly affect the profits shown on a hotel's **income statement.**

Essential RM Term

Income statement: A detailed listing of an operation's revenue and expenses for a specific time period. Also know as the statement of income and expense, profit and loss statement, or P&L.

When RMs excessively focus on RevPAR, they believe maximizing revenues take precedent over all other considerations. As a result, rooms could be sold at rates close to (or even below) variable operating costs because every incremental dollar of room revenue achieved increases RevPAR—no matter how low the room rate.

In previous chapters, you learned the importance of assessing the various distribution costs associated with selling rooms and the resulting net ADR yield on those sales. A RevPAR calculation ignores these costs. Thus, a room selling for $200, with a net ADR yield of 75 percent ($150 net ADR), impacts RevPAR more positively than a room sold for $159.00 with no channel distribution costs; despite the latter's room's higher profit margins.

Despite the shortcomings, maximized RevPAR can often correlate with achieving higher hotel profits.[*] The danger for RMs comes if they confuse correlation with causation. Big difference. To illustrate, there is a very strong correlation between the number of firemen fighting a fire and the amount of fire-related damage that occurs. Thus, the more firefighters present at a fire, the larger the fire will be. That's logical. It does *not* logically follow, however, that additional firefighters *cause* the damage. The correlation between the number of firefighters at a scene and the damage caused in a fire does not prove that more firefighters create more damage. Firefighters are sent to fires according to the severity of the fire. If there is a large fire, a greater number of firefighters are sent. Large fires cause more damage; additional firefighters would actually reduce the damage levels of severe fires.

In a similar manner, RevPAR increases can indicate improved profitability, but they do not always do so. Accepting and applying this truth requires some courage on the part of RMs because of the widespread industry belief that RevPAR is the ultimate measure of revenue generation success. It is not. Despite its current popularity, RMs would do well to recall business consultant and author Jim Rohn's statement, "Things that I felt absolutely sure of but a few years ago, I do not believe now. This thought makes me see more clearly how foolish it would be to expect all men to agree with me." [**] Many hoteliers would agree that RevPAR is the best measure of revenue optimization, but you should *not*. You now know better.

---

[*] http://www.hotel-online.com/News/PR2010_2nd/Apr10_RevPARImpact.html Retrieved 4/29/2010
[**] http://www.brainyquote.com/quotes/authors/j/jim_rohn.html Retrieved 4/29/2010

RevPOR

As a professional RM it is important for you to recognize that the RevPAR statistic used in a limited service hotel represents a very different concept than does the one used in a full-service hotel. This is so because RevPAR as traditionally calculated does not take into account revenue from other hotel services and revenue centers, such as restaurants, spas, golf courses, marinas, and casinos. As a result, RMs working in full-service hotels often calculate RevPOR to serve as an additional measure of their properties revenue generating ability. In Chapter 1, you learned that the formula for RevPOR is:

$$\frac{\text{Total (Rooms + Nonrooms) revenue}}{\text{Total occupied rooms}} = \text{RevPOR}$$

The hotel that generates significant nonrooms revenues will be very interested in measuring and evaluating its guests' spending patterns. Knowing about these patterns can be helpful, for example, when considering the relative merits of selling rooms to a group that will heavily utilize a hotel's meeting space, food service options, lounges, gift shops and the like, versus selling those same rooms (even at a higher ADR) to rooms buyers who are not expected to heavily utilize the hotel's revenue generating facilities. As an RM, you should be concerned about all of the revenue generated by your property, not merely the revenue generated by room sales.

Figure 9.1 lists some of the nonrooms revenue generators commonly found in full-service as well as some select-service hotels.

Not every hotel will generate revenue from each of these areas; however, as the number of nonrooms revenue generators increases, their potential impact on RevPOR increases as well. As a general rule, increases in RevPORs are to be desired and, as a result, RMs should regularly monitor and assess their property RevPORs.

Two legitimate issues are relevant to the calculation and assessment of RevPOR. The first issue relates to occupancy percentage. RevPOR does *not* consider the number of rooms

---

Figure 9.1 | Common Nonrooms Revenue Sources

- Food
- Beverages
- Meeting space
- Meeting/convention services
- Audio visual services
- Gift shop
- Casinos
- Admission fees (e.g., water parks and similar mixed use hotel facilities)
- Telecommunications

- Garage and parking
- Golf course
- Golf pro shop
- Guest laundry
- Health center/spa services
- Swimming pool
- Tennis
- Tennis pro shop
- Other operated departments
- Rentals and other income

sold. Conversely, recall that RevPAR calculations *are* directly affected by the quantity of rooms sold. In most cases, a hotel that operates with a very high RevPOR but a very low occupancy percent will not be profitable. For that reason, the authors suggest that some RMs working in full-service properties may prefer to modify the traditionally calculated RevPAR formula to include nonrooms revenue. Doing so creates a modified *Total RevPAR* statistic.

For many RMs, the computation and assessment of this newly proposed **Total RevPAR** statistic could be very useful.

Essential RM Term

Total RevPAR: The average rooms and nonrooms revenue generated by each available guest room during a specific period of time:

$$\frac{\text{Total (Rooms + Nonrooms) revenue}}{\text{Total rooms available for sale}} = \text{Total RevPAR}$$

The second significant concern surrounding RevPOR is more complex and relates directly to the measurement of a hotel's profitability rather than its revenue generation. This entire issue can best be understood by considering yet again how the airline industry is *different* from the lodging industry.

To calculate the actual costs of flying its passengers, airlines carefully consider the amortization cost of the plane, based on the number of hours it can fly in its useful life. They also assess the aircraft's maintenance, fuel, crew, and other costs. They then use all of that information to determine an operating cost-per-seat mile flown. Because today's airline passengers pay for additional luggage, drinks, meals, blankets, and pillows, the variable costs of adding additional passengers are very few and are essentially limited to the cost of any additional fuel needed to fly the incremental passenger.

It is important to recognize that when an airline seat goes unsold, it still has a real cost associated with flying that seat to its destination. Because that is so, virtually any revenue generated by the seat's sale helps to defray the airline's total cost, even if the revenue generated by the seat's sale is less than the fixed cost of flying the empty seat. In the airline industry, an empty seat represents a specific nonrecovered amount of cost and a lost revenue opportunity.

RMs in the lodging industry must take a different position regarding the costs associated with selling a guest room. Unlike their airline counterparts, lodging RMs must consider the cost to them of an empty room to be $0.00, because leaving a guest room *empty* causes the hotel to incur no incremental costs. Unlike an airplane that loses a small amount of its useful life when it flies an empty seat, leaving a guest room empty actually *extends* its life because there is reduced wear and tear on the furnishings and carpet, no additional usage of supplies or guest room amenities, and, in most cases, no incremental utilities cost.

Alternatively, putting one to four guests in the room for one night results in very definitive increased costs, including those associated with cleaning the room, replenishing room supplies (e.g., linens, towels, sheets, and the like), and the cost of any amenities included in the room's sale (e.g., soap, shampoo, lotions). If a complimentary breakfast is included, these costs, too, will be incurred. Additionally, wear and tear on the room must be considered.

Depending on the hotel's specific cost structure, the expense incurred in selling a room (including labor and supplies) can range from a modest to a very significant amount. Clearly, the incremental costs associated with selling a room in a budget hotel located in a rural area are much less than those related to selling an upscale room in the downtown area of a large city. In both cases, however, if the room is unsold for the night, these costs are not incurred. If the room is occupied, the hotel must seek to receive revenues in an amount at least equal to these **room-related occupation costs.**

Essential RM Term

Room-related occupation costs: Those rooms-related costs incurred directly as a result of selling a guest room. Examples include labor costs, room supplies, and room amenities.

Also referred to as room-related occupancy cost, occupied room cost, or cost per occupied room (CPOR).

You have previously learned that net ADR yield represents the amount of revenue remaining after subtracting costs related to the room's *sale*. You can now understand why experienced RMs know that the calculation of the minimum selling price that should be charged for a guest room must include additional costs if revenue is to exceed the total cost of the room's sale. These costs include all rooms-related occupancy costs *plus* the cost of any distribution channel commissions *and* any franchise-related fees and royalties that must be paid to create the sale.

To illustrate this, consider a hotel with a $40.00 per night rooms-related occupancy cost, or CPOR. Assume also that this hotel's highest cost distribution channel consists of a 20 percent commission and a 7 percent total franchise fee. Utilizing the **minimum ADR sales point formula**, the hotel would identify its absolute minimum room rate as $54.79.

Essential RM Term

Minimum ADR sales point formula: The lowest room rate that can be charged and still generate enough revenue to pay all rooms-related occupancy costs *plus* the cost of any distribution channel commissions and franchise-related fees and royalties paid to create the sale.

$$\frac{\text{Rooms-related occupancy costs}}{\text{Net ADR yield \%}} = \text{Minimum ADR sales point}$$

In this example, the calculation would be:

$$\frac{\$40.00}{1 - (0.20 + 0.07)} = \text{Minimum ADR sales point}$$

Or

$$\frac{\$40.00}{1 - (0.20 + 0.07)} = \frac{\$40.00}{1 - (0.73)} = \$54.79$$

In this illustration, any reservation sold above the minimum ADR sales point and delivered through the hotel's highest cost distribution channel would still cover the incremental rooms-related occupancy costs and selling costs associated with the room's sale. Room sales made at a rate below the minimum ADR sales point will increase RevPAR, but it will not increase profits.

Of course, guests staying at a property may also spend additional dollars in some of the hotel's other revenue-generating departments. In limited-service hotels, however, there may be very few sources of additional revenue beyond room night charges. In a full-service hotel, the additional nonrooms revenue typically generated by the sale of a room may be quite significant, and these revenues must be considered when assessing a minimum ADR sales point.

RMs should not, of course, actually seek to sell rooms at the minimum ADR sales point. Doing so would ignore the many other fixed costs of the hotel including debt service, mortgage, management fees, real estate taxes, utilities, and nonrooms labor. As you can imagine, the profit-related RevPOR issue takes on additional significance if an RM team seeks to increase rooms revenue via the last minute publication of reduced room rates.

When a hotel attempts to raise occupancy by reducing rates, it may do so at the cost of losing already booked business from group or transient sales. Many group rooms buyers and travel agencies monitor changes in rates for rooms they have previously booked. They will not hesitate to cancel previously booked reservations in favor of newer, less expensive ones. This resulting rebooking can reduce total rooms revenue, reduce the hotel's RevPOR, and depress the property's net profits.

GOPPAR

Despite the popularity of RevPAR and RevPOR among many RMs, more sophisticated RMs and the majority of hotel GMs prefer to monitor their property GOPPAR achievement because they know that an excessive RevPAR focus can actually harm a hotel's long-term profitability. This is especially so in times of severe weakness in rooms demand.***

In Chapter 1 you learned that GOPPAR represents a hotel's gross operating profit per available room. GOPPAR is the average **gross operating profit (GOP)** generated by each available guest room during a specific accounting period.

A close examination of the GOPPAR formula shown in Figure 9.2 reveals three significant reasons for its appeal to hotel GMs and owners.

Gross Operating Profit (GOP)

Gross operating profit (GOP): Total revenues less management-controllable operating expenses. GOP can be expressed in total dollars or as a percentage of total revenue.

1. The statistic is calculated using total, not rooms only, hotel revenue. This is an especially critical factor in full-service hotels.

2. A GOPPAR calculation includes expense as well as revenue but focuses only on those expenses that can be controlled by on site hotel managers and for which

Figure 9.2	**GOPPAR Formula**

$$\frac{\text{Total revenue} - \text{Management-controllable expense}}{\text{Rooms available to sell}} = \text{GOPPAR}$$

***

*** *Successful Tactics for Surviving an Economic Downturn: Results from an International Study,* Dr. Sheryl E. Kimes. Cornell Hospitality reports, April 2010: The Center for Hospitality Research, Cornell University. Retrieved 4/30/2010.

Figure 9.3	400-Room Hotel Alternative RevPAR Performances		
400-Room Property	**Higher Occupancy/ Lower ADR**	**Higher ADR/Lower Occupancy**	**Moderate ADR/ Moderate Occupancy**
Occupancy %	80%	60%	70%
Rooms sold	320	240	280
ADR	$ 199.99	$ 266.65	$ 228.55
Rev	$ 63,996	$ 63,996	$ 63,994
RevPAR	**$ 159.99**	**$ 159.99**	**$ 159.99**
Controllable operating costs @ $75.00 per room	$ 24,000.00	$ 18,000.00	$ 21,000.00
Gross operating profit	$ 39,996.80	$ 45,996.00	$ 42,994.00
GOPPAR	$ 99.99	$ 114.99	$ 107.49

these managers can be held accountable. Note that GOP is the numerator in the GOPPAR formula.

3. The calculation is based on the total number of *available* rooms in the property (as is RevPAR), and thus it avoids the limitations of those statistics, such as RevPOR, that are determined by the number of sold rooms only.

As you can see in Figure 9.3, hotels with identical RevPAR generation can vary widely in their GOPPAR production.

The difference in profit generation between hotels with identical RevPARs can be significant. Note in Figure 9.3 that the "higher ADR, lower occupancy" hotel generates 15 percent ($114.99 − $ 99.99)/$ 99.99 = 15%) greater profits than the "higher occupancy, lower ADR" hotel, and 7 percent ($114.99 − $ 107.49)/$ 107.49 = 7.0%) greater profits than the "moderate occupancy/moderate ADR" hotel, despite the fact that the respective RevPARs for each of the three hotels is identical.

Because of the number of factors used in its calculation, a GOPPAR maximization strategy is more sophisticated than a RevPAR maximization strategy. The influence of GOPPAR assessment on an RM's pricing and selling strategies should be clear. Consider, for example, that a strategy of selling rooms *below* the combined total of occupancy costs and selling costs should be avoided because implementing such a strategy would lead to a *decrease* in GOPPAR, although such a strategy would increase occupancy %, total room revenues, and the resulting RevPAR. Similarly, if a hotel decided to temporarily increase sales commissions to encourage room sales, this would be reflected in a reduced GOPPAR (but not a reduced RevPAR). A GOPPAR focus eliminates some of the negatives inherent in an undue focus on RevPAR.

Because a hotel's operating profit is divided by the number of available room nights, GOPPAR will increase as long as each incremental unit sale (whether rooms, F&B or other revenue) generates profits. Experienced RMs know that a GOPPAR focus may also help to resolve the traditional conflict between those in hotel operations (e.g., housekeeping and F&B staff) and a property's sales team. This conflict often arises because operations

RM AT WORK 9.1

"Run the numbers again," said Elijah, the FOM at the 400-room Radisson Riverview. "We need to make sure we are accurate about this."

"I ran them three times already," replied Jennifer. "Last year, in September, our RevPAR was $87.50. We ran a 70 percent occupancy and a $125 rate."

"And so far this September?" asked Elijah

"Like I said before, with three days left in the month, we are at a 69 percent occupancy and $129 rate. That's an $89.01 RevPAR," said Jennifer.

"And we were budgeted for a 4 percent RevPAR increase?" asked Elijah.

"Right, and that's the problem. We are at a 1.5 percent increase now. And as you know, if we don't make budget, we don't make our bonus."

"O.K. I got it. Now one more time, what did the New York booking agent say when you talked to him on the phone?" asked Elijah.

"He said the entire Lion King cast was displaced because of a booking error at the hotel they had reserved. He's scrambling for housing. He wants to bring the entire cast and crew here for four days, starting tonight. They want 100 rooms each day, but their budget is only $59.00 a night. If we take them, we'll be sold out for the rest of the month," said Jennifer.

Assume that, with three days left in the month, Elijah's best estimate is that if he agrees to take the Lion King group it would mean 100 sold rooms per night at $59.00 and assume further that his hotel would indeed sell all of its remaining rooms on those nights at the $129 ADR the property is currently averaging for the month.

1. If he takes the group, would Elijah achieve the RevPAR needed to be granted the performance bonuses offered to him and his assistant?

2. What additional factors would you advise Elijah to consider before he decides whether to accept the reservation for the rooms requested by the Lion King's booking agent?

3. If you were the RM at this property, would you advise Elijah to take the group? Why or why not?

---

staffs focus on departmental costs and profitability while sales staffs typically concentrate on increasing *total revenues regardless of costs*. This is especially so when sales staff salaries, bonuses, and other incentives are based on RevPAR generation.

It is important to note that cross-property assessments of GOPPAR must be made carefully. To illustrate, consider two hotels, each of which offers 400 rooms for sale. Assume further that the amount of meeting space and F&B capacity in hotel A greatly exceeds that available in hotel B. In such a case, it is very possible that its extra capacity results in the GOPPAR in hotel A exceeding that of hotel B. This could be true, however, even if hotel B does a better job of selling its available space profitably. It is for this reason that RMs working in full-service hotels must carefully consider the impact of meeting space and F&B sales and resulting profits on their hotels' overall profitability.

Flow-through

Flow-through is an accounting concept that may not be immediately recognizable as a significant revenue management issue. It is, however, extremely helpful in understanding the effect of revenue optimization strategies employed by a revenue management team. **Flow-through** is a measure of the ability of a hotel to convert increased revenue dollars to increased gross operating profit dollars.

Essential RM Term

Flow-through: The relative change in profit dollars expressed as a percentage of the change in revenue dollars.

Understanding the flow-through concept is critical, yet U.S. hoteliers have been somewhat slower than their European counterparts in measuring and reporting flow-through. This is readily demonstrated in the financial reporting of companies such as Accor, the French hotel group. Note the emphasis on flow-through given by Accor in this portion of a financial report on profit performance in its various international hotel groups:

As a result, earnings before interest, taxes, depreciation, amortization and rent (EBITDAR) margin in Europe was up 0.3 points with a flow-through rate of 49 percent. In Latin America, EBITDAR margin improved by 2.0 points and the flow-through rate reached 64 percent, overall and 77 percent in Brazil.[1]

Note both the emphasis on flow-through as well as its degree of variation within differing hotels. Increased or decreased flow-through rates carry significant amounts of information directly related to the performance of an RM team. As a result, it is likely your own revenue optimization performance will be assessed, in part, via the calculation of flow-through rates. Because that is so, you should understand the concept well and recognize the revenue management-related actions that will increase or decrease your own property's flow-through.

To better understand flow-through, consider the January operating performance of the 240-room Splash Town Water Park Resort. Figure 9.4 details the property's monthly operating performance Last Year (LY) and This Year (TY).

Using data from Figure 9.4, the Splash Town's flow-through for this January can be calculated by applying the following flow-through formula. In this example, the calculation would be:

$$\frac{\text{GOP this year } - \text{ GOP last year}}{\text{Total revenues this year } - \text{ Total revenues last year}} = \text{Flow-through}$$

or

$$\frac{\$627,990 - \$519,940}{\$2,100,150 - \$1,952,580} = \text{Flow-through}$$

or

$$\frac{\$108,050}{\$147,300} = 73.4\% \text{ Flow-through}$$

Figure 9.4	Splash Town Waterpark Income Statements

Splash Town Water Park Resort
Income Statements
For the Month Ended January 31, Last Year versus This Year

	Last Year (LY)	%	This Year (TY)	%
Revenue				
Rooms	1,105,000	56.6%	1,200,000	57.1%
Nonrooms	847,850	43.4%	900,150	42.9%
Total Revenue	1,952,850	100.0%	2,100,150	100.0%
Operated Department Expenses				
Rooms	335,890	17.2%	353,100	16.8%
Nonrooms	537,034	27.5%	558,300	26.6%
Total Operated Department Expenses	872,924	44.7%	911,400	43.4%
Total Operated Department Income	1,079,926	55.3%	1,188,750	56.6%
Total Undistributed Operating Expenses	559,986	28.7%	560,760	26.7%
Gross Operating Profit	**519,940**	**26.6%**	**627,990**	**29.9%**
Rent, Property Taxes, and Insurance	146,700	7.5%	146,700	7.0%
Depreciation and Amortization	105,000	5.4%	105,000	5.0%
Net Operating Income	268,240	13.7%	376,290	17.9%
Interest	106,000	5.4%	106,000	5.0%
Income Before Income Taxes	162,240	8.3%	270,290	12.9%
Income Taxes	64,896	3.3%	108,116	5.1%
Net Income	97,344	5.0%	162,174	7.7%

Because gross operating profit (GOP) is calculated as total hotel revenue less those expenses that are considered directly controllable by management, flow-through was created by managerial accountants to measure the ability of a hotel to covert increases in revenue directly to increases in GOP.

In this example, 73.4 percent of *incremental* revenue, or 73.4 cents of every additional revenue dollar, has been converted to gross operating profits. For most hotels, incremental revenue increases return disproportionably high profit levels because variable costs (see Chapter 2) are so low. If rooms are sold at too low rates, however, flow-through will be reduced despite the sale's positive impact on RevPAR.

Note that for the Splash Town property an increase in revenues of only 7.5 percent [($2,100,150 − $1,952,850)/$1,952,850 = 7.5%] over the prior year resulted in gross operating profit increases of 20.8 percent ($627,990 − $519,940)/$519,940 = 20.8%) because of that additional revenue.

Flow-through is computed to help managers identify the impact of increases in revenue on profitability. When it is high (typically over 50 percent), it reflects efficiency on the part of management in converting additional revenues into additional profits. For most hotels, flow-throughs that are less than 50 percent indicate relative inefficiency in converting additional revenues into additional profits. In most cases, increased revenues that yield low flow-through rates indicate the revenues generated were not of sufficient *quality* to enhance profits. This would be the case, for example, when, in an effort to enhance RevPAR, an RM team sells additional rooms at rates too low to significantly improve profit levels. This reinforces the point first made in Chapter 6 and examined again in Chapter 13 that not all revenue is created equal. Some revenue is good revenue and some revenue is simply not as good.

Reduced flow-through rates can also be the result of disproportionately high operating costs directly related to increases in revenues. To illustrate, consider the sales department of a hotel that creates a rooms package including many amenities (e.g., roses, chocolate, and wines) for a *Valentines Day Special* dinner and overnight stay. If, in this case, the number of incremental revenue dollars achieved from the sales effort are only modestly higher than the cost of the room and amenities provided, the hotel's RevPAR would increase, but would be offset by a very low flow-through rate resulting from the high cost of generating the modest increase in incremental revenue.

Understanding the flow-through characteristics of a specific hotel helps RMs better understand the importance of generating profitable incremental revenues and the importance of utilizing truly effective revenue optimization techniques.

Unfortunately, for some RMs, the availability of the actual data required to calculate GOPPAR and flow-through may be limited. Financial data such as that presented in Figure 9.4 simply may not be made available to them. This can be the case, for example, when only a hotel's owners, GM, and property accountants are privy to the hotel's overall operating performance. In cases such as these, the calculation of GOPPAR and flow-through may be performed only by people other than the RM, and distribution of the results may be highly restricted. As RMs increase in professional stature, and as hotel owners and managers better understand the important role flow-through data plays in their RMs' decision making, RMs will likely be given regular access to this important financial data.

STAR REPORTS

Figure 9.5 details information about the hotel operating statistics you have examined in this chapter. Note that each statistic possesses strengths and weakness when used to assess a hotel's operating performance.

Hotel owners, GMs, and their revenue management teams most often use several of the statistics in Figure 9.5 to evaluate their hotels' revenue optimization efforts. Even if all of these statistics are used, however, they are insufficient to fully evaluate the effectiveness of an RM's efforts.

The reasons why can be illustrated by assuming you are the RM for a hotel that achieved a 60 percent occupancy last month. This month, however, your occupancy percentage increased to 70 percent. Did you do well?

Consider, in this case, the importance of knowing which of the following alternative scenarios is true before you answer:

- This month, the average occupancy of the hotels with which you directly compete was 50 percent.

Figure 9.5	Hotel Operating Statistic Summary		
Statistic	**Measures**	**Strength**	**Weakness**
Occupancy %	Proportion of rooms sold	Easy to compute	Does not consider ADR
ADR	Rate at which rooms were sold	Easy to compute	Does not consider occupancy %
RevPAR	Rooms revenue generated per available room	Easy to compute	Does not consider nonrooms revenue or profitability
RevPOR	Total revenue generated per occupied room	Considers all hotel revenue generated	Does not consider the number of rooms sold or profitability
Total RevPAR	Total revenue generated per available room	Considers all hotel revenue generated (e.g rooms, F&B and meeting space)	Does not consider profitability
GOPPAR	GOP generated per available room	Assesses profitability of room sales effort	Results dependent on non-RM efforts; data may be unavailable
Flow-through	Proportion of revenue increase converted to gross operating profit increase	Assesses profitability of incremental revenues	Results dependent on non-RM efforts; data may not be readily accessible

- This month, the average occupancy of the hotels with which you directly compete was 70 percent.
- This month, the average occupancy of the hotels with which you directly compete was 90 percent.

It is easy to see that the performance of a single hotel can better be evaluated by comparing it to the performance of other hotels within its competitive set (see Chapter 1). Knowing the performance of your hotel's competitive set, or *comp set* for short, provides additional information that helps you better assess your own hotel's performance.

Hotel owners and GMs know the importance of monitoring the performance of the competition, but they also know what Indiana University social psychologist Norman Triplett discovered: "Bicyclists race faster against each other than against the clock."[2]

Just as Triplett's social facilitation experiments lead him to conclude that the presence of another contestant participating simultaneously in a bicycle race served to inspire all riders to pedal faster, hotel owners and GMs know that competition among hotels usually leads to improved revenue optimization performance. Unfortunately for free information exchange, however, most hotels are understandably hesitant to share their operating performance numbers with their direct competitors. To get around this confidentiality of data problem many hoteliers share their average room rate and occupancy figures in a creative and useful way.

In the lodging industry, ADR and occupancy performance data are communicated by participating RMs to independent third parties who perform the necessary comparative

RM IN ACTION 9.2: A RISING TIDES LIFTS ALL SHIPS?

It's often said that a rising tide lifts all ships. It has also been pointed out, however, that sometimes boats are stuck on the bottom in a rising tide. In such cases, the results are rarely good.

When economies are strong, hotel rates and occupancies typically increase. In significant economic downturns such as that experienced worldwide in late 2008, hotel rates and occupancies tend to decline. To illustrate, examine the headline and a brief excerpt from an article published in the *San Jose* (California) *Mercury News*.

> San Jose's Major Hotels Report 59% Occupancy; Down from 66% in October
> Prior Year Figures from the San Jose Convention and Visitors Bureau show the occupancy rate last month in the city's 14

major, full-service hotels was just under 59 percent, down from more than 66 percent in October 2007.

If you were the owner of a full-service hotel in San Jose and your own RM team managed to maintain October 2008 occupancies equal to those of October 2007, would you be pleased? Undoubtedly, you would be. Knowing how others are performing helps RMs better understand their own performance. The importance of doing well on comp set comparisons is not only known by hotel owners and GMs. It is also well known by those who may be asked to finance or lend money to those hoteliers in tough times.

Excerpted on 11/15/2008 from http://www.hotel-online.com/News/PR2008_4th/Nov08_SanJoseOccupancy.html

Essential RM Term

Market share: The portion (or percentage) of sales in a defined region that is controlled by a single company.

For example, in a region where 10,000 hotel rooms were sold last month, a single hotel having sold 2,300 rooms would have a 23 percent market share (i.e., 2,300/10,000 = 23%).

calculations and return competitive set-related performance data to the participating hotels. These third parties also inform hotels about their ranking in terms of **market share** capture.

The Smith Travel Research (STR) company is an industry leader in providing hoteliers competitive set data. In fact, every major U.S. hotel chain must provide the data used to prepare STR's competitive set reports.

Brands can mandate that their franchisees provide STR (or other data collection entities) with their occupancy and revenue information, but no franchisor requires a hotel's gross operating profit data to be shared. This means RevPAR and market share data are readily available for

▶ RM ON THE WEB 9.1

Smith Travel Research (STR) is the hotel industry's leading performance information and market data provider. You can view its web site at www.strglobal.com

It is important to recognize that the ability to read and understand STAR and other STR prepared reports is a skill needed by every hotel RM.

external comp set comparison; however, GOPPAR and flow-through comparisons cannot as readily be made.

Smith Travel Research (STR) produced reports, widely known as STAR reports, are generated for occupancy and average room rate figures on a daily as well as weekly, monthly, and annual basis. As a result, you will likely be provided with comparative RevPAR and market share data reports for your hotel on a continuous basis. With STAR reports, you can better determine if you are obtaining your fair share of the available business in your area and if your market share is growing or decreasing.

The format and content of STAR reports vary based on the specific type of report you will review, (i.e., daily performance, weekly performance, or area market reports). Your ability to properly read and analyze the reports, however, should not change. Learning how to analyze STAR reports begins with an understanding of the definitions used by STR in its report preparation. Figure 9.6 describes the most important of the terms you should know.

Figure 9.6 STR Terms and Definitions

Term	Definition
Average room rate	Average rate (ADR) at which a hotel's rooms are sold
Occupancy %	Ratio of rooms sold to rooms available for sale
RevPAR	Average Room Rate × Occupancy %
% Change	The percentage change in a rooms statistic from one performance period to another (i.e., January this year vs. January last year).
Index	A measure of a property's performance in relation to its competitive set. An index of "100" indicates that the property performed equal to its comp set's average. An index greater than 100 indicates a property is performing above the comp set's level; an index below 100 indicates the property is performing below its comp set's average.
Competitive set	A group of four or more properties selected by a hotel for purposes of comparison. A single hotel or brand can make up a maximum of 35 percent of the reporting rooms of any competitive set in order to protect proprietary data. For reports the competitive set data excludes the data from the subject (original) property.
Occupancy index	An index designed to measure a property's share of room's sold.
Average room rate index	A measure of a property's pricing performance in relation to its competitive set.
RevPAR index	A measure of a property's revenue generation performance in relation to its competitive set.
Market share (supply)	The proportion of the market's rooms controlled by the subject hotel.
Market share (demand)	The proportion of the market's total rooms sold that were sold by the subject hotel.
Market share (revenue)	The proportion of the market's rooms revenue captured by the subject hotel.

Other important terms used by STR include the following:

Census: The total number of hotel properties and rooms in a market segment.

Chain scale: Classifications based primarily on the actual, systemwide average room rates of the major chains. They are currently classified as:

- Luxury
- Upper upscale chains
- Upscale chains
- Midscale chains with food & beverage
- Midscale chains without food & beverage
- Economy chains

Market: A **Metropolitan Statistical Area**, a group of Metropolitan Statistical Areas, or a group of counties. STR analyzes over 150 U.S. markets.

Essential RM Term

Metropolitan Statistical Area (MSA): A geographic area (as designated by the U.S. Office of Management and Budget) that includes one or more counties or county equivalents that have at least one *urban core area* of at least 50,000 population, plus adjacent territory that has a high degree of social and economic integration.

Market price segments: The current classifications of a STR market, defined by estimated average room rate:

Luxury—top 15 percent average room rates

Upscale—next 15 percent average room rates

Mid-price—middle 30 percent average room rates

Economy—next 20 percent average room rates

Budget—lowest 20 percent average room rates

Market Share: Total room supply, room demand, or room revenue as a percent of a larger group.

Region: STR currently defines nine different regions in the United States:

1. New England (Maine, New Hampshire, Vermont, Massachusetts, Connecticut, Rhode Island)
2. Middle Atlantic (New York, Pennsylvania, New Jersey)
3. South Atlantic (Maryland, Delaware, West Virginia, Virginia, North Carolina, South Carolina, Georgia, Florida)
4. East North Central (Michigan, Wisconsin, Illinois, Indiana, Ohio)
5. East South Central (Kentucky, Tennessee, Alabama, Mississippi)
6. West North Central (Minnesota, North Dakota, South Dakota, Iowa, Nebraska, Missouri, Kansas)

7. West South Central (Arkansas, Oklahoma, Texas, Louisiana)

8. Mountain (Montana, Idaho, Wyoming, Colorado, Utah, Nevada, Arizona, New Mexico)

9. Pacific (Alaska, Washington, Oregon, California, Hawaii)

Sample: The number of properties and rooms from which data are received.

STR #: An identification code for the property that remains constant even if the property changes **flags** (brands).

Understanding the makeup of a competitive set is a key component of understanding and analyzing STR reports. A competitive set is simply a group of hotels used to establish a performance benchmark. To illustrate, assume that you manage a 400-room full-service property in a large metropolitan area. You compete for most of your customers with six other hotels in your area, each of which has approximately the same number of rooms, services, and quality level as your own property.

Essential RM Term

Flag: A hotel's franchise affiliation. Also commonly referred to as a *brand*.

Assume that you have chosen to identify these six properties to STR as the group you wish to consider as your competitive set. In nearly all cases, each of these hotels will, as will you, regularly submit their occupancy and rooms revenue data to STR. These data are then tabulated and returned to you in the form of a STAR report comparing your performance against that of the six hotels you chose to comprise the members of your comp set.

To ensure confidentiality, STR will only report the aggregate results of the competitive set; they will never release or divulge information on an individual property or brand in your comp set. STR reports can be customized but typically include date related to:

- Occupancy
- ADR
- RevPAR
- Market share
- Historical trends (changes from prior periods)
- Cumulative performance thru defined periods (i.e., 3-month trailing, 12-month trailing and year-to-date (YTD))

In a typical report, the subject (your) hotel's performance is compared to that of its competitive set, and the subject hotel's rank (e.g., first in the set, or second, third and so on) on each criteria is listed.

Examining a single segment of a STAR report related to hotel occupancy will help illustrate how a STAR performance report can be used to assess your own RM-related performance. To interpret Figure 9.7, assume that your hotel is the 400-room property referred to earlier. Your competitive set is the six similar hotels that you have identified as your competition. In Figure 9.7, the "Property" column refers to your hotel.

The Comp Set column in this STR Trend Report refers to the data from the six hotels you have chosen as your competitive set. The monthly occupancy percentages listed represent the occupancy rates, respectively, of your hotel and the combined (average) occupancy of your comp set.

Figure 9.7	STR Report: Occupancy Trend Segment		
Month	**Property**	**Comp Set**	**Index**
Jan	55.2	52.2	105.7
Feb	59.7	58.2	102.6
Mar	63.1	63.6	99.2
Apr	64.2	64.4	99.7
May	63.9	61.7	103.6
June	67.6	66.1	102.3
July	68.9	63.5	108.5
Aug	72.7	58.8	123.6
Sept	81.8	82.9	98.7
Oct	83.1	85.5	97.2
Nov	65.6	67.1	97.8
Dec	60.2	57.6	104.5

One of the most important features of a STAR performance report will be your hotel's index on various criteria. This occupancy, room rate, or RevPAR ratio is calculated as:

$$\frac{\text{Performance of subject (your) hotel}}{\text{Performance of competitive set hotels}} = \text{index}$$

For example, if your hotel achieved an occupancy of 70 percent last month, and your competitive set achieved an occupancy of 70 percent, your occupancy index would be computed as:

$$\frac{70\% \text{ occupancy (Subject hotel)}}{70\% \text{ (Comp set)}} = 100\% \text{ occupancy index}$$

If, however, your hotel achieved an occupancy of 70 percent last month, and your competitive set achieved an occupancy of 75 percent, your occupancy index would be computed as:

$$\frac{70\% \text{ occupancy}}{75\% \text{ occupancy}} = 93.3\% \text{ occupancy index}$$

In this scenario, your hotel achieved 93.3 percent of the average occupancy level achieved by the comp set. Room rate, occupancy, and RevPAR indexes will be important to you and to several other parties vitally interested in your revenue optimization performance:

- Your hotel's owners: Hotel owners and investors will want to know if the management team they have put in place is effective in competing in the marketplace.

- Your franchisor: Brand managers need to measure how well their brands compete in the marketplace because strong brand performance helps them sell additional franchises. Weak performance by the brand helps indicate where brand managers can modify the brand to improve its performance or provide help to an individual operator.

- Your management company (if applicable): These companies know that their effectiveness as managing consultants will be based in large degree on how well they perform on STR reported indexes. Good results are used to secure new business and demonstrate competency to their current clients.

- Your general manager and DOSM: GMs and DOSMs want to know the effectiveness of their marketing plans and sales abilities, as well as those of their competitors. In many cases, the performance bonuses of these executives will be based on STR reported indexes.

- The financial community: Those who may be asked to buy, invest in, or lend money to your property will, to some degree, evaluate the wisdom of the investment based on the hotel's STR reported indexes. Good relative performances, demonstrated by a strong STAR report, can help persuade investors to supply funding, whereas a weak STAR report will make it more challenging to secure external financial support.

STAR reports and others similar to them can provide a wealth of information to those RMs sophisticated enough to read and correctly analyze the important competitive set and market share data they contain.

COMPETITIVE SET ANALYSIS

Lodging industry RMs know that their hotels will perform better than some of their direct competitors and perhaps less well than others. Variations in a brand's reputation, a hotel's location, its age, the skills of the workers in its operating departments, and the decision making ability of its revenue management team members all combine to allow some hotels to charge more and to achieve above average occupancy rates. Alternatively, some hotels can charge more, but only at the expense of reduced occupancy levels. Other hotels achieve higher occupancy rates, but only by reducing rates. How a hotel ranks among its competitive set in terms of ADR, occupancy, and RevPAR generation can tell the property RMs much about how guests perceive the value proposition offered by their hotels' pricing structures and how future rate and inventory management decisions should be made.

A few RMs discount competitive set reports. They would argue that true success simply means meeting the goals they have set for themselves, regardless of the performance of others. They would point to Methodist Bishop Ernest A. Fitzgerald's comment: *"The real winners are not those at the top but those who have come the farthest over the toughest roads. Your victory may never make the headlines. But you will know about it, and that's what counts."*[3] While that sentiment may be true, it is also true that realistic goal setting related to revenue optimization can only be undertaken with a complete understanding of competitors and the market in which the RM team will operate. Competition and competitive results as a basis for evaluating the skills (and compensation packages) of RMs are facts of life, and it is important that RMs recognize it.

Those RMs who remain unconvinced of the importance of competition might wish to consider the insight of Bill Gates, Microsoft founder (and among the richest persons in the world) when he warned, *"Your school may have done away with winners and losers, but life has not. In some schools they have abolished failing grades; they'll give you as many chances as you want to get the right answer. This doesn't bear the slightest resemblance to ANYTHING."*[4]

Regardless of your own view of competitors, your personal performance philosophy, or your hotel's actual results ranking, it is important for you to remember that talent in revenue management decision making does not always make itself apparent by blowing away your competition. Sometimes talent is best displayed by the quiet resolve of an RM team to try again tomorrow, and to learn from the mistakes of today. To learn from their mistakes or to celebrate their victories, however, all RMs must be able to read and understand how to interpret the following performance indexes:

Occupancy Index Analysis

ADR Index Analysis

RevPAR Index Analysis

Occupancy Index Analysis

In all but the most unusual of circumstances, RMs want to achieve an occupancy rate higher than that of their competitors, and as a result, an occupancy index higher than 100. In addition, over time real increases, not decreases, in occupancy indexes are desirable. To illustrate, consider the data in Figure 9.8. In this scenario, your hotel's occupancy data for the years of 201W, 201X, and 201Y are presented. In the past 13 months, your occupancy index has ranged from a low of 55.0 percent (January 201Y), to a high of 98.3 percent (April 201Y).

A close review of Figure 9.8 reveals that the % Change column presents your hotel's performance change from its previous performance in the *same* time period. For example, the occupancy change for your property this October (201Y) versus last October (201X) was 5.0 percent (see line 1.13), while the change in the comp sets' performance for the same period was −10.5 percent.

An even closer review of the data in Figure 9.8 (see line 2.3) reveals that your own hotel, like your comp set, is experiencing an occupancy decline through the last three months ending October, 201Y compared to 201X; −5.0 percent for your hotel vs. −14.2 percent for your comp set. However, your occupancy is up 21.1 percent for the 12 months ending October, 201Y (see line 4.3), while your comp sets' occupancy is down 8.0 percent.

The portion of the monthly STAR trend report presented in Figure 9.8 is an example of the detail STR provides to RMs. A careful review of such data can help you improve your forecast ability because you can see when occupancy rates historically increase or decrease, monitor your hotel's performance, and set future goals for your RM team.

Figure 9.8	STAR Monthly Trend Report

Your Hotel
Monthly STAR Report
Occupancy
for October 201Z
Property # 23232

			Occupancy					
	Year	Month	Property	% Change	Comp Set	% Change	Index	% Change
Line 1.1	201X	October	47.8	47.5	65.0	3.2	73.5	43.0
Line 1.2	201X	November	35.1	72.1	51.2	−4.1	68.6	79.6
Line 1.3	201X	December	27.9	72.2	41.4	−3.7	67.4	78.8
Line 1.4	201Y	January	29.2	111.6	53.1	2.1	55.0	107.5
Line 1.5	201Y	February	39.0	54.8	59.3	−5.6	65.8	64.1
Line 1.6	201Y	March	45.0	45.6	61.6	7.1	73.1	36.1
Line 1.7	201Y	April	51.7	39.7	52.6	−8.5	98.3	52.9
Line 1.8	201Y	May	36.4	−10.3	53.8	−17.2	67.7	8.3
Line 1.9	201Y	June	43.7	43.3	54.6	−6.7	80.0	53.6
Line 1.10	201Y	July	38.4	−8.8	47.9	−11.3	80.2	2.8
Line 1.11	201Y	August	44.7	1.4	53.9	−17.6	82.9	23.0
Line 1.12	201Y	September	40.8	−20.8	48.7	−15.2	83.8	−6.6
Line 1.13	201Y	October	50.2	5.0	58.2	−10.5	86.3	17.4
Three Months—Ending October								
Line 2.1		201W	40.6	3.5	59.4	−9.5	68.4	2.3
Line 2.2		201X	47.7	17.5	62.6	5.4	76.2	11.5
Line 2.3		201Y	45.3	−5.0	53.7	−14.2	84.4	10.8
Year-To-Date—Ending October								
Line 3.1		201W	38.0	−18.5	59.7	−7.6	63.7	−11.7
Line 3.2		201X	36.2	−4.7	59.5	−0.3	60.8	−4.6
Line 3.3		201Y	41.9	15.7	54.3	−8.7	77.2	27
Twelve Months—Ending October								
Line 4.1		201W	34.3	−23.9	57.8	−6.9	59.3	−18.3
Line 4.2		201X	33.2	−3.2	57.6	−0.3	57.6	−2.9
Line 4.3		201Y	40.2	21.1	53.0	−8.0	75.8	31.6

Figure 9.9	Ranking Analysis		
Current Month	**Occupancy**	**ADR**	**RevPAR**
January 201X	5 of 7	3 of 7	5 of 7
February 201X	4 of 7	7 of 7	5 of 7
March 201X	5 of 7	6 of 7	6 of 7
April 201X	6 of 7	6 of 7	7 of 7

In addition to rankings of occupancy data, monthly STAR reports for ADR and RevPAR performance will indicate your property's ranking within the competitive set. Figure 9.9 illustrates how a hotel is ranked relative to other members in its comp set.

In this example, the subject hotel trails its comp set in most months and, of course, would seek to improve. Some RMs dream of becoming number one in their competitive sets for every reporting period, but the best RMs simply get out of bed every day and work hard at it.

ADR Index Analysis

As you have learned, an analysis of a hotel's occupancy rate without a simultaneous assessment of its ADR for the same time period can lead to serious mistakes regarding revenue optimization assessments. As a result, understanding a hotel's ADR index is just as important as understanding its occupancy index.

Figure 9.10 presents a simplified illustration of the possible results an RM team could experience when reviewing its weekly, monthly, quarterly, or annual ADR index. The figure also presents a reasonable *initial* assessment of those results.

The initial assessments presented in Figure 9.10 have significant meaning, of course, only in conjunction with an evaluation of the same property's occupancy index. It is as potentially dangerous for an RM to assess an ADR index without evaluating the concurrent occupancy index as it is to do the reverse. As a result, some RMs erroneously skip the individual ADR (and/or occupancy) index evaluation process and analyze only the RevPAR index (*Note:* Occupancy index $\times$ ADR index = RevPAR index). As you will learn in the next section, however, doing so is a significant mistake.

Figure 9.10	ADR Index Results and Initial Assessment
ADR Index Range	**Initial Assessment**
79% and below	Rates significantly below the comp set
80% –94%	Rates moderately below the comp set
95% –104%	Rates in keeping with the comp set
105% –119%	Rates moderately above the comp set
120% and above	Rates significantly above the comp set

Experienced RMs know that an ADR index can tell them much more than their relative standing regarding room rates charged. To better understand exactly what you can learn from a careful examination of an ADR index, assume that you are the RM for the hotel whose ADR-related data for the first week of October is presented in Figure 9.11.

Note that this important report reveals four key points:

1. The room rates you achieved during the first part of the week were *strong*; thus your ADR index Monday through Wednesday was above 100 percent and your index rank among your 7 member comp set was either 1 (first) or 2 (second).

2. The room rates you achieved during the latter part of the week were *weak* relative to the comp set. Your ADR index on Saturday, for example, fell to 75.5 percent, placing you last (7 of 7) in ADR rank for that day.

3. Your change (from prior year) in actual ADR ranged from a low of 1.6 percent (Tuesday) to a high of 3.1 percent (Thursday); however, your comp sets' range on this statistic was from −0.8 (Monday) to 8.5 (Friday).

4. While the increase in room rates charged at your hotel were fairly consistent through the week, your comp set significantly increased rate during the latter part of the week and especially on Friday and Saturday. Your RM team did not and as a result your property paid a price in reduced ADR and ADR index.

Careful readers could point out that the data in Figure 9.11 do not indicate the success (occupancy rate) achieved by your hotel or the comp set during the first week of October and thus only an incomplete look at the RM team's effectiveness is provided. They would be correct. Although an ADR index report can reveal much about a hotel's revenue-related decision making, it does *not* measure the rooms sold as a result of those rate decisions. Thus, in this example, your comp sets' occupancy rate for this entire period or any day in it could easily be the same, a good bit higher, or significantly lower than that of your hotel. The same careful readers would also recognize that the ability to assess the *overall* revenue generating performance of this hotel during the first week of October *cannot* be readily

Figure 9.11 ADR Index Summary (One Week)

October	Sun 1	Mon 2	Tues 3	Weds 4	Thurs 5	Fri 6	Sat 7
ADR Your property Comp set	186.52 179.85	206.45 196.55	201.98 197.85	182.45 192.12	188.45 202.45	199.84 235.66	201.56 266.85
ADR % Change Your property Comp set	2.3 2.7	1.6 −0.8	2.2 1.9	2.1 4.5	3.1 2.4	2.5 8.5	2.4 7.9
Index	103.7	105.0	102.1	95.0	93.1	84.8	75.5
Index % Change	2.2	1.6	1.4	−2.5	−3.6	−10.5	−12.2
Rank Index ADR	2 of 7 2 of 7	1 of 7 2 of 7	2 of 7 3 of 7	3 of 7 3 of 7	4 of 7 5 of 7	7 of 7 7 of 7	6 of 7 7 of 7

made without considering occupancy data as well as ADR index data. That is the function of the RevPAR index.

RevPAR Index Analysis

In Chapter 1 you learned that one formula for calculating RevPAR is:

$$\text{ADR} \times \text{Occupancy percentage} = \text{RevPAR}$$

In a similar manner, one formula for calculating RevPAR index is:

$$\text{ADR index} \times \text{Occupancy percentage index} = \text{RevPAR index}$$

Despite the simplicity of its calculation, the *analysis* of a RevPAR index can be quite complex. To illustrate, consider that your hotel achieves a 100 percent RevPAR index for a particular time period. Assume also that the members of your competitive set truly represent those hotels which are similar to yours and against which you directly compete. Figure 9.12 illustrates five very different scenarios that could produce a 100 percent RevPAR index as well as a possible explanation of how the results were achieved.

Note that in each scenario, the RevPAR index is 100 percent yet because of the revenue optimization strategies utilized, the impact on the hotel's profitability could vary widely. It is important for RMs undertaking a comp set analysis to recognize that such an evaluation gains credibility to the degree that a comp set fairly represents a hotel's competitors. When a hotel loads its comp set with weaker than realistic competitors, it can easily produce high indices. In a similar manner, if no true competitors exist (e.g., the case experienced by a full-service hotel in a city where nearly all of the other lodging properties are limited-service), a STAR report's index evaluation must be undertaken very carefully.

In Figure 9.12, the RevPAR index in all scenarios is 100 percent, but the more common situation would be that your hotel, due to variations in occupancy or ADR index, leads or lags your competitive set in some areas of RevPAR index. Figure 9.13 illustrates the most

Figure 9.12	100 percent RevPAR Index Assessment: Your Hotel			
Scenario	**Occ. Index**	**ADR Index**	**RevPAR Index**	**Possible Assessment**
1	75.5	132.5	100%	Exceptionally high rates leading to excessively reduced occupancy rate.
2	90.5	110.5	100%	Strong rates; but higher room-related occupation costs than in scenario 1.
3	100	100	100%	Exactly equal to the competitive set performance.
4	110.5	90.5	100%	Low rates, higher room-related occupation costs than in scenario 3.
5	132.5	75.5	100%	Exceptionally high room-related occupation costs occupancy resulting from too low rates yields reduced GOP.

Figure 9.13	Possible Variations from 100 percent RevPAR Index

RevPAR Index Above 100

Strong Occupancy/Average ADR index: Indicates that guests perceive strong value at current rate structure and that many likely would be willing to continue booking even at higher rates.

Average Occupancy/Strong ADR index: Indicates that guests perceive strong value at current rate structure. Increase discounted offerings during slack demand periods to fill more rooms.

Strong Occupancy/Strong ADR index: Indicates that guests perceive strong value at current room rates and the property's market position is strong. Increase rates (and service levels) during periods of highest demand to maintain and expand market dominance.

RevPAR Index Below 100

Weak Occupancy/Average ADR index: Indicates that the average guest does not perceive strong value at the current rate structure; carefully reexamine marketing efforts as well as service levels prior to seeking to expand customer base or increase rates.

Average Occupancy/Weak ADR index: Indicates that guests perceive value but only at reduced rates; carefully evaluate physical facility and service levels prior to seeking increased rates.

Weak Occupancy/Weak ADR index: Indicates very poor guest perception of product and service levels at the current rate structure. Reexamine marketing efforts, product service levels, and facility quality as well as brand affiliation prior to seeking significantly increased rates.

RM AT WORK 9.2

"Are you familiar with STAR monthly trend reports?" asked Mark, the outgoing RM at the newly refurbished Bradford Hampton Inn.

Mark was talking to Ja Lin, the newly hired RM for the property. Mark was retiring, and the hotel's GM had asked him to "show her the ropes" on his last day of work and her first day.

"I think I understand them pretty well," replied Ja Lin.

"That's great" said Mark, "performance is really important here. But you'll really like the freedom you'll have in this position. Our GM and DOSM are so busy with sales and their own to-do lists that rate and inventory management decisions will be pretty much left up to you. Since the renovation, we have always led the comp set. Our RevPAR index for

the month is 119.5 percent. That makes us first again. I'm really proud of that!"

Ja Lin reviewed the trend report document Mark had handed her to her. The competitive set's overall occupancy rate for the month was 61.5 percent. Her property's occupancy index for the month was 140.9 percent. Its ADR index was 84.8 percent.

"Of course, the owners always want more. Just between you and me, I'm not sure they will ever be satisfied. They are always pushing for us to do better," continued Mark as he shook his head.

"Do better?" asked Ja Lin.

"Yes, better. You know. Make them more money. Honestly, I just don't think they are very realistic," said Mark.

RM AT WORK 9.2 *(continued)*

1. What do you think has been the rationale behind Mark's revenue management strategy?

2. Do you think the current strategy is in the long-term best interests of the hotel's owners? Explain.

3. What actions would you advise Ja Lin to take to learn more about her hotel's relative placement within her competitive set and the customer value her hotel delivers?

---

common ways in which that could occur, as well as possible reasons for the RevPAR index variation when either the occupancy index or ADR index is strong (above 100) or weaker (below 100).

MARKET SHARE ANALYSIS

A complete competitive set evaluation must also include a market share analysis. For this important assessment, market share refers to the percentage of supply, demand, and revenue accounted for by a hotel property. To illustrate, in Figure 9.14 the subject hotel normally accounts for 10.7 percent of its comp set's total number of rooms available for sale (supply). Figure 9.14 also details the demand and revenue achieved by the subject property for the periods January through June.

In Figure 9.14, the terms supply, demand, and revenue are defined as follows:

Supply: Number of rooms available to sell × Number of days in the period

Demand: Number of rooms sold (excluding complimentary rooms)

Revenue: Total room revenue generated from the sale or rental of rooms

Close inspection reveals that these terms are virtually synonymous with similar terms listed in Figure 9.6 (STR terms).

Figure 9.14	Market Share Report		
MARKET SHARE			
Month	**Supply %**	**Demand %**	**Revenue %**
January	10.7	10.7	10.7
February	10.7	11.5	9.0
March	10.7	9.0	11.5
April	10.7	8.5	8.5
May	10.7	11.5	11.5
June	11.7	11.5	11.5

Figure 9.15	Supply Data	
Property	**Number of Available Rooms**	**% of Available Rooms (Supply)**
Subject Hotel	230	10.7
Comp Set member # 1	185	8.6
Comp Set member # 2	280	13.0
Comp Set member # 3	462	21.5
Comp Set member # 4	470	21.9
Comp Set member # 5	520	24.2
Total	**2,147**	**1.0**

As shown in Figure 9.15, the subject hotel in this illustration contributes 10.7 percent of the total rooms available to sell (230 rooms/2,147 total rooms = 10.7%). This ratio is calculated as:

$$\frac{\text{Available rooms subject hotel}}{\text{Available rooms comp set (including subject hotel)}} = \text{Supply share (\%)}$$

Similar calculations are undertaken to compute the subject hotel's demand and revenue generation displayed in Figure 9.14:

$$\frac{\text{Rooms sold by subject hotel}}{\text{Rooms sold by comp set (including subject hotel)}} = \text{Demand share (\%)}$$

$$\frac{\text{Rooms revenue generated by subject hotel}}{\text{Rooms revenue generated by comp set (including subject hotel)}} = \text{Revenue share (\%)}$$

RMs analyzing this portion of a monthly performance report (STR includes this specific report as part of their "Monthly STAR Summary") could encounter a variety of possible outcomes, each of which may be helpful in evaluating the hotel's revenue optimization performance. A close examination of Figure 9.14 reveals six key observations:

1. In January the subject hotel contributed 10.7 percent of the comp set's total rooms available to sell, captured 10.7 percent of demand (rooms sold) and achieved 10.7 percent of the comp set's total revenue. In many ways, this could be considered *average*, or expected performance if indeed the subject hotel was of average quality within its comp set. If, however, the hotel property could reasonably be considered as *above average* (e.g. superior brand, new property, extraordinary service features, or location), then the performance could be considered disappointing. For a hotel flying a less prestigious flag or with below average service or property features, however, this performance could be considered quite good.

2. In February the subject hotel contributed 10.7 percent of the comp set's total rooms available to sell, captured 11.5 percent of demand (rooms sold), but achieved only 9.0 percent of the comp set's total revenue. In this scenario, the hotel is not achieving its fair share of the revenue generated by the comp set, despite the fact that the number of rooms sold is more than in keeping with its share of supply. This is not a good situation both because room rates are depressed and because of the direct costs associated with selling "too many" rooms relative to the revenue generated. In this scenario, strong consideration should be given to reducing room discounts and/or raising rack room rates.

3. In March the subject hotel contributed 10.7 percent of the comp set's total rooms available to sell, captured 9.0 percent of demand (room sales) and achieved 11.5 percent of the comp set's total revenue. This set of results indicates aggressiveness in increasing or maintaining higher room rates, despite a depressing effect on the property's occupancy levels. This may be a very good situation because higher room rates help increase guests' perceptions of quality and because the direct costs associated with selling excess rooms relative to the revenue generated by the hotel are avoided. In this scenario, strong consideration should be given to increasing marketing efforts.

4. In April the subject hotel contributed 10.7 percent of the comp set's total rooms available to sell, captured only 8.5 percent of demand (room sales), and achieved only 8.5 percent of the comp set's total revenue. This difficult and unfortunate scenario could indicate a *below* comp set average property (e.g., inferior brand, older property, poor service, or quality levels). If the property is truly competitive, however, it indicates a too low room rate structure and ineffective marketing and/or servicing of current guests.

5. In May the subject hotel contributed 10.7 percent of the comp set's total rooms available to sell, captured 11.5 percent of demand (room sales) and achieved 11.5 percent of the comp set's total revenue. In this ideal scenario, the subject hotel leads the comp set in room sales and revenue generation. RMs encountering this very desirable circumstance can examine their opportunity to reduce discount rate offerings even further, increase selected rates (especially to less cost-sensitive guests) and work to ensure continued high levels of guest satisfaction. *Note:* A realistic reassessment of the composition of the competitive set may be in order if this performance level remains consistent. This would be done to ensure that the comp set has not been chosen, either intentionally or unintentionally, to artificially inflate the perceived performance of the subject property.

6. In June, the subject hotel contributed 11.7 percent of the comp set's total rooms available to sell, captured 11.5 percent of demand (room sales) and achieved 11.5 percent of the comp set's total revenue. The results of this month illustrate the importance of monitoring supply as well as demand and revenue. When a hotel's supply contribution changes, it is likely its demand and revenue performance will change as well. In this case, the subject hotel's market share increased, which could be the result of its adding more rooms, the closing of a competitor, or the offering of a reduced number of rooms (due to renovation) by one or more competitors. In scenarios such as this one, both demand and revenue results must be evaluated

in light of the variation observed in the subject hotel's supply contribution. In this case, the property's demand and revenue generation were equal to the prior month (May). However, because of its larger supply proportion, this would represent disappointing demand and revenue results because they are unchanged from those experienced in April.

ADDITIONAL ASSESSMENTS

A recurring theme of this book is that maximized revenue generation, by itself, is not the best measure of an RM team's effectiveness. As a result, while a continual assessment of occupancy, ADR, RevPAR, competitive set performance, market share and, if the data are available, GOPPAR and flow-through is important, at least three additional revenue-related areas of assessment are also important. These areas of examination and the specific questions they can answer are:

- Source of business: Who are our buyers?
- Distribution channels: At what cost do our buyers purchase from us?
- Web 2.0: What do our buyers say about their experiences with us?

For some RMs, the answers to these questions may be provided by an effective hotel sales and marketing department or the property's GM. This is so because the answers to these type questions are critical to effective hotel sales and operations, as well as to revenue optimization. The correct responses to these questions, however, are just as critical to revenue management teams because the answer to the question, "Who are our buyers?" will provide data essential to initial differential pricing decision making.

Knowing the distribution channels that deliver the majority of a hotel's rooms buyers and the costs of those channels is key to effectively opening and closing room discounts and to rooms inventory allocation. Also, better understanding guests' experiences during their stay can help an RM provide valuable assistance in product improvement, as well as in identifying areas in which a hotel excels and thus could gain marketing and perhaps pricing advantages.

Source of Business Assessment

In many hotels, answering the question, "Who are our customers?" falls to the sales and marketing department. As a result, fortunate RMs may be provided with detailed information about the proportion of a hotel's guests who are defined as transient, corporate, government, **SMERF**, other group, contract, or any of a number of alternative designations designed to assist in the selling of hotel rooms and services.

Those RMs working in environments in which answers to the question "*Who are our buyers?*" are not routinely provided to them can make use of a number of excellent hospitality-specific marketing management resources that can help them answer it.[5]

Essential RM Term

SMERF: Acronym used to describe **S**ocial, **M**ilitary, **E**ducational, **R**eligious, and **F**raternal buyers of hotel rooms and services. Some hoteliers prefer to use the term *Sports* as oppose to *Social* when identifying their market mix.

The European term in use is often MICE (**M**eeting, **I**ncentive, **C**onference, and **E**vent).

Essential RM Term

Marketing mix: The relative proportion of revenue contributed by each of a hotel's most important guest types (e.g., transient, group, or contract guests).

Essential RM Term

Ancillary revenue: Nonrooms income. Examples include guests's food and beverage purchases, meeting room rental, AV-related income, parking, spa charges, and activity fees. Also known as nonrooms revenue.

For RMs, the assessment and evaluation of sources of business are important for improved decision making. This is so because the **marketing mix** achieved by a hotel directly affects its revenue-generation ability and its profitability. Experienced RMs know a simple fact: *All customers are not created equally.*

The truth is that some customers are a good deal more desirable (worth more) than others. To illustrate, consider the value to a hotel of two different pieces of business, each staying two nights, each paying the same room rate of $199.99 per night and buying the same number of rooms (200 total room nights); but with very different nonrooms or **ancillary revenue** expenditures. In this example, attendees at a convention held by the Veterans of Foreign Wars (VFW) spend very differently than do equal numbers of leisure travelers.

In Figure 9.16, the revenue variance between these two groups is 32 percent. The variance is calculated as:

$$\frac{\$57{,}798 \,(\text{VFW revenue}) - \$43{,}798 \,(\text{Transient revenue})}{\$43{,}798} = \text{Revenue variance}$$

or

$$\frac{\$14{,}000}{\$43{,}798} = 32\% \text{ revenue variance}$$

Figure 9.16	Guest Revenue Contribution Calculation	
Group	**VFW Convention**	**Leisure Traveler**
Nightly rooms sold	100	100
ADR	$ 199.99	$ 199.99
Total room nights (2-night stay)	200	200
Total revenue @ ADR = $199.99	$ 39,998	$ 39,998
Daily per room ancillary revenue	$ 89.00	$ 19.00
Total ancillary revenue (Daily ancillary x 200)	$17,800	$ 380.00
Total Revenue 2-night stay	**$ 57,798**	**$ 43,798**
RevPOR	**$ 288.99**	**$ 218.99**
Revenue Variance	**+ 32%**	

In this example, it is easy to see that 200 VFW convention rooms are simply more valuable to the hotel's revenue optimization efforts than are 200 transient rooms even though the rooms are sold at the same room rate.

The importance of knowing the relative value of your guests is clear. In fact, frequent traveler or similar guest-rewards programs work mainly because they are designed to let customers know they are more valued than the average guest. Hotel companies know that the value of guests increase as they spend more and as they spend more *often*, and these type guests should be rewarded or treated in other special ways.

RMs must be able to recognize all of their most valuable customers. RMs must also understand the value of their current customers and, just as importantly, they must be able to assess the potential value of future customers. Figure 9.16 also demonstrates the significant limitations RMs would encounter if they used only ADR, rooms sold (occupancy), or RevPAR generation as the primary means of guest value assessment. Note that in such a limited assessment, both customer types in this illustration would, erroneously, be considered *equal* in value.

In addition to decisions related to rate determination (higher valued guests may be deserving of reduced room rates to encourage their continued business), RMs must understand the source and value of their guests if they hope to implement other revenue optimization strategies. To illustrate, consider Mitch and Sonia, two RMs whose hotels compete in the same market and routinely offer government workers a $99.00 room rate and corporate guests a $149.00 room rate.

Assume that Mitch elects, during the Thanksgiving holidays, to offer a 20 percent discount on his corporate travel rate. Sonia's RM team is considering the wisdom of offering a matching rate. Prior to doing so, it is critical that Sonia's team understand well the proportion of rooms they sell to this specific group. If Sonia's hotel generates 5 percent of her total room revenue from corporate travelers, the impact of this rate-management decision will be very different than if corporate travelers typically contribute 75 percent of her hotel's total revenue.

Those hospitality professionals with a foodservices background will recognize the similarity of this particular rooms-related challenge to the menu mix challenges they routinely face. This will be examined in Chapter 10. In a hotel, raising room rates significantly on *insignificantly* small sources of business will likely result in minimal revenue increases. Even minimal rate reductions or increases, however, for significantly *large* sources of business, can result in significantly increased or reduced total revenues.

Distribution Channel Assessment

Historically, the most common approach to the quality assessment of alternative distribution channels has been related to total revenue generation. The widely shared belief was that those distribution channels that contribute the most revenue volume (Room rate × Rooms sold) were considered best.

Increasingly, RMs understand that it is total revenue generation *less* channel distribution costs that characterizes a high-quality distribution channel. This is illustrated well by the advertisement for seminars and training offered by industry professionals specializing in revenue management. One popular revenue management consultant advertised one of her new Webcast seminars with the following headline:

Distribution Management

RevPAR is no longer the only metric. Revenue managers now must manage distribution channels based on the cost of reservation in order to achieve maximum revenue "flow-through."[6]

In Chapter 4 you learned that net ADR yield is the actual revenue realized by a hotel after subtracting the cost of fees and assessments associated with revenue generated by a specific. These "reservation costs" can, of course, be significant. You also learned that net ADR yield is a concept useful in determining differential price points and in managing pricing in such a manner as to move repeat buyers from higher cost to lower cost channels of distribution. Recall that the formula for net ADR yield is:

$$\frac{\text{Net room rate}}{\text{Standard ADR}} = \text{Net ADR yield}$$

In this formula; Standard ADR − Distribution channel costs = Net room rate

An effective assessment of alternative distribution channels requires RMs to again apply the net ADR yield concept. Figure 9.17 shows a typical variation from the average (mean) distribution channel performance that can occur when distribution channels with differing net ADR yields contribute to a hotel's total revenues.

As shown in Figure 9.17, even when the number of rooms sold and the rate at which they area sold is identical, variation in the cost of the channel can result in above or below average net revenue. To objectively assess the quality of a distribution channel, RMs must consider the standard ADR achieved in it, as well as the total number of rooms sold. They must also, however, carefully assess the channel's relative cost (Net ADR Yield) if they are to make informed revenue management-related decisions about its continued use.

Figure 9.17	Variation from the Average (mean) Distribution Channel Performance					
Source	**Net ADR Yield**	**Rate**	**Net Per Room**	**Rooms Sold**	**Net Revenue**	**+/− Average**
Channel 1	98%	$ 299.99	$ 293.99	100	$ 29,399	10%
Channel 2	95%	$ 299.99	$ 284.99	100	$ 28,499	6%
Channel 3	90%	$ 299.99	$ 269.99	100	$ 26,999	1%
Channel 4	88%	$ 299.99	$ 263.99	100	$ 26,399	−1%
Channel 5	85%	$ 299.99	$ 254.99	100	$ 25,499	−5%
Channel 6	80%	$ 299.99	$ 239.99	100	$ 23,999	−10%
Total				**600**	**$ 160,795**	
Average	**89%**	**$ 299.99**	**$ 267.99**	**100**	**$ 26,799**	**0%**

> ▶ **RM ON THE WEB 9.2**
>
> Information related to a hotel's market performance is typically provided by STR, a hotel's franchise company, and its own marketing intelligence information. TravelCLICK is another excellent source. TravelCLICK helps RMs by providing data regarding e-booking sources. Information supplied by their *Hotelligence* program helps RMs analyze competitive rates, target desirable travel agents and GDS sources, analyze the impact of their revenue optimization decisions, and create action plans for future months.
>
> To learn more about TravelCLICK you can review its web site at www.travelclick.net
>
> Since individual travelers and travel professionals increasingly utilize the Internet to book rooms, RMs must make strategic decisions about partnering with and supporting specific GDS companies and individual travel-related web sites. TravelCLICK carefully monitors and reports on these popular distribution channels.

Monitoring Web 2.0

Increasingly, potential guests seek information and make decisions about the hotels they will frequent via Internet user postings. As a result, RMs understand that they have an increasingly important role to play in closely monitoring travel social media sites like TripAdvisor and others like it that post travel reviews. In the 1940s, the flamboyant and controversial film actor Errol Flynn observed: *"It isn't what they say about you, it's what they whisper."*[7] Today, the Internet allows customers to *whisper* (or text and twitter!) about your hotel to millions of readers at a time. Although few people actually enjoy criticism, especially when it is unfairly delivered, good or bad comments from guests provide valuable information you can use to improve your product and services.

It is important to recognize that you cannot manage or control social media content. You can, however, carefully monitor it. One easy way to do so is to set up a free Google Alerts account for your property (www.google.com/alerts). Tools such as this one search news, blogs, videofile sharing sites, and others for your hotel's name and then notify you (via e-mail) of the search results.

TripAdvisor can set up a similar program to notify you of any comments about your property that have been posted on their site. Although it is important to monitor and respond to negative comments (see Chapter 8), it is also important to recognize that the majority of comments posted on social media sites are actually positive, not negative. For that reason, it makes sense to carefully monitor social media sites for positive posting about your property. These performance observations, obtained with the permission of the individuals posting the comment, can be posted on your own web site in the

> ▶ **RM ON THE WEB 9.3**

Savvy RMs increasingly rely on the Internet to better understand their customers' attitudes toward their hotel stays. One tactic that is gaining in popularity is that of replacing paper and pencil guest satisfaction surveys with Web-based surveys. In a Web-based survey system, hotel guests are sent an e-mail at the conclusion of their stay asking them to comment about the quality of their hotel room, performance of the hotel's staff, and their overall feelings about price paid versus value received. After the guest completes the survey, the data go directly into the hotel's customer experience management system, allowing properties to track guest satisfaction and identify any problem areas that need to be addressed.

Medallia is an industry leader in providing hoteliers web-based customer survey assistance and industry tracking data. You can view its web site at www.medallia.com

Hotels now utilizing Web-based customer survey systems report increased response rates, respondent-friendly surveys that are easier to complete, significant cost savings, and much faster guest feedback.

form of a testimonial list. Multiple positive comments such as these can have significant power with rooms buyers for the very reason that they are user generated, not property supplied.

COMMON-SENSE REVENUE OPTIMIZATION

For RMs working in the lodging industry, a continual evaluation of evolving revenue optimization strategies, tactics, and results is crucial. Revenue optimization techniques in the industry have advanced far beyond a simplistic "head-in-beds" approach that focused on maximizing a property's occupancy percentage. Such an approach all too often caused RMs to reduce their room rates in the false belief that doing so would increase demand and, as a result, maximize RevPAR.

As you have learned, today's best practices require RMs to establish differential room rates based on market segment acceptance; consider historic, current, and future demand; and manage room rates to reflect room supply and occupancy demand. Knowledge of pricing theory and understanding consumer perceptions of value are also of great importance to an RM's success.

Increasingly, the integration of profit maximization based on GOPPAR and flow-through assessment require RMs to consider opening and closing rate codes based on the level of *profitability* associated with each of a hotel's market segments. Doing so requires that RMs know their hotel's true costs of sales and that they accept increased responsibility for bottom-line profitability. Regardless of their job title or their personal impact on their hotels' departmental operations, however, RMs must ultimately establish their room rates based on their *customers'* perceptions of value received for price paid.

Experienced RMs know that room rates, because they are prices, set their guest's initial expectations for their hotels' products and services. Rates that are too high set unrealistic guest expectations. Rates that are too low undervalue the efforts of the hotel's staff and deprive the property of deserved profits. An overemphasis on Internet intermediaries (who seek their own revenue optimization strategies) as a hotel's primary selling tool risks product and brand commoditization and in too many cases has led to lack of pricing credibility. What is needed, of course, is a common-sense approach to room rate determination. While common sense is much too often uncommon, RMs would do well to recall the definition of common sense proposed by author (of *Uncle Tom's Cabin*) Harriet Beecher Stowe's son C. E. Stowe, who observed: "*Common sense is the knack of seeing things as they are, and doing things as they ought to be done.*"[8] RMs should be those hospitality industry leaders who see things as they are and ensure things are done as they ought to be done.

Those RMs in lodging who possess good amounts of common sense know that to do the *right* things they must:

- Understand the importance of accurate data when forecasting based upon historical, current, and future room demand.
- Recognize the impact of current guest demand or pace on rooms pricing.
- Carefully assess the impact of their pricing decisions on future guest demand and long-term guest loyalty.
- Avoid pricing practices that lead to the commoditization of rooms; the lodging industry's primary product.
- Take into account the impact of their revenue optimization decisions on each of their property's:
  - Transient markets
  - Group markets
  - Contracted rooms markets
- Consider all aspects of overbooking before applying it as an effective rooms inventory management strategy.
- Utilize sound and creative discounting and stay restrictions as supplements to differential rooms pricing strategies.
- Implement and regularly measure the effectiveness and costs related to their non-electronic distribution channel management strategies.
- Implement and regularly measure the effectiveness and costs related their electronic distribution channel management strategies including the:

- CRS
- GDS
- IDS
- Monitor guest experiences using Web 2.0.
- Calculate and analyze the statistics necessary to assess the RM team's decision-making effectiveness, including:
  - ADR
  - Occupancy
  - RevPAR (limited-service hotel) or Total RevPAR (full-service hotel)
  - RevPOR
  - GOPPAR
  - Flow-through
- Monitor the performance of competitors via the insightful analysis of a justifiable comp set.
- Take pricing risks when it is prudent to do so; and accept and learn from mistakes.
- Create realistic RevPAR and profit increase goals and broadly communicate those goals within their organizations.
- Resist the urge to discount rates as a means of increasing profitability because it is a counterproductive strategy.
- Communicate to the entire RM team that neither occupancy, ADR, or RevPAR is the end goal—rather, customer-centric and *profitable* revenue generation is the end goal.

Common sense and the right management assessment tools lead to revenue optimization success for RMs, their RM teams, and their hotels.

❖ ESSENTIAL RM TERMS

Statistic	Market share
Income statement	Metropolitan Statistical Area (MSA)
Total RevPAR	Flag
Room-related occupation costs	SMERF
Minimum ADR sales point formula	Marketing mix
Gross operating profit (GOP)	Ancillary revenue
Flow-through	

IIII➡ APPLY WHAT YOU KNOW

1. Antonio is the RM at the 180-room Hawthorne Suites. Disappointed in his occupancy rate last year, he decided to reduce his room rates this year by 10 percent to help increase sales and improve his RevPAR. This action resulted in an upswing in occupancy, from 75 percent last year, to 85 percent this year; an increase of 13.3 percent.

   Last year, Antonio's controllable operating costs were $61.00 per room. This year, they rose to $62.00 per room, an increase of only 1.6 percent. Help Antonio better understand the overall results of his rate reduction strategy by completing his hotel's May operating performance worksheet and then answering the questions that follow.

Hawthorne Suites May Performance

Statistics	Last May	This May
Occupancy %	75%	85%
Rooms sold		
ADR	$129.99	$116.99
Rooms revenue		
RevPAR		
Controllable operating costs		
Gross operating profit		
GOPPAR		

A. What was Antonio's RevPAR "Last May?" _____

B. What was Antonio's RevPAR "This May?" _____

C. What was Antonio's GOPPAR "Last May? _____

D. What was Antonio's GOPPAR change from last May to this May:

   In dollars? _____

   In %? _____

E. Compare Antonio's GOPPAR performance this year versus last year. How effective do you believe Antonio was in devising and implementing his revenue optimization strategy?

2. Paige Vincent is the RM at the City Center Novotel. For over 12 months, she has been working hard to improve the performance of her hotel. Paige just received the following performance data. Help her understand the revenue optimization trends for her property by completing the chart and then answering the questions that follow.

City Center Novotel Performance:			
Occupancy %	**Novotel**	**Comp Set**	**Index**
This month	57.2	58.1	
Last 3 months	55.1	57.7	
Last 12 months	51.3	55.6	
ADR			
This month	$266.57	$270.15	
Last 3 months	$244.91	$269.69	
Last 12 months	$231.45	$268.95	
RevPAR			
This month			
Last 3 months			
Last 12 months			

A. What was Paige's occupancy index this month? _____

B. What was Paige's ADR index for the last three months? _____

C. What was Paige's RevPAR index this month? _____

D. What was Paige's RevPAR for the last 12 months? _____

E. Compare Paige's property performance for the past 12 months to that of her competitive set. How effective do you believe Paige has been in devising and implementing her revenue optimization strategy?

3. Jamie Lynn is the RM at a 250-room full-service hotel property. Her comp set includes five full- and limited-service properties:

Property	**Number of Rooms**	**Supply**
Sheraton	235	
Radisson	220	
Holiday Inn Crown Plaza	271	
Hyatt Place	314	
Clarion	210	

The demand and revenue performance of Jamie Lynn's hotel for the time period January through May is listed below.

Month	Demand	Revenue
January	16.2	23.7
February	18.5	15.5
March	16.7	17.1
April	20.1	20.5
May	23.7	16.2

A. Assume there were no changes in the number of rooms offered by the comp set or by Jayme Lynn, during the period January to May. What was Jayme Lynn's proportion of the comp set's supply? _____

B. In which months did Jamie Lynn's occupancy rate exceed that of her comp set? _____

C. In which months did Jamie Lynn's ADR exceed that of her comp set? _____

D. Based on Jamie Lynn's January results, what rate-related advice would you give her?

E. Based on Jamie Lynn's May results, what rate-related advice would you give her?

4. Jerielle Pelley is the front office manager at the 125-room limited-service Best Stay Inn. She also serves as her property's RM. Jerielle has just taken a call from Lawrence, a friend and the RM at a hotel within her comp set. Because of an internal oversight, Lawrence's hotel is overbooked by 70 group rooms next Saturday. Lawrence would like to purchase that number of rooms from Jerielle at their previously agreed upon walk rate of $75.00. Jerielle's normal rack rate is $129.00. Currently, she has 55 occupied rooms (arrivals and stayovers) on the books for that day. She estimates that she could sell, at her normal ADR, another 30 rooms by Saturday. Complete the source of business worksheet and then answer the questions that follow.

Source of Business Calculation

Group	With Lawrence Walks	Without Lawrence Walks
Sold		
ADR	$	$129.00
Total revenue estimate	$	$
Daily per room ancillary revenue	$8.00	$8.00
Total ancillary revenue	$	$

(continued)

Source of Business Calculation (*continued*)

Group	With Lawrence Walks	Without Lawrence Walks
RevPOR	$	$
Total revenue		
Revenue Variance	Amount $	% +14.6

A. What would Jerielle's ADR be if she accepted all of Lawrence's walked rooms? ____ _____

B. What would be Jerielle's RevPOR *with* the walked rooms? _____

C. What would be Jerielle's RevPOR *without* the walked rooms? _____

D. What would be the dollar difference in her hotel's total revenue if Jerielle agreed to take the rooms? _____

E. What would be the % difference in her hotel's total revenue if Jerielle agreed to take the rooms? _____

F. If you were Jerielle, would you accept the walked rooms from Lawrence's hotel? Explain your answer.

5. Watson Walbert is on the corporate RM team for the Sunbird Hotel Corporation. Sunbird is the franchisor for Red Robin and Falcon hotels. Part of Watson's job is evaluating revenue and Net ADR Yields for the distribution channels used by the company franchisees. Sunbird charges its franchised hotels a total of 5 percent of gross room revenue for each room sale made. Additional fees (listed as a percentage of ADR) that are assessed for each distribution channel are presented in the following table. Calculate the information required to complete the chart Watson is working on and then answer the questions that follow:

Channel	ADR	Total Fees: 5% franchisor fee PLUS an additional;	Net ADR	Net ADR Yield
Third-party Web sites	$166.54	27%		
Franchisor Web site	$229.99	7%		
Proprietary Web site	$239.99	5%		
Travel agent	$209.59	11%		

A. Which source provides the hotels with their highest net ADR? _____

B. Which source provides the hotels with their lowest net ADR? _____

C. What is the net ADR yield on rooms delivered via this hotel group's franchisor operated web site? _____

D. What is the net ADR yield on rooms delivered to the hotels via travel agents? _____

E. Which source provides the franchisor with the highest per-room revenue? _____

F. Which site provides the franchisees with the highest per-room revenue? _____

KEY CONCEPT CASE STUDY

"Thanks for coming in, Damario," said Sofia Davidson, the GM at the Barcena Resort. Damario, the revenue manager at the 480-room Barcena Resort had now been on the job for 12 months.

"I've been reviewing the data from last month and I have to tell you, the owners are really pleased with our progress," said Sofia.

"I'm pleased, too," said Damario. "We've come a long way."

"Our occupancy index for the past three months has exceeded our comp set by 10 points, and you've managed to keep our rate index in the high 90s," said Sofia.

"That's a real credit to our RM team," Damario replied.

"You're being too modest. The forecast and pricing systems you designed and implemented for us are going great. The controller is happy, the DOSM is happy, and that makes me pretty happy too!" said Sofia. "What's next?

"We still have some real challenges," replied Damario, "but I think we are ready for the next big step."

"And what would that be?" asked Sofia.

"I want to get the *Strategic Pricing and Revenue Management Advisory Committee* to become more aggressive. I want to eliminate our lowest-yield channels and focus even more on our best customers," said Damario.

"Best as in highest rated? That does make sense," said Sofia. "But what exactly will that mean for us?"

"Rate increases, for one thing," replied Damario. "I believe we are ready for our first significant rate increase in a long time. I'm thinking an 8 percent RevPAR increase for next year is a realistic target. Based on our guest feedback results, I know we can do it. And I want to get more involved on the F&B pricing side. I think we can make great strides there as well."

For Your Consideration

1. What evidence in the conversation between Sofia and Damario would lead him to believe the property was ready to seek significant rate increases?

2. Assume you were on Damario's RM team. Since the property's room rates are below the competitive set's, what specific additional data would

be required to convince you that it would be a good time to raise your rack rates?

3. Assume you were in favor of increasing the RevPAR target next year by 8 percent. Would you be in favor of increasing rack rates, reducing discounts offered, or increasing the number of discounted rooms available for sale? What specific additional data would you want to see before making your decision?

4. Assume you were Sofia. Based on his current results, would you favor Damario's increased involvement in the hotel's F&B pricing systems?

ENDNOTES

1. Excerpt from Accor, August 2008 Report to shareholders; at http://www.accor.com/gb/upload/pdf/CP_S1_VA.pdf.

2. Joe Griffith, *Speaker's Library of Business* (Englewood Cliffs, NJ: Prentice Hall 1990), 65.

3. http://thinkexist.com/quotes/ernest_a._fitzgerald/. Retrieved 11/25/2008.

4. http://thinkexist.com/quotes/bill_gates/4.html/. Retrieved 11/26/2008.

5. Robert Reid and David Bojanic, *Hospitality Marketing Management*, 4th ed. (Hoboken, NJ: John Wiley and Sons, 2006).

6. http://www.carolverret.net/viral/readtopic.php?id=45. Retrieved 9/25/2009.

7. http://www.quotegarden.com/gossip.html. Retrieved 11/29/2008.

8. http://thinkexist.com/quotation/common_sense_is_the_knack_of_seeing_things_as/145812.html. Retrieved 11/15/2008.

PART III

REVENUE MANAGEMENT FOR FOODSERVICE OPERATORS

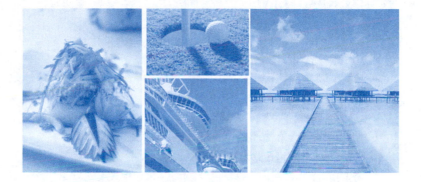

CHAPTER 10

Revenue Management for Food and Beverage Services

CHAPTER OUTLINE

TRADITIONAL FOODSERVICE PRICING METHODS

A designated position termed *revenue manager* is not as well recognized in the foodservice industry as it is in the lodging industry. In fact, many foodservice operators would equate the duties assigned to a revenue manager in foodservice with those of the person responsible for determining menu prices and, perhaps, for the marketing or advertising of the business.

Of course, the proper determination of menu prices is very important. Today's foodservice RMs should know that the careful examination of how industry professionals can best establish menu prices is not a new phenomenon. The first edition of Lendal Kotschevar's *Management by Menu* was released by the National Institute for the Foodservice Industry (NIFI) in 1975.[1] The first edition of Jack E. Miller's classic book *Menu Pricing & Strategy* was also published over 30 years ago (1980).[2]

Both of these texts are important because in them these two industry educators/leaders demonstrated considerable insight regarding the challenge of establishing menu prices. In that regard, they could be considered among the innovative RMs of their time. Both books have been continually revised and updated. A review of past (and present) best practices related to menu pricing strategies will inevitably lead you to two interesting conclusions. The first is that restaurateurs and hoteliers seemingly have very little in common when it comes to pricing. The second is that, despite some thoughtful suggestions to the contrary, the menu pricing techniques used by most foodservice operators have remained relatively unchanged during the past half century, while the industry itself has changed radically. Both of these conclusions deserve further examination.

The foodservice and lodging industries are both considered part of the larger hospitality industry, but the revenue management and pricing strategies used by most restaurateurs are worlds apart from those utilized by hoteliers. A few examples will illustrate some of the many differences.

Recall from Chapter 4 what the hotelier's likely response would be to the guest who wishes to purchase ten or more guest rooms for a single night. In most cases, such a guest would be referred to the hotel's group sales department where, because of the large number of rooms to be purchased, discounts off of full (rack rate) prices would be assumed by both parties. A price would be negotiated, an agreement made, and the rooms would be sold. Contrast that to the experience of a guest arriving at a restaurant seeking a table for ten

Essential RM Term

Table service: A restaurant style in which guests are served while seated in a dining area.

diners. In most **table service** restaurants, such a guest would be assessed a mandatory service charge of 10 to 20 percent. This charge would be automatically added to the customer's bill. The result is that the service charge effectively serves as a price increase (not decrease) for a larger sale. Hotels routinely discount for large sales. Restaurants either increase prices for large sales or leave their prices unchanged. They do not generally discount their prices for large sales.

For a second example of pricing differences, consider the situation that exists when, on a day in the future, it is common knowledge that all of the hotel rooms in an area will be sold out. Examples of such days might include those with large sporting events, festivals, or graduations. On days like these, you can be sure hoteliers have either increased their room prices or at the least have eliminated the ability of their guests to buy rooms at a discount. For restaurateurs, on the other hand, such a high demand day means two things will be true:

1. They will be very busy and thus customer waiting times to get in will be long.

2. They will maintain their normal menu pricing structure.

A final illustration of the differing revenue management strategies employed by restaurateurs and hoteliers is especially instructive. Consider that, on the slowest business day of the week or month, most hotel RMs aggressively employ their discount-oriented programs and distribution channels in an attempt to capture maximum market share. The wisdom of such actions may be questionable, but there is no doubt the tactic is commonly applied.

In contrast, on the slowest day of the week, most restaurateurs charge the exact same prices that they charge on the *busiest* day of the week. With few exceptions (i.e., two-for-one promotions or discount coupons good only at certain times), most restaurateurs and bars *do not* equate a change in guest demand for products with a rationale for modifying prices. Interestingly, this is true even for food and beverage operations located within hotels. As these three examples illustrate, foodservice operators apply very different pricing strategies than do lodging industry RMs. If you are to be a professional RM, the reasons why this is so are worthy of examination.

If you undertake a detailed review of how most foodservice industry experts suggest menu prices are to be determined, you will discover that their recommendations vary only slightly. In general, the experts suggest that menu prices be assigned on the basis of one of the following general concepts:

- Product cost percentage
- Product cost: plus
- Contribution margin

Product Cost Percentage

In 1936, George L. Wenzel, director of the Institute for Fine Cooking, published a large loose-leaf pamphlet titled the *American Menu Maker* in New York. This pamphlet would go on to be the forerunner of the 1,000+ page *Wenzel's Menu Maker*; the book that would become *the* standard for the teaching of foodservice operations for the next 35 years. In the first edition of Wenzel's *Menu Maker* (1947), the author explains the importance of food cost percentage with the beautiful clarity of the times: "Since the percentage of profit runs between 5 percent and 20 percent, any increase in food cost, payroll or other expense percent will decrease your net profit just that much."[3] Wenzel's advice to budding restaurateurs was quite logical and very direct: *Predetermine your desired food cost percentages, maintain them, and thus you maintain your desired profit levels.*

Essential RM Term

Product cost percentage (pricing method):
A pricing method that relies on product cost percentage targets when determining menu prices.

Those foodservice operators taught to utilize a **product cost percentage** pricing philosophy establish their selling prices based primarily on the prices they themselves pay for the ingredients that make up their menu items.

This pricing approach can be defended for two important reasons. The first is that successful restaurateurs know the value of serving good food. Good food usually costs more to produce than lower-quality food. As a result, it is only logical, for example, that an operator charge guests more for a 12-ounce USDA Prime New York strip steak than for a 4-ounce hamburger. The steak costs the operator more and thus must sell for more. This operator would further rationalize that knowledgeable diners would also *expect* to pay more for the steak than the burger. Thus, to some degree, the price expectations of guests are determined, in part, by the product purchased. The operator would even further reason that those menu items that cost the business more to buy must sell for more, and that guests will be willing to pay more for them.

The second piece of logic used by those who set menu prices based on product cost relates directly to the four cost categories of most importance to them. These are commonly identified by foodservice accountants as:

1. Products (food and beverages)
2. Labor
3. Other expenses
4. Profit

To illustrate how these four categories are viewed, assume that a single dollar of revenue represents 100 percent of the income that could be devoted to them. It follows that a portion of that dollar must go to pay for the products sold, another portion for the labor required to prepare and serve the item, another portion for all other expenses required to operate the business (i.e., dishes, napkins, rent, marketing, utilities, loan payments, and the like) and, as Wenzel clearly pointed out, a final amount representing the operation's profit must remain. If any of the first three categories take *too large* a percentage of the income dollar, not enough will be *left over* to pay planned profits to the owner of the business.

To ensure their pricing takes into account both of these concerns (the cost of the product and the product cost as a percentage of revenue), restaurateurs developed and utilize the following pricing formula that does just that:

$$\frac{\text{Cost of products sold}}{\text{All product sales}} = \text{Product cost \%}$$

This formula can be worded somewhat differently for a single (food) menu item:

$$\frac{\text{Item food cost}}{\text{Selling price}} = \text{Item food cost \%}$$

The principles of algebra allow operators to rearrange the formula as follows:

$$\frac{\text{Item food cost}}{\text{Item food cost \%}} = \text{Selling price}$$

It is easy to see that this method of pricing is based simply on the idea that an item's cost should be a *predetermined* percentage of its selling price. When operators apply the formula, they carefully determine the costs they will incur (the numerator), then use that information to determine target percentages (the denominator) for each cost category. When the targets have been established, the product percentage target dictates the menu pricing decision. Increases in costs in any category (e.g., food, beverages, labor, or other expense costs) can easily be factored into the percentage targets to create new (and lower) ratios that still yield profit-producing totals.

To illustrate the process, assume that an operator created the following cost category targets:

Cost Category	%Target
Products	40%
Labor	34%
Other expense	16%
Profit	10%
	100%

Assume also that the operator has developed a menu item that can be produced for $1.50 in ingredient costs. With a targeted product (food) cost percentage for that item of 40 percent, the pricing formula would be applied as:

$$\frac{\text{Item food cost}}{\text{Item food cost \%}} = \text{Selling price}$$

or

$$\frac{\$1.50}{40\%} = \$3.75$$

Thus, in this example, the recommended selling price with a $1.50 item food cost and a 40 percent targeted food cost percentage is $3.75.

Essential RM Term

Pricing factor (foodservice): A constant number used to help determine foodservice product menu prices.

Experienced foodservice operators know that a second formula for arriving at appropriate selling prices based on predetermined product cost percentage goals can also be employed. This method uses a **pricing factor** (multiplier) that can be assigned to each desired food cost percentage.

Figure 10.1	Pricing Factor Table
Desired Product Cost %	**Factor**
20	5.000
23	4.348
25	4.000
28	3.571
30	3.333
33 1/3	3.000
35	2.857
38	2.632
40	2.500
43	2.326
45	2.222

Thus, if you were attempting to price a product and achieve a product cost of 40 percent, the pricing factor would be calculated using the following formula:

$$\frac{\$1.00}{\text{Desired item food cost \%}} = \text{Pricing factor}$$

or

$$\frac{\$1.00}{40\%} = \$2.50$$

Figure 10.1 details a pricing factor table for desired item food cost percentages from 20 percent to 45 percent.

A pricing factor, when multiplied by the item's cost, will result in a selling price that yields the desired item cost percentage. For example, the pricing factor of 2.5 multiplied by an item food cost of $1.50 will yield a selling price that is based on a 40 percent food cost. The computation would be as follows:

$$\text{Pricing factor} \times \text{Item food cost} = \text{Selling price}$$

or

$$2.5 \times \$1.50 = \$3.75$$

Astute readers will recognize that these two methods of arriving at proposed selling prices yield identical results. Mathematically, one formula relies on division while the other relies on multiplication. With either approach, operators determine selling price based on the goal of achieving a predetermined food or beverage cost percentage for each product sold. When utilizing this pricing strategy, operators typically view those menu items with lower product cost percentages more favorably. This is the oldest and most traditional menu pricing system currently in use and it is still in widespread use today.

Product Cost: Plus

A **product cost: plus** menu pricing system simply considers an item's product cost, *plus* any number of additional cost-related factors, when determining selling price.

One of the most popular cost: plus pricing systems involves the calculation of a menu item's **prime cost**. A prime cost is simply the product cost of a menu item *plus* the cost of the labor required to produce it. The item's prime cost is then used to establish its selling price.

There are a variety of these cost: plus systems, but all have grown out of astute foodservice operators' recognition of some shortcomings of menu pricing systems based solely on product cost percentages. Figure 10.2 lists some of the cost categories that, either by percentage or dollar amount, are often added to a product's ingredients cost to aid operators in menu price determination.

All of the cost: plus pricing systems that have been developed result from the very logical effort by foodservice operators to include additional expense-related variables to their product pricing models.

The concept of actually modifying the product cost percentage approach to include additional costs (a fairly recent and quite radical idea at the time) was first proposed by Penn State University's hospitality professor James Keiser and industry consultant Elmer Kallio. In 1972, their newly published hospitality textbook included this revolutionary thought: *"Although meal pricing is based primarily on the cost of food . . . with the increased use of electronic data processing, it may soon be easier to include labor costs—and other costs—in the calculation of specific selling prices."*[4]

Today, of course, advanced computer programs exist to help operators easily consider any number of additional costs they desire when they calculate their menu prices, and the many operators who embrace the cost: plus pricing approach frequently do just that.

Figure 10.2 | **Alternative Components of Cost: Plus Pricing Systems**

Menu Price =	Product Cost	Plus	Variable labor cost
	Product Cost	Plus	Fixed labor cost
	Product Cost	Plus	Total item labor cost
	Product Cost	Plus	Selected controllable expenses
	Product Cost	Plus	Proportional overhead cost per item
	Product Cost	Plus	Desired per item gross profit

Contribution Margin

Interestingly, the next significant menu pricing-related development was initiated outside the hospitality industry by the Boston Consulting Group (BCG). BCG is a global management consulting firm founded by Harvard Business school alumnus Bruce Henderson in 1963. In the early 1970s, BCG created and popularized its *growth-share matrix*, a 2 × 2 chart (matrix) designed to assist large corporations in deciding how to allocate cash among their business units.

Using preestablished definitions of profitability, BCG showed businesses how to categorize each of their individual business units as a *"Star," "Cash Cow," "Question Mark,"* or *"Dog"* based on its ability to generate cash. The business's leaders would then use this information to allocate future financial resources among the business units accordingly.[5] The BCG growth-share model rapidly gained popularity in a variety of industries.

In 1982, Michigan State University School of Hospitality professors Michael Kasavana and Donald Smith published *Menu Engineering: A Practical Guide to Menu Pricing*. In it, Kasavana and Smith argue that **contribution margin (CM)** was a more important factor in identifying profitable (and properly priced) menu items than was product cost percentage.

Essential RM Terms

Contribution margin (CM): The profit (margin) that remains after a product's cost is subtracted from its selling price.

Selling price − Product cost = Contribution margin

Their approach, which they labeled *menu engineering*, touted the value of menu items that sold well and that had high CM levels. After defining *popularity* as the frequency of a menu item's sale and identifying those menu items with high (above average) or low (below average) popularity and CM levels, Kasavana and Smith modified Henderson's 2 × 2 matrix somewhat and proposed four categories of menu items (renaming some with catchy new titles!), as follows:

Stars: Menu items with high popularity and high CM

Plow horses: Menu items with high popularity and low CM

Puzzles: Menu items with low popularity and high CM

Dogs: Menu items with low popularity and low CM

To apply menu engineering, a foodservice operation's menu items are analyzed and, based on their calculated attributes, are placed into one of the boxes illustrated in Figure 10.3. Suggestions for how to promote, reprice, or replace individual menu items based on their matrix placement make up a large part of the information that has since been written about menu engineering.

Due in large part to the stature of its authors and partly because of its simple logic, menu engineering was embraced very quickly. Today most foodservice professionals will readily recognize the names of the categories used in its application, despite some academic debate about the best techniques to use when placing individual items within the matrix squares.

Figure 10.3	Menu Engineering Matrix		

		Popularity	
		Low	High
Contribution Margin	High	PUZZLE High contribution margin Low popularity	STAR High contribution margin High popularity
	Low	DOG Low contribution margin Low popularity	PLOW HORSE Low contribution margin High popularity

To a large degree, the system became popular because it was the first of many with a CM focus. A CM-based pricing system addresses the fundamental problem encountered by advocates of the older product cost percentage–based pricing methods. Proponents of product cost–based pricing systems had always struggled to answer questions such as: *"Is it better to sell a $10.00 chicken item with a 30 percent food cost or a $20.00 steak item with a 50 percent food cost?"*

Clearly, due to the $7.00 CM ($10.00 selling price − $3.00 product cost = $7.00 CM) achieved by the chicken sale, the steak sale, with its $10.00 CM ($20.00 selling price − $10.00 product cost = $10.00 CM) is the more desirable sale. Because restaurateurs take dollars (not percentages) to the bank, it was not too difficult to make contribution margin converts out of a great number of product cost percentage advocates.

A second and less recognized reason the new system was so quickly embraced is that it was so familiar. This was the case because a CM-based pricing system is simply a slight variation of the older, previously accepted product cost–based pricing system. When CM is used as the basis for pricing, the formula for determining selling price is:

Product cost + Contribution margin desired = Selling price

Notice that product cost is still an essential element in the determination of selling price. Establishing menu prices using a CM system is simply a matter of combining product cost with a predetermined dollar amount of contribution margin. The RMs task in such a system is simply to establish the target CM for each menu item. When using this approach, foodservice operators most often establish different target CMs for different groups of items. For example, in a restaurant where items are priced separately, entrées might be priced to achieve a contribution margin of $8.50 each, desserts a contribution margin of $2.25, and drinks, perhaps, a contribution margin of $1.75 each.

To illustrate the use of a CM pricing approach, assume $8.50 is an RM's desired CM for all entrées sold. Utilizing that target in the previous chicken and steak example, the pricing approach would be:

Menu Item	Product Cost	Desired CM	Selling Price
Chicken	$3.00	$8.50	$11.50
Steak	$10.00	$8.50	$18.50

> ► **RM ON THE WEB 10.1**
>
> Foodservice RMs will have no difficulty identifying a large number of publications detailing a variety of cost-based menu pricing techniques and strategies. To find a list of current publications, go to either the Amazon.com (www.amazon.com) or Barnes and Noble (www.bn.com) web sites.
>
> When you arrive, choose the *Books* category, then enter either *Menu Pricing* or *Food and Beverage Cost Control* to review the most recently published works related to the determination of food and beverage prices.

Those managers who rely on the contribution margin approach to pricing do so in the belief that the average contribution margin per item is a *more* important consideration in pricing decisions than is food cost percentage. They also believe that applying basic menu engineering techniques will significantly increase an operation's profitability.

Today, the calculation of product (food or beverage) cost percentage and product cost-plus pricing are standard content in all cost related hospitality textbooks. Despite some spirited debate about their pluses and minuses, the techniques used for applying menu engineering principles are also a standard topic in virtually every recently published pricing and cost related foodservice management text.[6] Most recently, some researchers/ writers have sought to modify and expand the CM-based pricing approach by examining the merits of combining food cost percentage analysis *with* CM,[7] or even through adding labor costs to the basic menu engineering model.[8]

The common feature in all three menu pricing approaches, however, remains their primary focus on what foodservice *operators* pay for the ingredients used to make their menu items.

THE CASE AGAINST COST-BASED FOODSERVICE PRICING

The debate over the *best* pricing method for use in foodservice is likely to continue for some time. Recall from Chapter 2, however, that utilizing cost as the major determinate in pricing a business's products is generally *not* a desirable approach. As a result, as a professional RM it should concern you that applying any of the three cost-based menu pricing strategies you have reviewed thus far is not likely to be an effective revenue optimization strategy.

In fact, applying a cost-based foodservice pricing strategy is, in most cases, (pardon the pun) a *recipe* for disaster. How bad is cost-based pricing? Internationally known management consultant Peter Drucker identified cost-driven pricing as one of the five deadly business sins. In an interview, Drucker pointed out five actions that must be avoided if a business is to be successful. He called these actions "deadly sins" and identified *cost-based pricing* as the third deadly sin. Commenting on the fallacy of believing that the role of a selling price is to recover an operator's costs and to ensure making a profit, he correctly states, *"Customers do not see it as their job to ensure manufacturers (or any other business) a profit."*[9]

RM IN ACTION 10.1: AND THE SPECIAL TONIGHT IS . . .

Ask a foodservice professional to explain the term "special" and they will likely tell you about the chef's latest creation—an item that requires special skill or is exceptionally unique. Lynne Nowick, a Republican politician in Suffolk (New York), sees it differently. According to a *Newsday* report published in *Restaurants and Institutions,* Ms. Nowick stated, "People hear the word special and they think it's going to be a bargain. Many times it's not. And sometimes people—young people on a first date or the elderly are too embarrassed to ask."

Based on her definition of "special," Nowick has proposed local legislation that requires prices on all food items, including specials, be listed on a printed page with the menu or posted in a way "readily observable."

Jerry Marlow, vice president of the Long Island chapter of the New York State Restaurant Association and owner of Collins and Main in Sayville, said the association has taken no stand on the bill. He instructs his own waiters, who verbally describe specials to customers, to detail their prices as well. Marlow's position reflects what should be the view of all customer-centric revenue managers: "We're not trying to hoodwink anybody; Nowick's proposal is fair to consumers."

Nowick's proposal does serve as a reminder that pricing must always be considered by guests to be *fair*, even when the guest may be confused about what an RM likely means when a term such as "special" is used.

Often, fairness in pricing is perceived as less about the amount charged than the way in which a price is communicated. Guests should not be placed in the uncomfortable position of having to ask the price of an item not included on a menu. Transparency and clarity in pricing should be a trademark of the revenue optimization decisions made by all customer-centric RMs.

———————

Excerpted on 12/01/2008 from www.rimag.com.

In a noncommodity industry, cost-based pricing, in any of its forms, has significant drawbacks. The fact is that if foodservice pricing were actually simple, even the least talented of foodservice professionals would be able to successfully calculate their costs, add a desired profit level (or CM), and determine menu prices that their guests would consider appropriate. Foodservice pricing is not simple. The failure rate for restaurants is among the highest of any business. This is due, in many cases, to inappropriate product pricing.

To better understand the difficulties inherent in implementing effective foodservice pricing strategies, RMs might consider an interesting fact. A review of today's most popular hospitality marketing texts finds that these publications always include a detailed discussion of hotel guest room pricing, but they do not address the specifics of food and beverage pricing. In fact, detailed food and beverage pricing strategies have historically been presented and debated in hospitality accounting or cost control courses; not marketing courses (Note: please reread this sentence now to ensure you understand its significance!).

This placement variance reflects the reality that, in most cases, hotel room pricing decisions are driven by a hotel organization's sales and marketing staff while foodservice pricing has primarily been the domain of F&B operations or accounting and finance specialists. These F&B specialists have been taught to rely on cost-related data to establish their prices.

Thus, a legitimate question for professionals in the emerging field of foodservice revenue optimization is rather stark in its simplicity:

"Is foodservice pricing essentially an accounting issue or a marketing function?"

The authors would answer the question as *neither.* We would propose that foodservice pricing and revenue optimization strategy is simply too important to be considered as only one, among many, of the important topics to be addressed by either operations, finance, or marketing professionals. Indeed, as much as any other business challenge, this very issue is one of the best possible arguments for designating highly trained RMs as the pricing experts within foodservice organizations. The lodging industry increasingly understands the importance of inventory management and strategic pricing and has embraced specially trained RMs. The foodservice industry should do likewise.

Essential RM Term

Sales volume (foodservice): The number of a single menu item sold during a defined accounting period.

To better understand the complexity of food and beverage pricing and exactly why trained pricing professionals are so needed, it is important to recognize that in foodservice, an important distinction must be made between total sales revenue and **sales volume**—or the number of units sold.

To illustrate, consider a bagel shop manager whose Monday business consists of $4,000 in total sales (revenue) because she sold 2,000 bagels (sales volume) at $2.00 (selling price) per bagel. Foodservice revenue and price are not synonymous terms. Revenue refers to the amount spent by *all* guests, while price refers to the amount charged to one guest. In the foodservice industry, total revenue is generated by the following formula:

$$\text{Selling price} \times \text{Number (volume) sold} = \text{Total revenue}$$

From this formula, the two important components of total foodservice revenue are easily identifiable. Selling price is one component; the other is the number of items sold. In foodservice, variation in selling price (menu prices) will directly affect the number of items sold. As is true in the lodging industry, selling price and number sold are interrelated in the foodservice industry.

Recall from Chapter 2 that in many cases, as price increases, the number of items sold at that price will decrease. Given sufficient demand, the opposite is also true—as price decreases, the number of items sold at that price will increase. For this reason, price increases (or decreases) must be evaluated based on their impact on *total* revenue generation and not on the number that represents the final selling price.

To illustrate, assume you are the RM for a chain of specialty coffee shops. Due to rising ingredient costs, you are considering raising the price of the breakfast pastries sold in your shops from $1.99 to $2.29. Figure 10.4 illustrates the possible effects of this price increase on your total revenue in a single unit that has been selling 200 pastries per day. Note especially that, in at least one scenario, increasing price has the effect of *decreasing* total revenue.

Experienced foodservice managers know that increasing prices due to their increased costs, without giving added customer value, will no doubt result in higher menu prices. Most frequently, however, it also results in lowered total revenue due to reduced guest

Figure 10.4	Possible Results of Pastry Price Increases			
Original Price		**Number Sold**	**Total Revenue**	**Revenue Result**
$1.99		200	**$398.00**	
New Price	**Potential Impact of New Price**			
$2.29	Increased customer count	250	$572.50	Increase
$2.29	No change in customer count	200	$458.00	Increase
$2.29	Decrease in customer count	173.8	**$398.00**	No Change
$2.29	Decrease in customer count	150	$343.50	Decrease

counts or guests' per-visit purchases. This is true simply because foodservice guests (like lodging industry room buyers), are not concerned about an operator's costs. Increased costs do not automatically equal to an increase in customer's perceived value. Buyers are, however, very concerned about those things that *do* impact their perceptions of a business's price/value offer.

So how important are costs? As co-authors of an internationally best selling book devoted solely to food and beverage cost control, the answer is that costs and their control are very important to profitability. However, *"No amount of effective expense (cost) control can solve the profit problems caused by inadequate revenue resulting from inferior food quality or service levels."*[10]

For some foodservice operators, inefficiency in cost control is passed on to guests in the form of higher prices. An increase in costs cannot be automatically allowed to decree an increase in selling price. In fact, the opposite should be true. An appropriate selling price for a product or service must *dictate* the item's cost. Savvy RMs working in foodservice learn that price comes first; then allowable costs can be calculated. Selling prices must accurately reflect consumer perceptions of value. When these types of prices are established first, a business can then compute the costs it can reasonably incur while still generating required profits.

If you recognize that two diamonds of the same size and quality will have equal value even if one was discovered accidentally on the ground and the other took the expense of a year's labor and equipment to uncover, then you can see why costs should not be allowed to dictate prices. For the foodservice industry, even more so than in the lodging industry, sound pricing must be based not on cost but on establishing a positive price/value relationship in the mind of the guest. This is essential, in large part due to the greater number of alternatives available to foodservice customers.

As illustrated in Figure 10.5, a foodservice organization chooses from two basic options when pricing its products. The first relies on cost and results in menu prices desired by the operator. The operator's *hope* in such a case is that guests will agree that the price is fair and represents good value. While hope is an appropriate strategy when playing slot machines or buying lottery tickets, as a business strategy, it is not one of the best. This is especially apparent

RM IN ACTION 10.2: RECONSIDERING THE VALUE PROPOSITION

Nation's Restaurant News (NRN) reported that after recording a 19-percent drop in second-quarter profits and warning of further declines in same-store sales for its two main brands, The Cheesecake Factory Inc. said today that it would try to reverse the downturn, in part by reconsidering the *value* perception of its namesake chain.

Interestingly, quarterly revenues for the same period were *up* 9 percent due to new restaurant openings. For RMs, an important lesson that can be learned is that additional stores (or even increased individual guest sales) do not *automatically* lead to greater profits.

In the report, David Overton, Cheesecake Factory chairman and chief executive, was quoted as saying:

The chain . . . will look at "tweaking" the Cheesecake Factory's value proposition by region. I think we're still seen as offering value, but you have to be careful in this environment.

Note Overton's use of the term; *value proposition.* As an RM, you must champion the concept within your organization that it is value delivered, not your production costs, that matter most to guests. In fact, it is the value you deliver to guests that ultimately determines your allowable prices. Those are the prices that must dictate your allowable costs if you are to be a profitable and viable foodservice organization.

Excerpted on 8/10/2008 from www.nrn.com.

when the hope is based on the questionable position that guests view the costs you incur as synonymous with the value you deliver. They do not.

Option B in Figure 10.5 recognizes that guests ultimately determine menu prices based on the value delivered to them. Note also, however, that this option includes recognition of allowable costs; which is the amount an organization can spend to produce a product given their own guests' perception of the product's value.

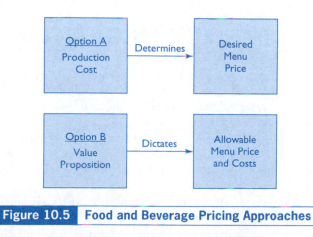

Figure 10.5   **Food and Beverage Pricing Approaches**

RM AT WORK 10.1

"$28.95—that's almost ten dollars more than we charged for it yesterday!" said Shana, the Dining Room manager at Chez Paul's restaurant. "It's even more than our highest priced steak!"

Shanna was discussing the day's dinner menu with Henri, the restaurant's chef. Henri had just delivered to Shanna the daily menu insert that her service staff would use that night. On the night's new menu she noticed that the price of Huachinango a la Veracruzana (Red Snapper with Spicy Red Sauce), one of the operation's signature dishes, had increased overnight. Yesterday it sold for $19.95. Today Henri had priced it at $28.95.

"Tell me about it," replied Henri, "our seafood supplier really jacked our price on the new shipment. Claimed there was a supply shortage. Price went up almost $7.00 per pound. Over $3.00 a portion. Might last for two or three weeks. You know how Mark is. If I don't keep a 36 percent food cost . . . or less, it could mean my job. With the new cost of snapper, I needed this increase to keep the food cost ratio in line."

Shanna knew it was true that Mark, the restaurant's manager, did keep the pressure on to control costs in both the front and back of the house. In this case, however, Shanna wasn't sure that her servers or the customers they would serve that night would be very happy with Henri's pricing decision. The snapper was a very popular item, and that meant tonight lots of customers would notice the price increase.

1. Assume you were a server at Chez Paul's on the night this new menu price was initiated. How would you respond to a returning guest who questioned the significant price increase on the snapper item?

2. Assume you were a regular customer at Chez Paul's, and that the snapper was your favorite item. How would you likely respond to the new menu price? If you bought it, would you consider the item to have delivered an extra $9.00 of value to your dining experience?

3. Do you think Henri's new menu price was a direct result of Mark's cost-based pricing philosophy? How would you have advised Henri to respond to the increase in red snapper cost?

APPLYING DIFFERENTIAL PRICING IN FOODSERVICES

In Chapter 4 you learned that differential pricing—the strategy of charging different prices to different buyers for the same, or for slightly different versions of the same product—is a powerful revenue optimization tool. It is a tool that, unfortunately, has been used too sparingly by some foodservice operators.

Historically, most restaurateurs have established a single price for the various menu items they sell and then have left the prices alone until the next time the menu was printed. At the time of a menu reprint, individual menu items would be added or removed based on their popularity or cost.

New menu items would be considered and, if added to the menu, their costs would be calculated. Based on these new costs, and using the restaurant's preferred menu pricing method, the new menu item's price would be established. Finally, revised menus or menu boards

RM IN ACTION 10.3: VALUE? . . . TO WHOM?

In 1989 Wendy's introduced its 99¢ Value menu. McDonald's created its Dollar Menu in 2002. Burger King rolled out its similarly priced BK Value Menu in 2006. These chains, as well as others, still offer a variety of value menu items at the same 99¢ to $1.00 price point. Some customers love value menus, as do franchise companies whose fees are based on a franchisee's gross sales; not the franchisee's profits. RMs in foodservice, however, must take a serious look at the long-term impact of selling food only on the basis of its "low cost." The times (unlike value menu prices) really do change. Unlike their selling prices, restaurants' costs of doing business have not remained fixed over the years. Minimum wage levels and food prices have increased, as have insurance, energy, and many other costs.

In 2008, the owners of four Manhattan Burger King franchised units filed suit against Burger King. These operators claimed they simply could not make money when offering *value menu* items in their Burger King franchised Manhattan stores (due to the high costs associated with operating in New York City). Referring to the lawsuit, Rich Gallucci, one of the franchisee's attorneys, was quoted in *Franchise Times* as saying:

> It's not a suggestion that the value menu doesn't benefit someone. Obviously, if you go in and purchase a hamburger for 99 cents, it benefits you as a consumer and

it benefits the corporation. But it does nothing to help the franchisee.

Some industry experts have mixed feelings about the true value of value meals because they are seen as a mixed blessing. Advocates state that value menus undoubtedly drive traffic to stores. They maintain that customers like these value menus and, the reasoning continues, customers must be given what they want.

Interestingly, General Motors (GM) made the same supposedly customer-oriented argument when asked by Congress why it sold so many large SUVs and trucks from 2000–2008. Prior to its bankruptcy filing, GM's CEO was vilified, chastised, and removed from his position for building the wrong car types despite his protests of *"that's what the customer wanted."*

The job of business leaders is to ensure the long-term viability of their businesses. Thus, it is not necessarily wrong for professional RMs in the foodservice industry to follow the lead of Burger King franchisees who, in 2009 twice voted against a franchisor recommended expansion of their value menu.[11] They, like all professional RMs, are right to legitimately question the long-term wisdom of any business strategy that seeks to increase top line revenues chiefly by selling items at prices so low they prevent the operation from making a reasonable profit on their sale.

_____

Excerpted on 12/08/2008 from www.franchisetimes.com.

Essential RM Term

Point of sale (POS) system: A computer system used to record and retain sales data.

with the updated prices would be created. The **point-of-sale (POS) system** would be reprogrammed to reflect the new prices and the updating process would be complete.

Today, significant advances in print, display technology and POS system programming could allow this historical procedure to change radically. Differential pricing based on guests' view of value and willingness to pay, however, has been implemented only warily as a revenue optimization strategy in foodservice. This is likely the case because a *"Set them and forget them"* mentality (the inevitable result of cost-based menu pricing) most often results in a *"we only change prices when our costs change"* mentality.

Unfortunately, too often an overemphasis on product cost results in the use of outdated and ineffective revenue optimization strategies. One example of this is the overdependence on low prices as a means of increasing revenue. RMs in foodservice, like their lodging industry counterparts, must be very careful to avoid commoditization of their products and services. Recall from Chapter 8 that commoditization is the process by which a branded product or service reaches a point in its development where the brand has no features that differentiate it from other brands. As a result, consumers buy on price alone.

Successful restaurateurs know that seeking to compete solely on the basis of low cost is a losing strategy. They also know that most foodservice operators face fairly similar costs when selecting the items they will sell. Whether the product sold is oranges or beer, whole-sale prices typically vary only slightly from one supplier to the next. The result, in too many cases, is that competing foodservice operations, all of which are paying nearly identical prices for their own goods, inevitably reduce quality to reduce their costs (and thus maintain or reduce their selling prices).

Unfortunately, this cost-based action frequently leads to reduced perceptions of the value they offer their customers. Such an approach is bad for an individual foodservice unit and bad for the entire foodservice industry. This is so because value is not just about attracting guests with low prices. It is about meeting guest expectations. In the foodservice industry, a good value is the right quality product in the right portion size accompanied by the right service for the right price. This concept was articulated well by Brad Nelson, corporate chef for Marriott International, when he stated: *"It still has to be value with quality; it is not just about making it cheaper. You have to stick with quality levels because, frankly, people are not going to waste [time and money] on poor-quality products."*[12]

You know that if you wanted to buy a car you would not likely purchase the car that sells for the very lowest price in your area. That car probably would not even start! Rather, you would look for the car that provided you the most value for the price you could afford. In a similar manner, if you were purchasing a clothing item, such as blue jeans, for yourself it is unlikely you would choose the absolutely lowest priced jeans you could find. Because you recognize there are quality differences in jeans, you are most likely to behave rationally and choose the jeans that provide the most value to you.

In many ways, the value offered by service providers is even more important than the value offered by product providers. If you are purchasing a car, you can inspect it and drive it prior to its purchase. You could try on jeans before purchasing them. As you learned in Chapter 3, however, the intangibility of services makes choosing service providers more difficult and less based on price. If, for example, you were choosing to hire a financial investment firm to help you manage your wealth, you would likely be very cautious about choosing a company that sought to win your account by proudly advertising it was the lowest priced supplier of investment advice in your area. In a similar manner, if one of your loved ones needed heart surgery, it is doubtful that a surgeon would win your confidence if they sought to win patients by offering to provide the lowest priced heart transplants in your area.

In any service industry, including foodservice, if the word *value* comes to be used interchangeably with the words *low price* rather than *higher quality*, significant problems will inevitably result. This is especially true in the sale of food and beverages. Hospitality professionals, more so than the average person, know it is absurd to believe that the quality of all foods and beverage ingredients are the same.

The quality of most products (cheese and wine are two excellent examples) vary a great deal. Seeking to sell such products at the lowest possible menu price, rather than at the highest possible value level, makes little sense. Yet it occurs all too frequently. Michael Pollan, popular author of *The Omnivore's Dilemma*, sagely observes: "*When you think about it, it is odd that something as important to our health and general well-being as food is so often sold strictly on the basis of price.*"[13]

In Chapter 5 you learned:

Strategic pricing is the application of data and insight to effectively match prices charged with individual buyer's perceptions of value and willingness to pay.

Certainly the specific food and beverage products sold in an operation have some impact on value perception and some guests' willingness to pay. As a result, a 20-year old Scotch may well demand a higher selling price than a 5-year-old Scotch. In the same manner, USDA Prime beef steaks will command a higher price than USDA Choice or USDA Select beef steaks.

It is important to recognize, however, that the increased quality of these products is not synonymous with increased value and customer willingness to pay. The 20-year-old Scotch or Prime steak will continue to be superior quality products regardless of the price at which you choose to sell them. If your pricing is perceived as excessive, however, the products will not provide good value, nor will your potential customers be willing to pay for them. This is a key point in better appreciating the restaurateur's common lament that "*my customers don't want to pay for quality.*" Customers do not pay for quality. They pay only for value.

For many, and perhaps most, foodservice customers, knowledge of quality differences in food and beverage products is too limited to be the main factor affecting their view of foodservice value. Foodservice operators who are often justly proud of the products they choose to sell often find that hard to accept. To prove it to yourself, however, simply ask a non hospitality friend or colleague to tell you the difference between Choice and Select beef. Or between Roquefort and Blue cheese. Or between Prosciutto and a sugar-cured smoked ham. In asking questions such as these, you will quickly find that the average American diner choosing to eat out is buying many things. These include such things as convenience, speed, unique products, social setting, escape, and even romance. But most do not choose their restaurant based on their vast knowledge of variance in the quality of the raw menu ingredients offered to them.

In fact, fully discerning the quality and cost differences in purchased food and beverage products may be as alien a concept to the average American diner as the intricacies of those diners' own various businesses would be to the foodservice operator. While this fact may be somewhat upsetting to restaurateurs who are passionate about the quality of food and beverages they serve, it is a reality that must be addressed by the foodservice operator. As a result, a skilled revenue manager can often more easily point out how creative pricing could be implemented in a foodservice operation than the operation's own food and beverage production specialists.

Foodservice customers do assess the value delivered to them. Most simply do not use product quality/cost to do so. Accepting the premise that many factors other than food and beverage quality are the major determinates of value perception for foodservice customers may require a significant change in thought process on the part of some restaurateurs. Change can be difficult; some would even say that it is only babies who truly look forward to change!

As an RM working in foodservice, however, you must recognize the critical factors that directly affect the value proposition you make to your own guests, as well as how they will respond to them. If that represents change on your part, it is a change you must make. Foodservice industry revenue managers should recognize the role that differential pricing could play in the industry. In the interest of providing revenue managers with additional menu pricing perspectives, we now consider the applicability of differential pricing in the foodservice industry.

You have learned that RMs in the lodging industry know the number of rooms they have to sell is fixed. Thus, room rates are adjusted based on demand. The same is true in the airline industry. In both industries, selling prices are higher during peak times and lower during off-peak periods. In both cases, customers have become accustomed to this variability. However, in foodservices, most operators have very rarely equated a fluctuation in demand of services with their ability to charge more or charge less. Perhaps this is because foodservice operators see themselves as selling food and beverage products rather than services.

As you have learned, consumers most often look unfavorably upon sellers who raise product prices simply because demand increases (recall the snow shovel example from Chapter 5). In fact, foodservice operators do not sell products as much as they sell capacity. The 100-seat restaurant sells the right to occupy one of the 100 seats for a period of time. Put another way, restaurateurs don't sell steaks; they rent seats to customers who buy steaks. The purchases made and the amount spent during the period the guest rents the seat dictate the revenues generated. This situation is actually quite similar to the hotelier selling a sleeping room. Both sell a unit of inventory (room or seat) for a period of time. Just as an unsold sleeping room represents revenue loss, so, too, does an unsold restaurant seat.

Actually, it is interesting that the foodservice industry has not fully embraced the willingness to pay pricing concept introduced earlier in this book and the differential pricing strategies that logically flow from that pricing approach. The hospitality industry has certainly borrowed other ideas from the airline industry. One example is the creation of frequent diner programs patterned after the airlines frequent flyer programs. In fact it is hard to find a successful restaurant today that doesn't offer some type of rewards program for its best customers. The concept of utilizing yield in pricing, however, has not been fully embraced by foodservice operators, despite, as shown in Figure 10.6, the several similarities between the ways in which restaurants, hotels, and airlines create gross revenues.

Just as hotels have rooms to fill, airlines have seats to fill and restaurants have a fixed number of chairs to fill. If the chairs are not filled with diners the costs associated with lighting, heating, mortgage, and staffing the operation are still incurred. Just as the lodging and airline industries take advantage of differential pricing, so too should restaurateurs consider expanding their use of this powerful revenue optimization strategy.

Those foodservice operators seeking to sell their products based on the prices they themselves pay for raw ingredients will have no difficulty finding a variety of excellent sources to help them with that process.[14] The authors propose, however, that RMs in foodservices take a more aggressive approach in the application of differential pricing. As the economic downturn that began in late 2008 demonstrated so clearly, those restaurants that seek to

Figure 10.6	Gross Revenue Generation: Foodservices/Lodging/Airlines			
Industry	**Constrained Supply?**	**Capacity Utilization Measure**	**Pricing Measure**	**Gross Revenue Measure**
Foodservices	Yes: seats	Customer count[a]	Menu prices/ Check average	Total INCOME (Customer count) Check Average)
Lodging	Yes: rooms	Occupancy %	ADR	RevPAR (Occ. × ADR)
Airlines	Yes: seats	Load %	Yield	Total Yield (Load × Yield)

[a]Note this measure is not expressed as a proportion (%) of available capacity, a significant weakness that will be addressed in the RevPASH section of the following chapter.

maximize revenues via the offering of low prices can easily lose customers to even lower-cost product providers, including grocery stores offering home meal replacement products at prices even lower than those that can be offered by restaurateurs.

Can differential pricing successfully be applied to foodservices? In many cases, the answer is a resounding *yes!* Consider how differential pricing might be applied to full-service restaurants. To do so, envision a scenario in which the restaurant is operated by a talented lodging industry RM. In such a case, that RM would likely first identify the operation's forecasted peak hours of demand. Assume that, like many restaurants, these high-demand times consisted of a three-hour period every Friday and Saturday night.

The lodging industry RM would ask several questions that would logically follow. Each question is worthy of thoughtful consideration:

Question 1. Can menu prices be higher on Friday and Saturday night?

Assuming no restrictions on the ability to reprint menus or to reprogram the operation's POS system, this is a legitimate question. Many traditional foodservice operators would be firmly against such an approach to pricing. They would state that their guests would have significant negative reactions. An RM advising the foodservice operator might point out, however, that these diners would be the same customers who routinely pay more to fly during busy periods, rent hotel rooms at a premium price during peak vacation periods, and readily pay more to golf on the weekend than through the week. It is important to realize that there is no contract with foodservice guests that states prices have to be the same every night of the week.

How could food and beverage prices reflect demand? Recognizing that guests prefer pricing discounts to surcharges, operators could take a lesson from their lodging industry counterpart and establish a "rack" menu price. This would be the menu price charged for items when no discounts are offered. It may represent, for example, a premium of 15 to 20 percent (or more) over current menu prices.

These rack menu prices could be the prices charged during the three-hour peak Friday and Saturday night dining periods. Discounts off these rack menu prices could then be offered for diners arriving significantly earlier or later than the peak three-hour period on Fridays and Saturdays, as well as those dining on slower days or during slower periods. The potential advantages of varying the discounts off rack menu prices are evident.

Given the traditional pricing practices of the hospitality industry, the implementation of such a rack menu price approach might or might not lead to a negative response from diners. Astute readers who recall Chapter 4 will recognize that this is simply an example of using time as a determining factor when implementing a differential pricing strategy. Half-price happy hours and early-bird dining specials are more traditional foodservice examples of this same time-based strategy.

This first reasonable revenue optimization question is presented here in its purest differential pricing form simply as an example of the type of out-of-the-box thinking that will be required if foodservice operators hope to move aggressively away from cost-based pricing systems and toward value-based pricing systems utilizing differential pricing. Additional and, to traditional foodservice operators, perhaps less threatening questions that might be asked by a lodging industry RM in this illustration include:

Question 2. Can *special* menu items be priced higher on Friday and Saturday night?

Assume overall menu prices are not increased as suggested in the first question. Are Friday and Saturday nights good days to offer higher-priced specials? The answer may be yes if guests see the specials as providing real value.

Just as hoteliers should seek to optimize revenue via the enhancement of value (and price) during high-demand days, so, too, should foodservice RMs. The value enhancements offered must, of course, reflect the style of restaurant, bar, or lounge operated. As a foodservice RM, it will be your job to identify, by applying data and insight, the best ways for your own operation to enhance diner value during high-demand periods. When you do, you may be able to adjust prices upward on special dishes to reflect that increased value. High-demand periods such as those identified in this scenario may be an excellent time to do so.

Question 3. Can *selected* menu items be priced lower on Friday and Saturday night?

Restaurateurs sell seating space as much as they sell menu items. As a result, the sale of those items that can be prepared and served quickly are simply more advantageous to the operation during a busy meal period than that same item's sale during a less busy period.

It would be logical to consider the impact on total revenues of reducing prices on quick preparation or quick-to-serve menu items to increase the total number of guests served on a day when such a strategy can be applied. Recall that the total revenue formula for a foodservice operation is:

$$\text{Selling price} \times \text{Number Sold} = \text{Total Revenue}$$

As you have learned, revenue optimization strategies utilizing differential pricing can often mean lowering prices to attract more customers; resulting in increased total revenues.

Question 4. Can *preferred* seating be offered at a higher price?

Both lodging and airline RMs know the advantages they gain by providing low-cost rooms and seats to those buyers who are price conscious while simultaneously offering upgraded rooms (with preferred amenities or larger size) and seats (for those in First Class or aisles) to the buyers who prefer to pay more to enhance their lodging or travel experience.

If, however, you ask the typical foodservice operator whether their customers would pay more to avoid waiting in a long line for a table on Friday or Saturday night, or to pay for the ability to choose the exact dining room seat they prefer in their favorite restaurant, your question might be met with an incredulous look. Ask guests the same questions, however, and you will undoubtedly get an enthusiastic *"Yes!"* from those select guests who highly value their time and/or the location of their seat.

This example again illustrates the power of differential pricing and its potential in foodservice. Note that there is no intent to charge all guests a higher price for the ability to bypass a waiting line or to choose their seat. The option could be offered only to those willing to pay more and, as a result, receive more personal value from their dining experience. In many cases, the problem in implementing differential pricing relates more to convincing the operation's staff that the enhanced value is worthy of a higher price than it does to convincing guests of the same thing.

Question 5. How could our yield be improved?

RMs in lodging understand the revenue generating power of operating at 100 percent occupancy. Although it is a financial management concept that has only recently been explored, a restaurateur's ability to fill increasing proportions of his or her available seating will also have a significant impact on the operation's revenue generating capacity. More guests served in the same time period result in more income and, as a result, yield more profit.

Assuming equal menu item preparation times among different operations, one of the easiest ways a restaurant can improve its revenue optimization (revenue yield) practices is to have a flexible seating system. That means being able to immediately create a **deuce**, a three-top, four-top, or larger table so lost seats are minimized (e.g., the result that occurs when seating two or three guests at four-top tables).

Optimizing table mix (the number and capacities of various tables) directly impacts an operation's ability to maximize table **turns**.

Essential RM Terms

Deuce: Restaurant industry jargon for a table that seats two guests.

Turn (table): The number of times a table (or seat) is used during the same dining period. The formula to calculate table turn is:

$$\frac{\text{Number of guests served}}{\text{Number of available seats}} = \text{Table turns}$$

For example: "We turned our tables 2.5 times last Saturday night"

Is it the role of an RM in foodservices to become so operationally involved that an issue such as table turns is important to them? Absolutely. In fact, while pricing menu items is an essential task for foodservice RMs, their greater role is the assessment of value offered to

> ▶ **RM ON THE WEB 10.2**

In the foodservice industry, revenue yields are a function of the proportion of seats that are filled by diners and the length of time each guest remains at the table. To better monitor and manage the guest seating process, savvy RMs increasingly recommend the use of a high-quality table management system.

Such systems interface with an operation's POS, provide the host or hostess a graphical floor plan that provides the visual information needed to manage floor activity and to accommodate special seating requests. The systems also calculate guest wait times and help maximize table turns.

Such systems automatically update an operation's available table status and can interface with pager systems to notify guests instantly when their table is ready. Real-time and historical reporting on guests served, serving times, server performance, and guest preferences are additional available features. To learn more about one such popular table management system, go to www.reserveinteractive.com

When you arrive at the home page, click *Table Management.*

guests. This includes the ability to maximize seating capacity during busy periods simply because most guests intensely dislike excessive waits. It also includes the identification of operations-specific differential pricing factors that can be applied to benefit guests and to optimize revenues.

Certainly the alternative pricing strategies that might be suggested by questions such as those posed by our hypothetical lodging industry RM are not exhaustive. Rather, they are offered as a means of encouraging foodservice RMs to question traditional cost-based pricing approaches and to ask themselves this most important question:

How can I effectively use differential pricing in my own food and beverage operation?

Foodservice RMs must understand their operations and their customers. They must also understand how those customers will react to the application of various revenue optimization techniques. Remember that a cost-based pricing system is simply not as effective as a more sophisticated differential pricing system. In Chapter 4 you learned that each of the following factors have been used by other industries when developing and implementing differential pricing strategies.

- Customer characteristic
- Location
- Time
- Quantity

- Distribution channel
- Product Version
- Bundling
- Payment terms

In addition to these important factors, RMs should recognize that there are additional foodservice-specific factors that affect food and beverage customers' perceptions of value and thus directly impact these customers' willingness to pay.

FACTORS AFFECTING VALUE PERCEPTIONS IN FOODSERVICES

Understanding the factors that affect guest perceptions of value is essential to creating differential pricing programs that will allow you to match your food and beverage prices with your customers' perceptions of value and their willingness to pay. One important job of RMs in foodservice is to carefully evaluate the revenue enhancement opportunities available to them. The proper application of strategies to optimize revenues will vary based on the individual operation, but should always be based on what you now know about price, value, and the desirability of differential pricing. While each foodservice operation is unique, for many RMs, key factors to be considered for their ability to influence revenue management strategy include:

- Competition
- Service levels/ delivery format
- Guest type
- Product quality
- Portion size
- Ambiance
- Meal period
- Location
- Image
- Sales mix

Competition

This factor is sometimes too closely monitored by foodservice operators. When competitors' prices are overemphasized, the common result is that the observer's own prices drop until they are the lowest or among the lowest price for similarly offered products. In fact, competitors' price monitoring makes sense only when it is performed with the goal of staying on the upper, not lower, end of the pricing scale. This is so because small variations in price simply make little difference to the average guest.

For example, if a group of young professionals goes out for pizza and beer after work, the major determinant in their location choice certainly will not be whether the selling price for the beer is $5.00 in one establishment and $5.50 in another. Successful foodservice operators spend their time focusing on building guest value in their own operation, not in attempting to mimic the pricing efforts of the competition. In fact, in the consumer's mind, higher prices are most often associated with higher-quality products or services and thus a better price/value relationship.

Service Levels/Delivery Format

In the foodservice industry, how a product is presented or delivered to customers often affects the customers' perceptions of value much more than the product itself. Guests are willing to pay more for the same product when service levels are higher. Consumers understand, for example, that a canned soda sold from most vending machines will generally be less expensive than an identical product served in a chilled glass by a friendly waitstaff member. In a similar manner, most guests expect and are quite willing to pay a bit extra for the opportunity to experience a tableside preparation of a Caesar salad or specialty coffee drink.

Increasingly, foodservice RMs are assessing their product delivery format when considering pricing. For example, many pizza chains now charge a lower price for a pizza that is picked up and taken away by the guest than for that same pizza eaten inside. Interestingly, however, most QSRs operating drive-throughs still charge their drive-through customers the same price as their dine-in customers. These pricing strategies clearly differ. As an RM, it will ultimately be your job to ensure the strategy used in your organization supports and reinforces the value message you seek to send.

Some RMs work in foodservice operations that have not traditionally enjoyed the drive-through, carry-out, and off-site delivery options available to other RMs. These RMs should still consider the options available for off-site product delivery. Many operators can drum up new and profitable business via the introduction of simple, streamlined, catering programs. Menu items chosen on the basis of their popularity, portability, and profitability make the most sense.

The hospitality industry is a service industry. Thus, as the personal level of service provided increases, prices should also be increased. This personal service may range from the delivery of products, as in the pizza example, to simply increasing the number of servers in a dining room and thus reducing the number of guests each employee must serve. Increased service levels can justify increased prices. This is not to imply that the additional revenues generated should be exclusively reserved to pay for the additional labor. Guests are willing to pay more for increased service levels and the higher prices paid should provide for extra profits as well. It is important to recognize that in the foodservice industry those companies that have been able to survive and thrive over the years have done so in large part because of their uncompromising commitment to levels of guest service that exceed those of their competitors, not because of their low price.

Guest Type

Every type of guest wants value for their money. If you recall the work of economists Milton and Rose Friedman (Chapter 3), however, you recognize that not all guests define value received in the same way. Understanding the Friedmans' work is especially important for the restaurant manager. For some guests, price will be critically important. For others guest types, status, image projected, and service levels delivered by the foodservice operation will be far more important.

Increasingly, guests are willing to pay for convenience and/or speed. An example of this can clearly be seen in the pricing decisions of convenience stores across the United States. In these facilities, food products such as sandwiches, fruit, drinks, cookies, and the like are sold at relatively high prices. The guests these stores cater to, however, value speed and convenience above all else. For this speed and convenience they are willing to pay a premium price.

Other factors are important to other guest types. For example, the couple that goes out for a romantic dinner on a special occasion certainly wants value for their money. The value

RM AT WORK 10.2

"The price paid would be the same," said Braylon.

"I know it seems that way, but I still think it's very different," replied Lynette.

Braylon, the kitchen manager at the Kingsford Steakhouse, was talking to Lynette, the restaurant's owner. They were discussing the special introductory pricing being developed for a new menu item that would soon be placed on their menu.

They were both excited about their chef's new creation (a beef filet and lamb chop combination served with a rosemary reduction sauce) and they had agreed it would be priced at $39.95. That was a full five dollars more than their 20-ounce veal chop, the next most expensive item on the Kingsford's menu. They had decided to implement an introductory pricing strategy for the new item to encourage their regular clientele to give it a try.

With its downtown location, USDA Prime beef steaks, and extensive wine list, the Kingsford was a very popular spot for business lunches. At dinner time, it attracted fine food enthusiasts from all around the immediate area.

"Look," continued Braylon, "with my idea, we put 50 percent off coupons on our web site. For the new item only. That way, the average selling price is essentially $15.00. With your "buy one/ get the second at no charge," it's still 50 percent off. It's the same."

"But my approach obscures the price reduction better than yours, so I guess I'm not convinced it is the same. Or that our typical guest is the type that clips coupons," said Lynette.

"I don't know about that," replied Braylon. "Remember that everybody likes a bargain."

1. Do you think the guests who would be attracted to Braylon's pricing strategy are the same type of guests as those that would be attracted to Lynette's pricing strategy? Why?

2. Do you agree with Braylon that all foodservice guests seek bargains when dining out?

3. Can the distribution method RMs use to advertise a specific price affect the profile of guests who respond to it? Do you see similarities between price distribution strategies in the foodservice industry and the various distribution channels managed by lodging industry RMs?

they seek, however, may be established much more by the mood and atmosphere experienced in a restaurant than by that restaurant's prices. The good news for RMs is that many factors that affect different guest types' view of value are directly subject to management's control.

Product Quality

In nearly every instance, a guest's quality perception of any specific product offered for sale in the foodservice business will range from very low to very high. This is not to say that their view of wholesomeness or the safety of the product should vary. These should not. But a guest's perception of product quality is based on a variety of factors, most of which have little, if anything, to do with the raw ingredient costs of a menu item.

For example, when typical foodservice guests think of a hamburger they actually think, not of one product, but a range of products. A hamburger may be correctly envisioned as a less-than-2-ounce burger patty placed on a regular bun, wrapped in paper and served in a sack. If so, its price will likely be low, the service provided with its sale limited, and its perceived quality may be low as well. If, however, a guest's thoughts turn to an 8-ounce flame-charred burger presented with avocado slices and alfalfa sprouts on a toasted whole-grain bun and elegantly served in a white-tablecloth restaurant, the product will be perceived as having higher quality, and if priced properly, deliver higher value. Note that in this example, the price per pound of the burger meat used to make the two alternative products was simply not the determining quality factor.

Foodservice managers routinely choose from a range of quality levels when developing product specifications and, consequently, planning menus and establishing prices. The product quality you choose is important. For example, if you select the market's cheapest bourbon as your well brand, you will likely be able to charge less for drinks made from it than your competitor who selects a better brand; but it is not the most important factor in pricing. The cheapest bourbon on the market, beautifully served in a sparkling clean glass, in an exciting atmosphere, by enthusiastic and helpful servers will always be perceived as a superior quality product, and worthy of higher drink prices, than will higher cost bourbon that has been poorly presented.

To be successful, RMs must understand how their guests view quality and resist the temptation to oversimplistically equate quality delivered with the price paid for a menu's raw ingredients. As you have learned, perceived product quality is critical in pricing. Raw ingredient costs are much less critical.

Portion Size

In a cost-based pricing system, portion size plays a large role in determining menu pricing because size directly affects costs. Portion size can also play a critical role in a value-based differential pricing system. Careful readers will recognize that variations in portion size are simply a form of product versioning (see Chapter 4), a classic differential pricing technique. Product versioning based on portion size, however, is too often applied in the form of bigger is better. That approach leads to increased food costs, increased food waste, and increased customer waists as well. Not good.

Great chefs have always known that guests eat with their eyes first. This relates to presenting food that is visually appealing. It also relates to portion size. A burger and fries that fill an 8-inch plate may well be lost on an 11-inch plate. Portion size, then, is a function of both product quantity and presentation. It is in the area of presentation that value perception can be increased with no increase in costs. It is no secret why successful cafeteria chains use smaller than average dishes to plate their food. For their guests, price and value statements come across loud and clear. In some dining situations, particularly in an all-you-care-to-eat operation, the presentation principle again holds true. The proper dish size is just as critical as the proper sized scoop or ladle when serving the food.

Increasingly, today's consumers prefer lighter food with more choices in fruits and vegetables. The portion sizes of these items can be increased at a fairly low increase in cost. At the same time, average sweetened beverage sizes are increasing, as are the size of some side items such as French fries. Again, these tend to be lower-cost items. Within responsible limits and with an eye toward customers' long-term good health, this can be good news for the foodservice RM if prices can be increased to match the larger sizes. In the very best restaurants, however, giving guests so much food they simple can't eat it all should not be the goal. Rather, the goal should be the delivery of high-quality food, beautifully presented and served in a manner that maximizes guests' perceptions of value.

Evaluation of portion size and presentation is an excellent example of how RMs can influence a foodservice organization's operational methods. In conjunction with production personnel, every menu item served should be analyzed with an eye toward determining if the quantity being served is the optimum quantity. Just as importantly, each item should be analyzed for its presentation before, not just after, its price is established.

Ambiance

If people ate out only because they were hungry, few restaurants would be open today. There are certainly lower-cost ways to avoid hunger. In fact, people eat out for a variety of reasons, many of which have very little to do with an operation's food or its costs. Fun, companionship, time limitations, adventure, and variety are just a few reasons diners cite for eating out rather than eating at home. For the RM whose operation provides an attractive **ambiance**, menu prices can reflect this.

The operator that provides a pleasing and popular ambiance is selling much more than food and thus will be able to justify increased prices. RMs must recognize, however, that foodservice operations that count on ambiance alone to carry their business generally start out well but are not ultimately successful. Ambiance may draw guests to a location the first time, but excellent product quality and outstanding service go much further over the long run than do overly clever restaurant designs. Interestingly, while many foodservice operators do understand the importance of visual design in establishing ambiance, too few fully understand the role their servers play.

The importance of quality servers in the process of creating and maintaining ambience was pointed out well by Starbucks CEO Howard Schultz. When asked in an interview with

Entrepenuer.com why turnover at his locations was less than a fifth of that experienced in the typical foodservice operation, Schultz stated:

> It's ironic that retailers and restaurants live or die on customer service, yet their employees have some of the lowest pay and worst benefits of any industry. That's one reason so many experiences are mediocre for the public. We pay our partners well at every level, compared to similar positions at other companies." In 1988, we did something no one else had done, which was to offer our part-time employees comprehensive health care; in 1991, we offered all employees stock options. These benefits have paid for themselves in increased productivity and commitment to the business on the part of our partners.[15]

Starbucks, of course, is not known as the lowest-priced provider of specialty coffee, but it is the most successful. This is due, in large part, to the ambiance created by its facilities and reinforced by its well-trained and well-paid staff.

Meal Period

In some cases, diners expect to pay more for an item served in the evening than for that same item served at a lunch period. Sometimes this is the result of a smaller luncheon portion size, but in other cases the portion size, as well as service levels, may be exactly the same in the evening as earlier in the day. You must exercise caution in this area. Guests should clearly understand why a menu item's price changes with the time of day. If this cannot be answered to the guest's satisfaction, it may not be wise to implement a **day part**-sensitive pricing structure.

> **Essential RM Term**
>
> **Day part:** A subsection of the day, during which a specific menu type may be served.
>   For example, the time period 6:00 A.M. to 10 A.M. (breakfast) vs. 11:00 A.M. to 2:00 P.M. (lunch). Used to target market and to precisely track sales levels.

Foodservice operators can, however, carefully assess those time periods that currently contribute little or no revenue to their operations. In doing so, they may find that traditionally slow meal periods can be targeted for the development of special menu items or special pricing that can assist in revenue optimization. Because many of a foodservice operation's costs are fixed, incremental revenue dollars generated through the extension of nontraditional meal periods (e.g., Taco Bell's promotion of "fourth meal" is a well-known example[16]) can be highly profitable dollars.

Location

Location can be a major factor in determining price. As an RM, you need look no further than America's many themed amusement parks or sports arenas to see evidence of this. Foodservice operators in these locations are able to charge premium prices because they have, in effect, a monopoly on food sold to the visitors. The only all-night diner on the interstate highway exit is in much the same situation. Contrast that with an operator who is one of ten seafood restaurants on a tourist town's **restaurant row**.

> **Essential RM Term**
>
> **Restaurant row:** Industry slang for a geographic area that contains multiple and competing foodservice operations.

RM IN ACTION 10.4: AND FOR DINNER . . . LET'S STOP AT DUNKIN DONUTS!

In addition to the revenue optimization potential of differential pricing, a new emphasis on previously neglected meal periods or day parts can provide the opportunity to expand overall sales levels.

Money online reported that Dunkin' Donuts, the coffee and baked goods chain synonymous with breakfast and fresh coffee, had decided to target the afternoon and evening crowds with new flatbread sandwiches and personal pizzas heated in convection ovens rather than microwaves. Prior to the roll-out, two-thirds of the company's sales in its 5,400 plus units came before noon, with most customers choosing snacks such as baked goods and breakfast sandwiches with coffee. Addressing his company's new revenue optimization strategy, Will Kussell, president and chief brand officer, was quoted in the article as saying:

> It speaks to changing consumption trends, with people having a lot more occasions to graze, and consumers'

desire to have what they want, when they want it.

Of course it also speaks to the company's desire to even sales volume among day parts. Interestingly, the company also hopes the new ovens will boost customer satisfaction with breakfast sandwiches (since microwaving can sometimes create limp eggs and mushy bread!)

Success is not guaranteed. Nor is it the first time Dunkin' Donuts has offered non-breakfast items. The chain offered soup and sandwiches in the 1980s with mixed results. The success of McDonald's in expanding business in its various day parts, Wendy's struggles in doing the same, and Subway's entry to the breakfast business, however, provide models of success and of challenge for foodservice RMs whose own operations struggle with uneven sales volume throughout the day.

Excerpted on 2/13/2008 from www.money.excite.com.

It used to be said of restaurants that success was due to three things: location, location, and location. This may have been true before so many operations opened in the United States. There is, of course, no discounting the value of a prime restaurant location, and location alone can certainly influence pricing decisions. It does not, however, guarantee success. Location can be an asset or a liability. If it is an asset, menu prices may be increased to reflect the fact that the location itself adds value. If a location is indeed a liability, menu prices may need to be lowered initially in an effort to provide the consumer value needed to attract sufficient clientele and ensure that the operation's revenue objectives are met.

Image

It has always been true that customers do not make a purchase unless they want the thing they are buying more than they want to keep their money. In the foodservice industry, the *thing* purchased is often much more than food and drink. In many cases, foodservice operations become popular because of the unique image they project. The exclusive night-club, the trendy bar, and the hard-to-get-into restaurant are just a few examples of facilities

> ▶ **RM ON THE WEB 10.3**

It is a gross oversimplification to equate formal dining with high-priced dining, or casual dining with lower menu prices. A unique image and the premium prices that can be commanded as a result of it are not the exclusive domain of any one service style.

You are likely familiar with Ruth's Chris Steakhouses, the upscale USDA Prime steakhouse founded by Ruth Fertel in 1965. The product quality, ambiance, and service levels provided allow Ruth's Chris to charge premium prices and deliver excellent value. Its web site (www.ruthchris.com) reflects the elegant dining experience provided.

You are likely less familiar with the equally pricy but extremely casual Zingerman's Deli (Ann Arbor, Michigan), where commonly sold items include English farmhouse cedar cheese ($40.00 per pound), Kentucky smoked breakfast sausage ($12.00 per pound), and deli sandwiches at prices approaching those of Manhattan's most popular 7th Avenue delicatessens.

Prices at Zingerman's reflect their carefully crafted, laid back image. That image consists of a commitment to providing a wide variety of extremely high-quality food products, exceptional customer service (in a very relaxed atmosphere), and as a result, outstanding value. To view this exceptional operation's site, go to www.zingermansdeli.com

that have captured the imagination of buyers because of the exclusive image they project. The facilities promise their customers that they will feel better about themselves simply because they were able buy. W. Edwards Deming, the American management consultant most famous for his work on quality enhancement, stated this simple fact clearly when he observed: "Profit in business comes from repeat customers, customers that boast about your product or service, and that bring friends with them."[17]

For RMs in foodservice, Deming's insightful comment holds much meaning because every facility has the opportunity to project a unique image if it first precisely identifies just what it wants its image to be. Cleanliness, friendliness, speed, décor (and even food!) can be a part of the unique image projected. In addition to these, effective pricing can help demonstrate to guests the desirability of coming and of bringing friends with them.

Sales Mix

Of all the factors mentioned thus far, sales mix is the one that most tests the abilities of foodservice RMs and is the one that should most heavily influence menu pricing decisions. To better understand why, consider again the very different challenges of lodging industry RMs and their food and beverage counterparts.

In most cases, the lodging customer chooses from among a fairly limited number of different room types when making a purchase. The number of alternative prices offered to guests is similarly rather limited. In addition, the direct costs associated with providing the alternative room products are fairly similar. For example, the cost of selling a king-bedded room with an ocean view is essentially identical to the cost of providing a king-bedded room with a garden view. This is so despite the fact that the selling price (ADR) associated with these two room types may, due to their location within the hotel, vary quite a bit.

The foodservice guest, by contrast, may well have the ability to choose from literally dozens or even hundreds of different menu items resulting in thousands of different meal combinations. The **menu mix** that will result from guests' choices is unknown ahead of time, but will dictate an operation's average sale per guest (**check average**).

Essential RM Terms

Menu mix: The total number of various food and beverage products (menu items) ordered by guests during a designated time period.

Check average: The mean amount spent per visit by each restaurant guest during a designated time period (e.g., by day part (lunch or dinner) or calendar period (daily, weekly, or monthly). The formula for calculating check average is:

$$\frac{\text{Total revenue}}{\text{Guests served}} = \text{Check average}$$

In most cases, the menu mix produced by guest orders will also directly influence total product costs. This is so because not all menu items cost the same to produce or are priced to achieve the same cost-to-selling-price ratio. Astute readers should recognize that, as a result of menu mix, it is the foodservice *guest* who determines an operation's average selling price; because of the specific menu items he or she selects, as well as the operation product costs, which are also a direct result of the menu mix.

Essential RM Term

Price blending (foodservice): The process of pricing food and beverage products with different cost ratios in such a way as to optimize revenues in a least cost manner.

Because the number of customers served and menu mix directly determines an operation's revenue generation and its profitability, can RMs use strategic pricing to alter an operation's customer count and menu mix? Absolutely! In fact, the best of foodservice RMs can become especially skilled at **price blending**.

Price blending simply refers to the process of strategically pricing food and beverage products with the intent of optimizing revenue. In many ways it is the equivalent of the lodging RMs' revenue optimization efforts.

The price blending process addresses the fact that the listed price of a menu item will directly affect an item's popularity and thus the frequency with which that item will be ordered. As you have learned, menu mix is the overall frequency with which different items are ordered and it directly affects an operation's revenue generation, its resulting product costs, and ultimately its profitability.

Figure 10.7	Unblended Pricing Structure		
San Diego Red's Burgers			
Item	**Item Cost**	**Desired Food Cost**	**Proposed Selling Price**
Hamburger	$1.50	40%	$3.75
French fries	0.32	40%	0.80
Soft drinks (12 oz.)	0.18	40%	0.45
Total	2.00	40%	5.00

To illustrate the price blending process, assume that you are the operations vice president and newly designated revenue manager for San Diego Red's, a chain of upscale hamburger restaurants. Assume also that you plan to achieve an overall food cost of 40 percent in your units. For purposes of simplicity, assume that Figure 10.7 illustrates the three products you sell and their corresponding selling price when each is priced to achieve exactly a 40 percent food cost.

Recall from earlier in this chapter that the formula for computing a product (food) cost percentage is:

$$\frac{\text{Cost of products sold}}{\text{All product sales}} = \text{Product cost \%}$$

The formula can be worded somewhat differently for a single menu item without changing its accuracy:

$$\frac{\text{Cost of a specific item sold}}{\text{Sales of that item}} = \text{Cost \% of that item}$$

It is important to understand that the sales value indentified in these formulas is synonymous with selling price when assessing the menu price of a single item. For a single menu item the principles of algebra allow you to rearrange the formula as follows:

$$\frac{\text{Cost of a specific item sold}}{\text{Cost \% of that item}} = \text{Selling price of that item}$$

Thus, in Figure 10.7, for example, the hamburger's selling price is calculated as

$$\frac{\$1.50}{40\%} = \$3.75$$

Note that in Figure 10.7 all products are priced to sell at a menu price that would result in a 40 percent food cost. Under this system, the operation's sales mix would have no effect on overall food cost percent. The resulting sales mix would, however, likely damage your profitability. The reason why is very simple. If you use the price structure indicated in Figure 10.7, your drink prices are too low.

Figure 10.8	Blended Price Structure		

San Diego Red's Burgers

Item	Item Cost	Proposed Food Cost %	Proposed Selling Price
Hamburger	$1.50	60.2%	$2.49
French fries	0.32	21.5%	1.49
Soft drinks (12 oz.)	0.18	16.5%	1.09
Total	2.00	39.4%	5.07

Most guests are willing to pay far in excess of 45 cents for a soft drink at a quick-service restaurant. You run the risk, in this example, of attracting many guests who are interested in buying only soft drinks at your restaurants. Your French fries may also be priced too low. Your burger itself, however, may be priced too high relative to your competitors. However, if you use the price-blending concept and if you assume that each guest coming into your restaurants will buy a burger, French fries, and a soft drink, you can create a different menu price structure and still achieve your overall cost objective, as seen in Figure 10.8.

Note that, in this example, you would actually achieve a total food cost slightly lower than 40 percent. Your hamburger price is now less than $2.50 and perhaps more in line with local competitors. Recall, however, that you have assumed each guest coming to your restaurant will buy one of each item. In reality, not all guests will select one of each item.

Some guests will not elect fries, while others may stop in only for a soft drink. It is for this reason that historical menu mix data are critical to menu pricing. These histories let you know exactly what your guests are buying when they visit your outlets. You can then use historical data to forecast menu mix and refine your pricing strategy.

To illustrate how this works, assume that you monitored a sample of 100 guests who came into one of your units and found the results presented in Figure 10.9.

Figure 10.9	Historical Sales Mix Data					

San Diego Red's Burgers

Total Sales: <u>$449.25</u> Guests Served: <u>100</u>
Total Food Cost: <u>$180.20</u> Food Cost %: <u>40.1%</u>

Item	Number Sold	Item Cost	Total Food Cost	Selling Price	Total Sales	Food Cost %
Hamburger	92	$1.50	$138.00	$2.49	$229.08	60.2%
French fries	79	$0.32	$25.28	$1.49	$117.71	21.5%
Soft drinks (12 oz.)	94	$0.18	$16.92	$1.09	$102.46	16.5%
Total			$180.20		$449.25	40.1%

As you can see from Figure 10.9, you can use the price-blending concept to achieve your overall cost objectives if you have a good understanding of how many people buy each menu item. In this example, you have achieved the 40 percent food cost you sought. Costs vary from a high of 60.2 percent (burger) to a low of 16.5 percent (soft drink). Those operators concerned with maintaining low food cost percentage may feel there could be danger if guests begin to order nothing but hamburgers. Those operators who focus on CM would, of course, not share the concern. In either situation, however, by monitoring what your guests buy and the menu mix that results, you can make needed price adjustments to optimize revenue while keeping overall costs within predetermine targets.

A word of caution regarding the manipulation of sales mix and price blending is in order, however. Since price itself is one of the primary factors that impact the proportion of guests selecting a specific item, a change in menu price may cause a significant change in an item's popularity. If, for example, in an effort to reduce overall product cost percentage you drastically increased the price of soft drinks at San Diego Red's, you may find that a higher percentage of guests would elect not to purchase a soft drink. This could have the effect of actually increasing your overall product cost percentage, since fewer guests would choose to buy the one item with an extremely low food cost percentage.

For RMs in foodservice, strategic pricing involves the exact same managerial process as that presented in the lodging industry chapters; namely, the application of data and insight to effectively match prices charged with buyer's perceptions of value and willingness to pay. It is critical that foodservice operators understand their costs are important, but they are much *less* important to pricing and their customer's perceptions of value than are sound and appropriately applied differential pricing and revenue optimization strategies.

❖ ESSENTIAL RM TERMS

Table service	Deuce
Product cost percentage (pricing method)	Turn (table)
Pricing factor (foodservice)	Ambiance
Product cost: plus (pricing method)	Day part
Prime cost	Restaurant row
Contribution margin	Menu mix
Sales volume (foodservice)	Check average
Point of sale (POS) system	Price blending (foodservice)

IIII➡ APPLY WHAT YOU KNOW

1. David Berger is the F&B director at the private membership Fox Ridge Country Club. He is implementing a new dining room menu and has calculated menu prices for the six new entrée items the menu will include. Review the worksheet below and then answer the questions that follow.

Menu Item	Selling Price	Product Cost	Per Serving Labor Cost
New York Strip	$26.95	$12.97	$1.95
1/2 Duckling	$25.95	$11.73	$2.55
Veal Chop	$31.95	$13.85	$1.95
Roasted Free-Range Chicken	$18.95	$6.53	$2.55
Pork Medallions	$24.95	$5.58	$3.10
Portabella Mushroom Pasta	$18.95	$3.85	$4.25

A. Which of David's items has:

   The lowest food cost %? _____

   The highest food cost %? _____

B. Which of David's items have:

   The lowest prime cost? _____

   The highest prime food cost ? _____

C. Which of David's items have:

   The lowest contribution margin? _____

   The highest contribution margin? _____

D. What would David's overall food cost % be if each of the six items sold on the menu were equally popular?

E. How crucial do you believe David's menu prices are to his potential diners' frequency of visit? Explain your answer.

2. Fawzia Mohamed is the GM and RM of a popular 300-seat family-style Italian restaurant open only for dinner. Nightly, she calculates a variety of statistics that help her better understand the revenue-generation abilities of her operation. Complete the revenue generation report she has developed using today's data and then answer the questions that follow.

Nightly Revenue Generation re-cap   Date: _Today_

Hour of Operation	Guests Served	Check Average	Revenue
5–6 P.M.	118	$11.25	
6–7 P.M.	251	$13.25	
7–8 P.M.		$13.97	$4400.55
8–9 P.M.	264	$12.98	
9–10 P.M.	102		$1,096.50
Total			
Table Turns = ___			

A. How many guests did Fawzia's serve on this night? _____

B. What was Fawzia's total revenue for the night? _____

C. What was Fawzia's check average for the night? _____

D. What would Fawzia calculate her restaurant's table turns for the night to be? _____ _____

E. What revenue management challenge does Fawzia face from 7–8 P.M.? _____ _____? What would you advise her to do about it?

3. The menu at _Lara's Salads and Subs_ consists of only four items. These are salads, subs, drinks, and chips. Lara's menu and the historical sales data she has collected over the past three months are presented as follows. Lara is considering the potential impact on revenues of creating a value meal by bundling a salad, sub, chips, and drink, and pricing the four item package at $ 9.99. Currently, her menu mix (based on a 1,000 guest sample) and selling prices are as shown:

Lara's Menu Mix

Menu Item	# Sold per 1,000 Guests	Selling Price
Salad	660	$3.49
Sub	812	$6.99
Chips	420	$.99
Drinks	940	$.99

A. Based on the historical data, for each 1,000 guests served, what would Lara's revenue be from:

Salad sales? _____

Sub sales? _____

Chip sales? _____

Drink sales? _____

All product sales? _____

B. What is Lara's historical check average? _____

Assume that the $9.99 packaged meal Lara proposes is put into place and that in the coming days, 1,000 new customers are served. Assuming no other changes to menu mix;

C. What would the operation's total revenue be if 25 percent of the guests select the value meal? _____

D. What would the operation's total revenue be if 50 percent of the guests select the value meal? _____

E. If you were Lara, how would you evaluate the wisdom of implementing the new meal package? _____

4. Assume you are the RM for a newly opened theme park in a major southwestern city. Your guests will consist primarily of families visiting the park, as well as schoolchildren on field trips and church youth groups. Yours is the only such park within 150 miles. Identify at least five noncost factors you would want to consider as you determine the prices that will be charged for the menu items you will sell. Explain why you selected each factor chosen.

5. Dino's Bar B Q serves only three dinner plates. These are Bar B Q chicken, beef brisket, and smoked sausage links. Dino's served 1,000 guests each day on Monday, Tuesday, and Wednesday of last week. Scott Larsen, the restaurant's manager tracked the percent of guests who chose each item on those three days. Each item's selling price and the operation's menu mix is detailed in the following table. Review Scott's operating information for the three days and then answer the questions that follow.

Item	Price	% Selected		
		Monday	**Tuesday**	**Wednesday**
Chicken	$14.95	30%	50%	20%
Brisket	$ 8.95	50%	30%	30%
Links	$11.95	20%	20%	50%

A. On Monday, what was Scott's:

Total revenue? _____

Check average? _____

B. On Tuesday, what was Scott's:

Total revenue? _____

Check average? _____

   C. On Wednesday, what was Scott's:

      Total revenue? _____

      Check average? _____

   D. For the combined three-day period, what was Scott's:

      Total revenue? _____

      Check average? _____

      Percent difference in revenue generated when comparing his lowest to his highest income day? _____

   E. Assume that Scott's restaurant is often full, and that he is not authorized to increase his menu prices. What specific steps would you advise him to take to increase his operation's total income?

KEY CONCEPT CASE STUDY

"So you want Sam to *lower* his prices during his busiest serving period to increase his revenues?" asked Sofia Davidson, the GM at the Barcena Resort.

"That's right," replied Damario, the resort's revenue manager, "but I'm convinced it will increase his profits as well."

Sam was the Barcena Resort's F&B director. He reported directly to Sofia. In his position, Sam was responsible for several food outlets inside the resort, including the poolside restaurant/ snack bar that was so popular with the resort's guests during the lunch period and early afternoon. It was that facility's pricing structure that was the topic of Damario and Sofia's meeting.

"Damario, I have to tell you that when I agreed you could take a look at our F&B department's pricing, I was really hoping that with your revenue management background, you could help us find areas where prices could be increased, not decreased," said Sofia.

"Sofia," replied Damario, "what we all want is to maximize revenue and profits. Listen . . . right

now, the pizzas at Sam's pool-side operation are the most popular item."

"Right" replied Sofia, "he does a great job with them. That's why they sell so well."

"And that's the problem," said Damario. "The pizzas take 20 minutes to bake. They can't be made ahead because the toppings vary. That means guests ordering pizzas are occupying the restaurant's tables, but no food is being served for at least 20 minutes. In fact, the average sit-down, order, wait for the order to be prepared, eat, and leave time for a family buying pizzas is nearly one hour."

"So?" replied Sofia.

"So," said Damario, "the number of table turns we can make during the peak lunch period is minimal. When people see the long lines of guests waiting to be seated during the busy times, they decide to skip lunch or go outside the resort to eat.

"So because the pizza is popular you want to lower the price of hot dogs?" asked Sofia.

"That's right. I'd like to offer a package special of hot dogs and soft drinks only.

And only during our busiest times. I want to price the package right. . . . and promote it well. Our hot dogs are preprepared so they can be served almost immediately. I've checked and the average total table time for hot dog buyers is less than 30 minutes," said Damario.

"Well if you want to reduce pizza sales, why not just raise pizza prices. That would slow their sales and increase their profitability," said Sofia.

"Our lunch time revenue issues at the pool are not price based," said Damario. "They are item selection and capacity based. I want to bundle hotdogs with drinks, offer them at a great price, and move a reasonable number of buyers away from pizza and to the special. Under my plan, we can do that without raising prices or making our menu prices appear even higher. And we will be providing even more value to budget-conscious families. Simply raising our pizza prices doesn't do that. "

"O.K. I understand your plan. And when you informally discussed this idea with Sam, what was his reaction?" asked Sofia.

"He said reducing prices on the hot dogs would decrease his margins and hurt his profits . . . especially if the new package became a good seller. I think he will be hesitant to try the idea. And that's why I wanted this meeting with you before the entire *Strategic Pricing and Revenue Management* committee meets and I present the idea to them," said Damario.

For Your Consideration

1. In this scenario, Damario presents a potentially controversial proposal to his boss *prior* to introducing it to the entire *Strategic Pricing and Revenue Management* committee. Why do you think Damario chose to do this? How important would Sofia's support likely be to Damario's success in gaining support for his proposal? As an RM, how important do you think administrative support will be to your own success as you seek to implement change?

2. Pricing decisions are often viewed in internal operational terms. Ultimately, however, external guests' reactions to pricing and revenue optimization strategies are of most importance. How do you think the resort's guests would respond to Damario's plan? Do you believe the plan is consistent with the development of a customer-centric revenue optimization strategy?

3. Damario appears to believe that optimization of food and beverage revenue is based primarily on menu mix and capacity maximization. Sam's position appears to be that profit optimization is a matter of maintaining proper product cost ratios (and thus the hesitancy to reduce prices on the hot dogs). Whose position most closely resembles your own view? Explain in detail why you would agree with Damario or with Sam.

4. Assume you were Sofia and that you supported trying out Damario's idea. What would you say to Sam? What specific measure(s) or operating statistics would you want to see after the plan's implementation that would help convince you (and Sam) of its effectiveness?

ENDNOTES

1. Lendal Kotschevar, *Management by Menu* (National Institute for the Foodservice Industry (NIFI), Chicago, IL, 1975).

2. Jack Miller and David Pavesic, *Menu Pricing and Strategy* (New York: CBI Publishing Co., 1980).

3. George Wenzel, *Wenzel's Menu Maker* (New York: Publication Press Inc., 1947), 13.

4. James Keiser and Frederick Kallio, *Controlling and Analyzing Costs in Foodservice Operations* (New York: John Wiley & Sons, 1974).

5. http://en.wikipedia.org/wiki/Boston_Consulting_ Group. Retrieved 12/5/2008.

6. Jack Ninemeier, *Menu Planning, Design, and Evaluation Managing for Appeal and Profit* (Richmond, CA: McCutchan Publishing, 2008), 291–297.

7. David Pavesic, "Cost-margin analysis: A Third Approach to Menu Pricing and Design," *International Journal of Hospitality Management* 2 (3), 1983: 127–134.

8. S. Lebruto, R. Ashley, and W. Quain, "Menu Engineering: A Model Including Labor," *FIU Hospitality Review* 13 (2), 1995: 41–50.

9. P. F. Drucker, "The Five Deadly Business Sins," *The Wall Street Journal* (1993, October 21), p. A20.

10. Lea Dopson, David Hayes, and Jack Miller, *Food and Beverage Cost Control*, 5th ed. (Hoboken, NJ: John Wiley, 2011), 5.

11. www.qsrweb.com article, "Burger King franchisees again vote down $1 dbl cheeseburger." Posted 7/14/2009.

12. "Tweaking Menus to Offer Value," *Hotels* Online; article posted 5/1/2009.

13. Michael Pollan, *The Omnivores Dilemma* (New York: Penguin Press, 2006), 244.

14. See Miller and Pavesic, Chapter 6: "Menu Pricing Strategies."

15. https://www.entrepreneur.com/magazine/ entrepreneur; posted article from May 1998 issue.

16. http://www.tacobell.com/fourthmeal. Retrieved 9/1/2009.

17. http://www.brainyquote.com/quotes/quotes/w/ wedwardsd131224.html.

Evaluation of Revenue Management Efforts in Food and Beverage Services

CHAPTER HIGHLIGHTS

1. Examination of the ways RMs analyze their sources of income by revenue center, day part, and service style.

2. Presentation of methods RMs use to accurately measure and assess increases and decreases in revenue generation.

3. Examination of three alternative methods RMs use to evaluate their efficiency in revenue generation.

FOOD AND BEVERAGE REVENUE ANALYSIS

The analysis of income generation in food and beverage operations has historically focused on the menu items you will sell to your guests. In such an analysis, the goal is the identification of your operation's most popular and most profitable menu items. The rationale for such an analysis is quite reasonable. Food and beverage operators should want to know which of their menu items sell best (are the most popular) and which contribute most to their bottom lines (generate the most profit). Knowing these two characteristics of menu items should guide RMs in the removal of items that are unpopular, unprofitable, or both, as well as toward the increased promotion of more popular and more profitable items.

Those RMs seeking detailed information on the mathematics and mechanics used to perform a detailed menu mix analysis (see Chapter 10) can choose from one or more of virtually dozens of such systems that have been proposed in the past few decades. Several of them may prove to be useful in your own specific operational situation. Despite the large number of systems proposed, however, there are basic commonalities among the most popular approaches to menu analysis.

Figure 11.1 presents details about four of the most well-known and frequently used menu analysis systems, as well as their most commonly used names. Each has its proponents and its detractors, but as a group they represent the major philosophical approaches to menu item analysis in use today. They are presented here chiefly as a means of providing serious foodservice RMs with the reference sources they need to acquire a working knowledge of these systems since they are the ones most likely to be encountered. The ability to understand each of these system's objectives and to apply, if appropriate, the specific factors they emphasize is one mark of an individual well prepared to assume the role of an RM in a variety of foodservice settings.

It is important to note that despite their differences, each of the analysis systems presented in Figure 11.1 assumes that revenue optimization in the foodservice industry is best viewed from the perspective of assessing the individual menu items purchased by customers.

As you learned in Chapter 10, menu mix data are extremely critical in the menu price determination process. The regular use of menu analysis is recommended for all RMs. Menu analysis, however, will not address all of a foodservice RM's most important income-related questions. Where the assessment of revenue generation in foodservice is concerned,

Figure 11.1	Major Menu Analysis Systems	
Key Factors Examined	**Goal**	**Common Name**
Menu item popularity and food cost %[1]	Minimize food cost %	Miller Matrix System
Menu item popularity and weighted contribution margin[2]	Maximize contribution margin	Menu Engineering
Menu item popularity, food cost %, and weighted contribution margin[3]	Maximize gross margin	Pavesic Matrix System
Menu item popularity, food cost %, selling price, and contribution to gross profit[4]	Include variable and fixed costs in menu item analysis to create menu item profit targets	Goal Value Analysis

an effective RM should have many questions. RMs should fully appreciate the wisdom of Anglican Bishop of London Mandell Creighton, who stated: *"The real object of education is to have a man in the condition of continually asking questions."*[5]

In your role as an RM, even the most sophisticated menu analysis system will not assist you in addressing such important revenue-related questions as these three:

1. Which of our revenue centers contribute the most to our sales?
2. Are our revenues increasing or decreasing? By how much?
3. How efficiently are we using our space and our staff as we generate sales?

To find answers to questions such as these, RMs use additional revenue assessment techniques. These supplemental assessment efforts can be grouped into three main activities:

- Examination of revenue sources
- Measurement of revenue change
- Evaluation of revenue generation efficiency

The remainder of this chapter will teach you how to utilize these three important activities to better understand how your business can optimize its revenue.

EXAMINATION OF REVENUE SOURCES

A recurrent theme of this book is that effective RMs use accurate data and their own insight in the application of disciplined tactics that predict buyer response to prices, optimize product availability, and yield the greatest profits. To do that, foodservice RMs must first have a clear understanding of how their operations generate income. As a foodservice RM, there are a variety of ways you could assess the sources of your revenue. In most cases, however, your income analysis efforts will be focused on one (or more) of the following:

Revenue centers

Day parts

Service styles

Revenue Centers

Most foodservice operations can benefit by examining their income producing ability based on its originating source, or revenue center. Recall from Chapter 1 that a revenue center is simply a business subsection or part that contributes to an operation's total income. Thus, for example, in a table service restaurant that also contains a bar area, the restaurant's dining room could be considered as one revenue center and the bar as a separate revenue center. Similarly, in a restaurant chain consisting of five separate operating units, each unit can be viewed as an individual revenue center. In nearly every case, understanding the sales-generating performance of an operation's various revenue centers will provide you with better information than knowing only about that operation's total sales performance.

To illustrate the importance of assessing revenues on the basis of revenue center, consider the situation faced by Darla Santiago. Darla is a district manager for Sub-city Sandwich shops. Her district (one of several in the company) consists of five individual units. On a companywide basis, the average shop generates $100,000 in revenue per month. In Darla's five-unit district, the stores' monthly average is only $80,000 per unit. Darla is rightfully concerned about her district's underperformance.

Figure 11.2 shows the actual revenue achieved by Darla's five shops last month. Note that the average store did indeed generate $80,000 in revenue ($400,000 total revenue/5 units = $80,000 per unit). Note also, however, that four of Darla's five stores actually exceeded the company's average of $100,000 in sales for the month.

Is there a revenue-generation problem in Darla's district? Yes. Is that problem present in each of her five units? Clearly it is not. Unit number 3 is the source of Darla's problem, and it is in that specific unit that Darla needs to assist the manager and take corrective action. In this illustration, it is easy to see that by analyzing her sales on the basis of individual revenue centers, Darla is in a much better position to correct her problem than if she had analyzed only the total revenue produced in her five-unit district.

Those RMs undertaking revenue center analysis typically seek to answer two important revenue source–related questions:

1. What was the dollar amount of revenue generated by each revenue source?
2. What proportion of total sales was contributed by each revenue source?

Figure 11.2	Darla's Sub-city District: Last Month's Revenue Performance
Unit Number	**Month's Revenue**
1	$120,000
2	105,000
3	$50,000
4	$115,000
5	$110,000
Total District Revenue	$400,000
Average Revenue Per Unit	$80,000

Figure 11.3	Il Cuoco Galante: Monthly Sales

This month

Revenue Center	Sales	Contribution
Pelligrino's	$245,000	31.2%
Artusi's	415,000	52.9%
Pomadoro's	125,000	15.9%
Total Revenue	**$785,000**	**100 %**

To illustrate the analysis process, consider the data in Figure 11.3. These numbers represent the $785,000 revenue generated last month by Il Cuoco Galante (the Courteous Cook) Italian restaurant. The restaurant operates on two levels of a renovated warehouse in the city center. On the first floor is Pelligrino's, a casual dining room that seats 200. On the upper floor is Artusi's, the 100-seat fine-dining room, as well as the 50-seat Pomadoro's Lounge.

This operation has three distinct revenue centers, each of which contributes a different proportion of revenue to the restaurant's total monthly sales. To calculate the proportional contribution level of each revenue center, the following formula is applied:

$$\frac{\text{Revenue center sales}}{\text{Total revenue}} = \text{Revenue center contibution \%}$$

Utilizing the formula and the data from Figure 11.3, the revenue center contribution achieved by Pelligrino's dining room would be calculated as follows:

$$\frac{\$245,000 \text{ Revenue center sales}}{\$785,000 \text{ Total revenue}} = 31.2\% \text{ Revenue center contribution \%}$$

For RMs operating multiple revenue centers, the ability to better understand the relative contribution of each center can be critical to assessing and evaluating income-producing effectiveness.

Day Parts

For those RMs who operate a single revenue center, as well as for those RMs whose operations include multiple revenue centers, an examination of sales contribution by day part will most often be very instructive. Recall from Chapter 10 that the term *day part* is most often used to indicate a meal period (i.e., breakfast, lunch, or dinner); however, a day part can consist of any definable time period that is of interest to the RM.

To calculate the proportional contribution level of each day part, apply the following formula:

$$\frac{\text{Day part sales}}{\text{Total revenue}} = \text{Day part contribution \%}$$

RM IN ACTION 11.1: DIPPING DINNER DAY PARTS

Monitoring day parts allows RMs to target problem areas that might not be easily identified when only an operation's total revenue generation is assessed. When *Nation's Restaurant News* (NRN) reported that a study found significant drop off in one geographic area's dinner traffic, it also reported what savvy operators in the area were doing in response to the dip in volume.

Some operators offered targeted menu price reductions during specific (dinner) time periods, while others took different approaches. Denver-based Vicorp, which operates the Baker's Square and Village Inn family-dining concepts, sought out innovative ways to increase its sluggish dinner day part traffic and sales without slashing prices.

Said Josh Kern, Vicorp's vice president of marketing, *"What we're trying to do is weave in a level of value that's not necessarily [about] price."*

Understanding precisely when an operation's volume originates, peaks, or declines is key to allowing RMs to implement targeted revenue optimization responses that can improve volume levels during those slack periods.

Excerpted on 1/15/2009 from www.nrn.com.

To illustrate, consider Big B's coffee shop located near the State University campus. This week it achieved a sales volume of $10,500 and was open daily from 6:00 A.M. to 9:00 P.M.

Figure 11.4 details this week's volume as generated during the three day parts established by the shop's owner for the purpose of analyzing the shop's sales.

Utilizing the day part contribution formula and the data from Figure 11.4 to illustrate the calculation process, we can calculate the revenue contribution achieved during the five-hour 11:00 A.M.–4:00 P.M. day part as follows:

$$\frac{\$1075 \text{ Day part sales}}{\$10,500 \text{ Total revenue}} = 10.2\% \text{ Day part contribution } \%$$

It is important to remember that a day part can consist of any defined time period of interest to you—including hours, meal periods, or even full operating days (e.g., Mondays, Tuesdays, Wednesdays, etc.) Given the data in Figure 11.4, it is easy to see that, given its relatively low contribution to overall sales, the potential for revenue improvement during the 11–4 time period is a challenge that should command the attention of Big B's RM.

Figure 11.4 **Big B's Coffee Shop Weekly Volume**

This Week

Day Part	Sales	Contribution
6:00 A.M.–11:00 A.M.	$ 5,550	52.9%
11:00 A.M.–4:00 P.M.	1,075	10.2%
4:00 P.M.–9:00 P.M.	3,875	36.9%
Total Revenue	**$10,500**	**100%**

Service Styles

You have now learned how to closely examine where your revenue is generated (revenue centers) and when it is generated (day parts). In many operations, it is just as important to analyze the service format utilized for revenue generation. Historically, a traditional restaurant served its guests in a dining room or other dining area. Dine-in service still constitutes a major delivery style. Increasingly, however, alternative service styles are popular with diners. Drive-through and carry out, also known as take-out or take-away services, may be important forms of revenue generation for your foodservice operation. If that is the case, a regular appraisal of the revenue contribution of these alternative delivery sources will be an important part of your RM duties.

Drive-through

Irvine California–based In-N-Out Burgers makes a good case for having originated the drive-through restaurant concept. In 1948, Harry and Esther Snyder opened the first In-N-Out Burger in Baldwin Park, California. Customers ordered their food through a two-way speaker box. Prior to that unit's opening, drive-in restaurant carhops typically took orders and delivered food to those guests who wanted to order from their car.[6]

Today, virtually every operation in the QSR segment offers guests a drive-through option. It is important to note that foodservice operators are not the only ones offering their products in a drive-through format. Banking at local branch banks, prescription drugs offered by drive-through pharmacies and retail beer, wine, and liquor sold at drive-through stores are all examples of products and services delivered in a drive-through environment.

In the foodservice industry, however, drive-through sales are so significant that some QSR operators routinely report as much as 70 percent of their total unit volume is derived from sales to their drive-through customers. In fact, some guests will even decide whether to eat in a QSR's dining area based on the number of cars in the operation's drive-through line (if too many cars are visible, potential guests will often go to a competitor's operation).

To maximize drive-through revenue generation, RMs understand that speed is essential. According to Matt Jennings, president of data management at Minnesota-based Restaurant Technologies, for every seven-second reduction in drive-through service time, sales will increase 1 percent over time.[7] The need for speed has resulted in a number of operationally oriented initiatives, including double lanes, the use of off-site call centers to speed guest orders, and the introduction of touch-screen systems designed to reduce ordering errors. In addition to speed, quality of communication (two-way radio or speaker quality) and order accuracy are the two factors most often mentioned as being of greatest importance to drive-through guests' perceptions of value delivered.

RMs in the QSR segment can expect continued evolution of the drive-through experience. Regardless of the operational form this service takes in the future, however, those RMs working in units that derive significant sales from drive-through customers should consistently monitor the revenue-generating levels of their drive-through services.

Carry-out

While the specific forms of carry-out services offered by restaurants vary greatly, carry-out services have historically differed from drive-through service in two important ways. The first is that customer orders for carry-out products can be received in multiple ways. Walk-in guest orders or guest preorders communicated by telephone are very common. However, carry-out preorders received from guests increasingly are delivered to the foodservice operation via fax, text message, e-mail, the store's web site, and, of course, cellular phones and apps.

In all cases, the improvement in communication method utilized is typically intended to shorten the time that guests must wait to pick up their orders. Reduction of waiting times is important because in today's advanced communications world, it is simply unrealistic to assume that guests would, for example, arrive at a carry-out pizza operation, place their order, and then wait 15-30 minutes for their pizza to be prepared. More common in a variety of food operations is the continued development of advanced preorder systems (e.g., Domino's and Papa John's text order system[8]), preprepared items ready for immediate customer take away (e.g., Little Caesars' Hot and Ready program[9]), or service styles that provide preprepared menus items that require only that onsite guests choose their items prior to those items immediate service and packaging for takeout (e.g., Panda Express and Sbarros, among others, illustrate this "dish on demand" style of takeout).

A second major difference between carry-out and drive-through is that the typical carry-out guest physically enters the foodservice operation's place of business. As a result, special parking areas and interior space for waiting guests, as well as specialized procedures for filling orders and accepting guest payment must be provided. In all cases, however, if your foodservice operation generates significant carry-out volume, that revenue should be tracked separately from your operation's other income-generating service styles.

Offsite Delivery

Although most foodservice customers equate delivery service with pizza and similar foods, RMs know that delivery service provides many operations with the opportunity to significantly increase revenue. In Chapter 10 you learned how, in many cases, a product's presentation and delivery affects customers' perceptions of value as much as the product itself. In many cases, guests are willing to pay a premium to have their food purchases delivered directly to them.

▶ RM ON THE WEB 11.1

Sometimes an RM's greatest challenge in increasing carry-out sales in a traditional dine-in operation relates to carryout (take out) food packaging. The napkins, service wear and condiments provided with an operation's take-out orders significantly impact guests' perceptions of value and thus should be of concern to RMs. Fortunately, members of the Food Packaging Institute (FPI) create and sell all the items RMs need to ensure modern packaging is readily available to meet their guests' needs.

To learn more about the FPI and its member organizations, go to www.fpi.org

When you arrive at the site, select *About Us*.

Essential RM Term

Offsite catered event: An occasion in which a foodservice operation provides food and beverage products, as well as any labor required to serve the products, at a location separate from its primary place of business.

When foodservice operators in the United States use the word *catering*, they are most often referring to the delivery of products to an offsite location. In most of the rest of the world, the term catering simply means the provision of food and beverage. Regardless of the term used, the delivery services provided by a food and beverage operation can range from the dropping off of a single menu item (e.g., a pizza) to a full **offsite catered event**.

Regardless of the distinctions and specific terminology used, if your foodservice operation provides offsite delivery or catering services (and in most cases it should!), you should separately track the revenue generated from those efforts.

Dine In

In many restaurants, the majority of all sales will take place within a traditional dining room setting. As a result, for many RMs, the analysis of sales made to dine-in guests will be among their most important tasks.

In many cases, a restaurant's dine-in seating area will consist of only one large room. Sometimes, however, an operation's total dine-in seating area will consist of two or more smaller and distinctly separate dining sections. In some cases, the sections may reflect an effort on the part of the operator to create uniquely different dining experiences. Thus, for example, one area in a facility may be designated for formal dining while another may be designed to attract a more casual dining customer.

Essential RM Term

Banquet room: A uniquely designated space available for privately hosted on-site catered events.

In other cases, separate dining areas may be created due to a restaurant's architectural design. In such cases, dining area separation may be the result of multifloor buildings, indoor versus outdoor designations, or even dining room versus bar dining areas. In some restaurants, one or more separate **banquet rooms** may be exclusively designated for overflow diners or for onsite catered events.

Foodservice RMs working in the lodging industry are very familiar with the banquet room arrangement as they routinely monitor the revenue production of their hotels' largest ballroom(s) or meeting rooms, as well as multiple, but smaller, banquet rooms commonly rented to guests hosting private meetings or meal events.

As an RM, you must decide how to segment your revenue sources to best track their income production. In most cases, greater detail will be more useful than lesser detail. As a result, any distinction or unique characteristic that logically leads you to believe the revenue-generating characteristics of one income source is different from another is sufficient reason to track its sales volume separately. Thus, you may find it advantageous to track your revenue on the basis of any unique combination of revenue center, day part, or service style.

MEASUREMENT OF REVENUE CHANGE

You have learned that RMs in foodservice must acquire the ability to examine their revenue generating sources with a great deal of specificity and accuracy. But why should you monitor your income so closely? The reasons for doing so are many, but all reflect a single

> **▶ RM ON THE WEB 11.2**

In some cases, RMs will find it challenging simply to properly identify their operations' distinct sources of revenue. To better understand why, examine the web site of Chicago's very successful Italian Village Restaurants. To view its web site, go to www.italianvillage-chicago.com

This popular and single-site facility opened in 1927. Today the total operation consists of Vivere, its upscale dining room, *The Village,* its casual dining area, and *LaCantina,* its basement level and wine cellar-styled steak and seafood house.

In addition, the restaurant offers delivery service, carry-out, and even private dining (on-site catering). It is easy to see that the RM responsible for monitoring revenue at the Italian Village must first make good revenue source-related decisions if he or she is to best understand each of the operation's varied income producing areas.

Essential RM Term

For-profit (foodservice): A foodservice operation whose continued operation is dependent on its ability to generate income in excess of expenses. Also referred to as commercial foodservice operation. Examples include most restaurants, bars, nightclubs, and lounges.

reality: A **for-profit foodservice** *operation that is not consistently* increasing *its revenues will cease to exist.*

A careful reading of the definition of a for-profit foodservice might lead an RM to believe that *decreasing* expenses would be equally as effective as increasing revenues when an operation seeks to ensure its income exceeded it expenses. If you recall that the accountant's profit formula presented earlier in this book was:

$$\text{Revenue} - \text{Expense} = \text{Profit}$$

It would certainly appear that from a mathematical perspective, a decrease in expense would indeed result in a larger profit number. That's true, but only in the short term.

Experienced RMs know that with increased sales volume comes increased expense. As a result, greater expense is more desirable than less expense. The idea that lower expense is somehow *better* than higher expense is illogical. When pressed on this point, cost-oriented foodservice managers would, of course, maintain that they seek to reduce expense while at the same time maintaining constant or even increasing revenues. From an RM's perspective, however, the problem with such a viewpoint is that it assumes expenses can be reduced with *no change* in the amount of total income. When foodservice expenses are reduced, that is almost never true. As you might predict, and despite the protests of very determined cost cutters, reducing expenses in foodservice nearly always leads to reduced guest perceptions of value, reduced revenues, and thus reduced profits.

Recall the profit definition utilized by RMs:

$$\text{Profit} = \text{The net value achieved by a seller } and \text{ a buyer in a business transaction}$$

It is fairly easy to see why reducing foodservice expenses in an effort to optimize profit is so often a failing strategy. There are two main reasons this tends to be so. In the typical expense reduction plan:

- All savings achieved are intended to go to the seller.
- The actions producing the savings typically reduce buyer's value.

To illustrate, consider the restaurateur whose menu features beef steaks and who faces rising beef steak costs. Assuming the facility is operating efficiently (with minimal waste), conventional foodservice wisdom would compel the operator facing increased beef prices to either: (1) reduce the size of steaks to maintain the operation's current menu prices) or (2) increase menu prices to maintain current steak portion sizes and cost ratios. Note that both actions would be intended to maintain profit levels. Note, however, that in both cases, any increase in benefits (e.g., more profit) is designed to go to the seller. Note also that when utilizing either approach, the value delivered to the buyer will be *reduced*, not enhanced. Recall the definition of *value* presented in Chapter 2:

> *In a buyer or seller transaction, value is the amount of perceived benefit gained minus the price paid.*

It is easy to see that neither smaller steaks (at the same price) nor the same-size steaks (at higher prices) are really very likely to *increase* a buyer's perceived benefit. As an RM, if you would defend the operator's action on the basis of rising beef costs, you have not yet grasped a critical concept presented earlier in this book, namely: *Buyers are indifferent to seller's costs and do not in any way feel obligated to ensure a seller's profits.* In fact, most buyers (including you!) are generally delighted to find they have acquired a wanted item at a retail cost close to or even *below* the seller's wholesale price.

Essential RM Term

Nonprofit (foodservice): A foodservice operation whose continued operation is not solely dependent on its ability to generate income in excess of expenses. Also referred to as a noncommercial foodservice operation or a subsidized operation.

Examples include those foodservice facilities operated in schools, colleges, hospitals, and extended-care facilities.

Because, in the long term, unwarranted expense reduction strategies typically result in decreased rather than increased revenue, even **nonprofit foodservice** operations find that strategies designed to increase revenues are more effective than those designed to reduce expenses because revenue-increasing strategies typically reduce these operations' required operating subsidies.

It is a truism that RMs must know how to measure their revenue increases or decreases with great accuracy. The reason it is important to do so was stated well by philosopher John Locke when he declared, *"The improvement of understanding is for two ends: first, our own increase of knowledge; secondly to enable us to deliver that knowledge to others."*[10]

RMs must monitor revenue change because it increases their own understanding of their operations and because it provides the information they need to encourage others in their organizations to undertake increasingly customer-centric revenue optimization strategies. Those strategies undertaken to increase customer perceptions of value are customer-centric. Those strategies designed to reduce expense *only* for the benefit of the operation may bring short-term expense relief, but generally are failing revenue optimization strategies for the long term. This is so because it is extremely difficult for a foodservice (or any other business) to disregard economist Milton Friedman's observation: *"The most important*

Figure 11.5	Drivers of Revenue Change Matrix

Check Average

		Increase	Decrease
Guests Served	**Increase**	Revenue increases	Revenue may increase or decrease
	Decrease	Revenue may increase or decrease	Revenue decreases

single central fact about a free market is that no exchange takes place unless both parties benefit."[11] Ignoring Milton's insight and decreasing customer value perceptions in an effort to reduce expense most often results in operators applying yesterday's strategies to today's customers in hopes of growing revenues tomorrow. That just doesn't work.

You have learned that revenue generation and thus changes in foodservice revenues can be viewed as being driven by the number of guests served and the amount purchased per guest (check average). Figure 11.5 graphically presents these drivers of revenue change for foodservice operators in a matrix format.

From Figure 11.5, it is easy to see that an increase in guests served in conjunction with an increase in check average will result in an increase in total revenue. Similarly, a decrease in guests served, accompanied by a decrease in check average, always results in a decrease in total revenue.

The impact on revenue is less clear when an increase in guests served occurs in conjunction with a decrease in check average, or when a decrease in the number of guests served is accompanied by an increase in check average. Because that is true, foodservice RMs must monitor sales both in terms of dollar sales *and* the number of guests served. In both of these mixed-results cases, an overall revenue increase is to be desired if profits are to grow and if concurrent increases in expenses such as food and labor are to be absorbed without profit reductions. Note that this is very similar to the situation in the lodging industry, where RMs must simultaneously monitor occupancy and ADR if they are to accurately assess total revenue generation.

Assessing Revenue Increases

When foodservice RMs maintain careful records of revenues achieved and guests served, any sales increase (or decrease) must be analyzed carefully if they are to fully understand the revenue direction of their businesses. To illustrate, consider the revenue data for Rodger's Restaurant, as detailed in Figure 11.6.

Note that the RM responsible for monitoring Rodger's revenue has identified two separate revenue centers (food sales and beverage sales) and has calculated the percentage of total sales revenue contributed by each of these sources. The actual dollar difference in total revenues achieved can be determined by simple subtraction using the formula:

This year total sales − Last year total sales = Total sales difference

Figure 11.6	Rodger's Revenue This Year versus Last Year			
Sales	**Last Year**	**% of Sales**	**This Year**	**% of Sales**
Food Sales	$1,891,011	82.0%	$2,058,376	81.0%
Beverage Sales	415,099	18.0	482,830	19.0
Total Sales	$2,306,110	100.0	$2,541,206	100.0

Certainly, knowing the absolute dollar amount of revenue increase or decrease is important. More effective RMs, however, would want to know the *percentage* change in total revenues as well. Based on the data in Figure 11.6, the overall sales percentage increase or (decrease) achieved by Rodger's is calculated using the following steps:

Step 1. Determine sales for this **accounting period**.

Step 2. Calculate the following: *This* accounting period's sales minus *Last* accounting period's sales.

Step 3. Divide the difference in Step 2 by *Last* accounting period's sales to determine the percentage variance.

To illustrate these three steps using the total sales data presented in Figure 11.6, the process is:

Essential RM Term

Accounting period: A defined period of time (e.g., a year, month, week, day, or hour) in which an RM wishes to report or analyze an operation's revenue generation.

Step 1. $2,541,206

Step 2. $2,541,206 − $2,306,110 = $235,096

Step 3. $235,096/$2,306,110 = 10.2%

Utilizing this same three-step process for the two separate revenue sources of food sales and beverage sales, the revenue variance (change) expressed in both its dollar amount and percentage change is presented in Figure 11.7.

From the data in Figure 11.7, it is easy to see that the overall change in revenue was 10.2 percent. RMs assessing the revenue-generating performance of Rodger's restaurant may be more challenged to answer the following question:

Did food sales increase more than beverage sales?

The question is not as easily answered as it may first appear. From a change in dollars generated perspective, food sales did indeed increase more than beverage sales ($176,365 food sales increase versus $67,731 beverage sales increase). From the perspective of percentage change, however, beverage sales are increasing at a faster rate than food sales (a 16.3 percent increase in beverage sales versus an 8.9 percent increase in food sales).

Figure 11.7	Rodger's Revenue Variance Data			
Sales	**Last Year**	**This Year**	**$ Variance**	**% Variance**
Food Sales	$1,891,011	$2,058,376	$167,365	+8.9
Beverage Sales	415,099	482,830	67,731	+16.3
Total Sales	2,306,110	2,541,206	235,096	+10.2

RM AT WORK 11.1

"It just doesn't make any sense to me," said Darryl, the new bar supervisor at the Smoke and Bones Bar-B-Que house.

"What doesn't make sense?" asked Kemina, the restaurant's dining room supervisor.

"In the staff meeting, Emesta said our bar sales went from $8000 last month to $10,000 this month. A 25 percent increase," replied Darryl.

"Yes, that's what I heard her say also," replied Kemina. She had attended the same month-end revenue management meeting that Darryl had attended. In these regularly scheduled meetings, Emesta Gamez, the restaurant's general manager, always updated the supervisors about the restaurant's monthly sales performance. To do so, she always announced the sales achievement of the bar and dining room, the restaurant's two revenue centers. "We had a nice increase in my dining room sales, as well. I heard Emesta say our increase was 5 percent," continued Kemina.

"And that's what doesn't make sense," replied Darryl. "Emesta said your dining rooms sales were up 5 percent. Well, 25 percent plus 5 percent is 30 percent, but Emesta said our total sales were only up 6.1 percent.

"Darryl, you can't add the 25 and 5 to get 30. You have to take the average," said Kemina.

"I did that too. I added 25 percent and 5 percent and then divided by 2. I got 15 percent, not the 6.1 percent overall increase Emesta said we hit!" said Darryl. "Like I said before, it just doesn't make any sense to me."

1. Describe the reason Darryl is having difficulty understanding the 6.1 percent sales increase announced by Emesta.

2. Do you think the misunderstanding Darryl is experiencing is a common one? Explain your answer.

3. What could Emesta do in her scheduled meetings to help resolve this confusion?

While it is clear from the data in Figure 11.7 that Rodger's achieved an overall increase in sales of 10.2 percent, Figure 11.5 would indicate that there are at least four ways the operation could have experienced that level of sales increase:

1. Served the same number of guests at a higher check average.
2. Served more guests at the same check average.
3. Served more guests at a higher check average.
4. Serve fewer guests, but at a much higher check average.

If the RM at Rodger's has carefully maintained records of both sales revenue and guests served, answers to questions of this type can be easily determined. If the RM has kept accurate guest count records, a check average (see Chapter 10) can be calculated. With this information, the RM can determine whether sales are up because Rodger's is serving more guests; because the same number of guests has been served but each one is spending more per visit; or in the best-case scenario, whether both events are occurring and more guests were served at a higher check average.

It is important to recognize that if each guest at Rodger's was spending quite a bit more per visit, the operation may actually have experienced a decrease in total guest count yet still achieved an increase in total sales. If this were the case, the RM at Rodger's would certainly want to know about it because it might be unrealistic to assume that revenue will continue to increase in the long run if the number of guests visiting the establishment is significantly declining.

If you were the RM at Rodger's and due to good recordkeeping you knew much about the impact of the number of guests served on your revenues totals, there would still be more you should know. Consider, for example, how you might address the following question:

> If menu prices at Rodger's were raised by 5 percent last year and if its revenues increased by 10.2 percent, how much did sales increase *beyond* the increase directly attributable to the increased prices? (Hint: the answer is *not* 5.2 percent.)

It is a fact in the foodservice business that menu prices are typically raised over time. Those increased selling prices, however, must not be confused with increased sales volume. For example, the restaurateur selling a single Delmonico steak in 1954 may have sold it for $5.00. An operator selling the same steak today might achieve revenues of $20.00 for its sale, despite the fact that in both case only one steak was sold. Clearly, today's operator in this example is not achieving four times the real sales volume of the 1950s operator.

Because menu price increases artificially inflate revenue gains over time RMs calculating real revenue increases in operations that have raised menu prices need to separate resulting sales increases into two parts—the part attributed to the price increase and the part that can be attributed to the real growth in sales. To do so, a sales adjustment technique must be applied.

To illustrate the use of the technique, assume that Rodger's menu prices for all food and beverage were indeed raised by 5 percent at the beginning of this accounting period. If this was the case, the operation's RM must take into account the impact of that 5 percent menu price increase. The procedure used to adjust sales variance to include known menu price increases utilizes the following three steps:

Step 1. *Increase* the prior accounting period sales by the percentage amount of the price increase.

Step 2. Subtract the result in Step 1 from this accounting period's sales.

Step 3. Divide the difference in Step 2 by the value of Step 1.

In this example, the RM at Rodger's would follow the three steps outlined here to determine the sales increase beyond that which can be attributed to increased menu prices. Using the example of total sales achieved (see Figure 11.7), the adjustment procedure would be applied as follows:

Step 1. $2,306,110 \times 1.05 = $2,421,415.50

Step 2. $2,541,206 - $2,421,415.50 = $119,790.50

Step 3. $119,790.50 \div $2,421,415.50 = 4.95\%

Figure 11.8 presents the data that would result from utilizing this same adjustment procedure for all three categories: food, beverage, and total sales. Figure 11.8 indicates that total sales at Rodger's increased by 4.95 percent after adjustment for a 5 percent menu price increase.

Figure 11.8	Rodger's Revenue Variance with 5% Adjustment for Menu Price Increase				
Sales	**Last Year**	**Adjusted Sales (Last Year × 1.05)**	**This Year**	**Variance**	**Variance %**
Food sales	$1,891,011	$1,985,561.60	$2,058,376	$ 72,814.40	+3.67
Beverage sales	$415,099	$435,853.95	$482,830	$46,976.05	+10.78
Total sales	$2,306,110	$2,421,415.50	$2,541,206	$ 119,790.50	+4.95

Assessing Revenue Decreases

Revenue managers working through the difficult process of accurately calculating the sources of any sales volume increases can at least be pleased that their **top-line revenues** are growing.

Those RMs whose operations face declining revenues are less fortunate but may take comfort in the position once expressed by Lewis Burwell "Chesty" Puller. Puller was an officer in the United States Marine Corps and holds the distinction of being the most decorated Marine in U.S. history. During a particularly difficult military operation, Puller issued the following report to his superior officers: *"We've been looking for the enemy for some time now. We've finally found him. We're surrounded. That simplifies things. Puller."*[12]

Essential RM Term

Top-line revenues: Foodservice jargon for an operation's total income. Used to differentiate the operation's gross revenue production from its *bottom line* or net income (profit) production.

Puller knew that sometimes things must be viewed differently, and more optimistically, than they might initially appear to others. This can sometimes be the case with RMs who calculate and seek to understand their operations' decreasing revenue levels.

Using the same three-step revenue change assessment procedure introduced previously in this chapter, RMs may, of course, find that their calculations produce a negative percentage change rather than a positive one. In some cases, an RM whose operation consists of multiple revenue sources may find revenues increasing in one or more of those sources while other sources are experiencing declining revenues. In still other cases, an apparent reduction in food-service revenue as calculated by an RM may be misleading or even completely erroneous.

To illustrate some of the many factors that must first be taken into consideration before you can correctly analyze a decrease (or an increase) in foodservice revenue, assume you were the RM for a restaurant located across the street from a professional basketball stadium. If you were to compare sales from this January to sales generated last January, the number of home basketball games in January for this professional team would have to be determined before you could make truly valid conclusions about your guest count, and thus your revenue increases or decreases. This is so because more homes games will likely mean more revenue; fewer home games would mean less revenue.

In a similar manner, if a foodservice facility is closed on specific days of the week, the number of operating days in two given accounting periods may be different. When this is the case, percentage increases or decreases in sales volume must be based on average *daily sales*, rather than the total revenues generated in the two accounting periods. To illustrate, consider Dilbert's, a mobile sandwich kiosk that operates in the downtown business

Figure 11.9	Dilbert's Revenue This January versus Last January			
	Last Year	**This Year**	**Variance**	**Variance %**
Total sales (January)	$17,710.00	$17,506.00	−$204	−1.2%
Number of operating days	22 days	21 days	1 day	
Average daily sales	$ 805.00	$ 833.62	+$28.62	+ 3.6%

district of a large city. Its clientele consist primarily of office workers, and it is open Monday through Friday only.

In January of this year, the kiosk was open for 21 days. Last year, however, because of the number of weekend days in January, the stand operated for 22 days. Figure 11.9 details the revenue comparison of the kiosk, assuming no increase in menu selling price this year compared with last year.

RM IN ACTION 11.2: . . . AND LAST QUARTER COMPANY REVENUES WERE UP! DOWN? BOTH!?

For multiunit foodservice operators, there are two ways to increase revenues: sell more at existing stores or increase the number of opened stores. Clearly, the first approach costs less to do than the second. When same-store (comp) sales are increasing, it means more guests are being served, guests are paying more for the same menu items they bought a year ago, or some combination of the two. In each case, sales are increasing without the added expense associated with building and operating new stores.

Increasing same-store sales also indicates effective marketing and a food and beverage concept that is popular with consumers. As experienced RMs know, however, in some cases foodservice organizations reporting their financial results tout *net revenue* gains rather than same-store sales increases. The results can be confusing to the uninitiated.

To see a clear example of this, consider that a careful reading of the nearly 1,000-word article (optimistically titled: "Starbucks Corp. Reports

12 Percent Net Revenue Gain In Second Quarter") includes the following four short (less than 50 words) but revealing sentences explaining the company's revenue trends:

1. Lower than expected revenue was driven by a mid-single-digit decline in U.S. comparable store sales; driven by decreased traffic.

2. For the quarter, U.S. revenues increased by 8 percent.

3. International total revenues expanded 27 percent.

4. Net earnings totaled $316.8 million—down 11 percent (from prior year).

Note the gentle reference to the *mid-single-digit* decline in comparable (same store) sales. Mid-single-digit in this article is financial reporting code for a decrease of between 4 and 8 percent. In this instance, the 8 percent increase in U.S. revenue was driven entirely by new store sales which, when combined with

RM IN ACTION 11.2: (Continued)

the 27 percent increase in international sales, resulted in the 12 percent net overall sales increase; despite significantly declining same store sales in the United States.

If you sense that from a long-term perspective all was not well with Starbucks at the time of this report (note the 11 percent net earnings decline!), you would be absolutely correct.

Experienced RMs know that when a company's comps are falling, it can mean one of several things. It could mean that the operation's appeal is weakening and fewer guests are stopping in. It could mean, as was true in this case, that the economy is worsening and people are less inclined to buy foodservice products from anyone. It could also mean that

in a failed effort to increase customer counts, menu prices have been reduced excessively. In all cases, however, falling same-store sales represent a problem. In such a situation, the question RMs must directly address is both simple and complex:

"Are we experiencing a short-term trend that will quickly reverse itself, or does this represent the beginning of a long-term downward spiral?"

The correct answer to the question may be simple but what to do about it is the part that is more complex.

Excerpted on 1/25/2009 from www.amonline.com/web/online/VendingMarketWatch.

Essential RM Term

Same-store sales: Sales revenues achieved by operations that have been open for more than one year. Also referred to as same-store revenue, comparable (comp) sales, or like for like (LFL) sales.

This statistic allows RMs and others to determine which portion of increased revenue has come from real sales growth and which portion from the opening of new units or stores. The distinction is important because in most cases a saturation point, at which time future sales increases must be driven by same store sales growth, will likely occur.

An examination of the data in Figure 11.9 reveals that total sales for Dilbert's in January declined by 1.2 percent when compared to January of the prior year. It would be a mistake, however, for Dilbert's owner to conclude that the kiosk's revenue is lower than the previous year. This is so because an examination of the average daily sales achieved by the kiosk reveals a revenue increase of 3.6 percent when compared to the prior year.

Are Dilbert's sales for January up or down? Clearly, the answer must be qualified in terms of monthly or daily sales. For this reason, RMs must be careful to consider all relevant factors before making determinations about variances in sales. These can include the number of operating meal periods or days, changes in menu prices, variation in guest counts, or change in check averages and the number of holidays and other special events. Only after carefully considering all relevant variables can RMs truly interpret their operations' revenue trends. For many RMs it will be average *daily* sales, *daily* customer count, and *daily* check average over a specific accounting period that will reveal the most accurate information regarding revenue increases or decreases. Precise understanding and interpretation of **same-store sales** trends is also critical if RMs are to make effective customer-centric revenue optimization and pricing decisions.

> ▶ **RM ON THE WEB 11.3**

Technomic Information Services (TIS) has been tracking the foodservice industry for over 40 years. It provides industry intelligence, financial forecasts, data and training support to manufacturers, operators and distributors, and others allied to the field. Many of its publications and digital products can help RMs monitor industrywide dining trends. One of its most recent product additions examines consumer response to various menu-pricing strategies. To learn more about this new and useful revenue optimization tool, go to www.technomic.com

When you arrive at the site, click *Reports and Newsletters,* and then click *Consumer Trend Reports. Under Market Trends,* click on *The Consumer Pricing Strategy Report.*

EVALUATION OF REVENUE-GENERATING EFFICIENCY

Unlike their colleagues in the lodging industry, most foodservice RMs do not have access to a widely distributed external measure of their revenue management-related effectiveness. No equivalent of a Smith Travel Research (STR) competitive set report (see Chapter 9) is freely shared among foodservice operations. As a result, external benchmarks of relative market share capture, capacity utilization, and pricing effectiveness are not readily available to restaurant and bar operators.

The National Restaurant Association does prepare an annual forecast of sales for eating and drinking places. That forecast seeks to predict changes in the total amount of food and beverage purchased away from home and can be helpful in gauging overall dining trends.[13] Also, within some QSR chains, sales-related data taken from company-affiliated stores are available to franchisees and company store operators. For the most part, however, foodservice industry RMs must devise and implement their own internal measures of revenue generating effectiveness.

One of the many challenges facing foodservice RMs relates to the identification of the specific factors that will indicate the presence of effective revenue optimization strategies. Recall that revenue optimization consists of disciplined tactics used by RMs to predict buyer response to prices, optimize product availability, and yield the greatest profits. Creative RMs can assess their ability to optimize revenues in a variety of ways. For most foodservice RMs, however, a comprehensive assessment of their operations' effectiveness means evaluating the three key revenue-related factors of facility usage, labor usage, and capacity management. How RMs measure and interpret performance in these three important areas is addressed in the remaining portion of this chapter.

Revenue per Square Foot

Foodservice operations vary in size. A large restaurant or bar can simply seat and serve more guests than a smaller operation. As a result, it makes sense that large operations usually generate more sales than smaller ones. Logic might dictate that to maximize sales, only

Essential RM Term

Revenue per square foot: An operation's total annual revenue divided by the number of square feet occupied by the operation. Also referred to as *sales per square foot.*

Essential RM Term

Occupation costs: Expenses related to occupying and paying for the physical facility that houses a foodservice unit. Some examples of occupancy costs include rent, utilities, and facility insurance.

large facilities should be built and operated. The problem, of course, is that larger operations are more expensive to build, manage, and maintain.

Because the revenue-generating ability of an operation is so directly related to its size, it can be extremely difficult to equitably compare the sales achieved by a large unit to those achieved by a smaller operation. **Revenue per square foot** is the industry term for the calculation used to address this problem. It is a statistic that relates an operation's physical size to its ability to generate income.

Operations with low revenue per square foot production have less ability to cover fixed expenses than do those with higher values. Those operations that produce high revenue per square foot values are more efficient and typically more profitable than those that achieve lower levels. Regardless of their current achievements, RMs measuring their operations' revenue generating ability would certainly want to see increasing (not decreasing) values in this metric.

The revenue per square foot concept is perhaps easiest to understand in the context of shopping centers and food courts located in retail shopping malls. In such settings, the total number of square feet a foodservice operation leases from the shopping mall's owner typically determines its **occupation costs**.

The formula used to calculate revenue per square foot is:

$$\frac{\text{Total revenue}}{\text{Total square footage occupied}} = \text{Revenue per square foot}$$

Thus, for example, in an operation that achieved annual sales of $900,000 while operating in a 1,500 square foot unit, the annual revenue per square foot calculation would be:

$$\frac{\$900,000}{1,500 \text{ ft}^2 \text{ occupied}} = \$600 \text{ revenue per square foot}$$

Revenue per square foot is a valuable statistic because it penalizes those operators who do not use their occupancy costs efficiently while rewarding those who maximize sales in smaller spaces. Foodservice operations can range in size from 1,500 square feet for a small coffee shop to over 10,000 square feet for an upscale full-service restaurant operation. Although it is impossible to identify one ideal revenue per square foot target for all restaurants due to the great variation in products sold, location, and selling prices, many operators find their results range between $200 and $1,000 per square foot.[14]

Revenue per square foot averages also vary by foodservice industry segment. The actual revenue-producing capacity of an upscale restaurant, for example, will likely be very different from that of a small corner tavern or carry-out pizza shop. Similarly, the typical revenue per square foot averages generated by operations in urban locations with higher occupancy cost and menu prices will likely vary from those located in lower-cost rural areas. In all cases, however, foodservice operators seek to maximize the sales they achieve in the space they occupy, and the revenue generated must make good business sense when compared to the operations' overall occupancy costs.

Most importantly, the individual responsible for RM tasks in each business would certainly want to know if this important measurement was increasing, decreasing, or staying the same. This is especially true for those operators seeking to expand the size of their current operation or those planning to open additional units.

In some cases, RMs may find it difficult to fairly assess the efficiency of their unit's revenue per square foot production. The reasons this can be true are varied and may even be beyond the immediate control of management. Consider, for example, the foodservice unit located in a shopping mall's food court. If one of the major (anchor) retail stores in the mall closes or is replaced with a less popular store, overall mall traffic may significantly decline. In such a case, it is also likely that the revenue generated per square foot for all the mall's stores may decline. With lower shopper volume, it is quite likely that every food operation located in the mall's food court will also experience a volume reduction and consequently a decline in revenue generated per square foot of occupied space. The fact that this measure can be affected by external variables, however, is actually one of the strongest arguments for an RM's careful and continual monitoring of it.

Revenue per Labor Hour

The calculation of a food cost percentage (see Chapter 10) seeks to relate revenue produced with the cost of the products required to generate those revenues. In a similar manner, revenue per square foot calculations seek to relate revenue produced in an operation with the operation's size and, to a certain degree, with the **other expense** incurred in occupying the operating space.

One of the most significant calculations used to help RMs evaluate their operations' revenue production effectiveness relates to efficiency in labor usage.

In fact, examining the use of labor is yet another area in which differences exist between RMs whose focus is on revenue production and the foodservice cost control specialist whose focus in on monitoring expense. Figure 11.10 lists some of the labor cost manager's most popular measurement tools.

The efficient use of labor is very important to those individuals with responsibility for an operation's P&L (profit and loss, or income) statement. The efficient use of labor is also important to RMs, but for different reasons.

Essential RM Term

Other expense (foodservice): Those operating costs that are neither food nor labor costs.

Figure 11.10	Popular Measures of Labor Cost	
Measurement	**Formula**	**Purpose**
Labor cost %	$\dfrac{\text{Cost of labor}}{\text{Revenue}}$	To examine the ratio of revenues achieved to labor expenditures
Labor dollars per guest served	$\dfrac{\text{Cost of labor}}{\text{Guests served}}$	To examine the labor-related costs of serving each guest in commercial and noncommercial (noncash) foodservice operations
Guests served per labor dollar	$\dfrac{\text{Guests served}}{\text{Cost of labor}}$	To examine the number of guests served for each labor dollar expended

If you have ever experienced very slow service in a restaurant, bar, or club, then you know that inadequate staffing can reduce the level of guest purchases. Those guests who are serviced slowly simply buy fewer items because they are not given the opportunity to purchase more. As well, the total number of guests who can be seated and served in a given time period will be reduced when insufficient servers, bartenders, or cooks are scheduled.

Just as more guests can be served in large facilities than in smaller ones, more revenue can be generated with an appropriate sized staff than with one that is too small. Like facility size, however, increases in staff size are accompanied by increased cost. Thus, RMs measure labor efficiency in terms of the amount of sales generated for each labor hour used. The formula for computing this measure of labor productivity is:

$$\frac{\text{Total revenue}}{\text{Labor hours used}} = \text{Revenue per labor hour}$$

Labor hours used is simply the sum of all labor hours paid for by an operation in a defined accounting (selling) period. To illustrate the calculation and use of the revenue per labor hour metric, consider the case of Ezat Moradi. Ezat operates a Middle Eastern-themed restaurant. The sales volume he has achieved in the past four weeks is detailed in Figure 11.11.

Note that revenue per labor hour in Ezat's operation ranged from a low of $37.80 in week three to a high of $44.95 in week four. From this example it is easy to see the variance in his staffing effectiveness and its resulting impact on sales.

Those RMs who carefully monitor revenue per labor hour do so because they feel it is a better measure of labor usage than the labor cost percentage. Indeed, while revenue per labor hour will vary with changes in menu selling price (as does the labor cost percentage), it will not vary based on changes in the price paid for labor. In other words, increases and decreases in the price paid per hour of labor do not affect this productivity measure. Because the revenue per labor hour ratio does not consider the hourly amount paid to employees, a foodservice unit paying its employees an average of $10.00 per hour could, when using this measure of productivity, achieve the same sales per labor hour efficiency as a similar unit paying $12.00 for each hour of labor used. In this scenario, the operation paying $10.00 per hour would have created a lower cost, yet equally productive, work force if the sales per labor hour used are the same in the two units.

Figure 11.11   Ezat's Four-Week Revenue per Labor Hour

Week	Revenue	Labor Hours Used	Revenue per Labor Hour
1	$ 18,400	410.00	$ 44.88
2	21,500	525.25	40.93
3	19,100	505.25	37.80
4	24,800	551.75	44.95
Total	**$ 83,800**	**1,992.25**	**$ 42.06**

To better understand the use of the revenue per labor hour measure, consider the decision you would face as the RM of a private golf course and country club. One of the services you would like to offer your members is beverage service while golfers are on the course. The question you must answer is, *"How many beverage carts should I place on the golf course at any given time of the day and day of week to adequately serve the club's members?"*

Too few beverage carts on the course will result in thirsty, unserved, and ultimately unhappy golfers; while too many carts will cause the club to incur excessive labor costs. In this situation, you would want to monitor your beverage cart revenues per labor hour utilized and make determinations on the number of carts that you should use at various times to ensure cost-effective, quality service.

It is relatively easy to compute revenue per labor hour used because both the numerator and the denominator of the formula are generated on a very regular basis. Sales per labor hour can be calculated based on the number of hourly workers scheduled, scheduled salaried workers, or both. It is important to recognize that the efforts of *both* salaried and hourly employees must be considered when computing a facility's overall revenue per labor hour used.

Revenue per labor hour can be calculated by revenue center, day part, or service style. RMs should, of course, seek increases in this important revenue measure without sacrificing quality service levels. Figure 11.12 details specific steps you can take to maximize your own operation's revenue per labor hour.

Figure 11.12 | **Six Strategies for Increasing Foodservice Revenues per Labor Hour**

1. Emphasize the relationship between revenues and a server's own income.

   Calculate exactly how much more your tipped waitstaff could earn in a week if they boosted check average by 10 percent. Explain that they have the power needed to make their income increase.

2. Set reasonable targets.

   Give servers a realistic goal to accomplish during their shift and have them report their progress during the shift. Make sure the goal is attainable, because if the goal is too high, you will be setting your staff up for failure, not success.

3. Publicize results.

   Waitstaff are competitive. Peer pressure can be a powerful motivator. Post shift-by-shift performance results where all servers can see them. Highlight strong performance as well as individual improvement.

4. Provide tangible rewards.

   Schedule your servers with the highest check averages during peak periods to reward them and to help maximize total revenues. Place your strongest staff on the schedule when they can have the greatest impact. Consider hourly wage increases for consistently strong performers.

(continued)

Figure 11.12 (*Continued*)

5. Train, train, train.

   One of an RM's most important tasks is helping service staff understand how their upselling (see Chapter 7) efforts directly impact revenue generation. Training in upselling and guest service skills should be ongoing and its effectiveness carefully measured.

6. Eliminate those servers who simply can't perform.

   Not every person has the ability or even the desire to be a highly effective server. Continually monitor those employees whose revenue generation per hour ranking is consistently in the bottom 20 percent of your staff. If well-designed training efforts do not improve their performance, reassign them to nonserver tasks or terminate their employment.

▶ RM ON THE WEB 11.4

Foodservice industry RMs can easily locate restaurant marketing-related texts and other publications. Most of the material in these publications, however, emphasize increasing the number of guests who frequent a business. That is a reasonable approach to growing revenues; however, experienced RMs know that increasing check average generation among current guests is also an extremely effective way to improve top-line revenues and increase revenue per labor hour with minimal incremental costs. The key to increasing per guest sales is an exceptionally well-trained staff.

You can find information about first-rate server training tools on the web site of the National Restaurant Association. To review or purchase these training aids go to www.restaurant.org

When you arrive at the site, click *Profitability* and *Entrepreneurship,* and then click *Opening a Restaurant* in the left margin. Then click on *How-to Series*.

Next click *Teaching Servers How to Sell*.

As the NRA site correctly points out in the introduction to this superb training tool:

> An effective server is much more than an "order taker." Rather, he or she can increase a restaurant's profits, receive more tips and ensure that guests leave the restaurant with nothing but good things to say about their experience. This program provides advice on teaching servers how to sell.

RM AT WORK 11.2

"You wanted to see me, sir?" said Marco to the clearly agitated guest seated at the six-top table in the corner of The Heidelberg, the upscale German-style restaurant that Marco managed.

"I've been waiting fifteen minutes for my waiter to bring us our check. And as slow as he's been, it will probably take another ten minutes to process my credit card. I just want to pay and get out of here. The food was great, but this is ridiculous!" said the guest.

"I'm really sorry Sir. I'll find your server," replied Marco as he glanced around the dining room. As he did, he noticed several unbussed tables that were littered with dirty dishes; as well as the hostess stand where the line of guests waiting to be seated hadn't gotten any smaller in nearly an hour.

When Marco entered the kitchen looking for the disgruntled guest's server, he was surprised to see several of the line cooks relaxing on the production line.

"How's it going back here tonight?" asked Marco as he glanced around the kitchen.

"Great. All our tickets are out," replied Sanjia, the sous chef in charge of the production line. "We're keeping up easily."

Assume that all of the front and back of house workers at the Heidelberg are well trained and highly motivated:

1. Do you think the restaurant's servers are likely doing their best to provide good service to the restaurant's guests? If so, then why was the guest in this scenario unhappy?

2. What do you think is the cause of a consistently long line of waiting diners when there are a large number of vacant, cluttered, but unbussed tables in the dining room?

3. The sous chef in this case said, "We're keeping up easily." Do you think that means the operation is being efficient at labor-related revenue optimization on this night? If you were the RM, how would you seek to solve this restaurant's guest-service related problems?

Revenue per Available Seat Hour (RevPASH)

The final assessment of revenue productivity presented here is one that RMs must understand. It is also one of the newest. In fact, references to this metric simply did not exist until hospitality professor Dr. Sheryl E. Kimes developed and advocated the continual monitoring of revenue per available seat hour (RevPASH) as a way to measure the efficiency with which table service restaurants generate income.

To best understand RevPASH, it is important for foodservice RMs to appreciate that they are in the business of selling space, as well as menu items. A restaurant has a fixed number of seats, each of which has the potential to generate larger or smaller amounts of revenue based on how many guests are seated, how long each guest remains in the seat, and how much is purchased by each seated guest. An increase in the number of guests seated will typically yield greater revenues. In a well-planned and properly managed operation, greater revenues should yield greater profits.

As you have already learned, revenue optimization in the hospitality industry is essentially a form of capacity (inventory) management in which inventory availability is manipulated by controlling its length of usage (e.g., in hotels this is the guest's length of stay), timing of the sale, purchase terms, and price. To optimize revenues, RMs monitor their product supply and their guests' demand for it. Prior to the publication of Dr. Kimes's work, those few industry professionals who addressed the issue of revenue capacity management in the restaurant industry focused exclusively on management of guest demand (guests served). Those RMs now utilizing the RevPASH measure recognize that the management of supply (seat availability) is just as important as the management of demand.

In Chapter 4 you learned that an important aspect of optimizing revenue is the optimization of product availability. Essentially, revenue optimization related to inventory management means setting prices based on guest willingness to pay and doing so in such a way that price-sensitive customers who are willing to purchase at off-peak or lower demand times can do so at lowered prices. At the same time, those who place greater value on a product or service pay a higher price to purchase its use at peak times.

Revenue optimization techniques work best when they are applied to businesses that have relatively fixed capacity (inventory), experience demand that is variable and uncertain, offer a perishable inventory, and attract customers of varying price sensitivity. These characteristics are certainly true of the restaurant industry and help explain why RevPASH is such a valuable tool.

Dr. Kimes's revenue management-related work is important both for its emphasis on supply management and its decidedly customer-centric orientation. This can be easily seen in her stated definition of restaurant revenue management:

> Restaurant revenue management can be defined as selling the right seat to the right customer at the right price and for the right duration. The determination of "right" entails achieving both the most revenue possible for the restaurant and also delivering the greatest value or utility to the customer. Without that balance, RM-type practices will in the long term alienate those customers who will feel that the restaurant has taken advantage of them.[15]

The effective monitoring and management of RevPASH is designed to increase revenue by focusing on the duration of guests' dining experiences, as well as the amount they spend. Duration is simply the length of time customers occupy a seat or table. Although RMs do not typically have the ability to control the specific menu items purchased by guests, the time it takes them to eat, or how long they linger at their table after eating, RevPASH monitoring can give RMs a good idea of the speed at which a kitchen produces food and the speed at which guests are served.

Recall from Chapter 1 that the formula for RevPASH is:

$$\frac{\text{Total revenue}}{\text{Available seat hours}} = \text{Revenue per available seat hour (RevPASH)}$$

To calculate RevPASH, RMs must be able to identify the number of diners served each hour, as well as the amount these guests spend (revenue). Typically, this information can be easily retrieved from an operation's POS system. Because modern POS systems record guest

Figure 11.13	Sara's Revenue

Per Available Seat Hour (RevPASH) For: Last Friday Night

Hour	Available Seats	Guests Served	Revenue	RevPASH
4–5 P.M.	0	0	0	0
5–6 P.M.	100	25	$1,500	$15.00
6–7 P.M.	100	75	3,700	$37.00
7–8 P.M.	100	100	5,200	$52.00
8–9 P.M.	100	100	5,150	$51.50
9–10 P.M.	100	100	4,800	$48.00
10–11 P.M.	0	0	0	0
Total	**500**	**400**	**$20,350**	**$40.70**

Seats Utilized = 400/500 = 80%   *Check Average = $20,350/400 = $50.88*

check opening and closing times, a reliable estimate of guest duration is also readily available. The POS also records the number of guests served and total revenue generation, thus allowing for ready calculation of check average. Finally, RMs must know the number of dining room seats available to their guests as well as the number of hours those seats were available for use.

To illustrate the application of RevPASH, consider the case of Sara's, a restaurant operation with 100 seats. The restaurant is open for dinner from 5:00 P.M. to 10:00 P.M. Figure 11.13 shows the revenue this operation generated during each of the hours it was open last Friday.

The RM for Sara's calculates the total available seat hours in the operation by multiplying the number of seats available for guest use times the number of hours these seats were available (Available seats × Hours of operation = Available seat hours). In this case, the calculation is 100 (available seats) × 5 hours (of operation) = 500 available seat hours.

Note that, overall, Sara served 400 guests and thus filled 80 percent of its seats, at a check average of $50.88. On this Friday night Sara's overall RevPASH was $40.70 ($20,350/500 = $40.70). Note also that RevPASH can be calculated on an hourly basis. On this day the operation was most efficient in generating revenue during the 7:00 P.M. to 10:00 P.M. time periods. During each of these time periods, the individual (hourly) RevPASH values achieved exceeded the operation's overall average of $40.70.

RMs reviewing the data in Figure 11.13 could come to several revenue-enhancing conclusions. First, if Sara's could add incentives to attract or move diners to earlier times (5:00 P.M. to 6:00 P.M.), or perhaps stay open later (10:00 P.M. to 11:00 P.M.), an increase in revenue and profit potential could be considerable. Second, when seats go unused, as they did between the hours of 6:00 P.M. to 7:00 P.M., RevPASH is reduced. Thirdly, if Sara's could increase its seat utilization ratio RevPASH would increase. This could be the case, for example, during the 7:00 P.M. to 10:00 P.M. period when all tables are full. Shorter duration periods for each diner could lead to increased seat usage—including, perhaps, the usage of more than 100 seats in one hour (the equivalent of a 100+ percent seat utilization).

RMs can affect their revenue generation and guest duration times in a variety ways. For example, promoting desserts early (before 7 P.M.) and late (after 10 P.M.) at Sara's might make good sense. The servers at Sara's could hold back on strong dessert promotion during peak

Figure 11.14 RevPAR and RevPASH Commonalities

Industry	Capacity Utilization Measure	Sales per Unit Measure	Formula Variation
Lodging	Occupancy %	Average daily rate (ADR)	Occupancy % × ADR = RevPAR
Foodservice	Seat utilization %	Check average	Seat utilization % × Check average = RevPASH

dining hours (7–10 P.M.) if the preferred emphasis is to be *less* on building check average and more on increasing seat utilization by getting waiting diners seated and served as quickly as possible.

Lastly, astute RMs should immediately recognize that less than complete utilization of seating capacity leads directly to reduced RevPASH. To illustrate this concept, consider that, if all of the tables at Sara's are four-tops, but those tables are used to serve parties of two or three diners, substantially less of the restaurant's revenue generating capacity would be utilized. The result would be a significant reduction in RevPASH. In most cases, RMs will find that a larger number of smaller tables allows greater seat utilization than a smaller number of larger tables.

Interestingly, the foodservice RM's goal of putting "Smiles in Seats" is nearly identical to that of the lodging industry RM who seeks to put "Heads in Beds." Those RMs with experience in the lodging industry will no doubt recognize the unmistakable commonalities between revenue per available room (RevPAR) and RevPASH. These parallels are detailed in Figure 11.14.

Referring to the data in Figure 11.13, it is easy to see that RevPASH at Sara's can be calculated with the original RevPASH formula, or with the following alternative RevPASH formula:

$$\text{Seat utilization \%} \times \text{Check average} = \text{RevPASH}$$

or

$$0.80 \times \$\,50.88 = \$\,40.70$$

Because of its mathematical similarities to RevPAR, RevPASH interpretation must be approached just as carefully by foodservice RMs as lodging industry RMs assess RevPAR. Figure 11.15 illustrates why this is true. Note that in each case, the RevPASH at Sara's is identical, despite significant differences in how the value is obtained.

Figure 11.15 Sara's Restaurant Alternative RevPASH Production

Seat Utilization %	Check Average	RevPASH
40	$101.92	$40.77
60	$ 67.95	$40.77
80	$ 50.88	$40.77
100	$ 40.77	$40.77

Astute readers will recall the following statement from Chapter 9:

"Any evaluation of a hotel's occupancy % or its ADR, without a simultaneous assessment of both concepts (RevPAR), is simply meaningless."

Savvy foodservice RMs will recognize that the same statement applies to RevPASH interpretation:

"Any evaluation of a restaurant's seat utilization % or its check average, without a simultaneous assessment of both concepts (RevPASH) is simply meaningless."

Because of the inherent truth in that statement, watch for increasing numbers of foodservice RMs to calculate and assess the RevPASH—a new and innovative revenue optimization tool.

Figure 11.16	Six Strategies for Increasing RevPASH

1. *Regularly monitor RevPASH by revenue center and day part.* Effective RMs measure what matters. Few things are more important to the success of a foodservice operation than its selling efficiency. Only when RevPASH is known and carefully scrutinized can revenue optimization steps be taken to improve it.

2. *Maximize table/seating flexibility.* Flexibility in seating arrangements is a key factor for increasing seat utilization %. Effectively utilize one of the many reputable computer-based table management systems now available. Minimize the seating of guests at tables where seat capacities exceed the size of the party being seated.

3. *Use targeted differential pricing discounts to promote volume in periods where seat utilization is low.* Lodging industry RMs understand the value of discounting when demand is reduced. In a similar manner, foodservice RMs should target periods of low seat utilization when designing specials and publicizing reduced priced food and beverage promotions.

4. *Use differential pricing to maximize the sales value of seats during high utilization periods.* While few restaurateurs actually increase prices during periods of high guest demand and maximum seat utilization, creative RMs can ensure that selected menu items that can be prepared and served quickly are featured and highly promoted during high demand periods to maximize seat turnover. Minimize the promotion of longer-preparation-time menu items during these periods.

5. *Manage reservations.* Ensure that advanced reservations taken for the right size group, at the right time period, are optimized. High-volume restaurants should use a computer-based reservation management system.

6. *Staff high seat utilization periods properly.* The maximization of seat utilization depends on preparing food in an efficient manner and then serving it promptly. The timely clearing and resetting of tables and processing of guest payment are additional areas in which appropriate staffing plays a critical role in maximizing seat utilization percentage.

RM IN ACTION 11.3: BOUNCE-BACK

Although the RevPASH concept is still relatively new to the hospitality management literature, astute RMs can find many references to its principles if they are perceptive industry observers. To illustrate, consider that most well-managed restaurants train staff to say, *"Thank you. Come again,"* to departing guests. Effective RMs should want their guests to *come again*—but at specific times and for very specific reasons.

You cannot assume your customers know that you are open later on Saturday night this month or that you are adding Créme Brulee to your menu next month. Bounce-back coupons and promotions are tools that can be used to inform guests about the future and by doing so increase revenue. Examples include:

- Inviting guests to return (bounce-back) with a friend (e.g., *Buy 1 get 1 or Buy 1 get the 2nd at 1/2 price*)
- Inviting guests to try a new product or service (e.g., *Try our new special event catering service and receive 10% off the price of your first event*)
- Giving guests a specific reason to return (e.g., *Free dessert with dinner for guests arriving between 4 and 6 p.m. only*)

Bounce-backs can be used to persuade guests to try new items, increase check average, increase party size, or increase frequency of visit. Note that all of these actions influence RevPASH. Best of all, you can stop any bounce-back offer at any time.

See if you can detect how the reference to bounce-back would impact RevPASH in the following statement posted on the Web by Quantified Marketing Group in their article "10 Tactics for Driving F&B Sales"

> All you do is offer incentives at the point of purchase on popular services to encourage the guest to try your restaurant another time. For instance, if you're busy for lunch and need to drive sales for dinner, offer bounceback certificates that can only be redeemed during dinner hours.

Bounce-backs can be personal invitations to your business's best friends—your current customers! Monitoring RevPASH and understanding precisely when your operation needs and can accommodate additional volume allows you to target promotions such as bounce-backs in a way that can significantly improve your operation's RevPASH performance.

Excerpted on 1/25/2009 from www.quantifiedmarketing. com/learning_center.

THE REVENUE EVALUATION PROCESS IN FOODSERVICES

Ask any cost-focused foodservice professional exactly how much time he or she spends monitoring the expense side of the business and the answer you will get will be some variation of the word "Plenty!" These professionals spend time monitoring expenses because they know the importance of properly controlling costs. In a similar manner, RMs carefully monitor top-line revenues because they know the importance to marketing, promotion, pricing, and staffing efforts of understanding exactly where and when an operation generates its sales.

Monitoring revenue generation in a foodservice is the key to revenue optimization and profit maximization. The process is systematic and does demand a significant portion of an RM's valuable time. The information gained, however, is valuable because it leads to improved decision making. Those RMs who might question the time and effort required to effectively monitor and then understand how their operations generate income would do well to recall the observation of eighteenth-century English poet and critic Samuel Johnson, who wrote, *"Those who attain any excellence commonly spend life in just one pursuit; for excellence is not often granted upon easier terms."*[16]

Effective RMS in foodservices can best assess their units' revenue generation effectiveness by following 12 important steps.

12 Steps for Evaluating Revenue Generation in Foodservice Operations

1. On at least a weekly basis, analyze revenue generated by each of the operation's revenue centers.

2. On at least a weekly basis, analyze revenue generation based on the day part producing the sale.

3. On at least a weekly basis, analyze revenue generation based on the service style used to produce the income.

4. On a monthly basis (or **28-day accounting period**), analyze revenue production based on revenue center, day part, and service style.

5. Regularly calculate and analyze both dollar amount changes and percentage changes (up or down) for all revenue sources.

6. Monitor alcoholic beverage sales separately from food sales.

7. Regularly monitor and assess the operation's revenue per square foot efficiency.

8. Regularly monitor and assess the operation's revenue per labor hour efficiency.

9. Consistently track the number of guest served as well as revenues generated and maintain accurate check average data.

10. Regularly monitor and calculate, on an hourly basis, the operation's seat utilization %.

11. Set RevPASH goals and systematically calculate and assess the operation's progress toward meeting those goals.

12. Continually monitor staffing levels, food production, and service standards that directly affect the operation's ability to optimize revenues.

Essential RM Term

28-day accounting period: An accounting device used by those foodservice operators who, for ease of data comparison, divide their operating year into 13 equal time periods, each of which consists of four full weeks (28 days).

❖ ESSENTIAL RM TERMS

Off-site catered event	Same-store sales
Banquet room	Revenue per square foot
For-profit (foodservice)	Occupation costs
Nonprofit (foodservice)	Other expense (foodservice)
Accounting period	28-day accounting period
Top-line revenues	

▶ APPLY WHAT YOU KNOW

1. Phillipi Chow is the owner of the Shanghi House Chinese restaurant. The Shanghi House consists of two distinct dining areas. Cheng's (dining room) provides an upscale dining experience designed to rival the finest of Hong Kong eateries. Lohr's (dining room) is a casual dining area that emphasizes moderately priced but very authentic menu items from a number of different Chinese provinces. Both dining areas are open for lunch and dinner. All items on Lohr's menu are also available for takeout. Last week, Phillipi's operation generated the following sales:

Cheng's Lunch	$ 23,250
Cheng's Dinner	$ 46,525
Lohr's Lunch	$ 34,500
Lohr's Dinner	$ 27,850
Carryout (Lunch)	$ 8,500
Carryout (Dinner)	$ 12,275

Help Phillipi answer the following questions about his operation (calculate your answers to one decimal place):

A. What was the total dollar amount and percentage (%) of last week's total sales generated by:

Cheng's? $ _____ %

Lohr's? $ _____ %

Carryout? $ _____ %

B. What was the total dollar amount of Philippi's lunch sales? $ _____.

What portion of his total revenues was achieved during lunch? $ _____ %

C. What portion of Philippi's total sales revenue this week was contributed by carryout sales made during the dinner period? _____%

D. What portion of the revenue generated in Cheng's dining room was achieved during its dinner service period? _____ %

E. What was the total dollar amount of Philippi's dinner sales? $ _____.

   What portion of this operation's total revenues last week was achieved during its dinner period? _____ %

2. Bonita Reya is the RM for the Mayfair hotel. She is comparing this February's food and beverage (F&B) sales to the F&B sales achieved at the hotel this past January. Sales were up in all of Bonita's revenue centers! The hotel has one dining room, a lounge, and accounts separately for banquet food and banquet beverage (alcoholic beverage) sales. Bonita has collected the following sales data, but some are missing. Complete her sales summary, calculating your percentage answers to one decimal place, and then answer the questions that follow:

Mayfair Hotel F&B Revenue: February This Year versus January This Year				
Revenue Source	**February**	**January**	**$ Variance**	**% Variance**
Dining room	$ _____	$ 15,000	$ _____	+ 20.0%
Lounge	_____	1,500	1,000	+ ___%
Banquet food	29,000	_____	4,000	+ 16.0%
Banquet bar	17,000	15,000	2,000	+ ___%
Total F&B	$ _____	$ _____	$ _____	+ ___%

A. What was the total dollar amount of sales achieved by the F&B department in:

   January ? _____

   February ? _____

B. What was the total dollar amount of increase achieved by the hotel's F&B operation in February when compared to January? _____

C. Which revenue source achieved the greatest dollar increase in sales? _____

D. Which revenue source achieved the greatest percentage increase in sales? _____

E. In February, what was the overall percentage increase in sales achieved by the Mayfair hotel's food and beverage operations? _____ %

3. Jack Sparrow is the owner of Captain Jack's Seafood. It is open seven days a week. Jack monitors three revenue sources in his operation. These three sources are the dining room, the bar, and his carryout operation. Jack finished tallying his February 2013 sales. He wishes to compare his revenue to that achieved in the prior year. Complete

his sales summary, calculating your percentage answers to one decimal place, and then correctly answer the questions that follow:

	Feb 2012	Feb 2013	$ Variance	% Variance
Captain Jacks				
Dining room	195,750	192,550		
Bar	35,550	36,520		
Carry-out	16,500	16,250		
Total Revenue				

A. What were the dining room revenue variances in February 2013 when compared to the prior February:

In dollars ? _____
In percent ? _____

B. What were the bar revenue variances in February 2013 when compared to the prior February:

In dollars ? _____
In percent ? _____

C. What were the carryout revenue variances in February 2013 when compared to the prior February:

In dollars ? _____
In percent ? _____

D. What were the total operational revenues variances in February 2013 when compared to the prior February:

In dollars ? _____
In percent ? _____

E. Are revenues at Captain Jack's increasing or decreasing when comparing revenue in February 2013 to the prior February? _____ Explain your answer.

4. Gene Monteagudo is a district manager for the Pizza Time chain of pizzerias. His promotion to regional manager means he must select one of his current unit managers to fill his district manager's (now vacant) position. Gene will choose from among the managers in the six units that make up his district. He would like to promote the unit manager who is most effective at generating revenue using his target of $290.00 annual revenue per square foot of operation size and a $45.00 revenue goal for each

hour of variable labor utilized. Each unit's size in square feet (SF), as well as its monthly variable labor hour usage and sales averages, are presented below:

Pizza Time District Results: Monteagudo District

Unit Location	Unit SF	Variable Labor Hours	Average Revenue
Chippewa Falls	780	710	$ 19,750
Altoona	1100	580	$ 26,750
White Creek	1550	800	$ 30,500
Cadot	1200	730	$ 9,750
Augusta	1400	910	$ 31,750
Clair	1225	495	$ 23,750

A. Which unit's manager achieved the highest revenue per square foot (SF)? _____

B. Which unit's manager achieved the highest revenue per variable labor hour used? _____

C. What is the district's average revenue production:

Per square foot? _____

Per variable labor hour? _____

D. Which unit's manager achieved the greatest revenue? _____

E. Based solely on their ability to efficiently generate revenue, which unit's manager would you promote? _____ Explain your answer.

5. José López married María Famosa. Their son Juan López Famosa graduated from hospitality school and assumed the management of the family-owned Havana House restaurant. The operation features Cuban foods and is open for lunch and dinner. The restaurant normally seats 100, but during portions of the busy dinner hour an additional 50 seats are made available by opening an attached banquet room. Juan uses a system he designed to carefully monitor RevPASH. Using last night's data, answer the questions Juan has about his operation's revenue generation. Calculate any required percentage answers to one decimal place.

A. What was the restaurant's total RevPASH yesterday? _____

B. What was the restaurant's seat utilization % and check average yesterday? _____

Seat utilization % _____

Check average _____

C. Assume lunch is served from 11–4. Dinner is served from 4–11.

What was the restaurant's lunchtime RevPASH yesterday? _____

What was the restaurant's dinnertime RevPASH yesterday? _____

Hour	Available Seats	Guests Served	Revenue	RevPASH
Lunch				
11 A.M–12 P.M.	100	45	$825	
12–1 P.M.	100	135	2,550	
1–2 P.M.	100	85	1,575	
2–3 P.M.	100	30	490	
3–4 P.M.	100	10	210	
4–5 P.M.	100	20	410	
5–6 P.M.	150	60	1,150	
7–8 P.M.	150	170	4,650	
8–9 P.M.	150	155	3,650	
9–10 P.M.	100	85	1,800	
10–11 P.M.	100	50	1,950	
Total				
Utilization %				
Check Average				

D. What was the restaurant's lunch time seat utilization % and check average yesterday?

Lunch seat utilization % _____

Lunch check average _____

E. What was the restaurant's dinner time seat utilization % and check average yesterday?

Dinner seat utilization % _____

Dinner check average _____

F. Based on yesterday's revenue performance, what RevPASH enhancement suggestions would you make to Juan?

For implementation during lunch? _____

For implementation during dinner? _____

KEY CONCEPT CASE STUDY

"Well, what do you think so far?" asked Damario, the revenue manager at the Barcena Resort.

Damario was talking with Sam, the resort's F&B director. They were standing outside the resort's pool-side dining area. It was noon and the operation was in full swing, with all tables and nearly every seat full. There was a short line of diners, mostly families, waiting to be seated.

"Well", replied Sam, "since we began the special promotion that you recommended, our lunch time check average is down and the lines to get in seem to be shorter than they used to. Especially during our peak periods. I'm not sure those are good things."

Damario and Sam were discussing the roll-out of a newly implemented program designed to move guests *away* from ordering the restaurant's very popular Pizza and Pop Special (one large pizza and four sodas for $29.99) and *toward* its newly initiated Dogs and Drinks Special (five hot dogs and four sodas for $24.99). Prior to the promotion, the five hot dogs and four sodas, if purchased separately, would have cost a family of four nearly $30.00, so a family purchasing the hot dog meal received savings of nearly $5.00. Because of the added value, when the new promotion began, the sale of pizzas had declined and the sale of hot dogs had increased substantially.

"Tell me again," said Damario, "how long does it take to cook a pizza?"

"About five minutes to make, about 20 minutes to cook," replied Sam.

"And the hot dogs?" continued Damario.

"Those are already cooked, so delivering them to a table takes us about five minutes," said Sam.

"And do I recall that we priced the hot dog special to yield a contribution margin similar to the pizza promo?" asked Damario.

"Yes, we did get close on the two specials, but actually the contribution margin on the hot dog special is about $1.00 less than on the pizza special. That's why I'm concerned about all these hot dog sales!" said Sam. "It's such a popular promotion, maybe when we are really busy like now, during our rush hour, we should raise the price back up closer to the pizza price. That might even out our sales of each special and increase our overall check average."

"Actually Sam," replied Damario, "that would be the last thing we would want to do. Let me tell you why."

For Your Consideration

1. Many foodservice professionals (like Sam) equate increased check average with increased profitability. For the typical foodservice operation, do you feel it makes more sense to grow profits via the maximization of check average or the optimization of seat utilization? What are the potential drawbacks of each approach?

2. What do you think will be the net effect of this hot dog promotion on the operation's revenue generation? On its net operating income?

3. In a foodservice operation the control of costs is important, but so is an analysis of revenue optimization efforts. How would a RevPASH calculation help Damario better explain the apparent impact of this new promotion to Sam?

4. This chapter included the key sentence: *Effective RMs measure what matters.* Revenue generation matters. List three specific dangers faced by a foodservice operation that does not carefully scrutinize the sales-related efficiency demonstrated by each of its revenue generation centers.

ENDNOTES

1. Jack Miller and David Pavesic, *Menu Pricing and Strategy*, 4th ed. (New York: John Wiley & Sons, 1996), 145–147.

2. Jack Ninemeier, *Menu Planning, Design, and Evaluation Managing for Appeal and Profit* (Richmond, CA: McCutchan Publishing, 2008), 291–297.

3. David Pavesic, "Cost-margin Analysis: A Third Approach to Menu Pricing and Design," *International Journal of Hospitality Management* 2 (3) (1983): 127–134.

4. David K. Hayes and Lynn Huffman, "Menu Analysis: A Better Way," *Cornell Hotel and Restaurant Quarterly*, 25 (4) (February 1985): 64–70.

5. http://thinkexist.com/quotes/bishop_creighton/. Retrieved 1/5/2009.

6. http://www.in-n-out.com/history.asp/. Retrieved 1/10/2008.

7. Mike Hughlett, "The Science of the Drive-Through Customer Experience," *Chicago Tribune* 12/07/2008. Retrieved 1/10/2009.

8. Julie Ross, "Domino's, Papa John's look to build clientele via text message ordering,"

Nation's Restaurant News 12/10/2007. Retrieved 1/10/2009.

9. http://www.littlecaesars.com/. Retrieved 1/12/2008.

10. http://thinkexist.com/quotation/the_improvement_of_understanding_is_for_two_ends/177056.html. Retrieved 1/11/2009.

11. http://www.woopidoo.com/business_quotes/profit-quotes.htm. Retrieved 1/15/2009.

12. http://en.wikipedia.org/wiki/Chesty_Puller. Retrieved 1/18/2009.

13. http://www.restaurant.org/pressroom/pressrelease.cfm?ID=1725. Retrieved 12/19/2008.

14. http://wiki.answers.com /Q/What_is_the_average_sales_per_square_foot_for_a_restaurant. Retrieved 10/10/2009.

15. Sheryl E. Kimes, "Implementing Restaurant Revenue Management," *Cornell Hotel and Restaurant Administration Quarterly* (June 1999): 16–21.

16. http://thinkexist.com/quotation/those_who_attain_any_excellence_commonly_spend/149481.html. Retrieved 5/20/2009.

PART IV

REVENUE MANAGEMENT IN ACTION

CHAPTER 12

Specialized Applications of Revenue Management

CHAPTER OUTLINE

CHARACTERISTICS OF ORGANIZATIONS APPLYING REVENUE MANAGEMENT

You have learned that after the deregulation of their industry in the 1970s, principles of yield management were first applied in the United States by airline companies. As the *yield management* tactics they developed were adopted by the hotel industry, those techniques became known as *revenue management*, and as they continued to evolve were commonly referred to as *revenue optimization*. Both hoteliers and restaurateurs apply revenue optimization principles, but other businesses in the **service industry** can utilize them as well.

Essential RM Term

Service industry: Those businesses that primarily sell their customers intangible goods. Also known as the service sector.

In fact, revenue optimization strategies can be applied in any business setting in which service capacity or inventory is limited or constrained and thus must be managed and allocated among interested buyers.

RMs in a variety of fields must address issues of capacity allocation among distribution channels. These same RM professionals must also determine when to sell their inventory, at what price, and to which potential customers. Making good inventory allocation decisions results in optimized customer satisfaction and revenue. Poor decisions will have the opposite effect.

If you are an RM in a hospitality-related industry, you can apply customer-centric revenue optimization strategies any time the product or service you sell is characterized by specific and identifiable features. For those revenue managers working in the hospitality industry, a review and better understanding of these features can help you recognize revenue optimization opportunities that exist in your own hospitality-related settings.

In general, revenue optimization strategies and tactics are applicable any time a service business is characterized by:

- Constrained supply
- High fixed costs

- Variable demand
- Versioning opportunities
- Perishable inventory
- Ability to manage differential pricing
- Ability to communicate efforts

Constrained Supply

When a relatively fixed supply of product or service capacity is available to sell, RM strategies can usually be applied. In some industries, inventory levels can be increased in anticipation of increased consumer demand. Thus, for example, an ice cream manufacturer can increase production during the hot summer months when demand is high and reduce production in the colder winter months when demand is reduced. In most service industries, however, revenue managers will encounter either hard or soft supply constraints (see Chapter 1).

Supply may be constrained due to physical limitations such as the number of chairs in a barbershop, rooms in a hotel, or seats at a concert. It may also be constrained by the duration of use, such as seat hours available in a restaurant, nights stayed in a hotel, or the number of hours spent using the facilities at a water park. In some cases, both physical and time-based constraints are in play. Massages provided by health spas are an easy-to-understand illustration of inventory supply affected by both physical constraints and by time-based constraints. In a typical resort's five-bed spa, the number of massages that can be sold daily is constrained by the number of beds, and thus the number of persons providing the massages, as well as by the length of each massage.

When inventory levels cannot easily be altered in response to increase demand customer-centric revenue optimization strategies should be applied. You have learned that even revenue managers managing hard constraint inventory can, over time, expand capacity. Restaurants can expand their dining rooms or add new units. Hotels can add more rooms and a car rental company can make the decision to increase the number of vehicles available to rent at a specific airport location. In most cases, however, the cost of permanently adding this increased supply of inventory is prohibitive. It is typically more cost-effective to become more adept at managing the supply that currently exists.

High Fixed Costs

In Chapter 2, you learned that a fixed cost, or fixed expense, is one that remains constant despite increases or decreases in sales volume. Variable costs are those incremental, or extra, costs associated with each additional sale. Thus, for example, the restaurateur incurs the fixed costs of rent, utilities, and insurance regardless of the number of guests served. As each additional guest is served, the restaurant incurs the incremental cost of the food and beverages that are sold to the guest.

Revenue optimization strategies work best in industries with relatively high fixed costs. Concert promotion and its associated ticket sales are an easy-to-understand illustration of this. Assume, for example, that a concert promoter reserved the new Yankee's Stadium for a Latin concert featuring singer Jennifer Lopez, Colombian artist Shakira, and Mexican vocal artist Paulina Rubino. The costs incurred by this concert promoter are largely fixed. They include the stadium rental, advertising for the event, and the payments to be made to the artists. The incremental cost incurred by the promoter for each additional ticket holder would be extremely small. In fact, with the additional revenues and profit generated from each ticket holder's likely merchandise, food and beverage purchases, the actual variable cost associated with each additional concert attendee could well be near zero. Note that this is a very different situation from that of the manufacturer who incurs a very real additional cost each time a manufactured item is sold.

If you are an RM whose fixed operating costs are relatively high and your variable (incremental) selling costs are low, you will nearly always be in a good position to manage your inventory in a way that permits revenue optimization.

Variable Demand

In Chapter 3, you learned that idle production capacity cost is often a large but necessary expense incurred by service providers. In restaurants, idle production capacity exists because in most cases, demand for meals is higher at lunch and dinner time than it is during **shoulder periods**.

Because the overall demand for the services of restaurateurs and hoteliers varies on a predictable basis, RMs can use that predictability to select from among varied customers whose willingness to buy varies as well. For many service businesses, groups of their varied buyers may be combined and viewed as representing a type of supply or distribution channel. As a result, and as illustrated in Figure 12.1, for a variety of service businesses multiple distribution (supply) channels all contribute to its total buyer demand.

Essential RM Term

Shoulder period: The time period just prior to, or just after, a peak demand period.

For example, in a restaurant, the period just before or just after lunch is a shoulder period. In a resort, the weeks just before and just after the resort's peak season are shoulder periods.

Some of the variance in demand experienced by service providers is time based and quite predictable (for example, the demand variance that regularly occurs because of the hour of the day or day of the week). Other variations in the demand exhibited by a specific supply channel will be unique to that channel or the customer type it attracts.

When demand varies and is predictable, RMs in any hospitality-related service industry can use that information to design pricing programs that segment buyers and provide them with maximum value. To illustrate, assume Figure 12.1 represents various travelers seeking **package tours** to the warm Caribbean islands.

Assume Channel 1 represents North American travelers and Channel 2 represents South American travelers. Interest in such tours by North American travelers peak in the winter months of November to March. South Americans' travel interest peaks on a different time frame because on that continent January is the warmest month of the year and June and July are most often the coldest.[1]

Essential RM Term

Package tour: A tour organized in advance by a travel company to whom the vacationer or tourist most often pays a single fee covering transportation, accommodations, meals, and entertainment. This is also known as a vacation package or tour package.

Variable and predictable buyer demand can be used by revenue managers to target differing groups of customers, utilize various channels of distribution, and establish effective differential pricing strategies.

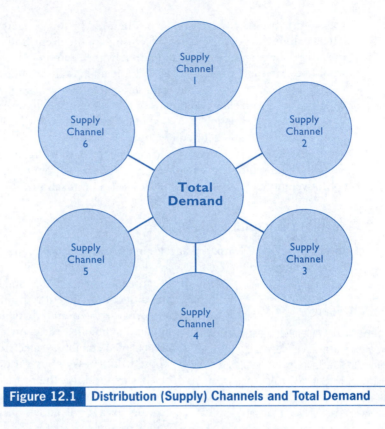

| Figure 12.1 | **Distribution (Supply) Channels and Total Demand** |

Versioning Opportunities

In Chapter 4, you learned that RMs can use different versions of the same products to vary the product's price. Thus, for example, hotels purposefully create room types with varying amenity levels and price the rooms accordingly. In this way, both price-conscious customers and those who prefer to pay more and receive more can both be accommodated.

Similarly, it is for this reason that a ticket behind home plate at a professional baseball game sells for more than a ticket for seating in the outfield. Creative revenue managers, however, often can find a number of ways to create versions of their basic product. That is why at least 13 of the 30 major league baseball teams offer "All-You-Can Eat" seats. These seats are usually located in distant outfield or upper-deck sections and, if not effectively priced, often remain empty game after game. For a fixed price, usually ranging from $30 to $55, baseball fans can eat as many hot dogs, nachos, peanuts, and soft drinks as they desire. Some teams also offer packages including beer, desserts, and candy.[2]

For nearly any service industry in which variations in the product or service offered for sale exist naturally or can be made available, revenue optimization opportunities exist. In many cases, innovative RMs can create product versions where their existence is not so readily apparent. Consider the inventive RM newly responsible for pricing tickets to a popular tourist venue such as an historic medieval castle and the extensive gardens attached to it. Historically, all-day admission tickets were the primary product sold to those seeking to visit the **attraction**.

In the hands of a creative RM, this attraction could be marketed and priced as having three product version alternatives, or zones. The first zone could be the castle itself. The second zone could be the gardens. The third zone could be access to both the castle and gardens. In such an arrangement, admission prices to visit this attraction could be versioned in such a way that:

- A ticket at a fixed price could allow access only to Zone 1.

- A ticket at the same or a different fixed price could allow access only to Zone 2.

- A ticket priced lower than the sum of the individual Zone 1 and Zone 2 ticket prices could be sold to allow access to both areas (Zone 3).

- Limited-time tickets (e.g., one or two hours rather than a full day) could be sold for any zone.

- Specific off-peak time periods (e.g., 8:00 A.M. to 10:00 A.M.) tickets could be sold for one or more zones.

- Season or return tickets could be priced attractively to encourage multiple return visits to one or more zones.

- An individual zone ticket could be packaged with other activities (e.g., restaurant meals, hotel stays, or other attractions) to create yet another product version.

When you consider that many hospitality-related service businesses have the characteristics of both versioning opportunities and variable demand for each form of product sold, the opportunities to apply revenue optimization strategies should be readily apparent to you.

Perishable Inventory

In many cases, when business persons think of product inventory they envision a physical item. It is true that in a retail environment, articles such as two-carat diamond rings, Maytag washing machines, Nintendo Wii consoles, or Jimmy Choo shoes represent tangible products. If any of these products is not sold on a particular day, it can usually be sold for the same price on the next day with no appreciable loss of quality or utility. That is simply not the way inventory must be viewed in the service industries. Fortunately, as author Anthony J. D'Angelo pointed out "You can learn a lot from the people who view the world differently than you do."[3]

Restaurant operators and hoteliers may have traditionally viewed their inventories as consisting of bottles of wine, prime steaks in the cooler, or reserve linen stocks, but savvy RMs in all service industries should view inventory as irreplaceable units of *time* in which their service is actually available for sale. Effective service-industry RMs sell time, not things.

It is easy to understand that the potential for an hotelier to sell a specific room on a specific night disappears forever if the room is not sold on that night. Viewed from that perspective, the hotelier's inventory is highly perishable because it disappears completely if it goes unsold.

Some restaurant operators regard perishability only as relating to physical products such as fruits, vegetables, and meats that are subject to spoilage. Effective RMs in the foodservice industry, however, recognize that what most restaurateurs actually sell is the amount of time guests occupy a dining room seat. Thus, it is not the total number of customers served or even the amount spent by each customer that is of most importance. True revenue optimization results from pricing products in a way that minimizes the number of available *seat hours* (see Chapter 12) that go unsold each day. In nearly all constrained supply service industries, it is their unique and specialized time-based inventory units that are most perishable and it is the sale of these time-based units that RMs in these industries must seek to optimize.

RMs working in hospitality-related service organizations must first clearly understand their inventory. This includes understanding the perishable nature of that inventory. Whether it is an unsold seat at a concert, an open tennis court time, an unreserved golf tee time, or an empty seat on a tour bus, unsold service inventory perishes immediately. When it does, the opportunity to optimize revenue from its sale perishes as well. Only after RMs understand fully the perishability of their salable products can they design and manage a differential pricing program that minimizes unsold inventory.

RM AT WORK 12.1

"I'm sorry Sir," said Javier "but all of our boats and our jet skis are out right now. I could get you a unit in about 45 minutes."

"Thanks anyway," said the disappointed couple as they walked away from the small beachfront watercraft rental business Javier operated with his partner Esperanza. Their stand was located on the beach in San Juan Del Sur, Nicaragua. Beach traffic was heavy in the daytime and especially in the early afternoon. That's when Javier and Esperanza's business was best.

"What did they want?" asked Esperanza as she walked over to the stand where Javier had been talking to the young couple.

"They wanted a two-person jet ski. I told them all our units were out on the water right now," said Javier.

Esperanza looked at her watch and said, "Typical. It's two o'clock. Prime time. Everybody wants to rent just after lunch and

before dinner. You should have told that couple to come back tomorrow morning, when it's slow!"

"Maybe we need to buy more jet skis," said Javier, "so we have more inventory available in the afternoon."

"More jet skis would just mean more cost," replied Esperanza. "Maybe what we really need to do is reexamine our pricing."

1. Assume that you were advising Javier and Esperanza on pricing. Would you suggest their units rent for the same amount before noon as they do in the afternoon?

2. Javier seems to believe that additional jet skis would expand the business's inventory. What exactly is the product sold by Javier and Esperanza? Is it perishable?

3. Assume that Javier and Esperanza wanted to implement a demand-based (differential) pricing structure. How would you advise them to do it?

Ability to Manage Differential Pricing

In Chapter 4 you learned that differential pricing is a powerful revenue optimization tool. While that is true, it is also true that as the number of prices to be managed increases, the managerial skill and sophistication required to manage them will increase as well.

Figure 12.2 presents this challenge graphically. As the number of prices to be managed increases, the difficulty of managing them also increases. Figure 12.2 also helps explain an important line written by Robert L. Phillips, Ph.D. Dr. Philips is a lecturer at Stanford University and the author of the excellent text *Pricing and Revenue Management*.

On that book's first page, Phillips writes to his student readers, "The book assumes familiarity with **probabilistic modeling** and optimization theory and comfort with basic calculus."[4]

Essential RM Term

Probabilistic modeling: The application of statistical formulas to past events for the purpose of predicting the likelihood of future events.

If you are not a Stanford University MBA student, as are most of Dr. Phillip's students, then you may not be familiar with probabilistic modeling, basic calculus, or even the term *optimization theory.* Perhaps this definition of that last term from the Wolfram Mathworld web site (www.mathworld.wolfram.com) can help. This math-related web site defines optimization theory as:

> A branch of mathematics which . . . includes the calculus of variations, control theory, convex optimization theory, decision theory, game theory, linear programming, Markov chains, network analysis, optimization theory, queuing systems, etc.[5]

If you are still not sure about applying optimization theory to your own differential pricing tasks, . . . you are not alone.

However, if your educational background includes calculus as well as training in advanced statistical methods including multiple regression analysis, you may be very comfortable implementing an extremely complex revenue optimization strategy involving the manipulation of hundreds or even thousands of prices. Certainly the approaches to pricing and revenue optimization taken by Ph.D.s teaching in elite business schools are not wrong. Those approaches may, however, be too complex to be easily implemented by many RMs working in many hospitality-related service industries.

Sophisticated mathematical models based on historical data can be very useful in predicting future events. But it is also good to acknowledge the observation of creative thinker and author

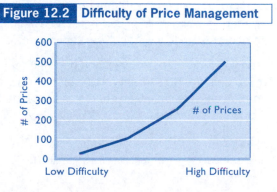

Figure 12.2 **Difficulty of Price Management**

Edward de Bono, who correctly pointed out, "There is never any justification for things being complex when they could be simple."[6] Of course, what is complex for one RM may be easy for another. Background, experience, and training can increase the ability of an RM to manage an increasingly complex pricing system. In nearly every case, however, a simple pricing is considerably more useful to an organization than an excessively complex system.

There are several reasons this is true. First, RMs in any service industry (including hospitality) must themselves understand how they arrive at their prices. Computer programs and mathematical models that take data RMs already understand and present that data in a more useful format are helpful. However, the purchase and implementation of highly advanced computer-based pricing programs that simply call for RMs to trust the program without first understanding precisely how it works or its potential impact on customers should be avoided in the same way investors should avoid putting their money into financial institutions or financial instruments they do not understand.

Nolan Wrentmore, Aimbridge Hospitality's corporate director of revenue management put it nicely when commenting on the lodging industry's possible overdependence on algorithm based forecast systems during the worldwide recession that began in 2008; "You're always going to need the human element, someone that will analyze the data ultimately . . . I personally like to understand how things work and where the projections are coming from."[*]

The implementation of an easily understandable and thus manageable pricing system is important for an additional key reason. Simply put, a seller's potential *customers* need to readily grasp the inherent fairness of that seller's pricing structure if a customer-centric revenue optimization system is to be implemented. If RMs find the pricing systems they employ are excessively complex, their ability to explain these systems to their own front-line employees is significantly reduced. When front-line employees do not understand their organization's pricing systems it is impossible for these key staff members to explain the organization's pricing rational to customers.

▶ RM ON THE WEB 12.1

Package tour operators sell products with virtually hundreds of versions and thousands of prices. Vacationers can choose from among a dizzying array of differing locations, departure dates, length of tour, flight arrangements, hotels, and vacation activities. A well-designed web site, however, can make it easy for buyers to know immediately the prices they will be charged and to understand why there is variation in price. To see an example of how such a well-designed site operates, go to www.applevacations.com.

When you arrive, create a vacation package that you would enjoy. Then see for yourself how RMs for this organization straightforwardly manage and communicate the thousands of prices associated with their buyer-customized products and services.

[*]Revenue management proves worth, but not a cure-all. Hotel Business magazine Vol 19 No.7 April 21 May 6, 2010. Page 24

Those organizations that manage prices in ways that RMs, employees, and customers believe are just and rationale can succeed in revenue optimization. The organizations that do not utilize differential pricing—as well as those whose pricing systems are excessively complex—will not generally have the same success.

Ability to Communicate Efforts

Even if a service business possesses each of the characteristics previously identified, its ability to utilize advanced revenue optimization strategies will be limited if it cannot readily communicate those initiatives to its potential customers. This critical communication process must be in place both externally and internally. For example, the hotel RM who reviews forecast information and elects to offer a significant discount for rooms on an upcoming Sunday night must be able to communicate that discount through the hotel's distribution channels. If not, potential customers simply will not know about the price change.

Essential RM Term

Buy-one, get-one: A promotional strategy that permits the buyer of an item to receive a second, identical item, for no additional charge.

In a similar manner, a restaurant RM who wants to promote a new menu item by offering it as a **buy-one, get-one** (BOGO) must communicate that message externally if he or she wishes to create new unit traffic because of the special promotion's existence.

In some service businesses, external signage, the use of a proprietary web site, a customer e-mail list, or traditional advertising may permit direct-to-buyer communication. In other industries, those approaches may not be readily available or may be to slow to be effective.

New customers may be attracted via the external communication of revenue optimization strategies such as discounting, bundling, or versioning, but it is likely those same customers may have detailed questions about the promotional offers upon arrival at the business. For that reason, effective internal communication systems must also be in place for those onsite staff members who will sell directly to buyers. Consider the real-life example of a hotel guest who, when driving by a hotel property, reads an external sign that proclaims "*Ask about our weekday special!*" Upon entering the hotel, the guest inquires about the special promotion.

"We have rooms at $89.00 and special rooms for $99.00," replied the front desk agent.

"What's the difference between the rooms?" asked the guest.

"With the $99.99 room, you get a free breakfast!" was the reply.

Clearly, in this real-life example, the internal seller (the front-desk agent) was not an effective advocate for the promotion. How much better would it have been if the front-desk agent had been trained to give the following alternative response to the guest's inquiry?

"Both rooms are lovely, but the $99.00 room includes a complimentary breakfast normally priced at $14.99. When you choose that room, we include the breakfast and you save more than $5.00 a night!"

In Chapter 2 you learned that a strategic price is a concept, not a number. In this hotel example, the desk agent knew the $99.00 number, but did not convey to the guest the $99.00 value concept.

Those hospitality-related service organizations that are able to successfully implement revenue optimization programs develop effective systems for rapidly, clearly, and accurately communicating their RM strategies and tactics to their external as well as their internal audiences.

SERVICE INDUSTRIES APPLYING REVENUE OPTIMIZATION STRATEGIES

You have learned that there are seven key characteristics of organizations that can successfully implement revenue optimization strategies. If you are an RM for a hospitality-related service business, you can readily assess your own organization's ability to implement revenue optimization strategies by using the Organizational Assessment format shown in Figure 12.3. To illustrate its use, information that would be utilized by a RM evaluating the

Figure 12.3	**Organizational Assessment: Public Golf Course**
1. Constrained supply	Yes: The number of golfers allowed on the course at one time must be restricted to ensure that speed of play is in keeping with industry norms and golfer expectations.
2. High fixed costs	Yes: The incremental cost of allowing each additional golfer on the course is minimal. If golfers purchase the use of electric carts, food and beverages, or golfing supplies from the Pro shop, each incremental golfer likely contributes additional revenue that exceeds his or her incremental costs.
3. Variable demand	Yes: In most cases demand is predictably highest on weekends and selected holidays. In most cases, demand is lowest in the very early weekday mornings and the very late afternoons.
4. Versioning opportunities	Yes: Traditional versioning includes offering 9-hole and 18-hole options. Creative RMs, however, can devise additional product versions based on a variety of factors such as tee-off time, frequency of customer visit, or age of golfers.
5. Perishable inventory	Yes: The saleable inventory unit consists of rounds of golf played per day. Like hotel room nights this inventory cannot be carried over from one day to the next.
6. Ability to manage differential pricing	Could be limited and thus restricting. The typical smaller course may not have sophisticated POS capability. In many cases, single employee staffing restricts the ability to effectively implement highly sophisticated or complex product pricing strategies.
7. Ability to communicate efforts	Beyond traditional price advertising, this could be limited and thus restricted. The typical golfer may visit a course's web site or hear of it through other golfers; however, call-in or walk-in golfers (buyers) are very common. External communications may be limited to electronic communication with those golfers who have previously used the facility or who have been exposed to the course's advertising. As a result, well-designed external and internal communication programs will be essential if an effective differential pricing program is to be implemented.

Figure 12.4	Service Industries Able to Utilize Revenue Optimization Strategies

- Bars
- Bed and breakfasts
- Campgrounds
- Car rentals
- Casinos
- Catering services
- Comedy clubs
- Concert halls
- Convention centers
- Cruise ships
- Dining clubs
- Golf courses

- Health clubs
- Hotels
- Janitorial services
- Live concerts/ performances
- Motels
- Night clubs
- Personal/fitness training
- Race tracks
- Recreational equipment rentals
- Resorts

- Restaurants
- Ski resorts/lifts
- Spas
- Sporting events
- Swimming clubs/pools
- Tanning services
- Theaters/cinemas
- Theme parks
- Timeshares (lodging)
- Uniform services providers
- Water parks

potential for applying revenue optimization strategies at an open-to-the-public golf course has been supplied.

While every business entity is unique, the hospitality-related service industries listed in Figure 12.4 are among those that, after careful assessment, are likely able to apply effective revenue management strategies to optimize their business income.

It is important to recall, however, that revenue optimization is not best viewed as a matter of price manipulation designed to extract the maximum amount of money from a business's customers. Revenue optimization is a customer-centric process designed to maximize your customers' value formula (and their profits) as the best means of increasing your own profits.

SPECIALIZED REVENUE MANAGEMENT DUTIES

Thus far, the revenue optimization tools and tasks presented in this book apply primarily to the duties and responsibilities of RMs who work at the individual property level. Those professionals certainly play a crucial role in the implementation of revenue optimization strategies. As you learned in Chapter 5, however, the job duties and titles of individual RMs in the hospitality industry can vary greatly.

Because you now know about the specific activities used by property level RMs to enhance their unit revenues, you can better appreciate the roles played by two different, but increasingly important, RM-related jobs. Both of these positions are designed to assist property-level RMs in their duties as well as to aid those operations that are too small to employ a full-time RM. Although the specific job titles for these positions vary, based on the organization that employs them, the positions themselves can be broadly classified as one of the following:

- Revenue managers with multiunit responsibilities
- Franchisor-based revenue managers

Revenue Managers with Multiunit Responsibilities

If you are an RM responsible for the income optimization efforts for more than one company unit, your job will be different from that of a property-level RM. At the multiunit or corporate level, your assigned tasks may involve communicating details about company-wide revenue optimization strategies and systems to the organization's individual operations or other administrative staff. Additional responsibilities of multiunit RMs may include the assessment of companywide sales data and revenue forecasting as well as the implementation of overall pricing strategies.

In addition to their corporate-level assignments most RMs with multiunit responsibilities are given the task of training, coordinating, and advising their companies' property-level RMs. In this role, the RM takes on the important job of coach. In some cases, RMs who are very talented at analyzing their own property-level data and applying their own experiences to data interpretation find it difficult to pass those same skills on to others. The best RM teachers are those who are successful in conveying to others their technical skills and their passion for the job. Experienced coaches in all fields know that it is their task to help individuals enhance their individual skills by providing needed information and tools. They must also encourage those they coach to do what must be done to realize their full potential. Legendary football coach Vince Lombardi pointed this truth out clearly when he stated, "Coaches who can outline plays on a blackboard are a dime a dozen. The ones who win get inside their player and motivate."[7]

Those RMs who are successful at the multiunit level take great satisfaction in motivating and shaping the professional development of their property-level staff. Figure 12.5 lists tasks that are typical of those assigned to a lodging industry RM responsible for multiple hotels.

Note in Figure 12.5 that an important responsibility of multiunit RMs is the maintenance of a positive relationship with their brand's managers. In Chapter 4 you learned that most hotels in the United States are affiliated with a brand (franchise). Restaurants too are highly franchised.

In the increasingly branded foodservice industry, many franchisors sell and manage only one brand. Thus, for example, the Burger King Corporation, founded in Miami, Florida in 1954, franchises only the Burger King brand. Of Burger King's over 11,000 stores, 90 percent are operated by franchisees, with many of those franchisees being multiunit operators.[8]

Alternatively, Louisville, Kentucky-based Yum Brands bills itself as the world's largest restaurant company. Yum's 36,000 restaurants include the well-known KFC, Pizza Hut, Taco Bell, and Long John Silvers brands. Nearly all of Yum's units are franchised and it is not uncommon for one franchisee to operate multiple YUM brands.

In the lodging industry, it is also common for franchisors to offer potential franchisees a variety of brand choices. At the time of this book's printing, for example, Wyndham Hotels' 7000+ franchised properties include units branded as Wyndham, Ramada, Day's

Figure 12.5	**Typical Multiunit RM Responsibilities**

- Overseeing, managing, and coordinating each property's guest room rates and effective inventory strategies designed for RevPAR growth
- Monitoring competitors' pricing and makes internal adjustments accordingly
- Responsible for setting property-level selling strategies and promoting team-based learning
- Creating and analyzing booking pace tools used at each property
- Maintaining strong relationships with all the company's E-Commerce distribution partners
- Knowing all GDS and IDS distribution channels, including the cost per reservation associated with each channel
- Analyzing property-level room revenue forecasts to ensure the ability to forecast within 5 percent accuracy
- Leading strategic thinking, which creates action plans that will result in an effective mix of business for each property
- Effectively measuring the impact and results of all revenue optimization strategies employed
- Providing critical analysis of company-wide strategies, room statistics and demand factors
- Reviewing property-level sales and call sheets and/or sales goals weekly/monthly
- Ensuring each hotel has a logical plan for taking on-site transient reservations
- Working directly with property-level RMs, directors of sales and general managers
- If managing franchised units, maintaining a strong relationship with the brand's revenue management professionals
- Conducting monthly and quarterly revenue meetings with their own immediate supervisor

---

Inn, Super 8, Wingate, Baymont, Microtel, Hawthorne Suites, Howard Johnson, Travelodge, Knights Inn and AmeriHost Inn. Choice Hotels International markets the Clarion, Comfort, Comfort Suites, Quality, Cambria Suites, Mainstay Suites, EconoLodge, Rodeway Inn, and Sleep Inn brands. Marriott, Hilton, and Carlson also franchise multiple brands. Thus, it is easy to see that an RM with multiunit responsibility in the lodging or foodservice industry might be responsible for the income optimization efforts of differently branded properties franchised by a single franchisor or by a number of different franchisors.

As is true in a number of other business areas, brand consolidation is shrinking the number of different brand operators (but not brands) in the hospitality industry. It is also true that the franchisor model so popular in foodservices and lodging will likely

RM IN ACTION 12.1: CORPORATE REVENUE MANAGER WANTED!

As recently as the early 2000s, use of the job title *Revenue Manager* was virtually nonexistent in the U.S. hospitality industry. By the mid-2000s, advertisements seeking *revenue managers* for positions in the lodging (but not foodservice) industry were quite common. The following is typical of the information contained in position announcements seeking individuals to work as a revenue manager for a *multiunit* hotel operator. As you read it, consider whether your own familiarity with revenue optimization activities lets you grasp the duties and responsibilities of this position.

Job Title: Corporate Revenue Manager

Job Description: Corporate Revenue Manager needed for large and expanding international hotel company. Position reports to the Corporate Director of Revenue. This unique opportunity combines hospitality/travel industry knowledge and Internet channel management into a single position. Position offers opportunities for advancement and has direct exposure to senior management.

Job Duties:

- Providing assistance to both corporate and property-level personnel

- Developing and delivering corporate and property-level analysis using data collection, data maintenance, and data querying skills

- Analyzing short- and long-term forecasting, analyzing trends in group inventories and rates

- Monitoring and analyzing the competition daily and weekly

- Analyzing booking pace; making recommendations for short- and long-term rate strategy

- Monitoring and implementing appropriate brand-initiated optimization strategies and tools

Skills Required: The best candidate will have the following skills or experiences:

- Hospitality technology familiarity in CRS, PMS, and/or RM systems

- Distribution technology familiarity in GDS

- Knowledge of MS Excel

- Business or hospitality/travel industry degree or comparable hotel-level experience in revenue management, front office, sales, or e-commerce

- Minimum of 2–3 years hotel or hospitality industry operations, sales, and/or revenue management experience

Education Required: College degree preferred, but a combination of education and experience that provides the required knowledge, skills, and abilities is also acceptable.

spread to other independently own hospitality-related businesses such as tanning salons, comedy clubs, health clubs, and ski resorts as these business owners seek the business advantages that accompany franchise affiliation. In all cases, however, it is important that a multiunit RM with responsibilities for branded properties understand well and take advantage of the revenue optimization tools and positive strategies employed by that brand's managers.

> ▶ **RM ON THE WEB 12.2**

The number of job openings for RMs of all types continues to increase. To view a current listing of property level, multiunit, and franchisor-based revenue management positions in the lodging segment of hospitality, go to www.hcareers.com

While you are there, choose *Restaurants* from the *Industry* category and then choose *Revenue Manager* from the *Management* positions drop-down menu. You will not get many listings. Watch for the number of advertisements seeking qualified RMs in foodservice to increase in the coming years, however, as more industry professionals recognize the importance of their customer-centric revenue management efforts.

Franchisor-based Revenue Managers

Although some hospitality industry observers view it positively and others view it quite negatively, the number of hospitality and hospitality-related businesses owners choosing to affiliate with franchisors is ever increasing. In the United States, the overwhelming majority of hotels are branded. As well, each year, an increasing proportion of restaurants that are opened are franchise units rather than independent operations. As a result of the popularity of franchising, increasing numbers of revenue managers are employed directly by franchisors. In those positions, RMs perform their jobs in one of three major areas:

> Internal brand support
>
> Brand partner support
>
> Franchisee support

Internal Brand Support

Those RMs who are employed directly by a brand may work at the franchisor's corporate headquarters, at a regional office, or even out of their own homes. These RM professionals are most commonly assigned to support-related jobs. In this role, they assist others within the corporation in the implementation of revenue management-related strategies, tactics, and tasks.

For a single illustration of the work performed by RMs at the corporate level, consider a scenario in which a hotel brand's corporate-level sales and marketing team is successful in securing a chainwide contract for a large corporation's travel business. In such a situation, the newly agreed-upon rate and its accompanying rate code must be appropriately loaded into the CRS serving each of the brand hotels' PMSs, as well as in the GDS, IDS, and any other distribution channel utilized by each of the properties affiliated with the brand. If this is not done promptly and accurately, the new client corporation's travel managers will not be able to easily book and receive the appropriate contracted rate when they call to make

RM IN ACTION 12.2: WANTED: ADVANCEMENTS IN RATE LOADING!

If you ask corporate travel managers across the country to identify one of their biggest complaints with the hotel industry, it would relate to the loading of negotiated (contracted) rates. Lodging industry RMs are aware of the difficulties. Despite that awareness, however, a variety of problems still prevent prompt and accurate loading of negotiated hotel rates into the GDS or into the CRSs of the brand's individual hotels.

The loading process is grueling, time-consuming, error prone, and often frustrating, as clearly indicated by the comments of one exasperated corporate rooms buyer reported by Management Travel reporter Lauren Darsen and posted on the Pro Media web site:

> "There is still a chronic delay in loading hotel rates," said Gilead Sciences Inc. corporate travel manager Rick Wakida. "I don't get the feeling that the process has improved. It doesn't matter if it is on the part of a chain or an independent hotel."

Annual negotiated rates typically expire December 31. If the newly renegotiated rate is not in the GDSs by January 1, room buyers or their travel management companies cannot access them, leaving the traveler to call the hotel directly for a rate quote. That rate is usually significantly higher than the negotiated rate.

In many cases, it takes weeks or even months to get a negotiated rate loaded for all of a large brand's many hotels. This is especially true when the brand consists of thousands of individually owned and operated hotels, many of whom, for a variety of reasons, do not respond immediately to requests or suggestions made by *corporate*!

According to vice president of worldwide sales strategy for Intercontinental Hotels Group (IHG) Jill Cady, a major contributor to the delay in hotel rate loading is the lengthy negotiation period, which occurs throughout the fall months but can extend beyond that. Cady suggests that individual buyers work out a more efficient approach in order to complete negotiations earlier in the year. That strategy and others employed by knowledgeable lodging industry RMs will no doubt help, but brand-level RMs will have to do even more to make this problem go away permanently. As a well-trained RM, what are your suggestions?

Excerpted on 2/10/2009 from www.management.travel.

room reservations for their traveling employees. This challenge is especially significant if the brand's portfolio consists of thousands of hotels operated by hundreds of different owners. If the brand's RMs cannot get the rate loaded properly, the successful hard work of the company's sales and marketing team will be greatly diminished.

In addition to supporting the sales effort, corporate-level RMs also assist those **internal customers** such as marketing, operations, data management, and even financial management staff as each functional area seeks to use its specialized expertise to enhance the reputation and value of the franchisor's brand(s).

Essential RM Term

Internal customer: A co-worker or another department who receives services produced elsewhere in the company to then create a product or service for the company's external customers.

Figure 12.6 **External Brand Management Efforts**

Partners ⟷ Brand Efforts ⟷ Franchisees

Brand Partner Support

In addition to those RMs serving internal customers, other franchisor-based RMs efforts are undertaken to enhance the brand image. These efforts are typically aimed at one of two external audiences. As illustrated in Figure 12.6, brand-specific RMs' external brand enhancement efforts can be directed toward either their brand partners or their franchisees.

If you are not familiar with the ways in which franchisors operate, it might surprise you to know about the varied business entities that are directly associated with them. Collectively known as **brand partners**, these businesses provide franchisors with the many products and services required for promoting and managing their brands.

Essential RM Term

Brand partner: A business entity utilized by a franchisor to achieve the goals of one or more of that franchisor's brands.

To illustrate this concept using an operations-related foodservice example, you would likely agree that McDonald's knows the importance of consistency when purchasing buns for its sandwich products. It is also true, however, that the McDonald's corporation does not purchase buns. Its franchisees purchase buns. As a result, one task of McDonald's operations-related brand managers is ensuring that each franchisee in its system has access to a bakery supplier that can provide sandwich buns of the size, quality, and consistency mandated by McDonald's. If this effort were not undertaken, bakery product uniformity across the brand could be reduced and the important consistency-related image of the McDonald's brand would be lessened. Franchisor-based RMs help the brand partners with which they work provide the same consistency of product and services, as do McDonald's purchasing and operations staff in this example.

Those RMs whose work is directly related to franchisee support seek to further the financial interests of their company's brand and its franchisees. To illustrate, consider the RM employed by a franchisor to ensure each of the brand's properties is given maximum exposure when potential customers browse the web. In this case, the franchisor-based RM might seek to develop effective partnerships with different web site operators perceived to be of benefit to the brand's franchisees. The specific online travel sellers of greatest importance, however, would likely be very different for RMs affiliated with branded hotels in the **economy hotel** segment (e.g., EconoLodge, Red Roof Inn, Motel 6, Super 8, and Travelodge) than

Essential RM Term

Economy hotel (segment): Those hotel properties providing limited amenities and no onsite food and beverage services (except for morning coffee and light breakfast). This industry category typically contains properties in the bottom 30 percent price tier of the local market.

Essential RM Term

Midscale hotel (segment): Hotels that offer some business and recreational amenities fall into the midscale category. Midscale hotels may or may not offer food and beverage services. This segment typically contains properties with ADRs between the 40th and 70th percentile of the room pricing structure of the local market.

those of importance to RMs affiliated with properties in the **midscale hotel** segment (e.g., Comfort Inn, Hampton Inn, Holiday Inn Express, and SpringHill Suites). The decisions made by each of these RMs will be important to the long-term success of their individual brands. Other partnerships important to RMs in all hotel segments include those related to the GDS, IDS, and each of a brand's other important distribution channel partners.

The specific brand partnerships maintained by a franchise company will vary based on the industry and industry segment associated with the brand. Today's common brand partnerships include those related to a wide variety of businesses serving the RM-related needs of hospitality industry businesses.

Essential RM Term

Franchise services representative (FSR): A franchisor representative assigned to assist franchisees in the operation of their franchised unit(s).

Franchisee Support

As brand executives increasingly recognize the importance of implementing revenue optimization strategies, the number of RM specialists they employ has increased. In many cases, the assignments of these RMs are to work directly with the company's franchisees as a **franchise services representative (FSR)**.

▶ RM ON THE WEB 12.3

In the lodging industry, third-party web site operators are one of a brand's most important partnership categories. Property placement on these web sites will directly affect the number of bookings received from the sites. To illustrate this fact, choose a mid- to large-sized city you would like to visit.

Now consider the franchisor-based RMs responsible for securing outstanding placement for their own franchisees on a popular third-party operated web site such as Expedia.com.

Each franchisor-based RM would like you to select one of their hotels when you visit your chosen city. Now go to www.expedia.com

When you arrive, choose a date for your visit, enter that date and notice the *order* of hotels listed on the results page. Each franchisor would, of course, prefer to see its partners list the hotels within its brand first. If you choose a career as a franchisor-based RM, it may someday be your job to help make that happen!

The actual job title used to identify a FSR varies by franchisor. One important task of all RMs serving in the FSR role, however, is that of helping to explain the franchisor's revenue optimization strategies and tools to their franchisees' property-level front office, sales, marketing, and other staff, including the property's GM.

If you are the property-level RM of a franchised business in the hospitality or hospitality-related industries you are likely to interact with your franchisor's FSRs whether you are responsible for a single property or for multiple properties. To fully appreciate the role of a franchisor-based RM, it is first important to understand that a franchisor's income derives from the gross revenues, not the net profits, of their franchisees. This fact could sometimes influence the advice given by an FSR, and it also means franchisees must always judiciously consider the guidance given by their FSRs.

In the lodging industry, the total fees charged by franchisors to franchisees typically range from 5 to 15 percent of gross sales. Although the specific fees charged to franchisees will vary by industry, those revenue-related fees charged by most lodging industry franchisors include:

Royalty fees: Charged for the use of the brand's name, logos, and other franchise services.

Advertising or marketing contribution fees: Charged for participation in national or regional advertising programs of various types.

Reservation fees: When the brand operates a reservation system, this fee is charged to offset the telephones, computers, and reservation-related staff required to operate the CRS.

Frequent traveler program fees: Most franchisors offer incentive programs designed to reward guests for frequent stays. This fee is assessed for each reservation made through the program and is charged to recover costs related to the program's operation and administration.

Other fees: These fees can relate to a variety of programs, including technical support for franchisor-mandated computer systems, national training programs, and regional or national meetings and conferences.

Those foodservice companies who sell franchises and manage specific restaurant brands have their own revenue-based fee structures. These fees can range from lows of 1 to 2 percent of gross sales to combined royalty and marketing fees as high as 8.5 percent for a popular restaurant brand such as a Burger King.[9] In the case of a highly sought after McDonald's franchise, total fees can exceed 12.5 percent of monthly revenues.[10]

Because franchisor income is based on revenue *generated* rather than franchisee profits realized, one too-little-discussed challenge faced by all franchisor-employed RMs is that of credibility. Questions related to the trustworthiness of franchisor actions are very common among franchisees of all brands. This is so because in the past it has been readily apparent that a franchisor's revenue enhancement initiatives, many times forced on its franchisees, viewed by the franchisees simply as an attempt to build franchisor revenues at the expense of franchisee profits.

As you have learned, a focus on building revenue is typically a very good thing for a business. You have also learned, however, that both buyer and seller must benefit in an economic exchange. If you are employed as a franchisor-based RM in the hospitality industry, your franchisees, not your franchisee's guests, are your customers. As a result, the

> **▶ RM ON THE WEB 12.4**
>
> If you have, or plan, an RM career as a franchisor's representative, it is good to stay current on the attitudes of the franchisees who will make up your own customers.
>
> Participation in chain-sponsored meetings and conferences is a good start, but these events expose you only to the views of your current customers. To stay abreast of the concerns and needs of your potential customers (franchisees), attendance at one or both of the two major lodging industry trade association annual meetings can be very helpful.
>
> The American Hotel and Lodging Association's (AH&LA) annual meeting is held each November in New York. You can learn more about this year's event by going to www.ahla.com
>
> The 20-year-old Asian American Hotel Owners Association's (AAHOA) 9,000-plus members include over 40 percent of all the U.S. lodging industry's property owners. It has been an extremely vocal and effective advocate for expanding the rights of lodging industry franchisees. Its annual meeting is held in April. You can learn more about this year's meeting by going to www.aahoa.com

Essential RM Term

Brand equity: The accumulated value of a brand's image or identity as perceived by consumers. In the hospitality industry, some important attributes of brand equity are consistency, quality, and value.

long-term value (profit) delivered to your franchisees must be the principal reason for implementing any new revenue enhancement program. If the revenue enhancement programs you seek to launch are not viewed in that manner, the **brand equity** you seek to enhance will not be increased but instead will actually diminish in the eyes of your current franchisees and your prospective franchisees.

REVENUE MANAGEMENT AND DESTINATION MARKETING

In Chapter 6 you learned that a CVB (convention and visitors bureau) is the short-hand term commonly used to identify the entity responsible for promoting travel and tourism in a specifically designated geographic area or destination. While it is true that the terms revenue management and destination marketing are *not* synonymous, for those industry professionals working in the area of destination marketing, the issues of constrained supply management, differential pricing, and communicating value for price paid are all present.

RM AT WORK 12.2

Angela Tuller is the CEO of Sandstone Hotels, a rapidly growing, privately held (owned) lodging company that owns 20 hotel properties and that manages, for other hotel owners, an additional 15 properties.

"I really like your brand," said Angela to Chuck Ledsing, the franchise sales representative for Sleep Well hotels. "As you know, our company already operates four Sleep Wells, and I'm pleased with the brand and how those properties perform in their markets."

"Then why are you considering Waterford Inns for your new property's flag?" asked Chuck. "Our Sleep Wells outperform Waterford's ADR in every market where we compete head to head with them."

"I know that's true," replied Angela, "but the Waterford's occupancy rate is higher, and it's a growing brand. Just like yours. And their franchise fees are 2 percent lower than yours!" replied Angela.

1. Assume you were the corporate RM responsible for leading ADR building efforts at Sleep Well hotels. What types of information do you think Chuck would need from you as he tries to sell Angela your company's brand for her new property?

2. Assume you were the corporate RM responsible for building occupancy percentage at Waterford Inns. What types of information do you think your own sales representative would want from you as he or she tries to sell Angela your company's brand for her new property?

3. Assume you were the Corporate RM at Angela's company. How important do you think your personal relationship with each brand's corporate-level RMs would be in obtaining from them the information Angela will likely need to get from you as she seeks to make this important decision?

As a result, those who seek to market a specific destination must understand very well the principles of revenue management presented in this book.

To illustrate, consider the hospitality professional working at a CVB whose responsibilities include seeking to attract increased numbers of visitors during their area's off-peak travel periods. For ski resort areas, this may be the warm summer months. For a beach location, it may be the colder winter months. In some cases, a metropolitan area itself, a local attraction, or even the local scenery may be the most important draw. In all these cases, however, an understanding of revenue management concepts will aid this professional's understanding of how to best assist area hotels, restaurants, and attractions as they jointly try to optimize their area's overall tourism-related revenue.

If you seek a career in the destination marketing area it is also important to recognize that most entities responsible for marketing geographic locations are governmental or quasi-governmental agencies. Because they receive public funding (typically via a tax on hotel rooms sold in the area), one important task of destination marketing professionals is that of communicating to their constituencies the responsible management of the funds they receive, as well as the positive financial impact of their activities on their local economies.

▶ RM ON THE WEB 12.5

The Destination Marketing Association International (DMAI) is a professional trade association of great interest to revenue managers working in the area of destination marketing. In addition to member education and other professional development activities, DMAI maintains online postings of position vacancies. To review the types of positions available and the varied geographic locations now seeking professionals with revenue management-related skills, go to www. destinationmarketing.org

When you arrive at the site, click on *Resources*; then click *DMAI Career Center* to see a list of currently available destination marketing positions and the specific duties associated with them.

RM IN ACTION 12.3: WHAT HAPPENED IN VEGAS. . .

In 2003, the Las Vegas ad shop R&R Partners conceived the line "What Happens Here Stays Here." The line became wildly popular and it fit the city's worldwide marketing efforts perfectly. Following a relatively unsuccessful mid-1990s attempt to increase its marketing among families, the new and somewhat risqué tag line described the Las Vegas experience in the 2000s exceptionally well. Destination marketers for Las Vegas promoted an image that was fun, exciting . . . and a bit extravagant. Visitors responded in record numbers.

Unfortunately for many travel destinations, the worldwide economic downturn that began in 2008 had a devastatingly negative effect on business and leisure travel. As the United States and the world's other major economies slowed in 2008 and the slowdown continued into 2009, Las Vegas too began to feel the economic pinch, and its RevPAR levels began to decline somewhat. But Vegas was still lots of fun . . . right?!

In early 2009, when newly-elected President Barack Obama cautioned banks and other institutions receiving monetary assistance from the federal government to spend that money carefully, Las Vegas found its fun-loving reputation worked against it. As reported in the February 15, 2009, global edition of the *New York Times*:

> "Anxiety among hotel executives in Las Vegas escalated when President Barack Obama told an audience in Elkhart, Indiana, that companies "can't go take a trip to Las Vegas or go down to the Super Bowl on the taxpayer's dime."

The president later stated he was not opposed to visiting Las Vegas specifically, but he did oppose "wasteful" spending. The result? Business meetings that were to be held in Vegas were canceled in record numbers. Data for the first four months of 2009 indicated convention attendance was down 23 percent and ADR was down 31.7 percent compared to the prior year. The projected image of excess, extravagance, and naughtiness was now working *against* Las Vegas.

Amid the increased cancellations of meetings, Las Vegas responded by utilizing new marketing tactics that emphasized its competitive costs and easy-to-reach location. Despite that effort, the weak economic climate caused RevPAR in Las Vegas to decline significantly in 2009.

The Las Vegas lesson is that destination marketing tactics must change when circumstances warrant. Both positive and negative external or internal events can affect the revenue optimization approaches utilized by those RMs working in this exciting, but very competitive and often volatile segment of the hospitality industry.

Excerpted on 2/15/2009 from www.iht.com/Las Vegas Sags As Conventions Cancel.

❖ ESSENTIAL RM TERMS

Service industry	Internal customer
Shoulder period	Brand partner
Package tour	Economy hotel (segment)
Attraction	Midscale hotel (segment)
Probabilistic modeling	Franchise services representative (FSR)
Buy-one, get-one	Brand equity

⫸ APPLY WHAT YOU KNOW

1. Kevin Sharp owns a five-bed tanning salon in Plant City, Florida. He is considering implementing an aggressive revenue optimization program. Help Kevin determine if such an approach might be right for his business by completing the following organizational assessment tool. If you are unfamiliar with Kevin's industry, discuss the assessment tool with a friend who is familiar with it, or visit a local tanning salon yourself.

Organizational Assessment: <u>Tanning Salon</u>	
1. Constrained supply	
2. High fixed costs	
3. Variable demand	

(*continued*)

Organizational Assessment: Tanning Salon (Continued)	
4. Versioning opportunities	
5. Perishable inventory	
6. Ability to manage differential pricing	
7. Ability to communicate efforts	

2. Mandy Davies is the newly appointed corporate RM for Saga Hotels. Saga owns and operates ten hotels consisting of three Holiday Inn Express properties, two Comfort Inns, one Hampton, one Residence Inn, one Motel 6, and two Country Inn and Suites. The hotels are located within 300 miles of each other. At the request of Mandy's boss (Saga's vice president of operations) Mandy is seeking to standardize the RM-related reporting of each property's RM-related activity.

   A. List five specific pieces of information you believe Mandy would need to receive monthly from each property if she wanted to effectively monitor the company's overall RM-related efforts and results.

   B. Explain your rationale for each of the pieces of information you believe Mandy should receive.

   C. Identify the names of all the franchise companies with which Saga is affiliated.

   D. What difficulties do you think Mandy may encounter due to the variety of franchisors with whom they affiliate?

   E. What potential advantages do you think Mandy could gain due to the variety of franchisors with whom they affiliate?

3. Wiredup.com is one of the hotel industries most popular discount booking sites. Dana Bash is the corporate RM for a hotel company franchising the upscale Lexor hotel brand. Dana works directly with her company's 50 franchisees, most of whom operate their properties in downtown metropolitan areas. Wiredup.com constitutes one of their largest sources of their Internet-delivered room reservations. Recently, Wiredup.com has begun to quote its online rates followed by the statement, *"Additional hotel fees may apply."*

   In nearly all of Dana's hotels, overnight parking is not free to guests and can constitute a significant expense. In some cases, the cost of providing parking can be as much as 25 percent of the heavily discounted rates charged by Wiredup. Increasingly, Dana's franchisees are reporting that some of their arriving guests are very upset upon hearing that parking charges are not included in their room rates. Wiredup. com does not refund room purchases once they have been made, so arriving guests cannot express their unhappiness by cancelling their rooms. Dana's franchisees have presented the problem to her.

A. Why do you believe this brand partner implemented the new pricing disclaimer? Explain your answer.

B. Is this brand partner operating in a manner that is detrimental to Dana's hotels? Explain your answer.

C. Is this brand partner operating in a manner that is detrimental to the guests arriving at Dana's hotels? Explain your answer.

D. What specific action do you think would be appropriate for Dana to take in this situation?

E. What other challenges might Dana face when utilizing intermediaries to help sell her properties' rooms?

4. National Hotels Company is the franchisor for the relatively new *Home Too* hotel brand. Currently, 30 franchisees operate approximately 70 hotels nationally. The National Hotels president is Ralph Hitz. Ralph is convinced that if he created an online revenue management training program, and if his current franchisees used it properly, the RevPAR increases achieved by each of the company's franchisees would approach double digits within 12 months. He further reasons that the improved performance experienced by current franchisees would increase his chances of making more sales to prospective *Home Too* franchises.

A. Ralph's company Controller feels any costs related to designing and implementing the new training program should be split equally among the current franchisees because they would be the ones to benefit most from an increase in RevPAR. Do you agree?

B. Ralph's vice president for franchise sales feels that to stay competitive, any costs related to the revenue management program should be waived for new franchisees who have not yet committed to buying the brand. Do you agree?

C. Ralph's vice president for marketing feels that all current and future franchises should be given free and unlimited access to the new program since it will increase the total revenue generated by the brand's franchisees. Do you agree?

D. How do you think the National Hotel Company generates its own revenue?

E. If you were Ralph, how would you proceed regarding the development and deployment of the new revenue management training tool? Explain your answer.

5. Tom Gaylon is the executive director of the Greater Pikesville CVB. Pikesville is a popular tourist destination noted for its vibrant downtown and area attractions. The 25 hotels in the Pikesville area average a 65 percent annual occupancy; with occupancies in the 80s and 90s during the summer, but falling to the 50s and 60s during the coldest winter months.

Pikesville has recently completed work on an expansion of their area convention center. Mr. Gaylon wants to utilize the convention center's extensive meeting space to attract group business and thus help increase area hotel occupancies throughout the year. Because of your knowledge of RM principles, he has asked if you can help his CVB sales staff better target their marketing efforts to optimize revenue at the convention center and in the area hotels.

A. In this scenario, what is the product or service being sold? Who is the seller? Who is the customer?

B. Describe the likely characteristics of Pikeville's competitive set. How important would it be for you and the CVB sales staff to be thoroughly familiar with each set member's features, benefits, and characteristics?

C. Based on your knowledge of the variation in occupancy experienced by Pikeville's hotels, do you think opportunities likely exist for applying differential pricing principles for the use of the convention center? Explain your answer.

D. How do you think potential users of the convention space would define *value* received during their visits to Pikeville?

E. Hotel room rates and menu prices are controlled by hotel and restaurant owners, not by an area CVB. What special revenue optimization-related challenges do you feel are present when a RM does not have the authority to determine prices? Explain your answer.

KEY CONCEPT CASE STUDY

"Thanks for meeting with me, Damario," said Pam, the DOSM for the Barcena Resort. "I truly appreciate it. I have a decision to make and I'd really like your input."

"No problem," replied Damario, the revenue manager at the Barcena Resort. "How can I help?"

"You know that I'm on the TDB Board," said Pam, referring to her position on the board of directors for the area's Tourism Development Bureau (TDB). The Bureau was the entity charged with the task of generating sales leads (primarily for group and meetings business) for all of the hotels operating in the Barcena's market area.

"Right. That's an important position for our property," said Damario.

"And that's why I wanted to talk to you," replied Pam. "The Bureau is asking all of its members to commit a significant amount of money to an ad campaign designed to promote travel to our area during the off season."

"That sounds reasonable," said Damario.

"It is reasonable," replied Pam, "but the catch is that no mention will be made in the ads of any specific property. The campaign targets our beaches and attractions, not the properties."

"And your question is whether you should commit to using part of your advertising budget to support the campaign?" asked Damario.

"No, not really. I am convinced all of the local properties can get a bigger bang for our advertising buck by pooling our resources. And you know we could use the extra volume during our slower periods."

"I certainly agree with that!" said Damario. "So where is your concern?"

"My concern relates to measuring the effectiveness of this campaign and our financial contribution to it. I want to know that if the campaign is implemented, we have the tools in place to track its effectiveness. I don't want to contribute this year and maybe again in future years without knowing the precise impact of what we are doing," said Pam. "That's where I need your help. Since you arrived, we have been doing a variety of things to help drive up our revenues. How will I know if increases in income we might achieve are due to those actions we are already taking or are due to this new campaign?"

"Now I see your problem," said Damario.

For Your Consideration

1. In this scenario, the resort's DOSM and RM work closely together to meet their respective goals. In many cases, the explicit goals of these two functional areas are identical. Identify two specific instances in which the interests of these two areas *could* be in conflict. How important do you think it is for a company's revenue manager and its sales and marketing functions to work closely together? Explain your answer.

2. Assume you were Damario; what specific ADR-related tools might you suggest Pam use to help measure the effectiveness of the proposed campaign?

3. Assume you were Damario; what occupancy percentage-related tools might you suggest Pam use to help measure the effectiveness of the proposed campaign?

4. If the proposed ad campaign is implemented and it is effective, what nonrooms-related revenue centers in the resort would likely be affected? How could Pam measure the campaign's affect on these areas?

ENDNOTES

1. http://www.nationsencyclopedia.com/Americas/Argentina-CLIMATE.html. Retrieved 2/2/2009.
2. "Eating Away the Innings in Baseball's Cheap Seats." *USA Today* (March 7–9, 2008), weekend edition.
3. http://thinkexist.com/search/searchquotation.asp?search=differently+. Retrieved 2/4/2009.
4. Robert L. Phillips, *Pricing and Revenue Management*, (Stanford, CA: Stanford Business Books, 2005).
5. http://mathworld.wolfram.com/OptimizationTheory.html. Retrieved 4/20/2009.
6. http://thinkexist.com/quotes/edward_de_bono/3.html. Retrieved 2/10/2008.
7. http://thinkexist.com/quotation/coaches_who_can_outline_plays_on_a_black_board/322630.html. Retrieved 2/10/2009.
8. http://www.bk.com/companyinfo/corporation/facts.aspx. Retrieved 2/10/2009.
9. http://www.bk.com/CompanyInfo/FranchiseOpps/Franchisee_FAQ_1108.pdf. Retrieved 2/10/2009.
10. http://money.howstuffworks.com/franchising1.htm. Retrieved 2/15/2009.

CHAPTER 13

Building Better Business

CHAPTER OUTLINE

CHAPTER HIGHLIGHTS

1. Detailed examination of the key strategies RMs use to build better business.

2. Examination of important revenue optimization issues when market conditions are moderate to strong.

3. Examination of important revenue optimization issues when market conditions are weak or distressed.

KEYS TO BUILDING BETTER BUSINESS

You have learned that RMs are responsible for more than simply achieving top-line revenue targets. As they implement customer-centric revenue optimization programs RMs must be more concerned with the *quality* of revenues achieved than with revenue *quantity.* Doing so requires an understanding of costs, profit margins, and the full impact of decision making on customers and the long-term reputation of the business.

Foodservice industry veteran Herman Zaccarelli has observed that life is often lived backwards. In his book *Management Without Reservations: Leadership Principles for the Manager's Life Journey,* he states:

> In most cases, you must be able to see your end goal before you can begin planning how to achieve it. Whether your management vision involves achieving financial objectives, enhancing your community, improving personal relationships at work, the achievement of specific service levels, or any other measurable objective, your vision should have definitive traits. It must be:
>
> Identifiable
>
> Communicable
>
> Inspiring
>
> Rewarding
>
> When your vision has these characteristics, you will know where you are going and be able to lead others there as well.[1]

If you seek to be a professional RM whose vision is the creation of high-quality revenue (better business) for your own organization, then you too will find that your vision must be identifiable and communicable. On a professional level, your view of customer-centric revenue management must inspire others with whom you work. When it does, you will find revenue management to be a rewarding career both from a professional and a personal perspective.

In the remainder of this chapter you will learn about some of the important keys to building higher-quality revenues for your organization as well as specific strategies you can use for building better business when business is good as well as when it is not so good.

There are very identifiable keys to building better, more profitable business:

- Championing revenue management
- Clearly defined areas of responsibility
- Effective price management
- Candid product and service self-assessment

Championing Revenue Management

If you seek a career as an RM, it is important to recognize that in the hospitality industry, the profession is extremely new. In fact, as recently as 1989, neither the term *revenue management* nor *revenue manager* was even included in the most widely respected and newly published lodging industry text books.[2] When you consider that the occupations of other hospitality professionals such as hotelier, restaurateur, and chef are centuries old, it is easy to see why many nonrevenue management professionals, even within the hospitality industry, do not clearly understand the role or function of a well-trained RM. It is for just that reason RMs who seek to establish their identity and the value of their profession must assume the role of revenue management champion.

In general usage, to champion a concept or cause is to support the cause and vigorously defend it (e.g., to champion liberty or freedom of speech). The word *champion* was first given a management twist when, in their book *In Search of Excellence*, Tom Peters and Robert Waterman argued that successfully innovative companies revolve around "fired-up champions."[3] Peters and Waterman further argued that to gain sustained success any new idea or concept needed a passionate champion; a specific individual within the organization who would defend a new idea and nurture it through its early days of emergence. Lacking such a person, they suggested, the new idea will likely die.

Experienced professionals understand why. Change invariably encounters institutional indifference or outright resistance. That is a reality that does *not* change. In fact, the observation, "There is nothing more difficult to take in hand, more perilous to conduct, or more uncertain in its success than to take the lead in the introduction of a new order of things,"[4] is as accurate now as it was in 1513 when Niccolo Machiavelli included it in *The Prince*, his classic treatise on the nature of man and management.

Champions do not usually have it easy. Their passion and efforts may be dismissed as unnecessary because the efforts have not been clearly recognized as needed in the past. They may be trivialized as a duplication of current efforts, because their responsibilities are not well-understood or defined. Finally, they may be considered wasteful of organizational resources because the costs associated with their activities have not previously been separately identified. All of these reactions can be daunting, but they will not discourage a true champion. The reason why was put nicely by boxing legend Muhammad Ali. He observed: "Champions aren't made in the gyms. Champions are made from something they have deep inside them—a desire, a dream, a vision."[5]

Interestingly, the best of champions may not be easy to work with themselves. They typically are bright, enthusiastic, and talented people. They may also be viewed as obnoxious, impatient, egotistic, and perhaps a bit irrational. If, however, revenue management is to advance as a legitimate hospitality industry occupation and as a legitimate field of hospitality study, it will need zealots to keep interest in it alive. Without such champions, it may ultimately be dismissed as simply another management fad (e.g., see MBO in the 1970s, TQM in the 1980s, Reengineering in the 1990s and, perhaps, Six Sigma in the 2000s).

The difficulty of helping to champion revenue management as an emerging and distinct discipline was certainly experienced by the authors as they worked to produce this book. The newness of the revenue management field triggered a range of reaction to the proposed book, from academicians and industry practitioners alike:

- There is no need for a book about revenue management because it's just a fad.
- A book would be O.K., but there would not be enough material to fill more than 50 pages.

- It could be useful, but only if the highest level quantitative aspects of revenue management are thoroughly presented to readers with advanced training in mathematics.

- It could be useful, but only if the highest-level quantitative aspects of revenue management and advanced mathematics are minimized.

- It could be useful, but only if the emphasis is on the marketing aspects of revenue management.

- It could be useful, but only if the emphasis is on the accounting and financial aspects of revenue management.

- It could be useful, but only if the emphasis is on how RMs utilize the Internet to sell hotel rooms.

- RM is just another name for marketing, we already know about marketing.

- RM is just another name for sales; we already know about sales.

- RM is just another name for channel management (or Internet distribution management). With advances in technology, the strategies and tactics related to these topics change too fast to be addressed in a book.

Fortunately, from some forward thinking professionals, the authors also encountered frequently the reaction of:

- **It's about time!**

Our efforts to accommodate the wide range of opinion regarding ideal content for the book were guided by the wisdom of Theodore Roosevelt, the twenty-sixth president of the United States, who observed: "In any moment of decision the best thing you can do is the right thing, the next best thing is the wrong thing, and the worst thing you can do is nothing!"[6]

In that spirit, it is the authors hope that this first edition of *Revenue Management for the Hospitality Industry* is viewed just as it we view it—a first effort at presenting important hospitality-related revenue optimization information in a cohesive, reader-friendly format. The addition and deletion of specific material in future editions is assumed because the revenue management field will no doubt continue to evolve. It is for just that reason, however, that the process of championing revenue management as a discipline worthy of specialized study is so critical. The authors welcome the constructive criticism of this text and trust that part of its value is to spur others to advance the revenue management field by their improvements on our initial effort. To flourish, the emerging field of revenue management very much needs knowledgeable champions just like you.

Clearly Defined Areas of Responsibility

One difficulty faced by some RMs relates to the specific job duties they are assigned by their own organization. In some organizations, the role of RM will be assumed by an individual who is also responsible for related tasks such as marketing, selling, channel management, and financial management. This is the case, for example, in a single unit restaurant or smaller lodging operation. In these cases, the property's general manager may assume all RM-related roles.

Essential RM Term

Ownership of responsibility: The individual or department with primary accountability for a defined task or mission.

In larger hospitality properties RM-related responsibilities may be shared among many individuals and across departments. Because of this diversified approach it can sometimes be confusing to clearly understand the specific role of each revenue management-related individual or department. Of course, each hospitality organization should assign revenue management-related tasks based on its own needs, but one good way to view the various functional areas that directly impact RM is by their **ownership of responsibility.**

You have learned that in larger organizations the optimization of revenue in a customer-centric manner requires the cooperation of many professionals. A RM's ability to effectively control and manage this coordinated endeavor is dependent on clearly understanding the responsibilities of each partner in the process. Although every hospitality organization is unique, in an effective revenue optimization effort each of the functional areas involved should understand their distinct and well-defined areas of ownership. When areas of responsibility begin to blur, it can be helpful to refocus an organization regarding exactly who owns what.

Sales

The sales department owns the customer *relationship*. In most cases, relationships are why customers first come to your business and then become repeat buyers. The relationship may be to a brand, be based on their own past buying experience, or be associated with a specific member of your organization's staff (e.g., a favorite bartender, server, or meetings and convention sales professional).

As you learned in Chapter 3, most buyers are happy to *buy*, but strongly resent being *sold*. The best RMs and salespersons understand this well. They succeed by helping customers see the benefits inherent in the products and services they sell. By doing so, they permit customers to make their own *buy* decisions. Effective RMs do not focus on their own selling. They focus on their targeted customers' buying behavior. They also understand that the most successful sales relationships are customer-focused, not product- or organization-focused. The key point to remember here is that it is the RMs' job to ensure pricing and inventory control decisions support and enhances sales relationships—not damage them.

Marketing

The marketing department owns the sales *message*. Effectively communicating the organization's value message is a process that begins with the identification of target customers. Understanding what, why, how much, and when these potential customers will buy allows those in marketing to craft and make known a cohesive organizational value message. It is that message that helps define the organization's image in the mind of potential buyers. Utilizing the tools of advertising, public relations, promotion, and publicity marketing professionals focus on sending messages designed to encourage target customers to buy. RMs who are doing a good job in pricing and inventory management help keep the sales message clear and easily understood by customers.

Accounting

The accounting department, or controller's office in a hotel, owns the revenue-related *data*. Useful, timely, and precise data are essential to revenue optimization decision making. Data accuracy is certainly important—however, its primary role is to communicate what RMs should *know*, rather than what they should do. As a result, data related to ADR, occupancy %, check average, head counts, sales per seat and the like must be precise but should not be allowed to dictate revenue management-related decision making. Accounting is, by definition, an internal assessment process. Because its focal point is an organization's buyers, customer-centric revenue optimization is essentially an *externally* focused process.

Distribution

Distribution owns the management of *channels*. As you learned in Chapter 8, channel distribution management is a means of influencing the way in which your customers buy from you. In the hospitality industry, distribution channels typically include both electronic and non-electronic types. Electronic forms can include an organization's own web site, blog, or twitter site, the web site of its franchisor, third-party online selling sites such as Travelocity, hotels.com and Expedia, travel agency sites, and various search engines, to name just a few elements.

Nonelectronic distribution channels can include onsite sales, telephone reservations, onsite group sales, and working with travel partners such as a local CVB. In all cases, the goal of effective distribution management is an expansion of your customer reach and as a result, an expanding number of potential buyers who can respond positively to your marketing message.

Operations

Operations owns the guest's *experience*. From the time guests decide to buy from you to the time they pay their bills and leave your business, guests will interact with a variety of your operations staff. Each of these employees plays an important role in confirming the wisdom of a buyer's purchase or in increasing a buyer's regret to have purchased from you.

A quality product or service that is properly priced but improperly delivered to guests works against an organization's revenue optimization effort. Experienced RMs know that a hospitality organization's operations staff is an integral part of the overall success achieved by a revenue optimization team. The operations team must be able to consistently deliver what the organization has promised to its customers in its value proposition.

Revenue Management

Revenue management owns *inventory and its price*. Using specific business data and information gathered from sales, marketing, accounting, distribution, and operations, RM professionals apply data and their insight to strategically price available inventory. You have learned that inventory management is the process of allocating the number of products available for sale at various prices through various distribution channels. As a result, RMs forecast customer demand, analyze trends and market segments, and make the best strategic pricing decisions possible. The process focuses on both top-line revenues and **bottom-line** results.

Essential RM Term

Bottom line: Industry slang for an organization's profits, or final outcomes.

All of the revenue-impacting functional areas of an organization must focus their efforts on maximizing value for customers. When the efforts are well-coordinated and executed, customer-centric revenue optimization can be the result.

While the emphasis on the revenue management process may seem to be new, the best hospitality professionals have recognized it for a long time. The relationship between value delivered and sales results was put nicely by Ralph Hitz, who in 1930 managed the largest chain of hotels in the United States. A marketing phenomenon, Hitz instituted many of the data collection and application processes used by effective RMs today. Hitz's early 1930s-era observation was pointed and accurate: "Give the customer value and you will get volume sales in return."[7]

RM AT WORK 13.1

"That's just a fantasy. There is no Santa Claus—or Easter Bunny, either," said Carl, the F&B director at the Harley Hotel.

"What do you mean?" asked Sandy, the hotel's DOSM.

Carl, Sandy, Matt, the hotel's controller, and Ali, the property's RM, were holding their weekly revenue management meeting. They were discussing a proposal from Sandy that the Crystal Room, which was the hotel's upscale dining room, participate in the local Chamber of Commerce's new "Dining Guide" coupon program.

Essentially, explained Sandy, the chamber would not charge participating restaurants or hotels for their ads. The participating businesses were simply required to offer a "two for one" coupon. According to Sandy, the idea was a no-brainer and a real winner. The coupons would bring new customers to the hotel. These customers would love the food and, on subsequent visits and without the coupons, would pay the full price. The customers would also tell all their friends. The "word of mouth" advertising would be invaluable for additional F&B sales as well as enhanced room sales to local residents for special events.

Carl was not convinced.

"What I mean is that it is unrealistic for you to assume that guests who use these coupons will come back and pay full price. These kind of people only buy when the can get a deal. From my experience, they will tip the staff based on the reduced meal price too!" said Carl

"But the program is free," said Matt. "Free advertising is worth something all by itself."

"Not to me it isn't, replied Carl. "The only time we'll see these customers again is when they have another coupon."

"Well, the program also supports our Chamber of Commerce efforts," said Sandy, "and that's important, too!"

"If you want to support the Chamber, then give them money from your budget, don't take it from mine," replied Carl.

Assume you were Ali:

1. Do you think Sandy makes a compelling case for participating in the Chamber's new promotion? Why?

2. Do you think Carl makes a compelling case for not participating in the Chamber's new promotion? Why?

3. Given your knowledge of differential pricing, would you recommend the hotel's participation in the program? Explain your answer.

Effective Price Management

You have learned that pricing is often an underappreciated means of growing revenues. It should not be. The fact that pricing has not typically been given the attention it deserves is actually somewhat surprising. The reasons for this unfortunate state of affairs in hospitality are varied, but include the following:

- *History.* Generations of managers have been taught to equate price with cost. But doing so makes pricing essentially a mathematical rather than managerial process. Until several generations of managers learn to equate price with value delivered to customers, a cost-based pricing approach may very well continue to dominate in the hospitality industry.

- *Limitations of measurement.* Financial managers and consultants most often assess a company's success based on its cost structure or its efficiency in utilizing inputs when producing outputs. The worth and profits that a business creates for its *customers* are crucial but is rarely measured because doing so can be very difficult. It is much easier to compute a cost ratio than to measure customers' perceptions of value delivered. Despite their irrelevance to buyers it is simply easier for managers to base pricing decisions on costs than it is to create and utilize the measurement tools and processes needed to base price on customer willingness to pay. This is an industry-wide weakness that should be better addressed by creative professionals in hospitality accounting.

- *Lack of understanding.* Examine a typical hospitality marketing textbook and you will readily see that, as a topic of study, pricing gets the least attention of any of the four Ps of marketing. Rarely is pricing viewed as more important than product, promotion or place, yet from a customer's perspective, it is price that most influences perceptions about each of these concepts. Companies must integrate pricing strategy into the highest levels of their organizations. They must also be willing to invest in the intellectual capital required to understand and apply advanced pricing-related business strategies. This means implementing RM-related training for key staff members in a variety of departments. When they do, pricing will attain the organizational stature it deserves.

- *Contempt for theory.* In the introductory pages of far too many hospitality textbooks the authors proudly state that their book "is very practical and as a result will not waste the reader's time with a bunch of impractical theory." Such authors do their readers a great disservice. While the original source of the statement is often in dispute, having been variously attributed to Albert Einstein, Kurt Lewin, and others, the maxim, *"There is nothing so practical as a good theory,"* clearly applies to pricing. In actuality, only useful and thus very practical theories help make sense of a complex world. To imply there is no theory involved in the thoughtful study of pricing is to demonstrate a lack of practical knowledge.

- *Misunderstanding of the industry.* Those who disdain theory appear to hold a belief that the nature of the hospitality industry is first and foremost hands-on, immediate, concrete, consistent and of course, very practical. By contrast, they believe theory is too abstract, irrelevant, and generalized and therefore not helpful for day-to-day decision making. In fact, experienced professionals know the hospitality industry is far from static or predictable. Practicing the art and science of hospitality involves the systematic organization and management of such human realities as beliefs, values, ethics, thoughts, intentions, purposes, feelings, actions, behaviors, and responses of your customers and your staff who serve them. Any potential manager who does not recognize the variant nature of these factors is simply not being very practical.

- *Misunderstanding the role of theory.* Predicting how complex relationships and values are interconnected is the task of theory. Having a systematic way of thinking about human dynamics that is coherent, informative, and grounded in actual experience is to possess a powerful tool (a theory) that can have very practical uses when responding to concrete situations created by an organization's customers. This concept was stated nicely by W. Edwards Deming, the renowned American statistician, professor, author, and consultant. Best known for his work in shaping Japanese manufacturing after World War II, he observed: "Rational behavior requires theory. Reactive behavior requires only reflex action."[8] Deming would agree with the authors that RMs who do not seek to understand pricing theory are simply not being very practical in helping their organizations optimize revenues and profits.

- *Underappreciation of immediate impact.* One of the biggest reasons that the implementation of effective pricing strategy has not gotten the attention it deserves is simply an underappreciation of the impact effective pricing can have on an organization's bottom line. Just how big an impact can be made by the application of an effective pricing strategy? To illustrate, consider Jack Lani. Jack is the owner of Jack's Hilo House Restaurant. Figure 13.1 illustrates the impact on profitability of a 1 percent increase in selling price in his operation.

    Note that a 1 percent increase in net selling price results in a 10.7 percent increase in Income Before Income Taxes. These results are not at all surprising. A detailed study of the Global 1200, a list of 1,200 large and publicly traded companies from around the world, found that for those companies, a net price increase of 1 percent would result in an average 11 percent increase in operating profits.[9]

    The 1 percent price increase to 11 percent profit improvement average holds true when prices are increased beyond 1 percent. Thus, for example, a 2 percent increase in net price would typically result in a 22 percent increase in profits (Net Income Before Income Taxes).

    Of course, a potential drawback any time prices are increased is that it may result in reduced customer demand. Consider, however, whether you honestly believe your current or future customers would select an alternative hotel or restaurant if you were doing an excellent job and your organization elected to raise its prices by 1 percent. If you do feel they would leave you, your major issue is more likely related to self-confidence in your own value proposition than to pricing. Unfortunately, if you do not have that self-confidence, you can be pretty sure that your staff (and customers) will not have it, either!

Effective price management requires RMs and their teams to understand six truths about pricing:

1. *Pricing communicates.* Pricing is often the first thing your customers will see and hear about your product offerings.

2. *Pricing establishes expectations.* Consumers automatically make a price/quality judgment when they see or hear an initial price. Just as a $70,000 automobile

Figure 13.1	Effect of 1% Price Increase on Restaurant Profitability

Jack's Hilo House Restaurant			
	With Current Prices	**With 1% Price Increase**	**Change%**
SALES:			
Food	$2,000,000	$2,020,000	1.0%
Beverage	500,000	505,000	1.0%
Total Sales	**2,500,000**	**2,525,000**	**1.0%**
COST OF SALES:			
Food	750,000	750,000	0.0%
Beverage	100,000	100,000	0.0%
Total Cost of Sales	**850,000**	**850,000**	**0.0%**
GROSS PROFIT:			
Food	1,250,000	1,270,000	1.6%
Beverage	400,000	405,000	1.3%
Total Gross Profit	**1,650,000**	**1,675,000**	**1.5%**
OPERATING EXPENSES:			
Salaries and wages	650,000	650,000	0.0%
Employee benefits	110,000	110,000	0.0%
Direct operating expenses	130,000	130,000	0.0%
Music and entertainment	2,500	2,500	0.0%
Marketing	45,000	45,000	0.0%
Utility services	75,000	75,000	0.0%
Repairs and maintenance	75,000	75,000	0.0%
Administrative and general	69,000	69,000	0.0%
Occupancy	125,000	125,000	0.0%
Depreciation	45,000	45,000	0.0%
Total Operating Expenses	**1,326,500**	**1,326,500**	**0.0%**
Operating Income	323,500	348,500	7.7%
Interest	90,000	90,000	0.0%
Income Before Income Taxes	**233,500**	**258,500**	**10.7%**
Prepared using **USAR**			

Essential RM Term

USAR: Short for Uniform System of Accounts for Restaurants. The standardized accounting procedures for the restaurant industry, including those related to the presentation of operating results in the Statement of Income and Expense (Income Statement).

will be perceived as being of higher quality than a $30,000 car, in the hospitality industry guest expectations of quality to be received *increase* as price increases. It is important to recall, however, that the terms *quality* and *value* are not always perceived by guests as synonymous. A high-quality wine can be offered for sale at a price so high its purchase does not represent a good value to diners. Similarly, a hotel may offer a room with amenities that are clearly of higher quality than its competitors but that its potential guests simply do not value highly.

3. *Pricing boosts profitability.* No additional costs are incurred when prices exactly match customer willingness to pay. As you have learned, small increases in net price charged can result in significant increases in organizational profitability.

4. *Accurate pricing increases forecasting ability.* A variety of areas within a hospitality organization need an accurate estimate of the number of customers that will be serviced in the future, as well as how much those guests will spend. Operations staff must forecast the amount of labor required to properly serve guests. Purchasing-related staff must ensure adequate supplies are on hand to serve anticipated guests.

RM IN ACTION 13.1: OFFER MORE: DON'T ASK FOR LESS

The tendency for organizations to reduce, rather than enhance, value delivered to guests can sometimes be very strong. This is especially the case when volume is reduced and hospitality managers seek to lower prices and costs. Effective managers know, however, that offering more, not giving less, is the key to long-term profitability.

Robert Logan is an experienced luxury hotel manager, having managed properties for The Peninsula Group, Four Seasons Resorts, and Sandy Lane Barbados. His properties consistently operate at 100 percent occupancy levels. In 2009, at the height of the global economic crisis, his responses to cost-related interview questions posed by *Hotels* magazine were especially insightful. In the interview, Logan was asked how hoteliers could control costs without negatively affecting guest experiences. His reply is instructive:

> We would never do anything to affect the guest experience, and that's where we have noticed and seen some reaction from other hotels internationally where they may pull back on amenities and services. We would never do that. Our key strategy is always to maintain rate integrity.

Logan goes on to emphasize maintaining, not reducing, rates by emphasizing to his staff the importance of creatively enhancing, not reducing, the value provided during each guest's stay as a way to ensure repeat business. Offering customers more value, not less, and at a fair price is the key to long-term success in the hospitality industry.

Excerpted on 3/28/209 from: www.hotelsmag.com posting of 3/10/2009.

Accounting staff must plan for the timing and wise use of cash receipts. When pricing accurately reflects market realities (i.e., guests' willingness to pay), precise sales forecasts can be developed.

5. *The pricing process is proactive, not reactive.* The best RMs understand that a price is a concept, not a number. They also know that strategic pricing is an ongoing process. The process is initiated and modified as data and insight shape RMs estimates of guest willingness to pay via the channels used to offer inventory for sale. These RMs act on, rather than merely react to, the fluctuating buying behavior of their customers.

6. *Appropriate pricing is a more powerful long-term strategy than cost cutting.* Effective managers should, of course, always ensure that their product, labor, supply, and overhead costs are managed wisely. Seeking to increase profits by cutting corners, however, typically ends up costing an organization more than it saves.

Eliminating services, reducing quality, and cheapening products is an unwise strategy to optimize profitability. The stripped-down product or service will likely cost less to make or deliver, but the savings typically comes at the customer's expense as their own profits are reduced. The net effect is a reduction in value offered for price charged. This can actually ruin a company's reputation, especially if the brand previously had a reputation for high quality and full-service products.

Candid Product and Service Self-Assessment

Over time, customers demonstrate an uncanny ability to discover those businesses that offer great value. In a city that has a fairly weak lodging market, one or two hotels will still be operating at extremely high occupancy levels. In a similar manner, while some restaurant operators in a specific area wonder if they will generate enough volume to stay in business next year, others in the same area are happily considering expansion of their seating capacity or the building of additional units.

▶ RM ON THE WEB 13.1

Pricing specialists represent one of the fastest-growing career fields in the United States. Pricing is always important, but in an economic downturn it is often viewed as even more important than normal. This is so because effective pricing strategies can help organizations differentiate themselves from their competitors and help them achieve success despite the economic difficulties they encounter. The Professional Pricing Society (PPS) is the professional association for those individuals who have primary responsibility for establishing the selling prices of their organizations' goods and services.

As part of its mission, the PPS offers its member certification as a *Certified Pricing Professional* (CPP). To review the requirements for this certification, go to www.pricingsociety.com

When you arrive, click on *Pricing Certification/Training* to learn more about the PPS and its CPP designation.

In too many cases, hospitality managers react to their own low volume levels with disbelief. Given our wonderful product and outstanding service, they reason, customers should be coming to us in droves. The fact that they are not coming in droves, in the opinion of these managers, reflects negatively on the customers' level of intelligence, not the manager's own product and service offerings.

These managers' typical responses are similar to the playwright whose stage production, amidst terrible reviews, closed only one day after opening. Asked the reason for the early closing, the playwright stated, "My play was a complete success. The audience was a failure."[10]

In the hospitality industry, failure could be defined as the inability of an organization to deliver on its value proposition (see Chapter 2). In the long run, those companies that disappoint their customers do not stay in business. It is also important to recognize, however, that if corrected in time, a service or product failure is not fatal. In business, as in life, failure should be a teacher, not an undertaker. Experienced RMs know that an honest assessment of failures can challenge organizations to new heights of accomplishments, not pull them to new depths of despair. From the honest assessment of failures to please guests can come valuable experience that will help prevent future shortcomings.

Not all failures in hospitality are the result of operational shortcomings. Sometimes the value message is not effectively delivered by those responsible for marketing. In other cases, the message is delivered extremely well but the guest experience actually provided by operations staff does not contain significant customer value. Most often, however, the marketing message of an organization pretty well matches what an organization's customers actually experience. The key to building better business in such situations is a candid self-assessment of the organization's ability to differentiate it products and avoid market commoditization.

In Chapter 8 you learned that commoditization results when a branded product or service has no features that differentiate it from other brands. When that happens, consumers buy on price alone. It does not have to happen. It often does, however, when a business cannot clearly define its value proposition. Vague promise statements such as, *"Good food served by friendly staff,"* or *"A great stay at a fair price,"* can quickly become meaningless to staff and customers alike if the organization does not have an effective system of evaluating their ability to deliver on those promises. In such cases, things are not going as planned simply because their never was a plan. Experienced RMs know that with nearly any desired business or customer-centric outcome, if you can't define it, you can't measure it, and if you can't measure it you can't improve it.

Too often, hospitality operators believe that a unique food item or new hotel location will be sufficient to attract a sustainable customer base. Their belief is that their uniqueness will also be sufficient to sustain profitability. These operators would do well to carefully consider the observations on innovation posed by artist and inventor Leonardo da Vinci. He observed: "Life is pretty simple. You do some stuff. Most fails. Some works. You do more of what works. If it works big, others quickly copy it. Then you do something else. The trick is the doing something else."[11]

In the hospitality industry the something else indicated by da Vinci typically results from an ongoing evaluation of your organization's ability to differentiate its products and services from the competition. It is virtually impossible to use differential pricing to address variances in your customers' views of unique value delivered to them, if they cannot easily identify that value.

When commoditization is present, downward pressure on prices is constant. Corn is a commodity. It would make no sense for a buyer of corn to pay more for a bushel of Farmer Bob's corn than for a bushel of Farmer Jane's. In such situations it is only when the potential buyer is unaware of alternative options that higher prices can be maintained.

Essential RM Term

Barriers to entry: Obstacles in the path of a business seeking to gain entrance to a new market.

In the hospitality industry, the use of the Internet makes hotel room rates and menu prices completely transparent to guests. As a result, it is not possible for an organization to artificially maintain high prices if it is viewed as selling a commodity. This is especially true when a hospitality operator is viewed as selling a commodity. In this situation, there will always be smaller operators, with lower cost structures, who seek to enter the lower-end/lower-price segment of that organization's market. In some industries, natural **barriers to entry** thwart such efforts.

For example, even if you knew that, due to commoditization, a large number of customers would respond positively to a small, two-door sports car, your ability to create, manufacture, distribute, and service the new cars you hope to build would come at a very high financial price to you. In the automobile industry, the mere cost of start-up and production is a significant barrier to entry.

Contrast that situation to the one faced by the Mrs. Fields cookie company, the 1980s product phenomenon that initially produced hundreds of franchises, thousands of stores, and dozens of direct competitors—and ultimately, the public announcement of its bankruptcy filing in 2008, as well as its subsequent 2009 acquisition by NexCen brands.[12]

Anyone who ever ate a freshly baked Mrs. Fields cookie could attest to their high quality. They taste great. Unfortunately, it was very easy for competitors to make an *almost as good* product. These competitors sold at a lower price to those buyers who were not convinced the value obtained when purchasing a Mrs. Field's cookie was sufficient to warrant paying more. Mrs. Fields clearly offered a superior product. That is not enough in the hospitality industry. In most cases, competitors' barriers to entry cost too little to prevent a significant copycat effect.

Menu items are easily duplicated, and new hotels routinely open in close proximity to those that are operating at high occupancy levels. Because that is true, hospitality organizations must continually and honestly assess their success or failure in sustaining their competitive advantages through product augmentation, service innovation, and execution.

The unpleasant reality that must be faced by nearly all hospitality operators is that a meal or a night's sleep are experiences that can be duplicated rather easily by others. In the hospitality industry, there are few unique products or patented operating procedures available to you that will not be available to your competitors. Unfortunately, that fact may lead some to conclude that the commoditization of hospitality staples such as hamburgers, mid-priced hotel rooms, draft beers, or meeting planning services are destined to be commoditized. That is not true.

What buyers purchase from a hospitality business is much more than a specific product or service. When they buy from a hospitality organization, they buy a shopping cart full of things including tangible items such as cleanliness, product size and presentation, speed of service, staff appearance, facility appearance, and ease of payment, to name just a few. Intangible items purchased include image, peace of mind, confidence in the expected experience, safety, product consistency, and fairness in complaint resolution to name but a few. The point for RMs to remember is that even if your product or service is identical to that of your competitors, strengthening service levels delivered allows for product differentiation.

When conceived, implemented, measured, and improved continually, creative product enhancements allow you to deliver your product or service in a way that makes it superior to your competitors. Value in a buyer's mind can be firmly established even when what you sell is *not* perceived as the very best available. For example, most hospitality industry experts would agree that McDonald's hamburgers rarely beat all of their competition in blind taste tests. These same experts would also agree, however, that McDonald's fanatical adherence to monitoring and measuring, and even regularly grading franchisees on their quality, service, cleanliness, and value (QSC&V) performance means that the largest numbers of QSR customers consistently choose to purchase from McDonald's when given a choice among quick service alternatives.

BETTER BUSINESS ISSUES IN MODERATE TO STRONG MARKETS

Although there are a variety of ways in which to examine the economic environments you may encounter during your career as an RM, one way to do so is by market strength. Using this approach, differing markets have specific characteristics that can be summarized as shown in Figure 13.2.

Experienced RMs know that some markets in which they work will be strong and vibrant while others will be weak or will be moderate, defined simply as a point between these two extremes of strong and weak.

Of course, it is possible that some sections of a country, a region, or even a specific metropolitan area will contain diverse market conditions. What is most important for RMs

Figure 13.2	**Characteristics of Diverse Market Conditions**			
Market Condition	**Common Characteristics**	**Impact on Lodging**	**Impact on Foodservice**	**Impact on Hospitality-related Businesses**
Strong	Strong economy, demand regularly exceeds supply	Historically high ADRs and occupancy rates	Increased customer counts and check average	Price increases acceptable due to robust demand
Moderate	Demand and supply in equilibrium	Newly opened facilities capture higher rates and occupancy levels	Menu price and customer count improvement reflect long-range population trends toward increased dining out	Ability to increase prices judiciously is present due to balanced supply
Weak/ Distressed	Weakened demand, oversupply of rooms	Lowered occupancy rates, downward pressure on ADR	Unit closures due to over-supply.	Downward pressure on price, closure of marginally profitable businesses

Essential RM Term

Cyclical (business): A business affected by identifiable but only marginally predictable fluctuations in economic activity.

Essential RM Term

Seasonal (business): A business affected by an identifiable and very predictable fluctuation in economic activity.

to recognize is that from an historical perspective, if you work in the hospitality industry you work in a **cyclical business.**

RMs employed by ski resorts are very familiar with the demand variation associated with their high/busy seasons and their low/slow seasons. Many hospitality businesses, including resort hotels, restaurants in tourist locations and golf courses can experience very predictable demand fluctuations. Such businesses are considered to be **seasonal.** These, too, however, can be subject to the larger cyclical nature of the overall business environment and economy.

Despite the pretentiousness of a good many experts, predicting the beginning and end of a business cycle is extremely difficult. Like a stock trader's ability to identify the top and bottom of a stock market cycle, the capability of predicting the beginning or the end of business cycles is, at best, an imperfect science.

This truth was well illustrated when, in January of 2008, hospitality industry experts were estimating that the U.S. lodging industry would experience year-end growth in RevPAR of +4.5 percent, a growth rate well above the historic average increase of 3.3 percent. By the end of the 2008, however, Smith Travel Research was reporting a predicted U.S. lodging industry RevPAR change of −1.9 percent for the year, with the decline in ADR and occupancy rate continuing to accelerate rapidly into 2009."[14]

Although the *timing* of business cycles may be hard to predict, the lodging (as well as restaurant) industry has experienced a fairly predictable business cycle occurrence. When occupancy levels are high, hotel developers are encouraged to build new hotels, thus adding to room supply and ultimately, because of the increased supply, reducing overall occupancy rates.

Essential RM Term

Pipeline (hotel): The lodging industry term used to describe those hotels that are in various phases of development but which have not yet opened.

Low periods of industrywide levels of occupancy have the opposite effect. In periods of low occupancy, neither developers nor lenders are encouraged to develop or fund new hotel construction. Because fewer hotels are placed into the **pipeline,** the number of available new rooms ultimately declines and, as a result, occupancy rates rise over time.

Figure 13.3 demonstrates the cyclical nature of occupancy rates using the most recently completed decade of the 2000s as an illustration. Note that the average occupancy in the decade ranged from a low of 56.4 (2009) to a high of 63.3 (2006), according to data from lodging industry monitor Price Waterhouse.[15]

The 12.2 percent variance between the highest and lowest occupancy rates periods [(63.3% −56.4%)/56.4% = 12.2%] is reasonably typical for the lodging industry. Occupancy variation within a specific geographic area may exhibit even greater variance. When you consider that declining occupancy rates often lead to room rate discounting, it is easy to see that the percentage variation in RevPAR generation within a single decade can easily reach 20 percent or more. As a result, lodging industry RMs, as well as those RMs in other hospitality-related industries, will most often find that over the length of their careers

Figure 13.3	A Decade of U.S. Hotel Occupancy Rates
Year	Occupancy %
2000	63.3%
2001	59.8%
2002	59.1%
2003	59.2%
2004	61.4%
2005	63.1%
2006	63.3%
2007	63.1%
2008	60.4%
2009	56.4%
2010	57.0%*

* Forecast on 9/1/2010.

Essential RM Term

Distressed market: An economic condition that results in revenue levels that are significantly (10 percent or more) below historic norms.

they will be faced with seeking better business when they encounter strong as well as weak or **distressed market** conditions.

The keys to better business in strong markets are different from those addressed in weak or distressed markets. When markets conditions are moderate to strong, busy RMs must focus on these key market condition-related issues:

■ Irrational exuberance
■ Revenue displacement analysis
■ Investment in training

Irrational Exuberance

The term *irrational exuberance* is derived from words that Alan Greenspan, chairman of the Federal Reserve Board in Washington, used in a speech titled "The Challenge of Central Banking in a Democratic Society" before the American Enterprise Institute at the Washington Hilton Hotel on December 5, 1996."[16] The term is now used to describe an almost euphoric sense that *the good times will last forever.* While originally used in reference to banking, Greenspan's words apply to those in the hospitality industry who also might believe strong markets last forever. They do not last forever, and RMs, as well as business owners must recognize that fact.

You have learned that the role of an RM is to manage inventory and pricing. In a strong market, the tendency too often is to increase the amount of available inventory rather than

Essential RM Term

Leveraging: The use of borrowed money to acquire business assets.

to better price existing inventory. That tendency results in strategies designed to build more sales units (e.g., hotels or restaurants), rather than build per unit sales. If the building expansion is heavily based on **leveraging**, the results that can occur during a downturn when the debt cannot be repaid can be disastrous.

The fallacy of excessive unit expansion approach is well illustrated by the case of Starbucks. When the first unit opened in Seattle in 1971, there was no doubt consumers loved Starbucks and its premium coffees. Twenty years later (1991), Starbucks had expanded to just over 100 units. Business continued to be good and profitable.

Between 1991 and 2001, Starbucks revenue growth averaged 47 percent per year.[17] By the end of 2001, Starbucks had grown to over 4,700 units and in March its stock price was $43.25 per share. In 2006, Starbucks operated or licensed 13,728 units with plans to open an additional 2,400 units in fiscal year 2007.[18] In October 2006, the stock was selling for $39.50 per share. Unfortunately, while *build it and they will come* made a great premise for the Academy Award nominated fantasy baseball movie *Field of Dreams*, it is markedly less effective as a long-term revenue optimization strategy.

The economic downturn of 2008 began seriously in the fall of that year. In March 2009, CEO Howard Schultz announced Starbucks would close 900 stores. At that point, the stock was selling at $11.50 per share and those investors who purchased it at its October 2006 levels had experienced a −66.89 percent return on their investment.[19]

Schultz' re-focus on per-unit sales allowed the stock to recover much of its lost value, but as Starbucks learned the hard way, adding excess supply in the lodging or restaurant industry can grow revenues significantly, but it grows significant expense and debt repayment as well. In an economic downturn, paying for excessive amounts of idle production capacity (see Chapter 3) is deadly.

The 2008 and 2009 RevPAR declines experienced by Orlando and Las Vegas and the business fallout resulting from those declines are lodging industry examples of room supply (inventory) exceeding sustainable growth in demand with very unfortunate but quite predictable results.

When a business downturn follows a strong market—and in the hospitality industry it always will—those companies that exuberantly expanded revenue via the addition of new inventory or capacity are inevitably damaged more than those who expanded more cautiously. Careful industry professionals recognize the wisdom of emphasizing inventory utilization and strategic pricing to optimize profits *first*, and unit expansion second.

The lessons for RMs are clear. Strong markets are a mandate for additional emphasis on identifying and targeting directly those customers with high willingness to pay levels rather than on additional customers exhibiting only average or low willingness to pay. In the restaurant industry, strong markets mean seating utilization percentage levels and RevPASH should be maximized (see Chapter 11). In the lodging industry, strong markets mean that 100 percent occupancy indexes and ADR indexes of 110 percent or more (see Chapter 9) should be the goal of effective revenue optimization teams. It also means hotel and restaurant developers, and their bankers, should avoid the business sin of irrational exuberance.

Revenue Displacement Analysis

When strong markets create significant inventory demand, RMs often have the option of choosing among several interested buyers, each of whom would like to purchase their available inventory. When that happens, RMs must have the ability to conduct an effective revenue **displacement analysis**.

Essential RM Term

Displacement analysis (revenue): A structured examination of the relative merits of choosing among alternative pieces of business for the purpose of identifying the piece that optimizes revenue.

In the lodging industry it is important to recognize that a displacement analysis may or may not result in choosing the piece of business that maximizes occupancy, ADR, or even total revenue. It may be for that very reason displacement analysis is not a topic addressed in even the most widely used hospitality marketing texts. Experienced RMs, however, recognize that revenue displacement analysis is an important process designed to choose among buyers. Its goal is to identify the sale that provides the business and its customers the greatest long-term benefit. The identified sale may or may not maximize revenue, but it will always optimize revenue.

The term *displacement* is used in this analysis process because it recognizes that to accept one piece of business means another piece of business must be rejected (displaced) or denied. To illustrate, consider the RM of a 300-room hotel that generally allocates 150 rooms to group sales and 150 rooms to transient sales. On a future date, all 150 group rooms have been sold to a group rooms buyer at a rate of $125.99 per night. 100 transient rooms for that date have been sold at an ADR of $179.99. In the hotel's weekly revenue optimization team meeting, the DOSM states that the group rooms buyer has requested an additional 50 rooms and that granting the request would add $6,299.50 (50 rooms @ $125.99 = $6,2990.50) to the hotel's room revenue total on that night.

When asked, the FOM states that in her opinion, 25 of the remaining 50 transient rooms could be sold at the current ADR of $179.99 if no reallocation of rooms is made. Figure 13.4 shows the displacement analysis method used to calculate the impact on room revenue that would occur if the DOSM's request for a group rooms reallocation is granted.

As shown in Figure 13.4, if the RM reallocates the 50 available rooms to group sales, the increase in hotel revenue is in fact $1,799.75, not $6,299.50. The smaller difference is due to the fact that some of the 50 additional group customers' revenue simply displaced revenue that would have been achieved from the sale of the 25 transient rooms if no reallocation had been made.

Experienced RMs know that a revenue displacement analysis process such as that illustrated in Figure 13.4 can be modified to include additional selling options (e.g., three, four, or even more alternatives) as well as forecasted income derived from meeting room rental, F&B sales, and other income-producing departments. Doing so can give a more complete picture of the total revenue potential of one piece of business when compared to its alternatives. Even more advanced assessments can and should consider the GOPPAR impact associated with alternative selling decisions. Doing so can help avert the common tendency of some sales staff members to sell at a too low price simply to maximize top line revenues (RevPAR). Certainly, a property's sales effort should not conflict with its revenue

Figure 13.4	Two-Option Displacement Analysis

Current Allocation		Requested Allocation	
Transient Rooms: 150	**Revenue**	**Transient Rooms: 100**	**Revenue**
Sold: 100 @ 179.99	$ 17,999.00	Sold: 100 @ 179.99	$ 17,999.00
Forecast: 25 @ 179.99	$ 4,499.75	Forecast: 0	$ —
Group Rooms: 150		**Group Rooms: 200**	
Sold: 150 @ 125.99	$ 18,898.50	Sold: 150 @ 125.99	$ 18,898.50
Forecast: 0		Forecast: 50 @ 125.99	$ 6,299.50
Total Room Revenue	**$ 41,397.25**	**Total Room Revenue**	**$ 43,197.00**
Rooms		Rooms	
Sold	275	Sold	300
ADR	$ 150.54	ADR	$ 143.99
Occ. %	91.7%	Occ. %	100.0%
RevPAR	**$ 137.99**	**RevPAR**	**$ 143.99**
		RevPAR Variance	**4.3%**
		Rooms Revenue Variance	**$ 1,799.75**

optimization efforts. If, however, incentive programs for sales staff are specifically designed to reward RevPAR generation rather than GOPPAR results, then these two efforts can be in conflict.

Revenue displacement analysis must do more than simply identify revenue variance or even GOPPAR impact. In Chapter 4, you learned that revenue optimization is the application of disciplined tactics that predict buyer response to prices, optimize product availability, and yield the greatest profits. Business profitability is a marathon, not a sprint. Effective RMs know that in the long term, greatest profits may not mean the greatest revenue today or even the greatest GOP this month. Indeed, the greatest profit may not be realized for months or even years. Leadership author and professor Warren G. Bennis made this point well when he observed: "The manager has a short-range view, the leader has a long-range perspective."[20] A protégé of Douglas McGregor, the management theorist who originally coined the terms *Theory* X and *Theory* Y to describe differing approaches to leadership, Bennis understood well that there is a significant difference between a revenue manager and a revenue optimization leader. Unlike short-term focused revenue managers, revenue optimization leaders always consider the long-term impact of their decisions on their businesses and their customers.

RM AT WORK 13.2

"That's just crazy," said Warren Calipari, the new FOM at the 400-room Courtyard Plaza hotel. "Of course we should hold all the rooms for transient. I was in Houston in 2011 when they hosted the NCAA finals. I saw the ADRs we ran. I don't think you understand basketball!"

"I understand basketball, but I don't think you understand this hotel or this customer," replied Andrea Stidham, the hotel's DOSM.

Warren and Andrea were discussing the NCAA's recently announced selection of their city as the site for a future NCAA's *Final Four* men's basketball championship tournament.

"We need to block the rooms for those dates now," continued Warren, "and put at least a four-day MLOS on them. Everything we have should be sold as transient. With this tournament in town we'll sell out easily."

"I already told you, that's the same weekend as the Pecan Growers annual conference. They have been coming to this property on that weekend for the past eight years. They take 85 percent of our rooms for three days. They have contracts in place now for the next two years. Each year when their conference is over they come in and extend their contract

for another year. That way they always stay booked two years out. The men's basketball final is three years out, but it falls on the same dates they will be requesting for that year," replied Andrea.

"That's great. They *don't* have a contract in place for the rooms right now. That means we can hold all of our rooms for the NCAA tournament. Your group should have booked further out. Just tell them you are sorry. You know Andrea, in this business, if you snooze you lose. How can you turn down a sell-out weekend at double our rack rate?" said Warren.

1. Assume you were the decision-making RM at the Courtyard Plaza. Would you agree to block the rooms for transient sales as Warren suggests, or would you follow Andrea's advice?

2. Assume you were the executive director of the Pecan Growers association. What do you think your reaction would be if you were told you needed to move your conference due to the NCAA tournament?

3. Is this a revenue management challenge that is best addressed with a revenue displacement analysis? Explain your answer.

RMs show leadership when they use data from revenue displacement analysis along with their own insight to reward customer loyalty, resist the temptation to take unfair advantage of short-term demand spikes, and consider their pricing decisions from a customer-centric perspective. It is important to do so because it is these same customers that will be critical to retain when market demand inevitably moderates.

Investment in Training

Managers in all areas of hospitality often claim they would like to better train their staff but they are simply too busy. When volume levels are high, staff members may also feel they are too busy to attend training sessions. In both cases, the individuals involved make the mistake

Figure 13.5	Benefits of Revenue Management-Related Training

Improved employee performance

Reduced operating costs due to reduced staff errors

More satisfied guests

Reduced work stress

Improved staff relationships

More professional staff

Fewer operating problems

Lower employee **turnover rates**

Increased morale

Higher levels of work quality

Easier to recruit new staff

Increased profits

Essential RM Term

Turnover rate (employee): The number of employees who leave an organization each year, expressed as a percentage of the average number of workers employed by the organization. High turnover rates typically mean less experienced employees.

of thinking you can find time to train. You cannot. You will never *find* time to train; you must *make* time to train.

When economic conditions are good, RMs will likely find that needed training resources such as money and time are in greater supply than when market conditions are weak. Because that is true, strong markets constitute an excellent time for training revenue management-related staff. The net benefits of effective training are always significant. Figure 13.5 lists some of the most important benefits of revenue management-related training for managers, supervisors, and line-level staff.

When training is increased, staff at all organizational levels can better serve guests. It simply makes sense that if guests are more satisfied they will return more often and total

▶ RM ON THE WEB 13.2

When occupancies and ADRs are strong in the lodging industry, conditions may be favorable for RMs to take the extra time required to strengthen their own skills. IDeaS Revenue Optimization is an SAS company that provides cutting-edge information on hospitality-related customer-centric revenue optimization. You can view its web site at www.ideas.com

When you arrive, click on *Resources* to review its webinars. These online educational programs may be able to assist your own decision making related to pricing, analyzing competitive set performance, forecasting demand, and managing your distribution channels.

revenues can increase. Due to work efficiencies resulting from better trained staff, labor and other operating costs are reduced as well. When that happens, there is a significant potential for increased profits.

In the long run, revenue management-related staff training must add value to the guest experience if the organization is to benefit. Too often managers seek to measure the value of training in terms of financial return to their own organization. Wrong approach. In a customer-centric revenue optimization system the training must ultimately enhance *buyer profits* because doing so is the best way to ensure the long-term success of the business. While the measurement of value delivered may not be easy to quantify, RMs should recognize that when done correctly, revenue management training doesn't cost, it pays.

BETTER BUSINESS ISSUES IN WEAK OR DISTRESSED MARKETS

If your career in the hospitality industry lasts very long, you will likely experience strong market periods, but you will also encounter those market conditions that are not so robust. Although there are no universally agreed-on definitions, most hospitality professionals would likely share the opinion that moderate markets are those in which a business's sales per customer and total sales are in keeping with fairly predictable historic norms.

In markets that are considered weak, however, revenue levels are typically 5 to 10 percent below historic levels. A distressed market is generally one in which revenue levels are 10 percent or more below historic levels. How bad can it get? In 2010, hospitality industry consulting firm PKF reported that the U.S. hotel market experienced a 20+ percent decline in revenue (and 34.5% decline in profits) from 2008 to 2009, the largest decline ever recorded by them.* RM-related decision making in weak or distressed markets such as these may not be any more difficult than it is during better times, but the impact of those decisions is most often much greater simply because the available opportunities for increasing revenues are so reduced. In distressed markets, the best RMs apply the "unofficial" mantra of the U.S. Marine Corps., "Improvise, Adapt, and Overcome."

In the lodging industry, there is not universal agreement among revenue managers about how to adapt when demand for rooms declines significantly. This is so because, when volume levels are low, RMs typically experience additional organizational pressure to fix the revenue problem. In some cases, they can. In other cases, the ability of a single RM to change the economic conditions impacting their business will be extremely limited.

For example, in the grim fall of 2001 following the 9/11 attacks, hotel occupancy levels in New York City plummeted, bottoming out in August 2002. It would take another 31 months (March 2005) before the city would recover and return to its historic occupancy levels.[21] RMs managing the revenue process in New York during that period could not single-handedly fix the problem that caused reduced room demand.

Seven years later, the worldwide economic recession that began in late 2008 would negatively impact hotels in virtually all areas of the United States, as well as most countries in the world. To consider just one example of how difficult it can get when business drops

---

*http://www.hotel-online.com/News/PR2010_2nd/May10_BottomsDown.html retrieved 5/5/2010.

off significantly, consider the impact of the 2008/2009 recession on the Irish hotel industry. In 1996, 30,000 hotel rooms were spread across that country. By 2008, there were 60,000 rooms available. When, in early 2009, travel to Ireland had dropped 15 to 20 percent, John Power, head of the Irish Hotels Federation (IHF) called for government assistance for the hotel industry stating, "50 per cent of (our) hotels are currently experiencing serious financial difficulties and most hotels are operating at a loss this year."[22]

Revenue managers facing difficult business conditions cannot single-handedly change the world's economies. They can however, carefully consider the key market issues they must directly address when making revenue optimization decisions in weak or depressed markets:

- Market assessment
- Price discounting
- Reassessment of training efforts

Market Assessment

Few owners want to open new businesses during a market downturn. Few operators of existing businesses enjoy managing during periods of slowed economic activity. The reality for both type managers, as well as RMs, is that they will at times experience down markets. Managing effectively in such an environment means these managers must begin with an assessment of how they got there in the first place.

Before undertaking an evaluation of market conditions, it is important to recognize that businesses can experience significantly reduced volume levels for several reasons. The first is simply that customers reject the business's value proposition. The solutions to such a critical problem are varied but they are not related to market conditions. Good businesses thrive in strong economies and they survive in distressed economies. Businesses that do not consistently provide profits to their customers, however, struggle to survive even when the economy is strong.

A **SWOT analysis** is a popular method for examining a business's environmental realities. It can help RMs better recognize if the volume problems faced by their businesses are related to its operational flaws or to economic conditions. SWOT (strengths, weaknesses, opportunities, and threats) analysis asks managers to examine their businesses and carefully consider:

- What are our Strengths?
- What are our Weaknesses?
- What are our Opportunities?
- What are the Threats we face in the future?

Essential RM Term

SWOT analysis: Strengths, Weaknesses, Opportunities, and Threats analysis—a systematic approach to assess an organization's current environment as part of the strategic planning process.

An internal SWOT analysis identifies *strengths* and considers how to increase and more fully utilize them. It identifies *weaknesses* and considers how to overcome them. Existing *opportunities* are explored to more fully take advantage of them. Finally, *threats* to an organization's long-term success are identified for the purpose of addressing and surmounting them.

A SWOT analysis may reveal that factors *other* than the economy have caused an operation's revenue decline. Examples are many but can include the weather, the opening of a new competitor, changes in consumer preferences (e.g., changes in what is popular and what is not), poor product quality or service delivery, or the need for the business to significantly upgrade its physical facility or technological capabilities.

Lodging industry RMs can identify the presence of an economic downturn through the careful monitoring of Smith Travel Research (STR) reports and similar data supplied by their franchisor, their local CVB, or others. Local, state, and national trade organizations may be the source of similar sales-related data in the foodservices and other industries. If SWOT analysis reveals that it is indeed an economic condition that threatens the revenue stream of a business, it is important to recognize that economic downturns can be classified as either short or long term. In many cases, a revenue decline based on very short-term economic conditions must simply be ignored.

The duration of the short-term condition may make overreaction a bigger threat than the economic condition itself. Consider, for example, the food and beverage operation located near a large manufacturing facility that was built five miles from the closest city. The majority of this operation's regular breakfast and lunch customers work at the facility.

Slowing sales of this manufacturer's products has resulted in an unplanned plant shutdown and employee layoff that will last two weeks. Despite the inevitable and significant impact on volume, the best advice for this restaurant operation's RM is likely to stay the course. In this case, the mere cost of publicizing significant changes to the operation's pricing or marketing structure likely outweigh any incremental revenues such actions might generate.

Of course, factors that make a significant short-term impact on a local or regional economy can linger and in some cases it may not be completely clear when the impact of a shorter-term economic difficulty will cease, moderate, or get worse. Figure 13.6 lists just some of the more common short-term and longer-term economic factors that can significantly affect an organization's ability to maintain its historic revenue levels.

Figure 13.6	**Economic Threats to Hospitality Businesses**
Shorter-term Threats	**Longer-term Threats**
Increased costs of travel/fuel	Terrorism attack or threat
Travel industry-related labor strike	Currency devaluation
Sensationalized local event (major crime, disaster, oil spill, or the like)	Prolonged economic recession in the local or regional area
Temporary plant or office closings	Permanent plant or office closings
Labor unrest/unionization efforts	Changing consumer demographics, trends, and preferences
Health epidemic or pandemic (e.g., Norovirus outbreak, H1N1 flu, bird flu); Eco-disasters (e.g. oil spills on beaches)	Anti-hospitality industry tax policies
Political upheaval	Guest perceptions of high crime rates in a country or region

RM IN ACTION 13.2: THE COLDER THE BETTER!

Will guests make hotel reservations even if they do not know at the time of the booking what their room rate will be? For winter travelers visiting the Washington, D.C., area, the answer in many cases is a resounding *yes!* In fact, for guests taking advantage of an innovative differential pricing program offered by hotels in Fairfax County, Virginia, cold weather is great news.

Offered from November 29 to December 27, guests booking a two-day weekend stay at over 13 participating Fairfax County hotels had their Saturday night rate "frozen" to match the Fahrenheit outdoor temperature recorded at Dulles International Airport at 12 noon on the Saturday of their stay. The official Saturday Dulles temperature was determined using the information posted on www.weatherbug.com.

As reported in *Hotels* magazine, the promotion is an example of a creative and memorable revenue optimization effort designed to market the entire Fairfax County, Virginia, area as a tourist destination. Details about the promotion (72-hour advanced booking restrictions, room availability, and minimum length of stay requirements), a list of participating hotels, and a listing of events and attractions located near Fairfax County are posted on the Visit Fairfax's web site (www.fxva.com). Why should guests stay in Fairfax?

"Fairfax County is a smart choice for travelers who want to experience every aspect of a big city weekend getaway without having to shell out the extra cash," says Barry Biggar, president and CEO of Visit Fairfax.

This promotion is included here as an excellent example of how innovative RMs, in conjunction with their local CVBs, can work together to design customer-centric optimization programs that are unique, memorable, serve to build property revenues, and deliver real value to potential guests in good economic times or bad.

Excerpted from: www.hotelsmag.com. Posted article on 03/28/2009.

It is important to recognize that a sales volume problem that was not caused by high prices can rarely be solved by lowering prices. Although the best inventory management and pricing advice for RMs facing very-short-term economic threats may be to remain creative and avoid radical change, appropriate organizational responses to longer-term conditions must also be considered.

Price Discounting

Any sustained economic downturn should raise the issue of how your business can best improvise, adapt, and overcome. If the subject of appropriate response is not raised by your company owners it will inevitably be raised by the managers or marketing and sales staff of your business. Historically, two principal business actions can be taken in response to an economic downturn:

1. Cut costs
2. Reduce prices

Facing significantly reduced revenues, the preferred response of far too many owners and managers is to undertake significant variable cost reduction. The rationale for cutting variable costs in a downturn is as straightforward as it is flawed. Fixed costs, those costs controlled primarily by the business's owners, cannot be easily reduced. Because variable costs are adjustable in the short term, these are the costs targeted for reduction. Actually, significant variable cost reduction in the face of an economic downturn could make good sense, but only if the following assumptions are met:

- The business was so poorly managed its variable costs have been significantly out of line in the past.
- The cost reductions instituted will have no negative effect on product quality or service levels.
- Reduced quality or service levels provided to loyal customers will, in the long term, produce an increase in buyers' perceptions of value and thus will create long-term increases in revenue.

Unfortunately, these assumptions are rarely met. In most cases:

- Well-managed businesses already have their variable costs in line.
- Despite pro-customer rhetoric to the contrary, variable cost reductions nearly always results in reduced, not increased, product quality or service levels (value) delivered to customers.
- Reduced value delivered to customers tends to *decrease*, not increase, any buyer's willingness to make future purchases When that happens, revenue does not increase, it declines further.

The irony of mandating massive variable cost cuts in a down economy is illustrated by the following tongue-in-cheek e-mail sent from a large hotel's DOSM to that property's GM:

Dear Boss, I am giving my full support to the cost-cutting initiatives you instituted at our staff meeting by instructing my sales team to leave their computers turned off during working hours. Also, I am checking with the hotel's chief engineer to estimate the savings that could be achieved by leaving the sales office lights off during the day. I'll keep you posted as I learn more about that.

For managers, the proper "cost-related" response to any economic downturn is best addressed in one of the many fine hospitality *operations* or *cost control* texts, and thus is not within the scope of this book.

A professional RM's response to proposed price discounting, however, is well within the scope of this book. One useful way to examine price discounting and its effectiveness is to do so from the perspective of individual customer sales and larger group sales.

Individual Sales

Just as cost cutting is justified by a set of assumptions, so too are assumptions made by those who advocate significant price reduction as an appropriate response to declining revenues caused by a weak economy:

- Reducing price will increase buyer demand.
- Prices can be easily returned to their higher levels when the economy improves.

■ The reduction of prices will help profits now and will cause no long-term damage to the profitability of the business.

In fact, these assumptions are rarely met. In nearly every case:

■ For most hospitality products, reducing price will not typically increase buyer demand in a down economy.

■ Widespread communication of reduced prices makes it extremely difficult to rapidly restore a buyer's reference price (see Chapter 5) to its previously higher level.

■ Short-term price reductions cause significant long-term damage to the reputation and profitability of well-managed businesses.

Trained RMs should be their organizations' pricing experts. Because that is true, these professionals have a responsibility to fully understand the impact of various pricing strategies. As well, they should be able to clearly explain the impact of alternative pricing approaches to others within their organizations. Perhaps at no time is this more important than when considering pricing strategy in a down economy.

The first thing an RM should know about significantly reducing prices in the face of a weak economy is that the strategy is generally employed by businesses who trail their segment's market leaders. Mark Lomanno, president of Smith Travel Research (STR), notes that during a significant economic downturn, some (hotel) operators do elect to reduce their rates. Observed Lomanno, "Yes, there will be hotel operators who discount, but, in general, it's the lower-performing properties that lead that charge.[23]

Lomanno correctly goes on to recommend that RMs follow their market *leaders*, not their market's worst performers, if they hope to maintain pricing integrity for their own products and services over a long period of time. This is easier to understand when you recognize that it should never be the goal of an RM to target customers who value price above all else. As an RM, your goal is to price in a way that appeals to customers who value your products and services not those who value low price alone. That is what market leaders do.

In a study released in 2009, Cornell University associate professor Linda Canina, co-author of the study, stated, "Based on a study of over 67,000 properties during a six-year period, hotels that maintained average daily rates *above* those of their direct competitors experienced lower occupancies compared to those other hotels, but they recorded higher relative RevPARs. This was true in all market segments."[24]

The study strongly indicates that the best way to have better revenue performance than your competitors is to maintain higher average rates and prices despite the conditions of the economy. This makes perfect sense when you recognize that in a significant economic downturn, those RMs who discount rates are trying to use low price to attract guests who have stopped buying for reasons that are in most cases totally unrelated to room prices. Those RMs who believe (incorrectly) that effective revenue management is simply synonymous with increasing prices in response to high demand naturally (though just as incorrectly), believe prices must be reduced in times of lessened demand.

It is sometimes easy for hospitality managers to justify discounting rates to capture as much market share as possible. Despite consistent results from studies such as that conducted

Essential RM Term

Distributable (expense): A cost that can be reasonably assigned to one specific department within an operation. Also referred to as a *distributed* expense. Examples in the lodging industry include the cost of rooms-related labor, amenities, and cleaning supplies—all expenses that are distributable to the property's rooms (housekeeping) department.

Essential RM Term

Undistributable (expense): A cost that cannot reasonably be assigned to only one specific department within an operation. Also referred to as an *undistributed* expense. Examples include rent, advertising, taxes, and insurance.

by Professor Canina, the rationale for such an approach continues to be, that in a shrinking market, lowered prices optimize income. That is likely a mind-set that will remain for many hotel and restaurant owners struggling with the very real problem of needing to generate the income required to meet their short-term variable and fixed cost obligations. As their organizations' pricing experts, however, RMs should recognize and share with management the very real short- and long-term consequences of discounting to maintain an organization's desired top-line revenue levels.

To illustrate, consider the case of Amanda Sipe. Amanda is the RM at the 200-room select service Fairmont Suites hotel. Last year Amanda's property achieved 69 percent occupancy and a $95.00 ADR. Her **distributable** CPOR (see Chapter 8) is $24.00 and the property's **undistributable** operating costs for the year were $10.00 per available room.

Amanda is convinced that the economy in her area is in decline and she fears the condition will last all through next year. Based on current pace reports, her estimate of reduced room demand in the coming year is in the range of 3 to 6 percent.

Assuming that Amanda feels she can offset the effect on occupancy of the downturn in the market via a $5.00 per room rate reduction, she faces two choices:

1. Maintain occupancy levels by reducing rate.
2. Maintain rate and experience reduced occupancy.

Figure 13.7 shows the financial impact on her property of the two alternative pricing strategies.

A close examination of Figure 13.7 reveals that if Amanda reduces her rate by $5.00 in an attempt to maintain her historical 69 percent occupancy level, her room revenue forecast is $4,533,300.

If instead Amanda sought to maintain her historical ADR, occupancy drops by 3.6 occupancy points (a 6.5 percent decline from the prior year) while the room revenue achieved is within $5.00 of the $4,533,305 forecast. Note, however, that because she would sell fewer rooms Amanda's reduced distributed expense would result in both an increase in GOP and GOP percent.

This example illustrates that in most situations, more *profit* can be made by seeking to maintain historical ADR levels than by seeking to maintain historical occupancy levels. It is critical that lodging industry RMs know and can clearly communicate this fact to others in the organization.

In the foodservice business, RMs face equally significant price discounting-related challenges. When market conditions are weak and customer counts decline, organizational pressure increases to retain volume through significant price reduction. While those managers in operations or in marketing may favor such an approach, foodservice RMs

Figure 13.7	Maintain Occupancy versus Maintain Rate

Maintain Occupancy		Maintain Rate	
ADR	$90	ADR	$95
Rooms	200	Rooms	200
Rooms available (12 months)	73,000	Rooms available (12 months)	73,000
Rooms sold (12 months)	50,370	Rooms sold (12 months)	47,719
Room revenue	**$4,533,300**	Room revenue	**$4,533,305**
Occupancy (Rooms sold/ Rooms available)	69.00%	Occupancy (Rooms sold/ Rooms available)	65.40%
Rooms sold	50,370	Rooms sold	47,719
Distributable CPOR	$24	Distributable CPOR	$24
Distributable operating expense (12 months)	$1,208,880	Distributable operating expense (12 months)	$1,145,256
Undistributable cost per available room	$16	Undistributable cost per available room	$16
Rooms available	73,000	Rooms available	73,000
Undistributable operating expense (12 months)	$1,168,000	Undistributable operating expense (12 months)	$1,168,000
Room revenue	$4,533,300	Room revenue	$4,533,305
Less Distributable CPOR	($1,208,880)	Less Distributable CPOR	($1,145,256)
Less Undistributable operating expense	($1,168,000)	Less Undistributable operating expense	($1,168,000)
Gross operating profit (GOP)	**$2,156,420**	Gross operating profit (GOP)	**$2,220,049**
GOP %	47.57%	GOP %	48.97%

Essential RM Term

Recession: A widespread and significant decline in economic activity and employment, typically lasting from six months to a year.

should be extremely cautious about such a tactic. The reasons why they must be cautious have little to do with customer counts, but much to do with customer perceptions. Discounting in a **recession** is most often a mistake because it can do significant damage to the reputation of a brand.

RM IN ACTION 13.3: ALMOST ALWAYS A BAD IDEA

In difficult economic times, many foodservice operators see a decline in their customer counts. A common reaction to declining customer counts is management's consideration of significant price reduction in an effort to maintain previous revenue levels. The question foodservice operators must ask themselves when considering a price reduction strategy as a way of increasing volume is very similar to the one that must be asked by lodging industry operators, namely:

"Are the short-term gains in customer count worth it in the long run?"

Chris Muller, professor at the University of Central Floridain Orlando provided a direct answer.

"It's almost always a bad idea."

Muller offered this reply when the question was posed to him by editors of *Restaurant and Institutions* magazine during the height of the 2009 worldwide recession. According to Muller, the reason foodservice operators must be cautious when using discounts to increase traffic to their units is the same reason hoteliers must use caution when reducing room rates. Unless customers see a clear and rationale reason for the price reduction (e.g.,

10 percent off drinks from 4 to 6 P.M., or half-price appetizers after 10:00 P.M.), excessive discounting can devalue a brand as well as customers' views of the value they receive for the money they spend.

For example, a $12.95 menu item offered for $5.99, even for a defined time period such as two weeks, can indeed cause buyers to feel they have received real value for their purchase. This is so because prior to the discount their reference price for the item was $12.95. Unfortunately, having made the purchase, their new reference price is $5.99 and any price above that in the future will be perceived as *not* representing good value. For menu items and for most other consumer products, it's simply hard to be willing to pay $12.95 today for an item you purchased for $5.95 the week before.

When a foodservice operation resorts to maintaining volume levels by lowering menu prices significantly, they train their guests to expect reduced prices and these customers will remember their lessons well, even after the economy rebounds.

Reference *Restaurants and Institutions,* 2009 edition, page 21.

To better understand why this is so, the results of a U.S. consumer study undertaken at the height of the 2009 recession are constructive. The study asked consumers what they assume when a brand lowers its prices during weak economic times. seventy percent of consumers responded, *"The brand is normally overpriced."*

In contrast, the same study asked buyers what they assume when a brand does *not* lower its prices during weak economic times—64 percent of those surveyed said that they assume *"the product is extremely popular,"* and 65 percent assume that *"the product is already a good value."* The study findings were summarized nicely by lead researcher J. Walker Smith, Ph.D., president of the Yankelovich MONITOR®. Dr. Walker explained simply, "Lowering prices during a recession clearly raises suspicions among consumers."[25]

Psychology plays an incredibly important role in price discounting. Massive price discounting is counterproductive for both hoteliers and restaurateurs. Can price discounting be used to generate incremental revenues? Of course. To better understand how talented RMs can skillfully conceive and market value-added services and reduce price without damaging brand reputation, consider the Regal Airport Hotel in Hong Kong. It offered a Valentine's Day romance package including dinner, wine, special bath amenities and in-room movie for HK $1,336. The same room *without* the extras was priced at HK $1,800. With this tactic, the hotel could lower prices without risking long-term rate damage, since the lower rate is clearly part of a special that could be eliminated when economic conditions improved.[26] If you understand that this initially counterintuitive approach is absolutely consistent with insightful pricing strategy, you may be ready to lead your own RM team.

RM IN ACTION 13.4: REVENUE OPTIMIZATION LESSONS FROM KETCHUP MAKERS

In their article "A Dynamic Model of Brand Choice When Price and Advertising Signal Product Quality" appearing in the INFORMS journal *Marketing Science,* Tülin Erdem of NYU, Michael P. Keane of the University of Technology Sidney, Australia and Arizona State University, and Baohong Sun of Carnegie Mellon University studied the impact of price reductions on brand image.

The researchers examined the pricing strategies of well-known ketchup brands (Heinz, Hunts, and Del Monte). Of the three, Heinz is perceived by consumers as being highest in quality and in price. The researchers were interested in the changes in consumer perceptions resulting from the price discounting of this highly regarded brand. Their findings?

> Recurring price promotions that reduce the perceived average price of a brand can feed back and adversely impact perceived quality . . . approximately one quarter of the increase in sales generated by a temporary price cut represents cannibalization of future sales due to the brand-equity-diluting effect of the promotion.

Reduced prices can increase short-term revenues, but they do so at the expense of brand equity. Frequent price cuts have a major adverse effect on brand equity, especially for well-respected brands. Higher sales revenue resulting from using price discounting to sell more of a brand's products or services actually come with a very high price tag. In fact, the higher the brand's perceived quality, the *more* damage is done by excessive price discounting. The researchers further state that buyers' perceptions of quality are based on four key factors: (1) price, (2) advertising frequency, (3) advertising content, and (4) consumer experience using the product. Of those, they report, price is *the most* important signal of brand quality.

From high-end hotel rooms, to restaurant meals, to cruise ship cabins, to ketchup, RMs advertising lowered prices must do so carefully and in a highly targeted (micro) manner or they risk increasing short-term revenues while at the same time significantly damaging their own long-term revenue-generating ability.

Excerpted from www.informs.org. Article posted on 2/8/2009.

Group Sales

If the pressure to reduce individual prices during a downturn is strong, the pressure to discount large volume or group business is even stronger. This is especially true in the lodging industry, where economic slowdowns can cause group rooms buyers to aggressively negotiate for lowered rates. For lodging industry RMs, it is essential to understand and be able to communicate to others in the organization the buying-related motives behind meetings and group rooms customers.

Group meetings and group room sales are, of course, perceived as big sales by most hotel sales departments. The sleeping rooms, meeting space, and F&B sales associated with securing a large group contract can be significant. As a result, in a distressed market, the tendency of some conference or group-oriented hoteliers is to radically reduce rates. They must resist that temptation and RMs need to be able to explain why they must.

Despite the inclination for buyers of all types to negotiate more aggressively in a downturned economy, it is important to recognize that for this specific market segment price is simply *not* the major factor in the purchase decision. Price is only the major factor when all other important factors are identical. RMs should be aware of the five factors that *do* strongly influence meetings buyers, listed here in order of importance:

1. *Location*: Whether the criteria includes proximity to area night life, golf, an airport, or other specific demand generator, research in this area has consistently shown that *location* is the single most important factor in property selection by meeting planners. Over 40 percent of planners surveyed in a recent study ranked it first in importance. Reducing sleeping room rates or the price of meeting space would, of course, have zero effect on this selection factor.

2. *History*: In many areas of business, past performance is the best predictor of future performance. Meeting planners know this as well. Hotels gain their meetings-related reputation based on how well they have cared for past groups. The quality of past performance is so important that over 20 percent of meeting planners base their location selections on previous successful experiences. Price reductions will not affect perceptions of historical performance.

3. *Unique meeting facility*: Having the physical space and specialized facilities (i.e., sufficient computer access, number of electrical outlets, ceiling height and the like) is important for those meeting planners with special needs. Facility features such as these are critical selection factors for over 15 percent of meeting planners, but price reduction cannot, of course, improve this aspect of a hotel's product and service offerings.

4. *Reputation*: For first-time rooms customers, the reputation of a hotel, or its brand can be highly influential. The recommendation made by a meeting planner's peers are part of that reputation. For 12 percent of meeting planners, referrals, references, and reputation of property are the top selection criteria. Reputations are built over time. They are not influenced by price reduction. In fact, as you have learned, significantly reducing price consistently leads buyers to *reduce* their perceptions of a product's quality.

5. *Cost*: Interestingly, prices rank as the fifth most important selection criteria. And only 6 percent of planners listed cost as the most important criteria for selecting event location.[27]

Despite the fact that price reduction will make a significant impact on less than 10 percent of buyers, in weak markets some RMs persist in the practice. They do so simply because in the short run, price is an easy factor to manipulate. Prices can be changed overnight. Location, history, facilities, and reputation cannot.

Effective RMs should, of course, make their products more attractive to buy when they encounter a slowed economic climate. But they must do so in a way that does not dilute their brand's value. As you will recall from Chapter 4, the use of product versioning, increased service levels, and variance in payment terms are three of the ways you can stay competitive in your market by offering price-sensitive group rooms buyers more value. You can use each of these revenue optimization strategies without eroding the worth of your product or changing your guests' reference price.

Reassessment of Training Efforts

Professional RMs know that successful companies facing weakened economic conditions do not ask for less; they offer their customers more. Recall from Chapter 5 that from a buyer's perspective value is defined as:

$$\text{Perceived benefit} - \text{Price} = \text{Value}$$

Offering more and better product and service features, and thus increasing perceived benefit, is a *better* way to increase value and revenues than is a reduction in price charged. For most hospitality businesses, product and service delivery enhancements provide the best chance to avoid commoditization and its related downward spiraling of prices. Employee training is the key to those enhancements.

In a down economy, hospitality businesses must not only do what they do well; they must do it better. And they must do new things. Using a lodging industry example to illustrate this fact, consider the hotel that has designed a very reasonable training program which must be completed by all newly hired desk agents. If there is a significant downturn in the economy, the program may be inadequate in providing sales staff and desk agents the skills and information they need to perform well. This is so because the program was not likely designed to address the very *specialized* front desk issues that accompany a down economy. These issues will be different than those that are emphasized in a moderate or strong economy.

Consider, for example, that when answering the reservations telephone in a down economy, hotel sales agents are much more likely to encounter callers who mention, by name, specific competitors who are offering lower rates. RMs must ensure their agents are carefully trained in a proper response (i.e., to avoid making negative statements about the competitor and instead emphasizing their own property's unique features).

In a similar manner, thrift-conscious callers may contact the hotel and, having referenced a price listed on a specific web site, ask whether they should book online or directly with the hotel. Savvy RMs know, "*Whichever you like,*" is not the best answer. In fact, an economic downturn creates an even greater rationale for ensuring sales or desk agents are well informed about the net ADR yields of various third-party web sites and online travel agencies used by the hotel.

A third economy-specific issue relates to price fences (see Chapter 4). This topic is important in a down economy because buyers may be more likely to increase their efforts to improperly skirt price fences. This will be happening at precisely the time RMs will be expanding their use of fences to carefully target specific customers. In this situation, it is especially critical that sales agents be well-trained in how to maintain rate fences by fully explaining all restrictions (e.g., MLOS, qualifications, or availability dates) at the time reservations are made.

As well, sales agents must help minimize the guest embarrassment or misunderstandings at check-in that can result when buyers do not qualify for a lowered rate they had previously booked. Sales agents and desk staff can do this if they are carefully trained to be especially clear, at the time reservations are made, when describing any rate qualification requirements that will be validated upon the guest's arrival. As this example illustrates, the need for RMs to become adept at implementing effective staff training programs is clear.

In a down market, the specific economy-related issues that will be important to you will vary based on your own industry segment and your area of responsibility. In all cases, however, a down economy should initiate a careful reassessment of your current training efforts. That examination should be undertaken with an eye toward enhanced training and service delivery in those very areas most affected or changed by the downturn.

This chapter began with a rationale for you to assume the role of RM champion. If you have successfully absorbed the lessons presented in this book and can complete the exercises it contains, then you are ready to do just that. That does not mean you must share the authors' views on every RM-related issue we have presented. In fact, it is more important that you do not! Remember that not all master chefs in the hospitality industry will make their sauces in an identical way. Nor would all talented DOSMs market their hotels in an identical manner. It is only through spirited debate and the open challenging of beliefs and opinions that current ideas are strengthened and new visions emerge. In most cases it is innovation, not conformity of thought, that should be your goal as an RM leader.

What *is* very important to the authors is your recognition that you are now well prepared to assume an RM leadership role in any organization fortunate enough to secure your services. You truly are an expert in the critically important RM-related topics of

▶ RM ON THE WEB 13.3

CHART is the acronym for the Council of Hotel and Restaurant Trainers. This professional association is comprised of more than 700 hospitality industry trainers responsible for the training needs of nearly five million hospitality employees, ranging from those in entry level positions to senior executives.

The mission of CHART is to advance (hospitality) industry training practices and improve operational results by providing access to education, tools, and resources. Those RMs who recognize the importance of employee training to the success of their own organizations should strongly consider membership in this organization. To learn more about joining CHART go to www.chart.org

When you arrive click on *Membership*, then choose *Application and Fees* to review the organization's eligibility requirements.

pricing (Chapter 2) and value (Chapter 3). You understand differential pricing (Chapter 4) and how ethical RMs can use it to create customer-centric revenue optimization programs (Chapter 5).

You have gained knowledge and you have gained skills. If your RM career is to be in the lodging industry, you understand well the importance of demand forecasting (Chapter 6). In addition, you are prepared to lead others in the essential areas of rooms pricing and inventory management (Chapter 7). You recognize the central issues to be addressed in the rapidly changing area of distribution channel management (Chapter 8) and most critically, you have learned how RMs assess the quality and impact of their own decision making (Chapter 9).

If your RM career is to be in the foodservice industry your understanding of traditional menu pricing systems as well as how you can apply differential pricing in a foodservice setting (Chapter 10) make you a very knowledgeable pricing professional. The fact that you are also prepared to evaluate your foodservice-related revenue management activities (Chapter 11) means you will be an extremely talented RM in an extremely competitive industry.

Regardless of the hospitality-related industry you may choose, you are now well-qualified to assess how differential pricing and inventory management can help your organization achieve its revenue optimization goals (Chapter 12). Because you have nearly completed the current chapter you better understand the specific actions and issues you must address to best serve your customers, build better business, and increase revenues in your organization, regardless of the economic conditions you may face in the future.

Because of your advanced training in the subject, you are well on your way to becoming a very accomplished revenue management professional. You are ready to succeed. As you face and successfully overcome the many challenges you will encounter in the future, the most fundamental request the authors can make of you is the same affirming one Christopher Robin made to Winnie-the-Pooh. Christopher Robin's appeal to Pooh, as penned by author A.A. Milne, was simply this:

Promise me you'll always remember: You're braver than you believe, and stronger than you seem, and smarter than you think![28]

Good luck!

❖ ESSENTIAL RM TERMS

Ownership of responsibility	Leveraging
Bottom line	Displacement analysis (revenue)
USAR	Turnover rate (employee)
Barriers to entry	SWOT Analysis
Cyclical (business)	Distributable (expense)
Seasonal (business)	Undistributable (expense)
Pipeline (hotel)	Recession
Distressed market	

▐▐▐➡ APPLY WHAT YOU KNOW

1. Karla Armbruster is the RM at a 200-room select service hotel near a major highway. Last year, her ADR was $149.99 and her property ran at 80 percent occupancy. Karla is considering the impact on her property of implementing programs that would increase her ADR by 5 percent and 10 percent. If she increases ADR by 5 percent, she anticipates a 77.5 percent occupancy next year. If prices are increased by 10 percent she forecasts her occupancy will decline to 70 percent. Finish the calculations she needs to complete the revenue analysis form below, then answer the questions that follow.

Karla's 200-Room Hotel: Revenue Analysis

200-Room Property	Last Year Pricing	5% ADR Increase	10% ADR Increase
Actual/Forecasted Occupancy %	80.0%	77.5%	70.0%
Rooms sold			
ADR	$ 149.99	$	$
Rev	$	$	$
RevPAR	$	$	$
RevPAR change	N/A		
Controllable operating costs @ $45.00 per room	$	$	$
Gross operating profit	$	$	$
GOPPAR	$	$	$
GOPPAR change	N/A		

A. What was Karla's RevPAR last year? _____

B. What would be the percent change in Karla's RevPAR with a 5 percent increase in ADR? _____

C. What would be the percent change in Karla's RevPAR with a 10 percent increase in ADR?_____

D. What was Karla's GOPPAR last year? _____

E. What would be Karla's forecasted percent change in GOPPAR with a 5 percent increase in ADR? _____

F. What would be Karla's forecasted percent change in GOPPAR with a 10 percent increase in ADR? _____

G. What would you advise Karla to do?_____. Explain your answer.

2. Jody Guilder is the Assistant GM for sales at the Caustic Bay Hotel. In response to a request from the hotel's GM, Jody supplied Poco Niller, the hotel's new RM, with STAR reports for the past 12 months.

   Jody claims business in the local area is down significantly because the Caustic Bay's occupancy is 15 percent less than it was last year. What specific data from the STR reports (see Chapter 9) should Poco analyze to determine if the decline in occupancy referred to by Jody is in fact due to declining economic conditions in the area or if it is due to other factors such as poor operations performance or a weak sales effort?

3. Teshia is the RM at the 250-room Springwood Suites hotel. The Springwood is a select service property whose F&B services consist only of complimentary breakfast. For a future date, Teshia has 100 rooms on the books and she forecasts that a total of 200 rooms can be sold that day at an ADR of $180.00.

   Teshia's DOS states that a large convention is coming to the area on that date and the group rooms buyer for the convention has requested the hotel offer the group a rate of $150.00 for 100 of the property's available rooms. The DOS believes the group will pick up all of its rooms and thus, with the 100 rooms already on the books and with only 50 of the additional room sales forecast by Teshia, the hotel will sell all 250 of its rooms on that day.

Original Forecast	
Rooms available	250
ADR	$180.00
Rooms sold	200
Room revenue	**$36,000**
Occupancy % (Rooms sold/Rooms available)	
Rooms sold	200
Distributable CPOR	$68
Distributable operating expense	
Undistributable cost per available room	$28
Rooms available	250

With Group Forecast	
Rooms Available	250
ADR	
Rooms sold	
Room revenue	
Occupancy % (Rooms sold/Rooms available)	
Rooms sold	
Distributable CPOR	
Distributable operating expense	
Undistributable cost per available room	
Rooms available	

(*continued*)

(Continued)

Original Forecast	
Undistributable operating expense	
Room revenue	$36,000
Less Distributable CPOR	
Less Undistributable operating expense	
Gross operating profit (GOP)	
GOP %	

With Group Forecast	
Undistributable operating expense	
Room revenue	
Less Distributable CPOR	
Less Undistributable operating expense	
Gross operating profit (GOP)	
GOP %	

A. If 100 rooms were committed at the requested group rate and the hotel indeed sold out, what would be the hotel's rooms revenue on this date? _____

B. What would be the hotel's GOP if no group rooms were allocated by Teshia and her original forecast of 200 sold rooms on this date were accurate? _____

C. What would be the hotel's GOP if 100 group rooms were allocated by Teshia and the revised forecast of 250 sold rooms on this date were accurate? _____

D. Would you advise Teshia to offer the group rooms at $150.00 per night?_____

E. What could be some reasons not related to this night's revenue that could motivate Teshia to offer the group the requested lower rate?

4. Adrian is the DOSM and also serves as the property RM at the Clarion Conference Center. Adrian is considering two alternative bid opportunities his hotel received from the local CVB. On a date in the future, two medical groups seek 150 rooms from his hotel, but he can accommodate only one of them.

The State Dentist's Association is willing to pay $199.00 per night for the 150 needed rooms ($29,850 total). This group will not hold its meetings onsite.

The State Doctor's Association will pay only $139.00 per night for the rooms but will spend an additional $30,000 for meals and $7,500 for meeting space. Adrian estimates the F&B-related GOP at $45.00 per room sold, and the meeting space-related GOP at $25.00 per sold room. Help Adrian decide which bid to pursue by completing the displacement worksheet he has begun then answer the questions that follow.

Dentists	
Rooms requested	150
ADR	$199.00
Rooms sold	150

Doctors	
Rooms available	150
ADR	$139.00
Rooms	

Room revenue	**$29,850**		Room revenue	
Rooms sold	150		Rooms sold	
Distributable CPOR	$75		Distributable CPOR	
Distributable operating expense	$11,250		Distributable operating expense	
Undistributable cost per available room	$30		Undistributable cost per available room	
Rooms available	150		Rooms available	
Undistributable operating expense	$4,500		Undistributable operating expense	
Room revenue	$29,850		Room revenue	
Less Distributable CPOR			Less Distributable CPOR	
Less Undistributable Operating Expense			Less Undistributable Operating Expense	
Gross operating profit (GOP): Rooms			Gross operating profit (GOP): Rooms	
			+ GOP: F&B	
			+ GOP: Meeting space	
TOTAL GOP			TOTAL GOP	
GOP per Sold Room	$		GOP per Sold Room	$

A. If 150 rooms were sold, what would be the total GOP if the hotel won the bid for the dentist's group? _____

B. If 150 rooms were sold, what would be the total GOP if the hotel won the bid for the doctor's group? _____

C. If 150 rooms were sold, what would be the GOP per sold room if the hotel won the bid for the dentist's group? _____

D. If 150 rooms were sold, what would be the GOP per sold room if the hotel won the bid for the doctor's group? _____

E. If you were Adrian, which of the medical group bids would you prefer to win? _____ _____. Explain your answer.

5. Danny is the owner of the Repas French restaurant. The restaurant does good volume but due to very weak local economy, Danny is considering promotions and price reductions next year that would, on average, reduce both his food and beverage prices by 5 percent. He is hoping that such price reductions can allow him to maintain his current sales level by attracting new customers as well as encouraging his current customers to dine with him more frequently. Danny's P&L for last year is shown. Using the cost-related assumptions that follow, complete this year's (current price) and next year's (with 5 percent price decrease) forecasted P&L, then answer the questions that follow.

Danny's assumptions with a 5 percent decrease in prices and very careful cost control are:

1. Food cost percent will increase from 28 percent to 30 percent of food sales.

2. Beverage cost percent will increase from 20 percent to 22 percent of beverage sales.

3. There will be no change in labor cost or other operating expense.

4. Due to increased numbers of guests served, there will be no reduction in total food and beverage revenue.

Repas P&L and 5% Price Reduction Forecasted P&L

	Current Price	With 5% Price Decrease	% Change
SALES:			
Food	$ 3,750,000		
Beverage	800,000		
Total sales	**$ 4,550,000**	**$ 4,550,000**	
Guests served	175,000		
Food check average	$ 21.43		
Beverage check average	$ 4.57		
COST OF SALES:			
Food (28%)	$ 1,050,000		
Food (30%)			—
Beverage (20%)	$ 160,000		
Beverage (22%)			—
Total Cost of Sales	$ 1,210,000	—	
GROSS PROFIT:			
Food	$ 2,700,000	—	
Beverage	$ 640,000	—	
Total Gross Profit	$ 3,340,000	—	
OPERATING EXPENSES:			
Salaries and wages (30%)	$ 1,365,000	$ 1,365,000	

Employee benefits	$ 410,000	$ 410,000	
Direct operating expenses	$ 130,000	$ 130,000	
Music and entertainment	$ 2,500	$ 2,500	
Marketing	$ 145,000	$ 145,000	
Utility services	$ 175,000	$ 175,000	
Repairs and maintenance	$ 105,000	$ 105,000	
Administrative and general	$ 169,000	$ 169,000	
Occupancy	$ 250,000	$ 250,000	
Depreciation	$ 85,000	$ 85,000	
Total Operating Expenses	**$ 2,836,500**	**$ 2,836,500**	
Operating Income	**$ 503,500**		
Interest	$ 190,000	$ 190,000	
Income Before Income Taxes	**$ 313,500**		
Per Guest Income Before Income Taxes			

A. What is Danny's current *Per Guest Income Before Income Taxes?* _____

B. If prices are reduced by 5 percent, how many guests must Danny serve to generate *Total Sales* equal to those he achieved last year? _____

C. If prices are reduced by 5 percent, what is the percentage change in guests needed to generate Total Sales equal to that of last year? _____

D. What would be Danny's *Per Guest Income Before Income Taxes* if he reduced prices and served the number of guests needed to generate *Total Sales* equal to last year? _____.

E. What would be the percentage change in Danny's *Per Guest Income Before Income Taxes* if he reduced prices and served the additional guests needed to generate Total *Sales equal* to last year? _____.

KEY CONCEPT CASE STUDY

"So Damario, what do you think now?" asked Sofia Davidson, the GM at the Barcena Resort.

Sofia was conducting the first annual performance review of Damario, the resort's revenue manager. Having concluded the past performance portion of his excellent review, Sofia and Damario were doing some planning and dreaming for the upcoming year.

"Well, I know it may be hard to believe, but I think that from a revenue optimization perspective, next year will be even better than this one," replied Damario.

"Why do you think so?" asked Sofia.

"Because many of the demand forecast and tracking systems we put in place last year are now starting to really help. We can look at current pace reports and compare them to prior year data. We couldn't do that last year because we didn't have the previous year data we needed," said Damario.

"The data collection systems you designed and implemented have really seemed to help us get a handle on our guests, where they come from, and what they want to buy most," said Sofia.

"Right. That helps with pricing and inventory management. The procedures we put in place over the last year are really beginning to help us make better decisions now," said Damario, "but we also have a secret weapon that I am counting on to drive improvements this year just as much or more than our systems did last year."

"You have secret weapon?. . . Really? Do tell. And what would that be?" asked Sofia.

"That would be our *Strategic Pricing and Revenue Management Committee*," replied Damario. "Now that we have been operating for nearly a year, we have finally gotten to a really good place. Now when we discuss pricing we don't have the controller's office automatically clamoring for increases. And sales and marketing can see past immediate revenue gains from low prices and focus on the profitability of their sales."

"And on our customers," said Sofia. "I've been really pleased at how our guest service metrics have ticked up."

"Me too," said Damario. "We are miles ahead of last year when it comes to factoring customer responses into all of our pricing and inventory management decisions."

"Your guidance has made the difference. You make the committee look good. And you've made me look good too!" said Sofia.

Thanks," said Damario with a smile, "I'm glad you're pleased. Now would this be a good time to talk about my raise for next year?"

"Why did I know this was coming?" said Sofia laughing. "And you're right. This is a good time."

For Your Consideration

1. Based on what you have learned in this and previous chapters in the book, do you think it is data collection and analysis or staff awareness and commitment that will most improve a hospitality organization's revenue optimization efforts?

2. In this case study, Sofia indicates that the customer-centric revenue optimization approach utilized by Damario has improved the resort's guest satisfaction scores. What do you think is the relationship between effective revenue management strategies and improved customer satisfaction? Why?

3. Damario indicated that the improved cohesiveness of his committee will be a "secret weapon" driving next year's results. Why is a unified organizational commitment to effective revenue optimization efforts so important? What specific actions can a revenue manager take to help build organizational cohesiveness?

4. Because they are so new, compensation programs for revenue managers continue to evolve. If you were Sofia, what specific factors would you consider when designing Damario's compensation package? How would you measure his effectiveness on each of those factors?

ENDNOTES

1. Brother Herman Zaccarelli C.S.C., *Management Without Reservations: Leadership Principles for the Manager's Life Journey* (IUniverse, Inc., 2007), 4–5.

2. Donald E. Lundberg, *The Hotel and Restaurant Business*, 5th. ed. (New York: Van Nostrand Reinhold, 1989).

3. Thomas J. Peters and Robert A. Waterman, *In Search of Excellence: Lessons from America's Best-Run Companies* (New York: Harper and Row, 1982).

4. http://www.brainyquote.com/quotes/quotes/n/niccolomac131418.html. Retrieved 3/15/2009.

5. http://www.loalibrary.com/Books/365-success-quotes-silvercitizen.pdf. Retrieved 3/16/2009.

6. http://www.brainyquote.com/quotes/authors/t/theodore_roosevelt.html. Retrieved 3/15/2009.

7. http://en.wikipedia.org/wiki/Ralph_Hitz. Retrieved 2/15/2009.

8. http://www.brainyquote.com/quotes/authors/w/w_edwards_deming.html. Retrieved 3/21/2009.

9. Michael V. Marn, Eric V. Roegner, and Craig C. Zwanda, *The Price Advantage* (Hoboken, NJ: John Wiley and Sons, 2004), 5.

10. http://quote.robertgenn.com/auth_search.php?authid=966. Retrieved 3/29/2009.

11. http://www.brainyquote.com/quotes/authors/l/leonardo_da_vinci_2.html. Retrieved 5/20/2009.

12. http://www.huffingtonpost.com/2008/08/15/mrs-fields-cookie-chain-t_n_119274.html. Retrieved 3/29/2009.

13. http://www.museumofhoaxes.com/hoax/weblog/comments/1448/. Retrieved 4/3/2009.

14. http://www.htrends.com/modules.php?op=modload&name=trends&file=detail&sid=36974. Retrieved 8/8/2009.

15. http://www.hotelsmag.com/article/CA6632412.html?nid=3457&rid=499702242. Retrieved 1/27/2009.

16. http://www.irrationalexuberance.com/definition.htm. Retrieved 3/31/09.

17. http://findarticles.com/p/articles/mi_qa4037/is_200203/ai_n9048368. Retrieved 3/31/09.

18. *Nation's Restaurant News*, 5/14/ 2007 issue.

19. http://finance.aol.com/quotes/starbucks-corporation/sbux/nas. Retrieved 3/31/09.

20. http://thinkexist.com/quotation/the_manager_has_a_short-range_view-the_leader_has/252312.html. Retrieved 4/2/2009.

21. http://www.hotelnewsnow.com/Articles.aspx?ArticleId=909&ArticleType=1&PageType=Similar. Retrieved 4/6/2009.

22. www.irishtimes.com/newspaper/breaking/2009/0806/breaking55.htm. Retrieved 8/9/2009.

23. Mark Lomanno, "Discounting Rates Lead To Decreased Product Value," *Hotel/ Motel Management* (December 8, 2008): 11.

24. www.hotelschool.cornell.edu/research/chr/pubs/reports/2009.html. Retrieved 8/8/2009.

25. www.thefuturescompany.com. The Dollars & Consumer Sense 2009 study was an RDD telephone survey conducted in January 2009 among 1,002 adults ages 18+. The margin of error at the 95 percent confidence level is +/–3.1%. Retrieved 4/10/2009.

26. Adam Kirby, ed., "Rather Than Slash Rates, Hotels Turn to Value-added Promos To Drive Bookings," *Hotels* magazine, Online edition (March 1, 2009). Retrieved 3/10/2009.

27. http://www.hotel-online.com/News/PR2007_4th/Nov07_SiteSelection.html. Top Five Reasons for Meeting Planner Site Selection. Retrieved 11/4/2007.

28. A.A. Milne, quoted at http://thinkexist.com/quotation/promise-me-you-ll-always-remember-you-re-braver/357150.html. Retrieved 4/6/2009.

INDEX